W9-BXZ-530

KOVELS'
DEPRESSION GLASS & DINNERWARE PRICE LIST

BOOKS BY RALPH AND TERRY KOVEL

American Country Furniture 1780–1875

A Directory of American Silver, Pewter, and Silver Plate

Kovels' Advertising Collectibles Price List

Kovels' American Art Pottery

Kovels' American Silver Marks: 1650 to the Present

Kovels' Antiques & Collectibles Fix-It Source Book

Kovels' Antiques & Collectibles Price List

Kovels' Bid, Buy, and Sell Online

Kovels' Book of Antique Labels

Kovels' Bottles Price List

Kovels' Collector's Guide to American Art Pottery

Kovels' Collector's Guide to Limited Edition Plates, Figurines,
Ingots, Paperweights, Etc.

Kovels' Collectors' Source Book

Kovels' Depression Glass & American Dinnerware Price List

Kovels' Depression Glass & Dinnerware Price List

Kovels' Dictionary of Marks—Pottery and Porcelain: 1650 to 1850

Kovels' Guide to Selling, Buying, and Fixing
Your Antiques and Collectibles

Kovels' Guide to Selling Your Antiques & Collectibles

Kovels' Illustrated Price Guide to Royal Doulton

Kovels' Know Your Antiques

Kovels' Know Your Collectibles

Kovels' New Dictionary of Marks—Pottery & Porcelain:
1850 to the Present

Kovels' Organizer for Collectors

Kovels' Price Guide for Collector Plates, Figurines,
Paperweights, and Other Limited Editions

Kovels' Quick Tips: 799 Helpful Hints on How
to Care for Your Collectibles

Kovels' Yellow Pages: A Collector's Directory

Kovels' Yellow Pages: A Resource Guide for Collectors

The Label Made Me Buy It: From Aunt Jemima to Zonkers—
The Best-Dressed Boxes, Bottles, and Cans from the Past

EIGHTH EDITION

KOVELS'
DEPRESSION GLASS & DINNERWARE PRICE LIST

Ralph and Terry Kovel

RANDOM HOUSE REFERENCE
NEW YORK TORONTO LONDON SYDNEY AUCKLAND

Published by Random House Reference, an imprint of the Random House Information Group, 1745 Broadway, New York, New York 10019.
Distributed by the Random House Information Group, a division of Random House Inc., New York, and simultaneously in Canada by Random House of Canada Limited, Toronto.
Random House is a registered trademark of Random House, Inc.
www.randomhouse.com

This book is available for special discounts for bulk purchases for sales promotions or premiums. Special editions, including personalized covers, excerpts of existing books, and corporate imprints, can be created in large quantities for special needs. For more information, write to Special Markets/Premium Sales, 1745 Broadway, MD 6-2, New York, NY, 10019 or e-mail *specialmarkets@randomhouse.com*

Printed in the United States of America

Library of Congress Cataloging-in-Publication Data
Kovel, Ralph M.
Kovels' depression glass & dinnerware price list / Ralph and Terry Kovel. — 8th ed.
p. cm.
Includes bibliographical references.
1. Depression glass—Catalogs. 2. Ceramic tableware—United States—History—20th century—Catalogs. I. Title: Depression glass & dinnerware price list. II. Title: Kovels' depression glass and dinnerware price list. III. Kovel, Terry H. IV. Title

ISBN 1-4000-4663-7

Eighth Edition

10 9 8 7 6 5 4 3 2 1

Contents

Acknowledgments

Prices and pictures in this book are compiled with the help of dealers, collectors, companies, and, of course, our staff. Some of our sources do not realize that their prices are included in the book. We want to thank the dealers and shops who knowingly or unknowingly helped determine the prices in the marketplace. Thank you to: AA Bit Depressed; Always Available Antiques and Collectibles; The Archive—Antiques & Collectibles; Attic Antiques; Backward Glances; Black Run Antiques; Blondie's Antiques; Cape Cod Glassware; Celebration Shoppe; Cheshire Cat Antiques & Collectibles; Classic Antiques, Inc.; Collector Online; Jane Cowan; Cyber Attic Antiques and Collectibles; Dgplace.com; Dishes Delmar; Ed & Judy's; Edie's Glassware; Mary D. Every; Fiftys-Dish; First Class Glass; Cindy Frank; Lorene Gable; Glass, Antique or Not; The Glass Cellar; Home Grown Antiques; Just Glass; Kaleidoscope; L & T Collectibles; Legacy Glass; Marwig Glass Store; My Glass Duchess; Nostalgic Glassware; Old Parsonage Antiques; Patty Ann's Depression Era Glassware; R & M Antiques; Recollections; Recollections—Maine; Robbins Nest; Sandra Rosenberg; Ruby Lane; Sarah's Glass Menagerie; Simple Pleasures; Sparkle Plenty Glass; Strawser Auctions; Suzman's Antiques; Time Was; Under the Influence; Waltz Time Antiques. Thanks also to the nameless dealers with booths filled with Depression glass or dinnerware who allowed us to record their prices for the book. David Stratton of the Salem Historical Society is just one of many experts who gave us extra attention. He kept searching until he found the official date of the demise of the Salem China Company. Special thanks also go to our friend Phil Davies of TIAS (The Internet Antique Shop at www.tias.com). He helped us locate many dealers and prices.

The pictures for the book came from many sources. Most of the glass and some of the ceramic and plastic dinnerware were photographed by Benjamin Margolit, who works with us on many books. This year he took new photos of many patterns because digital technology has made it possible to show even greater details of patterns. Special thanks to

Liam Sullivan and the imaging department at Replacements Ltd. They furnished many of the pictures of the dinnerware patterns from their huge stock of dishes. To find out if they have replacements for a glass or dinnerware pattern, call 1-800-REPLACE.

And of course we thank the staff at Random House Reference— Jeanne Kramer, publisher; David Naggar, president and publisher of Random House Information Group; Dorothy Harris, our editor; and Lindsey Glass, Beth Levy, Lisa Montebello, and Geraldine Sarmiento. Merri Ann Morrell at Precision Graphics once again created the pages from the electronic data.

Our amazing staff recorded the prices, assembled the pictures, and wrote and rewrote the paragraphs. Thanks to Linda Coulter, Grace DeFrancisco; Doris Gerbitz, Marcia Goldberg, Evelyn Hayes, Katie Karrick, Kim Kovel, Liz Lillis, Heidi Makela, Tina McBean, Nancy Saada, Julie Seaman, June Smith, and Cherrie Smrekar. The pictures come to us in many forms—drawings, black and white and color photographs, and digital images. Karen Kneisley turns all of them into clear pictures with no extra background. She can work magic. Gay Hunter is the major domo of the book. She keeps us all on schedule, reads and rereads the copy, researches and keeps track of all the changes in paragraphs, and handles any other problems that arise. We thank all of them for making this the best possible source for quick information. The cover of the book says Kovel, but that is only because there is not room for sixteen more names.

DEPRESSION GLASS

DEPRESSION GLASS

Introduction

This book is a price report. Prices are actual offerings in the marketplace during the last twelve months. They are not averages. The high and low prices represent different sales. There is sometimes a surprisingly large range of prices. Although only high and low are reported in the book, we may have recorded ten or more in-between prices that are not shown. Prices reported are not those from garage or house sales. They are from dealers and collectors who understand the Depression glass market and who sell at shops, at shows, on the Internet, or through national advertising.

This is a book for beginners as well as for serious collectors of Depression glass. We have included those patterns, both Depression and "elegant" patterns of glass, most often offered for sale. Each year the patterns chosen change slightly because collector interest is changing. There are more patterns of elegant glassware; kitchen glass by Hazel Atlas, Jeannette, Pyrex, and McKee; designer glassware that was made to go with ceramic dinnerware; and patterns by name designers like Russel Wright or Eva Zeisel. Most of the pattern names used are from the original glass factories' catalogs, but a few are just collectors' nicknames. We have gone beyond the exact definition of the term "Depression glass" and list patterns made between 1925 and 1970, including many newly popular patterns.

Opaque glass was popular in the 1930s. Each of the colors was given a special name by the company that produced it. "Monax" and "Ivrene" are opaque white glasswares. Opaque green glass was known by a variety of names. "Jade Green" is a generic name used by many companies. "Jade-ite" was the green used by Anchor Hocking; Jeannette Glass Company called their green kitchenware "Jadite." "Delphite," an opaque blue glass, is sometimes spelled "Delfite" in the ads, but we have chosen to always use the "Delphite" spelling.

A few forms are used consistently in the wording of entries. It is always a sugar & creamer, not a creamer & sugar. A pickle dish is listed as a pickle. An open salt dish is listed as a salt, but a saltshaker has its full name or is part of a salt and pepper set. Some pieces were made for dual use. A high sherbet may have been called a champagne goblet by some factories. We use the term preferred by the factory. Most glassware with a stem is called a goblet in this book, with the exception of sherbet and oyster cocktail glasses. A tumbler can have a flat or footed bottom but not a stem. A shot glass is listed here as a whiskey. We list not only the size of a plate, but also what it is commonly called; thus the listing would be "plate, dinner, 10 in." The size of a dinner plate varies slightly with each pattern, and we have used the actual size. A plate meant to sit under a sauce dish is listed as an underplate, not a liner. If there is a pair of candlesticks or salts or compotes, the word "pair" is included as the last word in the listing. Sometimes individual parts, like covers for butter dishes, are sold. These items are listed, for instance, as "butter, cover only." When a dealer says a piece is "Book One" or "Book Two," it is a pattern of glassware listed in *A Guidebook to Colored Glassware of the 1920s and 1930s* or *Colored Glassware of the Depression Era 2* by Hazel Marie Weatherman. (Book Two is still available. See References on page 137).

This book is not an in-depth study of Depression glass. The beginner who needs more information about patterns, manufacturers, color groups, or how and where to buy should use the bibliography, factory list, and club and publication list we have included. E-mail and website addresses are included if available. All of these lists follow the last glass price entries.

This year, if a reproduction of a pattern is known, we have tried to include it in the paragraph describing the pattern in the Depression glass listing. Hundreds of patterns, many not listed in other price books, are included here. The best way to learn about Depression glass is to attend the regional and national shows devoted to glass. Your local newspaper or the collectors' publications listed in this book will print the dates and locations.

Ceramic dinnerware, see pages 143–239.

Plastic dinnerware, see pages 241–253.

DEPRESSION GLASS

Color Names

Here are some of the names used by companies to describe the glass-ware colors:

AMBER	Apricot, Desert Gold, Golden Glow, Mocha, Topaz
BLUE-GREEN	Limelight, Teal Blue, Ultramarine, Zircon
CHARCOAL GRAY	Dawn, Smoke
CLEAR	Crystal
DEEP BLUE	Cobalt, Dark Blue, Deep Blue, Regal Blue, Ritz Blue, Royal Blue, Stiegel Blue
GREEN	Avocado, Emerald, Evergreen, Forest Green, Imperial Green, Moongleam, Nu-Green, Olive, Pistachio, Springtime Green, Stiegel Green, Verde
LIGHT BLUE	Azure, Moonlight Blue, Willow Blue
MEDIUM BLUE	Capri Blue, Madonna, Ritz Blue
OPAQUE BLACK	Black, Ebony
OPAQUE BLUE	Delphite
OPAQUE GREEN	Jade, Jade-ite, Jadite
OPAQUE OFF-WHITE	Azure-ite, Chinex, Clambroth, Cremax, Ivrene
OPAQUE PINK	Crown Tuscan, Shell Pink, Rose-ite
OPAQUE WHITE	Anchorwhite, Milk Glass, Milk White, Monax

PINK	Azalea, Cheri-Glo, Flamingo, LaRosa, Nu-Rose, Peach-Blo, Rose, Rose Glow, Rose Marie, Rose Pink, Rose Tint, Wild Rose
PURPLE	Alexandrite, Amethyst, Black Amethyst, Burgundy, Hawthorne, Heatherbloom, Moroccan Amethyst, Mulberry, Orchid, Wisteria
RED	Carmen, Royal Ruby, Ruby Red
YELLOW	Canary, Chartreuse, Gold Krystol, Marigold, Sahara, Topaz

1700 LINE

Anchor Hocking Glass Corporation, Lancaster, Ohio, made the 1700 line from 1946 to 1958. The plain dishes were made in Ivory, Jade-ite, and Milk White. Other related patterns are listed in the Fire-King section in this book.

Ivory
Cup & Saucer,
St. Denis 14.00

ADAM

Adam, sometimes called Chain Daisy or Fan & Feather, is a glass pattern made from 1932 to 1934 by the Jeannette Glass Company, Jeannette, Pennsylvania. Pink glass sets are the most common, but Crystal, Delphite, and Green pieces were also made. A few pieces are known in Yellow, but this does not seem to have been a standard production color. Reproductions have been made.

Crystal
Ashtray, 4 1/2 In. 25.00
Sugar, Cover 38.00
Green
Ashtray, 4 1/2 In. 25.00
Bowl, 7 3/4 In. 21.00

Bowl, Cereal,
5 3/4 In. . . . . . . 50.00 to 67.00
Bowl, Dessert,
4 3/4 In. . . . . . . 23.00 to 28.00
Bowl, Oval, 10 In. 53.00
Bowl, Vegetable,
7 3/4 In. 125.00
Butter, No
Cover . . . . 65.00 to 125.00
Cake Plate, Footed,
10 In. . . . . 33.00 to 37.00
Candlestick, 4 In., Pair . . 162.00
Coaster, 3 1/4 In. 20.00
Cup 30.00
Grill Plate,
9 In. . . . . 22.00 to 30.00
Plate, Dinner, Square,
9 In. . . . . 30.00 to 36.00
Plate, Salad, Square,
7 3/4 In. . . . . . . 17.00 to 25.00
Platter, Oval, 11 3/4 In. . . 46.00
Relish, 2 Sections,
8 In. . . . . 11.00 to 26.00
Saucer, Square, 6 In. 6.00
Sherbet, 3 In. 38.00
Sugar &
Creamer . . . . . . 60.00 to 77.00
Tumbler, 7 Oz., 4 1/2 In. . 39.00
Tumbler, Iced Tea, 9 Oz.,
5 1/2 In. . . . . . . 50.00 to 80.00
Vase,
7 1/2 In. . . . . 145.00 to 160.00
Pink
Ashtray, 4 1/2 In. 35.00
Bowl, 7 3/4 In. . . 30.00 to 40.00
Bowl, 9 In. . . . . . 19.00 to 35.00
Bowl, Cereal, 5 3/4 In. . . . 26.00
Bowl, Cover,
9 In. . . . . 69.00 to 78.00
Bowl, Dessert,
4 3/4 In. . . . . . . 15.00 to 25.00
Bowl, Sugar, Cover 60.00
Bowl, Vegetable, Oval,
10 In. . . . . 16.00 to 35.00
Butter, Cover . . 95.00 to 135.00
Butter, No
Cover . . . . 25.00 to 33.00
Cake Plate, Footed,
10 In. . . . . 15.00 to 40.00
Candlestick, 4 In.,
Pair . . . . 55.00 to 125.00
Candy Jar, 2 1/2 In. 61.00

Candy Jar, Cover,
2 1/2 In. . . . . 138.00 to 150.00
Coaster,
3 1/4 In. . . . . . . 17.00 to 19.00
Creamer . . . . 13.00 to 30.00
Cup . . . . 30.00 to 35.00
Cup & Saucer . . . 31.00 to 40.00
Grill Plate,
9 In. . . . . 15.00 to 26.00
Pitcher, Round, 32 Oz.,
8 In. 90.00
Pitcher, Square, 32 Oz.,
8 In. . . . . 46.00 to 60.00
Plate, Dinner, Square,
9 In. . . . . 26.00 to 45.00
Plate, Salad, Square,
7 3/4 In. . . . . . . 15.00 to 23.00
Plate, Sherbet,
6 In. . . . . 8.00 to 13.00
Platter,
11 3/4 In. . . . . . 25.00 to 46.00
Relish, 2 Sections,
8 In. . . . . 21.00 to 28.00
Salt & Pepper, Footed . . 110.00
Saltshaker, Footed 55.00
Saucer, Square, 6 In. 6.00
Sherbet, 3 In. . . 24.00 to 35.00
Sugar . . . . 23.00 to 45.00
Sugar, Cover . . . 37.00 to 59.00
Sugar, Cover
Only . . . . 28.00 to 30.00
Sugar & Creamer,
Cover . . . . 46.00 to 85.00
Tumbler, 7 Oz.,
4 1/2 In. . . . . . . 26.00 to 35.00
Tumbler, Iced Tea, 9 Oz.,
5 1/2 In. 90.00

ADDIE

Addie is the name collectors use for New Martinsville Glass Manufacturing Company's No. 34 pattern. Items were made in Black,

Cobalt, Crystal, Green,
Jade Green, Pink, Red,
and with silver encrusted
designs in the 1930s.
Amber and Amethyst
were made later by Viking
Glass Company.

Amber

Creamer	14.00
Cup	8.50
Plate, 8 1/4 In.	8.25
Sherbet, 2 In.	12.00
Sugar	14.00

Amethyst

Cup	14.00
Plate, 8 In.	12.00
Plate, 10 3/4 In.	40.00

Black

Sugar	18.00

Crystal

Cup & Saucer	12.00
Plate, 8 In.	12.00

Green

Cup & Saucer	12.00
Plate, 10 3/4 In.	22.00

Red

Cup & Saucer	24.00
Plate, 8 1/4 In.	20.00
Sugar & Creamer	65.00

AKRO AGATE

Picture a marble cake with
an irregular mixture of
colors running through
the batter. This is what
Akro Agate usually looks
like—a marbleized mix-
ture of clear and opaque
colored glass. The Akro
Agate Company, Clarks-
burg, West Virginia, originally made children's
marbles. The marbleized

children's sets and accessories were made in many
colors from 1932 to 1951.

Azure Blue

Creamer, Stacked Disc, 1 1/4 In.	35.00
Sugar, No Cover, Stacked Disc, 1 1/4 In.	35.00
Teapot, No Cover, Stacked Disc, 2 3/8 In.	15.00

Blue & White

Ashtray, Leaf	8.00
Cup & Saucer, Concentric Ring	30.00
Flowerpot, Rib Top, 2 1/4 In.	14.00

Blue Luster

Teapot, Cover, Interior Panel, 2 3/8 In.	75.00

Green & Brown

Flowerpot	22.00

Green & White

Cup, After Dinner, 2 1/8 In.	17.00
Cup & Saucer, Octagonal	22.00
Cup & Saucer, Stacked Disc & Interior Panel	35.00
Flowerpot, Flared, 4 In.	30.00
Flowerpot, Stacked Disc, 2 3/8 In.	22.00
Plate, Octagonal, 4 1/4 In.	10.00

Green Luster

Bowl, Cereal, Interior Panel, 3 3/8 In.	35.00
Cup, Interior Panel, 1 3/8 In.	8.00
Cup & Saucer, Interior Panel	30.00
Plate, 3 1/4 In.	9.00
Saucer, Interior Panel, 3 1/8 In.	7.00 to 8.00
Sugar, Interior Panel, 1 3/8 In.	45.00
Teapot, Cover, Interior Panel, 2 3/8 In.	45.00

Ivory

Saucer, Octagonal, 2 3/4 In.	4.00
Tumbler, Octagonal, 1 3/4 In.	20.00

Lilac

Cup, Chiquita, 1 1/2 In.	35.00

Opaque Blue

Pitcher, Stacked Disc, 2 3/8 In.	90.00
Saucer, Octagonal, 3 1/8 In.	16.00
Teapot, Stacked Disc, 2 3/8 In.	8.00

Opaque Dark Blue

Plate, Concentric Ring, 3 1/4 In.	10.00

Opaque Green

Cup, Chiquita, 1 1/2 In.	4.00
Cup, Interior Panel	18.00
Cup, Octagonal, 1 1/2 In.	16.00
Cup & Saucer, Chiquita	10.00
Cup & Saucer, Concentric Ring	18.00
Plate, Concentric Rib, 4 1/4 In.	8.00
Plate, Concentric Ring, 3 1/4 In.	5.00
Plate, Concentric Ring, 4 1/4 In.	6.00
Plate, Octagonal, 3 3/8 In.	5.00
Plate, Octagonal, 3 3/4 In.	7.50
Plate, Octagonal, 4 1/4 In.	8.00 to 9.00
Saucer	7.00
Saucer, Concentric Ring, 3 1/8 In.	4.00 to 7.00
Sugar & Creamer, Chiquita, 1 1/2 In.	20.00
Teapot, Interior Panel, 2 5/8 In.	15.00

Orange & White

Ashtray, Leaf, Stippled Band	12.00
Flowerpot, 3 In.	30.00
Flowerpot, Ribbed Top, 2 1/4 In.	15.00
Planter, 5 1/2 x 3 In.	15.00
Planter, Daffodils, 5 3/8 x 3 In.	22.00

Oxblood & White

Ashtray	35.00

Pink

Plate, Concentric Ring, 2 3/4 In.	12.00

Saucer, Octagonal,
2 3/4 In. 10.00

Teapot, Stacked Disc,
2 3/8 In. 30.00

Tumbler, Stacked Disc,
1 3/4 In. 16.00

Pumpkin
Cup, Octagonal, Open
Handle, 1 1/2 In. 35.00

Transparent Cobalt
Bowl, Cereal, Stacked
Disc & Interior Panel,
3 3/8 In. 60.00

Creamer, Stacked Disc
& Interior Panel,
1 1/4 In. . . . . . . 20.00 to 25.00

Cup, Chiquita, 1 1/2 In. . . . 4.00

Cup, Concentric Ring,
1 1/4 In. 65.00

Cup, Stacked Disc & Interior
Panel, 1 3/8 In. 4.00

Cup & Saucer, Chiquita . . 18.00

Cup & Saucer, Stacked
Disc & Interior Panel . . 50.00

Plate, Chiquita, 3 3/4 In. . . 12.00

Plate, Stacked Disc
& Interior Panel,
3 1/4 In. 25.00

Saucer, Chiquita,
3 1/8 In. 6.00

Saucer, Stacked Disc
& Interior Panel,
3 1/8 In. 15.00

Sugar, Chiquita, 1 1/2 In. . 18.00

Sugar, Cover, Interior
Panel, 1 1/4 In. 100.00

Teapot, Interior Panel,
2 3/8 In. . . . . . . 40.00 to 45.00

Teapot, Stacked Disc &
Interior Panel,
2 3/8 In. . . . . . . 65.00 to 75.00

Tumbler, Stacked Disc
& Interior Panel,
1 3/4 In. 30.00

Transparent Green
Bowl, Cereal, Interior
Panel, 3 3/8 In. 35.00

Creamer, Interior Panel,
1 1/4 In. 75.00

Creamer, Interior Panel,
1 3/8 In. 40.00

Cup, Stippled Band,
1 1/2 In. 15.00

Cup, Stippled Band,
1 1/4 In. . . . . . . 12.00 to 20.00

Cup & Saucer, Interior
Panel, 1 1/4 In. 32.00

Cup & Saucer, Stippled
Band, 1 1/4 In. 30.00

Plate, Interior Panel,
3 1/4 In. 15.00

Plate, Interior Panel,
4 1/4 In. 18.00

Plate, Stacked Disc & Interior
Panel, 3 1/4 In. 20.00

Saucer, Interior Panel,
3 1/4 In. 12.00

Saucer, Stippled Band,
3 1/4 In. 8.00

Saucer, Stippled Band,
3 1/8 In. 10.00

Sugar, Interior Panel,
1 3/8 In. 50.00

Teapot, Cover, Interior
Panel, 2 3/8 In. 50.00

Teapot, Cover, Interior
Panel, 2 5/8 In. 95.00

Teapot, Cover, Stippled
Band, 2 3/8 In. 45.00

Teapot, Stippled Band,
2 3/8 In. 30.00

Tumbler, Interior Panel,
2 In. 20.00

Tumbler, Stippled Band,
1 3/4 In. 11.00

Transparent Topaz
Bowl, Cereal, Interior
Panel, 3 1/2 In. 30.00

Bowl, Cereal, Interior
Panel, 3 3/8 In. 18.00

Creamer, Interior Panel,
1 1/2 In. . . . . . 32.00 to 40.00

Creamer, Stippled Band,
1 1/2 In. . . . . . 20.00 to 28.00

Cup, Interior Panel,
1 1/2 In. . . . . . 20.00 to 35.00

Cup, Interior Panel,
1 3/8 In. 25.00

Cup, Stippled Band,
1 1/2 In. 20.00

Cup & Saucer, Interior
Panel, 3 1/8 In. 32.00

Cup & Saucer, Interior
Panel, 3 1/4 In. 40.00

Cup & Saucer, Stippled
Band, 3 1/4 In. 20.00

Plate, Interior Panel,
3 1/4 In. 12.00

Plate, Interior Panel,
4 1/4 In. . . . . . 18.00 to 20.00

Plate, Stippled Band,
3 1/4 In. . . . . . . 6.00 to 10.00

Plate, Stippled Band,
4 1/4 In. 10.00

Saucer, Interior Panel,
3 1/8 In. 8.00

Saucer, Stippled Band,
3 1/4 In. 5.00

Sugar, Cover, Stippled Band,
1 1/2 In. . . . . . 35.00 to 50.00

Sugar, Interior Panel,
1 1/2 In. 60.00

Teapot, Cover, Interior
Panel, 2 3/8 In. 90.00

Teapot, Cover, Interior Panel,
2 1/2 In. . . . . . 70.00 to 95.00

Teapot, Cover, Stippled
Band, 2 3/8 In. 55.00

Teapot, Interior Panel,
2 3/8 In. 18.00

Teapot, Stippled Band,
2 3/8 In. 25.00

White
Saucer, Concentric Ring,
2 3/4 In. 6.00

Tumbler, Stacked Disc,
2 In. . . . . 16.00 to 17.00

Yellow
Creamer, Concentric
Ring, 1 1/4 In. 20.00

Creamer, Octagonal,
1 1/4 In. 25.00

Saucer, Concentric
Ring, 3 1/8 In. 7.00

Saucer, Octagonal,
3 1/8 In. 10.00

Tumbler, Octagonal,
1 3/4 In. 20.00

ALICE

An 8 1/2-inch plate, cup,
and saucer were appar-
ently the only pieces made
in the Alice pattern. The
pattern was made by the
Anchor Hocking Glass
Corporation, Lancaster,
Ohio, from 1945 to 1949
in Ivory, Jade-ite, and
Opaque White with a red
or blue border. Other
related patterns are listed

in the Fire-King section in this book.

Ivory
Cup & Saucer 10.00
Plate, Dinner, 9 1/4 In. . . . 26.00

Jade-ite
Cup & Saucer . . . 18.00 to 22.00
Plate, Dinner, 9 1/4 In. . . . 45.00

White
Cup & Saucer,
Blue Trim 12.50

AMERICAN

American is a pattern made to resemble the pressed glass of an earlier time. It was introduced by Fostoria Glass Company, Moundsville, West Virginia, in 1915 and remained in production until the factory closed in 1986. Most pieces were made of clear, colorless glass known as Crystal. A few pieces are known in Amber, Blue, Green, Milk Glass, Red, and Yellow. It is similar to Cubist pattern. Many pieces of American pattern were reproduced after 1987.

Blue
Handkerchief Box, Cover, 5 5/8
x 4 5/8 In. 830.00

Crystal
Appetizer Set, 10 1/2-In.
Tray, 7 Piece 350.00
Ashtray, 1 1/4 In. 28.00
Ashtray, Square,
2 7/8 In. . . . . 7.00 to 8.00

Ashtray, Square,
5 In. . . . . 35.00 to 85.00
Basket, Reeded Handle,
7 In. 95.00
Bowl, 3-Footed,
10 1/2 In. . . . . . 30.00 to 40.00
Bowl, Centerpiece, Footed,
9 1/2 In. . . . . . 80.00 to 110.00
Bowl, Cupped, 7 In. 50.00
Bowl, Deep, 4 3/4 In. 20.00
Bowl, Float, Oval,
11 3/4 In. 65.00
Bowl, Fruit, 13 In. 85.00
Bowl, Fruit, Footed,
12 In. 225.00
Bowl, Fruit, Footed,
16 In. 250.00
Bowl, Handle, Tricornered,
5 In. 12.00
Bowl, Oval, 4 1/2 In. 20.00
Bowl, Square, Handle,
4 1/2 In. 10.00
Bowl, Trophy, Handles,
8 1/2 In. 60.00
Bowl, Vegetable, Oval,
9 In. 25.00
Butter, Cover, 1/4 Lb. 25.00
Butter, Cover, 1 Lb. 120.00
Cake Stand, Round,
Pedestal, 10 In. 125.00
Cake Stand, Square,
Pedestal, 10 In. 310.00
Candle Lamp, Chimney,
4 5/8 In. 75.00
Candleholder, Bell
Base 165.00
Candlestick, 2-Light, 4 1/8 In.,
Pair . . . . 95.00 to 110.00
Candlestick, 8-Sided Foot,
6 In., Pair 50.00
Candlestick, Footed,
3 In., Pair 30.00
Candy Box, 3 Sections,
3 Sides 90.00
Coaster,
3 3/4 In. . . . . . . 9.00 to 12.00
Coaster Set, 3 3/4 In.,
8 Piece 125.00
Compote, 9 1/2 In. 75.00
Cookie Jar, Cover,
8 7/8 In. . . . . 250.00 to 285.00
Creamer . . . . . . 12.00 to 15.00
Creamer,
Individual . . . . . 9.00 to 12.00

Cruet, Stopper, 5 Oz. 54.00
Cup 9.00
Cup & Saucer . . . . 5.00 to 10.00
Decanter, Brandy,
7 1/4 In. 150.00
Decanter, Stopper, 24 Oz.,
9 1/4 In. . . . . . 75.00 to 100.00
Dish, Mayonnaise, 2 Sections,
Ladle 95.00
Dish, Sundae, Footed,
6 Oz. 8.00
Goblet, 6-Sided Foot,
10 Oz., 7 In. 12.00
Goblet, Iced Tea, Low Foot,
12 Oz., 5 3/4 In. 15.00
Goblet, Water, 6-Sided
Foot, 10 Oz.,
6 7/8 In. . . . . . 12.00 to 14.00
Goblet, Wine, 6-Sided
Foot, 2 1/2 Oz.,
4 3/8 In. . . . . . 12.00 to 22.00
Hat, 3 In. 25.00
Ice Tub,
6 1/2 In. . . . . . 55.00 to 80.00
Jam Jar, Cover,
6 3/4 In. . . . . . 35.00 to 40.00
Match Holder, 2 1/2 In. . . 25.00
Mug, Beer, 12 Oz. 75.00
Mug, Tom & Jerry,
5 1/2 Oz., 3 1/4 In. 40.00
Nappy, 5 In. 15.00
Nappy, Cover, 5 In. 25.00
Nappy, Handle,
4 1/2 In. . . . . . 10.00 to 13.00
Nappy, Handle, 8 In. 65.00
Oyster Cocktail,
4 1/2 Oz., 3 1/2 In. 18.00
Pickle Jar, Cover,
4 3/4 In. 330.00
Pitcher, 1 Pt., 5 3/8 In. . . . 35.00
Pitcher, 1/2 Gal.,
8 1/4 In. 195.00
Pitcher, Ice Lip, 3-Footed,
3 Pt., 6 1/2 In. 60.00
Pitcher, Ice Lip, Straight
Sides, 1/2 Gal. 105.00
Pitcher, Water, Ice Lip,
Sunburst Bottom,
1/2 Gal., 8 In. 120.00
Plate, Salad, 7 In. 10.00
Plate, Salad, 8 1/2 In. 6.00
Platter, Oval, 10 1/2 In. . . 50.00
Puff Box, Square,
3 In. 150.00

Punch Bowl, Stand,
    14 1/2 x 13 In. 700.00
Punch Cup . . . . . 11.00 to 13.00
Relish, Oval, 6 In. 13.00
Rose Bowl, 3 1/2 In. 24.00
Rose Bowl,
    5 In. . . . . 30.00 to 40.00
Salt & Pepper, 3 In. 20.00
Saltshaker, 3 In. 10.00
Sandwich Server, Center
    Handle, 9 In. 22.00
Sauceboat, Underplate . . . 55.00
Sauceboat, Underplate Only
    Oval, 8 In. 20.00
Saucer 5.00
Sherbet, 4 1/2 Oz.,
    4 1/2 In. . . . . 6.00 to 9.00
Sherbet, 5 Oz., 3 1/4 In. . . . 9.00
Sherbet, 5 Oz., 3 1/2 In. . . . 9.00
Sherbet, 6-Sided Foot,
    4 1/2 Oz., 4 3/4 In. 14.00
Sherbet, Flared, 4 1/2 Oz.,
    4 3/8 In. 9.00
Sherbet, Flared, 5 1/2 Oz.,
    3 1/4 In. . . . . 8.00 to 9.00
Strawholder, Cover,
    10 In. 35.00
Sugar, 2 1/4 In. 13.00
Sugar, 3 1/4 In. 12.00
Sugar Cuber, Silver
    Cover, Round, Tongs,
    6 1/4 In. . . . . 300.00 to 450.00
Sugar Shaker . . 75.00 to 125.00
Syrup, Bakelite
    Handle, 5 1/4 In. 225.00
Syrup, Sani-Cut
    Server, 6 1/2 Oz. 95.00
Torte Plate, 14 In. 75.00
Tray, Handles, 9 In. 20.00
Tray, Round, 12 In. 175.00
Tumbler, Cocktail,
    Cone, Footed, 3 Oz.,
    2 7/8 In. 20.00
Tumbler, Juice, Footed, 5 Oz.,
    4 3/4 In. . . . . . . 12.00 to 15.00
Tumbler, Water, 8 Oz.,
    4 1/8 In. 16.00
Tumbler, Whiskey, 2 Oz.,
    2 1/2 In. 10.00
Vase, Flared, 10 In. 260.00
Vase, Flared, Square Foot,
    9 In. 125.00

Wedding Bowl, Cover,
    6 1/2 x 8 In. 160.00
Green
Tray, Round, 12 In. . . . 115.00
Yellow
Bonbon, 3-Footed,
    7 In. 290.00

AMERICAN BEAUTY
See English Hobnail

AMERICAN HOBNAIL

Westmoreland Glass
Company made American
Hobnail, its version of the
popular hobnail design,
beginning in the early
1930s. Golden Sunset,
Brandywine Blue, Laurel
Green, and Milk Glass
pieces were made.

Milk Glass
Puff Box, 5 In. 27.00
Shaker, 4 1/4 In. 16.00
Sherbet 15.00

AMERICAN LADY

American Lady stemware
was made to complement

American tableware by
Fostoria Glass Company,
Moundsville, West Vir-
ginia, from 1933 to 1973.
Items were made in Crys-
tal or with Crystal bases
and Amethyst, Burgundy,
Empire Green, or Regal
Blue bowls.

Amethyst
Goblet, Water, 10 Oz.,
    5 1/2 In. 15.00
Goblet, Water, 10 Oz.,
    6 1/8 In. 22.00
Sherbet,
    4 1/8 In. . . . . . . 10.00 to 17.00
Crystal
Cordial 25.00
Platter, 3-Footed, Raised
    Rim, 12 In. 15.00
Sherbet . . . . 5.00 to 10.00
Regal Blue
Goblet, Water, 10 Oz.,
    6 1/8 In. . . . . . . 70.00 to 80.00
Sherbet, 5 1/2 Oz.,
    4 1/8 In. 85.00
Tumbler, Juice, Footed,
    5 Oz., 4 3/4 In. 125.00

AMERICAN MODERN

Morgantown Glass Works
made glassware to match
Russel Wright's American
Modern ceramic dinner-
ware in 1951. Stemware
and tumblers were made
in specially developed
colors: Chartreuse, Coral
(pink), Crystal, Seafoam
(light teal), and Smoke.

Chartreuse
Goblet, Cocktail, 3 Oz.,
    2 1/2 In. 43.00
Goblet, Cordial, 2 Oz.,
    2 In. 43.00
Tumbler, Juice, 8 Oz.,
    3 3/4 In. 43.00
Tumbler, Water, 12 Oz.,
    4 1/2 In. 43.00

Coral

Goblet, Cocktail, 3 Oz.,
2 1/2 In. 53.00

Sherbet, 5 Oz.,
2 3/4 In. 40.00

Tumbler, Iced Tea,
15 Oz., 5 1/4 In. 43.00

Tumbler, Water, 12 Oz.,
4 1/2 In. 43.00

Smoke

Goblet, Cocktail, 3 Oz.,
2 1/2 In. 38.00

Sherbet, 5 Oz.,
2 3/4 In. 35.00

Tumbler, Juice, 8 Oz.,
3 3/4 In. 40.00

AMERICAN PIONEER

Panels of hobnail-like protrusions and plain panels were used in the design of American Pioneer. It was made by Liberty Works, Egg Harbor, New Jersey, from 1931 to 1934. Crystal, Green, and Pink dishes are easily found. Amber is rare.

Crystal

Creamer 22.00

Cup & Saucer 15.00

Sugar 20.00

Sugar & Creamer 38.00

Green

Candy Jar, No Cover 95.00

Cup & Saucer 15.00

Plate, Luncheon, 8 In. 15.00

Pink

Candy Jar, Cover 101.00

Cup 15.00

Cup & Saucer 19.00

Plate, Handles,
11 1/2 In. 35.00

AMERICAN SWEETHEART

In 1930 Macbeth-Evans Glass Company introduced American Sweetheart. At first it was made of pink glass, but soon other colors were added. The pattern continued in production until 1936. Blue, Cremax, Monax, Pink, and Red pieces were made. Sometimes a gold, green, pink, platinum, red, or smoky black trim was used on Monax pieces. There is a center design on most plates, but some Monax plates are found with plain centers. One of the rarest items in this pattern is the Monax sugar bowl lid. The bowls are easy to find, but the lids seem to have broken.

Blue

Salver, 12 In. 200.00

Cremax

Bowl, Cereal, 6 In. 20.00

Monax

Berry Bowl, Master,
9 In. . . . . 60.00 to 77.00

Bowl, Cereal, 6 In. 19.00

Bowl, Vegetable, Oval,
11 In. . . . . 80.00 to 99.00

Chop Plate, 11 In. 25.00

Creamer,
Footed . . . . 8.50 to 12.00

Cup . . . . 10.00 to 15.00

Cup & Saucer . . . 10.00 to 17.00

Dinnerware Set,
42 Piece 600.00

Plate, Bread & Butter,
6 In. . . . . 5.00 to 8.00

Plate, Dinner,
9 3/4 In. . . . . . 20.00 to 36.00

Plate, Luncheon,
9 In. . . . . 10.00 to 19.00

Plate, Salad,
8 In. . . . . 10.00 to 15.00

Platter, 15 1/2 In. 250.00

Platter, Oval,
13 In. . . . . 42.00 to 89.00

Salt & Pepper,
Footed 525.00

Saltshaker,
Footed . . . . . 250.00 to 475.00

Salver, 12 In. . . . 22.00 to 30.00

Saucer . . . . 2.00 to 7.00

Sherbet,
4 1/4 In. . . . . . 22.00 to 25.00

Soup, Cream,
4 1/2 In. 140.00

Soup, Dish,
9 1/2 In. . . . 100.00 to 110.00

Sugar, Cover 625.00

Sugar, Footed . . . . 7.00 to 15.00

Sugar &
Creamer . . . . . . 24.00 to 28.00

Tidbit, 3 Tiers, Gold Trim,
15 1/2 In. 500.00

Pink

Berry Bowl,
9 In. . . . . 55.00 to 65.00

Berry Bowl, Flat,
3 3/4 In. . . . . . 85.00 to 110.00

Bowl, Cereal,
6 In. . . . . 12.00 to 24.00

Bowl, Vegetable, Oval,
11 In. . . . . 62.00 to 95.00

Creamer . . . . 11.00 to 24.00

Cup . . . . 18.00 to 20.00

Cup & Saucer . . . 18.00 to 30.00

Pitcher, 60 Oz.,
7 1/2 In. 1400.00

Don't use ammonia to clean glasses that have gold or silver decorations.

Pitcher, 80 Oz.,
8 In. 1100.00
Plate, Bread & Butter,
6 In. . . . . 6.00 to 8.00
Plate, Dinner,
9 3/4 In. . . . . . . 35.00 to 45.00
Plate, Salad,
8 In. . . . . 14.00 to 18.00
Platter, Oval,
13 In. . . . . 31.00 to 71.00
Salver, 12 In. . . . 25.00 to 38.00
Sherbet,
3 3/4 In. . . . . . . 22.00 to 36.00
Sherbet,
4 1/4 In. . . . . . . 10.00 to 26.00
Soup, Cream,
4 1/2 In. . . . . . 95.00 to 120.00
Soup, Dish,
9 1/2 In. . . . . . . 80.00 to 85.00
Sugar, Footed . . . 12.00 to 22.00
Tumbler, 5 Oz.,
3 1/2 In. . . . . 125.00 to 140.00
Tumbler, 9 Oz.,
4 1/4 In. . . . . . 77.00 to 110.00

Red
Creamer . . . . . 165.00 to 245.00
Cup . . . . 120.00 to 125.00
Plate, Salad,
8 In. . . . . 125.00 to 150.00
Salver, 12 In. 150.00
Saucer . . . . 35.00 to 40.00
Tidbit, 2 Tiers 405.00

ANNIVERSARY

Pink Anniversary pattern
was made from 1947 to
1949, but it is still considered Depression glass by
collectors. Crystal pieces
are shown in a 1949 cata-
log. In the 1970s, Crystal

and Iridescent, a carnival-
glass-like amber color,
were used. The pattern
was the product of the
Jeannette Glass Company,
Jeannette, Pennsylvania.

Crystal
Cake Plate, Chrome
Cover, 12 1/2 In. 21.00
Cup & Saucer 6.00
Plate, Dinner, 10 In. 3.00
Plate, Sherbet, 6 1/4 In. . . . 2.00
Relish, 4 Sections,
Ruffled Edge 25.00
Sandwich Server,
12 1/2 In. 13.00
Sherbet, Footed 5.00
Sugar, Cover 9.00
Vase, 6 1/2 In. 13.00

Iridescent
Berry Bowl, 4 7/8 In. 5.00
Plate, Dinner, 9 In. . . . . . . , 7.00

Pink
Candy Dish, Cover 50.00

APPLE BLOSSOM
see Dogwood

ARCADY

Fostoria Glass Company
made pieces decorated
with the Arcady etch from
1936 to 1954. The pattern
was available in crystal only.

Cake Plate, Handle, 10 In. 55.00
Candelabrum, 3-Light . . . 75.00
Goblet, Champagne,
5 1/2 Oz., 5 3/8 In. 27.00
Goblet, Claret, 4 Oz.,
5 3/8 In. 27.00
Tumbler, Iced Tea,
Footed, 12 Oz., 6 In. . . . 27.00

ARGUS

Argus was made by Fos-
toria Glass Company from
1963 to 1980 for the
Henry Ford Museum. It is
based on a nineteenth-
century pressed glass
pattern. Stemware and
accessories were made in
Cobalt Blue, Crystal, Gray,
Olive, and Ruby.

Cobalt Blue
Sherbet, 8 Oz., 5 In. 13.00

Olive
Candy Dish, Cover 45.00
Goblet, Water, 10 1/2 Oz.,
6 7/16 In. 20.00
Goblet, Wine, 4 Oz.,
4 3/4 In. 18.00
Sherbet, 8 Oz., 5 In. 10.00
Tumbler, Iced Tea,
Footed, 13 Oz.,
6 3/4 In. . . . . . . 16.00 to 20.00
Tumbler, Old Fashioned,
10 Oz., 3 7/8 In. 16.00

Ruby
Goblet, Water, 10 1/2 Oz.,
6 1/2 In. . . . . . . 24.00 to 28.00
Plate, 8 In. 12.00

❖

**Display groups of
at least three
collectibles to create a
decorating impact.**

❖

AUNT POLLY

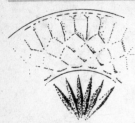

U.S. Glass Company, a firm with factories in Indiana, Ohio, Pennsylvania, and West Virginia, made Aunt Polly glass. Luncheon sets can be found in Blue, Green, and Iridescent. Pink pieces have been reported. The pattern was made in the late 1920s until c.1935.

Blue

Berry Bowl,
4 3/4 In. 23.00
Bowl, Oval,
8 3/4 In. . . . . . 29.00 to 40.00
Butter, Cover 165.00
Candy Dish, Handles,
Footed . . . . 25.00 to 55.00
Pickle, Oval, Handles,
7 1/4 In. . . . . . . 26.00 to 45.00
Pitcher, 48 Oz., 8 In. 235.00
Plate, Luncheon, 8 In. 25.00
Plate, Sherbet, 6 In. 14.00
Saltshaker 10.00
Sherbet . . . . 12.00 to 16.00
Tumbler, 8 Oz.,
3 5/8 In. . . . . . . 35.00 to 36.00
Vase, Footed,
6 1/2 In. 58.00

Green

Candy Dish, Handles,
Footed . . . . 10.25 to 21.50
Pickle, Oval, Handles,
7 1/4 In. . . . . . . 14.00 to 20.00
Sherbet 12.50

Iridescent

Butter, Cover 200.00
Sherbet 9.50

AURORA

The Hazel Atlas Glass Company made Aurora pattern glass in the late 1930s. Fewer than ten different pieces were made in Cobalt Blue and Pink, an even smaller quantity in Crystal and Green.

Cobalt Blue

Bowl, Cereal,
5 3/8 In. . . . . . . 7.00 to 19.00
Bowl, Deep,
4 1/2 In. . . . . . 70.00 to 83.00
Creamer, 4 1/2 In. 30.00
Cup & Saucer . . . 23.00 to 25.00
Plate, 6 1/2 In. . . 12.00 to 16.00
Saucer 6.00
Sherbet 30.00
Sugar & Creamer 10.00
Tumbler, 10 Oz.,
4 3/4 In. . . . . . . 11.00 to 28.00

Green

Bowl, Cereal, 5 3/8 In. . . . 11.00

Pink

Bowl, Cereal,
5 3/8 In. . . . . . 14.00 to 17.00
Cup 15.00

AVOCADO

Although the center fruit looks like a pear, the pattern has been named Avocado. It was made originally from 1923 to 1933 by the Indiana Glass Company, Dunkirk, Indiana, primarily in Green and

Pink. Some Crystal pieces were also produced. In 1974, Tiara reissued a line of pitchers and tumblers in Amethyst, Blue, Frosted Pink, Green, Pink, and Red. By 1982, pieces were made in Amber. The pattern is sometimes called Sweet Pear or No. 601.

Crystal

Bowl, 9 1/2 In. 18.00
Bowl, Handles, Oval,
8 In. . . . . 11.00 to 13.50
Bowl, Salad,
7 1/2 In. . . . . . . 6.00 to 25.00
Pickle, 9 In. 15.00

Green

Bowl, Deep, 9 1/2 In. . . . 150.00
Bowl, Handle,
7 In. . . . . 33.00 to 40.00
Bowl, Handles,
5 1/4 In. . . . . . 16.00 to 40.00
Creamer 38.00
Plate, Luncheon,
8 1/4 In. 60.00
Plate, Sherbet, 6 3/8 In. . . 24.00
Relish, Footed, 6 In. 35.00
Saucer 24.00
Sugar, Footed . . . 38.00 to 42.00

Pink

Plate, Luncheon,
8 1/4 In. 50.00
Sherbet 40.00

B PATTERN
see Dogwood

BALDA

Central Glass Works made Amber, Amethyst,

Green, and Pink pieces with the Balda etch in the 1920s and '30s.

Amethyst
Goblet, Cocktail 60.00
Goblet, Wine 60.00
Tumbler, Juice, Footed . . . 40.00

Green
Sherbet 16.00

Pink
Goblet, Cordial 60.00
Sandwich Server, Octagonal,
   Handle 55.00
Sherbet 60.00
Soup, Cream 60.00

BALLERINA
see Cameo

BAMBOO OPTIC

Bamboo Optic pattern was made by Liberty Works of Egg Harbor, New Jersey, about 1929. Pink and Green luncheon sets and other pieces were made. The pattern resembles Octagon.

Green
Creamer 10.00
Cup 5.00
Sherbet 3.50

Pink
Bowl, Rolled Edge,
   13 1/2 In. 95.00
Cup 5.00
Cup & Saucer 10.00
Plate, Luncheon, Octagonal,
   8 In. . . . . 6.00 to 8.00
Saucer 5.00

BANDED CHERRY
See Cherry Blossom

BANDED FINE RIB
See Coronation

BANDED PETALWARE
See Petalware

BANDED RAINBOW
See Ring

BANDED RIBBON
See New Century

BANDED RINGS
See Ring

BAROQUE

Fostoria Glass Company of Moundsville, West Virginia, made Baroque, or No. 2496, from 1936 to 1966. The dishes have molded fleur-de-lis—shaped handles and ridges. The pattern was made in Amber, Amethyst, Azure (blue), Cobalt Blue, Crystal, Green, Pink, Red, and Topaz (yellow). The same molds were used to make other glass patterns decorated with etched designs.

Azure
Bowl, 3-Footed, 7 In. 38.00
Creamer 25.00
Cup & Saucer 45.00
Goblet, Water, 9 Oz.,
   6 3/4 In. 45.00
Plate, Bread & Butter,
   6 In. 10.00
Plate, Dinner,
   9 1/2 In. 65.00
Plate, Salad, 7 1/2 In. 20.00
Relish, 3 Sections,
   10 In. 50.00
Sugar, 3 In. 25.00
Tumbler, Water, Footed,
   9 Oz., 5 1/2 In. 75.00
Vase, 7 In. 140.00

Crystal
Bowl, 3-Footed, 7 In. 45.00
Bowl, 4-Footed, Handles,
   10 1/2 In. . . . . . 35.00 to 38.00
Bowl, Flared, 12 In. 22.00
Bowl, Fruit, Tricornered,
   Handle, 4 In. 24.00
Bowl, Handle, 4 In. 13.00
Bowl, Handles, 10 In. 50.00
Candlestick, 2-Light,
   4 1/2 In. 35.00
Candlestick, Prisms,
   7 3/4 In., Pair 150.00
Compote, 4 3/4 In. 16.00
Creamer, 3 1/4 In. 10.00
Creamer, Footed,
   3 3/4 In. . . . . . . 10.00 to 18.00
Cup 10.00
Nut Dish, Footed, 7 In. . . . 20.00
Pickle, 3-Footed, 8 In. . . . 25.00
Plate, Bread & Butter,
   6 In. 3.00
Plate, Lady Finger,
   7 1/2 In. 19.00
Plate, Salad,
   7 1/2 In. . . . . 4.00 to 5.00
Relish, 3 Sections,
   10 In. 20.00
Salt & Pepper 135.00
Sandwich Server,
   Handle, 11 In. 20.00
Sherbet, 5 Oz.,
   3 3/4 In. . . . . . . 10.00 to 11.00
Sugar &
   Creamer . . . . . . 10.00 to 15.00
Tumbler, Water, 9 Oz.,
   4 1/4 In. 25.00
Tumbler, Water, Footed,
   9 Oz., 5 1/2 In. 24.00
Vase, 7 In. 95.00

Topaz
Bowl, Flared, 12 In. 40.00
Cake Plate, 10 In. 36.00
Candlestick, 5 1/2 In.,
   Pair . . . . 65.00 to 86.00
Cruet, Crystal Stopper,
   5 1/2 In. 30.00

Dish, Sweetmeat, Cover,
9 In. 138.00
Nut Dish, 3-Footed,
7 In. 45.00
Plate, Dinner,
9 1/2 In. 55.00
Relish, 3 Sections,
10 In. . . . . 28.00 to 36.00
Sauce Bowl 62.00
Vase, 7 In. 120.00

BASKET
See No. 615

BEADED BLOCK

Imperial Glass Company, Bellaire, Ohio, made Beaded Block from the 1920s to the 1950s. It was made in Crystal, Green, Ice Blue, Pink, Red, and White, as well as several opalescent colors, including Amber, Blue, Canary (vaseline), and Green. Iridescent Marigold pieces were also made. The molds originally had stippling in the blocks, leading collectors to call the early pieces Frosted Block. Some Iridescent Pink pieces made recently have been found marked with the IG trademark used from 1951 to 1977.

Blue
Vase, 5 1/4 In. 21.00
Vase, 6 In. . . . . . . 25.00 to 35.00

Canary
Plate, Square,
7 3/4 In. . . . . . . 26.00 to 50.00

Crystal
Bowl, Flared, 7 1/2 In. . . . 28.00
Creamer, Footed 18.00
Dish, Jelly, Flared,
Footed, 4 1/2 In. 20.00
Dish, Jelly, Footed,
4 1/2 In. . . . . . 18.00 to 21.00
Pitcher, 1 Pt.,
5 1/4 In. . . . . 50.00 to 100.00
Sugar, Footed 18.00

Green
Dish, Jelly, Footed,
4 1/2 In. 51.00
Pickle, Handles,
6 1/2 In. 18.00
Pitcher, 1 Pt., 5 1/4 In. . . 175.00
Plate, Square,
7 3/4 In. . . . . . 35.00 to 50.00
Sugar, Footed 12.00

Ice Blue
Celery Dish, 8 1/4 In. 60.00
Plate, Square, 7 3/4 In. . . . 43.00

Pink
Dish, Jelly, Handles,
4 1/2 In. 35.00
Tumbler, Juice,
5 1/4 In. 35.00
Vase, 6 In. . . . . . . 13.00 to 25.00

BEADED EDGE

Collectors call Westmoreland Glass Company's No. 22 pattern Beaded Edge. The dishes are a plain shape with "beads" around the edges. The pattern was produced mostly in Milk Glass from the late 1930s to the 1950s and is often decorated with enameled flowers, birds,

or fruit. Crystal and other colors can be found, too.

Crystal
Bowl, 7 1/2 In. 15.00
Bowl, Oval, Crimped,
Blackberries, 6 In. 20.00
Cake Plate, Zodiac, 15 In. 125.00
Cup 13.00
Plate, 7 1/2 In. 18.00
Plate, Dinner,
10 1/2 In. . . . . . 35.00 to 45.00
Plate, Luncheon,
8 1/2 In. 19.00
Saltshaker 40.00
Tumbler, Footed, 8 Oz. . . 18.00

Milk Glass
Bowl, Scalloped Rim,
6 1/2 In. 5.00
Compote, Cover,
6 1/2 In. 6.00
Creamer 35.00
Cup, Cherries 13.00
Cup & Saucer, Pears 13.00
Nappy, Cherry, Pear,
5 In. 16.00
Plate, Bread & Butter,
Fruit, 6 In. 9.00
Plate, Peaches, 7 1/2 In. . . . 3.25
Plate, Pears, 7 1/2 In. 10.00
Plate, Salad, 7 In. 22.00
Plate, Salad, Fruit, 7 In. . . 12.00
Plate, Salad, Peaches,
7 In. 15.00
Salt & Pepper 5.00
Sugar, Cover 35.00
Tumbler, Footed,
Cherries, Grapes 18.00

Red
Plate, Bread & Butter,
6 In. 10.00

BERWICK
See Bubble

BEVERAGE WITH
SAILBOATS
See White Ship

BIG RIB
See Manhattan

BLACK FOREST

Black Forest was first made in 1930 by Paden City Glass Manufacturing Company, Paden City, West Virginia. The etching pictures a moose and trees. The dishes were distributed by Van Deman & Son, New York City, and came in Amber, Black with gold, Cobalt Blue, Green, Light Blue, Pink, and Red.

Black
Vase, 6 1/2 In. 82.00
Vase, 10 In. 150.00

Pink
Console Set, 13-In. Bowl,
2 3/4-In. Candlesticks,
3 Piece 350.00

BLOCK
See Block Optic

BLOCK OPTIC

Block Optic, sometimes called Block, was made from 1929 to 1933 by the Hocking Glass Company, Lancaster, Ohio. Slight variations in the design of some pieces, like creamers and sugars, show that the pattern was redesigned at times. Green is the most common color, followed by Crystal, Pink, and Yellow. Amber and Blue examples are harder to find. Some pieces were made with a black stem or a black flat foot.

Crystal
Basket, 6 In. 12.00
Butter, Cover
Only . . . . 30.00 to 80.00
Goblet, 9 Oz.,
5 3/4 In. . . . . . . 10.00 to 28.00
Pitcher, 54 Oz.,
8 1/2 In. . . . . . 30.00 to 50.00
Pitcher, 80 Oz.,
8 In. . . . . 24.00 to 80.00
Sandwich Server,
10 1/4 In. . . . . 12.00 to 20.00
Sherbet, 5 1/2 Oz.,
3 1/4 In. . . . . . . 5.00 to 14.00
Sherbet, 6 Oz.,
4 3/4 In. . . . . . 10.00 to 11.00
Sugar & Creamer,
Cone Shape 10.00

Green
Berry Bowl,
4 1/2 In. . . . . . . 8.00 to 30.00
Berry Bowl, Master,
8 1/2 In. . . . . . 38.00 to 40.00
Bowl, Cereal,
5 1/4 In. . . . . . 16.00 to 21.00
Bowl, Salad, 7 1/4 In. . . . 130.00
Butter 85.00
Candlestick, 1 3/4 In. 60.00
Candy Jar, Cover Only . . . 45.00
Candy Jar, Cover,
2 1/4 In. 85.00
Candy Jar, Cover,
6 1/4 In. . . . . . 30.00 to 74.00
Console, Rolled Edge,
11 3/4 In. 100.00
Creamer, Cone
Shape . . . . 8.00 to 13.00
Creamer, Squat 18.00
Cup, Curly
Handle . . . . 7.00 to 8.00
Cup, Plain Handle 11.00
Cup & Saucer . . . 11.00 to 20.00

Cup & Saucer,
Frosted . . . . 16.00 to 17.00
Dish, Mayonnaise, Footed,
5 3/8 In. 100.00
Goblet, 9 Oz.,
5 3/4 In. . . . . . 18.00 to 45.00
Goblet, Cocktail, 4 In. . . . 45.00
Goblet, Wine,
4 1/2 In. . . . . . 12.00 to 45.00
Ice Bucket,
5 1/2 In. . . . . . 21.00 to 31.00
Ice Tub 39.00
Mug 45.00
Pitcher, 54 Oz.,
8 1/2 In. . . . . . 45.00 to 60.00
Pitcher, Bulbous, 54 Oz.,
7 5/8 In. 105.00
Plate, Dinner,
9 In. . . . . 20.00 to 30.00
Plate, Luncheon,
8 In. . . . . 7.00 to 8.00
Plate, Sherbet, 6 In. 3.00 to 7.50
Plate, Sherbet, Gold Trim,
6 In. 4.00
Salt & Pepper,
Footed . . . . 55.00 to 60.00
Salt & Pepper,
Squat . . . . . . 130.00 to 135.00
Saltshaker,
Footed . . . . 12.00 to 24.00
Sandwich Server,
10 1/4 In. 30.00
Saucer, 5 3/4 In. . . 7.00 to 12.00
Saucer, 6 1/8 In. 13.00
Saucer, Frosted,
5 3/4 In. 11.00
Sherbet, 5 1/2 Oz.,
3 1/4 In. . . . . . . 7.00 to 13.00
Sherbet, 6 Oz.,
4 3/4 In. . . . . . . 6.00 to 19.00
Sugar, Cone
Shape . . . . 13.00 to 18.00
Sugar, Squat . . . . 10.00 to 16.00
Sugar & Creamer,
Cone Shape 30.00
Sugar & Creamer,
Squat 28.00
Tumbler, 5 Oz.,
3 1/2 In. 29.00
Tumbler, 9 1/2 Oz.,
3 13/16 In. 18.00
Tumbler, 10 Oz., 5 In. . . . 17.00
Tumbler, 12 Oz.,
4 7/8 In. 15.00

Tumbler, Footed, 3 Oz.,
3 1/4 In. 85.00

Tumbler, Night Set 140.00

Vase, 5 3/4 In. 15.00

Pink

Bowl, Salad, 7 In. 125.00

Candlestick, 1 3/4 In. 45.00

Candlestick, 1 3/4 In.,
Pair 100.00

Candy Jar, No Cover,
2 1/4 In. 22.00

Coaster, Ruffled 24.00

Console, Rolled Edge,
11 3/4 In. . . . . 75.00 to 110.00

Creamer, Flat 35.00

Cup, Curly Handle 15.00

Cup, Plain
Handle . . . . 7.00 to 9.00

Cup & Saucer,
Curly Handle 18.00

Cup & Saucer,
Plain Handle 14.00

Dish, Mayonnaise,
Footed 103.00

Goblet, 9 Oz.,
5 3/4 In. . . . . . . 30.00 to 40.00

Goblet, Wine, 4 1/2 In. . . . 40.00

Ice Tub, Tab
Handles . . . . . 60.00 to 120.00

Pitcher, 80 Oz., 8 In. 31.00

Plate, Luncheon,
8 In. . . . . 5.00 to 8.00

Plate, Sherbet,
6 In. . . . . 3.00 to 5.00

Saltshaker, Footed 50.00

Sandwich Server,
10 1/4 In. 34.00

Sauce, 6 1/8 In. 8.00

Sherbet, 5 Oz.,
3 1/4 In. . . . . 6.50 to 8.00

Sherbet, 6 Oz.,
4 3/4 In. . . . . . . 17.00 to 20.00

Sherbet, Ruffled Edge,
Footed, 5 1/2 In. 35.00

Sugar, Cone Shape 18.00

Sugar, Squat 44.00

Sugar, Tall, Cone Shape . . . 7.00

Sugar & Creamer,
Cone Shape 35.00

Sugar & Creamer,
Squat 17.00

Tumbler, 11 Oz.,
5 In. . . . . 19.00 to 23.00

Tumbler, 12 Oz.,
4 7/8 In. . . . . . . 25.00 to 30.00

Yellow

Candy Dish, Cover,
2 1/4 In. 69.00

Creamer, Cone Shape 19.00

Cup 8.00

Plate, Dinner, 9 In. 45.00

Plate, Luncheon, 8 In. 10.00

Plate, Sherbet, 6 In. 3.50

Sherbet, 5 1/2 Oz.,
3 1/4 In. . . . . . . 20.00 to 25.00

Sherbet, 6 Oz.,
4 3/4 In. . . . . . . 15.00 to 23.00

Sugar, Cone
Shape . . . . 15.00 to 19.00

Sugar, Squat . . . . 12.00 to 16.00

BLUE MOSAIC

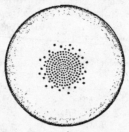

Blue Mosaic dinnerware
was made by Anchor
Hocking Glass Corpora-
tion, Lancaster, Ohio,
from 1966 to 1969. The
opaque white dishes have
a circular mosaic decal.
The cup, sugar, and
creamer are solid fired-on
blue and do not have a
decal. Other related pat-
terns are listed in the Fire-
King section in this book.

Snack Set, 8 Piece 83.00

BOOPIE
See Bubble

BOUQUET & LATTICE
See Normandie

BOWKNOT

The Bowknot pattern
remains a mystery,
although it probably dates
from the late 1920s. The
manufacturer is still un-
identified. The swags and
bows of the pattern were
mold-etched. There does
not seem to be a full
dinner set of this pattern.
Only the 7-inch plate, cup,
sherbet, two sizes of bowls,
and two types of 10-ounce
tumblers have been found.
Green pieces are found
easily. The pattern was
also made in Crystal.

Crystal

Tumbler, Footed, 10 Oz.,
5 In. 28.00

Green

Berry Bowl,
4 1/2 In. . . . . 9.00 to 24.00

Bowl, Cereal,
5 1/2 In. . . . . . . 34.00 to 40.00

Cup . . . . 8.00 to 10.00

Plate, Salad,
7 In. . . . . 8.50 to 20.00

Tumbler, 10 Oz.,
5 In. . . . . 11.00 to 34.00

Tumbler, Footed, 10 Oz.,
5 In. . . . . 22.00 to 30.00

BRIDAL BOUQUET
See No. 615

BUBBLE

Names of Depression
glass patterns can be
depressingly confusing.

Bubble is also known as Bullseye, the original name given by Anchor Hocking Glass Corporation, and as Provincial or Early American Line from 1960s ads. The stemware made to match the dishes was called Boopie, Berwick, or Inspiration in ads. The pattern was made from 1941 to 1968 in Crystal, Forest Green, Iridescent, Jade-ite, Pink, Royal Ruby, Sapphire Blue, White, and fired-on colors. Some Desert Gold (amber) pieces have been seen. The dishes, excluding items made in Forest Green and Royal Ruby, are heat-proof. The 4^1/$_2$- and 8-inch bowls were reissued in Royal Ruby by Anchor Hocking. They are marked with the anchor trademark. Other related patterns are listed in the Fire-King section in this book.

Crystal
Berry Bowl, 4 In. 3.00
Berry Bowl, Master,
    8 3/8 In. . . . . 6.00 to 10.00
Bowl, Cereal, 5 1/4 In. . . . 10.00
Bowl, Fruit,
    4 1/2 In. . . . . 3.00 to 10.00
Candlestick, 4 In.,
    Pair 11.00
Creamer 25.00
Goblet, Cocktail,
    3 1/2 Oz. . . . . 1.00 to 5.00
Goblet, Iced Tea,
    14 Oz. 10.00
Goblet, Water,
    9 Oz. . . . . 8.00 to 20.00
Grill Plate, 9 3/8 In. 18.00
Pitcher, Ice Lip, 64 Oz. . . 21.00
Plate, Bread & Butter,
    6 3/4 In. 7.00
Plate, Dinner, 9 3/8 In. 4.00
Platter, Oval, 12 In. 8.00

Sherbet, 6 Oz. 4.00
Soup, Dish,
    7 3/4 In. . . . . 9.50 to 20.00
Sugar . . . . 5.00 to 22.00
Tumbler, Iced Tea,
    12 Oz., 4 1/2 In. 12.00
Tumbler, Juice,
    5 Oz., 4 In. 20.00
Tumbler, Lemonade,
    16 Oz., 5 7/8 In. 18.00
Tumbler, Old Fashioned,
    Footed, 8 Oz.,
    3 1/4 In. . . . . . . 15.00 to 18.00

Forest Green
Berry Bowl, 4 In. 12.00
Berry Bowl, Master,
    8 3/8 In. 16.00
Bowl, Cereal,
    5 1/4 In. . . . . . . 11.00 to 25.00
Bowl, Fruit,
    4 1/2 In. . . . . 8.00 to 11.00
Creamer 10.00
Cup 7.00
Cup & Saucer 10.00
Goblet, 8 Piece 120.00
Goblet, 9 Oz.,
    5 1/2 In. . . . . . . 11.00 to 15.00
Goblet, Juice, 4 Oz.,
    4 1/2 In. . . . . . . 13.00 to 15.00
Pitcher, Ice Lip, 64 Oz. . . 25.00
Plate, Dinner,
    9 3/8 In. . . . . . . 10.00 to 30.00
Sherbet, 6 Oz. . . . . 7.00 to 10.00
Sugar 6.50
Sugar & Creamer 29.00

Iridescent
Berry Bowl, 4 In. 5.00
Bowl, Fruit, 4 1/2 In. 5.00
Nappy, Leaf Shape,
    7 1/4 In. 3.00

Jade-ite
Berry Bowl, Master,
    8 3/8 In. . . . . . . 10.00 to 23.00
Soup, Dish, 7 3/4 In. 23.00

Pink
Berry Bowl, Master,
    8 3/8 In. 26.00
Plate, Bread & Butter,
    6 3/4 In. 5.00

Royal Ruby
Berry Bowl,
    4 In. . . . . 7.00 to 12.00

Berry Bowl, Master,
    8 3/8 In. . . . . . . 23.00 to 29.00
Cup & Saucer . . . 12.00 to 15.00
Goblet, 9 Oz., 5 1/2 In. . . . 25.00
Pitcher, Ice Lip,
    64 Oz. . . . . 23.00 to 55.00
Plate, Dinner,
    9 3/8 In. . . . . . . 20.00 to 30.00
Sherbet, 6 Oz. . . . . 8.00 to 9.00
Tidbit, 2 Tiers, Center
    Handle . . . . 59.00 to 87.00
Tumbler, 12 Oz. 12.00
Tumbler, Iced Tea, 12 Oz.,
    4 1/2 In. . . . . . . 10.00 to 15.00
Tumbler, Juice, 5 Oz.,
    4 In. . . . . 8.00 to 10.00
Tumbler, Lemonade, 16 Oz.,
    5 7/8 In. . . . . . . 11.00 to 19.00
Tumbler, Water,
    9 Oz. . . . . 20.00 to 25.00

Sapphire Blue
Berry Bowl, 4 In. 16.00
Berry Bowl, Master,
    8 3/8 In. . . . . . . 16.00 to 32.00
Bowl, Cereal,
    5 1/4 In. . . . . . . 11.00 to 12.00
Bowl, Footed, 6 1/2 In. . . . 13.00
Bowl, Fruit,
    4 1/2 In. . . . . . . 11.00 to 15.00
Creamer . . . . 21.00 to 39.00
Cup . . . . 3.00 to 9.00
Cup & Saucer . . . . 6.00 to 12.00
Grill Plate, 9 3/8 In. 6.00
Plate, Bread & Butter,
    6 3/4 In. . . . . 3.00 to 9.00
Plate, Dinner,
    9 3/8 In. . . . . 5.00 to 15.00
Platter, Oval,
    12 In. . . . . 8.00 to 19.00
Soup, Dish,
    7 3/4 In. . . . . 9.00 to 30.00
Sugar . . . . 20.00 to 30.00
Sugar & Creamer 47.00

White
Berry Bowl, Master,
    8 3/8 In. . . . . 5.00 to 17.00
Creamer . . . . 15.00 to 45.00
Sugar . . . . 5.00 to 15.00
Sugar & Creamer . 7.00 to 13.00

BULLSEYE
See Bubble

BUTTERCUP

Buttercup is the name for Fostoria Glass Company's No. 340 etching. The dishes were made in Crystal from 1941 to 1960.

Bowl, Lily Pond, 12 In. . . 75.00
Candlestick, 3-Light, 8 In.,
    Pair . . . . 140.00 to 165.00
Cup 16.00
Goblet, Cordial, 1 Oz.,
    3 7/8 In. 48.00
Plate, 7 1/2 In. 15.00
Relish, 3 Sections,
    Gold Trim, Handle 95.00
Relish, 3 Sections,
    Handle . . . . 20.00 to 55.00

BUTTERFLIES & ROSES
See Flower Garden with
Butterflies

BUTTONS & BOWS
See Holiday

CABBAGE ROSE
See Sharon

CABBAGE ROSE WITH
    SINGLE ARCH
See Rosemary

CABOCHON

The bases of many Cabochon pieces look like cabochon-cut gemstones. A.H. Heisey & Company made the pattern from 1951 to 1957 in Crystal, Dawn (smoke), and Sultana (amber).

Crystal
Creamer 13.00
Goblet, 10 Oz. 38.00
Sugar, No Cover 9.00
Dawn
Creamer . . . . . . 45.00 to 60.00
Sugar 45.00

CAMBRIDGE SQUARE

Cambridge Glass Company's Square pattern was made from 1949 to 1955 mostly in Crystal. Some items were made in Carmen (red) and Ebony (black). Pieces have been reproduced by Imperial Glass Company and Boyd's Crystal Art, which each bought molds after Cambridge went out of business.

Crystal
Bowl, Salad, 11 In. 37.50
Candlestick, Pair 35.00
Goblet, Water 13.50
Relish, 3 Sections, 8 In. . . 25.00
Salt & Pepper 20.00
Tumbler, Cocktail,
    Footed 20.00
Tumbler, Water, Footed . . 10.00

CAMELLIA

Camellia etch often appears on Century blanks.

Fostoria Glass Company made the pattern in Crystal from 1951 to 1976.

Bowl, Salad, 10 1/2 In. . . . 15.00
Candlestick, 2-Light,
    7 In. 75.00
Plate, Luncheon,
    8 1/2 In. 8.00
Plate, Salad, 7 1/2 In. 16.00
Tumbler, Iced Tea, Footed,
    12 Oz., 6 1/8 In. 28.00

CAMEO

Cameo is also called Ballerina or Dancing Girl because the most identifiable feature of the etched pattern is the silhouette of the dancer. This pattern must have sold well when made by Hocking Glass Company from 1930 to 1934, because many different pieces were made, from dinner sets and servers to cookie jars and lamps. The pattern was made in Crystal, sometimes with a platinum trim, and in Green, Pink, and Yellow. In 1981, reproductions were made of both Green and Pink salt and pepper shakers. Children's dishes have recently been made in Green, Pink, and Yellow; there were never any old Cameo children's dishes.

Crystal
Cake Plate, 3-Footed,
    10 In. 35.00
Cup 7.00
Cup & Saucer . . . 20.00 to 22.00

Dish, Mayonnaise 55.00

Goblet, Wine, 3 1/2 In. . . . 95.00

Grill Plate,
10 1/2 In. . . . . . 15.00 to 25.00

Pitcher, Juice, 36 Oz.,
6 In. 95.00

Plate, Closed Handles,
10 1/2 In. 30.00

Plate, Dinner,
9 1/2 In. . . . . . . 20.00 to 30.00

Plate, Sherbet, 6 In. 7.00

Platter, Oval, Closed
Handles, 12 In. 25.00

Relish, 3 Sections, Footed,
7 1/2 In. . . . . . . 32.00 to 55.00

Sauce Bowl, 4 1/2 In. 7.00

Sherbet, Molded,
3 1/8 In. 20.00

Sugar, 3 1/4 In. 25.00

Tumbler, Juice, 5 Oz.,
3 3/4 In. . . . . . 20.00 to 42.00

Tumbler, Juice, Footed,
3 Oz. 83.00

Tumbler, Water, 9 Oz.,
4 In. 38.00

Vase, 8 In. 65.00

Green

Berry Bowl, Master,
8 1/4 In. . . . . . . 45.00 to 60.00

Bowl, Cereal, 5 1/2 In. . . . 39.00

Bowl, Salad,
7 1/4 In. . . . . . . 70.00 to 75.00

Bowl, Vegetable, Oval,
10 In. . . . . 28.00 to 55.00

Butter,
Cover . . . . . . 235.00 to 295.00

Cake Plate, 3-Footed,
10 In. . . . . 35.00 to 45.00

Candlestick,
4 In. . . . . 60.00 to 85.00

Candlestick, 4 In., Pair . . 140.00

Candy Jar, Cover,
4 In. . . . . 95.00 to 125.00

Candy Jar, No Cover,
4 In. . . . . 30.00 to 70.00

Compote, 5 In. 68.00

Console, 3-Footed,
11 In. . . . . 75.00 to 95.00

Cookie Jar,
Cover . . . . . . 50.00 to 71.00

Cookie Jar,
No Cover . . . . . 22.00 to 50.00

Creamer, 3 1/4 In. 23.00

Cup, Curly Handle 16.00

Cup, Oval, Handle 15.00

Cup & Saucer 19.00

Decanter,
Stopper . . . . . 65.00 to 210.00

Decanter, Stopper,
Frosted, 10 In. 100.00

Dish,
Mayonnaise . . . 39.00 to 65.00

Goblet, Water,
6 In. . . . . 75.00 to 95.00

Goblet, Wine,
4 In. . . . . 80.00 to 90.00

Grill Plate,
10 1/2 In. . . . . 12.00 to 20.00

Ice Bowl, Tab Handles, 3 x
5 1/2 In. . . . 225.00 to 330.00

Jam Jar, Cover 400.00

Pitcher, 36 Oz.,
6 In. . . . . 66.00 to 75.00

Pitcher, 56 Oz.,
8 1/2 In. . . . . . . 70.00 to 75.00

Plate, Closed Handles,
10 1/2 In. . . . . 12.00 to 35.00

Plate, Dinner,
9 1/2 In. . . . . . . 19.00 to 25.00

Plate, Luncheon,
8 In. . . . . 13.00 to 25.00

Plate, Salad, 7 In. 14.00

Plate, Sherbet,
6 In. . . . . 7.00 to 12.00

Plate, Square,
8 1/2 In. . . . . . . 60.00 to 75.00

Platter, Oval, Closed Handles,
12 In. . . . . . . 28.00 to 35.00

Relish, 3 Sections, Footed,
7 1/2 In. . . . . . . 17.00 to 50.00

Salt & Pepper . . 50.00 to 110.00

Saltshaker 40.00

Saucer, 6 In. 5.00

Sherbet,
3 1/8 In. . . . . . 15.00 to 38.00

Sherbet,
4 7/8 In. . . . . . 24.00 to 50.00

Sherbet, Molded,
3 1/8 In. 15.00

Soup, Cream, 4 3/4 In. . . 235.00

Soup, Rim,
9 In. . . . . 78.00 to 125.00

Sugar, 3 1/4 In. . . 20.00 to 33.00

Sugar, 4 1/4 In. . . 30.00 to 37.00

Sugar & Creamer,
3 1/4 In. 52.00

Syrup, 20 Oz.,
5 3/4 In. 425.00

Tray, Domino, 7 In. 275.00

Tumbler, Flat, 10 Oz.,
4 3/4 In. . . . . . . 30.00 to 42.00

Tumbler, Flat, 11 Oz.,
5 In. . . . . 40.00 to 52.00

Tumbler, Footed, 9 Oz.,
5 In. 30.00

Tumbler, Juice, 5 Oz.,
3 3/4 In. . . . . . . 30.00 to 60.00

Tumbler, Juice, Footed,
3 Oz. . . . . 65.00 to 75.00

Tumbler, Water, 9 Oz.,
4 In. . . . . 30.00 to 50.00

Vase,
5 3/4 In. . . . . 325.00 to 395.00

Vase, 8 In. . . . . . . 50.00 to 70.00

Pink

Console, 3-Footed,
11 In. . . . . 70.00 to 95.00

Goblet, Wine, 3 1/2 In. . . 860.00

Goblet, Wine, 4 In. 300.00

Yellow

Bowl, Vegetable, Oval,
10 In. . . . . 41.00 to 50.00

Console, 3-Footed,
11 In. 135.00

Creamer 25.00

Cup . . . . 7.00 to 10.00

Cup & Saucer . . . 12.00 to 13.00

Grill Plate, Closed Handles,
10 1/2 In. . . . . 12.00 to 14.00

Plate, Dinner,
9 1/2 In. . . . . . . 8.00 to 30.00

Plate, Sherbet,
6 In. . . . . 3.00 to 6.00

Soup, Cream, 4 In. 8.00

Sugar,
3 1/4 In. . . . . . . 20.00 to 22.00

Tumbler, Water, Footed,
9 Oz., 5 In. 25.00

CANDLELIGHT

Cambridge Glass Company used Candlelight etch

to decorate Crystal and Crown Tuscan glassware from the late 1930s through the early 1950s. Some pieces are gold-encrusted.

Crystal

Dish, Mayonnaise,
9 3/4 In. 25.00
Relish, Clover Shape,
3 Sections 60.00
Tumbler, Iced Tea,
Footed, 12 Oz. 80.00

CANDLEWICK

Candlewick was made by Imperial Glass Company, Bellaire, Ohio, from 1936 to 1984. A few pieces are still being made. Many similar patterns have been made by other companies. The beaded edge is the only design. Although the glass was first made in Crystal, it has also been produced in Black, Nut Brown, Sunshine Yellow, Ultra Blue, and Verde (green). Some pieces of Crystal are decorated with gold. Pieces have been found in Amber, Lavender, Pink, Red, and with fired-on gold, red, blue, or green beading. Some sets were made with cuttings, etchings, and hand-painted

designs. Reproductions have been made.

Black

Bowl, Rolled Edge,
Handles, 10 1/8 In. . . . 200.00
Tray, Handles,
8 1/2 In. 290.00

Crystal

Ashtray, 4 In. 8.00
Ashtray, 5 In. . . . . 8.00 to 10.00
Ashtray, Matchbook
Holder Center, 6 In. . . . 165.00
Ashtray Set, 4 Piece 40.00
Basket, Beaded Handle,
5 In. 350.00
Basket, Handle,
6 1/2 In. 22.00
Bowl, 2 Sections,
6 1/2 In. 25.00
Bowl, 3-Footed, 10 In. . . 175.00
Bowl, Bell Shape,
10 1/2 In. 60.00
Bowl, Float, 12 In. 40.00
Bowl, Handles,
8 1/2 In. 40.00
Bowl, Heart, Handle,
5 In. 20.00
Bowl, Heart, Handle,
9 In. 200.00
Bowl, Vegetable, Cover,
8 In. 300.00
Cake Plate, Birthday,
72 Candleholders,
14 In. 325.00
Candleholder, 2-Light . . . 35.00
Candleholder, 2-Light, Beaded
Stem, 4 1/2 In., Pair . . . 180.00
Candleholder, 3 1/2 In. 16.00
Candleholder, 3-Toed,
4 1/2 In., Pair 225.00
Candleholder, Flower,
Insert, 9 In. 150.00
Candleholder,
Mushroom, Pair 90.00
Candleholder, Rolled Edge,
3 1/2 In. 24.00
Candy Box, Cover,
3 Sections, 7 In. 175.00
Candy Box, Round,
Square Beaded Rim,
Cover, 6 1/2 In. 450.00
Celery Dish, Handles,
13 1/2 In. . . . . 35.00 to 45.00

Celery Dish, Oval,
8 3/8 In. 28.00
Chip & Dip, 2 Sections,
14 In. 650.00
Compote, 3-Bead Stem,
5 In. . . . . . . 145.00 to 230.00
Compote, 4 1/2 In. 30.00
Compote, 5 1/2 In. 34.00
Compote, Beaded Stem,
8 In. 125.00
Condiment Set, 4 Piece . . 75.00
Cordial, 1 Oz. 210.00
Creamer, Beaded Handle,
6 Oz. 8.00
Creamer, Flat, Beaded
Handle 9.00
Cup 8.00
Cup, After Dinner 15.00
Cup, Tea 8.00
Cup & Saucer 11.00
Cup & Saucer,
After Dinner 25.00
Dish, Mayonnaise, Cover,
Underplate, Ladle 85.00
Dish, Mayonnaise,
Ladle 28.00
Goblet, Amber Ball Stem
& Foot, 4 3/4 In. 10.00
Goblet, Champagne,
6 Oz. 18.00
Goblet, Cocktail,
4 Oz. . . . . 15.00 to 16.00
Goblet, Water,
10 Oz. . . . . 15.00 to 18.00
Goblet, Wine, 4 Oz. 40.00
Ice Tub, 5 1/2 x 8 In. . . . 125.00
Ladle, Marmalade,
3 Beads 18.00
Ladle, Mayonnaise,
6 1/4 In. 40.00
Parfait, 6 Oz. 80.00
Pitcher, Lilliputian,
16 Oz., 6 1/2 In. 285.00
Pitcher, Manhattan,
40 Oz., 9 1/2 In. 275.00
Plate, 4 1/2 In. 10.00
Plate, Canape,
6 In. . . . . 15.00 to 22.00
Plate, Handles,
7 1/2 In. . . . . . 25.00 to 45.00
Plate, Handles, Gold
Beads, 5 1/2 In. 12.00
Plate, Handles, Round,
10 In. 80.00

Plate, Luncheon, 9 In. 10.00

Plate, Salad,
7 1/2 In. . . . . . . 7.50 to 20.00

Plate, Salad, 8 In. 8.00

Plate, Salad, Kidney,
8 1/4 In. 11.00

Plate, Service, 14 In. 35.00

Platter, Oval,
16 1/2 In. 220.00

Punch Bowl, Cover,
Family 270.00

Punch Bowl, Ladle,
11 1/2 In. 150.00

Relish, 2 Sections,
6 1/2 In. . . . . . . 20.00 to 25.00

Relish, 3 Sections,
3-Footed, 10 In. 125.00

Relish, 3 Sections,
Rectangular, 12 In. 45.00

Relish, 5 Sections, Round,
Handles, 10 1/2 In. 40.00

Relish Set, 4 Piece 95.00

Salad Set, Etched Mallard,
10 1/4-In. Bowl,
4 Piece 250.00

Sauce Bowl,
Underplate 175.00

Saucer . , ... 3.00 to 18.00

Saucer, Tea 3.00

Sherbet, 6 Oz. . . . 14.00 to 25.00

Sherbet, High, 6 Oz. 24.00

Snack Set, Plate, Tumbler,
2 Piece 36.00

Soup, Cream,
5 In. . . . . 50.00 to 55.00

Sugar 8.00

Sugar & Creamer, Tray . . 39.00

Tray, 6 1/2 In. 18.00

Tumbler, 12 Oz.,
5 1/2 In. 22.00

Tumbler, Flared Rim,
12 Oz. 50.00

Tumbler, For Canape Set,
Monogram 5.00

Tumbler, Iced Tea,
12 Oz. 23.00

Tumbler, Juice, 5 Oz. 11.00

Tumbler, Juice, Etched
Mallard, 5 Oz. 55.00

Vase, Bud, Footed,
7 In. 375.00

Red

Goblet, Cocktail, 4 Oz. . . . 90.00

CANTERBURY

Duncan & Miller Glass Company, Washington, Pennsylvania, introduced Canterbury in 1937. The pattern was made in Cape Cod (opalescent blue), Chartreuse, Cranberry (opalescent pink), Crystal, Ebony, Jasmine (opalescent yellow), Ruby, Sapphire, and with etchings. Tiffin Glass Company bought some of Duncan's molds in 1955 and continued to make Canterbury.

Cape Cod

Bowl, Oval, 9 In. 60.00

Centerpiece, 10 In. 100.00

Vase, Crimped,
4 1/2 In. 45.00

Vase, Ruffled Edge,
8 1/2 In. 125.00

Chartreuse

Candy Dish, Cover,
3 Sections, 8 In. 75.00

Candy Dish, Cover,
6 1/2 In. 40.00

Goblet, Cocktail,
3 1/2 Oz., 5 1/4 In. 20.00

Relish, 3 Sections,
9 In. 48.00

Tumbler, 9 Oz.,
4 1/2 In. 14.00

Tumbler, Footed,
9 Oz., 5 1/2 In. 26.00

Vase, 5 In. 20.00

Crystal

Ashtray, 3 In. 8.00

Basket, Oval, 11 1/2 In. . . 70.00

Bowl, Crimped,
10 1/2 x 5 In. 30.00

Bowl, Fruit 7.50

Bowl, Handle, 6 x 2 In. . . 10.00

Bowl, Oval, 10 In. 39.00

Cake Plate, 14 In. 45.00

Cake Plate, Handles,
13 1/2 In. 25.00

Candleholder, 3 1/2 In.,
Pair 30.00

Candlestick, 6 In., Pair . . . 45.00

Celery Dish, Handles,
3 Sections, 10 1/2 In. . . . 30.00

Compote, Sterling Silver
Overlay, 5 1/2 In. 40.00

Cup 10.00

Cup & Saucer 15.00

Dish, Ice Cream,
6 Oz., 3 3/4 In. 6.00

Dish, Marmalade,
Underplate, 5 x 3 In. . . . 30.00

Dish, Mayonnaise, Underplate,
Handles, 7 1/2 In. 9.00

Finger Bowl, Underplate,
6 In. 30.00

Goblet, Water, 9 Oz.,
6 In. 12.50

Plate, 7 1/2 In. 10.00

Relish, 3 Sections, 3 Handles,
9 In. . . . . 18.00 to 30.00

Rose Bowl,
5 1/4 In. . . . . . . 25.00 to 35.00

Sandwich Server,
Handle, 11 In. 18.00

Saucer 3.00

Sherbet, 6 Oz., 4 1/2 In. . . . 9.00

Sugar, 3 Oz., 2 1/2 In. . . . 10.00

Sugar, 7 Oz., 3 In. 8.00

Vase, 8 1/2 In. 45.00

Ruby

Candy Dish, Cover, 3 Sections,
3 Handles, 8 In. 225.00

CAPE COD

Cape Cod was a pattern made by the Imperial Glass Company, Bellaire, Ohio, from 1932. It is usually found in Crystal, but was also made in Amber, Azalea (pink), Black, Evergreen, Heritage Blue, Milk Glass, Ritz Blue, Ruby, and Verde (green). In 1978 the dinner set was reissued. The cruet was reissued in 1986 without the rayed bottom.

Amber
Cruet, Stopper,
5 1/4 In. 16.00

Azalea
Sherbet, 6 Oz. 7.00

Crystal
Bowl, Baked Apple,
6 In. . . . . 9.00 to 10.00
Bowl, Dessert,
4 1/2 In. 12.00
Bowl, Oval,
9 1/2 In. 25.00
Bowl, Spider, 2 Sections,
Handle, 6 1/2 In. 15.00
Bowl, Spider, Handle,
4 1/2 In. 24.00
Butter, Cover, 1/4 Lb. . . . 110.00
Cake Plate, Square,
4-Footed, 10 In. 165.00
Cigarette Jar, Cover, Handle,
4 1/2 x 5 1/2 In. 50.00
Console, 13 In. 60.00
Cruet, Stopper,
5 1/4 In. 15.00
Cruet, Stopper, 8 In. 15.00
Cup & Saucer 8.00
Dish, Mayonnaise,
Cover, 3 3/4 In. 23.00
Dish, Sundae, 6 Oz. 8.00
Eggcup 55.00
Goblet, Cordial,
1 1/2 Oz. 8.00
Goblet, Water, 10 Oz.,
6 In. 9.00
Goblet, Wine, 3 Oz.,
4 1/2 In. . . . . 8.00 to 12.00
Nut Dish, Handle,
2 In. 15.00
Oyster Cocktail, 4 Oz.,
3 3/4 In. 8.00
Parfait, 6 Oz. 12.00
Parfait, 6 Oz., 8 Piece 85.00
Pitcher, Ice Lip, 40 Oz. . . 75.00
Plate, 7 1/4 In. 6.00

Plate, Bread & Butter,
6 1/2 In. . . . . 6.00 to 7.00
Plate, Dinner, 10 In. 45.00
Plate, Salad, 8 In. . . 8.00 to 9.00
Punch Cup 6.00
Relish, 3 Sections, Oval,
9 1/2 In. . . . . . . 15.00 to 35.00
Relish, 5 Sections,
11 In. . . . . 22.00 to 70.00
Salad Bowl, Fork,
Spoon 70.00
Salt & Pepper 7.00
Salt & Pepper, Footed . . . 15.00
Salt & Pepper, Footed,
Tall 30.00
Saltshaker, Pepper Mill . . 40.00
Sherbet, 6 Oz.,
5 In. . . . . 10.00 to 11.00
Sherbet, 6 Oz., Tall 18.00
Sugar, 4 1/8 In. 35.00
Sugar, Handles, 3 1/2 In. . . 4.00
Tray For Sugar &
Creamer 15.00
Tumbler, Juice, Footed,
6 Oz. . . . . 8.00 to 9.00
Tumbler, Water, Footed,
10 Oz., 5 1/2 In. 23.00

Heritage Blue
Goblet, 11 Oz. 40.00
Parfait, 6 Oz. 20.00

Ruby
Goblet, 9 Oz. 25.00
Mug, Footed, 12 Oz.,
5 In. 10.00
Nut Dish, 5 x 2 In. 8.00
Pitcher, Ice Lip, 40 Oz.,
8 1/4 In. 36.00
Sugar & Creamer 13.00

CAPRI BLUE

Capri Blue is the name of medium blue glass made in the 1960s by Hazel Ware, a division of Continental Can Company, Clarksburg, West Virginia. The modern-looking dishes were made in several shapes, including Daisy, El Dorado, Gothic, Moderne,

Scanda, Seashell, Simplicity, Skol, Spiral, Swirl, and Twist. Skol was made in other colors, too, and is listed in its own section in this book.

Ashtray, Round,
3 1/4 In. 4.00
Ashtray, Triangular,
6 5/8 In. 12.00
Bowl, Colony Swirl,
4 3/4 In. 14.00
Bowl, Oval, Colony Swirl,
9 1/2 In. . . . . . . 13.00 to 14.00
Bowl, Oval, Colony,
7 3/4 In. 15.00
Bowl, Square, Colony,
5 3/4 In. 11.00
Bowl, Swirl, 4 3/4 In. 20.00
Candy Dish, Cover,
Footed 32.00
Cup 5.00
Goblet, Water, 6-Sided Foot,
5 1/2 In. 25.00
Saucer 1.00

CAPRICE

Caprice was advertised in 1936 as the most popular crystal pattern in America. It was made until 1953. Over 200 pieces were included in the line. Frosted pieces are called Alpine Caprice, the name given by the maker, Cambridge Glass Company, Cambridge, Ohio. The sets were made in Amber, Amethyst, Blue, Cobalt Blue, Crystal, Emerald, Light Green, Milk Glass, Moonlight Blue, and Pink. Reproductions are being made in Cobalt Blue and Moonlight Blue.

Amethyst

Vase, 7 In. 95.00

Crystal

Bonbon, Square, Handles,
4 In. 20.00

Bowl, 4-Footed, Gold,
10 1/2 In. 55.00

Bowl, Ruffled Edge,
4-Footed, 12 In. 16.00

Bowl, Ruffled Edge,
4-Footed, 13 In. 35.00

Candlestick, 3-Light 40.00

Candlestick, 3-Light,
Pair 145.00

Candlestick, 7 In., Pair . . 195.00

Candy Dish, Cover,
3 Sections, 6 In. 90.00

Creamer, 4 Oz. 11.00

Cup 14.00

Goblet, Claret,
4 1/2 Oz. 60.00

Goblet, Wine, Blown,
2 1/2 Oz. 20.00

Ice Bucket, Alpine 110.00

Plate, Cabaret, 4-Footed,
14 In. . . . . 30.00 to 40.00

Plate, Luncheon,
8 1/2 In. 12.00

Relish, 3 Sections,
8 In. 18.00

Sandwich Server, Footed,
11 1/2 In. 60.00

Saucer 3.00

Sherbet, Blown, 6 Oz. . . . 30.00

Sherbet, High,
6 Oz. . . . . 12.00 to 20.00

Sherbet, Low, 6 Oz. 15.00

Sugar, 5 Oz. . . . . 10.00 to 12.00

Sugar & Creamer,
2 1/2 In. 19.00

Sugar & Creamer, 3 In. . . 20.00

Torte Plate, Cabaret,
Silver Overlay, 4-Footed,
11 1/2 In. 42.00

Tumbler, 8 Oz. 15.00

Tumbler, Footed, 10 Oz. . . 20.00

Tumbler, Iced Tea,
12 Oz. 60.00

Emerald

Plate, Luncheon,
8 1/2 In. 33.00

Moonlight Blue

Ashtray, 5 In. 25.00

Ashtray, Shell, 3-Footed,
2 1/4 In. 15.00

Bonbon, Oval, Footed,
6 In. 50.00

Bowl, 4-Footed, 13 In. . . 245.00

Bowl, Flared, Handles,
4-Footed, 12 1/2 In. 95.00

Bowl, Handle, Pedestal
Foot, 6 In. 65.00

Bowl, Ruffled Edge, 4-Footed,
10 In. . . . . 59.00 to 65.00

Bowl, Scalloped Edge,
4-Footed, 10 In. 85.00

Candlestick, 2 1/2 In. 45.00

Candlestick, 2-Light,
6 In., Pair 200.00

Candy Dish, Cover Only,
6 In. 58.00

Cigarette Box, Cover, 3 1/2 x
2 1/4 In. . . . . . 85.00 to 160.00

Compote,
5 1/2 x 6 1/2 In. 35.00

Compote, 7 In. 70.00

Cruet, Stopper,
8 In. . . . . 50.00 to 76.00

Cup & Saucer 43.00

Dish, Bridge, Diamond,
4 3/4 x 6 1/4 In. 125.00

Dish, Jelly, Handles,
5 In. 21.00

Dish, Lemon, Handles,
6 1/2 In. 20.00

Dish, Mayonnaise,
6 In. . . . . 45.00 to 55.00

Dish, Mayonnaise, Underplate,
6 In. . . . . 95.00 to 120.00

Goblet, Alpine, 10 Oz. . . . 60.00

Goblet, Claret,
4 1/2 Oz. 90.00

Goblet, Cocktail,
3 1/2 Oz. 55.00

Goblet, Cordial, 1 Oz. . . 150.00

Goblet, Water, 10 Oz. 54.00

Goblet, Wine, 2 1/2 Oz. . . 60.00

Plate, 6 In. 24.00

Plate, 8 1/2 In. 38.00

Plate, 16 In. 100.00

Plate, Cabaret,
11 1/2 In. 90.00

Plate, Cabaret, 4-Footed,
11 In. 55.00

Plate, Cabaret, 4-Footed,
14 In. 60.00

Plate, Salad, 7 1/2 In. . . . 28.00

Rose Bowl,
4 1/2 x 6 1/4 In. 168.00

Saucer 13.00

Sherbet, 6 Oz. 32.00

Sherbet, Tall, 6 Oz. 40.00

Sugar & Creamer 29.00

Sugar & Creamer,
Individual 30.00

Tumbler, Juice, Footed,
3 Oz. 125.00

Tumbler, Juice, Footed,
5 Oz. 55.00

Tumbler, Mushroom,
12 Oz. . . . . 55.00 to 65.00

Tumbler, Old Fashioned,
7 Oz. 100.00

Tumbler, Water, Footed,
10 Oz. 45.00

Vase, Ball, 4 1/2 In. 200.00

Vase, Ball, 8 1/2 In. 345.00

Vase, Ruffled Edge,
4 1/2 In. 175.00

CARCASSONE

Carcassone stemware and bar accessories were made by A.H. Heisey & Company from 1930 to 1941. Pieces can be found in Alexandrite (lavender), Cobalt Blue, Crystal, Flamingo (pink), Moongleam (green), and Sahara (yellow). The pattern was sometimes decorated with etchings and cuttings.

Alexandrite

Goblet, Cordial, 1 Oz. . . 195.00

Moongleam

Pilsner, 12 Oz. 149.00

Sahara

Goblet, Champagne,
  6 Oz. 34.00
Goblet, Claret, 4 Oz. 60.00
Goblet, Footed, 2 Oz. 72.00
Goblet, Wine, 4 Oz. 68.00
Oyster Cocktail, 3 Oz. ... 32.00
Sherbet, 6 Oz. 34.00
Tumbler, Footed, 6 Oz. .. 34.00
Tumbler, Footed,
  12 Oz. 34.00

CARIBBEAN

The rippled design of Caribbean is slick and modern in appearance and has attracted many collectors. It was made by Duncan & Miller Glass Company, Washington, Pennsylvania, from 1936 to 1955. Sets were made of Amber, Blue, Cobalt Blue, Crystal, Crystal with Ruby trim, and Red glass. The Duncan & Miller catalogs identify the line as No. 112.

Blue

Vase, Squat, Rolled Rim,
  7 In. 85.00

Cobalt Blue

Cigarette Box, Cover,
  3 1/2 In. 125.00

Crystal

Bowl, Flower, Oval,
  Handles, 10 3/4 In. 35.00
Candy Dish, Cover,
  7 In. 14.00
Punch Set, 12 Piece 350.00

CASCADE

Cambridge Glass Company made the Cascade pattern in the 1940s, mostly in Crystal. Crown Tuscan, Emerald, Mandarin Gold, and Milk Glass pieces can be found, too.

Crystal

Compote, 5 1/4 In. 35.00
Goblet, Cocktail 11.00
Goblet, Water 14.00
Sherbet 10.00
Sugar & Creamer 15.00
Tumbler, Footed,
  12 Oz. 15.00

CENTURY

Century pattern was made by Fostoria Glass Company from 1926 until 1986. It is a plain pattern with a slightly rippled rim. Full dinner sets were made of Crystal.

Bowl, 3-Footed, Triangular
  Shape, 7 1/8 In. 15.00
Bowl, Cereal, 6 In. 23.00
Bowl, Lily, 11 1/4 In. 33.00
Bowl, Oval,
  6 1/2 x 9 1/4 In. 11.00
Bowl, Oval, 9 1/2 In. 15.00
Butter, Cover ... 35.00 to 41.00
Creamer 12.00
Cup 13.00
Cup & Saucer 16.00

Dish, Mayonnaise 18.00
Pickle, Oval, 8 3/4 In. 15.00
Pitcher, 48 Oz.,
  7 1/8 In. ..... 85.00 to 160.00
Plate, Bread & Butter,
  6 1/2 In. 6.00
Plate, Luncheon,
  8 1/2 In. 14.00
Plate, Salad, 8 In. 9.00
Relish, 3 Sections, Oval,
  Handles, 11 1/8 In. 15.00
Relish, 3 Sections, Oval,
  Silver Overlay, Handles,
  11 1/8 In. 35.00
Salt & Pepper,
  Tray .... 18.00 to 24.00
Saucer .... 2.00 to 3.00
Sugar 12.00
Sugar & Creamer, Tray .. 45.00
Torte Plate,
  14 In. .... 25.00 to 35.00
Tray, Center Handle,
  11 1/2 In. 35.00
Vase, Bud, 6 In. 22.00

CHAIN DAISY
See Adam

CHANTILLY CAMBRIDGE

Cambridge Glass Company started decorating glassware with the Chantilly etch in 1936. The pattern is found mostly in Crystal, though there are pieces in Ebony encrusted with gold.

Crystal

Bowl, Flared, 4-Footed,
  12 In. 48.00

Cake Plate, Handles,
13 1/2 In. 55.00
Candlestick, Martha,
5 In. 25.00
Candy Dish, Cover,
7 In. 85.00
Candy Dish, Cover, Silver
Foot, Marked, 7 In. . . . 200.00
Creamer 13.00
Decanter, Footed 165.00
Goblet, Champagne,
6 Oz. 29.00
Goblet, Water,
9 Oz. . . . . 25.00 to 40.00
Pitcher, Martini, Stir Stick,
8 3/4 x 6 In. 300.00
Relish, Martha, 3 Sections,
9 In. 65.00
Sherbet, Low, 6 Oz. 15.00
Sugar & Creamer 25.00
Tumbler, Juice, Footed,
5 Oz. 20.00
Vase, Sterling Silver Base,
12 In. 215.00

CHARM

Charm is a pattern of Fire-King dinnerware made from 1950 to 1954. The square-shaped dishes were made by Anchor Hocking Glass Corporation of Lancaster, Ohio. The dinnerware was made in Azure-ite (opaque blue-white), Forest Green, Jade-ite (opaque green), and Royal Ruby. Collectors often refer to the color name rather than the pattern name when describing these pieces. It is sometimes called Square. Other related patterns are

listed in the Fire-King section in this book.

Azure-ite
Bowl, Dessert, 4 3/4 In. . . 10.00
Cup & Saucer . . . . . 5.00 to 8.00
Plate, Salad, 6 5/8 In. 9.00
Saucer 2.00

Forest Green
Bowl, Dessert,
4 3/4 In. . . . . 7.00 to 9.00
Bowl, Salad, 7 3/8 In. 15.00
Cup . . . . 2.00 to 5.00
Cup & Saucer . . . . . 7.00 to 9.00
Plate, Luncheon,
8 3/8 In. . . . . 8.00 to 11.00
Plate, Salad,
6 5/8 In. . . . . 8.00 to 10.00
Platter, 8 x 11 In. 27.00
Saucer . . . . 1.50 to 4.00
Soup, Dish, 6 In. 20.00
Sugar &
Creamer . . . . . . 15.00 to 22.00

Jade-ite
Soup, Dish, 6 In. 80.00

Royal Ruby
Bowl, Dessert, 4 3/4 In. . . . 8.00
Bowl, Salad, 7 3/8 In. 24.00
Cup 6.00
Cup & Saucer 9.00
Plate, Luncheon,
8 3/8 In. . . . . 9.00 to 15.00

CHECKERBOARD
See Old Quilt

CHEROKEE ROSE

The Tiffin glass factory can be traced back to the 1840s, when Joseph Beatty made glass in Steubenville, Ohio. The factory failed and was purchased by

Alexander Beatty in 1851. He was joined by his sons and moved to Tiffin, Ohio, in 1888. The company became part of U.S. Glass Company in 1892 and was still operating in 1963 when U.S. Glass went bankrupt. Employees bought the plant, and it went through several changes of ownership until it closed in 1980. Cherokee Rose was one of the popular glass patterns made by Tiffin in the 1940s and 1950s. The glass was made only in Crystal.

Goblet, Water, 9 Oz. 39.00
Sherbet 24.00
Tumbler, Footed, 8 Oz. . . 25.00

CHERRY
See Cherry Blossom

CHERRY BLOSSOM

Cherry Blossom is one of the most popular Depression glass patterns. It has been called Banded Cherry, Cherry, or Paneled Cherry Blossom by some collectors. The pattern was made by the Jeannette Glass Company, Jeannette, Pennsylvania, from 1930 to 1939. Full dinner sets, serving pieces, and a child's set were made in a wide range of colors.

Pieces were made in Crystal, Delphite (opaque blue), Green, Jadite, Pink, and Red. Molds were changed a number of times, resulting in several shapes and styles for some pieces. Reproductions have been made.

Crystal

Plate, Salad,
7 In. . . . . 21.00 to 30.00
Sugar, Handles, Scalloped
Rim, 3 1/2 In. 33.00
Sugar & Creamer 46.00
Tumbler, Flat, 4 Oz.,
3 3/4 In. 27.00
Tumbler, Flat, 12 Oz.,
5 In. 75.00
Tumbler, Footed, 9 Oz.,
4 1/2 In. 43.00

Delphite

Berry Bowl, Master,
8 1/2 In. . . . . . . 60.00 to 68.00
Bowl, Handles,
9 1/2 In. 25.00
Child's Set,
14 Piece . . . . 309.00 to 380.00
Creamer, Child's,
2 3/4 x 3 1/4 In. 40.00
Cup 18.00
Cup & Saucer 32.00
Cup & Saucer, Child's . . . 58.00
Plate, Child's,
6 In. . . . . 15.00 to 18.00
Plate, Dinner, 9 In. 26.00
Plate Set, Child's, 6 In. . . . 60.00
Sandwich Server,
Open Handles,
12 1/2 In. . . . . . 24.00 to 76.00
Saucer . . . . 7.00 to 15.00
Saucer, Child's . . . 8.00 to 10.00
Sugar 28.00
Sugar, Child's,
2 1/2 x 3 11/16 In. 40.00
Tumbler, Footed, 4 Oz.,
3 3/4 In. 24.00
Tumbler, Footed, 9 Oz.,
4 1/2 In. . . . . . 25.00 to 35.00

Green

Berry Bowl,
4 3/4 In. . . . . . 28.00 to 33.00

Berry Bowl, Master,
8 1/2 In. . . . . . 50.00 to 55.00
Bowl, Cereal,
6 In. . . . . 39.00 to 40.00
Bowl, Handles, 9 In. 70.00
Bowl, Vegetable, Oval,
9 In. . . . . 35.00 to 55.00
Butter,
Cover . . . . . 135.00 to 145.00
Butter, Cover Only 90.00
Cake Plate, 3-Footed,
10 1/4 In. . . . . 35.00 to 45.00
Coaster . . . . 8.00 to 20.00
Cup . . . . 10.00 to 25.00
Cup & Saucer . . . 29.00 to 37.00
Grill Plate, 9 In. . 33.00 to 38.00
Mug, 7 Oz. 375.00
Pitcher, 42 Oz.,
8 In. . . . . 70.00 to 85.00
Pitcher, Footed, 36 Oz.,
6 3/4 In. . . . . . 50.00 to 86.00
Pitcher, Footed, 36 Oz.,
8 In. 75.00
Plate, Dinner,
9 In. . . . . 30.00 to 40.00
Plate, Salad,
7 In. . . . . 16.00 to 30.00
Plate, Sherbet,
6 In. . . . . 6.50 to 12.00
Platter, Oval,
11 In. . . . . 50.00 to 66.00
Platter, Oval,
13 In. . . . . . . 85.00 to 100.00
Salt & Pepper 50.00
Sandwich Server, Handles,
10 1/2 In. . . . . 35.00 to 45.00
Saucer . . . . 7.00 to 10.00
Sherbet . . . . 14.00 to 30.00
Soup, Dish, 7 3/4 In. . . . 100.00
Sugar 18.00
Sugar, Cover . . . . 48.00 to 50.00
Sugar, Cover Only 30.00
Sugar & Creamer,
Cover . . . . 80.00 to 85.00
Tumbler, 4 Oz.,
3 1/2 In. 30.00
Tumbler, 9 Oz.,
4 1/4 In. 30.00
Tumbler, 12 Oz., 5 In. . . . 90.00
Tumbler, Footed, 4 Oz.,
3 3/4 In. . . . . . 16.00 to 30.00
Tumbler, Juice 33.00
Tumbler, Scalloped Foot, 8 Oz.,
4 1/2 In. . . . . . 40.00 to 48.00

Pink

Berry Bowl,
4 3/4 In. . . . . . 17.00 to 30.00
Berry Bowl, Master,
8 1/2 In. . . . . . 48.00 to 60.00
Bowl, Cereal,
5 3/4 In. . . . . . 40.00 to 65.00
Bowl, Fruit, 3-Footed,
10 1/2 In. . . . 105.00 to 113.00
Bowl, Handles,
9 In. . . . . 45.00 to 55.00
Bowl, Vegetable, Oval,
9 In. . . . . 44.00 to 65.00
Butter, Cover 105.00
Butter, Cover Only 80.00
Cake Plate, 3-Footed,
10 1/4 In. . . . . 35.00 to 75.00
Coaster . . . . 13.00 to 22.00
Creamer . . . . 14.00 to 28.00
Creamer, Child's 55.00
Cup . . . . 16.00 to 27.00
Cup, Child's 55.00
Cup & Saucer . . . 26.00 to 30.00
Cup & Saucer, Child's . . . 37.00
Grill Plate, 9 In. 18.00
Pitcher, 42 Oz.,
8 In. . . . . 70.00 to 79.00
Pitcher, Footed, 36 Oz.,
6 3/4 In. . . . . . 60.00 to 90.00
Pitcher, Footed, 36 Oz.,
8 In. . . . . 66.00 to 91.00
Plate, Dinner,
9 In. . . . . 23.00 to 40.00
Plate, Salad,
7 In. . . . . 28.00 to 32.00
Plate, Sherbet,
6 In. . . . . 9.00 to 12.00
Platter, Oval, 11 In. 45.00
Platter, Oval,
13 In. . . . . . . 85.00 to 150.00
Platter, Sections,
13 In. . . . . 95.00 to 99.00
Salt & Pepper 104.00
Sandwich Server, Handles,
10 1/2 In. . . . . 23.00 to 45.00
Saucer . . . . 5.00 to 8.00
Saucer, Child's 12.00
Sherbet . . . . 13.00 to 25.00
Sherbet,
Footed . . . . 21.00 to 30.00
Soup, Dish, 7 3/4 In. 95.00
Sugar . . . . 8.00 to 18.00
Sugar, Child's 55.00

Sugar, Cover .... 33.00 to 55.00

Sugar & Creamer,
Cover .... 65.00 to 80.00

Tumbler, 4 Oz.,
3 1/2 In. ...... 18.00 to 25.00

Tumbler, 8 Oz.,
4 1/2 In. 42.00

Tumbler, 12 Oz.,
5 In. .... 75.00 to 90.00

Tumbler, Footed, 4 Oz.,
3 3/4 In. ...... 12.00 to 24.00

CHERRY-BERRY

Two similar patterns, Cherry-Berry and Strawberry, can be confusing. If the fruit pictured is a cherry, then the pattern is called Cherry-Berry. If a strawberry is used, then the pattern has that name. The dishes were made by the U.S. Glass Company around 1927 in Crystal, Green, Iridescent Amber, and Pink.

Crystal
Bowl, 7 1/2 In. 22.00
Goblet, 5 3/4 In. 16.00

Green
Berry Bowl 35.00
Sherbet 12.00
Sugar, Cover 110.00

Iridescent Amber
Bowl, 7 1/2 In. 20.00

Pink
Butter, Cover 9.00
Plate, 6 In. .... 3.75 to 12.00
Salt & Pepper, 4 1/2 In. .. 11.00
Sherbet 13.00

CHERRY-BERRY
See also Strawberry

CHEVRON

Hazel Atlas made Ritz Blue breakfast accessories with chevron stripes in the 1930s.

Ritz Blue
Breakfast Set, 3 Piece 60.00
Creamer 15.00
Pitcher, Milk 26.50
Sugar 15.00
Sugar & Creamer 26.00

CHINEX CLASSIC

Chinex Classic and Cremax are similar patterns made by the Macbeth-Evans Division of Corning Glass Works from about 1938 to 1942. Chinex and Cremax are both words with two meanings. Each is the name of a pattern and the name of a color used for other patterns. Chinex is ivory-colored; Cremax is a bit whiter. Chinex Classic, the dinnerware pattern, has a piecrust edge, and just inside the edge is an elongated feathered scroll. It may have a floral or scenic decal in the center, colored edging, or both. The Cremax pattern has the piecrust edge, but no scroll design.

Ivory
Bowl, Cereal, 5 3/4 In. 8.25
Bowl, Vegetable, 7 In. ... 26.50
Bowl, Vegetable, 9 In. ... 18.50
Creamer 10.00
Cup & Saucer 8.25
Plate, Bread & Butter,
6 1/4 In. 6.50
Plate, Dinner,
9 3/4 In. 7.00
Sandwich Server,
11 1/2 In. 15.00
Sherbet 17.50
Soup, Dish, 7 3/4 In. 24.00
Sugar 10.00
Tumbler, 5 1/2 In. 35.00

Ivory With Decal
Bowl, Cereal, Castle,
Pink Trim, 5 3/4 In. 30.00
Bowl, Cereal, Flowers,
Blue Trim, 5 3/4 In. 9.50
Bowl, Vegetable, Flowers,
9 In. 33.00
Cup, Flowers 4.00
Cup, Flowers,
Blue Trim 12.50
Cup & Saucer, Castle,
Pink Trim 40.00
Plate, Dinner, Castle,
9 3/4 In. 25.00
Plate, Dinner, Castle,
Blue Trim, 9 3/4 In. 19.50
Plate, Dinner, Castle,
Pink Trim, 9 3/4 In. 35.00
Plate, Dinner, Flowers,
9 3/4 In. 13.50
Plate, Sherbet, Castle,
Blue Trim, 6 1/4 In. 9.50
Plate, Sherbet, Castle,
Pink Trim, 6 1/4 In. 15.00
Sandwich Server, Flowers,
11 1/2 In. 26.00
Saucer, Flowers,
Pink Trim 5.75
Sherbet, Castle,
Blue Trim .... 15.00 to 36.00

Sherbet, Castle,
  Brown Trim 25.00

Soup, Dish, Castle,
  Pink Trim, 7 3/4 In. 55.00

CHINEX CLASSIC
See also Cremax

CHINTZ

Several companies made
etchings named Chintz.
Fostoria Glass Company,
Moundsville, West Virginia,
used a Chintz etching on
Baroque, No. 338, and
other blanks. The allover
etched design pictures
branches of leaves and
flowers. Fostoria made
Crystal pieces from 1940
to 1973. Other Chintz
patterns, featuring flowers
and butterflies, were made
by A.H. Heisey & Com-
pany from 1931 to 1938 in
Alexandrite (orchid), Crystal, Flamingo (pink), Moongleam (green), and Sahara
(yellow). Tiffin Glass Company made stemware with
a Chintz etching. Pieces
listed in this book are
Fostoria Chintz.

Bonbon, Tricornered,
  Handle, 4 5/8 In. 15.00
Bowl, Flared,
  11 1/2 In. . . . . . 55.00 to 95.00
Bowl, Handles,
  10 1/2 In. 70.00
Bowl, Vegetable,
  Oval, 9 1/2 In. 245.00

Candlestick, 2-Light, 3 1/2 In.,
  Pair . . . . 50.00 to 75.00
Candlestick, 3-Light, 6 In.,
  Pair 65.00
Candlestick, 5 1/2 In. 35.00
Cheese & Cracker Plate,
  Footed 38.00
Creamer,
  Footed . . . . . . 12.00 to 14.00
Cup & Saucer 29.00
Goblet, Champagne, 6 Oz.,
  5 1/2 In. . . . . . . 22.00 to 25.00
Goblet, Claret, 4 1/2 Oz.,
  5 3/8 In. 40.00
Goblet, Cocktail, 4 Oz.,
  5 In. . . . . 23.00 to 25.00
Goblet, Water, 9 Oz.,
  7 5/8 In. . . . . . . 30.00 to 38.00
Ice Bucket, Handle,
  Tongs 160.00
Jug, Footed, 48 Oz. 725.00
Plate, Dinner, 9 1/2 In. . . . 72.00
Plate, Lady Finger, 3-Footed,
  7 3/4 In. 15.00
Sherbet, 6 Oz.,
  4 3/8 In. . . . . . . 18.00 to 27.00
Sugar, Footed 12.00
Sugar & Creamer 36.00
Torte Plate, Scalloped
  Edge, 14 In. 55.00
Tumbler, Juice, Footed,
  5 Oz., 4 3/4 In. 23.00
Tumbler, Water, 9 Oz.,
  7 5/8 In. 33.00

CHRISTMAS CANDY

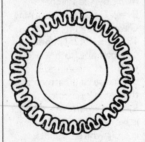

Christmas Candy, some-
times called Christmas
Candy Ribbon or No. 624,
was made by the Indiana

Glass Company, Dunkirk,
Indiana, in 1937. The pattern, apparently only made
in luncheon sets, was made
in Crystal, dark Emerald
Green, a light green called
Seafoam Green, and a
bright blue called Teal Blue.

Crystal
Creamer 10.00
Cup 6.00
Plate, Bread & Butter,
  6 In. 4.00
Plate, Luncheon,
  8 1/4 In. 10.00
Saucer 2.00
Sugar &
  Creamer . . . . . 20.00 to 26.00

Emerald Green
Bowl, 5 3/4 In. 10.00

Teal Blue
Cup & Saucer 54.00
Plate, Bread & Butter,
  6 In. 15.00
Saucer 12.00

CHRISTMAS CANDY
RIBBON
See Christmas Candy

CIRCLE

Circles ring the Circle
pattern made by Hocking
Glass Company, Lancaster,
Ohio, beginning in 1929. It
is found in Crystal, Green,
and Pink. It can be distinguished from the similar
Hocking pattern called
Ring by the number of
groupings of rings—Circle
has only one set, Ring has

several sets with four rings in each group.

Crystal

Sherbet, 3 1/8 In. 13.00
Tumbler, Juice, 4 Oz.,
   3 1/2 In. 4.00

Green

Bowl, 4 1/2 In. 13.00
Bowl, Flared,
   5 In. . . . . 18.00 to 23.00
Cup . . . . 5.00 to 7.00
Cup, Flared . . . . 5.00 to 6.00
Cup, Oval Handle 8.00
Cup & Saucer . . . 13.00 to 18.00
Goblet, Water, 8 Oz.,
   5 3/4 In. 13.00
Goblet, Wine,
   4 1/2 In. . . . . . . 16.00 to 23.00
Goblet, Wine, Gold Trim,
   4 1/2 In. 18.00
Plate, Luncheon,
   8 1/4 In. . . . . 6.00 to 7.00
Plate, Sherbet,
   6 In. . . . . 4.00 to 6.50
Saucer 4.00
Sherbet, 3 1/8 In. . . 5.00 to 7.00
Sherbet, 4 3/4 In. . 7.00 to 12.00
Tumbler, Water,
   10 Oz., 5 In. 20.00

Pink

Creamer 28.00
Cup 11.00
Plate, Luncheon,
   8 1/4 In. 9.00
Saucer 5.00
Sherbet, 3 1/4 In. . . 8.00 to 9.00
Sugar 28.00

CIRCULAR RIBS
See Circle

CLASSIC
See Chinex Classic

❖

Store glasses right-side up to protect the rims. Don't stack glasses.

❖

CLEO

In 1930 the Cambridge Glass Company, Cambridge, Ohio, introduced an etched pattern called Cleo. Many pieces are marked with the Cambridge C in a triangle. Sets were made in Amber, Crystal, Gold Krystol, Light Emerald, Peach-Blo, and Willow Blue.

Amber

Creamer, Footed 20.00
Plate, Luncheon, Decagon,
   8 1/2 In. 10.00

Crystal

Candy Dish, Cover,
   Footed 35.00
Goblet, Wine, 3 1/2 Oz. . . 30.00

Light Emerald

Bonbon, 6 1/4 In. 20.00
Bowl, Vegetable, Cover,
   Oval, 8 1/2 In. 325.00
Candy Dish, Cover, Footed,
   Handle 175.00
Compote, 6 x 12 In. 49.00
Plate, Ringed, 6 1/2 In. . . 100.00
Saucer 15.00

Peach-Blo

Bowl, Footed,
   10 3/4 In. 135.00
Console,
   1 5/8 x 8 3/8 In. 200.00
Tumbler, 10 Oz.,
   4 3/4 In. 65.00

Willow Blue

Pickle, Oval, 8 1/2 In. . . . 100.00

CLOVERLEAF

Three-leaf clovers form part of the border of Cloverleaf pattern made by Hazel Atlas Glass Company from 1930 to 1936. It was made in Black, Crystal, Green, Pink, and Topaz (yellow).

Black

Ashtray, 4 In. 65.00
Creamer . . . . . . 22.00 to 25.00
Creamer, Footed 22.00
Cup 20.00
Cup & Saucer . . . 19.50 to 30.00
Plate, Luncheon,
   8 In. . . . . 15.00 to 18.00
Salt & Pepper . . 95.00 to 115.00
Sherbet 23.00
Sugar, Footed . . . 16.50 to 25.00
Sugar &
   Creamer . . . . . . 27.00 to 45.00

Crystal

Sherbet 8.00

Green

Bowl, 8 In. 105.00
Bowl, Dessert,
   4 In. . . . . 20.00 to 35.00
Bowl, Salad, 7 In. 80.00
Cup . . . . 6.50 to 14.00
Cup & Saucer . . . 12.00 to 13.00
Grill Plate,
   10 1/4 In. 30.00
Plate, Luncheon,
   8 In. . . . . 10.00 to 16.00
Saltshaker . . . . . . 26.00 to 36.00
Sherbet . . . . 10.00 to 13.00

Pink

Cup & Saucer . . . 12.00 to 18.00
Plate, Luncheon,
   8 In. . . . . 10.00 to 11.00
Saucer . . . . 3.00 to 8.00
Sherbet . . . . 10.00 to 15.00

Topaz
Creamer 10.00
Saltshaker 50.00
Sherbet 10.00
Sugar 11.00

COIN

Fostoria Glass Company, Moundsville, West Virginia, made the Coin pattern from 1958 to 1982. It resembles the early pressed glass patterns, U.S. Coin and Columbian Coin. Dishes and accessories were made in Amber, Blue, Crystal, Empire Green, Olive, and Ruby. The four coins, usually frosted, depict a torch, a colonial man, an eagle, and the Liberty Bell. Lancaster Colony reissued some Coin pieces without frosted coins in the 1990s.

Amber
Ashtray, 4 x 3 In. 10.00
Bowl, Oval,
9 In. . . . . 20.00 to 25.00
Cake Plate, Footed,
10 In. 75.00
Candlestick, 4 1/2 In.,
Pair 13.00
Candlestick, 8 In., Pair . . . 26.00
Candy Jar, Cover, 6 In. . . . 50.00
Candy Jar, Cover,
12 1/2 In. . . . . . 26.00 to 40.00
Console, Footed,
8 1/2 In. 6.50
Creamer . . . . 8.50 to 11.00
Cruet, Underplate 128.00
Dish, Jelly 9.50
Pitcher, 32 Oz.,
6 1/4 In. . . . . . . 33.00 to 50.00
Salt & Pepper 10.00
Sugar & Creamer 27.00

Blue
Ashtray, 3 x 4 In. 20.00
Ashtray, 7 1/2 In. 35.00

Bowl, 8 In. 30.00
Bowl, Footed, 8 1/2 In. 35.00
Candlestick, 4 1/2 In.,
Pair . . . . 27.00 to 35.00
Candy Box, Cover,
9 In. 39.00
Candy Jar, Cover, 7 In. . . . 17.00
Cigarette Urn,
3 3/8 In. . . . . . . 38.00 to 41.00
Lamp, Oil, 4 In. 70.00
Nappy, 5 1/4 In. 10.00
Salt & Pepper 30.00
Sugar & Creamer 43.00
Vase, Bud, 8 In. 50.00

Crystal
Bowl, Footed, 8 1/2 In. . . . 42.00
Bowl, Oval,
9 In. . . . . 13.00 to 29.00
Cake Plate, Footed,
10 In. 135.00
Candlestick, 8 In., Pair . . . 55.00
Candy Box, Cover,
9 In. 16.00
Candy Jar, Cover,
6 3/8 In. 30.00
Creamer 8.50
Dish, Jelly . . . . 9.50 to 11.00
Nappy, 5 1/2 In. . . 8.50 to 10.00
Punch Cup 45.00
Punch Set, 10 Piece 595.00
Spooner, 5 In. 67.00
Sugar & Creamer 26.00
Urn, Cover, 12 3/4 In. . . . 72.00
Vase, Bud, 8 In. 8.00

Empire Green
Candlestick, 4 1/2 In.,
Pair 99.00
Candy Jar, Cover,
6 3/4 In. 125.00
Nappy,
5 1/2 In. . . . . . 21.00 to 35.00
Pitcher, 32 Oz.,
6 1/4 In. 204.00
Urn, Cover, 12 3/4 In. . . 155.00
Wedding Bowl, Cover . . 115.00

Olive
Bowl, 8 In. 15.00
Bowl, Oval,
9 In. . . . . 15.00 to 33.00
Candlestick, 4 1/2 In. 15.00
Candy Box, Cover,
6 1/4 In. . . . . . . 15.00 to 20.00

Candy Jar, Cover, Footed,
8 In. 16.00
Cigarette Urn,
3 3/8 In. . . . . . . 10.00 to 23.00
Pitcher, 32 Oz.,
6 1/2 In. 36.00
Salt & Pepper . . . 17.00 to 25.00
Sugar, Cover 35.00
Sugar & Creamer, Tray . . 21.00
Urn, Cover, 12 3/4 In. . . . 40.00
Vase, Bud,
8 In. . . . . 12.00 to 28.00

Ruby
Ashtray, 7 1/2 In. 23.00
Ashtray, Round, 5 In. 24.00
Bowl, 8 In. 22.00
Bowl, Footed,
8 1/2 In. . . . . . . 30.00 to 33.00
Bowl, Oval, 9 In. 32.00
Candlestick, 4 1/2 In.,
Pair 31.00
Candy Box, 6 1/2 In. 13.00
Dish, Jelly . . . . 8.50 to 16.00
Goblet, 9 Oz., 5 1/4 In. . . . 95.00
Nappy, 5 1/2 In. 16.00
Pitcher, 32 Oz.,
6 3/4 In. 164.00
Salt & Pepper 41.00
Tumbler, Iced Tea,
14 Oz., 5 1/4 In. 74.00
Tumbler, Old Fashioned,
10 Oz., 5 3/8 In. 55.00
Urn, Cover, 12 1/2 In. . . . 80.00
Vase, Bud,
8 In. . . . . 20.00 to 32.00

COLONIAL

Sometimes this pattern is called Knife & Fork, although Colonial is the more common name. It was made by Hocking Glass Company, Lancaster, Ohio, from 1934 to 1938. Crystal, Green, and Pink pieces are more common than Opaque White.

Crystal
Berry Bowl,
  9 In. . . . . 30.00 to 45.00
Butter, Cover . . . 44.00 to 49.00
Butter,
  Cover Only . . . 12.00 to 20.00
Creamer 16.00
Cup . . . . 4.00 to 8.00
Goblet, Cocktail, 3 Oz.,
  4 In. . . . . 12.00 to 15.00
Goblet, Cordial, 1 Oz.,
  3 3/4 In. . . . . . . 10.00 to 25.00
Goblet, Wine, 2 1/2 Oz.,
  4 1/2 In. 10.00
Pitcher, 68 Oz.,
  7 3/4 In. 35.00
Pitcher, Ice Lip, 68 Oz.,
  7 3/4 In. 30.00
Plate, Dinner,
  10 In. . . . . 30.00 to 32.00
Plate, Sherbet, 6 In. 3.00
Saltshaker 37.00
Sherbet, 3 3/8 In. 8.00
Sugar, 4 1/4 In. 11.00
Sugar, Cover . . . . 10.00 to 30.00
Tumbler, Footed, 3 Oz.,
  3 1/4 In. 13.00
Tumbler, Footed, 5 Oz.,
  4 In. 22.00

Green
Berry Bowl,
  4 1/2 In. . . . . . . 18.00 to 22.00
Berry Bowl,
  9 In. . . . . 30.00 to 60.00
Bowl, Vegetable,
  Oval, 10 In. 36.00
Butter, Cover . . . 55.00 to 60.00
Butter, Cover
  Only . . . . 20.00 to 23.00
Cheese Dish, Cover 465.00
Goblet, Claret, 4 Oz.,
  5 1/4 In. 25.00
Goblet, Cocktail, 3 Oz.,
  4 In. 28.00
Goblet, Cordial, 1 Oz.,
  3 3/4 In. 30.00

Goblet, Water, 8 1/2 Oz.,
  5 3/4 In. 33.00
Goblet, Wine, 2 1/2 Oz.,
  4 1/2 In. 25.00
Grill Plate,
  10 In. . . . . 25.00 to 29.00
Pitcher, Ice Lip, 54 Oz.,
  7 In. 77.00
Pitcher, Milk, 16 Oz.,
  5 In. 11.00
Plate, Dinner, 10 In. 85.00
Plate, Luncheon,
  8 1/2 In. . . . . 9.00 to 13.00
Plate, Sherbet, 6 In. 8.00 to 9.00
Platter, Oval,
  12 In. . . . . 25.00 to 30.00
Saltshaker, Footed 7.00
Saucer 8.00
Sherbet,
  3 3/8 In. . . . . . . 12.00 to 15.00
Soup, Dish, 7 In. 65.00
Spoon Holder 140.00
Sugar,
  4 1/2 In. . . . . . . 15.00 to 18.00
Sugar, Cover 48.00
Tumbler, Footed,
  3 Oz., 3 1/4 In. 25.00
Tumbler, Footed,
  5 Oz., 4 In. 45.00
Tumbler, Whiskey,
  1 1/2 Oz., 2 3/8 In. 20.00

Pink
Bowl, Vegetable, Oval,
  10 In. 40.00
Cup & Saucer . . . 17.00 to 20.00
Pitcher, Milk, 16 Oz.,
  5 1/4 In. 57.00
Plate, Dinner,
  10 In. . . . . 62.00 to 65.00
Plate, Luncheon,
  8 1/2 In. . . . . . . 11.00 to 12.00
Sherbet, 3 In. 25.00
Sherbet,
  3 3/8 In. . . . . . . 12.00 to 16.00
Sugar, 4 1/2 In. 20.00
Tumbler, 11 Oz.,
  5 1/8 In. 40.00
Tumbler, Footed, 5 Oz.,
  4 In. 36.50
Tumbler, Footed, 10 Oz.,
  5 1/4 In. 50.00
Tumbler, Water, 9 Oz.,
  4 In. 25.00

Tumbler, Whiskey, 1 1/2 Oz.,
  2 1/2 In. . . . . . . 16.00 to 18.00

COLONIAL BLOCK

A small set of dishes, mostly serving pieces, was made in Colonial Block pattern by Hazel Atlas Glass Company, a firm with factories in Ohio, Pennsylvania, and West Virginia. The dishes were made in the 1930s in Black, Crystal, Green, and Pink, and in the 1950s in White.

Crystal
Butter, No Cover 10.00
Candy Jar, Cover 19.00
Powder Jar, Cover,
  Frosted 40.00

Green
Bowl, 4 In. 11.50
Bowl, 7 In. 22.00
Butter, Cover 48.00
Butter, Cover
  Only . . . . 34.00 to 35.00
Butter, No Cover 24.00
Candy Jar, Cover Only . . . 25.00
Goblet, 5 1/2 In. . . 9.00 to 15.00
Sherbet . . . . 8.00 to 10.00
Sugar, Cover Only 15.00
Sugar, No Cover 15.00

Pink
Creamer 15.00
Goblet,
  5 1/2 In. . . . . . . 15.50 to 38.00
Sugar, Cover Only 16.50
Sugar, No Cover 12.00

White
Sugar, Cover 15.00
Sugar, No Cover 6.00

COLONIAL FLUTED

Federal Glass Company made Colonial Fluted or Rope pattern from 1928 to 1933. Luncheon sets were made primarily in Green, although Crystal pieces were also produced.

Green

Berry Bowl, Master,
7 1/2 In. 22.00
Creamer 13.00
Cup & Saucer 9.00
Plate, Luncheon,
8 In. . . . . 8.00 to 10.00
Plate, Sherbet,
6 In. . . . . 4.00 to 6.00
Saucer 4.25
Sherbet 5.00
Sugar & Creamer 16.00
Sugar & Creamer, Cover . 45.00

COLONY

Colony was made by Fostoria Glass Company from 1926 to 1979. It evolved from an earlier Fostoria pattern, Queen Anne. Red candlesticks and bowls were sold in the 1980s under the Maypole name, and matching vases and other pieces were made by Viking. Colony was originally made in Amber, Blue, Crystal, Green, and Yellow. Reproductions have been made.

Crystal

Bowl, Flared,
11 In. . . . . 30.00 to 45.00
Bowl, Low, Footed,
10 1/2 In. 79.00
Cake Plate, Footed,
12 In. 95.00
Candlestick, Prisms,
7 1/2 In. 80.00
Candlestick, Prisms,
9 3/4 In., Pair 110.00
Cheese & Cracker Plate . . 70.00
Compote, Cover, Low,
6 1/2 In. . . . . . . 38.00 to 54.00
Console, Rolled Edge,
9 In. 65.00
Creamer 14.00
Cup 10.00
Dish, Mayonnaise,
Underplate 38.00
Goblet, Water, 9 Oz.,
5 1/4 In. . . . . . . 14.00 to 17.00
Goblet, Cocktail,
3 1/2 Oz., 4 In. 10.00
Pickle, Oval, 9 1/2 In. 25.00
Pitcher, Ice Lip, 2 Qt. 85.00
Plate, Salad,
7 In. . . . . 9.00 to 10.00
Platter, 12 In. . . . 45.00 to 50.00
Relish, 2 Sections,
Handles, 7 In. 22.00
Relish, 3 Sections, Handles,
10 1/2 In. . . . . . 20.00 to 30.00
Salt & Pepper, Tray 25.00
Sandwich Tray, Handle . . 30.00
Sherbet, 5 Oz.,
3 5/8 In. . . . . . . 9.00 to 10.00
Soup, Cream 85.00
Sugar, Footed, 3 3/8 In. . . 12.00
Sugar &
Creamer . . . . . . 11.00 to 25.00
Torte Plate, 13 In. 57.00

Tray, For Sugar & Creamer,
6 In. 10.00
Tray, Muffin, Handles,
9 3/4 In. . . . . . . 32.00 to 57.00
Tumbler, Footed,
12 Oz., 5 3/4 In. 30.00
Tumbler, Juice, 5 Oz.,
3 5/8 In. . . . . . . 24.00 to 30.00
Tumbler, Water, 9 Oz.,
3 7/8 In. 22.00
Vase, Cornucopia, 9 In. . . 150.00
Vase, Flared, 6 In. 60.00

COLUMBIA

Columbia pattern can be found in Crystal but is rare in Pink. It was made by Federal Glass Company, Columbus, Ohio, from 1938 to 1942.

Crystal

Bowl, Cereal,
5 In. . . . . 17.00 to 20.00
Bowl, Ruffled Edge,
10 1/2 In. . . . . . 18.00 to 20.00
Bowl, Salad, 8 1/2 In. 20.00
Bowl, For Snack Plate . . . 10.00
Butter, Cover 20.00
Chop Plate,
11 In. . . . . 15.00 to 20.00
Cup 8.50
Cup & Saucer . . . 10.00 to 11.00
Plate, Bread & Butter,
6 In. . . . . 3.00 to 6.00
Plate, Luncheon,
9 1/2 In. . . . . . . 10.00 to 22.00
Saucer . . . . 2.00 to 3.00
Snack Plate, 8 3/4 In. 35.00
Soup, Dish,
8 In. . . . . 25.00 to 26.00

CONSTELLATION

Indiana Glass Company first made the Constellation pattern in the 1940s. Originally, the pattern was made in Crystal, Amber, Amberina, Green, Milk Glass, and Red. It was reissued in Sunset (Amberina) and Yellow Mist by Tiara Home Products in the 1980s.

Crystal
Sherbet 10.00

Green
Bowl, Oval, Handles,
   11 In. 12.00

CONTOUR

Contour pattern was made by Fostoria Glass Company from 1955 to 1977. Pieces were made in Crystal and Pink.

Crystal
Bowl, Fruit, 2 1/4 In. 22.00
Bowl, Vegetable, Oval,
   9 In. 50.00
Cake Stand, Round,
   Pedestal 36.00
Candlestick, 6 In. 30.00
Celery Dish, 8 7/8 In. 30.00

Celery Dish, Rose Cutting,
   9 In. 14.00
Coaster, 4 3/4 In. 12.00
Creamer, Flat, 3 1/2 In. . . 16.00
Cup & Saucer, Flat,
   2 3/8 In. 20.00
Goblet, Cordial, 3 In. 36.00
Goblet, Water, 5 7/8 In. . . 28.00
Goblet, Wine, 4 1/2 In. . . . 38.00
Jam Jar, 6 In. 34.00
Pickle, 7 1/4 In. 26.00
Pitcher, 1 Pt., 5 1/4 In. . . . 48.00
Pitcher, 7 1/8 In. 50.00
Plate, Dinner, 10 In. 28.00
Plate, Salad, 7 1/4 In. 15.00
Plate, Square, 8 3/8 In. . . . 18.00
Punch Bowl, Footed,
   12 7/8 In. 80.00
Relish, 2 Sections,
   7 1/2 In. 28.00
Relish, 3 Sections,
   10 3/4 In. 36.00
Sugar & Creamer 10.00
Sugar & Creamer, Tray . . 60.00
Tumbler, Iced Tea,
   6 1/8 In. 28.00
Tumbler, Juice,
   4 1/2 In. 20.00

Pink
Goblet, Cordial, 3 In. 45.00
Goblet, Water, 5 7/8 In. . . 28.00
Goblet, Wine, 4 1/2 In. . . . 36.00
Sherbet, 4 1/2 In. 27.00
Tumbler, Iced Tea,
   6 1/8 In. 28.00
Tumbler, Juice, 4
   1/2 In. 30.00

CORINTH

Crystal pieces of the Corinth pattern, made by Cambridge Glass Company from 1928 to 1933, were used for many etchings. Corinth jugs and tumblers were made in other colors.

Crystal
Candlestick, 5 In., Pair . . . 30.00

Goblet, Water, 9 Oz. 8.00
Sherbet 5.50
Tumbler, 10 Oz. 5.50
Tumbler, 13 Oz. 7.50

CORONATION

Coronation was made, primarily in berry sets, by Anchor Hocking Glass Corporation, Lancaster, Ohio, from 1936 to 1940. Most pieces are Pink, but there are also Crystal, Green, and Royal Ruby sets. The pattern is sometimes called Banded Fine Rib or Saxon. Some of the pieces are confused with those in Old Colony pattern.

Crystal
Cup, 4 1/2 In. 9.00
Goblet, Cocktail, 3 Oz. . . . 25.00

Pink
Cup . . . . 7.00 to 8.00
Cup & Saucer 15.00
Plate, Luncheon,
   8 1/2 In. 15.00
Plate, Sherbet,
   6 In. . . . . 5.00 to 10.00
Sherbet, Footed 10.00

Royal Ruby
Berry Bowl, 4 1/2 In. 9.00
Berry Bowl, Handles,
   4 1/2 In. . . . . 7.00 to 11.00
Berry Bowl, Master,
   8 In. 24.00
Berry Bowl, Master,
   Handles, 8 In. 15.00
Nappy,
   6 1/2 In. . . . . . . 15.00 to 20.00

CORSAGE

Fostoria Glass Company used the Corsage etch on Crystal stemware and dinnerware from 1935 to 1959. Many of the pieces are Lafayette and Baroque shapes.

Cup & Saucer 25.00
Oyster Cocktail, 4 Oz.,
   3 3/4 In. 17.00
Plate, 7 1/2 In. 10.00
Tumbler, Water, Footed,
   9 Oz., 5 1/2 In. 22.00

CRACKED ICE

Cracked Ice is an Art Deco–looking geometric pattern made by Indiana Glass Company in the 1930s. It was made in Green and Pink.

Pink

Plate, 6 1/2 In. 12.50
Sugar & Creamer, Cover,
   3 1/4 In. 180.00

CRAQUEL

Craquel was made by the U.S. Glass Company in 1924. It has an overall stippled finish. Pieces were made in Crystal with green trim and in Blue and Yellow.

Crystal

Sherbet, Green Trim,
   3 1/2 In. 9.00
Tumbler, Green Trim, 9 Oz.,
   3 3/4 In. 12.50

CREMAX

Cremax and Chinex Classic are confusing patterns. Cremax dishes have a pie-crust edge, but no scroll design like the one on Chinex. Also, the names Cremax and Chinex refer to colors as well as patterns. Cremax, made by the Macbeth-Evans Division of Corning Glass Works, was made from 1938 to 1942. It is a cream-colored opaque glass, sometimes decorated with floral or brown-tinted decals or with a colored rim.

Cup & Saucer, After
   Dinner . . . . 12.00 to 15.00
Cup & Saucer, Blue
   Trim 5.00
Pitcher 48.00
Sandwich Server, Pink Trim,
   11 1/2 In. . . . . . . 5.00 to 10.00
Saucer, Flower Decal 5.00
Saucer, Green Trim 3.00
Sugar 10.00

CRINOLINE
See Ripple

CRISS CROSS

The Criss Cross pattern is named for the embossed intersecting lines on the outside of the pieces. Kitchen items were made in Crystal, Green, Pink, and Ritz Blue by Hazel Atlas Glass Company in the 1930s. Some Crystal pieces are coated with fired-on colors.

Crystal

Bottle, Water, Label,
   64 Oz. 60.00
Butter, 1/4 Lb. 20.00
Butter, 1 Lb. . . . . 25.00 to 35.00
Butter, Chrome Cover
   & Tray . . . . 30.00 to 34.00
Butter, Cover Only,
   1/4 Lb. 10.00
Butter, No Cover, 1 Lb. . . 14.00
Creamer . . . . 20.00 to 35.00
Mixing Bowl,
   9 5/8 In. . . . . . . 25.00 to 30.00
Nappy, 4 1/2 In. 40.00
Reamer . . . . 12.00 to 19.50
Refrigerator Dish, Cobalt Blue
   Cover, 4 x 8 In. 53.00
Refrigerator Dish, Cover
   Only, 4 x 8 In. 10.00
Refrigerator Dish, Cover
   Only, 8 x 8 In. 14.00
Refrigerator Dish, Cover,
   4 x 4 In. 40.00

Green

Butter, Cover Only,
   1 Lb. 27.00
Butter, Cover,
   1 Lb. . . . . 50.00 to 75.00

Creamer 50.00
Reamer . . . . . . 40.00 to 50.00
Refrigerator Dish, Cover
Only, 4 x 8 In. 28.00
Refrigerator Dish, Cover,
4 x 4 In. 40.00
Refrigerator Dish, Cover,
4 x 8 In. 60.00

Pink
Reamer, Orange 375.00
Refrigerator Dish, No
Cover, 4 x 4 In. 19.00
Vase, 7 In. 35.00

Ritz Blue
Refrigerator Dish, Cover
Only, 4 x 4 In. 28.50
Refrigerator Dish, Cover
Only, 4 x 8 In. 58.00
Refrigerator Dish, Cover,
4 x 4 In. 125.00
Refrigerator Dish, No
Cover, 4 x 4 In. 54.00

CROW'S FOOT

Crow's Foot is the popular name for Paden City Glass Manufacturing Company's Lines 412 and 890. The pattern was made in the 1930s in Amber, Amethyst, Black, Crystal, Pink, Ritz Blue, Ruby, White, and Yellow. See the Nora Bird and Peacock & Wild Rose sections for Crow's Foot pieces with etchings.

Amber
Soup, Cream 10.00

Amethyst
Candlestick, 5 3/4 In. 53.00

Black
Candlestick, Mushroom,
2 1/2 In., Pair 80.00
Ice Bucket, Wicker Handle,
6 3/4 x 7 In. 290.00
Plate, 8 5/8 In. 15.00

Crystal
Bowl, Oval,
10 3/4 x 7 In. 55.00

Candlestick, Sterling
Silver Overlay,
5 3/4 In., Pair 65.00
Candy Dish, Cover, 3 Sections,
Engraved Leaves,
6 1/2 In. 45.00
Candy Dish, Cover, 3 Sections,
Sterling Silver Fruit,
6 1/2 In. 80.00

Pink
Cup & Saucer, Footed . . . 12.00
Plate, Square, 8 1/2 In. 8.00

Ritz Blue
Candlestick, Mushroom,
2 1/2 In., Pair 90.00
Cup, Footed 17.50
Sugar & Creamer, Sterling
Silver Overlay, 3 In. . . . 75.00

Ruby
Compote, 6 1/2 In. 75.00
Creamer, Footed 18.00
Cup & Saucer 25.00
Plate, Handles,
10 1/2 In. 45.00
Saucer 12.00
Soup, Cream 27.50
Sugar . . . . 18.00 to 20.00
Vase, 9 3/4 x
6 5/8 x 4 1/2 In. 150.00

CRYSTOLITE

A.H. Heisey & Company made Crystolite from 1938 to 1957. The extensive pattern line was made mostly in Crystal. A few pieces can be found in Sahara (yellow) and Zircon (light turquoise). Many pieces are marked with the Diamond H logo.

Crystal
Basket, 8 In. 328.00
Bowl, Conserve, 2 Sections,
8 In. 31.00
Bowl, Flared, 11 1/2 In. . . 20.00
Bowl, Gardenia, Flared,
4 x 12 In. 25.00
Bowl, Oval, Footed,
13 In. 80.00
Cake Stand, Pedestal Foot,
10 In. 820.00
Candleholder, Square Block,
2 1/2 In., Pair 40.00
Candlestick, 2-Light,
6 In. 36.00
Candy Box, Cover,
7 In. 60.00
Candy Dish, Cover,
3 Sections, 6 3/4 In. 40.00
Candy Dish, Cover,
7 In. 27.00
Candy Dish, Cover,
Shell, 5 1/2 In. 40.00
Celery Dish, Oval,
13 In. 50.00
Celery Dish, Oval, Handle,
7 In. 35.00
Celery Tray, 12 In. 19.00
Cheese Dish, Footed,
5 In. 35.00
Cigarette Box, Cover,
4 In. . . . . 20.00 to 35.00
Cigarette Box, Cover, Footed,
4 1/2 In. . . . . . . 30.00 to 40.00
Cruet, Stopper, 2 Oz. 25.00
Cruet, Stopper, 3 Oz. 40.00
Cup & Saucer . . . 20.00 to 30.00
Dish, Jelly, Footed,
5 In. 20.00
Dish, Preserve,
6 3/4 In. 21.00
Dish, Mayonnaise, 5 In. . . 33.00
Goblet, Cocktail,
3 1/2 Oz. 20.00
Mustard, Cover,
2 1/2 In. 40.00
Nappy, 5 1/2 In. 11.00
Plate, Coupe, 7 1/2 In. . . . 25.00
Plate, Dinner, 10 1/2 In. . . 71.00
Plate, Salad, 7 In. 10.00
Plate, Star Bottom,
8 In. 20.00
Puff Box, Cover,
4 x 4 3/4 In. 26.00

Punch Cup 10.00

Punch Set, 15 Piece 230.00

Relish, 2 Sections, Center
Handle . . . . 26.00 to 33.00

Relish, 5 Sections,
10 In. 40.00

Relish, Leaf Shape,
9 In. 16.00

Relish, Oval, 3 Sections,
9 In. 25.00

Salt & Pepper 35.00

Sherbet, 6 Oz., 3 7/8 In. . . 18.00

Sugar, 2 In. 10.00

Sugar,
3 1/2 In. . . . . . . 15.00 to 18.00

Sugar & Creamer,
Round 60.00

Sugar & Creamer,
Tray . . . . . . 35.00 to 40.00

Torte Plate, 11 In. 35.00

Torte Plate, 14 In. 40.00

Tray, Oval, 12 1/2 In. 25.00

Tumbler, Barrel, 10 Oz. . . 95.00

Tumbler, Blown,
10 Oz. . . . . , 40.00

Vase, Flared, 5 In. 16.00

CUBE
See Cubist

CUBIST

Cubist, or Cube, molded
with the expected rectan-
gular and diamond pattern,
was made by Jeannette
Glass Company from 1929
to 1933. It was made first
in Crystal and Pink. Later,
Green replaced Crystal,
and Amber, Blue, Canary

Yellow, Pink, Ultramarine,
and White were added.
Various shades of some of
the colors were made. It
has been made recently in
Amber, Avocado, and
Opaque White.

Crystal

Bowl, Gold Trim,
4 1/2 In. 5.00

Plate, Sherbet,
6 In. . . . . 2.00 to 3.00

Sugar, 2 1/2 In. 4.00

Sugar & Creamer 3.00

Tray, For Sugar & Creamer,
8 1/4 x 7 1/4 In. 6.00

Green

Bowl, Deep,
4 1/2 In. . . . . 5.00 to 8.00

Bowl, Dessert, Pointed
Edge, 4 1/2 In. 13.00

Butter, Cover . . . 58.00 to 60.00

Butter, Cover Only 40.00

Butter, No Cover 30.00

Candy Jar, Cover 45.00

Candy Jar, Cover,
Footed, 6 In. 19.00

Coaster,
3 1/4 In. . . . . 8.00 to 10.00

Creamer, 3 9/16 In. 10.00

Cup 12.00

Pitcher, 45 Oz.,
8 3/4 In. 200.00

Plate, Luncheon,
8 In. . . . . 12.00 to 13.00

Plate, Sherbet,
6 In. . . . . 4.00 to 8.00

Powder Jar 29.00

Salt & Pepper . . . 35.00 to 50.00

Sherbet, Footed . . . 9.00 to 10.00

Sugar, Cover 30.00

Sugar & Creamer,
Cover 42.00

Tumbler, 9 Oz., 4 In. 80.00

Pink

Bowl, Deep, 4 1/2 In. 10.00

Bowl, Salad, 6 1/2 In. 14.00

Butter, Cover . . 79.00 to 100.00

Butter, No Cover 23.00

Candy Jar, 6 1/2 In. 18.00

Candy Jar, Cover,
6 1/2 In. . . . . . . 30.00 to 40.00

Coaster, 3 1/4 In. 10.00

Creamer, 2 5/8 In. 5.00

Creamer, 3 9/16 In. 12.00

Cup 7.00

Pitcher, 45 Oz.,
8 3/4 In. . . . . 235.00 to 350.00

Plate, Luncheon, 8 In. 15.00

Plate, Sherbet,
6 In. . . . . 4.00 to 9.00

Powder Jar, Cover,
3-Footed . . . . . 35.00 to 39.00

Powder Jar, No Cover . . . 10.00

Saltshaker . . . . . . 15.00 to 17.00

Saucer 2.50

Sugar, 2 3/8 In. 5.00

Sugar, 3 In. . . . . . . 7.00 to 8.00

Sugar, Cover, 3 In. 28.00

Sugar & Creamer,
Cover 32.00

Sugar & Creamer,
Small . . . . 8.00 to 11.00

Tumbler, 9 Oz.,
4 In. . . . . 65.00 to 85.00

CUPID

There is an etched pair of
Cupids on the pattern
with the name Cupid. The
pattern was made in the
1930s by the Paden City
Glass Manufacturing Com-
pany of Paden City, West
Virginia. It was made in
Black, Green, Light Blue,
Pink, and Yellow. Some
pieces have gold trim.

Green

Creamer, Footed,
4 1/2 In. 120.00

Dish, Mayonnaise,
6 In. 145.00

Dish, Mayonnaise, Underplate,
Ladle 220.00

Sugar & Creamer 345.00

Pink

Ice Tub, 4 1/2 In. 400.00

Sugar 150.00

DAISY
See No. 620

DAISY PETALS
See Petalware

DANCING GIRL
See Cameo

DECAGON

Decagon, named for its 10-sided outline, was made by the Cambridge Glass Company of Cambridge, Ohio. The pattern, dating from the 1930s, was made in Amber, Amethyst, Carmen (red), Ebony, Emerald, Moonlight Blue (light blue), Peach-Blo (pink), and Royal Blue.

Amber
Cup & Saucer 12.00
Goblet, Cocktail,
  3 1/2 Oz. 12.00
Goblet, Cordial, 1 Oz. . . . 50.00
Gravy Boat,
  2 Spouts . . . . . . 70.00 to 75.00
Plate, Salad, 8 1/2 In. 10.00
Sugar 15.00
Sugar & Creamer 48.00
Tray, Oval, 11 In. 65.00
Tumbler, Footed, 8 Oz. . . 12.00

Crystal
Bowl, Fruit, 5 1/2 In. 6.00
Creamer 8.50
Plate, Bread & Butter,
  6 In. 4.00

Ebony
Ice Bucket, 5 3/4 In. 20.00

Emerald
Gravy Boat 5.50
Soup, Dish, Flat Rim,
  8 1/2 In. 70.00

Moonlight Blue
Bowl, 12 In. 60.00

Creamer 20.00
Cup & Saucer 15.00
Goblet, Champagne,
  6 Oz. 25.00
Goblet, Water, 9 Oz. 30.00
Plate, 8 1/2 In. 15.00
Sandwich Server, Center
  Handle, 12 In. 50.00
Sugar 20.00
Sugar & Creamer 30.00
Sugar & Creamer, Tray,
  Center Handle, Lightning
  Bolt Handles 130.00
Tumbler, Footed, 8 Oz. . . 30.00

Peach-Blo
Creamer 12.00
Cruet, 6 Oz. 155.00
Cup & Saucer 8.00
Ice Bucket, Handle,
  Tongs 60.00
Sugar, Lightning Bolt
  Handles 16.00

DECORATED TUMBLERS

Decorated tumblers have been made by Anchor Hocking, Federal, Hazel Atlas, Libbey, and other companies since the 1930s, when the pyroglaze process of printing was introduced. The barware and other glasses feature drinking jokes, characters, or decorative geometric patterns. Sportsman Series, Swankyswig, White Ship, and Windmill patterns are listed in their own categories.

Tumbler, Animal, Elephant,
  York, 4 3/4 In. 10.00
Tumbler, Animal, Kicky
  Kangaroo Kicking Field
  Goal, Yellow, Black,
  1940s, 4 3/4 In. 20.00
Tumbler, Animal, Tricky
  Tiger Doing Magic,
  Orange, Black, Federal,
  1940s, 4 3/4 In. 20.00
Tumbler, Antique Autos . . . 3.00
Tumbler, Bicycle Built For
  Two, Forest Green, Anchor
  Hocking, 6 1/4 In. 16.00
Tumbler, Black Rectangles, Gold
  Lines, 6 In. 2.00
Tumbler, Deco Star, Federal,
  5 1/2 In. 2.00
Tumbler, Famous Americans,
  Thomas Jefferson, Author
  & Statesman, Black,
  5 3/8 In. 3.00
Tumbler, Game Of Croquet,
  Forest Green, Anchor Hocking,
  5 In. 16.00
Tumbler, Iced Tea, Blue
  Leaf, Anchor Hocking,
  14 Oz. 5.00
Tumbler, Iced Tea, Civil War
  Centennial, Crossed
  Confederate Flags 5.00
Tumbler, Iced Tea, Colorado
  Centennial, Discovery Of Gold
  At Little Dry Creek 3.00
Tumbler, Iced Tea, Currier &
  Ives, White, Blue Decal, Hazel
  Atlas, 12 Oz., 5 In. 12.00
Tumbler, Iced Tea, Horse Car,
  Royal Ruby, Anchor Hocking,
  13 Oz., 5 In. 12.00
Tumbler, Iced Tea, Kansas,
  Chisholm Trail,
  6 1/2 In. 5.00
Tumbler, Iced Tea, Kansas,
  Dodge City Marshal,
  3 3/4 In. 4.00
Tumbler, Iced Tea,
  Kansas, Santa Fe Trail,
  3 3/4 In. 4.00
Tumbler, Iced Tea, Lime Green,
  Yellow, Brown Circles,
  Black Lines, Federal,
  6 3/4 In. 8.00
Tumbler, Iced Tea, Missouri,
  Capitol, Jefferson City,
  6 1/2 In. 5.00

Tumbler, Iced Tea, Missouri,
Tom Sawyer, 3 3/4 In. . . . 4.00

Tumbler, Iced Tea, Ohio
Indians, Pontiac The Red
Napoleon 5.00

Tumbler, Iced Tea,
Ohio Indians, Tecumseh,
Shawnee 4.00

Tumbler, Iced Tea, Snowflake,
Federal, 7 In. 5.50

Tumbler, Juice, Tomato Vines,
Hazel Atlas, 5 Oz. 3.00

Tumbler, Michigan, Traverse
City, Famous Sugar Sand
Miracle Mile, Frosted,
6 In. 3.00

Tumbler, New Year's, Baby
New Year, Federal, 1950s,
4 3/4 In. 15.00

Tumbler, New Year's, Clock At
Midnight, Federal, 1950s,
4 3/4 In. 15.00

Tumbler, Nursery Rhymes,
Hickety Pickety, Ribbed,
Yellow, Hazel Atlas,
4 1/8 In. 24.00

Tumbler, Nursery Rhymes,
Jolly Old Pig, Ribbed,
White, Hazel Atlas,
4 1/8 In. 29.00

Tumbler, Nursery Rhymes,
Little Boy Blue, Dark Blue,
Federal, 5 In. 6.00

Tumbler, Nursery Rhymes,
Little Miss Muffet, Libbey,
Red, 4 5/8 In. 8.00

Tumbler, Nursery Rhymes,
Mary Had A Little Lamb,
Ribbed, White, Hazel
Atlas, 4 1/8 In. 20.00

Tumbler, Nursery Rhymes,
Queen Of Hearts, Ribbed,
Yellow, Hazel Atlas,
4 1/8 In. 14.00

Tumbler, Nursery Rhymes,
Tom, Tom, Piper's Son,
Ribbed, White, Hazel
Atlas, 4 1/8 In. 20.00

Tumbler, Pink Elephant,
5 In. 6.00

Tumbler, Surrey, Forest
Green, Anchor Hocking,
5 In. 16.00

Tumbler, Thanksgiving,
Campfire, Brown, Green,
Yellow, Federal, 1950s,
4 3/4 In. 15.00

Tumbler, Thanksgiving,
Pilgrim Hats, Haystacks,
Federal Glass Co.,
4 3/4 In. 15.00

Tumbler, Thanksgiving, Pilgrim
Hats, Turkeys, Federal Glass
Co., 4 3/4 In. 15.00

Tumbler, Thanksgiving,
Pilgrim, Brown, Green,
Yellow, Federal, 1950s,
4 3/4 In. 15.00

Tumbler, Whiskey, Say When,
Hazel Atlas,
4 Oz. . . . . 2.00 to 4.00

Tumbler, Wild Birds, Federal
Glass, Frosted 25.00

Tumbler & Coaster Set, Silver
Heraldic Shields, Chrome
Holder, 9 Piece 20.00

Tumbler Set, Hi-Ball,
Gold Leaf, Metal Holder,
7 Piece 25.00

Tumbler Set, Hi-Ball, Pheasant,
4 Piece 10.00

Tumbler Set, Hi-Ball, Pheasant,
Frosted, West Virginia Glass,
6 Piece 5.00

Tumbler Set, Rocks, Black,
Gold Coins, Georges Briard,
4 Piece 10.00

DELLA ROBBIA

Della Robbia is a heavy glass pattern with raised pears and apples as part of the design. It was made by Westmoreland Glass Company, Grapeville, Pennsylvania, from 1926 to the 1960s. The pattern was made mostly in Crystal. Amber, Green, Milk Glass, and Roselin were also found. Crystal pieces

often have fruit stained in natural colors.

Crystal

Bowl, Belled, Footed,
Red Flashed, 12 In. . . . 125.00

Cake Stand, 14 In. 150.00

Candy Jar,
Cover . . . . 95.00 to 115.00

Compote, 3 5/8 In. 52.00

Creamer 12.00

Goblet, Water, 8 Oz.,
6 In. . . . . 23.00 to 45.00

Plate, Dinner,
10 1/2 In. 9.00

Plate, Luncheon,
9 In. . . . . 25.00 to 35.00

Plate, Salad, 7 1/4 In. 22.00

Sugar, Deep 18.00

Sugar, Footed 17.00

Sugar, Red Flashed 12.00

Torte Plate,
14 In. . . . . 90.00 to 140.00

Tumbler, Footed, 8 Oz.,
4 3/4 In. . . . . . . 15.00 to 29.00

Tumbler, Ginger Ale,
5 Oz. 25.00

Tumbler, Iced Tea, Belled,
Flared Rim, 12 Oz. 63.00

Tumbler, Iced Tea, Footed,
6 x 3 3/8 x 2 3/4 In. 43.00

Milk Glass

Candy Jar, Footed, Cover,
7 1/2 In. 15.00

DELPHITE

The term Delphite is used to describe opaque light blue glass. Jeannette Glass Company used the name Delphite for kitchenware and some dinnerware made in the 1920s and '30s. All of the pieces of kitchenware made of Delphite by Jeannette were also made of Jadite. Jadite pieces are listed in their own category in this book.

Collectors also call other companies' opaque light blue glass Delphite. McKee's similar pieces in Chalaine Blue and Seville Yellow are listed in the Kitchen category in this book.

Ashtray, Cowboy Hat,
  4 1/2 In. 37.00
Ashtray, Match Holder,
  3 1/4 In. 185.00
Bowl, Horizontal Ribs,
  9 3/4 In. 250.00
Bowl, Vertical Ribs,
  9 In. 175.00
Canister, Tea, 20 Oz. . . . 300.00
Drip Jar, Cover Only,
  4 3/4 In. 75.00
Match Holder,
  3 1/4 In. 125.00
Measuring Cup, 8 Oz. . . 125.00
Measuring Cup Set,
  3 Piece 275.00
Measuring Cup Set,
  4 Piece 325.00
Refrigerator Dish, Cover,
  4 x 8 In. . . . . 155.00 to 170.00
Refrigerator Dish,
  Cover, Round,
  32 Oz. . . . . . 115.00 to 170.00
Shaker, Pepper, Square . . 125.00
Vase, Bud 38.00

DEWDROP

Dewdrop was made in 1954 and 1955 by Jeannette Glass Company, Jeannette, Pennsylvania. It is available only in Crystal.

Bowl, Vegetable,
  8 1/2 In. 12.00
Cup 4.00
Pitcher, 7 1/4 In. 11.00
Plate, 11 1/2 In. 13.00
Punch Bowl, 10 1/2 In. . . . 25.00
Punch Bowl Base 12.00
Punch Set, Bowl, Base,
  Cups, 14 Piece 75.00

Relish, Leaf Shape,
  Handle 8.00
Snack Set, 2 Piece 8.00
Tray, 13 In. . . . . 10.00 to 22.00
Tray, Lazy Susan, 13 In. . 43.00

DIAMOND
See Windsor

DIAMOND PATTERN
See Miss America

DIAMOND POINT

Diamond Point is a newer version of the nineteenth-century Mitered Diamond pressed glass pattern. Indiana Glass Company first made the pattern in the 1960s in Amber, Crystal, Crystal with Ruby Stain, Milk Glass, and other colors. From 1971 to 1983, Indiana produced Diamond Point for Tiara Exclusives in Blue Etched, Cameo (black), Crystal, Gold Carnival, Horizon Blue, and Teal.

Amber
Candlelamp, 5 3/8 In. 12.00

Crystal
Candlelamp, 5 3/8 In. 12.00
Candy Dish, Cover 12.00
Candy Jar, Cover 22.00
Compote,
  7 1/4 In. . . . . . . 10.00 to 15.00
Creamer 8.00
Creamer, Footed 10.00
Goblet 15.00
Ice Tub 8.00
Punch Cup 13.00
Sugar & Creamer 10.00
Vase, Footed,
  8 In. . . . . 10.00 to 12.00

Ruby Stain
Candy Dish, Cover 12.00
Compote, 7 1/4 In. 13.00

DIAMOND QUILTED

Collectors use the names Diamond Quilted or Flat Diamond for the No. 414 line made by Imperial Glass Company, Bellaire, Ohio, in the 1920s and early 1930s. It was made in Amber, Black, Blue, Crystal, Green, Pink, and Red. Dinner sets, luncheon sets, and serving pieces, including a large punch bowl, were made, but not all items were made in all colors.

Black
Bowl, Handle, 5 1/2 In. . . . 18.00
Bowl, Ruffled Edge,
  7 In. 20.00
Candlestick 25.00
Creamer . . . . 11.00 to 17.00
Cup 17.00
Saucer 6.00
Sugar 17.00

Blue
Bowl, 7 In. 20.00
Candlestick 25.00
Cup 18.00
Plate, Sherbet, 6 In. 8.00

Green
Candlestick . . . . . 15.00 to 25.00
Candy Jar, Cover 45.00
Compote, Cover,
  11 1/2 In. 140.00
Plate, Luncheon,
  8 In. . . . . 8.00 to 12.00
Plate, Sherbet, 6 In. 4.00
Sherbet 8.00
Sugar 10.00

Pink
Bowl, 7 In. 20.00

Bowl, Handle, 5 1/2 In. . . . 15.00
Bowl, Ruffled Edge,
7 In. 9.00
Candlestick,
Pair . . . . 16.00 to 30.00
Creamer 12.00
Plate, Luncheon,
8 In. . . . . 10.00 to 12.00
Sugar 10.00

DIANA

Diana is one of the many
Depression glass patterns
with swirls in the glass.
Federal Glass Company,
Columbus, Ohio, made
this pattern, sometimes
called Swirled Sharp Rib,
from 1937 to 1941. It was
made in Amber, Crystal,
Green, and Pink, and can
be distinguished from
other swirled patterns by
the two sets of swirls
used—one in the center
of the piece, another on
the rim. A Pink bowl was
reproduced in 1987.

Amber
Bowl, Fruit,
11 In. . . . . 18.00 to 28.00
Candy Jar, Cover 48.00
Cup & Saucer 4.25
Plate, Dinner, 9 1/2 In. . . . 60.00
Platter, 12 In. . . . 12.00 to 22.00
Sandwich Server,
11 1/2 In. . . . . . 15.00 to 28.00
Sherbet 12.00
Soup, Cream, 5 1/2 In. . . . 20.00

Crystal
Bowl, Cereal,
5 In. . . . . 5.00 to 6.00
Bowl, Flared, Scalloped
Edge, 12 In. . . . 15.00 to 18.00

Candlestick, 2-Light, Keyhole,
Stem, Pair 85.00
Candy Dish, Cover,
3 Sections 100.00
Cocktail Icer, Insert 80.00
Cup, After
Dinner . . . . 5.00 to 7.00
Cup & Saucer 5.00
Cup & Saucer,
After Dinner . . 10.00 to 13.00
Plate, Bread & Butter,
6 In. 4.00
Plate, Dinner, 9 1/2 In. 8.00
Relish, 2 Sections, 6 In. . . 25.00
Sandwich Server,
11 3/4 In. 15.00
Saucer 2.00
Saucer, After
Dinner . . . . 4.00 to 6.00
Sherbet, Green Trim 45.00
Soup, Cream,
5 1/2 In. . . . . . . 8.00 to 13.00

Pink
Bowl, Cereal,
5 In. . . . . 7.00 to 9.00
Bowl, Handles,
10 In. 225.00
Bowl, Salad, 9 In. 25.00
Candy Dish,
Cover . . . . 25.00 to 63.00
Creamer 12.00
Cup & Saucer, After
Dinner 35.00
Plate, Bread & Butter,
6 In. . . . . 5.00 to 8.00
Plate, Dinner,
9 1/2 In. . . . . . . 15.00 to 20.00
Platter, Oval, 12 In. 30.00
Saucer 5.00
Sherbet 12.00

DOGWOOD

Dogwood is decorated
with a flower that has
been given many names.
Collectors have called this

pattern Apple Blossom, B
pattern, Magnolia, or Wildrose. It was made from
1930 to 1934 by Macbeth-
Evans Glass Company. It is
found in Cremax, Crystal,
Green, Monax, Pink, and
Yellow. Some Pink pieces
are trimmed with gold.
Some pieces were made
with such thin walls, the
factory redesigned the
molds to make the pieces
thicker.

Crystal
Plate, Luncheon,
8 In. . . . . 14.00 to 20.00
Sugar, Thick, Footed 19.00

Green
Bowl, Cereal, 5 1/2 In. . . . 35.00
Cup . . . . 40.00 to 45.00
Cup & Saucer 53.00
Grill Plate, 10 1/2 In. 17.50
Plate, Bread & Butter,
6 In. . . . . 7.50 to 12.00
Plate, Luncheon,
8 In. . . . . 7.50 to 22.00
Saucer 7.25
Sugar 23.00
Tumbler, 10 Oz., 4 In. . . . 28.00

Monax
Salver,
12 In. . . . . 15.00 to 35.00

Pink
Berry Bowl, Master,
8 1/2 In. . . . . . . 54.00 to 75.00
Bowl, Cereal,
5 1/2 In. . . . . . . 30.00 to 38.00
Creamer, Footed,
3 1/4 In. 24.00
Creamer, Thin,
2 1/2 In. . . . . . . 20.00 to 25.00
Cup . . . . 17.00 to 24.00
Cup & Saucer,
Thick . . . . 24.00 to 28.00
Cup & Saucer,
Thin . . . . 18.00 to 35.00
Grill Plate,
10 1/2 In. . . . . . 19.50 to 40.00
Luncheon Set,
12 Piece 135.00

Plate, Bread & Butter,
6 In. . . . . 6.00 to 9.50

Plate, Dinner,
9 1/4 In. . . . . . . 33.00 to 45.00

Plate, Luncheon,
8 In. . . . . 6.75 to 15.00

Platter, Oval, 12 In. 730.00

Salver, 12 In. . . . 35.00 to 49.00

Saucer, Thick 8.00

Saucer, Thin 7.00

Sherbet . . . . 31.00 to 40.00

Sugar, Thick,
3 1/4 In. . . . . . . 18.00 to 20.00

Sugar, Thin, 2 1/2 In. 20.00

Sugar & Creamer, Thick, Footed,
3 1/4 In. . . . . . . 38.00 to 45.00

Sugar & Creamer, Thin . . 38.00

Tumbler, 9 Oz., 4 In. 10.00

Tumbler, 10 Oz., 4 In. . . . 16.00

Tumbler, 11 Oz.,
4 3/4 In. . . . . . . 18.50 to 30.00

Tumbler, 12 Oz.,
5 In. . . . . 51.00 to 80.00

Tumbler, Juice, 5 Oz.,
3 1/2 In. 24.00

DOLLY MADISON

Fostoria Glass Company's Dolly Madison pattern features cut flutes around the bases of the stemware and the borders of plates and accessories. It was made from 1939 to 1973 in Crystal.

Champagne, 6 Oz.,
4 7/8 In. 18.00

Goblet, 9 Oz., 6 3/8 In. . . . 20.00

Goblet, Cordial, 1 Oz.,
3 3/8 In. 30.00

❖

Re-key all locks when you move to a new house or apartment or if you lose a key.

❖

Goblet, Wine, 4 Oz.,
4 3/4 In. 24.00

Tumbler, Iced Tea, Footed,
12 Oz., 5 3/4 In. 19.00

Tumbler, Juice, Footed,
5 Oz., 4 1/2 In. 17.00

DOLORES

Dolores etch was used on Crystal items made by Tiffin Glass Company (Factory R of U.S. Glass Company) from 1923 to 1929.

Compote, Graduated Bead
Stem, 6 1/2 In. 49.00

Console, Beaded & Scalloped
Edge, 13 x 3 In. 85.00

Decanter, Stopper, Bell,
11 In. . . . . , . . 140.00

Goblet, Cocktail,
4 3/8 In. 26.00

Goblet, Water, 6 5/8 In. . . 30.00

Pitcher, Water, 2 Qt. 250.00

Relish, 3 Sections, Beaded
& Scalloped Edge,
12 1/2 x 10 1/2 In. 65.00

Sherbet, 3 1/4 In. 28.00

Sherbet, 5 In. 28.00

Sugar & Creamer 49.00

Tumbler, Flat, 2 5/8 In. . . 26.00

Tumbler, Juice,
3 1/2 In. 26.00

DORIC

Doric was made by Jeannette Glass Company, Jeannette, Pennsylvania, from 1935 to 1938. The molded pattern has also inspired another name for the pattern, Snowflake. It was made in Delphite

(opaque blue), Green, Pink, and Yellow. A few White pieces may have been made.

Delphite

Candy Dish,
3 Sections 9.00

Sherbet . . . . 6.00 to 14.00

Green

Berry Bowl,
4 1/2 In. . . . . . . 9.00 to 16.00

Berry Bowl, Master,
8 1/4 In. 36.00

Berry Set, 7 Piece 100.00

Bowl, Handles, 9 In. 25.00

Bowl, Vegetable, Oval,
Handles, 9 In. 44.00

Butter, Cover 125.00

Cake Plate, 3-Footed,
10 In. 22.50

Candy Dish,
Cover . . . . 44.00 to 55.00

Cup . . . . 10.00 to 13.00

Grill Plate,
9 In. . . . . 21.00 to 28.00

Plate, Dinner,
9 In. . . . . 18.00 to 30.00

Plate, Sherbet,
6 In. . . . . 5.00 to 8.25

Platter, Oval, 12 In. 22.00

Relish, Handles,
4 x 4 In. 19.00

Relish, Handles,
4 x 8 In. . . . . . . 21.00 to 23.00

Salt & Pepper . . . 42.00 to 60.00

Saucer . . . . 3.00 to 5.25

Sherbet . . . . 12.00 to 23.00

Soup, Cream, 5 In. 50.00

Sugar, Cover Only 32.00

Tray, Handles,
10 In. . . . . 20.00 to 27.00

Tray, Square, 8 In. 37.00

Pink

Berry Bowl,
4 1/2 In. . . . . . . 9.00 to 12.00

Berry Bowl, Master,
8 1/4 In. 32.00

Berry Set, 7 Piece 109.00

Bowl, Cereal, 5 1/2 In. . . . 90.00

Bowl, Handles, 9 In. 42.00

Bowl, Vegetable, Oval,
9 In. . . . . 28.00 to 47.00

Cake Plate, 3-Footed,
   10 In. . . . . 30.00 to 32.00
Candy Dish,
   3 Sections . . . . 13.00 to 15.00
Candy Dish,
   Cover Only 20.00
Candy Dish, Cover,
   8 In. . . . . 24.00 to 48.00
Cup & Saucer . . . 13.00 to 18.00
Grill Plate,
   9 In. . . . . 24.00 to 27.00
Pitcher, 32 Oz.,
   5 1/2 In. 42.00
Plate, Dinner,
   9 In. . . . . 14.00 to 30.00
Plate, Sherbet, 6 In. 10.00
Platter, Oval,
   12 In. . . . . 29.00 to 34.00
Relish, Handles,
   4 x 8 In. 22.00
Salt & Pepper . . . 50.00 to 56.00
Saltshaker 16.00
Sherbet . . . . 10.00 to 23.00
Sugar 21.00
Sugar, Cover 38.00
Sugar, Cover Only 19.00
Tray, Handles,
   10 In. . . . . 19.00 to 32.00
Tray, Square, Handles,
   8 In. . . . . 43.00 to 50.00
Tumbler, 9 Oz.,
   4 1/2 In. . . . . . . 45.00 to 80.00

DORIC & PANSY

Doric & Pansy features the
snowflake design of Doric
alternating with pansies. It,
too, was made by Jean-
nette Glass Company, but
only in 1937 and 1938. It
was made in Crystal, Pink,
and Ultramarine. The
Ultramarine varied in

color from green to blue.
Collectors pay more for
the blue shades. A set of
child's dishes called Pretty
Polly Party Dishes was
made in this pattern.

Pink
Creamer,
   Child's . . . . 39.00 to 50.00
Cup & Saucer, Child's . . . 48.00
Saucer, Child's 10.00
Sugar, Child's 39.00
Sugar & Creamer,
   Child's 90.00

Ultramarine
Berry Bowl, 4 1/2 In. 25.00
Child's Set,
   14 Piece . . . . 255.00 to 300.00
Creamer 65.00
Cup . . . . 22.00 to 60.00
Cup & Saucer . . . 25.00 to 35.00
Plate, Child's 18.00
Plate, Dinner, 9 In. 37.00
Plate, Sherbet,
   6 In. . . . . 13.00 to 20.00
Salt &
   Pepper . . . . . 326.00 to 400.00
Saucer 13.00
Saucer, Child's . . . . 5.00 to 8.00
Sugar 65.00
Sugar & Creamer 250.00
Tray, Handles, 10 In. 33.00
Tumbler, 10 Oz.,
   4 1/4 In. 500.00

DORIC WITH PANSY
See Doric & Pansy

DOUBLE SHIELD
See Mt. Pleasant

DOUBLE SWIRL
See Swirl Jeannette

DRAPE & TASSEL
See Princess

DUTCH
See Windmill

DUTCH ROSE
See Rosemary

EARLY AMERICAN PRESCUT

Early American Prescut
was made by Anchor
Hocking Glass Corpora-
tion, Lancaster, Ohio,
from 1960 to 1998. The
pieces have an imitation
cut glass design and were
made in Crystal, Honey
Gold, Laser Blue, Royal
Ruby, and with tints
(Amber, Avocado, Blue,
and Ruby). There are
other imitation cut glass
patterns that are easily
confused with Early Amer-
ican Prescut. All of the
pieces in Anchor Hocking's
pattern have ten-point
stars except the punch
cups and Lazy Susan
inserts.

Crystal
Ashtray, 7 3/4 In. 15.00
Bowl, 3-Footed,
   6 3/4 In. . . . . 4.00 to 6.00
Bowl, 4 1/4 In. 18.00
Bowl, 5 1/4 In. . . . . 2.00 to 6.00
Bowl, 7 1/4 In. 8.50
Bowl, Cover, 4 1/4 In. 8.00
Bowl, Gondola, 9 3/8 In. . . 8.00
Bowl, Salad,
   10 3/4 In. . . . . . 10.00 to 18.00
Bowl, Scalloped Rim,
   5 1/4 In. 7.00
Bowl, Scalloped Rim,
   7 1/4 In. 20.00
Bowl, Scalloped Rim,
   8 3/4 In. 11.00
Butter, Cover . . . . 3.50 to 10.00
Candlestick, 2-Light,
   5 1/2 x 7 In. . . . 15.00 to 20.00

Candy Dish, Cover,
  5 1/4 In. 10.00
Candy Dish, Cover,
  7 1/2 In. 18.00
Chip & Dip 33.00
Console, 9 In. 8.50
Creamer . . . . 4.00 to 7.00
Cruet, Stopper 8.00
Cup 3.00
Egg Plate,
  11 3/4 In. . . . . . 25.00 to 65.00
Jam Jar, Cover 72.00
Juice Set, Pitcher, Tumblers,
  12 Oz., 7 Piece 23.00
Lazy Susan, Cover,
  13 1/2 In. 35.00
Pitcher, 18 Oz. 8.00
Pitcher, 60 Oz.,
  8 1/2 In. . . . . . . 25.00 to 45.00
Pitcher, Milk,
  12 Oz. . . . . 6.00 to 8.00
Pitcher, Square, 40 Oz.,
  5 1/2 In. 45.00
Pitcher, Square, 48 Oz.,
  6 In. 25.00
Plate, 11 In. . . . . . 10.00 to 14.00
Platter,
  13 1/2 In. . . . . . 13.00 to 15.00
Platter, Round, 11 In. 10.00
Punch Bowl, 7 x 14 In. 9.50
Punch Bowl Base,
  6 1/2 x 8 1/2 In. 40.00
Punch Set, 13 3/4 In.,
  15 Piece 35.00
Relish, 2 Sections,
  10 In. . . . . 3.00 to 10.00
Relish, 3 Sections,
  11 7/8 In. 14.00
Relish, 4 Sections, Swirl
  Dividers, 11 In. 90.00
Relish, 5 Sections,
  13 1/2 In. 15.00
Salad Set, Fork, Spoon,
  Box, 4 Piece 60.00
Salt & Pepper,
  Metal Tops 6.00
Snack Set, Cup & Plate,
  6 3/4 In., 2 Piece 65.00
Snack Set, Cup & Plate,
  10 In., 2 Piece 8.00
Sugar, Cover, Turquoise
  Tint 35.00
Sugar & Creamer 5.00
Syrup . . . . 12.00 to 20.00

Tray, Scalloped,
  12 x 6 1/2 In. . . . 8.00 to 14.00
Tumbler, 10 Oz.,
  4 1/2 x 3 In. 8.00
Tumbler, Iced Tea, 15 Oz.,
  6 In. . . . . 13.00 to 20.00
Tumbler, Juice, 5 Oz.,
  4 In. . . . . 2.00 to 4.00
Vase, 10 In. . . . . . . 8.00 to 17.00
Vase, Basket Block,
  8 1/4 x 5 1/2 In. 17.00

Honey Gold
Sugar 32.00

Royal Ruby
Ashtray, 7 3/4 In. 7.00

EARLY AMERICAN ROCK CRYSTAL
See Rock Crystal

EARLY AMERICAN SANDWICH GLASS
See Sandwich Duncan & Miller

ELAINE

Cambridge Glass Company decorated crystal stemware and dinnerware with the Elaine etch from 1934 to 1953.

Basket, 5 In. 150.00
Candy Dish, Cover,
  3 Sections 105.00
Compote, 7 In. 75.00
Creamer, Sterling
  Silver Base 50.00
Cup 20.00
Saucer 3.50
Sherbet, High, 6 Oz. 19.00
Tumbler, Footed,
  10 Oz. 38.00
Vase, Gold Encrusted Flowers,
  13 1/2 x 6 3/8 In. 470.00

EMPRESS

A.H. Heisey & Company made the Empress pattern in Flamingo (pink), Moon-

gleam (green), and Sahara (yellow) from 1930 to 1938. Some items can be found in Alexandrite, Cobalt Blue, and Tangerine, too. After 1938, the Empress molds were changed slightly and the pattern was renamed Queen Ann. Queen Ann items were made only in Crystal and are listed in their own section in this book.

Alexandrite
Bowl, Flower Cutting,
  11 In. 625.00

Flamingo
Bowl, 4 1/2 In. 25.00
Bowl, Dolphin Footed,
  6 In. 40.00
Candlestick, Dophin
  Footed, 6 In. 75.00
Compote, Oval, 7 In. 90.00
Pitcher, Dolphin Footed,
  3 Pt. 175.00
Plate, Square, 7 In. 20.00
Platter, Oval, 14 In. 65.00
Sherbet, 4 Oz. 40.00
Sugar & Creamer 110.00
Tumbler, 8 Oz. 60.00

Sahara
Bowl, Deep, 8 In. 60.00
Bowl, Dolphin Footed,
  3 x 8 1/2 In. 50.00
Candlestick, Dolphin
  Footed, 6 In. 120.00
Cup 30.00
Ice Bucket, Handle 125.00
Mustard, Cover 150.00
Pitcher, Dolphin Footed,
  3 Pt. 185.00
Plate, Salad, 8 1/8 In. 45.00
Plate, Square, 8 In. 20.00
Platter, Oval, 14 In. 70.00
Sugar, 3 Handles, Dolphin
  Footed . . . . 40.00 to 50.00

Sugar & Creamer,
Individual 75.00

ENGLISH HOBNAIL

Westmoreland Glass Company, Grapeville, Pennsylvania, made English Hobnail pattern from the 1920s through 1983. It is similar to Miss America except for more-rounded hobs and the absence of the typical Hocking sunburst ray on the base. English Hobnail was made in Amber, Blue Pastel, Brandywine Blue, Crystal, Green, Laurel Green, Light Green, Milk Glass, Pink, Ruby, and Turquoise. Some pieces were trimmed with black or ruby. There is much variation in the shading, and a darker amber was reissued in the 1960s. Cobalt Blue, Red, and Pink reproduction pieces were made in the 1980s.

Amber

Bowl, Rolled Console,
  11 In. 30.00
Nappy, Square, 6 In. 11.00
Nut Dish, Open Foot 23.00
Plate, 8 In. 15.00
Plate, 10 1/2 In. 18.00

Blue Pastel

Bottle, Cologne,
  Stopper ...... 50.00 to 75.00
Goblet, Water, Footed,
  8 Oz. 50.00

Brandywine Blue

Bowl, Handles, Footed,
  8 x 5 3/4 In. 157.00
Candy Dish,
  5 5/8 x 6 In. 54.00
Compote,
  5 1/2 x 6 3/4 In. 58.00
Sugar, 8-Sided Foot,
  4 1/4 In. 55.00

Crystal

Basket, Ruby Trim 165.00
Bonbon, Handle 15.00
Bowl, 4 In. 15.00
Bowl, Ivy, 6 1/2 In. 25.00
Candlestick Lamp 36.00
Candy Jar, Cover,
  9 In. .... 35.00 to 50.00
Centerpiece, Footed,
  Handles, 6 x 8 In. 50.00
Coaster 8.00
Compote,
  7 1/4 x 10 1/2 In. 60.00
Creamer, Square
  Foot .... 9.00 to 10.00
Cruet, 6 Oz. 65.00
Cup & Saucer 11.00
Cup & Saucer, After
  Dinner 38.00
Goblet, Cocktail, Footed,
  3 Oz. 5.00
Goblet, Cordial, Stem,
  1 Oz. .... 15.00 to 17.00
Goblet, Water, Square Foot,
  8 Oz. .... 10.00 to 11.00
Goblet, Wine, Footed,
  2 Oz. 9.00
Goblet, Wine, Square Foot,
  2 Oz. 24.00
Jam Jar, Cover,
  Underplate 34.00
Nut Dish,
  Open Foot ..... 8.00 to 10.00
Parfait, Footed 15.00
Plate, 8 In. .... 8.00 to 10.00
Plate, Sherbet, 6 1/2 In. ... 6.00
Plate, Square, 5 1/2 In. 7.00
Punch Set, Bowl, Underplate,
  Cups, 14 Piece 445.00
Rose Bowl, 5 In. 18.00
Sherbet, Black Foot 9.00
Sherbet, Footed .... 7.00 to 9.00
Sherbet, Footed, High 10.00

Sherbet, Square Foot,
  High 12.00
Sherbet, Square Foot,
  Low 10.00
Soup, Cream, 5 In. 29.00
Straw Jar, 10 In. 135.00
Sugar, 6-Sided, Foot 10.00
Tumbler, Iced Tea,
  Square Foot, 12 Oz. 12.00
Tumbler, Square Foot,
  5 Oz. .... 17.00 to 19.00
Tumbler, Water, Square
  Foot, 8 Oz. 12.00

Green

Nut Dish, Open Foot,
  2 In. .... 12.00 to 14.00
Plate, 8 In. .... 15.00 to 25.00
Salt & Pepper, Footed ... 45.00
Laurel Green
Bottle, Stopper 58.00
Bowl, Flared, 6-Point
  Star Base, 7 In. 25.00
Candleholder, 3 3/4 In.,
  Pair 78.00
Candlestick, 3 1/2 In. 22.00
Candlestick, 9 In. 190.00
Candlestick, Round,
  3 1/2 In. 22.00
Candlestick, Square,
  5 3/4 In. 35.00
Candy Dish, Footed,
  5 1/4 In. 36.00
Candy Jar, Cover, 9 In. ... 65.00
Compote, 5 x 7 In. 56.00
Finger Bowl, 4 1/2 In. ... 25.00
Goblet, Water, Round
  Footed, 8 Oz. 33.00

Milk Glass

Bowl, Oval, Crimped,
  10 In. 20.00
Butter, Cover 60.00
Candy Jar, Cover, 9 In. ... 30.00
Jam Jar, Cover, Spoon,
  5 In. 45.00
Pitcher, Ice Lip, 7 In. 45.00
Sugar & Creamer 30.00
Vase, 6 In. 30.00

Pink

Bottle, Cologne,
  Stopper 25.00

Candy Dish, Footed,
11 3/4 x 4 1/2 In. 70.00
Celery Dish, Oval, 9 In. . . 45.00
Creamer, Footed,
5 3/4 In. 30.00
Lamp 150.00
Nappy, 4 1/2 In. 13.00
Plate, 8 In. 18.00
Sugar & Creamer,
6-Sided Foot 68.00
Urn, 7 1/8 x 4 1/2 In. . . . 30.00

EVERGLADES

Cambridge Glass Company of Cambridge, Ohio, made Everglades about 1934. The glassware was made in Amber, Crystal, Eleanor Blue, and Forest Green. Plates have a wide border of leaves and a plain center design. Other pieces look like they were made of layers of leaves.

Amber
Creamer 50.00

Crystal
Bowl, Swan Handles,
14 In. 125.00
Plate, 16 In. 125.00
Sugar & Creamer 90.00

FAIRFAX

Fairfax was made by Fostoria Glass Company, Fostoria, Ohio, from 1927 to 1960. The name Fairfax refers to a glass blank and to an etching pattern. The same glass blanks were used for other etched designs including June,

Trojan, and Versailles. The undecorated blank, also known as No. 2375, is popular with collectors. The same shapes were used to make other patterns with etched designs. The glass was made in Amber, Azure (blue), Crystal, Ebony, Gold Tint, Green, Orchid, Rose (pink), Ruby, Topaz, and Wisteria.

Amber
Candy Dish, Scalloped Edge,
3-Footed, 6 1/2 In. 13.00
Cup & Saucer 9.00
Plate, Canape 8.00
Plate, Salad, 8 3/4 In. 5.00
Saucer 3.00

Azure
Bonbon, Handles 12.00
Bouillon, Footed 22.00
Bowl, Centerpiece,
Rolled Edge, 12 In. 30.00
Coaster 9.00
Compote, 7 In. 65.00
Cup, Footed 10.00
Cup & Saucer . . . 20.00 to 22.00
Nut Cup 25.00
Pitcher 300.00
Plate, Bread & Butter,
6 In. 5.00
Plate, Salad, 7 1/2 In. . . . 12.00
Saucer 5.00
Soup, Dish, 7 In. 66.00
Sugar, Footed 9.00
Sugar & Creamer 20.00
Whipped Cream Bowl . . . 65.00

Crystal
Bowl, Vegetable, Oval,
9 In. 49.00
Salt & Pepper 50.00
Sauceboat 62.00
Tumbler, Water, Footed,
9 Oz., 5 1/4 In. 24.00
Tumbler, Whiskey,
Footed, 2 1/2 Oz. 26.00

Ebony
Sugar & Creamer 20.00

Green
Cocktail Icer 15.00
Compote, 5 In. 25.00
Compote, 7 In. 54.00
Cup,
After Dinner . . 15.00 to 23.00
Cup & Saucer,
After Dinner 22.00
Ice Bowl, Underplate 32.00
Nut Cup 22.00
Relish, 2 Sections,
11 1/2 In. 30.00
Sugar & Creamer 85.00

Orchid
Salt & Pepper 125.00

Rose
Butter, Cover 30.00
Creamer, Footed 12.00
Cup 6.00
Cup, Footed 12.00
Cup & Saucer 15.00
Dish, Mayonnaise 35.00
Goblet, Water, 10 Oz.,
8 1/4 In. 35.00
Goblet, Wine, 3 Oz.,
5 1/2 In. 28.00
Pitcher 235.00
Plate, Salad,
7 1/2 In. 5.00
Relish, 11 1/2 In. 23.00
Salt & Pepper 51.00
Saucer 4.00
Sugar 12.00
Tumbler, Footed, 5 Oz.,
4 1/2 In. 16.00

Ruby
Sugar & Creamer 38.00

Topaz
Bowl, Cereal, 6 In. 15.00
Bowl, Fruit, 5 In. 8.00
Cocktail, Icer, Liner,
2 Piece 35.00
Cup 5.00
Cup & Saucer, Footed . . . 14.00
Plate, Salad,
7 1/2 In. 5.00
Saucer 4.00
Soup, Cream 25.00

FAN & FEATHER
See Adam

FASCINATION

Fostoria Glass Company's Fascination pattern was made from 1958 to 1982 in Crystal, Lilac, and Ruby. Some items are decorated with cuttings.

Lilac

Goblet, Wine, 4 Oz.,
5 1/8 In. 25.00

Ruby

Goblet, Claret, 6 Oz.,
5 3/4 In. 42.00

Goblet, Water, 10 Oz.,
6 3/4 In. 38.00

Sherbet, 7 Oz., 4 3/4 In. . : 28.00

Tumbler, Juice, Footed,
5 Oz., 4 1/4 In. 22.00

FERN

Walter von Nessen designed the Fern pattern for A.H. Heisey & Company in 1937. Pieces were made in Crystal until 1941. Some items can be found in Zircon (turquoise).

Crystal

Bonbon, Handle 25.00

Candlestick, 7 1/4 In.,
Pair 75.00

Zircon

Cheese Tray, Handle,
6 In. 150.00

Dish, Jelly, 12 In. 125.00

FINE RIB
See Homespun

FIRE-KING

Fire-King Oven Glass, Fire-King Ovenware, and the related Anchorglass

dinnerware were all made by Anchor Hocking Glass Corporation, Lancaster, Ohio, from 1941 through 1992. Most of the glass is heat resistant. Fire-King Oven Glass was made in plain Ivory or in Ivory, Jade-ite, and transparent Sapphire Blue with an embossed lacy pattern. A matching dinnerware set, called Philbe, is harder to find. It was made in Blue, Crystal, Green, and Pink. Fire-King Ovenware was made by Anchor Hocking from the late 1940s through the 1960s. Plain dinnerware listed in this section is also known as Restaurant Ware. It was made in Azure-ite, Crystal, Ivory, Jade-ite, Pink, Rose-ite, and White (later called Anchorwhite). Some pieces were decorated with gold trim, fired-on colors, or decals. Anchorglass dinnerware sets were made in patterns named 1700 Line, Alice, Blue Mosaic, Bubble, Charm, Early American Prescut, Fleurette, Game Bird, Gray Laurel, Jane-Ray, Meadow Green, Peach Lustre, Primrose, Soreno, Swirl Fire-King, Turquoise Blue, Wexford, and Wheat. These are listed in this book in their own sections.

Crystal

Beverage Set, Pink & Black
Wrought Iron, Decal,
7 Piece 69.00

Casserole, 12 x 7 In. 15.00

Casserole, Cover,
11 x 7 In. 18.00

Casserole, Square, 8 In. . . 22.00

Table Server, Hot Plate,
Ovenware, 1 Pt. 10.00

Ivory

Bowl, Oval, 8 x 12 In. . . . 15.00

Egg Plate, Gold Trim,
10 In. 10.00

Mixing Bowl Set, Black Dots,
Graduated, 3 Piece . . . 110.00

Mixing Bowl Set, Red Dots,
Graduated, 3 Piece . . . 110.00

Mixing Bowl Set, Tulip,
Graduated, 3 Piece . . . 225.00

Salt & Pepper,
Black Dots 65.00

Jade-ite

Batter Bowl 45.00

Bowl, 4 3/4 In. . . 22.00 to 48.00

Bowl, Cereal, Flanged Edge,
8 Oz. 38.00

Bowl, Chili, 5 In. 20.00

Bowl, Fruit, 4 3/4 In. 20.00

Candy Dish,
Maple Leaf 25.00

Candy Dish, Seashell 30.00

Creamer 11.00

Cup, Straight Sides,
6 Oz. . . . . 6.00 to 11.00

Cup & Saucer 18.00

Cup & Saucer, Heavy,
7 Oz. 15.00

Custard Cup,
1 7/8 x 2 In. 35.00

Eggcup 38.00

Grill Plate, 3 Sections 40.00

Grill Plate, 5 Sections,
9 5/8 In. 42.00

Mixing Bowl, Beaded Edge,
6 In. 25.00

Mixing Bowl, Beaded Edge,
7 In. 25.00

Mixing Bowl, Swedish Modern,
1 Pt., 5 In. 78.00

Mixing Bowl, Swedish Modern,
1 Qt., 6 In. 195.00

Mixing Bowl, Swedish Modern,
2 Qt., 7 1/4 In. 165.00

Mixing Bowl, Swedish Modern,
3 Qt., 8 3/8 In. 150.00

Mixing Bowl, Swirl,
9 In. 45.00

Mug, Hot Chocolate, Slim,
6 Oz. . . . . 25.00 to 30.00

Pitcher, Milk, 20 Oz.,
4 1/4 In. 125.00

Plate, Dinner, 9 In. 16.00

Platter, Oval,
11 1/2 In. 50.00

Platter, Oval, Football,
9 3/4 x 8 In. 90.00

Refrigerator Dish, Cover,
4 x 8 In. 50.00

Refrigerator Dish, Cover, Philbe,
5 1/8 x 9 1/2 In. 120.00

Skillet, 1 Spout,
7 In. .... 110.00 to 143.00

Skillet, 2 Spouts,
7 In. 189.00

Soup, Dish, 9 1/2 In. 150.00

Soup, Dish, Flat Rim,
9 1/4 In. 155.00

Sapphire Blue

Binky Nipple Cap,
Embossed 225.00

Bowl, Cereal,
5 3/8 In. ...... 18.00 to 22.00

Bowl, Utility, 1 1/2 Qt.,
8 3/8 In. 22.00

Casserole, Cover, 10 Oz.,
4 3/4 In. ...... 10.00 to 14.00

Casserole, Cover, 1 Pt.,
5 5/8 In. 10.00

Custard Cup, 6 Oz.,
3 3/8 In. 5.00

Loaf Pan, 9 x 5 In. 25.00

Measuring Cup, 1 Spout,
8 Oz. 25.00

Mug, Thick, 7 Oz. 30.00

Mug, Thin, 7 Oz. 45.00

Pie Plate,
9 1/2 In. .... 9.00 to 12.00

Pie Plate, Juice Saver, Philbe,
10 1/4 x 1 3/4 In. 175.00

Refrigerator Dish, Cover,
5 x 9 In. 20.00

Table Server, Tab
Handles 39.00

White

Batter Bowl 20.00

Beverage Set, Hobnail,
5 Piece 48.00

Bowl, Grapes, Vines,
Gay Fad, 5 3/4 In. 23.00

Candy Dish, Grapes, Vines,
Gay Fad, Footed 16.00

Casserole, Cover, Table Server,
Gold, Green, 2 Qt. 40.00

Cookie Jar, Cover,
Hobnail 25.00

Cruet, Fruit, Gay Fad 6.75

Gravy Boat, Handle,
11 1/2 x 7 1/4 In. 43.00

Jardiniere, Hobnail, Scalloped
Rim, 5 1/2 In. 12.00

Mixing Bowl, Peach Blossom,
Gay Fad, 7 3/16 In. 12.00

Pitcher, Hobnail,
72 Oz. 16.00

Relish, 3 Sections, Gold Trim,
9 3/4 In. 12.00

Relish, 3 Sections, Lace Edge,
13 In. 15.00

Relish, 3 Sections, Oval,
Gold Trim, 11 1/8 In. .. 12.00

Tumbler, 1890s Theme,
Rhyming Toasts, Gay Fad,
6 In., 6 Piece 108.00

Vase, Hobnail, Flared,
9 1/2 In. 12.00

FIRST LOVE

First Love, probably the most popular Duncan & Miller Glass Company pattern, was made from 1937 until the factory closed in 1955. It is an etched floral pattern on Crystal.

Ashtray, Square,
3 1/2 In. 20.00

Bowl, Floral, Flared,
12 In. 65.00

Candlestick, 2-Light,
Pair 75.00

Cigarette Box, Cover,
4 3/4 x 3 5/8 In. 130.00

Compote, 6 3/4 In. 35.00

Cruet 275.00

Dish, Mayonnaise,
5 1/2 In. 35.00

Goblet, Champagne,
5 Oz., 5 In. 20.00

Goblet, Cocktail,
3 1/2 Oz., 4 1/2 In. 20.00

Goblet, Water, 10 Oz.,
5 3/4 In. 33.00

Goblet, Wine, 3 Oz.,
5 1/4 In. 30.00

Plate, 8 1/2 In. .. 23.00 to 25.00

Plate, Handles, 8 In. 15.00

Plate, Handles, 11 In. 30.00

Relish, 3 Sections, 7 In. .. 25.00

Saucer 8.50

Sugar 15.00

Tumbler, Iced Tea, Footed,
12 Oz., 5 1/2 In. 35.00

Vase, 8 1/2 x 6 In. 90.00

FLANDERS

Flanders dinnerware was made at the U.S. Glass Company's Tiffin, Ohio, plant from 1914 to 1935. It was made in Crystal and in Mandarin (yellow) or Pink with crystal trim.

Pink

Goblet, 9 Oz.,
8 1/4 In. 65.00

Tumbler, Iced Tea, Footed,
12 Oz., 5 7/8 In. 140.00

FLAT DIAMOND
See Diamond Quilted

FLEURETTE

Fleurette is a white Fire-King pattern with decal decoration. It was made by Anchor Hocking Glass Corporation, Lancaster, Ohio, from 1958 to 1961. Other related patterns are listed in the Fire-King section in this book.

Cup, 5 Oz. 3.00
Cup & Saucer 5.00
Plate, Dinner,
   9 1/8 In. . . . . 5.00 to 6.00
Plate, Salad, 7 3/8 In. 10.00
Saucer, 5 3/4 In. 1.00
Sugar, Cover 10.00
Sugar & Creamer 4.00

FLORAGOLD

The iridescent marigold color of carnival glass was copied in this 1950s pattern made by Jeannette Glass Company, Jeannette, Pennsylvania. The pattern is called Floragold or Louisa, the name of the original carnival glass

pattern that was copied. Pieces were made in Crystal, Ice Blue, Iridescent, Reddish Yellow, and Shell Pink.

Crystal
Berry Bowl, Master, Square,
   8 1/2 In. 10.00
Berry Bowl, Square,
   4 1/2 In. . . . . 5.00 to 6.00
Bowl, Cereal, 5 1/2 In. . . . 23.00
Bowl, Fruit, Ruffled Edge,
   5 1/2 In. . . . . 8.00 to 10.00
Bowl, Ruffled Edge,
   9 1/2 In. 43.00
Bowl, Ruffled Edge,
   12 In. 9.00
Butter, 1/4 Lb. 35.00
Butter, Cover, Square,
   5 1/2 In. 25.00
Candy Dish, 4-Footed,
   5 1/4 In. . . . . . . 7.00 to 10.00
Candy Dish, Cover,
   6 3/4 In. 55.00
Candy Dish, Handle,
   5 In. 10.00
Creamer 10.00
Cup . . . . 5.00 to 6.00
Cup & Saucer . . . 18.00 to 22.00
Pitcher, 64 Oz. . . 34.00 to 39.00
Pitcher, Ice Lip, 64 Oz. . . 53.00
Plate, Dinner,
   8 1/2 In. . . . . . . 23.00 to 40.00
Saucer 12.00
Sherbet, Low 16.00
Sugar &
   Creamer . . . . . . 15.00 to 19.00
Sugar & Creamer,
   Cover 40.00
Tray, 13 1/2 In. 25.00
Tumbler, Water, Footed,
   10 Oz. . . . . 19.00 to 20.00

Iridescent
Ashtray, 4 In. . . . . . 6.00 to 7.00
Berry Bowl, Square,
   4 1/2 In. 4.25
Bowl, Deep, 9 1/2 In. 20.00
Bowl, Ruffled Edge,
   9 1/2 In. 15.00
Bowl, Ruffled Edge,
   12 In. 7.00
Creamer . . . . 5.50 to 6.50
Pitcher, 64 Oz., 9 In. 19.00

Plate, Dinner, 8 1/2 In. . . . 28.00
Platter, 11 1/4 In. 25.00
Sugar & Creamer 12.00
Tray, 13 1/2 In. . . 13.00 to 21.00
Tray, Indent, 13 1/2 In. . . . 80.00
Tumbler, Footed,
   10 Oz. . . . . 18.00 to 20.00

Reddish Yellow
Bowl, Fluted Edge, Iridescent,
   12 x 3 1/4 In. 23.00
Platter, Iridescent,
   13 1/2 In. 50.00

Shell Pink
Compote, 6 1/2 In. 21.00

FLORAL

Poinsettia blossoms are the decorations on Floral patterns made by Jeannette Glass Company from 1931 to 1935. Green is the most common color, although the pattern was also made in Amber, Crystal, Delphite, Green, Jadite, Pink, Red, and Yellow. Reproductions have been made.

Crystal
Bowl, Vegetable, Cover,
   8 In. 50.00
Pitcher 50.00
Plate, Dinner, 9 In. 25.00
Plate, Sherbet, 6 In. 9.00
Relish, 2 Sections 25.00
Salt & Pepper, 6 In. 65.00
Sherbet 20.00
Tumbler, Juice, Footed,
   5 Oz., 4 In. 24.00

Tumbler, Water, Footed,
7 Oz., 4 3/4 In. 25.00

Green

Berry Bowl, 4 In. 30.00
Bowl, Salad,
7 1/2 In. . . . . . . 27.00 to 35.00
Bowl, Vegetable,
Cover Only 35.00
Bowl, Vegetable, Cover,
8 In. . . . . 49.00 to 56.00
Bowl, Vegetable, No Cover,
8 In. 40.00
Bowl, Vegetable, Oval,
9 In. . . . . 28.00 to 39.00
Butter,
Cover . . . . . 130.00 to 180.00
Butter, No Cover 25.00
Candlestick, 4 In., Pair . . 110.00
Candy Dish,
Cover Only 35.00
Candy Dish, No Cover . . . 22.00
Candy Jar,
Cover . . . . 42.00 to 48.00
Coaster,
3 1/4 In. . . . . . 14.00 to 17.00
Creamer,
3 1/2 In. . . . . . 15.00 to 35.00
Cup . . . . 14.00 to 15.00
Cup & Saucer . . . 22.00 to 27.00
Lamp, 4 1/4 In. 535.00
Lamp, Frosted,
4 1/4 In. 290.00
Pitcher, Cone Foot, 32 Oz.,
8 In. . . . . 45.00 to 50.00
Plate, Dinner,
9 In. . . . . 16.00 to 27.00
Plate, Salad,
8 In. . . . . 12.00 to 14.00
Plate, Sherbet,
6 In. . . . . 8.00 to 10.00
Platter, Oval,
10 3/4 In. . . . . . 25.00 to 30.00
Refrigerator Dish, Cover,
Square, 5 In. 90.00
Relish, 2 Sections, Handles,
Oval 23.00
Relish, 3 Sections, Handles,
Oval 30.00
Salt & Pepper, Footed,
4 In. . . . . 45.00 to 70.00
Saltshaker, Footed,
4 In. . . . . 24.00 to 35.00
Saucer . . . . 10.00 to 12.00
Sherbet . . . . 12.00 to 21.00

Sugar, Cover . . . . 43.00 to 60.00
Sugar,
Cover Only . . . 25.00 to 30.00
Sugar, No Cover 12.00
Sugar & Creamer,
Cover . . . . 60.00 to 62.00
Tumbler, Juice, Footed,
5 Oz., 4 In. 25.00
Tumbler, Lemonade, Footed,
9 Oz., 5 1/4 In. 60.00
Tumbler, Water, Footed, 7 Oz.,
4 3/4 In. . . . . . 28.00 to 35.00
Vase, Flared, 3-Footed . . 460.00

Jadite

Refrigerator Dish, Cover,
4 x 4 In. 75.00

Pink

Berry Bowl, 4 In. 25.00
Bowl, Salad, 7 1/2 In. . . . 24.00
Bowl, Vegetable, Cover,
8 In. . . . . 55.00 to 69.00
Bowl, Vegetable, Cover,
9 In. 16.00
Bowl, Vegetable,
No Cover, 8 In. 25.00
Bowl, Vegetable, Oval,
9 In. 30.00
Butter,
Cover . . . . . 110.00 to 135.00
Candlestick, 4 In., Pair . . . 90.00
Candy Jar, Cover 36.00
Coaster, 3 1/4 In. 12.00
Creamer 16.00
Cup . . . . 12.00 to 15.00
Cup & Saucer . . . 22.00 to 27.00
Pitcher, Cone, 32 Oz.,
8 In. . . . . 40.00 to 50.00
Pitcher, Lemonade, Footed,
48 Oz., 10 1/4 In. 350.00
Plate, Dinner,
9 In. . . . . 20.00 to 28.00
Plate, Salad,
8 In. . . . . 10.00 to 17.00
Plate, Sherbet,
6 In. . . . . 8.00 to 10.00
Platter, 11 In. 65.00
Platter, Oval,
10 3/4 In. . . . . . 20.00 to 26.00
Relish, 2 Sections, Handles,
Oval 22.00
Salt & Pepper, 6 In. 65.00
Salt & Pepper, Footed,
4 In. . . . . 52.00 to 60.00

Saltshaker,
6 In. . . . . 30.00 to 55.00
Saltshaker, Footed,
4 In. 10.00
Sherbet . . . . 20.00 to 25.00
Sugar, Cover . . . . 40.00 to 45.00
Sugar, No Cover 18.00
Sugar & Creamer,
Cover 62.00
Tumbler, Juice, Footed,
5 Oz., 4 In. 28.00
Tumbler, Lemonade,
Footed, 9 Oz.,
5 1/4 In. . . . . . 54.00 to 65.00
Tumbler, Water, Footed, 7 Oz.,
4 3/4 In. . . . . . 22.00 to 29.00

FLORAL & DIAMOND BAND

Floral & Diamond Band
was made by the U.S.
Glass Company from the
late 1920s until c.1937. It
features a large center
flower and an edging of
pressed diamond bands.
Luncheon sets were made
in varying shades of Green
and Pink, but Black, Crystal, and Yellow were also
used. Some Crystal pieces
are Iridescent Marigold.

Crystal

Berry Bowl, 8 In. 20.00
Sugar & Creamer 19.00

Green

Butter, Cover 135.00
Butter, Cover Only 75.00
Compote,
5 1/2 In. . . . . . 20.00 to 28.00

Pitcher, 42 Oz., 8 In. 145.00
Plate, Luncheon, 8 In. 45.00
Sherbet . . . . 8.00 to 10.00
Sugar, 5 1/4 In. 20.00
Tumbler, Iced Tea,
    5 In. 55.00
Tumbler, Water, 4 In. 25.00

Pink
Butter, Cover Only 75.00
Sugar, Cover 75.00

FLORAL RIM
See Vitrock

FLORENTINE NO. 1

Florentine No. 1, also called Poppy No. 1, is neither Florentine in appearance nor decorated with recognizable poppies. The plates are hexagonal and have scalloped edges, differentiating them from Florentine No. 2, which has round pieces. The pattern was made by the Hazel Atlas Glass Company from 1932 to 1935 in Cobalt Blue, Crystal, Green, Pink, and Yellow. Reproductions have been made.

Cobalt Blue
Nut Bowl, Ruffled Edge,
    5 In. 98.00
Sugar & Creamer, Ruffled
    Edge 190.00

Crystal
Creamer 9.00
Creamer, Ruffled Edge . . . 45.00
Cup . . . . 5.00 to 9.00
Plate, Dinner,
    10 In. . . . . 12.50 to 15.00
Plate, Salad,
    8 1/2 In. . . . . 6.50 to 8.50
Platter, Oval,
    11 1/2 In. . . . . . 13.50 to 29.00
Saltshaker 20.00
Saucer 3.00
Sherbet . . . . 10.00 to 11.50
Sugar, Metal Cover 19.00
Sugar, Ruffled Edge 35.00

Green
Berry Bowl, 5 In. 19.00
Berry Bowl, Master,
    8 1/2 In. 45.00
Bowl, Vegetable, Oval,
    9 1/2 In. . . . . . . 46.00 to 50.00
Butter, Cover 150.00
Butter, Cover Only 75.00
Creamer . . . . 8.50 to 10.00
Cup . . . . 8.00 to 11.00
Cup & Saucer 18.00
Pitcher, 36 Oz.,
    6 1/2 In. 48.00
Plate, Dinner,
    10 In. . . . . 15.00 to 27.00
Plate, Salad,
    8 1/2 In. . . . . . 10.00 to 15.00
Plate, Sherbet, 6 In. 9.00
Salt & Pepper 41.00
Saucer 4.00
Sherbet, 3 Oz. . . . 12.00 to 15.00
Sugar 10.00
Sugar, Cover 40.00
Tumber, Water, Footed,
    10 Oz., 4 3/4 In. 32.00
Tumbler, Juice, Footed, 5 Oz.,
    3 3/4 In. . . . . . . 16.00 to 23.00
Water Set, 5 Piece 155.00

Pink
Berry Bowl, Master,
    8 1/2 In. 45.00
Creamer . . . . 20.00 to 22.00
Cup 13.00
Cup & Saucer . . . 15.00 to 18.00
Grill Plate, 10 In. 11.25
Nut Bowl, Ruffled Edge,
    5 In. . . . . 20.00 to 25.00

Pitcher, Footed, 36 Oz.,
    6 1/2 In. 40.00
Plate, Dinner, 10 In. 35.00
Plate, Salad, 8 1/2 In. 14.00
Saltshaker 29.00
Sherbet . . . . 11.00 to 17.00
Soup, Cream, 5 In. 20.00
Sugar 16.00
Sugar, Ruffled Edge 60.00
Sugar &
    Creamer . . . . . 35.00 to 42.00
Tumbler, Lemonade, 9 Oz.,
    5 1/4 In. 65.00

Yellow
Pitcher, 36 Oz.,
    6 1/2 In. . . . . . . 31.00 to 55.00
Plate, Dinner, 10 In. 25.00
Plate, Salad, 8 1/2 In. 16.00
Sherbet, 3 Oz. . . . . 6.00 to 15.00
Tumbler, Juice, Footed,
    5 Oz., 3 3/4 In. 25.00
Water Set, 6 Piece 225.00

FLORENTINE NO. 2

Florentine No. 2, sometimes called Poppy No. 2 or Oriental Poppy, was also made by Hazel Atlas Glass Company from 1934 to 1937. It has round plates instead of hexagonal plates, and larger and more prominent flowers than Florentine No. 1. It was made in Amber, Cobalt Blue, Crystal, Green, Ice

Blue, Pink, and Yellow. Reproductions have been made.

Amber

Berry Bowl, Master,
8 In. 23.00

Bowl, Vegetable, Cover,
Round, 9 In. 40.00

Coaster,
3 3/4 In. . . . . . . 18.00 to 22.00

Pitcher, 48 Oz.,
7 1/2 In. . . . . . 34.00 to 41.00

Pitcher, Cone Foot,
28 Oz., 7 1/2 In. 19.00

Plate, Dinner, 10 In. 21.00

Salt & Pepper,
Footed 40.00

Sherbet . . . . 14.00 to 15.00

Tumbler, Footed, 5 Oz.,
3 1/4 In. 23.00

Crystal

Berry Bowl, 4 1/2 In. 7.00

Berry Bowl, Master,
8 In. . . . . 30.00 to 45.00

Candlestick, 2 1/2 In.,
Pair 48.00

Coaster, 3 3/4 In. 18.00

Creamer 9.00

Cup . . . . 7.00 to 8.25

Cup & Saucer 18.00

Gravy Boat,
Underplate 150.00

Grill Plate, 10 1/4 In. 20.00

Parfait, Footed,
6 In. . . . . 15.00 to 28.00

Plate, Dinner,
10 In. . . . . 12.00 to 15.00

Plate, Salad,
8 1/2 In. . . . . 8.25 to 9.00

Plate, Sherbet, 6 In. 3.00

Platter, Oval, 11 In. 15.00

Saltshaker, Footed 15.00

Saucer . . . . 5.00 to 6.00

Sherbet 13.00

Soup, Cream,
4 3/4 In. . . . . . . 11.00 to 14.00

Tumbler, Juice, 5 Oz.,
3 1/2 In. 16.00

Tumbler, Juice, Footed, 5 Oz.,
3 3/8 In. . . . . . . 13.00 to 14.00

Tumbler, Water, 9 Oz.,
4 In. 13.00

Green

Berry Bowl,
4 1/2 In. . . . . . . 14.00 to 20.00

Berry Bowl, Master,
8 In. 25.00

Bowl, 5 1/2 In. 40.00

Bowl, Vegetable, Cover,
Oval, 9 In. 70.00

Bowl, Vegetable, Oval,
9 In. 30.00

Butter, Cover 115.00

Candy Jar, Cover 130.00

Coaster, 3 1/4 In. 16.00

Coaster, 5 1/2 In. 19.00

Creamer 7.00

Cup . . . . 8.00 to 10.00

Cup & Saucer 15.00

Luncheon Set, Box,
22 Piece 375.00

Plate, Dinner, 10 In. 20.00

Plate, Salad,
8 1/2 In. . . . . . . 11.00 to 13.00

Plate, Sherbet,
6 In. . . . . 7.00 to 8.00

Platter, Oval, 11 In. 22.00

Salt & Pepper, Footed . . . 45.00

Saucer . . . . 4.00 to 8.00

Sherbet . . . . 10.00 to 15.00

Soup, Cream,
4 3/4 In. . . . . . . 18.00 to 20.00

Sugar, No Cover 10.00

Tumbler, 5 Oz.,
3 3/8 In. 12.00

Tumbler, Footed,
3 7/8 In. 7.00

Tumbler, Footed, 5 Oz.,
4 In. . . . . 13.00 to 15.00

Tumbler, Juice, Footed,
5 Oz., 3 3/8 In. . . 13.00 to 15.00

Tumbler, Water, 9 Oz.,
4 In. . . . . 20.00 to 22.00

Water Set, 5 Piece 35.00

Pink

Candy Dish, Cover 100.00

Pitcher, 48 Oz. 155.00

Soup, Cream,
4 3/4 In. . . . . . . 12.00 to 24.00

Tumbler, 6 Oz.,
3 1/2 In. 34.00

Tumbler, Juice, 5 Oz.,
3 3/8 In. . . . . . 10.00 to 17.00

Tumbler, Water, 9 Oz.,
4 In. 29.00

Yellow

Berry Bowl, Master,
8 In. . . . . 32.00 to 47.00

Bowl, 4 1/2 In. 23.50

Bowl, Vegetable, Cover,
Oval, 9 In. 100.00

Butter,
Cover . . . . . . 140.00 to 175.00

Butter,
No Cover . . . . . 68.00 to 80.00

Candlestick,
2 3/4 In. . . . . . . 19.50 to 36.00

Candlestick, 2 3/4 In.,
Pair 75.00

Coaster,
3 3/4 In. . . . . . . 20.00 to 27.00

Coaster, 5 1/2 In. 35.00

Creamer 15.00

Cup . . . . 9.00 to 10.50

Cup & Saucer . . 14.00 to 20.00

Custard Cup 120.00

Gravy Boat 65.00

Gravy Boat,
Underplate . . 145.00 to 180.00

Grill Plate,
10 1/2 In. . . . . . 16.00 to 19.00

Parfait, Footed,
6 In. . . . . 59.00 to 70.00

Pitcher, 48 Oz.,
7 1/2 In. 296.00

Pitcher, Cone Foot, 28 Oz.,
7 1/2 In. . . . . . . 29.00 to 40.00

Plate, Dinner,
10 In. . . . . 16.00 to 20.00

Plate, Salad,
8 1/2 In. . . . . . . 12.00 to 15.00

Plate, Sherbet,
6 In. . . . . 5.00 to 8.00

Platter, Oval,
11 In. . . . . 22.00 to 30.00

Relish, 3 Sections,
10 In. . . . . 29.00 to 39.00

Salt & Pepper, Footed . . . 65.00

Saltshaker,
Footed . . . . . . 25.00 to 30.00

Saucer . . . . 5.00 to 8.00

Sherbet . . . . 12.00 to 15.00

Soup, Cream, 4 3/4 In. . . . 30.00

Sugar . . . . 10.00 to 11.00

Sugar, Cover 40.00

Sugar, No Cover 12.00

Tumbler, Footed, 5 Oz.,
4 In. . . . . 17.00 to 28.00

Tumbler, Footed, 9 Oz.,
  5 In. 40.00
Tumbler, Iced Tea, 12 Oz.,
  5 In. 38.00
Tumbler, Iced Tea, Footed,
  12 Oz., 5 In. 50.00
Tumbler, Juice, 5 Oz.,
  3 3/8 In. 17.00
Tumbler, Juice, 5 Oz.,
  4 3/8 In. 27.00
Water Set, 7 Piece 175.00

FLOWER
See Princess Feather

FLOWER & LEAF BAND
See Indiana Custard

FLOWER BASKET
See No. 615

FLOWER GARDEN WITH BUTTERFLIES

There really is a butterfly hiding in the flowers on this U.S. Glass Company pattern called Flower Garden with Butterflies, Butterflies & Roses, Flower Garden, or Wildrose with Apple Blossom. It was made in the late 1920s in a variety of colors, including Amber, Black, Blue, Blue-Green, Canary Yellow, Crystal, Green, and Pink.

Blue
Dish, Mayonnaise, Footed,
  Ladle, 4 1/2 In. 175.00
Blue-Green
Plate, 8 1/4 In. 45.00

Crystal
Candy Dish, Cover, Cone Shape,
  Gold Trim, Footed 100.00
Green
Candlestick, 3 1/4 In. . . . 100.00
Compote, 2 7/8 x 5 In. . . . 65.00
Pink
Candy Dish, Cover, Cone
  Shape, Footed 175.00
Saucer 26.50
Tray, Dresser,
  10 1/8 In. 60.00

FLOWER RIM
See Vitrock

FOREST GREEN

Its Forest Green color identifies this pattern. Anchor Hocking Glass Corporation, Lancaster, Ohio, made this very plain pattern from 1950 to 1965. Other patterns were also made in this same deep green color, but these are known by their pattern names. Related Anchor Hocking patterns are listed in the Fire-King section in this book.

Ashtray, Square,
  4 5/8 In. . . . . 6.00 to 8.00
Ashtray, Square,
  5 3/4 In. . . . . 8.00 to 10.00
Batter Bowl, Tab Handle, Spout,
  7 5/8 In. . . . . . . 25.00 to 32.00
Bowl, Bulb, Cupped,
  6 1/4 In. 15.00

Bowl, Bulb, Ruffled Edge,
  7 1/4 In. 12.00
Bowl, Crimped,
  7 1/2 In. 15.00
Bowl, Deep,
  5 1/4 In. . . . . . 15.00 to 19.00
Bowl, Dessert, Maple
  Leaf 12.00
Bowl, Dessert, Seashell,
  7 In. 10.00
Bowl, Scalloped,
  6 1/2 In. 10.00
Compote, 3-Footed,
  6 1/2 In. 15.00
Mixing, Bowl, White Ivy,
  7 1/8 x 3 3/4 In. 18.00
Mixing Bowl, Ribbed,
  4 3/4 In. 8.00
Mixing Bowl, Ribbed,
  7 1/2 In. 40.00
Pitcher, Ice Lip, 36 Oz.,
  9 In. 46.00
Pitcher, Juice, 22 Oz. 30.00
Pitcher, Whirly Twirly,
  86 Oz., 9 In. 50.00
Punch Cup 4.00
Punch Set, Bowl, Stand,
  Cups, 10 Piece 88.00
Saucer 1.50
Tumbler, 9 1/2 Oz.,
  4 5/8 In. . . . . . . 10.00 to 14.00
Tumbler, Bicycle For 2,
  13 Oz., 6 1/2 In. 16.00
Tumbler, Bicycle For 2,
  15 Oz. 11.00
Tumbler, Iced Tea,
  Label, 13 Oz.,
  6 1/2 In. . . . . . . 12.00 to 15.00
Tumbler, Iced Tea, Whirly
  Twirly, 12 Oz. 15.00
Tumbler, Lily Of The Valley,
  11 Oz., 5 1/4 In. 9.00
Tumbler, Long Boy, Bicycle
  For 2, 15 Oz. 11.00
Tumbler, Long Boy, Gas
  Buggy, 15 Oz. 14.00
Tumbler, Open Sleigh,
  13 Oz., 6 1/2 In. 16.00
Tumbler, Pagoda, Footed,
  10 Oz., 4 1/2 In. 9.00
Tumbler, Polka Dots,
  11 Oz., 5 1/4 In. 12.00
Tumbler, Roly Poly,
  Bicycle For 2 . . . . 15.00

Tumbler, Roly Poly, Prairie
Schooner 15.00
Tumbler, Water, 8 Oz.,
6 In. 15.00
Vase, 6 1/2 In. 25.00
Vase, Pineapple, 9 In. 22.00
Vase, Ruffled, 3 3/4 In. . . . 4.00
Water Set, White Dots,
5 Piece 55.00

FORTUNE

Anchor Hocking Glass
Corporation, Lancaster,
Ohio, made Fortune pat-
tern in 1937 and 1938.
The simple design was
made in Crystal or Pink.

Crystal
Candy Dish,
Cover . . . . 14.00 to 28.00
Tumbler, Water, 9 Oz.,
4 In. . . . . 10.00 to 13.00

Pink
Berry Bowl, 4 In. . . 4.00 to 5.50
Bowl, Dessert, 4 1/2 In. . . . 9.00
Bowl, Handle,
4 1/2 In. . . . . . . 3.50 to 10.00
Candy Dish,
Cover . . . . 15.00 to 35.00

❖

**Window-sash locks are
available at hardware
stores for less than
$10 each. Keep your
windows closed and
locked when you are
out of the house.**

❖

Cup 10.00
Tumbler, Juice, 5 Oz.,
3 1/2 In. . . . . . . 9.00 to 15.00
Tumbler, Water, 9 Oz.,
4 In. . . . . 6.00 to 17.00

**FROSTED BLOCK
See Beaded Block**

FRUITS

Pears, grapes, apples, and
other fruits are displayed
in small bunches on pieces
of Fruits pattern. Hazel
Atlas Glass Company and
several other companies
made this pattern about
1931 to 1933. Pieces are
known in Crystal, Green,
Iridescent finish, and Pink.

Green
Cup . . . . 8.00 to 10.00
Cup & Saucer . . . 13.00 to 25.00
Plate, Luncheon, 8 In. 10.00
Saucer 6.00

Iridescent
Tumbler, 4 In. 12.00
Tumbler, Combination
Fruits, 4 In. 25.00

Pink
Cup 12.00
Sherbet 10.00
Tumbler, 4 In. 15.00
Tumbler, Combination
Fruits, 4 In. 23.00

FUCHSIA

Fuchsia etch appears
mostly on Crystal pieces.
Some stemware has

Wisteria-colored bases.
It was made by Fostoria
beginning about 1931.

Bowl, 12 In. 65.00
Candlestick, 2-Light 70.00
Goblet, Cocktail, 3 Oz. . . . 38.00
Relish, 3 Sections,
9 1/4 x 9 In. 25.00
Sherbet, 5 Oz., 4 1/8 In. . . 15.00

GAME BIRD

Game Bird, sometimes
called Wild Bird, was
made by Anchor Hocking
Glass Corporation, Lan-
caster, Ohio, from 1959
to 1962. The opaque
white glass was decorated
with a decal of a Canada
goose, mallard duck, ring-
necked pheasant, or ruf-
fled grouse. Other related
patterns are listed in the
Fire-King section in this
book.

Canada Goose
Mug, 8 Oz. 9.00
Tumbler, Crystal,
4 1/2 In. 20.00
Tumbler, Iced Tea,
11 Oz., 5 In. 6.00
Mallard Duck
Mug, 8 Oz. 9.00
Ring-Necked Pheasant
Mug, 8 Oz. . . . . . . 2.50 to 9.00
Tumbler, Iced Tea,
11 Oz., 5 In. 6.00
Ruffled Grouse
Mug, 8 Oz. 9.00

Tumbler, Iced Tea,
11 Oz., 5 In. 7.00

GAZEBO

Paden City Glass Manufacturing Company made glass with the Gazebo etching in the 1930s. It looks like the Ardith etching, but has a gazebo between the flowers. Dishes were made in Black, Blue, Crystal, and Yellow.

Crystal

Bowl, Low, Flat, 14 In. . . 38.00
Bowl, Salad,
12 x 3 3/4 In. 80.00
Candy Dish, Cover,
10 1/4 In. 70.00
Candy Dish, Cover,
Heart Shape, Gold Trim,
3 Sections 65.00
Console, 4-Footed,
12 In. 60.00
Dish, Mayonnaise,
Underplate 20.00
Plate, 6 In. 6.00
Server, Center Handle,
11 In. 55.00
Torte Plate, Inset Ring,
10 1/2 In. 48.00

GEORGIAN FEDERAL

Georgian, also known as Lovebirds, was made by the Federal Glass Com-

pany, Columbus, Ohio, from 1931 to 1936. The pattern shows alternating sections with birds in one and a basket of flowers in the next. Some dishes have no lovebirds. Dinner sets were made mostly in Crystal, although Green pieces were also manufactured. Notice that it is mold-etched and in no way resembles the Fenton glass pattern called Georgian. Reproductions have been made.

Crystal

Berry Bowl, 4 1/2 In. 10.00
Bowl, Cereal, 5 3/4 In. . . . 20.00
Pitcher, 80 Oz. 55.00
Platter, Closed Handles,
11 1/2 In. 54.00
Saucer 4.00

Green

Berry Bowl,
4 1/2 In. . . . . 7.00 to 12.00
Berry Bowl, Master,
7 1/2 In. . . . . . . 78.00 to 80.00
Butter, Cover . . . 75.00 to 85.00
Butter, Cover
Only . . . . 38.00 to 40.00
Butter, No Cover 45.00
Creamer, Footed,
3 In. . . . . 11.00 to 18.00
Creamer, Footed,
4 In. . . . . 17.00 to 24.00
Cup . . . . 7.50 to 11.00
Cup & Saucer . . . . 8.00 to 18.00
Plate, Dinner, 9 1/4 In. . . . 26.00
Plate, Luncheon,
8 In. . . . . 5.00 to 19.00
Plate, Salad, 8 1/2 In. 4.50
Plate, Sherbet,
6 In. . . . . 7.00 to 15.00
Saucer . . . . 5.50 to 7.00
Sherbet . . . . 7.50 to 12.00
Sherbet, Underplate 23.00
Sugar, Cover,
3 In. . . . . 37.00 to 50.00
Sugar, Footed,
3 In. . . . . 8.00 to 14.00

Sugar, Footed,
4 In. . . . . 14.00 to 24.00
Sugar & Creamer, Cover,
Footed, 3 In. 80.00
Sugar & Creamer, Footed,
4 In. . . . . 33.00 to 35.00
Tumbler, 9 Oz., 4 In. 82.00
Tumbler, 12 Oz.,
5 1/4 In. 99.00

GEORGIAN FENTON

Fenton Glass Company made this Georgian pattern tableware from about 1930. It came in many colors, some pale but others in popular dark shades. Look for Amber, Crystal, Ebony, Green, Jade Green, Milk Glass, Rose, Royal Blue, and Ruby. It is very different from the Georgian or Lovebirds pattern made by the Federal Glass Company.

Amber

Bowl, Cereal, 6 3/4 In. . . . 16.00
Plate, Salad, 8 In. 16.00
Tumbler, 3 Oz.,
2 1/2 In. 8.00
Tumbler, 6 Oz., 3 In. 8.00

Crystal

Tumbler, Footed, 9 Oz.,
5 1/2 In. 12.00

Green

Tumbler, 2 1/2 Oz.,
2 1/2 In. . . . . . . 10.00 to 12.00

Rose
Tumbler, 9 Oz., 4 In. 10.00

Ruby
Goblet, Water, 8 Oz. 25.00
Sugar, Cover 45.00
Tumbler, 5 Oz., 3 In. 8.00
Tumbler, 9 Oz.,
   4 1/4 In. 15.00
Tumbler, Footed, 9 Oz.,
   5 1/2 In. 18.00

GEORGIAN PADEN CITY

Paden City Glass Manufacturing Company first made its version of the Georgian pattern in 1934. Pieces were made in Amber, Cheriglo, Crystal, Forest Green, Green, Light Blue, Light Green, Mulberry, Royal Blue, Ruby, and Yellow.

Crystal
Tumbler, 12 Oz.,
   4 3/4 In. 12.00

Light Green
Pitcher, 54 Oz., 8 In. 59.00
Tumbler, 12 Oz.,
   4 3/4 In. 12.00

Mulberry
Pitcher, 54 Oz., 8 In. 78.00
Tumbler, 9 Oz.,
   4 1/4 In. 15.00

Royal Blue
Tumbler, 9 Oz.,
   4 1/4 In. 18.00

Ruby
Goblet, Wine, 2 Oz. 25.00
Peach Melba, 10 Oz. 35.00
Sherbet, 5 Oz. 25.00
Tumbler, 12 Oz.,
   6 In. .... 23.00 to 25.00
Tumbler, Footed, 12 Oz.,
   5 5/8 In. 20.00

GLADIOLA
See Royal Lace

GOLDEN GLORY

Golden Glory is opaque white glass decorated with 22K gold leafy branches that looks almost like china dinnerware. Federal Glass Company made the pattern from 1959 to 1966 and again in 1978 and 1979.

Bowl, Dessert,
   4 7/8 In. 5.00
Bowl, Vegetable,
   8 1/2 In. 12.00
Creamer 4.00
Cup & Saucer 3.00
Luncheon Set, Gold Trim,
   Plates, Cups, Saucers,
   Platter, Sugar, Creamer,
   15 Piece 52.00
Plate, Dinner, 10 In. 6.00
Platter, Oval, 12 In. 11.00
Soup, Rim, 6 3/8 In. 8.00
Sugar 3.00
Sugar, Cover 6.00

❖

If it seems too good to be true, it usually is! Trust your instincts when buying antiques. Experienced collectors notice many little signs of repair or reproduction, often without realizing it.

❖

GOLF BALL

Morgantown Glass Works, Inc., Morgantown, West Virginia, made Golf Ball stemware and accessories in the late 1920s and early 1930s. The items came in a wide variety of colors with crystal stems and feet. The pattern name comes from the faceted ball that is part of the stem.

14K Topaz
Goblet, Wine, 4 1/4 In. 40.00

Caramel
Goblet, Cocktail, 3 1/2 Oz.,
   4 1/8 In. 20.00

Crystal
Goblet, Cordial, 1 1/2 Oz.,
   3 1/2 In. 40.00

Old Amethyst
Goblet, 3 1/2 Oz.,
   4 1/8 In. 20.00
Ivy Bowl, Footed, 4 In. .. 50.00

Ritz Blue
Goblet, Champagne, 5 1/2 Oz.,
   5 In. .... 48.00 to 55.00
Goblet, Cocktail, 3 1/2 Oz.,
   4 1/8 In. ...... 26.00 to 45.00
Goblet, Cordial, 1 1/2 Oz.,
   3 3/8 In. 42.00
Goblet, Water, 9 Oz.,
   6 3/4 In. ...... 45.00 to 60.00
Goblet, Wine, 3 Oz.,
   4 3/4 In. 50.00
Sherbet, 5 1/2 Oz.,
   4 1/8 In. 30.00
Tumbler, Iced Tea,
   12 Oz., 6 3/4 In. 65.00
Tumbler, Juice, Footed,
   5 Oz., 4 3/4 In. 35.00

Spanish Red
Candlestick, 4 1/8 In. 70.00
Candlestick, 4 1/8 In.,
   Pair 125.00
Goblet, Champagne, 5 1/2 Oz.,
   5 In. .... 35.00 to 41.00
Goblet, Cocktail, 3 1/2 Oz.,
   4 1/8 In. ...... 21.00 to 44.00
Goblet, Cordial, 1 1/2 Oz.,
   3 3/8 In. 23.00

Goblet, Water, 9 Oz.,
6 3/4 In. ...... 25.00 to 55.00
Goblet, Wine, 3 Oz.,
4 3/4 In. 43.00
Oyster Cocktail,
4 Oz., 4 1/8 In. 38.00
Sherbet, 5 1/2 Oz.,
4 1/4 In. 39.00

Stiegel Green
Goblet, Water, 9 oz.,
6 3/4 In. 26.00

GRAPE

Grape design is sometimes confused with the pattern known as Woolworth. Both have grapes in the pattern. Grape was made by Standard Glass Manufacturing Company, Lancaster, Ohio, in the 1930s. Full dinnerware sets were made in Green, Rose, and Topaz.

Green
Console, 12 3/4 In. 110.00
Vase, 8 In. 95.00

GRAPE & LEAVES
See Harvest

GRAY LAUREL

Gray Laurel is a Fire-King dinnerware made by Anchor Hocking Glass Corporation in 1953. The pattern has a laurel leaf design around the edge of the plates and bowls and on the side of the cups.

The pieces are Gray. The same pattern of laurel leaves was made in a lustrous orange-yellow color from 1952 to 1963 and was known as Peach Lustre.

Plate, Salad, 7 3/8 In. 8.00
Sugar & Creamer 16.00

GREEK KEY

Greek Key is one of A.H. Heisey & Company's oldest and most easily recognizable patterns. Some pieces were made until 1938. Other companies made glassware with a similar border, but most Heisey pieces are marked with the Diamond H logo.

Bowl, Handles,
5 1/2 In. ...... 36.00 to 39.00
Celery Dish, 9 In. 65.00
Creamer, Individual,
2 3/4 In. ...... 21.00 to 32.00
Cruet, Stopper 80,00
Dish, Banana Split,
Footed, 9 In. 17.00
Goblet, Water, 7 Oz.,
5 1/4 In. 105.00
Goblet, Water, 9 Oz.,
6 1/4 In. ...... 35.00 to 43.00
Hair Receiver 36.00
Ice Tub, Tab Handles,
5 5/8 In. 114.00
Nut Dish, Footed,
1 3/4 x 2 3/4 In. 16.00
Plate, 4 1/2 In. 17.00
Plate, 6 In. 8.00
Punch Bowl, 18 In. 168.00
Punch Bowl, Base,
15 x 14 3/4 In. 365.00
Sherbet .... 10.00 to 12.00

Sherbet, Flared,
4 1/2 In. 27.00
Sugar, Individual,
2 3/4 In. 27.00
Sugar, Oval, Hotel 60.00
Tumbler, 6 1/2 In. 8.00

HAIRPIN
See Newport

HANGING BASKET
See No. 615

HARP

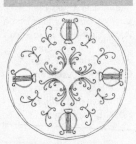

The pattern name Harp describes the small lyre-shaped instruments that are included on the borders of these pieces of glass. This Jeannette Glass Company pattern was made from 1954 to 1957. Pieces are found in Crystal, Crystal with gold trim, Light Blue, Pink, Shell Pink (opaque), and White.

Crystal
Ashtray .... 5.00 to 7.00
Ashtray, Gold Trim 18.00
Cake Stand,
9 In. ...... 15.00 to 26.00
Cake Stand, Gold Trim,
9 In. .... 23.00 to 30.00
Coaster .... 4.00 to 6.00
Coaster, Gold Trim 15.00
Cup 35.00
Plate, 7 In. 12.00
Plate, Gold Trim, 7 In. ... 18.00
Saucer 12.00

Tray, Handles, Gold Trim,
15 1/2 x 10 In. . . 25.00 to 36.00
Vase, 7 1/2 In. . . . 20.00 to 25.00
Vase, Gold Trim,
7 1/2 In. 27.00

Light Blue
Cake Stand, 9 In. 50.00

Pink
Cake Stand, Gold Trim,
9 In. 35.00

Shell Pink
Cake Stand, 9 In. 61.00
Tray, Handles,
15 1/2 x 10 In. 92.00

HARVEST

Indiana Glass Company made its Harvest pattern (also called Grape & Leaves) in Crystal and Milk Glass in the 1960s. In 1971, the company introduced iridescent colors and marketed the pattern as carnival glass.

Crystal
Bowl, Piecrust Border, Handles,
10 x 8 1/2 In. 35.00
Compote, Cover,
7 x 3 1/2 In. 35.00
Punch Set, Chrome Base,
12 x 6 1/2 In.,
14 Piece 45.00

Milk Glass
Creamer, Footed, 5 In. . . . 45.00
Pitcher, Footed, 8 Sides,
7 x 4 1/2 In. 45.00
Planter,
7 1/2 x 3 1/4 In. 22.00

Punch Bowl,
12 x 6 1/2 In. 28.00
Vase, 6 3/4 x 6 In. 45.00

HAWAIIAN

The Hawaiian pattern is made from Amber-colored glass with a freeform edge of another color. Fostoria Glass Company made the pattern from 1961 to 1964.

Basket, Peacock Blue
Trim 50.00
Bowl, Deep, Peacock Blue
Trim, 8 In. 55.00
Bowl, Deep, Peacock Blue
Trim, 11 1/2 In. 65.00
Bowl, Floral, Peacock
Blue Trim, 8 In. 48.00
Bowl, Peacock Blue Trim,
Oval, 15 In. 75.00
Plate, Cracker, Brown
Trim 45.00
Shrimp & Dip Set,
2 Piece 110.00
Vase, Ruffled Edge,
6 3/4 In. 45.00

HEATHER

Heather etch was used on Crystal blanks by Fostoria

Glass Company from 1949 to 1976.

Bowl, Lily, 9 In. 48.00
Goblet, Water, 9 Oz.,
7 7/8 In. 26.00
Sugar & Creamer 35.00
Tray, Handles 65.00
Tray, Muffin, Handle,
9 1/2 In. 35.00
Vase, Oval, 8 1/2 In. 85.00

HEIRLOOM

Heirloom is a ribbed, freeform pattern made in various colors, some with opalescent rims. It was made by the Fostoria Glass Company, Moundsville, West Virginia, in the 1950s and '60s. The pieces were pressed in molds and then stretched with tools.

Blue Opalescent
Bowl, 6 1/2 In. 85.00
Bowl, Oval, 15 In. 70.00
Candleholder, 3 x 3 1/2 In.,
Pair 35.00
Candleholder, Flora,
3 7/8 In. 95.00
Vase, 8 In. 37.00
Vase, 9 1/2 In. 50.00
Vase, 13 1/2 In. 55.00

Green Opalescent
Vase, Pitcher Shape 95.00

Pink Opalescent
Bowl, 14 1/2 x 6 1/2 In. . . 42.00
Bowl, Crimped, 11 In. . . . 40.00
Vase, Bud, 6 In. 23.00

Red
Bowl, Crimped Edge,
11 In. 65.00
Bowl, Oblong, 14 In. 75.00
Candlestick, 2 1/2 In.,
Pair 45.00
Vase, Pitcher Shape 110.00

Topaz
Bowl,
13 x 6 In. . . . . . 41.00 to 75.00

Vase, 10 In. 67.00

White Opalescent

Bowl, Oval, 15 In. 65.00

Candleholder, 3 1/2 In.,
  Pair 67.00

Vase, Winged Handles,
  11 In. 125.00

HEISEY ROSE
See Rose Etch

HERITAGE

Federal Glass Company, Columbus, Ohio, made Heritage from the 1930s through the 1960s. Evidently the serving pieces were made in Blue, Light Green, and Pink, but the plates and dinnerware pieces were made only in Crystal. Amber and Crystal reproduction bowls were made in 1987.

Crystal

Berry Bowl,
  5 In. . . . . 3.00 to 16.00

Berry Bowl, Master,
  8 1/2 In. . . . . . . 40.00 to 45.00

Bowl, Fruit,
  10 1/2 In. . . . . . 20.00 to 27.00

Creamer 30.00

Cup 7.00

Cup & Saucer . . . . 8.00 to 12.00

Plate, Dinner,
  9 1/4 In. . . . . . . 12.00 to 13.00

Plate, Luncheon,
  8 In. . . . . 5.50 to 18.00

Saucer 4.00

Sugar, Footed . . . 23.00 to 25.00

HERMITAGE

Fostoria Glass Company modeled its Hermitage pattern to look like nineteenth-century pressed glass. It was made from 1932 to 1944 in Amber, Azure, Crystal, Gold Tint, Green, Topaz, and Wisteria.

Crystal

Cocktail Icer, Amber
  Liner, 4 Oz. 20.00

Cup & Saucer 10.00

Decanter, Stopper,
  28 Oz. 55.00

Plate, Dinner, 10 In. 12.00

Plate, Salad, Crescent,
  8 In. 20.00

Tumbler, Whiskey, 2 Oz.,
  2 1/2 In. 10.00

Topaz

Goblet, Water, 9 Oz.,
  5 1/4 In. 19.00

Oyster Cocktail, 4 Oz.,
  3 In. 13.00

Sherbet, 5 1/2 Oz.,
  3 1/4 In. 10.00

HEX OPTIC
See Hexagon Optic

HEXAGON OPTIC

Hexagon Optic, also called Honeycomb or Hex Optic,

has an accurate, descriptive name. Green or Pink sets of kitchenware were made in this pattern by Jeannette Glass Company, Jeannette, Pennsylvania, from 1928 to 1932. Around 1960, some Iridescent sets and some Ultramarine (blue-green) pieces were made.

Green

Butter, Cover . . . 35.00 to 60.00

Creamer 15.00

Cup 5.00

Cup & Saucer 11.00

Ice Tub, Spout . . 30.00 to 39.00

Pitcher, 70 Oz., 8 In. 295.00

Pitcher, Sunflower, 32 Oz.,
  5 In. . . . . 22.00 to 28.00

Pitcher, Sunflower, 36 Oz.,
  5 1/2 In. 27.00

Plate, Luncheon, 8 In. 14.00

Plate, Sherbet, 6 In. 5.00

Refrigerator Dish, Cover,
  4 1/2 x 5 In. 22.00

Salt & Pepper . . . 16.00 to 30.00

Saltshaker 6.25

Tumbler, Footed,
  5 3/4 In. . . . . . . 7.00 to 10.00

Iridescent Marigold

Pitcher, Footed, 48 Oz.,
  9 In. 55.00

Tumbler, 9 Oz., 3 3/4 In. . . 3.00

Tumbler, 12 Oz., 5 In. 4.00

Pink

Berry Bowl, Ruffled Edge,
  4 1/2 In. 40.00

Ice Tub 65.00

Mixing Bowl, 8 1/4 In. . . . 13.00

Mixing Bowl, 9 In. 28.00

Plate, Sherbet, 6 In. 3.00

Refrigerator Dish,
  Cover 21.00

Saltshaker 25.00

Saucer 2.00

Tumbler, Flared, 12 Oz.,
  5 In. 8.00

Tumbler, Footed, 7 In. . . . 12.00

Tumbler, Footed, 7 Oz.,
  4 3/4 In. 7.00

Ultramarine
Tumbler, Flared, 12 Oz.,
5 In. 24.00

HINGE
See Patrician

HOBNAIL
See also Moonstone

HOBNAIL DUNCAN & MILLER

Many companies have made similar patterns with hobbed decorations since the nineteenth-century. Duncan & Miller Glass Company made its Hobnail pattern from 1930 to 1955 in Amber, Cape Cod Blue (opalescent blue), Cranberry Pink (opalescent pink), Crystal, Green, Rose, and Ruby.

Cape Cod Blue
Basket, 10 x 4 3/4 In. . . . 115.00
Ivy Ball, Footed,
7 x 4 1/2 In. . . . 70.00 to 95.00
Ladle,
10 3/4 x 3 3/8 In. 150.00
Cranberry Pink
Basket, Oval, 12 In. 275.00
Crystal
Goblet, 9 Oz., 6 In. 13.00
Goblet, Champagne,
5 Oz., 4 1/2 In. 16.00
Ivy Bowl, Footed,
7 1/2 In. 35.00
Plate, Bread & Butter,
6 In. 9.00

Plate, Dessert, 7 1/2 In. . . 12.00
Green
Candy Dish, Cover,
5 1/2 In. 12.00

HOBNAIL FENTON

Hobnail is one of Fenton Art Glass Company's most popular patterns. It was first made in 1940 in French Opalescent (opalescent crystal). Pieces can be found in opalescent colors (Blue, Cranberry, Emerald Green, Green, Lime, Plum, and Topaz), solid pastel colors (Blue, Green, Rose, and Turquoise), satin colors (Blue, Lavender, Lime, and Rose), overlay colors (Apple Green, Coral, Honey Amber, Opaque Blue, and Wild Rose), Blue, Colonial Green, Milk Glass, Orange, Peach Blow (white with an opaque pink interior), and Ruby. Pieces were made through the 1970s and in 1982 and 1983 for Levay Distributing Company.

Blue Opalescent
Bowl, 11 In. 95.00
Blue Satin
Vase, 3 In. 75.00
Vase, Fan, 4 In. 75.00

Cranberry Opalescent
Basket, 10 In. 165.00
Bride's Basket, Silver Plated
Frame, 11 1/2 In. 300.00
Vase, Tulip, 7 1/2 In. 70.00
French Opalescent
Jug, 80 Oz. 200.00
Vase, 8 In. 65.00
Lime Opalescent
Basket, 4 3/4 In. 110.00
Compote,
5 3/4 x 6 1/2 In. 25.00
Milk Glass
Basket, Oval, 12 In. 60.00
Bell 20.00
Bonbon, Handle, 6 In. . . . 18.00
Bowl, Scalloped Edge & Base,
3 1/2 x 8 1/2 In. 25.00
Candle Bowl 45.00
Candy Box, Cover,
Footed 25.00
Cigarette Box,
No Cover 20.00
Cigarette Holder, Top Hat,
3 1/4 x 4 1/2 In. 25.00
Cologne Bottle 20.00
Compote, 6 In. 12.00
Cruet, Stopper, 5 In. 25.00
Epergne, 3 Lilies 145.00
Pitcher, 1/2 Gal., 8 In. . . . 35.00
Pitcher, 5 In. 16.00
Pitcher, 72 Oz. 23.00
Relish, 3 Sections 15.00
Relish, Center Handle,
5 x 7 In. 23.00
Spooner 95.00
Toothpick 15.00
Tray, 2 Sections, Center
Handle 15.00
Tumbler, Footed 22.00
Tumbler, Water, Footed,
9 Oz., 5 1/2 In. 15.00
Vase, 8 In. 23.00
Vase, 9 1/2 x 5 In. 15.00
Vase, Bud, 10 In. 23.00
Wedding Bowl, Cover . . . 35.00
Plum Opalescent
Compote 145.00
Ruby
Bonbon, 8 In. 25.00

Topaz Opalescent
Basket, 10 In. 280.00
Vanity Set, 3 Piece 275.00

Turquoise
Bowl, 1 1/4 x 4 In. 85.00

HOBNAIL HOCKING

Hocking Glass Company, Lancaster, Ohio, made its Hobnail pattern from 1934 to 1936. It can be distinguished from other hobbed patterns by a honeycomb design with long sides and pointed ends. Mostly Crystal or Pink beverage sets were made. Some pieces have red rims or black feet.

Crystal
Cup 3.00
Cup & Saucer . . . . . 5.00 to 7.00
Decanter, Stopper, 32 Oz.,
    11 In. 35.00
Pitcher, 72 Oz. 17.00
Pitcher, Iced Tea, 13 Oz.,
    4 3/4 In. 18.00
Pitcher, Milk, 18 Oz.,
    5 1/4 In. 9.00
Plate, Luncheon,
    8 1/2 In. . . . . 4.00 to 6.00
Tumbler, Juice,
    5 Oz. . . . . 3.00 to 4.00
Tumbler, Juice, Red Trim,
    Footed, 5 Oz. 7.00
Tumbler, Water, 10 Oz.,
    3 3/4 In. 12.00
Water Set, 6 Piece 18.00

Pink
Plate, 6 In. . . . . 4.00 to 5.00
Plate, Luncheon,
    8 1/2 In. . . . . 5.00 to 11.00

Saucer 4.00
Sherbet, Footed,
    3 1/4 In. 5.00
Sherbet, Underplate 15.00

HOLIDAY

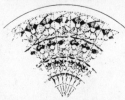

Holiday is one of the later Depression glass patterns. It was made from 1947 through 1949 by Jeannette Glass Company. The pattern is found in dinnerware sets of Crystal, Iridescent, and Pink. A few pieces of opaque Shell Pink were made. The pattern is sometimes also called Buttons & Bows or Russian.

Crystal
Pitcher, 52 Oz.,
    6 3/4 In. 40.00
Sherbet 25.00
Tumbler, Water, 10 Oz.,
    4 In. 28.00

Pink
Berry Bowl, 5 1/4 In. 15.00
Berry Bowl, Master,
    8 1/2 In. 48.00
Bowl, Vegetable, Oval,
    9 1/2 In. . . . . . . 20.00 to 38.00
Butter, Cover . . . 55.00 to 90.00
Butter, No
    Cover . . . . 10.00 to 25.00
Candlestick, 3 In. 55.00
Candlestick, 3 In.,
    Pair . . . . . . 110.00 to 150.00
Console, 10 3/4 In. 165.00
Creamer,
    Footed . . . . 6.00 to 15.00
Cup . . . . 6.00 to 10.00
Cup & Saucer . . . 12.00 to 20.00

Pitcher, Milk, 16 Oz.,
    4 3/4 In. . . . . . . 70.00 to 75.00
Pitcher, Water, 52 Oz.,
    6 3/4 In. . . . . 45.00 to 85.00
Plate, Dinner,
    9 In. . . . . 15.00 to 24.00
Plate, Sherbet,
    6 In. . . . . 10.00 to 11.00
Platter, Oval,
    11 3/8 In. . . . . . 20.00 to 30.00
Sandwich Server,
    10 1/2 In. 25.00
Sherbet 14.00
Sherbet, Rayed Foot 10.00
Soup, Dish, Flat,
    7 3/4 In. . . . . . . 65.00 to 75.00
Sugar, Cover . . . . 30.00 to 55.00
Sugar, Cover Only 12.00
Sugar & Creamer 30.00
Sugar & Creamer,
    Cover . . . . 60.00 to 65.00
Tumbler, Iced Tea, Footed,
    12 Oz., 6 In. 200.00
Tumbler, Water, 10 Oz.,
    4 In. . . . . 20.00 to 25.00
Tumbler, Water, Footed, 5 Oz.,
    4 In. . . . . 40.00 to 60.00

Shell Pink
Pitcher, Milk, 16 Oz.,
    4 3/4 In. 35.00

HOMESPUN

Homespun, often called Fine Rib, is a cause of confusion. Jeannette Glass Company made Crystal and Pink pieces in this pattern in 1939 and 1940. Similar pieces made by Hazel Atlas Glass Company are listed in the Homespun Lookalike section. Homespun made by Jeannette Glass Company is listed here.

Crystal
Berry Bowl, Handles,
4 1/2 In. 8.00
Cup & Saucer 33.00
Platter, 13 In. 35.00
Sherbet 35.00

Pink
Berry Bowl, Handles,
4 1/2 In. . . . . . . 13.00 to 18.00
Butter, Cover . . . 20.00 to 58.00
Cup 20.00
Cup & Saucer . . . 15.00 to 30.00
Plate, Child's . . . 20.00 to 28.00
Plate, Dinner,
9 1/4 In. . . . . . . 16.00 to 25.00
Plate, Sherbet, 6 In. 6.00
Saucer 10.00
Sugar 15.00
Teapot, Cover, Child's . . 250.00
Tumbler, 9 Oz.,
4 1/4 In. . . . . . . 25.00 to 30.00
Tumbler, Juice, Footed,
5 Oz., 4 In. . . . . . 9.00 to 12.00

HOMESPUN LOOKALIKE

Hazel Atlas Glass Company made tumblers and pitchers with fine ribs that are confused with the Homespun pattern by Jeannette. Homespun lookalikes were made in Crystal, Pink, and Ritz Blue in the 1930s. Homespun by Jeannette is listed

in its own section in this book.

Crystal
Pitcher, Ice Lip, 2 Qt.,
9 In. 112.00
Tumbler, Scotch & Soda,
11 1/2 Oz. 22.00

Ritz Blue
Ashtray, 5 1/2 In. 29.00
Tumbler, Iced Tea,
4 In. 30.00

HONEYCOMB
See Hexagon Optic

HORIZON

Horizon is a modern-looking pattern made by Fostoria Glass Company from 1951 to 1958. Cinnamon (brown), Crystal, and Spruce Green items were made.

Cinnamon
Sugar & Creamer 18.00

Spruce Green
Bowl, Cereal 20.00
Console, 12 In. 48.00
Sugar & Creamer 28.00

HORIZONTAL FINE RIB
See Manhattan

HORIZONTAL RIBBED
See Manhattan

HORIZONTAL ROUNDED
BIG RIB
See Manhattan

HORIZONTAL SHARP
BIG RIB
See Manhattan

HORSESHOE
See No. 612

IMPERIAL GRAPE

Imperial Glass Company introduced its Grape pattern in carnival glass in 1914. The pattern was reissued in several iridescent colors and Milk Glass in the 1960s.

Milk Glass
Candy Dish, Cover, 8 Sides,
8 x 5 1/2 In. 18.00
Punch Bowl, Footed, 8 Sides,
9 1/2 x 5 1/2 In. 15.00
Snack Plate,
10 1/8 x 8 1/4 In. 9.00
Snack Set, 10 In.,
4 Piece 20.00

IMPERIAL HUNT SCENE

Cambridge Glass Company decorated glass with the Imperial Hunt Scene etch during the late 1920s and early '30s. Items were made in Amber, Black, Crystal, Emerald, Peach-Blo, and Willow Blue.

Emerald
Goblet, Cocktail, 3 Oz.,
2 1/2 In. 55.00
Tumbler, Mushroom 70.00

Peach-Blo
Finger Bowl 45.00
Goblet, Claret, Gold Encrusted,
4 1/2 Oz., 5 1/2 In. . . . 170.00
Goblet, Wine, Emerald Green
Foot, 2 1/2 Oz. 115.00

IMPERIAL PINCH

Russel Wright designed Pinch tumblers to match his Iroquois Casual dinnerware line in 1951. The tumblers were made by Imperial Glass Company in Cantaloupe (amber), Chartreuse, Seafoam (teal blue), Smoke (brown), and Verde (dark olive green). Ruby and Pink tumblers can be found, too, but it is unclear whether these colors were part of Wright's original line.

Chartreuse
Tumbler, Iced Tea,
　14 Oz. 43.00
Tumbler, Water, 11 Oz. . . 45.00

Smoke
Tumbler, Iced Tea,
　14 Oz. 43.00
Tumbler, Water, 11 Oz. . . 43.00

Verde
Tumbler, Iced Tea,
　14 Oz. 45.00
Tumbler, Juice, 6 Oz. 45.00
Tumbler, Water, 11 Oz. . . 45.00

INDIANA CUSTARD

This design makes its original pattern name, Flower & Leaf Band, clear, but collectors prefer to call this pattern Indiana Custard. It is an opaque glassware of Custard, or Ivory, made by the Indiana Glass Company. Primarily luncheon sets were made from the 1930s to the 1950s. Some pieces have

bands that are decorated with pastel colors or decal designs. The same pattern was made of Milk Glass in 1957. It was called Orange Blossom.

Berry Bowl,
　5 1/2 In. . . . . . . 11.00 to 15.00
Bowl, Cereal,
　6 1/2 In. 24.00
Bowl, Vegetable, Oval,
　9 1/2 In. 24.00
Creamer . . . . 10.00 to 22.00
Cup 16.00
Cup & Saucer 29.00
Plate, Dinner,
　9 3/4 In. 36.00
Plate, Luncheon,
　8 7/8 In. 21.00
Saucer 10.00
Sugar, Cover . . . . 37.00 to 52.00
Sugar, Cover Only 25.00
Sugar,
　No Cover . . . . . . 7.50 to 15.00
Sugar & Creamer 40.00

INSPIRATION
See Bubble

IPSWICH

Ipswich is one of several A.H. Heisey & Company patterns inspired by Sandwich glass designs. It was made from 1931 to 1946 in Moongleam, Flamingo, and Sahara and in Crystal from 1951 to 1953. The candle vase can be found in Cobalt Blue. Candy jars and bowls were reissued by Imperial Glass Company in Amber, Antique Blue, Heather (lavender), Mandarin Gold, Moonlight Blue, and Verde (olive green), and a jar was made in Milk Glass. Most pieces, even the reissued items,

are marked with the Diamond H logo.

Crystal
Goblet, Water, 10 Oz. 30.00

Moongleam
Candlestick Vase,
　Pair 200.00
Candy Jar, Cover,
　1/2 Lb. 695.00
Sherbet, 4 Oz. 45.00

Sahara
Candlestick Vase, Pair . . 175.00
Plate, Square, 7 In. 60.00

IRIS

The design of Iris is unusually bold for Depression glass. Molded representations of stalks of iris fill the center of a ribbed plate. Other pieces in the pattern show fewer irises, but the flower is predominant. Edges of pieces may be ruffled or beaded. It was made by Jeannette Glass Company, Jeannette, Pennsylvania, from 1928 to 1932 and then again in the 1950s and 1970s. Early pieces were made in Crystal, Green, Iridescent, and Pink. Later, Crystal and White pieces were decorated with Blue-Green and Red-Yellow two-tone stains. Solid Red-stained after-dinner cups and saucers can be found. The pattern is also called Iris & Herringbone. Reproduction candy vases and coasters have been made in a variety of colors since 1977.

Crystal

Berry Bowl, Beaded Edge,
4 1/2 In. ...... 35.00 to 60.00

Berry Bowl, Master,
Beaded Edge, 8 In. 70.00

Berry Set, 8 Piece 70.00

Bowl, Cereal,
5 In. .... 95.00 to 150.00

Bowl, Fruit, 11 In. 65.00

Bowl, Fruit, Ruffled Edge,
11 1/2 In. ..... 10.00 to 25.00

Bowl, Salad, Ruffled Edge,
9 1/2 In. ..... 10.00 to 20.00

Butter, Cover ... 40.00 to 70.00

Butter,
Cover Only ... 26.00 to 35.00

Butter,
No Cover ..... 12.00 to 20.00

Candlestick,
2-Light .... 20.00 to 25.00

Candlestick, 2-Light,
Pair .... 40.00 to 50.00

Candy Jar,
Cover ...... 195.00 to 235.00

Candy Jar, No Cover 60.00

Coaster,
3 1/4 In. ..... 90.00 to 140.00

Creamer,
Footed .... 11.00 to 16.00

Cup & Saucer ... 18.00 to 33.00

Cup & Saucer,
After Dinner 240.00

Goblet, 4 Oz.,
5 1/2 In. ...... 25.00 to 33.00

Goblet, Cocktail, 4 Oz.,
4 1/2 In. ...... 21.00 to 30.00

Goblet, Water, 8 Oz.,
5 1/2 In. ...... 16.00 to 28.00

Goblet, Wine, 3 Oz.,
4 1/2 In. ...... 12.00 to 33.00

Nut Set, Bowl, Metal Base,
6 Picks, 11 3/4 In. 130.00

Pitcher, Footed,
9 1/2 In. ...... 28.00 to 70.00

Plate, Dinner,
9 In. .... 25.00 to 49.00

Plate, Luncheon,
8 In. .... 100.00 to 280.00

Plate, Luncheon, Frosted,
8 In. .... 35.00 to 70.00

Plate, Sherbet,
5 1/2 In. .... 8.00 to 20.00

Sandwich Server,
11 3/4 In. ..... 35.00 to 44.00

Sandwich Server, Frosted,
11 3/4 In. 20.00

Sauce, Ruffled Edge,
5 In. .... 7.00 to 12.00

Sherbet,
2 1/2 In. ...... 25.00 to 30.00

Sherbet, 4 In. .... 9.00 to 30.00

Soup, Dish, Flat,
7 1/2 In. .... 135.00 to 180.00

Sugar, Cover .... 23.00 to 25.00

Sugar, Cover Only 16.00

Sugar, No Cover 13.00

Sugar & Creamer 45.00

Sugar & Creamer,
Cover 46.00

Tumbler,
4 In. ...... 100.00 to 160.00

Tumbler, Footed,
6 1/2 In. ...... 11.00 to 42.00

Tumbler, Footed,
6 In. .... 18.00 to 34.00

Tumbler, Iced Tea,
6 1/2 In. 28.00

Tumbler, Iris On Foot,
6 1/2 In. ..... 95.00 to 200.00

Vase, 9 In. ...... 22.00 to 42.00

Iridescent

Berry Bowl, Beaded
Edge, 4 1/2 In. ... 6.50 to 9.00

Berry Bowl, Beaded Edge,
Master, 8 In. .. 14.00 to 40.00

Berry Set, 7 Piece 131.00

Bowl, Fruit, 11 In. 10.00

Bowl, Fruit, Ruffled Edge,
11 1/2 In. ..... 14.00 to 20.00

Bowl, Salad, Ruffled Edge,
9 1/2 In. .... 5.50 to 13.00

Butter, Cover ... 33.00 to 65.00

Butter, Cover Only 40.00

Candleholder, 2-Light,
Pair 66.00

Creamer .... 3.00 to 12.00

Cup .... 14.00 to 16.00

Cup & Saucer, After Dinner,
Rose Tint 350.00

Pitcher, Footed,
9 1/2 In. ...... 40.00 to 50.00

Plate, Dinner,
9 1/2 In. ...... 16.00 to 48.00

Plate, Sherbet,
5 1/2 In. ...... 14.00 to 15.00

Sandwich Server,
11 3/4 In. ..... 23.00 to 38.00

Sauce, Ruffled Edge,
5 In. .... 4.75 to 30.00

Saucer .... 5.25 to 11.00

Sherbet,
2 1/2 In. ...... 15.00 to 21.00

Soup, Dish, Flat,
7 3/4 In. ...... 50.00 to 60.00

Sugar, Cover Only 11.00

Sugar & Creamer,
Cover 10.00

Tumbler, Footed,
6 In. .... 18.00 to 25.00

Vase, 9 In. ...... 27.00 to 40.00

IRIS & HERRINGBONE
See Iris

JADITE

The term Jadite is used to describe opaque light green glass made by several companies. Jeannette Glass Company used the name Jadite for its kitchenware made from 1936 to 1938. McKee Glass Company called its opaque light green glass Jade or Skokie Green. All of the pieces of kitchenware made of Jadite by Jeannette were also made of a blue glass called Delphite. Delphite pieces are listed in their own category in this book. McKee made similar pieces in Chalaine Blue and Seville Yellow, which may be listed in the Kitchen category in this book. The opaque green made by Anchor Hocking Glass Corporation is called Jade-ite and is listed in the Fire-King category.

Ashtray, 6 Sides, Match
Holder, Jeannette 30.00

Batter Bowl, Spout,
McKee 54.00

Butter, Cover, McKee,
1 Lb. 100.00

Butter, Ribbed, McKee,
1 1/4 Lb. 175.00

Canister, Coffee, Round,
Jeannette, 40 Oz. 355.00

Canister, Coffee, Square,
McKee, 28 Oz. 355.00

Canister, Cover, Round,
Jeannette, 48 Oz.,
5 3/4 In. 50.00

Canister, Cover, Sugar,
Square, Jeannette,
4 1/4 x 5 In. 295.00

Canister, Cover, Tea,
Square, Jeannette,
4 1/4 x 5 In. 265.00

Canister, Round, Jeannette,
32 Oz. 135.00

Canister, Sugar, Round, Dark,
Jeannette, 40 Oz. 395.00

Canister, Sugar, Round, Light,
Jeannette, 40 Oz. 335.00

Canister, Tea, Round, Jeannette,
16 Oz. ..... 215.00 to 225.00

Drippings Jar,
Cover Only 25.00

Grease Jar, Jeannette ... 250.00

Measuring Cup, 2 Spouts,
McKee 275.00

Measuring Cup, Jeannette,
2 Oz. .... 40.00 to 45.00

Measuring Cup, Jeannette,
4 Oz. .... 30.00 to 55.00

Measuring Cup, Jeannette,
8 Oz. .... 60.00 to 75.00

Measuring Cup, Sunflower,
Jeannette, 16 Oz. 81.00

Measuring Cup Set, Jeannette,
4 Piece 275.00

Mixing Bowl, McKee,
7 1/2 In. 100.00

Mixing Bowl, Vertical
Ribbed, Jeannette,
4 1/2 x 9 In. .... 55.00 to 90.00

Mug, Tom & Jerry,
3 5/8 In. 72.00

Punch Set, Bowl, Cups, Hangers,
Stand, Ladle, Pine Cones,
Fir Branches 645.00

Reamer 45.00

Reamer, Lemon 65.00

Refrigerator Dish, Cover,
McKee, 4 x 5 In. 50.00

Refrigerator Dish, Cover,
McKee, 5 x 8 In. 75.00

Refrigerator Dish, Cover,
McKee, 6 1/4 In. 149.00

Refrigerator Dish, Jeannette,
4 x 8 In. 75.00

Saltshaker, Black Letters,
Jeannette, 6 Oz. 60.00

Shaker, Pepper, Round,
Ribbed, Jeannette,
8 Oz. .... 52.00 to 54.00

Shaker, Round, Ribbed,
Jeannette, 6 Oz. 25.00

Shaker, Spice, Round, Ribbed,
Jeannette, 6 Oz. 30.00

Sugar, 5 x 2 3/8 In. 113.00

Sugar Shaker, Round, Ribbed,
Jeannette, 8 Oz. 45.00

Tumbler, Flat 55.00

Vase, 6 1/4 In. 30.00

Vase, Bud, Jeannette 18.00

Water Bottle, Stopper,
McKee 500.00

Water Dispenser, Short,
McKee 225.00

JAMESTOWN

Jamestown was made by the Fostoria Glass Company from 1958 to 1982. It was made in Amber, Amethyst, Blue, Brown, Crystal, Green, Pink, and Ruby.

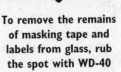

To remove the remains of masking tape and labels from glass, rub the spot with WD-40 lubricating and penetrating oil.

Amber
Goblet, Wine, 4 Oz.,
4 1/4 In. 10.00

Pitcher, 48 Oz.,
7 1/4 In. 65.00

Sherbet, 6 1/2 Oz.,
4 1/4 In. 6.00

Tumbler, Iced Tea,
Footed, 11 Oz., 6 In. ... 10.00

Tumbler, Juice, Footed,
5 Oz., 4 3/4 In. 10.00

Blue
Creamer 25.00

Goblet, Water, 9 1/2 Oz.,
5 3/4 In. 22.00

Goblet, Wine, 4 Oz.,
4 1/4 In. 24.00

Pitcher, 48 Oz.,
7 1/4 In. 135.00

Sherbet, 6 1/2 Oz.,
4 1/4 In. 16.00

Tumbler, Iced Tea, Footed,
11 Oz., 6 In. 25.00

Tumbler, Juice, Footed,
5 Oz., 4 3/4 In. 26.00

Crystal
Goblet, Water, 9 1/2 Oz.,
5 3/4 In. ...... 16.00 to 25.00

Tumbler, Iced Tea,
Footed, 11 Oz., 6 In. ... 22.00

Tumbler, Juice, Footed,
Barcelona Cutting, Footed,
5 Oz., 4 3/4 In. 14.00

Tumbler, Water, 12 Oz.,
5 1/8 In. 35.00

Green
Sherbet, 6 1/2 Oz.,
4 1/4 In. 13.00

Pink
Goblet, Water, 9 1/2 Oz.,
5 3/4 In. ...... 16.00 to 24.00

Plate, 8 In. 29.00

Ruby

Goblet, Wine, 4 Oz.,
4 1/4 In. 24.00
Sherbet, 8 Oz., 5 In. 18.00
Tumbler, Iced Tea,
Footed, 12 Oz., 6 In. . . . 25.00

JANE-RAY

Jane-Ray is a plain dinnerware with ribbed edge
made mostly in Jade-ite
from 1945 to 1963 by
Anchor Hocking Glass
Corporation, Lancaster,
Ohio. Crystal, Ivory, Peach
Lustre, and Vitrock pieces
were also made. Other
related patterns are listed
in the Fire-King section in
this book.

Ivory

Bowl, Dessert, 4 7/8 In. . . 25.00

Jade-ite

Bowl, Dessert,
4 7/8 In. . . . . . 12.00 to 16.00
Bowl, Oatmeal,
5 7/8 In. . . . . . . 10.00 to 14.00
Bowl, Vegetable,
8 1/4 In. . . . . . . 13.00 to 48.00
Creamer . . . . 10.00 to 38.00
Cup 5.00
Cup, After Dinner 25.00
Cup & Saucer . . . . 9.00 to 13.00
Cup & Saucer,
After Dinner 75.00
Plate, Dinner,
9 1/8 In. . . . . 6.00 to 15.00
Plate, Salad,
7 3/4 In. . . . . 5.00 to 16.00
Platter, Oval,
12 In. . . . . 13.00 to 35.00
Saucer . . . . 3.00 to 6.00

Soup, Dish, Flat,
7 1/2 In. . . . . . . 11.00 to 19.00
Soup, Dish, Flat, 9 In. . . . 495.00
Sugar 10.00
Sugar, Cover . . . . 23.00 to 36.00
Sugar & Creamer,
Cover . . . . 26.00 to 41.00

JANICE

Janice was made by New
Martinsville Glass Com-
pany, New Martinsville,
West Virginia, from 1926
to 1944. Dishes came in
Amethyst, Cobalt Blue,
Crystal, Emerald, Light
Blue, and Ruby. Viking
Glass Company purchased
the New Martinsville fac-
tory in 1944 and contin-
ued to make Janice pieces
until 1970. Dalzell-Viking
made Janice pieces from
1996 to 1998. The recent
pieces were made in
Cobalt Blue, Crystal, and
Red.

Cobalt Blue

Basket, Crystal Handle,
6 1/2 x 9 In. 145.00
Condiment Tray, Oval,
Handles 40.00

Crystal

Basket, 12 In. 85.00
Bowl, Centerpiece, 3-Footed,
11 x 3 3/4 In. 45.00
Bowl, Crimped, 12 In. . . . 50.00
Bowl, Oval, Cobalt Blue
Swan Handles,
12 1/2 x 5 1/2 In. 32.00
Bowl, Ruffled, 11 In. 14.00
Bowl, Silver Overlay,
8 In. 20.00

Bowl, Swan, Cobalt Blue Neck
& Head, 10 In. 50.00
Candlestick, 2-Light, 5 In.,
Pair . . . . 41.00 to 51.00
Candlestick, 6 In., Pair . . . 35.00
Candy Dish, Curved,
Handles, 7 1/2 In. 15.00
Candy Dish, Handles,
Footed, 6 In. 16.00
Cruet, Stopper, 5 Oz. 40.00
Plate, Handles, 12 In. 25.00
Plate, Open Handles,
7 In. 8.00
Plate, Salad, 8 1/2 In. 13.00
Platter, 14 In. 23.00
Relish, 2 Sections, 22K Gold
Rose Overlay, 6 In. 25.00
Relish, 2 Sections, Handles,
6 In. . . . . 14.00 to 15.00
Sugar 10.00

Light Blue

Bonbon, Upturned Handle,
7 In. 18.00
Cake Plate, Handles,
13 1/2 In. 40.00
Plate, Open Handles,
7 In. 18.00

Ruby

Bowl, Cupped, 3-Footed,
10 3/4 In. 75.00
Plate, Handles, 11 In. 55.00
Plate, Handles, Sterling
Overlay, 13 In. 65.00

JUBILEE

In the early 1930s, the
Lancaster Glass Company,
Lancaster, Ohio, made this
luncheon set decorated
with cut flowers. It was
made in Crystal, Pink, and
a yellow shade called
Topaz. Collectors will find
many similar patterns.
Most original Lancaster

Jubilee pieces have twelve petals and an open center on each flower. The 8-ounce sherbet and candy jar have only eleven petals.

Pink

Vase, 12 In. 200.00

Topaz

Bowl, 3-Footed,
   11 1/2 In. 200.00

Cake Plate, Open Handles,
   11 In. 31.00

Creamer 20.00

Cup . . . . 14.00 to 15.00

Cup & Saucer . . . 13.00 to 22.00

Goblet, Champagne,
   7 Oz., 5 1/2 In. 125.00

Plate, 3-Footed, 14 In. . . 157.00

Plate, Luncheon,
   8 3/4 In. . . . . . . 10.00 to 18.00

Plate, Salad,
   7 In. . . . . 11.00 to 14.00

Saucer . . . . 8.00 to 11.00

Sugar . . . . 18.00 to 20.00

Sugar &
   Creamer . . . . . . 20.00 to 23.00

Tray, Handles, 11 In. 36.00

JUNE

June is one of very few patterns that can be dated with some accuracy from the color. Fostoria Glass Company, Fostoria, Ohio, made full dinnerware sets in various colors. From 1928 to 1944, the glass was Azure, Green, or Rose. Crystal was made

from 1928 to 1952. If your set is Topaz, it dates from 1929 to 1938. Gold-tinted glass was made from 1938 to 1944. Color pieces with crystal stems or bases were made only from 1931 to 1944. Reproductions have been made in Azure (blue), Crystal, Rose (pink), and Topaz (yellow).

Azure

Cup & Saucer 45.00

Sherbet, 6 Oz., 4 1/4 In. . . 33.00

Tumbler, Footed, 12 Oz.,
   6 In. 85.00

Crystal

Bowl, Cereal, 6 1/2 In. 30.00

Candlestick, Grecian, 5 In.,
   Pair 110.00

Cup & Saucer 23.00

Goblet, Water, 10 Oz.,
   8 1/4 In. . . . . . . 36.00 to 45.00

Plate, Luncheon,
   8 3/4 In. 22.00

Sherbet, 6 Oz., 6 In. 22.00

Rose

Cup, After Dinner 98.00

Plate, Salad, 7 1/2 In. 20.00

Topaz

Bottle, Embossed Oil
   & Vinegar 550.00

Bouillon, Footed,
   Handles . . . . . . 25.00 to 65.00

Bowl, Centerpiece,
   3-Footed, 12 In. 99.00

Candlestick, Scroll, 5 In.,
   Pair 110.00

Cheese & Cracker Set,
   2 Piece 120.00

Cup & Saucer,
   After Dinner 55.00

Dish, Mayonnaise,
   Underplate, Ladle 120.00

Goblet, Claret, 4 Oz.,
   6 In. 75.00

Goblet, Cocktail, 3 Oz.,
   5 1/4 In. . . . . . . 36.50 to 38.00

Goblet, Wine, 3 Oz.,
   5 1/2 In. 65.00

Plate, Bread & Butter,
   6 In. 15.00

Plate, Dinner, 9 1/2 In. 35.00

Plate, Salad, 7 1/2 In. 15.00

Platter, 15 In. 150.00

Salt & Pepper, Footed . . 200.00

Soup, Dish, 7 In. 25.00

JUNE NIGHT

June Night etched crystal was made by Tiffin Glass Company (Factory R of U.S. Glass Company) in the 1940s and '50s.

Goblet, Champagne,
   5 1/2 Oz. 22.00

Goblet, Cocktail,
   3 1/2 Oz. 20.00

Goblet, Sherry, 2 Oz. 39.00

Goblet, Water, 9 Oz. 32.00

Goblet, Wine, 3 1/2 In. . . . 30.00

Parfait, 4 1/2 Oz. 30.00

Sherbet, 5 1/2 Oz. 15.00

Tumbler, Juice, Footed,
   5 Oz. 20.00

KING'S CROWN

King's Crown was originally known as Thumbprint when Tiffin Glass Company (U.S. Glass Company Factory R, Tiffin, Ohio) introduced it in 1891. Tiffin started to call the pattern King's Crown in the 1940s and continued to make it until the 1960s. In the 1970s, Indiana Glass Company bought the molds and changed them slightly. The Tiffin items came in Cobalt Blue; Crystal; Crystal with ruby, cranberry, or amber stain; Green; and Mulberry. Indiana items came in Amber, Avocado Green, Cobalt Blue, and iridized carnival colors. Tiara Exclusives sold King's Crown in Imperial Blue.

Amber

Cup 8.00
Plate, Bread & Butter,
  5 In. 6.00
Plate, Salad, 7 3/8 In. 3.00
Sherbet, 5 1/2 Oz. 6.00
Snack Plate, 10 3/8 In. . . . 15.00
Snack Set, 2 Piece 12.00
Tumbler, Juice, Footed,
  4 Oz. 4.00

Avocado Green

Breakfast Set,
  24 Piece 90.00
Sugar & Creamer 15.00

Crystal

Ashtray, Square,
  5 1/4 In. 45.00
Candleholder,
  Ruby Stain . . . . 30.00 to 33.00
Candy Box, Cover, Ruby
  Stain, Footed, 6 In. 55.00
Compote, 5 In. 8.00
Compote, Gold Trim,
  5 In. 22.50
Compote, Platinum Trim,
  7 In. 40.00
Compote, Ruby Stain,
  5 In. 30.00
Compote, Ruby Stain,
  7 In. 49.00
Cup, Ruby Stain 8.00
Cup & Saucer,
  Ruby Stain . . . . 14.00 to 22.00
Finger Bowl, 4 In. 18.00

Goblet, Claret, Cranberry
  Stain, 4 Oz. . . . 12.00 to 14.00
Goblet, Water, Ruby Stain,
  9 Oz. 13.00
Goblet, Wine,
  2 Oz. . . . . 5.00 to 9.00
Plate, Bread & Butter,
  6 In. 8.00
Plate, Bread & Butter,
  Ruby Stain, 6 In. 10.00
Plate, Salad, Ruby Stain,
  7 3/8 In. 12.00
Sherbet, 5 1/2 Oz. 6.00
Sherbet, Cranberry Stain,
  5 1/2 Oz. . . . . . . 8.00 to 10.00
Sherbet, Ruby Stain,
  5 1/2 Oz. . . . . . . 8.00 to 10.00
Torte Plate, 14 In. 45.00
Tumbler, Juice, Cranberry
  Stain, 4 1/2 Oz. 12.00
Tumbler, Juice, Ruby
  Stain, 4 Oz. . . . 10.00 to 15.00
Tumbler, Ruby Stain,
  8 1/2 Oz. 13.00
Wedding Bowl, Cover,
  Footed, Ruby Stain,
  10 1/2 In. 165.00

KITCHEN

Many of the same companies that made glass dinnerware also made accessories for the kitchen. The items were usually marketed without pattern names, and it can be difficult to identify the manufacturer. Where possible, the company name is included in the listings below. Jadite and Delphite colored pieces are listed in their own categories in this book, as is Fire-King kitchenware made by Anchor Hocking.

Bowl, White, 3-Footed,
  McKee, 3 x 7 In. 20.00
Butter, Cover, Seville Yellow,
  McKee, 1 Lb. 135.00

Butter, Cover, Ultramarine,
  Jennyware, Jeannette,
  7 x 4 In. 125.00
Butter, Cover, White, Red
  Ships, McKee, 1 Lb. . . 185.00
Canister, Cover, Cereal, Ivory,
  McKee, 48 Oz. 145.00
Canister, Cover, Ivory,
  McKee, 10 Oz. 75.00
Canister, Diagonal Ridges,
  Forest Green, Owens-Illinois,
  40 Oz. 50.00
Canister, Glass Cover,
  Transparent Green,
  Hocking, 47 Oz. 95.00
Canister, Metal Cover,
  Transparent Green,
  Hocking, 47 Oz. 40.00
Canister, No Cover, Ivory,
  McKee, 48 Oz. 50.00
Canister, Sugar, Ivory,
  McKee, 48 Oz. 145.00
Canister, Tea, Ivory,
  McKee, 48 Oz. 145.00
Carafe, White, Black
  Plastic Lacing On Neck,
  Glass Stopper, McKee,
  6 3/4 In. 25.00
Casserole, Cover, Crystal,
  Round, Fry, 8 In. 30.00
Casserole, Cover, Crystal,
  Round, Tab Handles,
  McKee, 5 In. 7.00
Casserole, Cover, Opalescent,
  Oval, Fry, 7 In. 18.00
Casserole, Cover, White, Black
  & Gold Diamonds, Federal,
  2 1/2 Qt. . . . . . 16.00 to 26.00
Cruet, Stopper, Green,
  U.S. Glass, 6 1/2 In. . . . 40.00
Custard Cup, Crystal,
  Marked 1927 & 1936,
  Fry, 6 Oz. 12.00
Eggbeater Bowl, White, Black
  Decal, McKee 68.00
Ice Tub, Cobalt Blue, Hazel
  Atlas, 7 5/8 In. 48.00
Knife, Crystal, Daisies On
  Handle, Cryst-O-Lite,
  No. 24, Federal, Box,
  8 1/2 In. 40.00
Measuring Cup, Cobalt Blue,
  3 Spouts, Hazel Atlas,
  8 Oz. 350.00
Measuring Cup, Crystal, 3
  Spouts, Federal, 8 Oz.,
  3 1/2 In. 22.00

Measuring Cup, Seville
Yellow, Footed, McKee,
4 Cup 185.00

Measuring Cup, White,
Hocking, 16 Oz. 80.00

Measuring Cup Set,
Ultramarine, Jennyware,
Jeannette, 3 Piece 210.00

Measuring Cup Set,
Ultramarine, Jennyware,
Jeannette, 4 Piece 295.00

Mixing Bowl, Horizontal Ribs,
McKee, 9 3/4 In. 250.00

Mixing Bowl, Pink,
Jennyware, Jeannette,
65 Oz., 8 1/4 In. 55.00

Mixing Bowl, Transparent
Green, Hocking,
7 1/2 In. 35.00

Mixing Bowl, Transparent
Green, Hocking,
10 1/4 In. 65.00

Mixing Bowl, Ultramarine,
Jennyware, Jeannette,
3 3/8 x 6 In. 60.00

Mixing Bowl, White, Blue
Chickens, Federal,
9 1/2 x 4 1/4 In. 15.00

Mixing Bowl, White, Red
Ships, McKee, 6 In. 37.00

Mixing Bowl, White, Red
Ships, McKee, 8 In. 53.00

Mixing Bowl, White,
Snowflakes, Federal,
1 1/2 Qt., 6 1/2 In. 8.00

Mixing Bowl, White,
Snowflakes, Federal,
2 1/2 Qt., 8 In. 11.00

Mixing Bowl Set, White,
Red Ships, Mckee,
4 Piece 185.00

Mug, Ivory, Little Bo Peep,
Red, McKee, 8 Oz.,
3 x 3 1/8 In. 15.00

Watch burning candles
in glass candlesticks.
If the candle burns
too low, the hot wax
and flame may break
the glass.

Mug, Tom & Jerry, Clambroth,
McKee, 3 1/2 x 4 In. . . . 18.00

Pie Plate, Crystal, Fry,
9 1/2 In. 20.00

Pitcher, Cobalt Blue,
Harpo 125.00

Pitcher, White, Red Ships,
Hocking, 86 Oz. 85.00

Reamer, Crystal, Frosted,
Baby's Orange, Westmoreland,
4 1/4 In., 2 Piece 75.00

Reamer, Crystal, Loop Handle,
Jennyware, Jeannette,
5 1/2 In. 135.00

Reamer, Grapefruit, Chalaine
Blue, McKee 950.00

Reamer, Grapefruit, Seville
Yellow, McKee 425.00

Reamer, Grapefruit, Transparent
Green, Hocking 1150.00

Reamer, Green, Ribbed, Loop
Handle, Anchor Hocking,
6 In. 25.00

Reamer, Green, Slick Handle,
Servmor Juice Extractor,
U.S. Glass, 2 Piece 55.00

Reamer, Ivory, Saucer Type,
Loop Handle, McKee,
5 1/2 In. 35.00

Reamer, Lemon, Crystal,
2 1/2 x 6 In. 15.00

Reamer, Lemon, Ivory,
McKee 60.00

Reamer, Opaque Green, Tall
Pointed Cone, Embossed
Saunders, 6 In. 1600.00

Reamer, Pink, 2-Cup Measure,
Hazel Atlas, 5 3/8 In.,
2 Piece . . . . . 160.00 to 195.00

Reamer, Saucer, Small Loop
Handle, Cambridge,
4 1/8 In. 20.00

Reamer, Sunkist,
Green 105.00

Reamer, Sunkist,
Ivory 95.00

Reamer, Sunkist, Opalescent
White, Marked Pat. No. 18764,
USA, 6 In. 150.00

Reamer, Sunkist, Opaque Pink,
Marked Pat. No. 18764,
USA, 6 In. 225.00

Reamer, Sunkist, Seville
Yellow 95.00

Reamer, Sunkist, Transparent
Green 95.00

Reamer, Sunkist, White,
Block Letters 115.00

Reamer, Valencia, Crystal,
Square Loop Handle,
6 In. 225.00

Reamer, Vaseline, Fry,
3 1/8 x 7 1/4 In. 130.00

Reamer, Vitrock,
8 3/4 In. 22.00

Reamer, White, Sunkist,
Thatcher Glass,
8 1/2 x 3 1/2 In. 22.00

Reamer, Yellow, 2-Cup
Measure, Hazel Atlas,
5 3/8 In., 2 Piece 395.00

Refrigerator Dish, Cover,
Clambroth,
4 1/2 x 5 In. 35.00

Refrigerator Dish, Cover,
Ivory, McKee,
2 1/2 x 8 x 5 In. 40.00

Refrigerator Dish, Cover, Ivory,
McKee, 4 x 5 In. 36.00

Refrigerator Dish, Cover,
Round, Pink, Jennyware,
16 Oz. 70.00

Refrigerator Dish, Cover,
Ultramarine, Jennyware,
Jeannette, 4 x 4 In. 45.00

Refrigerator Dish, Cover,
Ultramarine, Jennyware,
Jeannette, 4 x 8 In. 60.00

Refrigerator Dish, Cover,
Ultramarine, Jennyware,
Jeannette,
5 x 8 In. . . . . . . 68.00 to 72.00

Refrigerator Dish, Cover,
White, Colonial Couple,
Hocking, 32 Oz. 59.00

Refrigerator Dish, Cover,
White, Red Ships, McKee,
4 x 5 In. . . . . . . 17.00 to 39.00

Salad Fork, Crystal,
Imperial 25.00

Salad Spoon, Crystal,
Imperial 25.00

Salt & Pepper, Footed,
Pink, Jennyware,
Jeannette . . . . . 65.00 to 85.00

Salt & Pepper, Footed,
Ultramarine, Jennyware,
Jeannette 60.00

Salt & Pepper, Light Bulb Shape,
Crystal, 5 1/2 In. 20.00

Salt & Pepper, Transparent
Green, Hocking 87.00

Salt & Pepper, White, Black
Letters, Hocking 75.00

Salt & Pepper, White, Black
Letters, McKee 75.00

Salt & Pepper, White, Colonial
Couple, Hocking 99.00

Salt & Pepper, White, Dutch
Skaters, Hazel Atlas ... 28.00

Salt & Pepper, White, Green
Letters, Hocking 85.00

Salt & Pepper, White, Red Ships,
McKee 70.00

Saltshaker, Roman Arch,
Black, McKee 25.00

Saltshaker, White, Red Letters,
Hocking 45.00

Shaker, Blue Circle, Flour,
Anchor Hocking 45.00

Shaker, Chili, White, Black
Letters, Hocking 18.00

Shaker, Crystal, Hazel
Atlas 8.00

Shaker, Flour, Ivory,
McKee 58.00

Shaker, Flour, Seville Yellow,
McKee 65.00

Shaker, Flour, White, Red
Letters, Hocking 45.00

Shaker, Flour, White, Red
Ships, McKee 39.00

Shaker, Ginger, White, Black
Letters, Hocking 18.00

Shaker, Pepper, Ivory,
McKee 59.00

Shaker, Pepper, Roman
Arch, Black,
McKee .... 25.00 to 38.00

Shaker, Pepper,
Roman Arch, Custard,
Red Dots, McKee 72.00

Shaker, Pepper, White, Black
Letters, Green Stripes,
Hocking 50.00

Shaker, Pepper, White,
Dutch Boy Decal, Red,
Hocking 49.00

Shaker, Pepper, White,
Red Letters,
Hocking ...... 45.00 to 49.00

Shaker, Pepper, White, Red
Ships, McKee 35.00

Shaker, Pink, Hazel
Atlas 22.00

Shaker, Waffle, Pink, Hazel
Atlas 22.00

Shaker Set, Blue Circle, Anchor
Hocking, 4 Piece 125.00

Straw Jar, Manhattan,
Crystal 215.00

Straw Jar, Zipper,
Crystal 155.00

Sugar, Cover, Apple Shape,
Milk Glass, 4 In. 15.00

Sugar, Cover, Strawberry Shape,
Milk Glass, 4 In. 15.00

Sugar Shaker, Ivory,
McKee 59.00

Sugar Shaker, White,
McKee 40.00

Tumbler, Cobalt Blue,
Harpo, 4 1/8 In. 19.00

Tumbler, Cobalt Blue,
Harpo, 5 1/8 In. 28.00

Tumbler, White, Red Ships,
Hocking, 9 Oz., 4 5/8 In.,
6 Piece 165.00

KNIFE & FORK
See Colonial

LACE EDGE
See Old Colony

LACED EDGE

Imperial Glass Company,
Bellaire, Ohio, made Laced
Edge in the early 1930s.
The pattern is similar to
Hocking's Old Colony.
The biggest difference is
the shape of the lace. The
openings around Imperial's
edges are triangular, while
Hocking's are circular.
Laced Edge often has a
waffle design on the out-
side of the dishes and
comes in Amber, Crystal,
Green, Ritz Blue, Rose
Pink, Sea Foam (opalescent
green or blue), and Stiegel
Green. In the 1940s,
Laced Edge was sold as
Crocheted Crystal by
Sears, Roebuck & Com-
pany. Imperial continued
to make Laced Edge until
the 1970s.

Crystal

Bowl, Vegetable,
9 1/4 In. 15.00

Candlestick, 2-Light,
Pair 10.00

Plate, Bread & Butter,
6 1/2 In. 4.00

Plate, Salad, 8 1/4 In. 7.00

Soup, Dish, 7 In. 4.50

Sugar 8.00

Sea Foam Blue

Bowl, Fruit, 4 3/4 In. 36.00

Bowl, Oval, Divided,
11 In. 190.00

Bowl, Vegetable, 9 In. 40.00

Cup .... 28.00 to 41.00

Dish, Mayonnaise,
3 1/2 x 5 In. 51.00

Dish, Mayonnaise, Underplate
Only, 6 3/8 In. 39.00

Plate, Dinner, 9 In. 65.00

Plate, Dinner, 10 In. 128.00

Plate, Salad,
8 In. .... 35.00 to 51.00

Saucer 27.00

Vase, 4 5/8 In. 35.00

Vase, 5 In. 16.00

Sea Foam Green

Bowl, 6 In. 26.00

Saucer 41.00

Stiegel Green

Bowl, Cupped, 6 1/2 In. .. 30.00

Plate, Salad,
7 1/4 In. ...... 15.00 to 20.00

LACY DAISY
See No. 618

LAFAYETTE

Fostoria Glass Company made its Lafayette pattern from 1931 to 1960 in Amber, Burgundy, Crystal, Empire Green, Gold Tint, Green, Regal Blue, Rose, Ruby, Topaz, and Wisteria. Crystal Lafayette items were used for many of Fostoria's etchings.

Burgundy
Cup & Saucer 65.00

Crystal
Sugar & Creamer,
Wisteria Feet 55.00

Green
Torte Plate, 14 In. 45.00

Topaz
Bowl, 7 In. 40.00

Wisteria
Cup & Saucer 28.00
Plate, 6 In. 22.00
Plate, 7 1/2 In. 24.00
Plate, 10 1/2 In. 125.00

LAKE COMO

At first glance, Lake Como looks more like ceramic than glass. It is Opaque White with blue decal decorations picturing a lake and part of an ancient

ruin. It was made by Hocking Glass Company from 1934 to 1937.

Bowl, Cereal, 6 In. 25.00
Platter, Oval, 11 In. 57.00
Salt & Pepper 26.00
Sugar, Footed 33.00

LARIAT

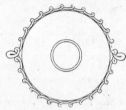

A.H. Heisey & Company, Newark, Ohio, made the Lariat pattern in Crystal from 1941 to 1957. The design is named for the looped "rope" around the border of the dishes. Heisey made the pattern to compete with Imperial's Candlewick. Lariat was produced by Imperial for six years after the Heisey factory closed in 1957.

Bowl,
12 x 4 In. . . . . . 26.00 to 39.00
Bowl, 8 In. 28.00
Bowl, Camellia,
9 1/2 In. 30.00
Bowl, Moonglo Cutting,
7 In. 50.00
Candlestick, 4 1/8 In.,
Pair . . . . 20.00 to 30.00
Candy Dish, Cover,
5 In. 60.00
Coaster, 4 In. 9.00
Creamer 18.00
Dish, Mayonnaise, 2 Sections,
7 In. . . . . 25.00 to 30.00
Finger Bowl Underplate,
6 In. 7.50
Goblet, Cocktail, Moonglo
Cutting, 3 1/2 Oz. 26.00

Nappy, Silver Overlay
Flowers, 7 In. 35.00
Oyster Cocktail,
4 1/4 Oz. 20.00
Plate, Salad, 7 In. 12.50
Punch Cup 8.00
Sandwich Server, 14 In. . . 45.00
Sugar 20.00
Sugar & Creamer 35.00
Vase, Fan, Footed, 7 In. . . 50.00

LAUREL

Opaque glass was used by McKee Glass Company, Jeannette, Pennsylvania, to make Laurel dinnerware in the 1930s. The pattern, with a raised band of flowers and leaves as the only decoration, is sometimes called Raspberry Band. A few pieces have decals of a dog in the center. That group is called Scottie Dog. The dinnerware was made in French Ivory, Jade Green, Powder Blue, or White Opal. A child's set was made with a colored rim.

French Ivory
Berry Bowl,
4 3/4 In. . . . . . . 8.00 to 10.00
Bowl, 11 In. 55.00
Bowl, Vegetable, Oval,
9 3/4 In. . . . . . . 25.00 to 30.00
Candlestick,
4 In. . . . . 15.00 to 24.00
Candlestick, 4 In.,
Pair . . . . 40.00 to 46.00
Cheese Dish, Cover 135.00
Children's Set,
14 Piece 575.00
Cup & Saucer 10.00
Plate, Red Rim, Child's,
6 In. 16.00

Plate, Sherbet,
6 In. . . . . 5.00 to 9.00
Platter, Oval,
10 3/4 In. . . . . . 25.00 to 35.00
Saltshaker 30.00
Sugar 12.00
Sugar, Red Trim 100.00
Sugar & Creamer,
Red Trim 200.00

Jade Green
Berry Bowl,
4 3/4 In. . . . . . . 14.00 to 16.00
Candlestick, 4 In., Pair . . . 55.00
Cheese Dish, Cover 375.00
Child's Set, 14 Piece . . . 595.00
Cup & Saucer 18.50
Plate, Dinner, 9 1/8 In. . . . 25.00
Plate, Salad, 7 1/2 In. 15.00
Platter, Oval, 10 3/4 In. . . 44.00
Saucer 8.50
Sherbet 35.00
Sugar. 35.00

White Opal
Creamer, Red Trim,
Child's 50.00
Plate, Yellow Trim,
8 In. 18.00
Sugar, Red Trim,
Child's 50.00

LELA BIRD

Paden City Glass Manufacturing Company, Paden City, West Virginia, made dishes with the Lela Bird etching in the 1930s. It was made in a variety of colors.

Crystal
Bowl, Flared, Footed,
9 In. 71.00

Green
Plate, 10 In. 75.00

LIDO FEDERAL

Lido pattern was made by the Federal Glass Company of Columbus, Ohio, in the mid-1930s. The glass was offered in Crystal, Golden Glow, Green, or Rose Glow. The pattern of the same name by Fostoria is listed separately in this book.

Golden Glow
Pitcher, 65 Oz. 65.00
Tumbler, 12 Oz.,
5 1/4 In. 22.00
Tumbler, Iced Tea,
10 Oz., 4 1/2 In. 18.00
Tumbler, Juice,
3 1/2 In. 10.00
Tumbler, Water, 8 Oz.,
4 In. 14.00

LIDO FOSTORIA

The Lido pattern made by Fostoria Glass Company is very different from the

Lido made by Federal Glass Company. Fostoria's Lido etch was made from 1937 to 1960 in Azure and Crystal.

Crystal
Bowl, Cupped, 3-Footed,
6 1/4 In. 20.00
Candlestick, 2-Light,
Flame, 7 In. 75.00
Candlestick, 4 In., Pair . . . 32.00
Compote, 5 3/4 In. 20.00
Plate, 8 1/2 In. . . 10.00 to 14.00
Plate, Sherbet, 6 In. 6.00
Sugar 9.00
Tumbler, Iced Tea, Footed,
14 Oz., 6 1/2 In. 22.00

LINCOLN DRAPE
See Princess

LINCOLN INN

Lincoln Inn was made by the Fenton Glass Company, Williamstown, West Virginia, from 1928 until about 1936. The ridged dinnerware sets were made in Amber, Amethyst, Black, Cobalt Blue, Crystal, Green, Jade Green, Light Blue, Pink, and Red. A recent copy of the Lincoln Inn pitcher was made by Fenton Glass Company in Iridescent carnival glass.

Cobalt Blue
Creamer 64.00
Cup & Saucer 31.00
Goblet, Water, 5 3/4 In. . . 43.00
Goblet, Wine, 4 In. 32.00

Plate, Bread & Butter,
6 1/2 In. 13.00
Plate, Salad, 8 In. 19.00
Sherbet,
4 1/4 In. ...... 15.00 to 30.00
Sugar 66.00

Light Blue
Goblet, Water, 5 3/4 In. .. 24.00
Sherbet, 4 1/4 In. 22.00

Red
Finger Bowl, 4 In. 35.00
Tumbler, Footed, 12 Oz.,
6 In. 50.00

LINE 191
See Party Line

LINE 300
See Peacock & Wild Rose

LITTLE HOSTESS
See Moderntone Little
Hostess Party Set

LOOP
See Old Colony

LORAIN
See No. 615

LOUISA
See Floragold

LOVEBIRDS
See Georgian

LYDIA RAY
See New Century

MADRID

Madrid has probably had
more publicity than any

other Depression glass
pattern. It was originally
made by the Federal Glass
Company, Columbus,
Ohio, from 1932 to 1939,
using the molds developed
for Sylvan, an earlier Federal pattern. Madrid was
made first in Green, then
in Amber; Madonna Blue
and Pink pieces were
made for a limited time. In
1976 Federal Glass re-
worked the molds and
made full sets of amber
glass called Recollection.
These can be identified by
a small "76" worked into
the pattern. In 1982, Crystal pieces of Recollection
were made. In more
recent years, Blue, Crystal,
and Pink pieces have been
reproduced by the Indiana
Glass Company. Madrid is
sometimes called Paneled
Aster, Primus, or Winged
Medallion.

Amber
Berry Bowl, Master,
9 3/8 In. 25.00
Bowl, Vegetable, Oval,
10 In. .... 19.00 to 30.00
Butter, Cover ... 65.00 to 70.00
Butter, Cover Only 35.00
Candlestick,
2 1/4 In. ...... 11.00 to 14.00
Candlestick, 2 1/4 In.,
Pair .... 22.00 to 55.00
Console, 11 In. 14.00
Cookie Jar, Cover Only .. 20.00
Creamer .... 8.00 to 17.00
Creamer, Footed 12.00
Cup .... 6.00 to 8.50
Cup & Saucer .... 9.00 to 15.00
Grill Plate, 10 1/2 In. 15.00
Mold, Jell-O,
2 1/8 In. ...... 10.00 to 17.00
Pitcher, Square, 80 Oz.,
8 1/2 In. 85.00

Plate, Dinner,
10 1/2 In. ..... 70.00 to 80.00
Plate, Luncheon,
8 7/8 In. .... 9.00 to 10.00
Plate, Salad,
7 1/2 In. .... 8.00 to 11.00
Plate, Sherbet, 6 In. 7.00
Platter, Oval,
11 1/2 In. ..... 15.00 to 18.00
Relish, 5 Sections,
10 1/4 In. ..... 22.00 to 25.00
Salt & Pepper, 3 1/2 In. .. 41.00
Saltshaker,
3 1/2 In. ...... 20.00 to 26.50
Sauce Bowl,
5 In. .... 6.00 to 12.00
Saucer .... 4.00 to 6.00
Sherbet .... 7.00 to 15.00
Sherbet, Cone Shape,
2 3/4 In. 7.00
Soup, Cream, 4 3/4 In. ... 19.50
Soup, Dish,
7 In. .... 13.00 to 25.00
Sugar .... 7.00 to 20.00
Sugar, Cover 70.00
Sugar & Creamer,
Cover .... 60.00 to 75.00
Tumbler, 5 Oz.,
3 7/8 In. ...... 12.00 to 15.00
Tumbler, 9 Oz.,
4 1/4 In. 15.00
Tumbler, 12 Oz.,
5 1/2 In. ...... 15.00 to 25.00
Tumbler, Footed, 10 Oz.,
5 1/2 In. ...... 19.50 to 30.00
Tumbler, Juice, Footed,
5 Oz., 4 In. .... 45.00 to 48.00
Tumbler, Water, 9 Oz.,
4 1/4 In. 15.00

Crystal
Bowl, Salad, 8 In. 14.00
Hot Plate, Indent,
5 In. .... 30.00 to 38.00
Platter, Oval, 11 1/2 In. .. 16.00
Saucer 18.00
Sherbet, Cone Shape 7.50
Sugar 30.00
Sugar, Cover 85.00
Sugar & Creamer 13.00

Green
Cup & Saucer 20.00
Plate, Luncheon,
8 7/8 In. 15.00

Platter, Oval, 11 1/2 In. . . .65.00
Saltshaker . . . . . . 40.00 to 72.00
Sauce, 5 In. 10.00
Sherbet 14.00
Sherbet, Cone Shape 11.00
Sugar, Cover 82.00
Sugar & Creamer,
Cover 85.00
Tumbler, 9 Oz., 4 1/4 In. . 25.00

Madonna Blue
Cup & Saucer 35.00
Plate, Dinner,
10 1/2 In. . . . . 60.00 to 100.00
Sherbet 18.00
Soup, Dish, 7 In. 60.00

Pink
Butter, Cover 12.40
Cake Plate, 11 1/4 In. 30.00
Creamer 12.00
Plate, Dinner, 10 1/2 In. . . 17.50
Plate, Sherbet, 6 In. 18.00
Saucer . . . . 1.00 to 7.00
Tumbler, 9 Oz.,
4 1/4 In. . . . . . . 20.00 to 28.00

MAGNOLIA
See Dogwood

MANHATTAN

Manhattan is another modern-looking pattern with a design of molded circles. It was made by Anchor Hocking Glass Corporation from 1938 to 1941, primarily in Crystal. A few Green, Iridescent, Pink, and Royal Ruby pieces also are known. The pattern has been called many names, such as Horizontal Fine Rib,

Horizontal Ribbed, Horizontal Rounded Big Rib, Horizontal Sharp Big Rib, and Ribbed. A similar line, called Park Avenue, was made in Crystal and Sapphire Blue by Anchor Hocking from 1987 to 1993.

Crystal
Ashtray, Metal Topper . . . 30.00
Ashtray, Round,
4 In. . . . . 11.00 to 12.00
Berry Bowl, Handles,
5 1/2 In. 17.00
Berry Bowl, Master, Handles,
7 1/2 In. . . . . . 24.00 to 25.00
Bowl, Fruit, Footed, Open
Handles, 9 1/2 In. 35.00
Bowl, Salad, Handles,
9 In. 25.00
Candleholder, Square,
4 1/2 In. . . . . . . 7.50 to 11.00
Coaster,
3 1/2 In. . . . . . 20.00 to 25.00
Compote, Sauce Bowl,
Handle, 4 1/2 In. 8.00
Cup 18.00
Cup & Saucer . . 22.00 to 28.00
Pitcher, 24 Oz. . . 32.00 to 39.00
Pitcher, Tilted, 80 Oz. . . . 45.00
Plate, Dinner,
10 1/4 In. . . . . 20.00 to 28.00
Plate, Salad, 8 1/2 In. 15.00
Plate, Sherbet,
6 In. . . . . 7.00 to 8.00
Relish, 5 Sections,
14 In. . . . . 20.00 to 30.00
Relish Insert . . . . . 6.00 to 11.00
Relish Set, 14 In.,
7 Piece 75.00
Relish Set, Royal Ruby
Inserts, Handle, 14 In.,
7 Piece 85.00
Salt & Pepper, Square,
2 In. . . . . 18.00 to 40.00
Sauce Bowl, Handles,
4 1/2 In. . . . . . . 9.00 to 12.00
Saucer 7.00
Sherbet 12.00
Sugar . . . . 12.00 to 18.00
Tumbler, Footed, 10 Oz.,
5 1/4 In. . . . . . 15.00 to 20.00

Vase, 8 In. . . . . . . 30.00 to 33.00
Pink
Berry Bowl, Handle,
5 3/8 In. . . . . . 25.00 to 35.00
Bowl, Fruit, Footed,
Open Handles,
9 1/2 In. . . . . . . 44.00 to 55.00
Candy Dish, 3-Footed,
6 1/4 In. . . . . . 14.00 to 18.00
Compote,
5 3/4 In. . . . . . 55.00 to 70.00
Creamer . . . . 15.00 to 22.00
Pitcher, Tilted,
80 Oz. . . . . . . 65.00 to 95.00
Saltshaker, Square,
2 In. 24.00
Sugar 16.50
Sugar & Creamer 40.00
Tumbler, Footed, 10 Oz.,
5 1/2 In. . . . . . 17.00 to 30.00
Royal Ruby
Relish Insert 7.00

MANOR

Manor etch appears on Crystal, Green, and Topaz dinnerware and on Crystal stemware with Wisteria feet. It was made by Fostoria Glass Company from 1931 to 1943.

Crystal
Dish, Lemon, Handles . . . 40.00
Topaz
Plate, Luncheon, 8 Oz. . . . 22.00
Tumbler, Footed, 10 Oz.,
5 1/8 In. 30.00
Wisteria
Cordial, 1 1/4 Oz.,
3 3/8 In. 145.00

MANY WINDOWS
See Roulette

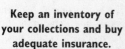

Keep an inventory of your collections and buy adequate insurance.

MARTHA WASHINGTON

The Cambridge Glass Company of Cambridge, Ohio, started manufacturing Martha Washington pattern in 1932. The glass was made in Amber, Crystal, Forest Green, Gold Krystol, Heatherbloom (lavender), Royal Blue, and Ruby.

Crystal

Cup & Saucer 23.00
Goblet, Champagne,
4 5/8 In. 22.00
Goblet, Cocktail,
4 1/4 In. 18.00
Goblet, Water, 6 1/8 In. . . 20.00
Plate, Luncheon, 8 In. 20.00
Tumbler, Juice,
4 3/8 In. 18.00

MAYFAIR
See Rosemary

MAYFAIR FEDERAL

The Mayfair patterns can easily be recognized, but if you are buying by mail, the names are sometimes confusing. Mayfair Federal is the pattern sometimes called Rosemary Arches. It was made in Amber, Crystal, or Green by Federal Glass Company in 1934 but was discontinued because of a patent conflict with Hocking's Mayfair pattern, referred to as Mayfair Open Rose.

Amber

Creamer 10.00
Cup 12.25
Plate, Dinner, 9 1/2 In. . . . 17.50
Platter, Oval, 12 In. 48.00
Sugar 14.25
Tumbler, 9 Oz.,
4 1/2 In. 30.00

Crystal

Cup 5.00
Cup & Saucer 18.00
Plate, Dinner, 9 1/2 In. . . . 12.00

Green

Sugar . . . . 10.00 to 23.00

MAYFAIR OPEN ROSE

Mayfair Open Rose was made by Hocking Glass Company from 1931 to 1937. It was made primarily in Light Blue and Pink, with a few Green and Yellow pieces. Crystal examples are rare. The cookie jar and the whiskey glass have been reproduced since 1982.

Crystal

Bowl, Vegetable, 10 In. . . 34.00
Cup, Yellow & Green
Stain 155.00
Tumbler, Iced Tea, Footed,
15 Oz., 6 1/2 In. 75.00

Green

Bowl, Fruit, Scalloped,
12 In. 48.00
Bowl, Low,
11 3/4 In. . . . . . 73.00 to 95.00
Bowl, Vegetable, Oval,
9 1/2 In. . . . . . 85.00 to 135.00
Creamer 20.00
Sandwich Server, Center Handle,
11 1/2 In. . . . . 35.00 to 65.00

Light Blue

Bowl, Cereal, 5 1/2 In. . . . 55.00
Bowl, Fruit, Scalloped,
12 In. . . . . . . 105.00 to 125.00
Bowl, Vegetable, 10 In. . . 80.00
Bowl, Vegetable, Cover,
10 In. 185.00
Bowl, Vegetable, Oval,
9 1/2 In. 80.00
Butter, Cover 335.00
Cake Plate, Footed,
10 In. . . . . 75.00 to 93.00
Cake Plate, Handles,
12 In. . . . . . . 85.00 to 100.00
Candy Dish,
Cover . . . . . . 325.00 to 365.00
Celery Dish, 2 Sections,
10 In. . . . . 65.00 to 85.00
Cup . . . . 55.00 to 70.00
Cup & Saucer 88.00
Goblet, 9 Oz.,
7 1/4 In. . . . . 140.00 to 200.00
Grill Plate,
9 1/2 In. . . . . . . 55.00 to 70.00
Pitcher, 80 Oz.,
8 1/2 In. 295.00
Plate, 5 3/4 In. . . 25.00 to 30.00
Plate, Dinner, 9 1/2 In. . . . 90.00
Plate, Luncheon,
8 1/2 In. . . . . . . 60.00 to 63.00
Plate, Sherbet,
6 1/2 In. . . . . . . 30.00 to 40.00
Platter, Open Handles, Oval,
12 In. . . . . 80.00 to 85.00
Relish, 4 Sections,
8 3/8 In. . . . . . . 65.00 to 75.00
Salt & Pepper 335.00
Sandwich Server, Handle,
11 1/2 In. 94.00
Saucer 25.00
Sherbet,
4 3/4 In. . . . . 100.00 to 105.00
Sherbet, Flat, Underplate,
2 1/4 In. . . . . 225.00 to 325.00

Sugar 90.00
Tumbler, 5 Oz.,
  3 1/2 In. 150.00
Tumbler, 9 Oz.,
  4 1/4 In. 135.00
Tumbler, Footed, 10 Oz.,
  5 1/4 In. 160.00
Tumbler, Iced Tea,
  Footed, 15 Oz.,
  6 1/2 In. . . . . 300.00 to 310.00
Vase, Sweet Pea,
  8 1/2 In. . . . . 135.00 to 175.00

Pink

Bowl, Cereal,
  5 1/2 In. . . . . . . 30.00 to 45.00
Bowl, Fruit, Scalloped,
  12 In. . . . . 75.00 to 90.00
Bowl, Low,
  11 3/4 In. . . . . . 70.00 to 88.00
Bowl, Vegetable, 7 In. . . . 40.00
Bowl, Vegetable,
  10 In. . . . . 35.00 to 40.00
Bowl, Vegetable, Cover,
  10 In. . . . . . 150.00 to 160.00
Bowl, Vegetable, Frosted,
  7 In. 19.00
Bowl, Vegetable, Oval,
  9 1/2 In. . . . . . 44.00 to 50.00
Butter, Cover . . 82.00 to 100.00
Cake Plate, Footed,
  10 In. . . . . 33.00 to 48.00
Cake Plate, Handles,
  12 In. . . . . 55.00 to 80.00
Candy Dish, Cover,
  5 1/2 In. . . . . . . 55.00 to 75.00
Celery Dish,
  10 In. . . . . 45.00 to 60.00
Celery Dish, Sections,
  10 1/2 In. 290.00
Cookie Jar,
  Cover . . . . 50.00 to 65.00
Cookie Jar,
  No Cover . . . . . 20.00 to 40.00
Creamer . . . . 25.00 to 35.00
Cup . . . . 18.00 to 25.00
Cup & Saucer 35.00
Cup & Saucer,
  Cup Ring . . . . . 60.00 to 62.00
Decanter,
  Stopper . . . . 210.00 to 450.00
Goblet, Cocktail, 3 Oz.,
  4 In. . . . . 100.00 to 170.00
Goblet, Water, 9 Oz.,
  5 3/4 In. 75.00

Goblet, Wine, 3 Oz.,
  4 1/2 In. . . . . 100.00 to 135.00
Grill Plate, 9 1/2 In. 50.00
Pitcher, 37 Oz.,
  6 In. . . . . 55.00 to 70.00
Pitcher, 60 Oz., 8 In. 85.00
Pitcher, 80 Oz.,
  8 1/2 In. . . . . 130.00 to 135.00
Pitcher, Water 75.00
Plate, 5 3/4 In. . . 11.00 to 18.00
Plate, Dinner,
  9 1/2 In. . . . . . . 30.00 to 60.00
Plate, Luncheon,
  8 1/2 In. . . . . . . 30.00 to 40.00
Platter, Oval, Handles,
  12 In. . . . . 27.00 to 35.00
Relish, 4 Sections,
  8 3/8 In. . . . . . . 37.00 to 45.00
Salt & Pepper . . . 80.00 to 90.00
Sandwich Server, Center Handle,
  11 1/2 In. . . . . . 55.00 to 75.00
Saucer . . . . 8.00 to 14.00
Saucer,
  Cup Ring . . . . . 35.00 to 45.00
Sherbet,
  3 1/4 In. . . . . . . 15.00 to 25.00
Soup, Cream,
  5 In. . . . . 65.00 to 75.00
Soup, Dish, 7 In. 30.00
Sugar 30.00
Sugar, Frosted 30.00
Sugar &
  Creamer . . . . . . 68.00 to 70.00
Tumbler, Footed, 10 Oz.,
  5 1/4 In. 60.00
Tumbler, Iced Tea,
  Footed, 15 Oz.,
  6 1/2 In. . . . . . . 45.00 to 60.00
Tumbler, Juice, 5 Oz.,
  3 1/2 In. 57.00
Tumbler, Water, 9 Oz.,
  4 1/4 In. . . . . . . 37.00 to 50.00
Vase, Sweet Pea,
  8 1/2 In. . . . . 195.00 to 300.00

MAYFLOWER

Fostoria Glass Company decorated crystal tableware and stemware with Mayflower etch from 1938 to 1957.

Bowl, 12 In. 50.00
Bowl, Vegetable, 10 In. . . 32.00
Bowl, Vegetable, Oval,
  9 In. 32.00
Cake Plate, Footed,
  10 In. 65.00
Candy Dish, Cover 20.00
Celery Dish, Sections,
  10 In. 43.00
Cookie Jar, Cover 40.00
Creamer 25.00
Cup 20.00
Decanter, Stopper 250.00
Goblet, 9 Oz., 7 1/4 In. . . . 25.00
Goblet, Champagne, 6 Oz.,
  5 1/2 In. . . . . . . 20.00 to 25.00
Pitcher, Milk 60.00
Plate, 7 1/2 In. 10.00
Salt & Pepper 70.00
Sandwich Server, Handle . 50.00
Sherbet, 6 Oz., 4 5/8 In. . . 16.00
Sugar . . . . 10.00 to 18.00
Sugar & Creamer 35.00
Tumbler, 4 In. 35.00
Tumbler, 5 1/4 In. 60.00
Tumbler, Iced Tea, Footed,
  12 Oz., 6 3/8 In. 43.00
Tumbler, Juice, Footed, 5 Oz.,
  4 7/8 In. . . . . . . 18.00 to 20.00

MEADOW FLOWER
See No. 618

MEADOW GREEN

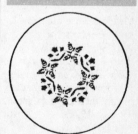

Anchor Hocking Glass Corporation, Lancaster, Ohio, made Meadow Green dinnerware and ovenware from 1967 to 1977. Most of the items are made of opaque white glass and have green and golden yellow floral decals. The cup, creamer, and sugar have a solid fired-on avocado green coating. Other related patterns are listed in the Fire-King section in this book.

Bowl, Dessert, 4 5/8 In. . . . 5.00
Cake Pan, Round, 9 In. . . . 10.00
Cake Pan, Square,
  8 5/8 In. 10.00
Casserole, Cover, 1 1/2 Qt.,
  11 In. 8.00
Casserole, Handle, Individual,
  5 In. 5.00
Casserole, No Cover, 1 Pt.,
  7 5/8 In. 6.00
Casserole, No Cover, 1 Pt.,
  9 In. 6.00
Casserole, No Cover,
  1 1/2 Qt., 11 In. 6.00
Mug, 3 1/2 In. 6.00
Plate, Dinner, 10 In. 9.00
Plate, Salad, 7 3/8 In. 5.00
Sugar, Cover, 4 In. 7.00

MEADOW ROSE

Meadow Rose etch appears on the same glassware shapes as Navarre. Both were made by Fostoria Glass Company. Meadow Rose was made in Crystal and Azure from 1936 to 1978.

Crystal

Bonbon, 3-Footed,
  7 In. 39.00
Cup & Saucer 30.00
Goblet, Water, 9 Oz.,
  6 3/4 In. . . . . . . 30.00 to 42.00
Pitcher, Footed, 48 Oz. . . 415.00

Sherbet, 6 Oz.,
  4 3/8 In. . . . . . 24.00 to 26.00
Sugar, Footed 20.00
Torte Plate, 14 In. 38.00

MIDNIGHT ROSE

Fostoria Glass Company decorated crystal tableware and stemware with Midnight Rose etch from 1933 to 1957.

Bowl, Oval 175.00
Candlestick, 2-Light,
  5 1/2 In. 38.00
Candlestick, 2-Light,
  5 1/2 In., Pair 125.00
Cup & Saucer 31.00
Dish, Lemon, 5 1/2 In. . . . 10.00
Dish, Sweetmeat, Handles,
  4 1/2 In. 18.00
Goblet, Water, 9 Oz.,
  7 5/8 In. . . . . . . 20.00 to 30.00
Relish, 5 Sections,
  12 In. 75.00
Sherbet, 5 1/2 Oz.,
  4 3/8 In. 20.00

MILANO

Anchor Hocking Glass Company made Milano tableware and accessories in the 1950s and '60s.

Items came in Amethyst, Aqua, Avocado Green, Blue, Crystal, Forest Green, and Honey Gold.

Aqua

Pitcher, 9 In. 45.00
Tumbler, 5 1/2 In. 20.00

Avocado Green

Pitcher, 96 Oz.,
  8 1/4 In. 20.00
Tumbler, Iced Tea,
  14 Oz., 6 1/2 In. 12.00
Tumbler, 12 Oz.,
  5 1/2 In. 10.00
Tumbler, Juice, 5 Oz.,
  3 7/8 In. 5.00

Honey Gold

Pitcher, 9 In. . . . . 33.00 to 35.00
Pitcher, 96 Oz.,
  8 1/4 In. 20.00
Tumbler, Iced Tea,
  14 Oz., 6 1/2 In. 6.00
Tumbler, Juice, 5 Oz.,
  3 7/8 In. 6.00

MINUET

Minuet etch features a colonial lady on one side of the pieces and her dancing partner on the other. A.H. Heisey & Company made the pattern from 1939 to 1957 in Crystal. Some accessory pieces can be found in Sahara (yellow).

Crystal

Goblet, Champagne,
  6 Oz. 25.00
Goblet, Cordial, Symphone,
  1 Oz. 125.00
Goblet, Wine, 2 1/2 Oz. . . 38.00
Plate, Luncheon, 8 In. 30.00
Sandwich Server, 15 In. . . 89.00
Sherbet, 6 Oz. 22.00
Tumbler, Iced Tea, Footed,
  12 Oz. 60.00

Sahara

Tumbler, Footed,
  10 Oz. 32.00

MISS AMERICA

Miss America, or Diamond Pattern, was made by Hocking Glass Company from 1933 to 1936 in many colors, including Crystal, Green, Ice Blue, Jade-ite, Pink, Red, and Ritz Blue. It is similar to English Hobnail, but can be distinguished by the typical Hocking sunburst base and hobs that are more pointed than those of the Westmoreland pattern. In 1977, some reproduction butter dishes were made of Amberina, Crystal, Green, Ice Blue, Pink, and Red. Saltshakers, pitchers, and tumblers are also being reproduced.

Crystal

Bowl, Cereal,
   6 1/4 In. . . . . 5.00 to 10.00
Bowl, Curved In, 8 In. . . . 60.00
Bowl, Vegetable, Oval,
   10 In. 18.00
Butter, Cover, Chrome . . . 20.00
Cake Plate, Footed,
   12 In. . . . . 25.00 to 45.00
Celery Dish,
   10 1/2 In. . . . . . 14.00 to 19.00
Coaster,
   5 3/4 In. . . . . . . 15.00 to 20.00
Compote, 5 In. . . 14.00 to 19.00
Creamer . . . . 7.00 to 10.00
Cup 8.00
Cup & Saucer . . . 10.00 to 16.00
Goblet, Juice, 5 Oz.,
   4 3/4 In. . . . . . . 21.00 to 27.00

Goblet, Water, 10 Oz.,
   5 1/2 In. 18.00
Goblet, Wine, 3 Oz.,
   3 3/4 In. 22.00
Grill Plate,
   10 1/4 In. . . . . 10.00 to 12.00
Pitcher, Ice Lip, 65 Oz.,
   8 1/2 In. 85.00
Plate, Dinner,
   10 1/4 In. . . . . 15.00 to 20.00
Plate, Salad, 8 1/2 In. . . . 37.00
Plate, Sherbet,
   5 3/4 In. . . . . 6.00 to 8.00
Platter, Oval,
   12 1/4 In. . . . . 15.00 to 16.00
Relish, 4 Sections,
   8 3/4 In. . . . . 11.00 to 25.00
Relish, 5 Sections,
   11 3/4 In. . . . . 25.00 to 35.00
Salt & Pepper . . . 35.00 to 40.00
Saltshaker 22.00
Saucer . . . . 4.00 to 5.00
Sherbet . . . . 7.00 to 22.00
Sugar . . . . 8.00 to 10.00
Sugar & Creamer 19.00
Tumbler, Juice,
   5 Oz., 4 In. 17.00
Tumbler, Water, 10 Oz.,
   4 1/2 In. . . . . . 18.00 to 55.00

Green

Cup 18.00
Plate, 6 3/4 In. 15.00
Salt & Pepper 250.00
Tumbler, Water, 10 Oz.,
   4 1/2 In. . . . . . 30.00 to 39.00

Pink

Bowl, Cereal,
   6 1/4 In. . . . . . 30.00 to 40.00
Bowl, Curved In,
   8 In. . . . . . . 138.00 to 175.00
Bowl, Fruit,
   8 3/4 In. . . . . . 60.00 to 80.00
Bowl, Vegetable, Oval,
   10 In. . . . . 45.00 to 70.00
Cake Plate 80.00
Candy Jar, Cover,
   11 1/2 In. . . . 175.00 to 195.00
Celery Dish, Oval,
   10 1/2 In. . . . . 30.00 to 44.00
Compote, 5 In. . . 35.00 to 50.00
Creamer 25.00
Cup . . . . 28.00 to 30.00
Cup & Saucer . . . 30.00 to 50.00

Goblet, Water, 10 Oz.,
   5 1/2 In. . . . . . 48.00 to 60.00
Goblet, Wine, 3 Oz.,
   3 3/4 In. . . . 120.00 to 125.00
Grill Plate,
   10 1/4 In. . . . . 25.00 to 55.00
Pitcher, Ice Lip, 80 Oz.,
   8 1/2 In. 300.00
Plate, Dinner, 10 1/4 In. . . 60.00
Plate, Salad,
   8 1/2 In. . . . . . 30.00 to 48.00
Plate, Sherbet,
   5 3/4 In. . . . . . 13.50 to 30.00
Platter, Oval,
   12 1/4 In. . . . . 35.00 to 47.00
Relish, 4 Sections,
   8 3/4 In. . . . . . 33.00 to 35.00
Saltshaker 37.00
Saucer . . . . 7.00 to 16.00
Sherbet . . . . 18.00 to 25.00
Sugar . . . . 25.00 to 27.00
Sugar & Creamer 50.00
Tumbler, Water, 10 Oz.,
   4 1/2 In. . . . . . 45.00 to 83.00

MISS AMERICA
See also English Hobnail

MODERNE ART
See Tea Room

MODERNTONE

Moderntone, or Wedding Band, was made by Hazel Atlas Glass Company from 1935 to 1942. The simple pattern is popular today with Art Deco enthusiasts. It was made of Amethyst, Cobalt Blue, Crystal, and Pink glass. Green tumblers can be found, too. It was also made of an opaque, almost white glass called Platonite, which is listed here under Moderntone Platonite.

Amethyst

Berry Bowl,
5 In. . . . . 24.00 to 27.00
Berry Bowl, Master,
8 3/4 In. . . . . . . 45.00 to 55.00
Creamer . . . . 11.00 to 18.00
Cup . . . . 11.00 to 14.00
Cup & Saucer . . . 15.00 to 20.00
Plate, Dinner,
8 7/8 In. . . . . . . 14.00 to 15.00
Plate, Luncheon,
7 3/4 In. 12.00
Plate, Sherbet,
5 7/8 In. . . . . 6.00 to 8.00
Saucer . . . . 4.00 to 7.00
Soup, Cream,
4 3/4 In. . . . . . . 20.00 to 25.00
Soup, Dish, 7 1/2 In. 225.00
Sugar . . . . 15.00 to 18.00
Tumbler, Iced Tea,
12 Oz., 5 1/4 In. 155.00

Cobalt Blue

Berry Bowl,
5 In. . . . . 22.00 to 38.00
Berry Bowl, Master,
8 3/4 In. . . . . . . 46.00 to 60.00
Bowl, Cereal,
6 1/2 In. 75.00
Butter, Metal Cover 95.00
Cheese Dish, Metal Cover,
Wood Base 395.00
Creamer . . . . 11.00 to 12.00
Cup . . . . 11.00 to 13.00
Cup & Saucer . . . 14.00 to 22.00
Custard Cup . . . . 21.50 to 30.00
Plate, Dinner,
8 7/8 In. . . . . . . 14.00 to 20.00
Plate, Luncheon,
7 3/4 In. . . . . . . 12.00 to 15.00
Plate, Salad,
6 3/4 In. . . . . . . 12.00 to 15.00
Plate, Sherbet,
5 7/8 In. . . . . 6.00 to 10.00
Platter, Oval, 11 In. 45.00
Salt & Pepper . . . 27.00 to 47.00
Saltshaker . . . . . 19.00 to 23.00

Sandwich Server,
10 1/2 In. . . . . 60.00 to 100.00
Saucer . . . . 5.00 to 6.00
Sherbet . . . . 11.00 to 15.00
Soup, Cream,
4 3/4 In. . . . . . . 22.00 to 25.00
Soup, Dish, 7 3/4 In. 75.00
Sugar . . . . 11.00 to 18.00
Sugar &
Creamer . . . . . . 14.00 to 30.00
Tumbler, Juice, 5 Oz.,
3 3/4 In. . . . . . . 48.00 to 60.00
Tumbler, Water, 9 Oz.,
4 1/8 In. . . . . . . 37.00 to 50.00
Tumbler, Whiskey,
1 1/2 Oz. . . . . . 45.00 to 65.00

Crystal

Creamer . . . . 10.00 to 18.00
Sugar 10.00
Tumbler, Whiskey,
1 1/2 Oz. . . . . . . 7.00 to 10.00

Green

Plate, Luncheon,
7 3/4 In. 6.00
Sugar 8.50
Tumbler, Juice, 5 Oz.,
3 3/4 In. . . . . 6.00 to 7.25
Tumbler, Water, 9 Oz.,
4 1/8 In. 8.00

Pink

Ashtray, 7 3/4 In. 95.00
Berry Bowl, Master,
8 3/4 In. 35.00
Soup, Cream, 4 3/4 In. . . . 18.00
Sugar 15.00
Sugar & Creamer 45.00

MODERNTONE LITTLE HOSTESS PARTY SET

The Moderntone Little Hostess Party Set was also made by Hazel Atlas Glass Company in the late 1940s. This is a child's set of dishes made in Platonite with fired-on colors. We have seen Beige, Blue, Burgundy, Chartreuse,

Gray, Green, Pink, Rust (orange), Turquoise, Yellow, and pastels, but other colors were probably made.

Blue

Plate, 5 1/4 In. . . . 8.50 to 12.00

Burgundy

Cup 14.00
Plate, 5 1/4 In. . . . 8.00 to 13.00
Teapot,
3 1/2 In. . . . . . . 29.00 to 46.00

Gray

Cup . . . . 10.00 to 12.00
Cup & Saucer 20.00
Plate, 5 1/4 In. . . . . 5.00 to 9.00
Saucer, 3 7/8 In. 5.00

Green

Cup . . . . 7.50 to 12.00
Plate, 5 1/4 In. . . . 8.50 to 12.00
Saucer, 3 7/8 In. . . . 6.25 to 8.00

Mixed Colors

Tea Set, Dark Colors, Box,
16 Piece . . . . 325.00 to 375.00
Tea Set, Pastels,
14 Piece . . . . 125.00 to 140.00

Pink

Cup 30.00
Cup & Saucer 20.00
Plate, 5 1/4 In. . . . 5.00 to 12.50
Saucer, 3 7/8 In. . . 6.25 to 10.00
Sugar, 1 3/4 In. . . 13.00 to 16.00

Rust

Creamer,
1 3/4 In. . . . . . . 13.00 to 15.00
Cup . . . . 10.00 to 12.00
Plate, 5 1/4 In. . . . . 5.00 to 9.00
Saucer, 3 7/8 In. 5.00
Sugar, 1 3/4 In. . . 12.00 to 15.00
Sugar & Creamer 25.00

Turquoise

Cup 15.00
Plate, 5 1/4 In. . . . 8.25 to 13.00
Saucer, 3 7/8 In. 5.00
Teapot, 3 1/2 In. 29.00

White

Cup 30.00
Cup & Saucer 50.00
Saucer, 3 7/8 In. 12.00

Sugar & Creamer 25.00

Yellow
Cup .... 9.00 to 16.00
Cup & Saucer ... 20.00 to 22.00
Plate, 5 1/4 In. ... 5.00 to 12.00
Saucer, 3 7/8 In. .. 6.25 to 10.00
Sugar 19.50

MODERNTONE PLATONITE

Moderntone Platonite was made by Hazel Atlas Glass Company from 1940 to the early 1950s. Platonite, an almost white glass, was covered with a variety of bright fired-on colors, including Black, Light or Dark Blue, Light or Dark Green, Red, Rust, Yellow, and White trimmed with a small colored rim. Clear glass pieces are listed in this book under Moderntone.

Burgundy
Cup 10.00
Plate, Sherbet, 6 3/4 In. ... 8.00
Sugar 12.50

Chartreuse
Plate, Sherbet, 6 3/4 In. ... 8.50

Dark Blue
Creamer 8.00
Cup & Saucer 7.00
Plate, Dinner, 8 7/8 In. ... 12.00
Saltshaker 10.00

Dark Green
Sherbet 5.00
Soup, Cream, 4 3/4 In. 7.00

Gray
Berry Bowl, 5 In. 11.00
Cup 8.00
Plate, Sherbet, 6 3/4 In. ... 8.50

Light Blue
Creamer 6.00
Plate, Dinner, 8 7/8 In. ...... 12.00 to 14.00
Plate, Sherbet, 6 3/4 In. 4.00
Saucer 1.00
Sherbet 10.00

Light Green
Plate, Sherbet, 6 3/4 In. ... 7.00
Sherbet 8.00
Sugar 20.00

Pink
Berry Bowl, 5 In. 6.00
Berry Bowl, Rim, 5 In. 5.00
Bowl, Rim, 8 In. 14.00
Cup & Saucer 5.00
Plate, Dinner, 8 7/8 In. ... 12.00
Platter, Oval, 12 In. 15.00
Salt & Pepper ... 16.00 to 23.00
Saucer 7.00
Sherbet .... 5.00 to 10.00
Soup, Cream, 4 3/4 In. .... 7.00 to 17.00
Sugar 20.00

Rust
Cup 15.00
Cup & Saucer 25.00
Plate, Dinner, 8 7/8 In. ... 10.00
Salt & Pepper 25.00
Saucer 2.00
Sugar .... 5.00 to 18.00
Sugar & Creamer 35.00

Turquoise
Cup & Saucer 11.00
Salt & Pepper 23.00
Sugar 23.00
Tumbler, 9 Oz., 4 1/8 In. 17.50

White
Plate, Dinner, 8 7/8 In. .... 7.00 to 9.00
Plate, Sherbet, 6 3/4 In. ... 5.00
Salt & Pepper 14.00
Saltshaker .... 7.00 to 10.00
Sherbet .... 5.00 to 12.00

Sherbet, Red Stripes 5.50
Sugar 4.00
Sugar, Red Stripes 10.00
Sugar & Creamer 10.00
Sugar & Creamer, Red & Black Stripes 15.00
Tumbler, 9 Oz., 4 1/8 In. 10.00
Tumbler, Cone Shape, Footed, Red Stripes, 4 1/2 Oz. .... 4.00 to 8.00

Yellow
Creamer .... 8.00 to 20.00
Cup 8.75
Cup & Saucer ..... 5.00 to 7.00
Plate, Dinner, 8 7/8 In. .... 9.00 to 12.00
Plate, Sherbet, 6 3/4 In. ... 8.50
Platter, Oval, 12 In. .... 10.00 to 22.00
Sherbet .... 5.00 to 10.00
Soup, Cream, 4 3/4 In. .... 7.00 to 10.00
Sugar 5.00

MOONDROPS

The New Martinsville Glass Manufacturing Company, New Martinsville, West Virginia, made Moondrops, Line No. 37, from 1932 until late 1936. Collectors like the pieces with fan-shaped knobs or stoppers. The pattern was made in Amber, Amethyst, Black, Cobalt Blue, Crystal, Evergreen, Ice Blue, Jade, Light Green, Medium Blue, Pink, Rose, Ruby, and Smoke.

Amber
Bowl, Concave, Footed, 8 3/8 In. 25.00

Console, Footed,
9 1/2 In. 30.00

Creamer,
3 3/4 In. . . . . . 10.00 to 12.00

Goblet, Cordial, 3/4 Oz.,
2 7/8 In. 15.00

Pitcher, 22 Oz.,
6 7/8 In. 125.00

Pitcher, 32 Oz.,
8 1/8 In. 135.00

Pitcher, Ice Lip, 53 Oz.,
8 1/8 In. 125.00

Sugar & Creamer 25.00

Tumbler, Shot, 2 Oz.,
2 3/4 In. 10.00

Amethyst

Bowl, Oval, Handles,
9 3/4 In. 55.00

Candlestick, 4 3/4 In. . . . 45.00

Creamer, 3 3/4 In. 15.00

Cup 10.00

Cup & Saucer 14.00

Plate, Dinner, 9 1/2 In. . . . 16.00

Tumbler, 9 Oz.,
4 1/2 In. 11.00

Cobalt Blue

Butter, Cover,
6 In. . . . . 165.00 to 250.00

Candy Dish, Metal Cover,
Bird Finial, 8 In. 150.00

Casserole, Cover,
9 3/4 In. 250.00

Goblet, Cordial, 3/4 Oz.,
2 7/8 In. 60.00

Crystal

Candlestick, 3-Light,
5 1/2 In. 50.00

Creamer, 3 3/4 In. 45.00

Cup & Saucer 25.00

Sugar, 2 3/4 In. 22.00

Tumbler, Footed, 5 Oz.,
3 5/8 In. 20.00

Tumbler, Shot, 2 Oz.,
2 3/4 In. . . . . . . 23.00 to 25.00

Evergreen

Cup 9.00

Cup & Saucer 20.00

Decanter, Rocket, Beehive
Stopper, 10 1/2 In. 150.00

Salt & Pepper 45.00

Pink

Tumbler, Shot, 2 Oz.,
2 3/4 In. 15.00

Tumbler, Shot, Handle,
2 Oz., 2 3/4 In. 28.00

Ruby

Ashtray, Footed 35.00

Butter, No Cover 75.00

Celery Dish, 11 1/2 In. . . . 17.00

Creamer,
3 3/4 In. . . . . . 16.00 to 20.00

Cup 16.00

Cup & Saucer . . . 20.00 to 25.00

Decanter Set,
5 Piece 240.00

Goblet, Cordial, 3/4 Oz.,
2 7/8 In. . . . . . 45.00 to 55.00

Goblet, Metal Stem, 3 Oz.,
5 1/8 In. 16.00

Goblet, Water, 8 Oz.,
5 3/4 In. 21.00

Goblet, Wine, 4 Oz.,
4 In. . . . . 25.00 to 30.00

Plate, Dinner, 9 1/2 In. . . . 25.00

Relish, 3-Legged, Ruffled,
8 1/2 In. 50.00

Sherbet . . . . 17.00 to 18.00

Soup, Dish,
6 3/4 In. . . . . . 80.00 to 90.00

Sugar, 2 3/4 In. 9.00

Sugar, 3 3/4 In. . . 16.00 to 18.00

Sugar & Creamer 40.00

Tumbler, 9 Oz.,
4 7/8 In. 22.00

Tumbler, Shot, 2 Oz.,
2 3/4 In. . . . . . 15.00 to 18.00

MOONSTONE

The opalescent hobnails on this crystal pattern give it the name Moonstone. It was made by Anchor Hocking Glass Corporation, Lancaster, Ohio, from 1941 to 1946. A few pieces are seen in Green.

Reproductions have been made.

Berry Bowl,
5 1/2 In. . . . . . 10.00 to 25.00

Bowl, 2 Sections, Ruffled Edge,
7 3/4 In. . . . . . 20.00 to 35.00

Bowl,
Cloverleaf . . . . 22.00 to 38.00

Bowl, Handles, Ruffled Edge,
6 1/2 In. . . . . . 15.00 to 22.00

Bowl, Ruffled Edge,
9 1/2 In. . . . . . 25.00 to 50.00

Candleholder,
4 1/2 In. . . . . . 12.00 to 16.00

Candy Jar, Cover Only 5.00

Candy Jar, Cover, Handles,
6 In. . . . . 28.00 to 40.00

Cup & Saucer . . . 12.00 to 17.00

Plate, Luncheon,
8 3/8 In. 15.00

Plate, Luncheon, Ruffled
Edge, 8 3/8 In. 30.00

Puff Box, Cover 50.00

Sandwich Server, Ruffled
Edge, 10 3/4 In. 30.00

Sherbet 7.00

Sugar 9.00

Sugar &
Creamer . . . . . . 16.00 to 30.00

Vase, Bud, 5 1/2 In. 15.00

Vase, Ruffled Edge,
5 1/2 In. 35.00

MOROCCAN AMETHYST

Moroccan Amethyst is the name of a color, not a shape. The smoky-purple glass was made by Hazel Ware, a division of Continental Can Company, Clarksburg, West Virginia, in the 1960s. The modern-looking dishes were made in several shapes, including Apple, Moderne, Seashell, Simplicity, Square, Starlite, Swirl, Swirl Colonial, and Vanity. Alpine punch sets and snack sets are a combination of Moroccan Amethyst and Opaque White pieces. Many of these shapes were made in the color Capri Blue, which is listed in its own category in this book.

Bowl, 10 3/4 In. 30.00
Bowl, Oval, 7 3/4 In. 14.00
Bowl, Round, 6 In. 10.00
Candy Dish, Cover,
   Short 35.00
Celery Dish, Rectangular,
   9 1/2 In. 16.00
Cocktail, Stirrer, 16 Oz.,
   6 1/4 In. 32.00
Cocktail Shaker, Swirl,
   Aluminum Cover 29.00
Goblet, Water, 9 Oz.,
   5 1/2 In. 10.00
Goblet, Wine, 4 1/2 Oz.,
   4 In. 10.00
Plate, Dinner, 9 3/4 In. 9.00
Punch Cup 6.00
Punch Set, White Bowl,
   Amethyst Cups &
   Base 110.00
Sandwich Server, Metal Handle,
   12 In. . . . . 25.00 to 30.00
Sherbet, 7 1/2 Oz.,
   4 1/4 In. 8.00
Tumbler, Iced Tea,
   16 Oz., 6 1/2 In. 22.00
Tumbler, Juice, 4 Oz.,
   2 1/2 In. 9.00
Tumbler, Old Fashioned, 8 Oz.,
   3 1/4 In. . . . . . . 12.00 to 14.00
Vase, Ruffled Edge,
   8 In. 15.00

MT. PLEASANT

Mt. Pleasant, sometimes called Double Shield, was made by L.E. Smith Company, Mt. Pleasant, Pennsylvania, from the mid-1920s to 1934. The pattern was made in Amber, Black Amethyst (a very deep purple that appears black unless held in front of a strong light), Cobalt Blue, Crystal, Green, Pink, and White. Some pieces have gold or silver trim.

Black Amethyst
Bonbon, Rolled Up Edge,
   Handle, 7 In. 23.00
Bowl, Cup, 3-Footed,
   5 3/4 In. 25.00
Candlestick, 2-Light,
   Pair 48.00
Creamer . . . . . . 20.00 to 22.00
Cup 12.00
Cup & Saucer 15.00
Dish, Mayonnaise, 3-Footed,
   5 1/2 In. 28.00
Dish, Mint, Center Handle,
   6 In. . . . . 22.50 to 25.00
Plate, Square, Handles,
   7 In. . . . . 13.00 to 15.00
Sandwich Server, Center
   Handle . . . . 16.00 to 37.50
Saucer 4.00
Server, Handle, 9 In. 40.00
Sherbet 17.50
Sugar 22.00

Cobalt Blue
Bowl, Fruit, Square,
   Footed, 4 7/8 In. 30.00
Candlestick 23.00
Candlestick, 2-Light,
   Pair 70.00
Cup & Saucer . . . 20.00 to 25.00
Plate, Leaf,
   8 In. . . . . 20.00 to 25.00
Sherbet . . . . 16.00 to 20.00
Sugar & Creamer 40.00
Tumbler,
   Footed . . . . 28.00 to 33.00
Vase, 7 1/4 In. 40.00

Crystal
Sherbet 16.00

MT. VERNON

Mt. Vernon was made in the late 1920s through the 1940s by the Cambridge Glass Company, Cambridge, Ohio. It was made in Amber, Carmen (red), Crystal, Emerald, Heatherbloom (lavender), Royal Blue, and Violet.

Amber
Cake Plate, Handles,
   11 1/2 In. 50.00

Carmen
Sherbet, 4 1/2 Oz.,
   4 1/8 In. 12.00

Crystal
Candy Dish, Cover,
   Footed, 5 1/2 In. 5.00
Compote, 7 1/2 In. 25.00
Creamer, Footed 10.00
Cup . . . . 6.50 to 7.50
Decanter Set, 5 Piece . . . 115.00
Finger Bowl 13.00
Goblet, Cocktail, 3 Oz.,
   5 1/4 In. 13.00
Goblet, Water,
   10 Oz. . . . . 15.00 to 23.00
Goblet, Wine, 3 Oz. 15.00
Plate, Bread & Butter,
   6 In. 4.00
Plate, Salad, 8 1/2 In. 7.50
Relish, 5 Sections,
   12 In. 26.00
Saucer . . . . 7.50 to 8.50
Sherbet, 6 1/2 Oz. 10.00
Sugar, Footed 10.00
Tumbler, 5 Oz. 12.00
Tumbler, 10 Oz. . 10.00 to 14.00

Tumbler, 14 Oz. 25.00

Tumbler, Footed, 5 Oz. . . 12.00

Tumbler, Iced Tea, Footed,
12 Oz. 23.00

Tumbler, Juice, Footed,
3 Oz. 9.00

NATIONAL

National pattern, by Jeannette Glass Company, is sometimes confused with Heisey's Crystolite pattern. The difference shows up on pieces with handles. Jeannette's pattern features open rectangular handles shaped like crossed logs. National was made from the late 1940s through the mid '50s in Crystal, Blue, Pink, and Shell Pink (opaque).

Crystal

Pitcher, 64 Oz., 8 In. 27.00

Sugar 5.50

Sugar &
Creamer . . . . . . 10.00 to 25.00

Tray, Sugar & Creamer,
Handles, 8 In. 8.00

Vase, 9 In. 45.00

NAVARRE

Fostoria Glass Company, Fostoria, Ohio, made Navarre pattern glass from 1937 to 1980. It is an etched pattern. Some of the pieces were made on

the Baroque glass blank, others on more modern shapes. It was originally made only in Crystal. A few pieces were made in the 1970s in Blue, Green, or Pink.

Blue

Bowl, Crown, 9 In. 125.00

Goblet, Champagne, 6 Oz.,
5 5/8 In. . . . . . . 45.00 to 70.00

Goblet, Claret, 4 1/2 Oz.,
6 1/2 In. 90.00

Crystal

Bowl, 3-Footed, Tricornered,
Handle, 4 5/8 In. 17.00

Bowl, Flame, Oval,
12 1/2 In. 115.00

Bowl, Footed, Handles,
10 1/2 In. 95.00

Bowl, Handles, 4 3/8 In. . . 20.00

Cake Plate, Handles,
10 In. . . . . 50.00 to 65.00

Candlestick, 2-Light, 4 1/2 In.,
Pair . . . . 65.00 to 90.00

Candlestick, 2-Light, 5 In.,
Pair 100.00

Candlestick, 3-Light,
6 In. 60.00

Candlestick, 3-Light, 6 In.,
Pair 135.00

Creamer 20.00

Cup & Saucer 34.00

Goblet, Champagne, 6 Oz.,
5 5/8 In. . . . . . . 26.00 to 30.00

Goblet, Cocktail, 3 1/2 Oz.,
6 In. . . . . 25.00 to 30.00

Goblet, Water, 10 Oz.,
7 5/8 In. . . . . . . 40.00 to 45.00

Oyster Cocktail, 4 Oz.,
3 5/8 In. 34.00

Plate, Dinner, 9 In. 84.00

Plate, Salad, 7 1/2 In. 18.00

Saucer 7.00

Sherbet, 6 Oz., 4 3/8 In. . . 18.00

Sugar, Footed, 3 5/8 In. . . 19.00

Sugar, Individual 26.00

Tidbit, 3-Footed,
8 1/4 In. 35.00

Torte Plate,
14 In. . . . . 30.00 to 55.00

Vase, Footed, 10 In. 275.00

NEO CLASSIC

Fostoria Glass Company used the Neo Classic stemware line for several cuttings and etchings from 1934 to 1964. Stemware was made in Amber, Amethyst, Burgundy, Crystal, Empire Green, Iridescent, Regal Blue, Ruby, and Silver Mist.

Amethyst

Goblet, 10 Oz., 6 3/8 In. . . 24.00

Burgundy

Goblet, 10 Oz., 6 3/8 In. . . 33.00

Goblet, Brandy, 1 Oz.,
4 In. 38.00

Goblet, Champagne,
5 1/2 Oz., 4 3/4 In. 28.00

Goblet, Cocktail, 3 Oz.,
4 5/8 In. 33.00

Goblet, Wine, 3 Oz.,
5 In. 33.00

Sherbet, 3 1/4 In. 23.00

Tumbler, Iced Tea, Footed,
13 Oz., 5 3/8 In. 33.00

Tumbler, Juice, Footed,
5 Oz., 3 7/8 In. 28.00

Empire Green

Tumbler, Iced Tea, Footed,
13 Oz., 5 3/8 In. 35.00

❖

Use coasters under glasses and flower vases on marble-topped tables. Marble can stain easily.

NEW CENTURY

New Century used to be called Lydia Ray by some collectors. It was made by Hazel Atlas Glass Company, a firm with factories in Ohio, Pennsylvania, and West Virginia, from 1930 to 1935. It has a series of ribs in the glass design. It is found in Amethyst, Cobalt Blue, Crystal, Green, and Pink. Ovide, another Hazel Atlas pattern, is sometimes incorrectly called New Century.

Amethyst
Tumbler, 9 Oz.,
  4 1/4 In. 20.00
Tumbler, 12 Oz.,
  5 1/4 In. 25.00
Tumbler, Juice, 5 Oz.,
  3 1/2 In. 15.00

Cobalt Blue
Pitcher, 80 Oz.,
  8 In. . . . . 70.00 to 120.00
Tumbler, 5 Oz.,
  3 1/2 In. . . . . . . 15.00 to 17.00
Tumbler, 8 Oz.,
  3 1/2 In. 12.00
Tumbler, 9 Oz.,
  4 1/4 In. 19.00
Tumbler, 10 Oz.,
  5 In. . . . . 22.50 to 30.00
Tumbler, 12 Oz.,
  5 1/4 In. 28.00
Tumbler, Footed, 5 Oz.,
  4 In. 25.00

Crystal
Butter, No Cover 15.00

Goblet, Cocktail, 3 1/4 Oz.,
  4 1/8 In. 29.00
Plate, Dinner, 10 In. 17.00
Plate, Salad, 8 1/2 In. 9.50
Platter, Oval,
  11 In. . . . . 21.50 to 23.50
Salt & Pepper 36.00
Salt & Pepper,
  Red Trim 47.00
Sugar 11.00

Green
Butter, No Cover,
  6 3/4 In. 40.00
Creamer 20.00
Cup & Saucer 12.00
Goblet, Wine, 2 1/2 Oz. . . 33.00
Plate, Dinner, 9 In. 30.00
Plate, Salad, 8 1/2 In. 15.00
Saltshaker 25.00
Sherbet 14.00
Sugar 10.00
Sugar, Cover 40.00
Tumbler, 9 Oz., 4 1/4 In. . . 8.50

Pink
Tumbler, 9 Oz.,
  4 1/4 In. . . . . . . 19.00 to 25.00

NEWPORT

Newport, or Hairpin, was made by Hazel Atlas Glass Company from 1936 to 1940. It is known in Amethyst, Cobalt Blue, Pink, Platonite (white), and a variety of fired-on colors. Reproductions have been made.

Amethyst
Berry Bowl, 3 1/4 In. 20.00

Bowl, Cereal,
  5 1/4 In. . . . . . . 15.00 to 45.00
Creamer 18.00
Cup 8.00
Cup & Saucer . . . 15.00 to 17.00
Plate, Dinner,
  8 13/16 In. 30.00
Plate, Luncheon,
  8 1/2 In. 12.00
Sandwich Server,
  11 3/4 In. . . . . . 10.00 to 45.00
Saucer 5.00
Sherbet . . . . 8.00 to 18.00
Soup, Cream,
  4 3/4 In. . . . . . . 11.00 to 20.00
Sugar 18.00
Sugar & Creamer 38.00
Tumbler, 9 Oz.,
  4 1/2 In. 50.00

Cobalt Blue
Berry Bowl, Master,
  8 1/4 In. 50.00
Bowl, Cereal, 5 1/4 In. . . . 45.00
Cup . . . . 5.00 to 14.00
Cup & Saucer 19.00
Plate, Dinner,
  8 13/16 In. 27.00
Plate, Luncheon,
  8 1/2 In. 20.00
Plate, Sherbet,
  5 7/8 In. . . . . 7.50 to 12.00
Platter, Oval, 11 3/4 In. . . 50.00
Sandwich Server,
  11 3/4 In. 50.00
Saucer 5.00
Sherbet 18.00
Soup, Cream 23.00
Sugar . . . . 16.00 to 20.00
Sugar &
  Creamer . . . . . . 36.00 to 45.00
Tumbler, 9 Oz.,
  4 1/2 In. . . . . . . 30.00 to 50.00

Pink
Berry Bowl,
  4 3/4 In. . . . . . . 10.00 to 28.00

Platonite
Berry Bowl, Red,
  4 3/4 In. 7.50
Berry Bowl, Yellow,
  4 3/4 In. 7.50
Creamer 5.00
Plate, Luncheon, 8 1/2 In.   11.00

Plate, Luncheon, Green,
8 1/2 In. 8.00

Plate, Luncheon, Yellow,
8 1/2 In. 8.00

Saltshaker 15.00

Sandwich Server,
11 3/4 In. 9.00

Sandwich Server, Yellow,
11 3/4 In. 17.50

Sherbet 8.00

Soup, Cream 6.00

Soup, Cream,
Gold Edge 11.00

Sugar 5.00

Sugar, Orange . . . . . 5.00 to 9.50

Sugar & Creamer 8.00

Sugar & Creamer,
Orange 15.00

Tumbler, Aqua, 9 Oz.,
4 1/2 In. 30.00

Tumbler, Green, 9 Oz.,
4 1/2 In. 24.00

Tumbler, Pink, 9 Oz.,
4 1/2 In. . . . . . . 22.00 to 24.00

Tumbler, Tan, 9 Oz.,
4 1/2 In. 22.00

Tumbler, Yellow, 9 Oz.,
4 1/2 In. . . . . . . 22.00 to 30.00

NO. 414
See Diamond Quilted

NO. 601
See Avocado

NO. 610

Many patterns are listed
both by the original pat-
tern number and by a
name. No. 610 is often
called Pyramid or Rex. It
was made from 1926 to
1932 by the Indiana Glass

Company. Green and Pink
were used more than
Crystal, White, and Yel-
low. In 1974 and 1975,
Tiara reissued the pattern
in Black and Blue.

Green

Pickle, Oval, 9 1/2 In. 40.00

Sugar & Creamer,
Tray 150.00

Tumbler, Footed, 8 Oz. . . 60.00

Pink

Pickle, 9 1/2 In. 60.00

Sugar 50.00

Sugar & Creamer 85.00

Sugar & Creamer,
Tray 140.00

Tumbler, Footed, 8 Oz. . . 65.00

Yellow

Berry Bowl, 4 3/4 In. 60.00

Berry Bowl, Master,
8 1/2 In. 100.00

Pickle, Oval,
9 1/2 In. 85.00

Tumbler, 8 Oz. 95.00

NO. 612

Indiana Glass Company,
Dunkirk, Indiana, called
this pattern No. 612, but
collectors call it Horse-
shoe. It was made from
1930 to 1933 primarily in
Green and Yellow, with a
smaller number of Pink
pieces. Sugar and creamer
sets were also made in
Crystal. Plates came in
two styles, one with the
center pattern, one plain.

Green

Berry Bowl, Master,
9 1/2 In. 45.00

Butter, Cover 1200.00

Creamer, Square Foot 22.00

Cup . . . . 12.00 to 15.00

Cup & Saucer . . . 15.00 to 20.00

Grill Plate,
10 3/8 In. . . . 125.00 to 145.00

Plate, Luncheon,
9 3/8 In. 15.00

Plate, Salad,
8 3/8 In. . . . . . . 14.00 to 15.00

Plate, Sherbet,
6 In. . . . . 9.50 to 12.00

Relish, 3 Sections,
Footed 25.00

Saucer . . . . 5.00 to 10.00

Sherbet 15.00

Sugar, Square Foot,
3 3/4 In. . . . . . . 16.00 to 22.00

Tumbler, 9 Oz.,
4 1/4 In. 15.00

Tumbler, Footed, 9 Oz. . . 45.00

Tumbler, Water, Footed, 9 Oz.,
4 1/2 In. . . . . . . 25.00 to 35.00

Yellow

Berry Bowl, 4 1/2 In. 26.00

Berry Bowl, Master,
9 1/2 In. 50.00

Bowl, Cereal, 6 1/2 In. . . . 28.00

Creamer, Square
Foot . . . . 21.00 to 28.00

Cup . . . . 14.00 to 17.00

Cup & Saucer 21.00

Plate, Luncheon,
9 3/8 In. . . . . . . 16.00 to 17.00

Plate, Salad, 8 3/8 In. 13.00

Plate, Sherbet, 6 In. 9.00

Platter, Oval, 10 3/4 In. . . 28.00

Relish, 3 Sections,
Footed . . . . 40.00 to 45.00

Sandwich Server,
11 1/2 In. . . . . . 23.00 to 32.00

Saucer 5.00

Sherbet . . . . 18.00 to 21.00

Sugar 28.00

Sugar, Square
Foot . . . . 17.00 to 20.00

Sugar & Creamer, Square
Foot 30.00

Tumbler, Footed,
9 Oz. . . . . 28.00 to 35.00

NO. 615

No. 615 is often called Lorain. Others call it Basket, Bridal Bouquet, Flower Basket, or Hanging Basket. It was made by the Indiana Glass Company from 1929 to 1932 in Crystal, Green, and Yellow. Sometimes Crystal pieces have blue, green, red, or yellow borders. Reproduction pieces were made in Milk Glass or Olive Green.

Crystal
Creamer 20.00
Cup & Saucer 30.00
Plate, Luncheon,
  8 3/8 In. 9.50
Plate, Luncheon, Blue Trim,
  8 3/8 In. 25.00
Plate, Salad, 7 3/4 In. 7.00
Relish, 4 Sections,
  8 In. . . . . 12.00 to 18.00
Sugar 18.00
Tumbler, Footed, 9 Oz.,
  4 3/4 In. 40.00

Green
Berry Bowl, Master,
  8 In. 50.00
Cup & Saucer . . . 18.00 to 20.00
Plate, Dinner, 10 1/4 In. . . 50.00
Plate, Luncheon,
  8 3/8 In. 15.00
Plate, Salad,
  7 3/4 In. . . . . 8.00 to 11.00
Platter, Oval,
  11 1/2 In. . . . . . 20.00 to 25.00
Sherbet . . . . 23.00 to 28.00
Tumbler, 9 Oz.,
  4 3/4 In. 19.00

Yellow
Bowl, Vegetable, Oval,
  9 3/4 In. . . . . . . 39.00 to 76.00

Creamer 30.00
Cup 20.00
Cup & Saucer . . . 19.00 to 30.00
Plate, Luncheon,
  8 3/8 In. . . . . . . 25.00 to 38.00
Plate, Salad,
  7 3/4 In. . . . . . . 15.00 to 28.00
Plate, Sherbet, 5 1/2 In. . . 14.00
Platter, 11 1/2 In. 75.00
Platter, Oval, 11 1/2 In. . . 55.00
Relish, 4 Sections,
  8 In. . . . . 39.00 to 48.00
Saucer . . . . 5.00 to 24.00
Sherbet . . . . 32.00 to 35.00
Sugar 28.00
Sugar & Creamer 60.00
Tumbler, Footed, 9 Oz.,
  4 3/4 In. . . . . . . 32.00 to 35.00

NO. 616

No. 616 is called Vernon by some collectors. It was made by Indiana Glass Company from 1930 to 1932. The pattern was made in Crystal, Green, and Yellow. Some Crystal pieces have a platinum trim.

Crystal
Creamer, Footed 12.00
Sugar, Footed . . . 18.00 to 30.00
Tumbler, Footed,
  5 In. . . . . 15.00 to 16.00

Yellow
Cup 18.00

NO. 618

Another Indiana Glass Company pattern made from 1932 to 1937 was

No. 618, or Pineapple & Floral. The pattern was made in Amber, Crystal, and fired-on Green and Red. Reproductions were made in Olive Green in the late 1960s.

Amber
Cup 10.00
Cup & Saucer . . . 13.00 to 15.00
Plate, Salad, 8 3/8 In. 9.00
Saucer 5.00
Sugar & Creamer 20.00

Crystal
Ashtray, 4 1/4 In. 30.00
Bowl, Cereal, 6 In. 20.00
Bowl, Salad,
  7 In. . . . . 5.00 to 10.00
Bowl, Vegetable, Oval,
  10 In. 30.00
Compote . . . . 7.00 to 10.00
Creamer 15.00
Cup 11.00
Cup & Saucer . . . . 9.00 to 15.00
Plate, Dinner,
  9 3/8 In. . . . . . . 16.00 to 25.00
Relish, 2 Sections,
  11 1/2 In. 20.00
Saucer 4.00
Sherbet . . . . 14.00 to 22.00
Tumbler, Water, 8 Oz.,
  4 1/4 In. . . . . . . 30.00 to 38.00

NO. 620

No. 620, also known as Daisy, was made by Indiana Glass Company. In 1933 the pattern was made in Crystal, and in 1940 in Amber. It was reissued in the 1960s and 1970s in Dark Green and Milk Glass. Some pieces have a fired-on red color.

Amber

Berry Bowl,
4 1/2 In. . . . . 9.00 to 11.00
Berry Bowl, Master,
7 1/4 In. 10.00
Berry Bowl, Master,
9 1/4 In. 35.00
Bowl, Cereal, 6 In. 26.00
Bowl, Vegetable, Oval,
10 In. . . . . 10.00 to 23.00
Creamer . . . . 4.00 to 9.00
Cup . . . . 6.00 to 8.00
Cup & Saucer . . . . 8.00 to 14.00
Plate, Dinner,
9 3/8 In. . . . . 4.00 to 10.00
Plate, Salad,
7 3/8 In. . . . . 7.00 to 9.00
Plate, Sherbet,
6 In. . . . . 4.00 to 5.00
Platter, Oval,
10 3/4 In. . . . . . 16.00 to 18.00
Relish, 3 Sections,
8 3/8 In. . . . . . . 24.00 to 35.00
Sandwich Server,
11 1/2 In. . . . . . 15.00 to 22.00
Saucer . . . . 4.00 to 6.00
Sherbet . . . . 8.00 to 10.00
Soup, Cream,
4 1/2 In. . . . . 6.00 to 12.00
Sugar . . . . 5.00 to 10.00
Sugar &
Creamer . . . . . . 16.00 to 25.00
Tumbler, Iced Tea, Footed,
12 Oz. 40.00
Tumbler, Water, Footed,
9 Oz. . . . . 20.00 to 30.00

Crystal

Bowl, Vegetable, Oval,
10 In. 20.00
Cup & Saucer 12.00
Grill Plate,
10 3/8 In. . . . . . . 7.00 to 15.00
Plate, Salad, 7 3/8 In. 9.00
Relish, 3 Sections,
8 3/8 In. . . . . . . 13.00 to 25.00
Sandwich Server,
11 1/2 In. 15.00
Sherbet 5.00

Dark Green

Berry Bowl, Master,
7 3/8 In. . . . . 8.00 to 9.00
Creamer 10.00
Cup & Saucer 5.00
Plate, Dinner, 9 3/8 In. 7.00
Plate, Salad, 7 3/8 In. 7.00
Soup, Cream 6.00

NO. 622
See Pretzel

NO. 624
See Christmas Candy

NORA BIRD

The Nora Bird etching, made by Paden City Glass Manufacturing Company, Paden City, West Virginia, is a smaller version of the Peacock & Wild Rose etching by the same company. It was produced from 1920 to the 1930s in Amber, Black, Cobalt Blue, Crystal, Green, Light Blue, Pink, and Red.

Black

Vase, 8 In. 300.00

Crystal

Candlestick, Mushroom,
5 x 1 7/8 In. 55.00

Green

Candlestick, Pair 85.00
Dish, Mayonnaise,
Underplate 125.00

Pink

Candlestick 25.00
Compote, 6 x 8 In. 75.00

NORMANDIE

A few Depression glass patterns were made in Iridescent Marigold color, which has been collected as carnival glass. Normandie products made in this iridescence, called Sunburst, appear in the carnival glass listings as Bouquet & Lattice; when the pattern is in the other known colors, it is called Normandie. Look for it in Amber, Crystal, Pink, and Spring Green, as well as in the Iridescent color. Normandie was made by the Federal Glass Company from 1933 to 1940.

Amber

Berry Bowl, Master,
8 1/2 In. 17.50
Creamer, Footed 9.00
Cup 4.00
Plate, Luncheon,
9 1/4 In. . . . . . . 10.00 to 27.00
Salt & Pepper . . . 60.00 to 62.00
Sugar 6.00
Tumbler, Iced Tea, 12 Oz.,
5 In. 65.00
Tumbler, Juice, 5 Oz.,
4 In. 43.00

Crystal

Berry Bowl, Master,
8 1/2 In. . . . . . . 22.00 to 24.00
Bowl, Vegetable, Oval,
10 In. 20.00
Cup 12.00
Cup & Saucer 15.00

Grill Plate, 11 In. 16.00
Sugar & Creamer 12.00
Tumbler, Iced Tea, 12 Oz.,
   5 In. 65.00

Iridescent
Berry Bowl, 5 In. 6.50
Bowl, Cereal, 6 1/2 In. 9.00
Bowl, Serving, Round,
   8 3/4 In. 24.00
Bowl, Vegetable, Oval,
   10 In. 23.00
Cup & Saucer 11.00
Grill Plate, 11 In. 10.00
Plate, Dinner,
   11 In. . . . . 14.00 to 18.00
Plate, Sherbet, 6 In. 5.00
Platter, Oval, 11 3/4 In. . . 23.00
Saucer 3.00
Sherbet 8.00

Pink
Cup . . . . 9.00 to 12.00
Cup & Saucer . . . 12.00 to 27.00
Pitcher, 80 Oz., 8 In. 225.00
Plate, Salad, 7 3/4 In. 14.00
Saucer 5.00
Sherbet . . . . 9.00 to 11.00
Sherbet, Underplate 13.00

NUDE

Of all the stemware featuring a nude stem, the pattern by Cambridge Glass Company is probably the best-known. The pattern was first made in Crystal in 1936. The most desirable Nude stemware features a colored bowl

with a Crystal stem. Carmen (Red), Crown Tuscan (opaque light pink), Heatherbloom (lavender), Royal Blue, and other colored bowls can be found for high prices.

Amber
Ivy Ball, Crystal Stem & Foot,
   6 3/8 In. 485.00

Crystal
Compote,
   8 1/4 x 6 3/4 In. 195.00
Compote, Shell Shape,
   5 1/2 x 5 1/4 In. 275.00
Goblet, Brandy, 1 Oz. . . . 375.00

Forest Green
Ivy Ball, Crystal Stem
   & Foot, 6 3/8 In. 325.00

Gold Krystol
Goblet, Wine, Crown Tuscan
   Stem & Foot, 3 Oz. . . . 175.00

Heatherbloom
Goblet, Champagne, Crystal
   Stem & Foot, 6 Oz. . . . 650.00

Mocha
Goblet, Brandy, Crystal Stem
   & Foot, 1 Oz. 250.00
Goblet, Cocktail, Crystal Stem
   & Foot, 3 Oz. 200.00

Royal Blue
Compote, Crystal Stem &
   Foot, 6 3/8 In. 410.00
Goblet, Brandy, Crystal Stem
   & Foot, 1 Oz. 295.00

Smoke
Goblet, Brandy, Crackle
   Bowl, Crystal Stem &
   Foot, 1 Oz. 1200.00

OATMEAL LACE
See Princess Feather

OCTAGON

Octagon, sometimes called Tiered Octagon or U.S. Octagon, was made by the U.S. Glass Company from 1927 to 1929. It

was used by the Octagon Soap Company as a premium. The pieces were made in Crystal, Green, and Pink. Some pieces are found marked with the glass company trademark.

Crystal
Salt & Pepper, 2 7/8 In. . . 12.00

Green
Nut Bowl 20.00
Plate, Salad, 7 In. 15.00

OLD CAFE

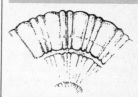

Old Cafe was made by the Hocking Glass Company, Lancaster, Ohio, from 1936 to 1940. Pieces are found in Crystal, Pink, and Royal Ruby.

Crystal
Berry Bowl, 3 3/4 In. 9.00
Bowl, Cereal, 5 1/2 In. . . . 20.00
Candy Dish, Handles,
   8 In. . . . . 8.00 to 14.00
Candy Jar, Royal Ruby,
   Cover 20.00
Relish, Tab Handles,
   Metal Bail 18.00
Saucer 3.00
Vase, 7 1/4 In. . . 15.00 to 25.00

Pink
Bowl, Open Handles,
   6 1/2 In. 25.00
Candy Dish, Handles,
   8 In. . . . . 15.00 to 25.00
Cup 10.00
Olive Dish,
   6 In. . . . . 10.00 to 13.00
Plate, 10 In. 76.00
Sherbet, Low Foot 16.00

Royal Ruby

Bowl, Cereal, 5 1/2 In. 30.00
Candy Dish, Handles,
 8 In. . . . . 18.00 to 25.00
Candy Jar, Cover Only . . . 20.00
Cup . . . . 10.00 to 12.00

OLD COLONY

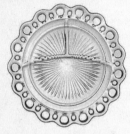

To add to the confusion in
the marketplace, this pattern, which was advertised
as Old Colony, has also
been called Colony, Lace
Edge, Loop, Open Lace, or
Open Scallop. In addition,
the pattern is often con-
fused with other similar
patterns, such as Imperial's
Laced Edge. Cups or tum-
blers may also be mixed
up with Queen Mary or
Coronation. The pattern
listed here, made by Hocking Glass Company, Lan-
caster, Ohio, from 1935
to 1938, can usually be
identified by the familiar
sunburst base common to
many of Hocking's designs.
Most pieces of Old
Colony are Pink, although
Crystal is also found.

Crystal

Bowl, Cereal,
 6 3/8 In. . . . . . 10.00 to 28.00
Bowl, Plain, 9 1/2 In. 33.00
Bowl, Ribbed,
 9 1/2 In. 38.00

Grill Plate, 10 1/2 In. 40.00
Platter, 12 3/4 In. 50.00
Relish, 3 Sections,
 10 1/2 In. . . . . 29.00 to 30.00

Pink

Bowl, 8 1/4 In. 30.00
Bowl, 9 1/2 In. 34.00
Bowl, Cereal,
 6 3/8 In. . . . . . 28.00 to 32.00
Bowl, Flower, Crystal
 Frog . . . . 25.00 to 45.00
Bowl, Plain,
 9 1/2 In. . . . . . 28.00 to 33.00
Bowl, Ribbed,
 9 1/2 In. . . . . . 30.00 to 45.00
Butter, Cover . . 95.00 to 120.00
Candlestick, Frosted 55.00
Candy Jar, Cover,
 Ribbed 57.00
Compote, 7 In. . . 33.00 to 45.00
Console, 3-Footed 275.00
Console, Frosted, 3-Footed,
 10 3/4 In. 80.00
Cookie Jar,
 Cover . . . . . . 70.00 to 105.00
Cookie Jar, No Cover 45.00
Creamer 33.00
Cup & Saucer 65.00
Grill Plate,
 10 1/2 In. . . . . 25.00 to 27.00
Plate, Dinner,
 10 1/2 In. . . . . 38.00 to 40.00
Plate, Luncheon,
 8 1/4 In. . . . . . 25.00 to 35.00
Plate, Salad,
 7 1/4 In. . . . . . 30.00 to 35.00
Platter, 12 3/4 In. 45.00
Platter, 5 Sections,
 12 3/4 In. . . . . 29.00 to 42.00
Relish, 3 Sections,
 7 1/2 In. 90.00
Relish, 3 Sections,
 10 1/2 In. . . . . 25.00 to 35.00
Relish, Solid Lace, 4 Sections,
 13 In. . . . . 65.00 to 80.00
Saucer . . . . 12.00 to 18.00
Sherbet . . . . . 120.00 to 150.00
Sugar &
 Creamer . . . . . 75.00 to 80.00
Tumbler, 9 Oz.,
 4 1/4 In. . . . . . 26.00 to 29.00
Tumbler, Footed,
 10 1/2 Oz., 5 In. 110.00

OLD ENGLISH

Old English, or Threading,
was made by the Indiana
Glass Company, Dunkirk,
Indiana, in the late 1920s
and early 1930s. It was
first made in Amber, Crystal, and Forest Green. Pink
was a later color.

Amber

Tumbler, Footed,
 4 1/2 In. 25.00

Crystal

Eggcup . . . . 7.00 to 12.00

Forest Green

Vase, Ruffled Edge, Footed,
 4 1/2 In. 18.00

OLD FLORENTINE
See Florentine No. 1

OLD QUILT

Old Quilt, or Checker-
board, is an older pattern
first made by Westmore-
land Glass Company,
Grapeville, Pennsylvania,
around 1910. In the 1940s,
Westmoreland reintro-
duced Old Quilt in Milk
Glass. The pattern was
made in limited editions of

other colors, but the most commonly available pieces are in Milk Glass.

Antique Blue
Candy Dish,
　6 1/2 x 4 3/4 In. 43.00
Pitcher, 42 Oz.,
　8 1/2 In. . . . . . . 40.00 to 75.00

Milk Glass
Box, Cover, Square,
　5 x 4 In. 40.00
Cake Plate, Footed,
　12 1/2 In. 40.00
Celery Vase, 6 1/2 In. 20.00
Compote, 7 1/4 x 8 In. . . . 65.00
Jardiniere, Footed, Ribbed,
　6 1/2 x 6 In. 60.00
Sugar 29.00
Sugar &
　Creamer . . . . . . 55.00 to 60.00
Vase, Fan, 8-Sided Foot,
　9 In. 25.00
Vase, Hand Painted,
　6 1/2 In. 50.00

OLD SANDWICH

Old Sandwich looks like the Pillar and Paneled Thumbprint patterns made in the mid-1800s. A.H. Heisey & Company, Newark, Ohio, introduced it in 1931 in Flamingo (pink), Moongleam (green), and Sahara (yellow). Some pieces in Cobalt, Tangerine (orange), and Zircon (light turquoise) can be found. Most items are marked with the Diamond H logo.

Cobalt
Ashtray, Square,
　2 1/4 In. 50.00
Goblet, 10 Oz., 5 3/4 In. . . 25.00

Flamingo
Dish, Sundae, Footed,
　6 Oz. 30.00

Moongleam
Goblet, Cocktail, 3 Oz.,
　4 3/8 In. . . . . . . 33.00 to 37.00
Plate, Square, 8 In. 30.00

Sahara
Mug, 12 Oz. 60.00
Oyster Cocktail, 4 Oz. . . . 15.00
Pitcher, 1/2 Gal., 7 In. . . . 75.00
Pitcher, Ice Lip, 1/2 Gal.,
　8 1/2 In. 55.00
Plate, Square, 8 In. 50.00
Salt, Square 10.00
Tumbler, 8 Oz. 20.00

OPALESCENT HOBNAIL
See Moonstone

OPEN LACE
See Old Colony

OPEN ROSE
See Mayfair Open Rose

OPEN SCALLOP
See Old Colony

OPTIC DESIGN
See Raindrops

ORANGE BLOSSOM

Indiana Glass Company made Orange Blossom in

1957. The pattern is the same as Indiana Custard, but the Milk Glass items are called Orange Blossom.

Bowl, Dessert, 5 1/2 In. . . . 5.00
Creamer 5.00
Cup & Saucer 5.00
Sugar 4.50
Sugar & Creamer 10.00

ORCHID ETCH

A.H. Heisey & Company, Newark, Ohio, used the Orchid etching on several shapes of glass, including Waverly and Queen Ann. The pattern was made in Crystal from 1940 to 1957.

Ashtray, 3 In. . . . 24.00 to 30.00
Bowl, Crimped, Waverly,
　12 In. 75.00
Butter, Cover, Waverly,
　1/4 Lb. 165.00
Candlestick, 3-Light,
　Cascade, Pair 215.00
Candlestick, Mercury,
　4 In. 35.00
Candlestick, Queen Ann,
　Prisms 200.00
Candy Dish, Cover,
　Wave Finial, 5 In. 210.00
Cigarette Holder, Cover,
　Footed, Waverly 165.00
Cup & Saucer, Waverly . . 75.00
Decanter, Sherry, Oval, Silver
　Plated, Stopper, 1 Pt. . . 335.00
Dish, Mayonnaise,
　Flared, Footed,
　5 1/2 In. . . . . . . 68.00 to 70.00
Goblet, 10 Oz. 50.00

Goblet, Champagne,
6 Oz. .... 30.00 to 40.00

Goblet, Cocktail, 4 Oz. 35.00

Goblet, Cordial, 1 Oz. ... 21.00

Goblet, Juice, Footed,
5 Oz. 53.00

Goblet, Wine, 3 Oz. 85.00

Nut Dish, Oval, 7 In. 45.00

Pitcher, Donna,
1/2 Gal. 625.00

Plate, Salad, 7 In. 20.00

Plate, Salad, 8 In. 40.00

Relish, 3 Sections, Oblong,
11 In. .... 70.00 to 73.00

Sandwich Server, 14 In. .. 60.00

Saucer 15.00

Sherbet, 6 Oz. ... 24.00 to 40.00

Sugar & Creamer 26.00

Torte Plate, Rolled Edge,
14 In. 50.00

Tumbler, Iced Tea,
12 Oz., 6 1/2 In. 75.00

ORIENTAL POPPY
See Florentine No. 2

OVIDE

Hazel Atlas Glass Company made Ovide pattern from 1929 to the 1950s. Early pieces were made in transparent Green. Opaque Black was introduced in 1932. By 1935, Platonite, an opaque white glass, was used with fired-on colors. Pieces were made with colored rims, overall fired-on colors, or decorations like birds, windmills, or Art Deco

geometrics. Ovide is sometimes incorrectly called New Century.

Black

Candy Dish, Cover 46.00

Creamer 9.50

Cup & Saucer 14.00

Plate, Luncheon, 8 In. 14.00

Salt & Pepper ... 28.00 to 35.00

Sherbet .... 7.00 to 11.00

Sugar 9.50

Sugar & Creamer 18.00

Tumbler 29.00

Green

Berry Bowl, 4 3/4 In. 8.00

Bowl, Cereal, 5 1/2 In. ... 12.00

Creamer 9.50

Goblet, Fruit Cocktail 7.00

Platter, 11 In. 19.00

Salt & Pepper 26.00

Sugar 9.50

Tumbler 29.00

Platonite

Berry Bowl, Fired-On Red,
4 3/4 In. 5.00

Berry Bowl, Fired-On
Yellow, 4 3/4 In. 5.00

Bowl, Cereal, Black
Flowers, 5 1/2 In. 10.00

Creamer, Fired-On
Butterscotch 11.00

Creamer, Fired-On Pink
& Black 12.00

Cup & Saucer, Black
Flowers 17.50

Cup & Saucer, Fired-On
Yellow 7.00

Plate, Dinner, Black
Flowers, 9 In. 20.00

❖

Do not wash or rinse iridescent glass with very hot water or strong soap. It will remove some of the color.

❖

Sugar , ... 9.00

Sugar & Creamer,
Red Trim 32.00

OYSTER & PEARL

Anchor Hocking Glass Corporation, Lancaster, Ohio, made only accessory pieces in the Oyster & Pearl pattern from 1938 to 1940. The first pieces were Crystal or Pink. Those made in White with a fired-on pink or green interior were made later, as were Royal Ruby pieces.

Crystal

Bowl, Heart Shape Handle,
5 1/4 In. .... 9.00 to 14.00

Candleholder, 3 1/2 In. ... 15.00

Candleholder, 3 1/2 In.,
Pair .... 25.00 to 35.00

Pink

Bowl, Deep, Handles,
6 In. 22.00

Bowl, Heart Shape,
Handle, 5 1/4 In. 15.00

Relish, 2 Sections,
10 1/2 In. ..... 18.00 to 25.00

Royal Ruby

Bowl, Deep, Handles,
6 1/2 In. 22.00

Bowl, Fruit, 10 1/2 In. ... 60.00

Candleholder, 3 1/2 In.,
Pair .... 49.00 to 65.00

White

Bowl, Heart Shape, Handle,
Fired-On Green 11.00

PANELED ASTER
See Madrid

PANELED CHERRY
BLOSSOM
See Cherry Blossom

PANELED GRAPE

Crystal Paneled Grape with stained decorations was originally made by Jenkins Glass Company, Kokomo, Indiana, from 1903 to the 1930s. Westmoreland Glass Company, Grapeville, Pennsylvania, started making Paneled Grape in Milk Glass in the 1940s and continued until the factory closed in 1984. Some of Westmoreland's pieces have hand-painted swags, called Roses & Bows, or grapes. Westmoreland also made Paneled Grape in Crystal and other colors from the 1950s until 1984. Another company made a similar pattern, Panel Grape, in various colors, but not Milk Glass, for distributor L.G. Wright. A reproduction canister was made by Summit Art Glass Company.

Crystal
Creamer . . . . 18.00 to 23.00
Cruet, 2 Oz. 25.00
Pitcher, 16 Oz. 50.00
Pitcher, 32 Oz. 45.00

Golden Sunset
Compote, 7 In. 32.00
Cup & Saucer 30.00

Laurel Green
Basket, 11 x 7 1/4 In. . . . 175.00

Milk Glass
Appetizer Set, Bowl, Plate,
  Ladle 60.00
Basket,
  11 x 7 1/4 In. 150.00 to 170.00
Basket, Oval, Split Handle,
  6 1/2 In. . . . . . .30.00 to 60.00
Basket, Ruffled Edge,
  8 In. 100.00
Bowl, Bell Shape, Footed,
  9 1/2 In. 99.00
Bowl, Footed, 8 1/2 In. . . . 60.00
Bowl, Lip, 9 1/2 In. 60.00
Bowl, Lip, Skirted
  Foot, 9 In. 65.00
Bowl, Oval, 11 1/2 In. . . . 75.00
Candlestick, 3-Light, Skirted
  Edge, Pair 390.00
Candlestick, 4 In.,
  Pair . . . . 25.00 to 28.00
Candlestick,
  5 In. . . . . 29.00 to 35.00
Candlestick, 8 1/2 In. . . . 160.00
Candy Jar, 6 1/4 In. 43.00
Compote, Cover, 7 In. . . . 48.00
Compote, Crimped, Footed,
  9 In. . . . . 46.00 to 75.00
Creamer, Large 23.00
Crimped, 4 1/2 In. 25.00
Cup 14.00
Cup & Saucer 23.00
Dish, Mayonnaise,
  Underplate 30.00
Dish, Mayonnaise,
  Underplate, Ladle 35.00
Dish, Sleigh Shape,
  9 In. 55.00
Egg Plate Set, Plate,
  Bowl, Spoon 275.00
Epergne, Vase Only,
  8 1/2 In. 40.00
Goblet, Water, 8 Oz. 20.00
Jardiniere, 4 In. 30.00
Jardiniere, 5 In. 40.00
Jardiniere, 6 1/2 In. 45.00
Nut Dish, Oval, Footed,
  6 1/2 In. 30.00
Pickle, Oval 175.00
Pitcher, Footed,
  1 Qt. . . . . 35.00 to 45.00
Pitcher, Footed, 16 Oz. . . . 31.00
Planter,
  5 x 9 In. . . . . . . 30.00 to 35.00

Planter, Square,
  4 1/2 In. 30.00
Plate, Dinner, 10 1/2 In. . . 45.00
Plate, Luncheon,
  8 1/2 In. 25.00
Puff Box, Cover,
  4 1/2 In. 35.00
Sauceboat, Underplate . . . 70.00
Saucer 9.00
Soap Dish . . . . 110.00 to 145.00
Sugar & Creamer 45.00
Vase, Bell Shape, 6 In. . . . 12.00
Vase, Bud, 13 In. 113.00
Vase, Crimped Edge,
  9 In. 50.00
Vase, Footed,
  9 1/2 In. . . . . . . 35.00 to 40.00
Vase, Ivy Ball, Footed . . . 50.00
Vase, Swung, 14 In. 34.00
Wedding Bowl, Square,
  Cover, 9 In. 25.00

PANSY & DORIC
See Doric & Pansy

PARK AVENUE ANCHOR HOCKING

Many collectors mistake pieces of Park Avenue for the earlier Manhattan pattern. There are slight differences between the items. Anchor Hocking Corporation made Park Avenue in Crystal and Blue from 1987 to 1993.

Blue
Dessert, Footed, 13 Oz. . . 28.00
Tumbler, Iced Tea,
  16 Oz. 18.00

Crystal

Dessert, Footed, 13 Oz. ... 9.00

Tumbler Set, 10 Oz.,
  8 Piece 35.00

Vase, 9 3/4 In. 15.00

PARK AVENUE FEDERAL

Federal Glass Company's Park Avenue is nothing like the pattern of the same name by Anchor Hocking. The bases of the items are square and the ribbed sections are vertical. The pattern was made from 1941 through the early '70s in Crystal and Yellow. Some pieces have gold trim.

Crystal

Ashtray, Square, 3 1/2 In. .. 6.00

Bowl, 8 1/2 In. 8.00

Bowl, Dessert, 5 In. 5.00

Tumbler, 4 In. 5.00

Tumbler, 9 Oz., 4 3/8 In. .. 8.00

Tumbler, Juice, 4 1/2 Oz.,
  3 1/2 In. ..... 4.00 to 5.00

Tumbler, Whiskey,
  2 1/8 In. 5.00

PARROT
See Sylvan

PARTY LINE

Party Line was made by Paden City Glass Manufac-

turing Company, Paden City, West Virginia. It had many names, including Line 191, Tiered Semi Optic, and Tiered Block. It is a durable pattern advertised in 1928 for home, restaurant, hotel, and soda fountain use. The dishes were made in Amber, Black, Blue, Cheriglo (pink), Crystal, Green, and Mulberry.

Amber

Compote,
  3 3/4 x 6 3/4 In. 14.00

Saltshaker 25.00

Sherbet 8.00

Sugar & Creamer 26.00

Cheriglo

Cup 10.00

Sugar 12.00

Tumbler, Footed,
  3 1/2 Oz. 8.00

Tumbler, Soda, Footed,
  8 Oz. .... 15.00 to 18.00

Green

Berry Bowl, 4 1/2 In. 10.00

Creamer 12.00

Cup 9.00

Ice Bucket ..... 20.00 to 28.00

Parfait, Footed, 5 Oz. 16.00

Pitcher, Measuring,
  Reamer, 36 Oz. 52.00

Sherbet 10.00

Sherbet, High, 6 Oz. 12.50

Tumbler, Soda, Footed,
  12 Oz. 25.00

PATRICIAN

Federal Glass Company, Columbus, Ohio, made

Patrician, sometimes called Hinge or Spoke, from 1933 to 1937. Full dinner sets were made in Golden Glo and Green, and smaller quantities in Crystal and Pink. Yellow pieces were produced later.

Crystal

Berry Bowl, 5 In. 15.00

Berry Bowl, Master,
  8 1/2 In. 50.00

Bowl, Vegetable, Oval,
  10 In. 42.00

Cookie Jar, Cover 90.00

Grill Plate, 10 1/2 In. 15.00

Grill Plate, Experimental
  Iridescent, 10 1/2 In. .. 130.00

Sherbet 13.00

Soup, Cream 15.00

Tumbler, Juice, 5 Oz.,
  4 In. 38.00

Golden Glo

Berry Bowl,
  5 In. .... 12.00 to 14.00

Berry Bowl, Master,
  8 1/2 In. ...... 42.00 to 43.00

Bowl, Cereal,
  6 In. .... 18.00 to 27.00

Bowl, Sugar 22.00

Bowl, Vegetable, Oval,
  10 In. .... 31.00 to 40.00

Butter, Cover .. 80.00 to 100.00

Butter, Cover
  Only .... 35.00 to 45.00

Cookie Jar,
  Cover .... 80.00 to 115.00

Creamer 15.00

Cup 9.00

Cup & Saucer ... 16.00 to 20.00

Grill Plate, 10 3/4 In. 14.00

Pitcher, Applied Handle,
  75 Oz., 8 1/4 In. 150.00

Pitcher, Molded Handle,
  75 Oz., 8 In. .. 95.00 to 135.00

Plate, Dinner,
  10 1/2 In. ...... 8.00 to 15.00

Plate, Luncheon,
  9 In. .... 10.00 to 18.00

Plate, Salad,
  7 1/2 In. ...... 17.00 to 18.00

Platter, Oval,
  11 1/2 In. ..... 29.00 to 33.00

Salt & Pepper 58.00
Saltshaker 25.00
Saucer 9.50
Sherbet . . . . 9.00 to 13.00
Soup, Cream . . . . 15.00 to 22.00
Sugar 15.00
Sugar, Cover . . . . 65.00 to 90.00
Sugar, Madrid Cover,
　Round Knob 250.00
Sugar & Creamer 19.00
Tumbler, 9 Oz.,
　4 1/4 In. 30.00
Tumbler, 14 Oz.,
　5 1/2 In. . . . . . . 30.00 to 55.00
Tumbler, Footed, 8 Oz.,
　5 1/4 In. . . . . . . 55.00 to 70.00

Green
Berry Bowl, 5 In. 15.00
Bowl, Vegetable, Oval,
　10 In. 40.00
Butter,
　Cover . . . . . . 125.00 to 170.00
Butter, No Cover 80.00
Creamer . . . . 12.00 to 13.00
Cup . . . . 9.00 to 13.00
Cup & Saucer 19.00
Grill Plate, 10 1/2 In. 17.00
Plate, Dinner, 10 1/2 In. . . 60.00
Plate, Luncheon, 9 In. 13.00
Plate, Salad, 7 1/2 In. 20.00
Salt & Pepper 75.00
Saltshaker . . . . . . 38.00 to 44.00
Sherbet . . . . 12.00 to 17.00
Soup, Cream . . . . 22.00 to 30.00
Sugar 12.00
Sugar & Creamer 37.00
Tumbler, Footed, 8 Oz.,
　5 1/4 In. 75.00

Pink
Berry Bowl, Master,
　8 1/2 In. 37.00
Platter, Oval, 11 1/2 In. . . 35.00

PATRICK

Patrick pattern was made by the Lancaster Glass Company of Lancaster, Ohio, about 1930. The pattern was etched in Rose or Topaz colored glass.

Rose
Creamer . . . . . 53.00 to 100.00
Dish, Mayonnaise,
　Footed, Underplate,
　Ladle, 3 Piece 165.00
Plate, Luncheon, 8 In. 68.00
Sugar 100.00

Topaz
Dish, Mayonnaise,
　Footed 150.00
Goblet, Water, 10 Oz.,
　6 In. . . . . 70.00 to 80.00
Plate, Sherbet, 7 In. 20.00
Sandwich Server, Handles,
　11 In. . . . . 60.00 to 65.00
Sugar 53.00

PEACH LUSTRE

Peach Lustre is both a pattern and a color name used for Fire-King dinnerware made by Anchor Hocking Glass Corporation from 1952 to 1963. The pattern has a laurel leaf design around the edge of plates and bowls and the side of cups. The pieces are a lustrous orange-yellow color. The same pattern of laurel leaves was made in 1953 in gray and is known as Gray Laurel pattern. Other related patterns are listed in the Fire-King section in this book.

Plate, 8 In. 18.00
Sugar & Creamer . 8.00 to 18.00
Vase, 7 1/4 In. 10.00

PEACOCK & ROSE
See Peacock & Wild Rose

PEACOCK & WILD ROSE

Line 300 was the name used by Paden City Glass Manufacturing Company, Paden City, West Virginia, for the pattern now called Peacock & Wild Rose. It was made in the 1930s of Amber, Black, Cobalt Blue, Crystal, Green, Light Blue, Pink, and Red. A few of the lists call this pattern Peacock & Rose. A similar pattern, Nora Bird, is listed in its own section in this book.

Black
Vase, 10 In. 275.00

Crystal
Cake Plate,
　10 1/4 x 1 1/4 In. 130.00
Console, 14 In. 95.00
Vase,
　10 1/8 x 6 1/4 In. 290.00

Green
Bowl, Fruit, Handles,
　10 1/2 In. 300.00
Candleholder, 5 In. 85.00
Cheese & Cracker
　Underplate, 10 1/2 In. . . 95.00
Console, 14 In. 130.00
Sandwich Server, Center
　Handle, 10 1/2 In. 130.00
Sugar . . . . 70.00 to 90.00

Pink
Bowl, Footed, 10 1/2 In. . . 67.00
Bowl, Fruit, 10 1/2 In. . . 165.00
Bowl, Pedestal Foot,
　8 1/2 In. 265.00
Candlestick, 5 In., Pair . . 180.00

Cheese & Cracker Underplate,
10 1/2 In. 70.00
Compote, 6 1/4 In. 175.00
Console, 11 In. 165.00
Console, 14 In. 130.00
Dish, Mayonnaise,
6 x 3 In. 50.00
Sandwich Tray, Center
Handle, 10 1/2 In. 195.00
Vase, 10 In. 380.00

PEACOCK & WILD ROSE
See also Crow's Foot

PEBBLE OPTIC
See Raindrops

PENNY LINE

Paden City Glass Manufac-
turing Company, Paden
City, West Virginia, made
Penny Line in Amber,
Cheriglo, Crystal, Green,
Royal Blue, and Ruby. It
was No. 991 in the 1932
catalog.

Amber
Tumbler, Iced Tea,
12 Oz. 8.00

Cheriglo
Goblet, Cordial,
1 1/4 Oz. 15.00

Green
Goblet, Cocktail,
3 1/2 Oz. 5.00

Royal Blue
Plate, Luncheon, 8 In. 14.00
Saucer 4.00
Tumbler, Juice, 5 Oz. 15.00

Ruby
Bowl, Finger . . . . 18.00 to 20.00
Creamer 19.00
Cup . . . . 10.00 to 12.00
Decanter, 22 Oz.,
11 In. 165.00
Dish, Grapefruit, Footed,
18 Oz., 4 1/2 In. 20.00
Goblet, 10 Oz. 15.00
Goblet, Cordial,
1 1/4 Oz. . . . . 13.00 to 30.00
Goblet, Low Foot,
10 Oz. 35.00
Plate, 6 In. 12.00
Plate, 8 In. . . . . . . 12.00 to 15.00
Sandwich Server, Center Handle,
10 1/2 In. . . . . . 31.00 to 60.00
Saucer . . . . 4.00 to 9.00
Sherbet, 6 Oz. 12.00
Sugar 20.00
Tumbler,
2 1/2 Oz. . . . . . 10.00 to 15.00
Tumbler, 5 Oz. 12.00
Tumbler, 9 Oz. 15.00
Tumbler, Iced Tea,
12 Oz. 15.00
Tumbler, Water, 10 Oz. . . 12.00

PETAL SWIRL
See Swirl Jeannette

PETALWARE

Macbeth-Evans Glass
Company made Petalware
from 1930 to 1940. It was
first made in Crystal and
Pink. In 1932 the dinner-
ware was made in Monax,
and in 1933 in Cremax.
The pattern remained

popular, and in 1936
Cobalt Blue and several
other variations were
made. Some pieces were
hand-painted with pastel
bands of green, ivory, and
pink. Some pieces were
decorated with gold or
red trim. Flower or fruit
designs in bright colors
were used on others.
Bright bands of fired-on
blue, green, red, and
yellow were used to deco-
rate some wares. Collec-
tors have given some of
these patterns their own
names, including Banded
Petalware, Daisy Petals,
Diamond Point, Petal,
Shell, and Vivid Bands.

Cobalt Blue
Mustard, No Cover 8.00

Cremax
Bowl, Cereal, 5 3/4 In. . . . 10.00
Cup 8.50
Cup, Gold Trim 10.00
Cup & Saucer 12.50
Cup & Saucer, Fired-On
Red 13.00
Cup & Saucer, Pastel
Bands 20.00
Plate, Dinner, Gold Trim,
9 In. 8.00
Plate, Dinner, Pastel Bands,
9 In. 26.00
Plate, Salad, 8 In. . . 5.00 to 9.00
Plate, Salad, Gold Trim,
8 In. 10.00
Plate, Salad, Pastel Bands,
8 In. 15.00
Salver, 11 In. 9.00
Salver, Gold Trim,
11 In. 28.00
Salver, Pastel Bands,
11 In. 30.00
Salver, Pastel Bands,
12 In. 30.00
Saucer . . . . 3.00 to 4.00
Saucer, Gold Trim 3.50

Saucer, Pastel
  Bands . . . . 6.00 to 7.00
Sugar, Pastel Bands 20.00
Sugar & Creamer,
  Gold Trim 18.00

Crystal
Berry Bowl, Master,
  9 In. 10.00
Butter, Round 25.00
Cup . . . . 3.00 to 5.00
Cup & Saucer 15.00
Plate, Dinner, 9 In. 9.00
Salver, 11 In. 10.00
Tidbit, 2 Tiers, Silver
  Handle & Base 38.00

Monax
Cup & Saucer,
  Gold Trim 13.50
Plate, Dinner,
  9 In. . . . . 8.00 to 15.00
Plate, Dinner, Gold Trim,
  9 In. 16.00
Plate, Dinner, Japanese
  Garden Scene, 9 In. 24.00
Plate, Dinner, Pastel
  Bands, 9 In. 15.00
Plate, Salad, Gold Trim,
  8 In. 10.00
Plate, Salad, Strawberries,
  Gold Trim, 8 In. 20.00
Saucer . . . . 3.00 to 6.00
Soup, Cream,
  4 1/2 In. 12.00
Sugar . . . . 6.00 to 11.00

Monax Florette
Creamer 12.00
Cup 11.00
Cup & Saucer . . . 12.00 to 15.00
Luncheon Set,
  15 Piece 175.00
Plate, Dinner, 9 In. 20.00
Plate, Salad,
  8 In. . . . . 9.00 to 15.00
Plate, Sherbet, 6 In. 10.00
Platter, Oval, 13 In. 25.00
Salver, 11 In. . . . 18.00 to 30.00
Saucer . . . . 3.00 to 5.00
Soup, Dish, 7 In. 93.00
Sugar & Creamer 26.00

Pink
Berry Bowl, Master,
  8 1/2 In. 28.00

Bowl, Cereal, 5 3/4 In. . . . 20.00
Creamer . . . . . . 15.00 to 16.00
Cup 7.50
Cup & Saucer . . . 10.00 to 12.00
Plate, Dinner,
  9 In. . . . . 15.00 to 19.00
Plate, Salad, 8 1/2 In. 12.00
Platter, Oval, 13 In. 20.00
Salver, 11 In. 20.00
Sugar . . . . 8.00 to 16.00
Sugar & Creamer 32.00

PETTICOAT
See Ripple

PIE CRUST
See Cremax

PILLAR FLUTE

Pillar Flute was made by
Imperial Glass Company,
Bellaire, Ohio, in Amber,
Blue, Crystal, Green, and a
pink called Rose Marie. It
was made about 1930.

Green
Cup 15.00
Pitcher, 60 Oz.,
  8 1/2 In. 85.00
Plate, 8 In. 7.00
Sherbet 20.00
Tumbler, Whiskey,
  1 1/2 Oz. 18.00

Rose Marie
Cake Plate, Footed,
  12 In. 31.00
Cup 15.00
Tumbler, Whiskey,
  1 1/2 Oz. 18.00

PINEAPPLE & FLORAL
See No. 618

PINWHEEL
See Sierra

PIONEER FEDERAL

Pioneer, by Federal Glass
Company, Columbus,
Ohio, was first made in
Pink in the 1930s. In the
1940s, the dishes were
made in Crystal. The
pattern continued to be
produced until 1973.

Crystal
Bowl, Ruffled Edge,
  11 In. 15.00
Nut Bowl, Chrome
  Pedestal, Pick Holder &
  Handle, 4 1/2 In. 75.00
Plate, Fruit, 12 In. 18.00
Plate, Ruffled Edge,
  12 In. 20.00
Plate, Ruffled Edge,
  Smoke Tint,12 In. 15.00

Pink
Bowl, 10 1/2 In. 14.00

PIONEER FOSTORIA

Fostoria Glass Company's
Pioneer pattern was made
in Amber, Azure, Blue,
Burgundy, Ebony, Empire
Green, Green, Regal Blue,
Rose, and Ruby. Most
pieces were made be-
tween 1926 and 1941,
although a few were made
until 1960.

Green
Bowl, 8 In. 12.00
Cup 6.00
Cup & Saucer 10.00
Relish, 3 Sections 40.00
Vase, 7 7/8 In. 170.00

PLANTATION

Plantation was made by A.H. Heisey & Company, Newark, Ohio, from 1948 to 1957. The stemware has a faceted pineapple stem, and other pieces have embossed pineapple borders. The pattern was made in Crystal, some with the Plantation Ivy etching.

Bowl, Ivy Etch,
12 1/2 In. 75.00
Cup & Saucer 70.00
Goblet, 10 Oz. . . 45.00 to 57.00
Goblet, Claret, 4 Oz. 50.00
Goblet, Cocktail, Ivy Etch,
3 1/2 Oz. 70.00
Goblet, Wine, 3 Oz. 50.00
Plate, 8 In. 38.00
Relish, 3 Sections,
11 In. . . . . 58.00 to 75.00
Snack Tray, Cup, 7 In. . . 425.00
Sugar, Footed 40.00
Syrup, Cover 160.00
Tumbler, Iced Tea,
12 Oz. 85.00
Tumbler, Juice, Footed,
5 Oz. 48.00

POINSETTIA
See Floral

POPPY NO. 1
See Florentine No. 1

POPPY NO. 2
See Florentine No. 2

PORTIA

Portia was made by Cambridge Glass Company from 1932 until the early 1950s. It was made in Amber, Crown Tuscan, Crystal, Green, Heatherbloom (lavender), and Yellow.

Crown Tuscan
Candlestick, 2-Light,
Gold Encrusted, Keyhole,
6 In. 150.00
Vase, Gold Encrusted,
6 1/8 x 7 In. 230.00

Crystal
Bonbon, Handles,
5 1/4 In. 25.00
Bowl, Footed, Handles . . . 27.00
Compote, Nude Stem,
8 1/4 x 6 1/2 In. 1330.00
Cup & Saucer 28.00
Goblet, 10 Oz., 8 1/4 In. . . 45.00

❖

If you receive a package of glass antiques during cold weather, let it sit inside for a few hours before you unpack it. The glass must return to room temperature slowly or it may crack.

❖

Goblet, Champagne,
7 Oz., 6 5/8 In. 15.00
Goblet, Wine, 2 1/2 Oz.,
7 3/4 In. . . . . . . 21.00 to 25.00
Pitcher, Doulton,
80 Oz. . . . . . 355.00 to 385.00
Relish, 5 Sections,
12 In. 52.00

Heatherbloom
Bowl, Open Handles,
6 1/2 In. 50.00

PRELUDE

Viking Glass Company introduced the Prelude etch about 1945, after the company took over the New Martinsville Glass Company. The etch was used on Crystal items made from New Martinsville molds.

Bowl, Ruffled Edge,
12 In. . . . . 55.00 to 85.00
Candlestick, 2-Light,
5 In., Pair 65.00
Candy Dish, Cover,
6 3/4 In. 90.00
Compote, 5 1/2 In. 29.00
Creamer 15.00
Pitcher, 78 Oz. 250.00
Plate, 14 In. 45.00
Tray, Center Handle,
11 In. 35.00
Tumbler, Iced Tea, Footed,
13 Oz. 23.00

PRETTY POLLY PARTY
DISHES
See Doric & Pansy

PRETZEL

Pretzel, also called No. 622 or Ribbon Candy, was made by Indiana Glass Company, Dunkirk, Indiana, in the 1930s. Avocado, Crystal, and Teal pieces were made. Some reproductions appeared in the 1970s in Amber and Blue.

Avocado
Celery Dish, 10 1/4 In. 6.00

Crystal
Berry Bowl, 9 3/8 In. 20.00
Bowl, Fruit, 4 1/2 In. 5.00
Celery Dish, 10 1/4 In. 3.00
Creamer . . . . 5.00 to 7.00
Cup 5.00
Cup & Saucer . . . . 7.00 to 10.00
Plate, Dinner,
 9 3/8 In. . . . . 8.00 to 13.00
Plate, Dinner, Fruit
 Center, 9 3/8 In. 20.00
Plate, Salad,
 8 3/8 In. . . . . 6.00 to 7.00
Plate, Tab Handle,
 6 In. . . . . 3.00 to 4.00
Sandwich Server,
 11 1/2 In. . . . . . 11.00 to 13.00
Saucer 1.00
Snack Plate, Square, Indent,
 7 1/4 In. 8.00
Soup, Dish,
 7 1/2 In. . . . . 8.00 to 14.00
Soup, Dish, Frosted,
 7 1/2 In. 12.00
Sugar 7.00
Sugar & Creamer 13.00
Tumbler, 9 Oz.,
 4 1/2 In. 50.00
Tumbler, 12 Oz.,
 5 1/2 In. 110.00

PRIMO

Green and Mandarin Yellow are the two colors of Primo advertised in the 1932 U.S. Glass Company catalog.

Green
Ashtray 10.00
Cup 12.00
Mandarin Yellow
Plate, 7 1/2 In. 15.00
Tumbler, Footed, 9 Oz. . . 22.00

PRIMROSE

Primrose was a pattern made by Anchor Hocking Glass Corporation, Lancaster, Ohio, from 1960 to 1962. The white opaque glass was decorated with a red primrose. Other related patterns are listed in the Fire-King section in this book.

Bowl, Dessert, 4 5/8 In. . . . 4.00
Cake Pan, 8 In. 16.00
Casserole, Cover,
 1 1/2 Qt. 12.00
Cup, 8 Oz. 3.00

Cup, Snack, 5 Oz. 2.00
Custard Cup, 6 Oz.,
 3 3/4 In. 4.00
Loaf Pan, 5 x 9 In. 15.00
Plate, Dinner, 9 1/8 In. 9.00
Platter, Oval, 12 In. 10.00
Saucer 1.00
Snack Set, Box,
 8 Piece 30.00
Snack Tray, 11 x 6 In. 3.00
Soup, Dish, 6 5/8 In. 10.00
Sugar 5.00
Sugar, Cover 10.00

PRIMUS
See Madrid

PRINCESS

Hocking Glass Company, Lancaster, Ohio, made the popular Princess pattern from 1931 to 1935. The first sets were made in Green and two shades of yellow, Apricot and Topaz, so if you are assembling a set, be careful of the color variations. Pink was added last. Blue pieces are found in the West. Some pieces have a frosted finish, some are decorated with hand-painted flowers. Green is sometimes trimmed with gold; other colors are sometimes trimmed with platinum. This pattern is also called Drape & Tassel, Lincoln Drape, or Tassel.

Reproductions have been made.

Apricot

Cup . . . . 7.00 to 10.00
Cup & Saucer 9.00
Grill Plate, Closed Handle,
　10 1/2 In. 10.00
Plate, Dinner,
　9 1/2 In. . . . . . 15.00 to 19.00
Plate, Sherbet, 5 1/2 In. . . . 4.00
Tumbler, Footed, 10 Oz.,
　5 1/4 In. . . . . . 21.00 to 30.00
Tumbler, Iced Tea,
　13 Oz., 5 1/2 In. 39.00

Green

Berry Bowl,
　4 1/2 In. . . . . . 30.00 to 40.00
Bowl, Cereal,
　5 In. . . . . 45.00 to 50.00
Bowl, Hat Shape,
　9 1/2 In. . . . . . 50.00 to 85.00
Bowl, Salad, 8 Sides,
　9 In. . . . . 55.00 to 65.00
Bowl, Vegetable, Oval,
　10 In. . . . . 35.00 to 50.00
Butter,
　Cover . . . . . . 120.00 to 150.00
Butter, No Cover 35.00
Cake Stand,
　10 In. . . . . 30.00 to 50.00
Candy Dish,
　Cover Only 40.00
Candy Dish, Cover,
　9 In. . . . . 65.00 to 70.00
Cookie Jar,
　Cover . . . . 56.00 to 75.00
Cookie Jar, Cover Only . . 38.00
Cookie Jar, No Cover 20.00
Cup . . . . 10.00 to 19.00
Cup & Saucer . . . 19.00 to 26.00
Grill Plate, 9 1/2 In. 20.00
Pitcher, Juice, 37 Oz.,
　6 In. 70.00
Pitcher, Water, 60 Oz.,
　8 In. . . . . 60.00 to 70.00
Plate, Dinner,
　9 1/2 In. . . . . . 28.00 to 45.00
Plate, Salad, 8 In. 25.00
Plate, Sherbet, 5 1/2 In. . . . 8.00
Platter, Handles,
　12 In. . . . . 30.00 to 55.00
Salt & Pepper, 4 1/2 In. . . 80.00
Saltshaker, 4 1/2 In. 25.00

Sandwich Server, Handles,
　10 1/4 In. 65.00
Saucer . . . . 10.00 to 11.00
Sherbet . . . . 20.00 to 30.00
Spice Shaker, 5 1/2 In.,
　Pair . . . . 55.00 to 60.00
Sugar,
　Cover Only . . . 35.00 to 40.00
Sugar & Creamer,
　Cover 75.00
Tumbler, Juice, 5 Oz.,
　3 In. 40.00
Tumbler, Water, 9 Oz.,
　4 In. . . . . 35.00 to 38.00
Vase, 8 In. . . . . . . 45.00 to 65.00

Pink

Berry Bowl, 4 1/2 In. 33.00
Bowl, Cereal, 5 In. 47.00
Bowl, Cereal, Frosted,
　5 In. 35.00
Bowl, Hat Shape,
　9 1/2 In. . . . . . 65.00 to 80.00
Bowl, Salad, 8 Sides,
　9 In. 65.00
Bowl, Vegetable, Oval,
　10 In. . . . . 35.00 to 45.00
Butter, Cover 130.00
Butter, No
　Cover . . . . 30.00 to 35.00
Cake Stand,
　10 In. . . . . 50.00 to 85.00
Candy Dish, Cover,
　9 In. . . . . 60.00 to 78.00
Candy Dish, No Cover . . . 20.00
Candy Jar, Cover Only . . . 40.00
Cookie Jar, Cover 60.00
Cookie Jar, Frosted 65.00
Creamer 15.00
Cup . . . . 12.00 to 15.00
Cup & Saucer . . 22.00 to 24.00
Grill Plate, 9 1/2 In. 16.00
Grill Plate,
　10 1/2 In. . . . . 12.00 to 15.00
Pitcher, Juice, 37 Oz.,
　6 In. 80.00
Pitcher, Water, 60 Oz.,
　8 In. 78.00
Plate, Dinner,
　9 1/2 In. . . . . . 25.00 to 45.00
Plate, Salad, 8 In. 22.00
Plate, Sherbet,
　5 1/2 In. . . . . . . 8.00 to 10.00
Platter, Handles, 12 In. . . . 25.00

Sherbet . . . . 24.00 to 28.00
Tumbler, Footed, 10 Oz.,
　5 1/4 In. 35.00
Tumbler, Footed,
　12 1/2 Oz., 6 1/2 In. . . 130.00

Topaz

Bowl, Cereal, 5 In. 45.00
Cup . . . . 9.00 to 15.00
Cup & Saucer . . . 12.00 to 23.00
Grill Plate,
　9 1/2 In. . . . . . 10.00 to 15.00
Plate, Dinner,
　9 1/2 In. . . . . . 25.00 to 30.00
Plate, Salad,
　8 In. . . . . 12.00 to 22.00
Plate, Sherbet,
　5 1/2 In. . . . . . . 8.00 to 10.00
Sherbet . . . . 25.00 to 48.00
Sugar 20.00
Sugar & Creamer 40.00
Sugar & Creamer,
　Cover 52.00
Tumbler, Footed, 10 Oz.,
　5 1/4 In. . . . . . 22.00 to 30.00
Tumbler, Iced Tea,
　13 Oz., 5 1/4 In. 30.00

PRINCESS FEATHER

Westmoreland Glass Company made Princess Feather pattern from 1939 through 1948. It was originally made in Aqua, Crystal, Green, and Pink. In the 1960s a reproduction appeared in an amber shade called Golden Sunset. The pattern is sometimes called Early

American, Flower, Oatmeal Lace, or Scroll & Star. Reproductions have been made.

Crystal

Basket, Handle,
7 1/4 In. 125.00
Goblet, Champagne,
5 Oz. 9.00
Goblet, Water, 8 Oz. 7.00
Nappy, 6 3/4 In. 10.00
Plate, 8 In. 12.00
Punch Set, 12 Piece 269.00
Saltshaker 7.00
Sandwich Server,
13 1/2 In. 9.50
Sherbet, 5 Oz. 5.00

Pink

Compote 27.00

PRISMATIC LINE
See Queen Mary

PROVINCIAL

Provincial pattern, originally named Whirlpool, was made by A.H. Heisey & Company from 1939 to 1957. Pieces were first made in Crystal, then in Limelight (an alternate name for the turquoise Zircon color) after 1956. Beverage ware and a few table accessories were reissued by Imperial Glass Company in Amber, Cobalt Blue, Crystal, Heather (lavender), Nut Brown, Ruby, Stiegel Green, Sunshine Yellow, Ultra Blue, and Verde (olive green),

Crystal

Goblet, 10 Oz. 15.00
Sherbet, 5 Oz. 12.00
Tumbler, Juice, Footed,
5 Oz. 11.00

Limelight

Relish, 4 Sections,
10 In. 225.00
Tumbler, Iced Tea,
12 Oz. 95.00

PYRAMID
See No. 610

PYREX

Pyrex Ovenware was introduced in 1915 by the Corning Glass Works of Corning, New York. The early heat-resistant cookware was made of clear glass. Pyrex Flameware was introduced in 1936 for stove-top cooking. In 1947, Corning started making opaque white Pyrex cookware and dinnerware. The outside of the dishes had printed decorations, colored bands, or were covered with fired-on colors, such as Dove Gray, Flamingo (red orange), Lime (chartreuse), Regency Green, and Turquoise Blue.

Crystal

Refrigerator Dish, Cover,
No. 620, 1 1/2 Qt. 30.00

White

Bowl, Tab Handle, Fired-On
Brown, 1 1/2 Pt. 4.00
Casserole, Cover, Blue, Bluebird
Decal, 2 1/2 Qt. 32.50

Mixing Bowl, Fired-On
Pink, 2 1/2 Qt. 25.00
Mixing Bowl, Fired-On
Turquoise, 8 1/2 In. 15.00
Refrigerator Dish, Cover, Fired-
On Brown, 1 1/2 Pt. 6.00
Refrigerator Dish, Cover, Fired-
On Red, 1 1/2 Cup 3.00
Refrigerator Dish, Cover, Fired-
On Turquoise, 1 1/2 Pt. .. 6.00
Refrigerator Dish, Cover, Fired-
On Yellow, 1 1/2 Qt. 6.00
Refrigerator Dish, Cover,
Turquoise, Butterprint
Decal, 1 1/2 Qt. 7.50

QUEEN ANN

The Queen Ann pattern was made in Crystal by A.H. Heisey & Company from 1938 to 1957. Pieces are often confused with Heisey's Empress pattern. There are two differences. Empress was not made in Crystal and Queen Ann has an undulating interior surface.

Bowl, Dressing, Dolphin
Footed, 6 3/4 In. 25.00
Bowl, Floral, 8 In. 25.00
Candlestick, 8 In., Pair .. 175.00
Punch Cup 15.00
Soup, Cream 20.00

QUEEN MARY

Queen Mary, sometimes called Prismatic Line or Vertical Ribbed, was made

by Anchor Hocking Glass Corporation from 1936 to 1943. It was first made in Pink, later in Crystal. Ashtrays were made in Forest Green and Royal Ruby in the 1950s.

Crystal

Ashtray, 3 1/2 In. 2.00
Ashtray, Oval,
   2 x 3 3/4 In. 3.00
Candlestick, 2-Light,
   4 1/2 In. 8.00
Candlestick, 2-Light,
   4 1/2 In., Pair .. 15.00 to 25.00
Candlestick, 3-Light 45.00
Candy Dish,
   Cover .... 22.00 to 25.00
Coaster, 3 1/2 In. 3.00
Compote, 5 3/4 In. 15.00
Creamer, Oval ... 5.00 to 10.00
Cup, Large 12.00
Cup & Saucer 15.00
Plate, Dinner, 9 3/4 In. ... 23.00
Plate, Salad, 8 3/4 In. 6.00
Plate, Sherbet 5.00
Sandwich Server,
   12 In. .... 11.00 to 28.00
Saucer 3.00
Sugar, Oval .... 6.00 to 7.00
Sugar & Creamer 15.00

Pink

Berry Bowl,
   4 1/2 In. .... 9.00 to 10.00
Berry Bowl, 5 In. 9.00
Berry Bowl, Master,
   8 3/4 In. 16.00
Bowl, 4 In. 8.00
Bowl, Cereal, 6 In. 23.00
Bowl, Flared Top,
   2 3/4 x 2 1/2 In. 15.00
Bowl, Handle,
   4 In. .... 8.00 to 12.00
Bowl, Handles, 5 1/2 In. .. 18.00
Bowl, Vegetable, Vertical
   Ribbed, 8 1/4 In. 53.00
Butter, No Cover 40.00
Celery Dish, Oval 33.00
Creamer, Oval .. 10.00 to 18.00
Cup, Large ...... 7.00 to 12.00
Cup, Small ...... 8.00 to 15.00

Cup & Saucer, Large 12.00
Plate, Bread & Butter,
   6 1/2 In. 10.00
Plate, Dinner, 9 3/4 In. ... 65.00
Saucer .... 5.00 to 8.00
Sherbet .... 7.00 to 11.00
Sugar, Oval .... 12.00 to 15.00
Sugar & Creamer 25.00
Tumbler, Juice, 5 Oz.,
   3 1/2 In. ...... 12.00 to 20.00
Tumbler, Water, 9 Oz.,
   4 In. .... 15.00 to 24.00

RADIANCE

New Martinsville Glass Company, New Martinsville, West Virginia, made Radiance pattern, Line No. 42, from 1936 to 1939. It was made in Amber, Crystal, Emerald Green, Ice Blue, Pink, and Red. A few rare pieces were made in Cobalt Blue. A pattern by the same name was made by Cambridge.

Amber

Punch Set, Bowl, Cups,
   13 Piece 275.00

Cobalt Blue

Goblet, Cordial,
   1 Oz. .... 40.00 to 55.00

Crystal

Bowl, 2 Sections, Ruffled
   Edge, 7 In. 19.00
Butter, Cover 100.00
Celery Dish, Oval,
   10 In. 28.00
Compote, 6 In. 20.00
Punch Cup 35.00
Relish, Gold Encrusted,
   3 Sections, Handles,
   7 In. 20.00
Sugar & Creamer 33.00

Sugar & Creamer,
   Rose Etch 25.00
Sugar & Creamer, Tray,
   Etched Flowers 95.00
Vase, Flared, 10 In. 45.00

Ice Blue

Bonbon, 6 In. 40.00
Bowl, Flared, 10 In. 75.00
Candlestick, 2-Light,
   Pair 175.00
Cheese & Cracker Set, Enameled
   Flowers 195.00
Creamer, Meadow Wreath
   Etch 45.00
Cup & Saucer 28.00
Nut Bowl, 5 In. .. 30.00 to 33.00
Punch Cup ..... 12.00 to 15.00

Red

Bonbon, 6 In. ... 35.00 to 40.00
Goblet, Cordial, 1 Oz. ... 40.00
Plate, Luncheon, 8 In. 18.00
Punch Bowl 125.00
Punch Cup 15.00
Punch Set, Bowl, Cups,
   11 Piece 435.00
Relish, 2 Sections, 7 In. .. 58.00
Relish, 3 Sections, 8 In. .. 48.00
Tumbler, 9 Oz. .. 45.00 to 50.00
Vase, Crimped,
   10 In. 170.00

RAINBOW

Rainbow's name comes from the fired-on colors that coat the glassware. Anchor Hocking Glass Company made color-coated crystal pieces from 1938 through the early '50s. Pastel and primary colors were made.

Blue

Creamer, Footed 14.00
Cup 10.00
Plate, Sherbet, 6 1/4 In. .. 10.00
Tumbler, 9 Oz. 19.00

Dark Blue

Bowl, Deep, 5 1/4 In. 12.00
Platter, 11 In. 100.00

Dark Green
Bowl, Deep, 5 1/4 In. 12.00
Dark Yellow
Bowl, Deep, 5 1/4 In. 12.00
Green
Plate, Dinner, 9 1/4 In. . . . 16.00
Tumbler, 9 Oz. . . 18.00 to 19.00
Red
Bowl, Deep, 5 1/4 In. 12.00
Bowl, Fruit, 6 In. 9.00
Creamer, Footed 14.00
Cup 10.00
Jug, Ball, 80 Oz. 80.00
Plate, Salad, 7 1/4 In. 10.00
Sherbet, Footed 14.00
Sugar, Footed 14.00
Tumbler, 9 Oz. 19.00
Yellow
Cup 10.00
Plate, Dinner, 9 1/4 In. . . . 16.00
Plate, Salad, 7 1/4 In. 10.00
Sherbet, Footed 14.00
Tumbler, 9 Oz. 19.00

RAINBOW STARS
See Thousand Line

RAINDROPS

Watch out for confusion between Raindrops and another pattern called Pear Optic or Thumbprint. The rounded, fingernail-shaped impressions of the Raindrops pattern are on the inside of the pieces; the other pattern has hexagonal depressions on the outside. Federal Glass Company made Crystal and Green Raindrops luncheon sets from 1929 to 1933.

Crystal
Tumbler, Whiskey, 1 Oz.,
   1 7/8 In. 7.00
Green
Bowl, Cereal, 6 In. 15.00
Cup & Saucer 12.00
Sugar 10.00
Tumbler, 5 Oz.,
   3 7/8 In. . . . . 7.00 to 12.00

RAMBLER

Rambler etch features a climbing rose bush. Fostoria Glass Company used the etch from 1935 to 1957 on Burgundy, Crystal, Empire Green, Iridescent, Regal Blue, and Ruby glassware.

Crystal
Goblet, Champagne, Platinum
   Rim, 6 Oz., 7 1/2 In. . . . 42.00
Goblet, Water, 10 Oz.,
   6 7/8 In. 22.00
Relish, 6 Sections,
   13 1/2 In. 40.00
Sherbet 23.00
Ruby
Bowl, 10 1/2 In. 85.00
Vase . . . . : . 50.00

RASPBERRY BAND
See Laurel

REEDED

Reeded, or Spun, was made by Imperial Glass Company, Bellaire, Ohio, in 1935 in Aqua, Cobalt Blue, Crystal, Fired-On Orange, Red, Stiegel Green, and other colors.

Amber
Sugar & Creamer 22.00
Cobalt Blue
Creamer 25.00
Crystal
Pitcher 45.00

Tumbler 7.00
Stiegel Green
Creamer 25.00
Pitcher, Ice Lip, Applied
   Crystal Handle, 8 In. . . . 95.00
Sugar & Creamer 55.00
Vase, Bud, 6 In. 35.00

RESTAURANT WARE
See Fire-King

REX
See No. 610

RIBBED
See Manhattan

RIBBON

Black, Crystal, Green, and Pink pieces were made in Ribbon pattern in the 1930s. The pattern was made by the Hazel Atlas Glass Company.

Green
Candy Dish 45.00
Candy Dish, Cover 75.00
Creamer, Footed 15.00
Cup & Saucer 8.00
Plate, Luncheon,
   8 In. . . . . 10.00 to 12.00
Plate, Sherbet,
   6 1/4 In. . . . . 3.00 to 4.00
Salt & Pepper . . . 28.00 to 38.00
Sherbet, Footed . . 6.00 to 14.00
Sugar, Footed 15.00
Sugar & Creamer,
   Footed 36.00

RIBBON CANDY
See Pretzel

RIDGELEIGH

A.H. Heisey & Company, Newark, Ohio, made Ridgeleigh from 1935 to 1944. The pattern has narrow, prismlike vertical ribs and is similar to Anchor Hocking's Queen Mary and Fenton's Sheffield patterns. Many of the Heisey pieces are marked with the Diamond H logo. Items were made mostly in Crystal, although some pieces are available in Sahara (yellow) and Zircon (light turquoise).

Crystal

Ashtray, Square	10.00
Ashtray Set, Bridge, Diamond, Heart, Spade, Club, 4 Piece	125.00
Box, Cover, 6 In.	21.00
Candlestick, 2 In.	125.00
Candlestick, 2-Light, Bobeche, Prisms, Pair	140.00
Candlestick, Prisms, 10 In.	51.00
Celery Dish, 12 In.	40.00
Cheese Dish, Handles, 6 In.	25.00
Creamer	17.00
Creamer, Individual	20.00
Dish, Lemon, No Cover, 5 In.	8.00
Dish, Mayonnaise, Underplate	19.00 to 25.00
Goblet, Champagne, Blown, 5 Oz.	25.00
Jam Jar, Cover	35.00

Nappy, Scalloped Edge, 4 1/2 In.	10.00
Nut Dish, Tab Handles, 4 1/2 In.	8.00
Plate, 6 In.	9.00
Plate, Salad, 8 1/4 In.	15.00 to 18.00
Plate, Salad, Square, 8 In.	24.00
Plate, Square, 6 In.	15.00
Relish, 3 Sections, 11 In.	24.00
Salt, Individual	4.50
Sherbet, 6 Oz.	15.00
Sugar	15.00
Sugar & Creamer	40.00 to 50.00
Torte Plate, 13 In.	45.00
Tray, 10 1/2 In.	10.00 to 13.00
Tumbler, Whiskey, 2 1/2 Oz.	32.00 to 40.00
Vase, 9 In.	90.00

Sahara

Bowl, Fruit, 12 In.	90.00
Vase, 8 In.	150.00

Zircon

Ashtray, Square	46.00

RING

Hocking Glass Company made Ring from 1927 to 1933. The pattern, also known as Banded Rings, sometimes has colored rings added to the Crystal, Green, Mayfair Blue, Pink, or Red glass. The colored rings were made in various combinations of black, blue, orange, pink, platinum, red, and yellow. Platinum trim is on some pieces. Some solid red pieces also were made. The design is characterized by several sets of rings, each composed of four rings. Circle, a similar Hocking pattern, has only one group of rings.

Crystal

Berry Bowl, 5 In.	4.25
Cocktail Shaker, Cover	95.00
Cup & Saucer	5.95
Decanter	10.00
Decanter, Colored Rings, Stopper	45.00
Decanter, Gold Rings, Stopper	42.00
Decanter, Stopper	23.00 to 35.00
Goblet, Water, 9 Oz., 7 1/4 In.	7.00 to 10.00
Goblet, Water, Platinum Rim, 9 Oz., 7 1/4 In.	15.00
Ice Tub	18.00 to 24.00
Pitcher, 60 Oz., 8 In.	18.00
Pitcher, 80 Oz., 8 1/2 In.	30.00
Pitcher, Multicolored Rings, 60 Oz., 8 In.	95.00
Plate, Platinum Rim, 60 Oz., 8 In.	22.55
Plate, Sherbet, 6 1/4 In.	15.00
Saucer	1.00
Sherbet, Footed, 4 3/4 In.	7.00 to 10.00
Soup, Dish, Platinum, 7 In.	8.50
Sugar	15.00
Tumbler, 4 Oz., 3 In.	4.00
Tumbler, 5 Oz., 3 1/2 In.	3.00 to 5.00
Tumbler, 10 Oz., 4 3/4 In.	5.00
Tumbler, Gold Rim, 10 Oz., 4 3/4 In.	9.00
Tumbler, Iced Tea, Footed, Platinum Rim, 6 1/2 In.	10.00
Tumbler, Juice, Footed, Gold Rim, 3 1/2 In.	6.00 to 8.00

Tumbler, Whiskey,
1 1/2 Oz., 2 In. 9.00
Vase, 8 In. 45.00

Green

Pitcher, 80 Oz.,
8 1/2 In. 125.00
Plate, Off-Center Ring,
6 1/2 In. . . . . 5.00 to 21.00
Sugar 8.00
Vase, 8 In. . . . . . . 31.00 to 35.00

RING-DING

Ring-Ding was made in
1932 by Hocking Glass
Company of Lancaster,
Ohio. Painted bands of
green, orange, red, and
yellow decorate the clear
glass and gave the pattern
its name.

Pitcher, 80 Oz.,
8 1/4 In. 60.00
Tumbler, 10 Oz., 4 In. . . . 15.00

RIPPLE

Ripple was made by Hazel
Atlas Glass Company in
the early 1950s. The
dishes are Platonite, an
almost-white glass, with
fired-on pink and blue
coatings. Collectors used
to call the pattern Crinoline or Petticoat because
the plates and bowls have
ruffled edges.

Berry Bowl, Fired-On Pink,
5 In. . . . . 3.00 to 7.50
Bowl, Cereal, Fired-On Pink,
5 5/8 In. 8.00
Creamer, Fired-On Blue . . . 4.50
Cup & Saucer, Fired-On
Blue 7.00
Cup & Saucer, Fired-On
Pink 15.00
Luncheon Set, Fired-On Pink,
Box, 16 Piece 135.00
Plate, Luncheon, Fired-On Blue,
8 7/8 In. 7.50
Plate, Luncheon, Fired-On Pink,
8 7/8 In. 9.00
Plate, Salad, 6 7/8 In. 4.50

ROCK CRYSTAL

Rock Crystal, sometimes
called Early American
Rock Crystal, was made in
many solid colors by
McKee Glass Company.
Amber, Amberina, Blue-
Green, Cobalt Blue, Crys-
tal, Green, Pink, Red, and
Yellow pieces were made
in the 1920s and 1930s.

Amber

Goblet, 7 Oz. 25.00
Goblet, Champagne,
6 Oz. 20.00
Goblet, Cocktail,
3 1/2 Oz. 24.00
Parfait, Footed, 3 1/2 In. . . 33.00

Pitcher, Fancy
Tankard . . . . 595.00 to 650.00
Sandwich Server, Center
Handle, 10 3/4 In. 45.00
Vase, Footed, Gold Trim,
11 In. 150.00

Amberina

Goblet, Wine, 3 Oz. 50.00

Crystal

Bowl, Center, Footed,
12 1/2 In. . . . . . 55.00 to 75.00
Candlestick,
2-Light . . . . 20.00 to 25.00
Candlestick, 2-Light,
Pair . . . . 55.00 to 65.00
Candlestick, 5 1/2 In.,
Pair 45.00
Celery Dish, 12 In. 32.00
Compote, 7 In. 35.00
Dish, Ice 45.00
Dish, Sundae, Footed,
6 Oz. 12.00
Eggcup 65.00
Finger Bowl,
Underplate 35.00
Goblet, Champagne,
6 Oz. . . . . 16.00 to 20.00
Goblet, Cocktail,
3 1/2 Oz. 18.00
Goblet, Cordial,
1 Oz. . . . . 20.00 to 25.00
Goblet, Water,
8 Oz. . . . . 16.00 to 23.00
Goblet, Wine,
2 Oz. . . . . 18.00 to 20.00
Goblet, Wine, 3 Oz. 23.00
Pitcher, 48 Oz.,
9 In. . . . . 145.00 to 230.00
Plate, Dinner, Scalloped Edge,
10 1/2 In. 100.00
Plate, Scalloped Edge,
7 1/2 In. . . . . 8.00 to 12.00
Plate, Scalloped Edge,
8 1/2 In. 10.00
Plate, Scalloped Edge,
11 1/2 In. 20.00
Relish, 2 Sections,
11 1/2 In. . . . . . 26.00 to 32.00
Relish, 5 Sections,
12 1/2 In. . . . . . 30.00 to 45.00
Sherbet 14.00
Tumbler, Concave,
12 Oz. 35.00
Tumbler, Juice, 5 Oz. 24.00

Tumbler, Whiskey,
2 1/2 Oz. . . . . . 20.00 to 25.00
Water Set, 6 Piece 300.00

Green
Bowl, Center, Footed,
12 1/2 In. 120.00
Goblet, Champagne,
6 Oz. 25.00
Pitcher, Fancy Tankard,
9 In. 600.00
Plate, 7 1/2 In. 12.00
Relish, 2 Sections,
11 1/2 In. 60.00
Sandwich Server, Center
Handle, Black Trim,
10 3/4 In. 35.00
Vase, Footed, Gold Trim,
11 In. 125.00

Pink
Compote, 7 In. 75.00
Dish, Sundae, Footed,
6 Oz. 18.00

Red
Candy Dish, Cover,
Footed, 9 1/4 In. 110.00
Candy Jar, Cover,
16 Oz. 165.00
Compote, 7 In. 95.00
Dish, Sundae,
Footed, 6 Oz. 35.00
Finger Bowl,
5 In. . . . . 60.00 to 70.00
Finger Bowl,
Underplate 75.00
Goblet, Water,
8 Oz. . . . . . 65.00 to 110.00
Plate, 7 1/2 In. 20.00
Plate, 8 1/2 In. 30.00
Plate, Scalloped Edge,
11 1/2 In. 175.00

❖

**Rotate your dining
room, kitchen, and
coffee tables on your
birthday. If you
remember to do this
each year, the furniture
will fade evenly.**

❖

Sugar 45.00
Tray, 13 In. 125.00
Tumbler, Whiskey,
2 1/2 Oz. 50.00

ROMANCE

Fostoria Glass Company,
Moundsville, West Vir-
ginia, made items with the
Romance etching from
1942 to 1986. The pattern
is easily confused with June,
another Fostoria pattern
with an etching, because
both etchings include a
bow. The Romance etch-
ing is used on heavier
blanks, and the border
between the floral sprays
is a different design.
Romance pieces are
always Crystal.

Candlestick, 2-Light,
5 1/2 In. 40.00
Candlestick, 3-Light,
8 In., Pair 145.00
Cup & Saucer 25.00
Dish, Mayonnaise,
Underplate 40.00
Goblet, Champagne, 6 Oz.,
5 1/2 In. . . . . . 11.00 to 17.00
Goblet, Cocktail, 3 1/2 Oz.,
4 7/8 In. . . . . . 20.00 to 24.00
Goblet, Wine, 3 Oz.,
5 1/2 In. 39.00
Plate, 6 In. 10.00
Plate, 7 In. 12.00
Plate, 8 In. 21.00
Sherbet, 4 1/2 In. 15.00
Sugar 17.00
Torte Plate,
14 In. . . . . 45.00 to 50.00
Tumbler, Juice, Footed,
5 Oz., 4 3/4 In. 18.00
Tumbler, Water, Footed,
9 Oz. 22.00

ROOSTER

Roosters were all the rage
for barware in the 1930s
and '40s. Morgantown
Glass Works made its
cocktail set with rooster
stems and a rooster stop-
per for the shaker. Many
colors were used for the
bowls of the cocktail
goblet, combined with a
crystal stem and foot.

Amber
Goblet, Cocktail, 3 Oz.,
3 7/8 In. 50.00

Amethyst
Goblet, Cocktail, 3 Oz.,
3 7/8 In. 45.00

Crystal
Cocktail Set, Red
Stopper, Tumblers,
5 Piece . . . . 75.00 to 90.00
Goblet, Cocktail, 3 Oz.,
3 7/8 In. 50.00
Goblet, Cocktail, Frosted,
3 Oz., 3 7/8 In. 75.00

Green
Goblet, Cocktail, 3 Oz.,
3 7/8 In. 45.00

Light Blue
Goblet, Cocktail, 3 Oz.,
3 7/8 In. 50.00

Mocha
Cocktail, Morgantown,
3 1/2 In. 33.00

ROPE
See Colonial Fluted

ROSALIE

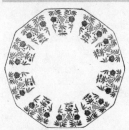

Rosalie etching was made by Cambridge Glass Company, Cambridge, Ohio, in the late 1920s and 1930s. Dishes were made in Amber, Bluebell, Carmen (red), Crystal, Emerald, Heatherbloom (lavender), Peach-Blo, Topaz, and Willow Blue.

Crystal
Cocktail Icer, Insert 35.00
Sugar & Creamer 40.00
Emerald
Bowl, Handles,
    8 1/2 In. 25.00

ROSE CAMEO

Rose Cameo was made by the Belmont Tumbler Company, Bellaire, Ohio, in 1933. It has been found only in Green and only in six different pieces, three of them bowls.

Berry Bowl, 4 1/2 In. 11.00
Bowl, Cereal, 5 In. 22.00
Plate, Salad,
    7 In. . . . . 12.00 to 15.00
Sherbet . . . . 12.00 to 16.00

Tumbler, Flared, Footed,
    5 In. 25.00
Tumbler, Footed, 5 In. . . . 25.00

ROSE ETCH

Rose Etch, also known as Heisey Rose, was made by A.H. Heisey & Company, Newark, Ohio, from 1949 to 1957. The etching was used on Crystal items, mostly from the Waverly and Queen Ann patterns. Most of the pieces are not marked.

Bowl, Floral, 12 In. 41.00
Butter, Cabochon,
    1/4 Lb. 325.00
Cake Plate, Footed,
    15 In. . . . . . . 275.00 to 310.00
Candy Dish, Cover Only,
    Bow Finial, 6 In. 165.00
Cheese Dish, Footed,
    6 1/2 In. 30.00
Compote, Oval,
    5 3/8 x 7 1/4 In. 50.00
Goblet, Champagne,
    6 Oz. . . . . 30.00 to 40.00
Goblet, Cocktail, 4 Oz. . . . 35.00
Goblet, Cordial, 1 Oz. . . 150.00
Goblet, Water, 9 Oz. 45.00
Plate, Dinner, 10 1/2 In. . . 97.00
Plate, Salad,
    8 In. . . . . 30.00 to 32.00
Relish, 3 Sections, 7 In. . . 50.00
Salt & Pepper, Footed . . . 80.00
Sandwich Server, Center
    Handle, 14 In. 219.00
Sandwich Server, Waverly,
    11 In. 65.00

Sugar 35.00
Torte Plate,
    11 In. . . . . 50.00 to 80.00
Torte Plate, 14 In. 100.00
Tumbler, Iced Tea, Footed,
    12 Oz. 68.00
Tumbler, Juice, Footed,
    5 Oz. 58.00
Vase, Violet, Footed,
    4 x 3 1/4 In. 50.00

ROSE LACE
See Royal Lace

ROSE POINT

Rose Point was made by the Cambridge Glass Company of Cambridge, Ohio, from 1936 to 1953. The elaborate pattern was made in Crystal and Crystal with gold trim. A few pieces were made in colors.

Amethyst
Wine, 4 1/2 Oz. 50.00
Crown Tuscan
Plate, Shell, 5 1/2 In. 35.00
Crystal
Basket, 5 In. 325.00
Basket, 10 x 6 3/4 In. . . . 895.00
Basket, Wallace Sterling
    Silver Holder, 6 In. . . . 195.00
Bonbon, Handles,
    6 1/2 In. . . . . 40.00 to 65.00
Bonbon, Handles, Footed,
    7 In. 77.00
Bowl, 4-Footed,
    13 In. . . . . . . 110.00 to 145.00
Bowl, Crimped, Footed,
    10 In. 125.00
Bowl, Handles, Footed,
    10 In. 125.00
Candlestick, 3-Light,
    6 In. 110.00

Candlestick, 3-Light,
6 In., Pair 250.00

Candlestick, 4 In. 45.00

Candlestick, Ram's Head,
4 1/2 x 4 3/4 In. 195.00

Candy Dish, Cover, 3 Sections,
Gold Trim, 8 In. 150.00

Candy Dish, Cover,
5 1/2 In. 230.00

Candy Dish, Cover, Footed,
High, 5 1/2 In. 185.00

Compote, 4-Footed,
6 In. . . . . 55.00 to 65.00

Compote, Blown,
5 3/8 In. . . . . . 85.00 to 100.00

Cup & Saucer 50.00

Decanter, Footed,
14 Oz. 525.00

Decanter, Tall, 28 Oz. . . 795.00

Goblet, Claret,
4 1/2 Oz. 110.00

Goblet, Cocktail, 3 Oz. . . . 25.00

Goblet, Cordial,
1 Oz. . . . . . . 77.00 to 85.00

Goblet, Parfait, Low,
5 Oz. 115.00

Goblet, Water,
10 Oz. . . . . . . 48.00 to 50.00

Goblet, Wine,
3 1/2 Oz. . . . . 65.00 to 75.00

Pitcher, Ball,
80 Oz. . . . . . 355.00 to 400.00

Pitcher, Doulton,
80 Oz. 575.00

Pitcher, Ice Lip,
20 Oz. 395.00

Plate, 7 In. 15.00

Plate, Dinner,
10 1/4 In. 200.00

Plate, Handles, 11 In. 70.00

Plate, Salad,
8 1/2 In. . . . . . 20.00 to 27.00

Relish, 2 Sections, Gold
Trim, 7 In. 31.00

Relish, 3 Sections,
Handles, 11 In. 85.00

Relish, 3 Sections, Handles,
Gold Trim, 10 In. 100.00

Relish, 3 Sections, Wallace
Sterling Silver Base,
6 3/8 In. 195.00

Relish, 5 Sections,
12 In. 75.00

Salt & Pepper, Ball,
2 In. 170.00

Salt & Pepper, Ball, Wallace
Sterling Silver Base,
2 In. 495.00

Salt & Pepper,
Egg Shape 195.00

Sandwich Server, Center Handle,
Square, 10 3/4 In. 230.00

Saucer . . . . 7.00 to 10.00

Sherbet, Low,
6 Oz. . . . . 25.00 to 30.00

Sugar 18.00

Torte Plate, Gold Trim,
14 In. 55.00

Tumbler, Footed,
7 1/2 In. 35.00

Tumbler, Iced Tea, Footed,
Low, 13 Oz. 55.00

Tumbler, Iced Tea, Footed,
Tall, 12 Oz. 145.00

Tumbler, Water, Footed,
Low, 10 Oz. 35.00

Vase, 5 In. 150.00

Vase, Bud, 6 1/8 In. 190.00

Vase, Bud, Footed, 6 In. . . 65.00

Forest Green
Goblet, Wine, 3 1/2 Oz. . . 85.00

Moonlight Blue
Celery Dish, 3 Sections,
2 1/4 x 13 In. 250.00

ROSEMARY

Rosemary, also called
Cabbage Rose with Single
Arch or Dutch Rose, was
made by Federal Glass
Company from 1935 to
1937. It was made in
Amber, Green, Iridescent,
and Pink. Pieces with
bases, like creamers or
cups, are sometimes con-
fused with Mayfair Federal
because the molds used
were those originally

designed for the Mayfair
pattern. The lower half of
the Rosemary pieces are
plain; the lower half of
Mayfair Federal has a band
of arches.

Amber
Creamer 9.00

Cup & Saucer 12.50

Plate, Dinner,
9 1/2 In. . . . . . 10.00 to 13.00

Plate, Salad,
6 3/4 In. . . . . 5.00 to 6.00

Saucer 5.00

Soup, Cream,
5 1/2 In. 18.00

Sugar 7.00

Tumbler, 9 Oz.,
4 1/4 In. . . . . . 28.00 to 31.00

Green
Sugar 14.00

Pink
Creamer 34.00

Plate, Salad,
6 In. . . . . 15.00 to 19.00

Soup, Cream,
5 In. . . . . 65.00 to 80.00

Sugar 33.00

Tumbler, 9 Oz.,
4 1/4 In. 50.00

ROSEMARY
See also Mayfair Federal

ROSES & BOWS
See Paneled Grape

ROULETTE

Hocking Glass Company
made Roulette pattern

from 1935 to 1939. Green luncheon and beverage sets were manufactured, as well as Pink beverage sets and some Crystal pieces. Collectors originally called the pattern Many Windows.

Green

Bowl, Fruit, 9 In.	. . . . 75.00
Cup	. . . . 7.00 to 14.00
Cup & Saucer	. . . 10.00 to 15.00
Plate, Luncheon, 8 In.	. . . . . 10.00
Plate, Sherbet, 6 In.	. . . . . . 5.00
Sandwich Server, 12 In.	. . 65.00
Saucer	. . . . 5.00 to 11.00
Sherbet	. . . . 8.00 to 10.00
Tumbler, Juice, 5 Oz., 3 1/4 In.	. . . . 24.00

Pink

Tumbler, Water, 9 Oz., 4 1/8 In.	. . . . 30.00

ROXANA

Hazel Atlas Glass Company made Roxana pattern in 1932. It was made in Crystal, White, and Yellow.

Yellow

Sherbet	. . . . 9.00 to 15.00
Tumbler, 9 Oz., 4 1/4 In.	. . . . 24.00

ROYAL

Royal etch is a border design of oak leaves and fleur-de-lis. Fostoria Glass Company used the decoration on Amber, Blue, Ebony, and Green dinnerware and accessories from 1925 to 1932.

Amber

Candy Dish, Cover, Footed, 1/4 Lb.	. . . . 75.00
Plate, Bread & Butter, 6 In.	. . . . 7.00

Blue

Candy Dish, Cover, 1/2 Lb.	. . . . 155.00
Plate, Canape, 8 3/4 In.	. . 59.00

Green

Candy Dish, Cover, 3 Sections	. . . . 135.00
Cup & Saucer, Footed	. . . 16.00
Plate, Canape, 8 3/4 In.	. . . . 35.00
Plate, Luncheon, 8 1/2 In.	. . . . 9.00
Soup, Dish, 8 1/2 In.	. . . . . 25.00

ROYAL LACE

Royal Lace was made from 1934 to 1941. The popular pattern by Hazel Atlas Glass Company was made in Cobalt Blue, Crystal, Green, and Pink, and in limited quantities in Amethyst. It is sometimes called Gladiola or Rose Lace. Reproductions have been made.

Amethyst

Toddy Jar, No Cover	. . . . 50.00
Toddy Set, 11 Piece	. . . . 500.00

Cobalt Blue

Berry Bowl, Master, 10 In.	. . . . 80.00 to 100.00
Bowl, 3-Footed, 10 In.	. . . . . . 125.00 to 175.00
Bowl, 3-Footed, Rolled Edge, 10 In.	. . . . 1200.00
Bowl, Vegetable, Oval, 11 In.	. . . . . . 105.00 to 113.00
Butter, Cover	. . . 750.00 to 900.00

Candlestick, Pair	. . . . 135.00
Candlestick, Rolled Edge, Pair	. . . . 600.00
Candlestick, Ruffled Edge, Pair	. . . . 595.00
Cookie Jar, No Cover	. . . . 78.00
Creamer	. . . . 65.00 to 68.00
Cup	. . . . 44.00 to 55.00
Cup & Saucer	. . . 55.00 to 60.00
Grill Plate, 9 7/8 In.	. . . . . 45.00
Pitcher, 48 Oz.	. . . . . 175.00 to 245.00
Pitcher, Ice Lip, 68 Oz., 8 In.	. . . . 500.00
Pitcher, Ice Lip, 96 Oz., 8 1/2 In.	. . . . 650.00
Plate, Dinner, 9 3/4 In.	. . . . . . .48.00 to 65.00
Plate, Luncheon, 8 1/2 In.	. . . . . . 50.00 to 65.00
Plate, Sherbet, 6 In.	. . . . 15.00 to 18.00
Platter, Oval, 13 In.	. . . . 95.00 to 110.00
Salt & Pepper	. . . . 375.00
Saltshaker	. . . . 390.00
Saucer	. . . . 14.00 to 15.00
Sherbet	. . . . 42.00 to 58.00
Sherbet, Chrome Base	. . . . 40.00 to 45.00
Soup, Cream, 4 3/4 In.	. . . . . . 50.00 to 55.00
Sugar, No Cover	. . . . . 50.00 to 68.00
Sugar & Creamer	. . . . . 85.00 to 140.00
Tumbler, 9 Oz., 4 1/8 In.	. . . . . . 50.00 to 57.00
Tumbler, 12 Oz., 5 3/8 In.	. . . . 145.00 to 195.00
Tumbler, Juice, 5 Oz., 3 1/2 In.	. . . . . . 60.00 to 88.00

Crystal

Bowl, 3-Footed, Ruffled Edge, 10 In.	. . . . 95.00 to 105.00
Bowl, Vegetable, Oval, 11 In.	. . . . 35.00
Butter, Cover	. . 80.00 to 125.00
Creamer	. . . . 55.00
Cup	. . . . 45.00
Grill Plate, 9 7/8 In.	. . . . . 15.00
Pitcher, 48 Oz.	. . . . 195.00

Pitcher, Ice Lip, 96 Oz.,
   8 1/2 In. .... 100.00 to 150.00
Plate, Sherbet, 6 In. 7.00
Salt & Pepper ... 45.00 to 60.00
Saltshaker 30.00
Sherbet 9.00
Soup, Cream, 4 3/4 In. ... 12.00
Sugar, Cover 90.00
Sugar, No
   Cover .... 10.00 to 15.00
Sugar & Creamer 24.00
Tumbler, 5 Oz.,
   3 1/2 In. 23.00
Tumbler, 9 Oz.,
   4 1/8 In. ...... 10.00 to 25.00

Green

Bowl, Vegetable, Oval,
   11 In. 85.00
Butter,
   No Cover ... 120.00 to 200.00
Cookie Jar, Cover 130.00
Creamer .... 25.00 to 30.00
Cup .... 20.00 to 30.00
Cup & Saucer 34.00
Pitcher, 64 Oz., 8 In. 195.00
Plate, Dinner, 9 3/4 In. 40.00
Plate, Luncheon,
   8 1/2 In. 45.00
Plate, Sherbet,
   6 In. .... 8.00 to 15.00
Salt & Pepper .. 75.00 to 138.00
Sherbet .... 20.00 to 36.00
Soup, Cream,
   4 3/4 In. ...... 32.00 to 40.00
Sugar, Cover 195.00
Sugar,
   No Cover ..... 22.00 to 45.00
Sugar &
   Creamer ...... 45.00 to 90.00
Tumbler, 5 Oz.,
   3 1/2 In. ...... 51.00 to 60.00
Tumbler, 9 Oz.,
   4 1/8 In. ...... 41.00 to 45.00

Pink

Berry Bowl,
   5 In. .... 58.00 to 75.00
Berry Bowl, 10 In. 30.00
Bowl, 3-Footed,
   10 In. .... 65.00 to 80.00
Bowl, 3-Footed, Rolled Edge,
   10 In. ...... 185.00 to 225.00
Bowl, 3-Footed, Ruffled
   Edge, 10 In. 105.00
Bowl, Vegetable, Oval,
   11 In. 75.00
Butter, Cover Only 100.00
Candlestick, Rolled Edge,
   Pair 140.00
Cookie Jar,
   Cover ...... 95.00 to 98.00
Cookie Jar, No Cover 40.00
Creamer 22.00
Cup 20.00
Cup & Saucer ... 30.00 to 32.00
Pitcher, 64 Oz., 8 In. 160.00
Pitcher, Ice Lip, 96 Oz.,
   8 1/2 In. 240.00
Plate, Sherbet, 6 In. 12.00
Platter, Oval,
   13 In. .... 48.00 to 65.00
Salt & Pepper .. 85.00 to 125.00
Sherbet 30.00
Sugar, Cover 110.00
Sugar,
   No Cover ..... 15.00 to 25.00
Sugar & Creamer,
   Cover 150.00
Tumbler, 5 Oz.,
   3 1/2 In. 60.00
Tumbler, 9 Oz.,
   4 1/8 In. 25.00
Water Set, 7 Piece 275.00

ROYAL RUBY

This pattern is identified
by its bright red color.
Many pieces have plain

shapes. Anchor Hocking
Glass Corporation made it
from 1938 to 1967 and
again from 1973 to 1977.
The same shapes were
made in Forest Green.
These items are listed in
this book under Forest
Green. Reproduction tum-
blers were made in 1977
and 1978.

Ashtray, Round, 3-Footed,
   4 In. 5.00
Ashtray, Square, 3 1/2 In. .. 7.00
Ashtray, Square,
   4 5/8 In. 10.00
Ashtray, Square,
   5 3/4 In. 15.00
Beer Bottle, 12 Oz.,
   8 In. 39.00
Berry Bowl, Master,
   8 1/2 In. ...... 20.00 to 30.00
Bowl, Fruit, 4 1/4 In. 6.00
Bowl, Salad, 11 1/2 In. ... 45.00
Bowl, Vegetable, Oval,
   8 In. .... 23.00 to 25.00
Candy Dish, Cover 23.00
Cigarette Box, Cover,
   6 In. 15.00
Creamer .... 5.00 to 8.00
Creamer, Footed 9.00
Cup .... 5.00 to 6.00
Cup & Saucer .... 8.00 to 10.00
Dish, Maple Leaf,
   6 5/8 In. 10.00
Plate, Dinner,
   9 In. .... 10.00 to 11.00
Plate, Salad, 7 3/8 In. 7.00
Plate, Sherbet, 6 1/4 In. ... 6.00
Punch Bowl 40.00
Punch Cup .... 3.00 to 4.00
Sandwich Server,
   13 1/4 In. 35.00
Saucer 3.00
Sherbet .... 8.00 to 11.00
Sherbet, Ball
   Stem .... 8.00 to 12.00
Soup, Dish,
   7 3/4 In. ...... 12.00 to 16.00
Sugar 10.00
Sugar, Footed .... 7.50 to 10.00

**A mixture of white
vinegar and water can
be used to clean glass.**

Sugar &
  Creamer ...... 16.00 to 18.00
Sugar & Creamer,
  Footed 20.00
Tumbler, 5 Oz. .... 6.00 to 8.00
Tumbler, 9 Oz. 25.00
Tumbler,
  10 Oz. .... 10.00 to 15.00
Tumbler, 13 Oz. .. 9.00 to 13.00
Tumbler, Crinkled,
  16 Oz. 15.00
Tumbler, Footed,
  12 Oz. .... 13.00 to 15.00
Tumbler, Hoe Down 75.00
Tumbler, Water, 9 Oz. 6.50
Tumbler, Wine, Footed,
  2 1/2 Oz. ..... 12.00 to 22.00
Vase, 6 3/8 In. .. 10.00 to 13.00
Vase, 9 In. 20.00
Vase, Coolidge, 6 3/8 In. .. 8.00
Vase, Crimped, 9 In. 18.00
Vase, Crimped, 12 In. 10.00
Vase, Hand Painted Scene
  Of Niagara Falls,
  6 3/8 In. 18.00
Vase, Harding, 6 3/8 In. ... 8.00
Vase, Hoover,
  9 In. .... 18.00 to 22.00
Vase, Ivy, Ball,
  4 In. .... 8.00 to 12.00
Vase, Provincial, 9 In. ... 35.00
Vase, Whirly Twirly,
  4 In. 12.00
Vase, Wilson, Scalloped
  Edge, 6 3/8 In. 25.00

RUSSIAN
See Holiday

S PATTERN

Macbeth-Evans Glass
Company made S Pattern,
or Stippled Rose Band,
from 1930 to 1935. It was

made before 1932 in
Crystal, Pink, Topaz, and
Crystal with blue, gold, or
platinum trim. The 1934
listing mentions Green,
Monax, and Red. Other
pieces were made in
Amber, Ritz Blue, Yellow,
and Crystal with many
colors of trim, including,
amber, green, platinum,
red, rose, silver, or white.

Amber
Plate, Luncheon,
  8 1/4 In. 5.00

Crystal
Cake Plate, 11 3/4 In. 40.00
Creamer 6.00
Creamer, Gold Trim 7.00
Creamer, Silver Trim 6.00
Cup & Saucer 6.00
Cup & Saucer, Platinum
  Trim 7.00
Cup & Saucer, Silver
  Trim 6.00
Grill Plate,
  10 1/4 In. ...... 6.00 to 15.00
Grill Plate, Platinum
  Trim, 10 1/4 In. 9.00
Pitcher, 80 Oz. 75.00
Plate, Luncheon,
  8 1/4 In. .... 5.00 to 8.00
Plate, Luncheon, Gold
  Trim, 8 1/4 In. 7.00
Plate, Luncheon, Platinum
  Trim, 8 1/4 In. 6.00
Plate, Luncheon, Silver
  Trim, 8 1/4 In. 5.00
Saucer .... 2.00 to 3.00
Sugar, Silver Trim 6.00
Sugar & Creamer,
  Pink Trim 12.00
Tumbler, 5 Oz., 3 1/2 In. .. 5.00
Tumbler, 9 Oz., 4 In. 7.00
Tumbler, 10 Oz.,
  4 3/4 In. 9.00
Tumbler, 12 Oz., 5 In. 9.00

Monax
Plate, Sherbet, 6 In. 23.00

Pink
Tumbler, 9 Oz., 4 In. 65.00

Yellow
Cup 5.00
Plate, Luncheon,
  8 1/4 In. .... 4.00 to 6.00

SAIL BOAT
See White Ship

SAILING SHIP
See White Ship

SANDWICH ANCHOR HOCKING

Many glass companies
used the name Sandwich
for one of their patterns.
The three most popular
patterns were made by
Anchor Hocking Glass
Corporation, Indiana Glass
Company, and Duncan &
Miller Glass Company.
The Anchor Hocking
Sandwich pattern was
made from 1939 to 1964
and can be distinguished
by the three lines around
the edge of each flower
petal. It was made in Royal
Ruby in 1938 and 1939;
and in Pink from 1938 to
1940. Crystal was made
from 1939 to 1966 and
again from 1977 to 1993;
Forest Green and White
(opaque) date from 1956
to the 1960s; Desert Gold
from 1961 to 1964. A

reproduction line was introduced in 1977 by another company in Amber, Blue, Crystal, and Red.

Crystal

Bowl, Oval, 8 1/4 In. 7.00
Bowl, Salad, 9 In. 23.00
Bowl, Scalloped Edge,
  6 1/2 In. . . . . . . 7.00 to 12.00
Butter, Cover 45.00
Butter, No Cover 25.00
Creamer . . . . . . 6.00 to 8.00
Cup & Saucer . . . . 4.00 to 10.00
Custard Cup 7.00
Custard Cup, Crimped
  Edge, 5 Oz. 15.00
Plate, 8 In. 10.00
Plate, Dinner,
  9 In. . . . . 12.00 to 20.00
Punch Bowl,
  9 3/4 In. . . . . . 20.00 to 30.00
Punch Bowl,
  Stand . . . . 55.00 to 60.00
Punch Bowl,
  Stand Only 30.00
Punch Cup . . . . 3.00 to 5.00
Saucer 4.00
Sherbet 8.00
Sugar . . . . 8.00 to 10.00
Sugar &
  Creamer . . . . . . 12.00 to 18.00
Sugar & Creamer,
  Gold Trim 15.00
Tumbler, Juice,
  3 Oz., 3 3/8 In. 15.00
Tumbler, Water,
  9 Oz. . . . . 8.00 to 12.00

Desert Gold

Bowl, 6 1/2 In. 15.00
Bowl, Salad, 9 In. 35.00
Cookie Jar,
  Cover . . . . 45.00 to 55.00
Cup 3.00
Plate, Dinner, 9 In. 9.00

Forest Green

Bowl, 4 5/16 In. 6.00
Cookie Jar, No Cover 25.00
Custard Cup 8.00
Custard Cup,
  Underplate Only 3.00

Tumbler, Juice, 5 Oz.,
  3 1/4 In. . . . . . . 8.00 to 15.00
Tumbler, Water,
  9 Oz. . . . . 10.00 to 12.00

Royal Ruby

Bowl, Scalloped Edge,
  5 1/4 In. 15.00

White

Punch Set 100.00

SANDWICH DUNCAN & MILLER

Duncan & Miller Sandwich is easy to recognize. It has long been said the pattern was designed by Mr. Heisey's son-in-law and that he added the diamond and H mark used by Heisey as part of the border design. New research suggests this is not true and that the so-called diamond and H mark is really a mold flaw. The plates in this series have ground bottoms. The star in the center of the plate does not go to the edge of the circle. Duncan & Miller Glass Company, Washington, Pennsylvania, named its pattern No. 41 Early American Sandwich Glass in 1925. The glass was made in Amber, Cobalt Blue, Crystal, Green, Pink, and Red. The pattern

remained in production until 1955, when some of the molds were bought by other companies. Lancaster Colony made pieces in Amberina, Blue, and Green in the 1970s. Tiffin made Milk Glass pieces. Reproductions have been made.

Crystal

Basket, Loop Handle,
  6 In. 85.00
Candlestick, 3-Light,
  16 In., Pair 575.00
Candlestick, 4 In.,
  Pair . . . . 8.00 to 14.00
Coaster 15.00
Creamer 9.00
Cup & Saucer 11.00
Dish, Ice Cream,
  4 1/4 In. 12.00
Dish, Mayonnaise,
  Footed 12.00
Dish, Mint, Handle,
  7 In. 25.00
Dish, Sundae, 5 Oz.,
  3 1/2 In. 12.00
Egg Plate,
  12 In. . . . . 50.00 to 75.00
Goblet, Champagne,
  5 Oz., 5 1/4 In. 12.00
Goblet, Cocktail, 3 Oz.,
  4 1/4 In. . . . . . 12.00 to 15.00
Goblet, Water, 9 Oz.,
  6 In. . . . . 15.00 to 19.00
Goblet, Wine, 3 Oz.,
  4 1/4 In. 19.00
Nappy, 2 Sections, 6 In. . . 15.00
Nappy, Heart Shape, Ring
  Handle, 6 In. 50.00
Parfait, 4 Oz., 5 1/4 In. . . . 30.00
Plate, Salad, 8 In. 10.00
Relish, 3 Sections,
  12 In. 15.00
Sugar 9.00
Sugar & Creamer,
  Underplate 5.00
Tray, Oval, 8 In. 20.00
Tumbler, Iced Tea, Footed,
  12 Oz., 5 1/2 In. 35.00
Tumbler, Juice, Footed,
  5 Oz., 3 3/4 In. 12.00

Vase, Footed, 9 3/4 In. 70.00

Pink

Dish, Grapefruit, Footed,
  5 1/2 In. 25.00

Nappy, Opalescent,
  6 In. 36.00

Sandwich Server, Handle,
  11 In. 70.00

Tumbler, Iced Tea, Footed,
  12 Oz., 5 1/2 In. 30.00

SANDWICH INDIANA

Another Sandwich pattern was made by the Indiana Glass Company, Dunkirk, Indiana, from the 1920s through the 1980s. It can be distinguished by the single line around the flower petals. The colors changed through the years. Amber was made from the late 1920s to the 1980s, Crystal from the late 1920s to the 1990s, Light Green and Pink from the 1920s to the 1930s, Red from 1933 to the 1970s, Teal Blue from the 1950s to the 1980s, Opaque White in the 1950s, and Smoky Blue in 1976 and 1977. The scroll design varies with the size of the plate. Tiara Home Products sold Sandwich in Red (1969), Amber (1970), and Crystal (1978), and in Amber, Chantilly Green,

and Crystal in the 1980s. Tiara also sold a few pieces from redesigned molds. A Teal Blue butter dish was also made. Reproductions have been made.

Amber

Goblet, 9 Oz.,
  5 1/2 In. . . . . 9.00 to 10.00
Plate, Dinner, 10 1/2 In. . . 10.00
Snack Set, 2 Piece 11.00

Crystal

Candlestick, 3 1/2 In.,
  Pair 65.00
Celery Dish, 10 1/2 In. . . . 16.00
Cup 3.00
Cup & Saucer 7.50
Decanter, Stopper 22.00
Goblet, 9 Oz.,
  5 1/2 In. . . . . 9.00 to 12.00
Plate, Luncheon,
  8 3/8 In. . . . . 5.00 to 8.00
Sandwich Server, Center Handle,
  13 In. . . . . 15.00 to 18.00
Sherbet . . . . 6.00 to 9.00
Sherbet, Underplate 10.00
Snack Set, 8 Piece 35.00
Sugar 8.00
Sugar & Creamer 18.00
Tumbler, Iced Tea,
  Footed, 12 Oz. 12.00
Tumbler, Water, Footed,
  8 Oz. . . . . 9.00 to 10.00

Light Green

Wine Set, Decanter, Tray,
  Goblets, 8 Piece 265.00

Pink

Ashtray, Heart Shape 10.00

❖

In the case of a major theft, keep careful records. You may be able to deduct part of the uninsured loss from your income tax.

❖

Teal Blue

Sherbet 6.00

SAXON
See Coronation

SCROLL & STAR
See Princess Feather

SEASHELL

Seashell accessories and plates were made by Cambridge Glass Company from the mid 1920s to 1953. Crown Tuscan items are especially popular. Many were etched or gold-encrusted. Amber, Amethyst, Carmen (red), Crystal, Ebony, Emerald, Mandarin Gold, Milk Glass, Mocha, and Windsor Blue pieces were made, too.

Crystal

Bowl, 9 In. 12.00
Sugar & Creamer 100.00

Emerald

Dish, Oval, 4-Footed,
  8 In. 50.00
Vase 45.00

Mandarin Gold

Dish, Oval, 4-Footed,
  8 In. 65.00

SEVENTEEN HUNDRED LINE
See 1700 Line

SEVILLE

Seville etch is similar to Royal, except that a daisy replaces the fleur-de-lis. Fostoria Glass Company made Seville etched pieces from 1920 to 1933 in Amber, Blue, Crystal, Green, and Rose.

Amber

Console, Rolled Edge,
12 In. 30.00
Dish, Grapefruit, Insert,
2 Piece 55.00
Plate, Dinner,
10 1/2 In. 24.00
Tumbler, Footed,
12 Oz. 15.00

Green

Bowl, Cereal, 6 1/2 In. . . . 22.00

SHAMROCK
See Cloverleaf

SHARON

Sharon, or Cabbage Rose, was made by the Federal Glass Company from 1935 to 1939. The pattern was made in Amber, Crystal, Green, and Pink. A cheese dish was reproduced in 1976 in Amber, Blue, Dark Green, Light Green, and Pink. Other items have been reproduced in various colors.

Amber

Berry Bowl,
5 In. . . . . 9.00 to 10.00
Berry Bowl, Master,
8 1/2 In. . . . . 6.00 to 8.00
Bowl, Cereal, 6 In. 25.00
Bowl, Fruit, 10 1/2 In. . . . 21.00
Bowl, Vegetable, Oval,
9 1/2 In. . . . . . . 14.00 to 20.00
Butter, Cover . . 45.00 to 56.00
Cake Plate, Footed,
11 1/2 In. 30.00
Candy Jar,
Cover . . . . 40.00 to 65.00
Creamer 14.00
Cup . . . . 10.00 to 12.00
Cup & Saucer . . . 15.00 to 20.00
Pitcher, Ice Lip,
80 Oz. 165.00
Plate, Bread & Butter,
6 In. . . . . 5.00 to 7.00
Plate, Dinner,
9 1/2 In. . . . . . . 10.00 to 15.00
Plate, Salad,
7 1/2 In. . . . . . . 15.00 to 20.00
Platter, Oval,
12 1/2 In. . . . . . 16.00 to 22.00
Salt & Pepper . . . 35.00 to 40.00
Saltshaker . . . . . 23.00 to 45.00
Saucer 5.00
Sherbet . . . . 11.00 to 16.00
Soup, Cream, Handles,
5 In. . . . . 24.00 to 30.00
Soup, Dish,
7 3/4 In. . . . . . . 55.00 to 58.00
Sugar 9.00
Sugar &
Creamer . . . . . 22.00 to 28.00
Sugar & Creamer,
Cover 45.00
Tumbler, Thick, 9 Oz.,
4 1/8 In. . . . . . . 35.00 to 40.00
Tumbler, Thick, 12 Oz.,
5 1/4 In. 62.00
Tumbler, Thin, 9 Oz.,
4 1/8 In. . . . . . . 26.00 to 30.00
Tumbler, Thin, 12 Oz.,
5 1/4 In. 138.00

Crystal

Berry Bowl, 5 In. 17.00
Cake Plate, Footed,
11 1/2 In. . . . . . 8.00 to 12.00
Cup & Saucer 25.00

Plate, Bread & Butter,
6 In. 10.00
Plate, Dinner, 9 1/2 In. . . . 23.00
Platter, Oval, 12 1/2 In. . . 37.00
Sugar 20.00

Green

Berry Bowl,
5 In. . . . . 16.00 to 25.00
Berry Bowl, Master,
8 1/2 In. 42.00
Bowl, Fruit, 10 1/2 In. . . . 50.00
Butter, Cover . . 92.00 to 145.00
Candy Jar, Cover 185.00
Creamer . . . . . . 20.00 to 27.00
Cup . . . . 20.00 to 23.00
Cup & Saucer 28.00
Jam Dish, 7 1/2 In. 80.00
Plate, Bread & Butter,
6 In. . . . . 8.00 to 12.00
Plate, Dinner,
9 1/2 In. . . . . . . 30.00 to 45.00
Platter, Oval,
12 1/2 In. . . . . . 32.00 to 35.00
Salt & Pepper 75.00
Saltshaker 40.00
Saucer 15.00
Soup, Cream, Handles,
5 In. 64.00
Sugar & Creamer 60.00
Tumbler, Thick, 12 Oz.,
5 1/4 In. 100.00

Pink

Berry Bowl,
5 In. . . . . 12.00 to 20.00
Berry Bowl, Master,
8 1/2 In. . . . . . . 33.00 to 40.00
Bowl, Cereal,
6 In. . . . . 30.00 to 38.00
Bowl, Fruit,
10 1/2 In. . . . . . 45.00 to 65.00
Bowl, Vegetable, Oval,
9 1/2 In. . . . . . . 35.00 to 38.00
Butter, Cover . . 55.00 to 70.00
Butter, Cover Only 45.00
Butter, No Cover 30.00
Cake Plate, Footed,
10 1/2 In. 45.00
Candy Jar, Cover 45.00
Creamer . . . . . . 18.00 to 24.00
Cup . . . . 14.00 to 22.00
Cup & Saucer . . . 20.00 to 30.00
Jam Dish, 7 1/2 In. 290.00

Pitcher 180.00

Pitcher,
Ice Lip . . . . . 200.00 to 210.00

Plate, Bread & Butter,
6 In. . . . . 7.50 to 10.00

Plate, Dinner,
9 1/2 In. . . . . . . 19.00 to 25.00

Plate, Salad, 7 1/2 In. 35.00

Platter, Oval,
12 1/2 In. . . . . . 30.00 to 35.00

Salt & Pepper 45.00

Saucer . . . . 14.00 to 15.00

Sherbet . . . . 16.00 to 20.00

Soup, Cream, Handles,
5 In. . . . . 45.00 to 60.00

Soup, Dish,
7 3/4 In. . . . . . . 55.00 to 65.00

Sugar . . . . 14.00 to 20.00

Sugar, Cover . . . . 30.00 to 55.00

Sugar & Creamer 35.00

Sugar & Creamer, Cover . 75.00

Tumbler, Footed, 15 Oz.,
6 1/2 In. 65.00

Tumbler, Thick, 9 Oz.,
4 1/8 In. . . . . . . 45.00 to 55.00

Tumbler, Thick, 12 Oz.,
5 1/4 In. . . . . . 75.00 to 105.00

Tumbler, Thin, 9 Oz.,
4 1/8 In. . . . . . . 45.00 to 55.00

Tumbler, Thin, 12 Oz.,
5 1/4 In. 50.00

SHEFFIELD
See Chinex Classic

SHELL

Shell is a Fire-King dinnerware pattern made by Anchor Hocking Glass Corporation, Lancaster, Ohio, from 1965 to 1976. It is similar to Swirl, but the edges of Shell items are noticeably scalloped. Dishes were labeled

Golden Shell (white with gold trim), Jade-ite Shell, and Lustre Shell (peach lustre). Plain white and iridized white pieces can be found, too. Some collectors use the name Shell for Petalware, which is listed in its own section in this book.

Jade-ite
Bowl, Cereal, 6 3/8 In. . . . 33.00

Bowl, Vegetable,
8 1/2 In. . . . . . . 29.00 to 48.00

Plate, Dinner,
10 In. . . . . 25.00 to 30.00

Saucer 7.00

Soup, Dish, 7 5/8 In. 38.00

Sugar & Creamer 55.00

Golden Shell
Bowl, Dessert, 4 3/4 In. . . . 4.00

Creamer 5.00

Cup & Saucer 5.00

Plate, Dinner, 1964-1965
World's Fair Decal,
10 In. 35.00

Lustre Shell
Bowl, Vegetable,
8 1/2 In. 30.00

Cup & Saucer,
After Dinner 18.00

SHELL PINK

Jeannette Glass Company made many accessories in its popular Shell Pink (opaque pink) color from 1957 to 1959. The same pieces were made in Milk Glass, Ultramarine, and clear Pink. See also Floragold, Holiday, and National.

Bowl, Berries, Footed,
Napco 15.00

Candleholder, Bird,
3 1/8 x 3 7/8 In. 85.00

Candy Dish, Grapes,
5 In. 20.00

Goblet, Thumbprint,
8 Oz. 15.00

Goblet, Thumbprint, Footed,
8 Oz., 6 1/4 In. 20.00

Pitcher 35.00

Powder Jar,
4 3/4 In. . . . . . . 50.00 to 75.00

Punch Cup 5.00

Punch Set, Box,
15 Piece 450.00

Relish, Sections,
12 1/2 In. 95.00

Snack Set, 2 Piece 30.00

Sugar, Cover 28.00

Sugar, Cover, Baltimore Pear,
Handles, 5 1/2 In. 38.00

Sugar & Creamer,
Cover, Footed, Baltimore
Pear . . . . 40.00 to 45.00

Tray, Venetian, 6 Sections,
16 1/2 In. 40.00

Tumbler, Footed, 5 Oz. . . 35.00

Vase, 7 In. 35.00

Vase, Cornucopia, 5 In.,
Pair 30.00

Vase, National, 9 In. 165.00

Wedding Bowl, Cover,
8 In. 23.00

Wedding Bowl, Cover,
Square, 8 1/2 In. 28.00

SHIPS
See White Ship

SHIRLEY TEMPLE

Shirley Temple is not really a pattern, but the dishes with the white enamel decoration picturing Shirley have become

popular with collectors. The most famous were made as giveaways with cereal from 1934 to 1942. Several companies, including Hazel Atlas Glass Company and U.S. Glass, made the glassware. Sugars and creamers, bowls, plates, and mugs were made. The milk pitcher and mug have been reproduced since 1982, and the bowl has been reproduced since 1986. Other items with the Shirley Temple decal include a Fostoria Mayfair Green sugar bowl and teacup, a White mug, and an 8 7/8-inch Moderntone Cobalt Blue plate. In 1972 Libbey Glass Company made tumblers in six sizes.

Cobalt Blue
Bowl, Cereal, 6 1/2 In. . . . 30.00
Butter, No Cover, Scalloped
 Edge 20.00
Mug, 4 In. 27.00
Pitcher, Milk,
 4 1/2 In. . . . . . 38.00 to 50.00

SIERRA

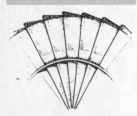

Sierra, or Pinwheel, was made by Jeannette Glass Company from 1931 to 1933. It is found in Green, Pink, and Ultramarine.

Green
Berry Bowl, Master,
 8 1/2 In. . . . . . 40.00 to 55.00
Berry Set, 5 Piece 95.00

Bowl, Cereal,
 5 1/2 In. . . . . . 16.00 to 25.00
Butter, Cover . . 85.00 to 105.00
Cup & Saucer 25.00
Plate, Dinner, 9 In. 24.00
Salt & Pepper 60.00
Saltshaker 32.00
Saucer 10.00
Sugar, Cover 55.00
Sugar & Creamer 60.00
Sugar & Creamer,
 Cover 85.00

Pink
Berry Bowl, Master,
 8 1/2 In. 40.00
Bowl, Cereal,
 5 1/2 In. . . . . . 15.00 to 20.00
Bowl, Vegetable, Oval,
 9 1/2 In. 65.00
Butter, Cover . . . 60.00 to 63.00
Cup 15.00
Cup & Saucer 22.00
Pitcher, 32 Oz.,
 6 1/2 In. 155.00
Plate, Dinner,
 9 In. . . . . 21.00 to 30.00
Platter, Oval,
 11 In. . . . . 55.00 to 65.00
Salt & Pepper 60.00
Sandwich Server, Handles,
 10 1/4 In. . . . . . 25.00 to 30.00
Saucer . . . . 8.00 to 10.00
Sugar 25.00
Sugar, Cover 48.00
Sugar & Creamer, Cover . 65.00

SKOL

Skol is a Swedish-modern pattern made in the late 1950s and 1960s by Hazel Atlas, then a division of Continental Can Company, Clarksburg, West Virginia. Some collectors call the pattern Dots because of the embossed circles on the outside of the pieces. Items were made in Avocado, Capri Blue, Crystal, and Harvest Gold.

Capri Blue
Bowl, Dessert, 4 7/8 In. . . 16.00
Cup & Saucer 5.00
Sherbet, 3 In. 16.00
Tumbler, 4 Oz.,
 3 In. . . . . 15.00 to 16.00
Tumbler, 8 Oz., 4 In. 17.00
Tumbler, 9 Oz.,
 5 1/4 In. . . . . . . 4.00 to 18.00
Tumbler, Old Fashioned,
 8 Oz., 3 3/8 In. 15.50

Crystal
Bowl, Dessert, 4 7/8 In. . . . 7.00
Cup 7.00
Cup & Saucer 9.00
Tumbler, 4 Oz.,
 3 In. . . . . 6.00 to 7.00
Tumbler, 6 Oz., 3 5/8 In. . . 6.00

Harvest Gold
Tumbler, 9 Oz., 5 1/4 In. . . 5.00

SMOCKING
See Windsor

SNOWFLAKE
See Doric

SORENO

Soreno was made by Anchor Hocking Glass Corporation, Lancaster, Ohio, from 1966 to 1970. The pattern has textured horizontal ribs and was made mostly in Avocado and Honey Gold, although pieces in Aquamarine, Aurora (iridescent crystal), Lustre (various colors), and Mardi-Gras can be found. Other related patterns are listed in the Fire-King section in this book.

Aquamarine
Pitcher, 28 Oz., 7 In. 13.00

Avocado
Bowl, Salad, 8 1/2 In. 15.00
Pitcher, 64 Oz., 9 1/2 In. . . 13.00
Snack Set, 8 Piece 28.00
Honey Gold
Pitcher, 64 Oz., 9 3/4 In. . . 4.00
Lustre
Ashtray, 4 1/4 In. 2.00

SPIRAL

It is easy to confuse Spiral, a Hocking Glass Company pattern, with Twisted Optic, made by Imperial Glass Company. Ask to be shown examples of each, because even a picture will not be much help. Looking from the top to the base, Twisted Optic spirals right to left; Spiral twists left to right. There are a few pieces that are exceptions. Spiral pattern beverage and luncheon sets were manufactured from 1928 to 1930 in Crystal, Green, and Pink. It is also sometimes called Spiral Optic or Swirled Big Rib.

Crystal
Ice Tub 18.00
Salt & Pepper 55.00
Green
Butter Tub 30.00
Jam Jar, Cover . . 25.00 to 35.00
Pitcher, 54 Oz.,
 7 5/8 In. 55.00
Plate, Luncheon,
 8 In. . . . . 2.25 to 4.55
Sherbet . . . . 5.00 to 10.00
Tumbler, Footed,
 5 3/4 In. . . . . . . 35.00 to 42.00

Vase, 5 3/4 In. 75.00

SPIRAL FLUTES
See Swirl Duncan & Miller

SPIRAL OPTIC
See Spiral

SPOKE
See Patrician

SPORTSMAN SERIES

Hazel Atlas Glass Company made this unusual pattern in the 1940s. It was made in Amethyst, Cobalt Blue, or Crystal with fired-on decoration. Although the name of the series was Sportsman, designs included not only golf, sailboats, hunting, and angelfish, but a few odd choices like windmills. We list White Ship and Windmill separately, although they are sometimes considered part of this pattern.

Cobalt Blue
Cocktail Shaker, Angelfish,
 Bakelite & Chrome
 Base . . . . 85.00 to 123.00
Cocktail Shaker Set,
 Tally Ho, 5 Piece 220.00
Ice Bowl, Skier 38.00
Tumbler, Angelfish,
 9 Oz., 4 5/8 In. 20.00

Tumbler, Fox Hunt,
 9 Oz., 3 3/4 In. 25.00
Tumbler, Hunting Dog,
 9 Oz., 4 5/8 In. 25.00
Crystal
Cocktail Shaker, Polar
 Bear 48.00
Ice Bowl, Polar Bear 38.00
Tumbler, Polar Bear,
 12 Oz. 13.00
Tumbler, Polar Bear, Old
 Fashioned, 8 Oz. 11.00

SPUN
See Reeded

SQUARE
See Charm

STANHOPE

A.H. Heisey & Company won an award in a plastics competition for its Stanhope pattern. The designer, Walter Von Nessen, created Bakelite inserts for the circular handles on the glassware. Stanhope was made from 1936 to 1941 in Crystal. Heisey's blown stemware line of the same name was also made in Zircon (turquoise).

Crystal
Goblet, 9 Oz., 6 In. 30.00

❖

Keep your collection of glassware away from the speakers of your sound system. The heavy bass and high-pitched sounds can crack the glass.

❖

Relish, 4 Sections, Red
Bakelite Knobs, 12 In. . . 65.00
Sugar & Creamer, Black
Bakelite Knobs 150.00

Zircon
Champagne, Saturn Optic,
5 1/2 Oz. 100.00

STAR

Federal Glass Company,
Columbus, Ohio, made
the Star pattern in the
1950s. All of the pieces
have a central star motif
and were made in Amber
and Crystal. The tumblers,
creamer, and sugar have
star-shaped bases.

Amber
Bowl, Dessert, 4 5/8 In. 5.50
Creamer 10.00
Saucer 4.00
Sugar 10.00
Sugar, Cover 21.00
Tumbler, Iced Tea, 12 Oz.,
5 1/8 In. 24.00
Tumbler, Juice, 4 1/2 Oz.,
3 3/8 In. 10.00
Tumbler, Water, 9 Oz.,
3 7/8 In. 13.00

❖

**Store glass dishes
carefully. Stand each
piece upright, not
touching one another.
Never nest pieces.**

❖

Tumbler Set, Box, 9 Oz.,
10 Piece 95.00
Crystal
Ashtray, 4 In. 10.00
Bowl, Dessert, 4 5/8 In. . . 18.00
Butter, Cover 125.00
Creamer . . . . 3.00 to 5.00
Pitcher, Ice Lip, 85 Oz.,
9 1/2 In. 18.00
Sugar 25.00
Tumbler, Juice, Yellow
Bands, 4 1/2 Oz.,
3 3/8 In. . . . . 6.00 to 7.00
Tumbler, Whiskey,
1 1/2 Oz., 2 1/4 In. 5.00

STARLIGHT

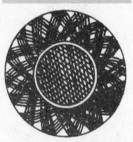

Starlight was made by the
Hazel Atlas Company of
Wheeling, West Virginia,
from 1938 to 1940. Full
table settings were made
of Cobalt Blue, Crystal,
Pink, and White. The
pattern is pressed, not
etched.

Crystal
Creamer 10.00
Plate, Dinner, 9 In. 8.00
Plate, Luncheon,
8 1/2 In. 5.00
Salt & Pepper 35.00
Saltshaker 9.00
Sugar &
Creamer . . . . . . 16.00 to 22.50
White
Cup . . . . 5.00 to 7.00
Plate, Dinner,
9 In. . . . . 7.00 to 8.00
Saucer 2.00

STARS & BARS
See Thousand Line

STARS & STRIPES

Stars & Stripes is a clear
glass pattern made about
1942 by Anchor Hocking
Glass Corporation. The
pieces have appropriate
wartime patriotic designs
of stars, stripes, and
eagles.

Plate, 8 In. . . . . . 18.00 to 35.00
Sherbet 20.00
Tumbler 35.00

STIPPLED
See Craquel

STIPPLED ROSE BAND
See S Pattern

STRAWBERRY

Strawberry and Cherry-
Berry are similar patterns.
The U.S. Glass Company
made luncheon sets with
strawberry decoration in

the early 1930s. Green and Pink were the most commonly used colors, although Crystal and Iridescent Marigold pieces were also made.

Crystal
Pitcher, 7 3/4 In. 300.00

Green
Berry Bowl, Master,
   7 1/2 In. . . . . . . 40.00 to 43.00
Butter,
   Cover . . . . . 225.00 to 240.00
Creamer, 3 3/4 In. 43.00
Sherbet . . . . 7.00 to 14.00
Sugar 42.00

Pink
Compote, 5 3/4 In. 30.00
Sherbet . . . . 10.00 to 13.00

STRAWBERRY
See also Cherry-Berry

SUN RAY

Sun Ray has embossed panels of vertical ribs that fan out like rays of the sun. Fostoria Glass Company, Moundsville, West Virginia, made the pattern mainly in Crystal from 1935 to 1944. Pieces in Blue, Green, Red, and Yellow have been seen, too. Items with frosted panels are called Glacier.

Crystal
Bonbon, Handle 20.00

Bowl, Handles, 9 1/2 In. . . 49.00
Bowl, Handles, 12 In. 50.00
Compote 25.00
Cruet 42.00
Cup & Saucer 15.00
Ice Bucket, Handles 80.00
Nappy, Handles 12.00
Nappy, Tricornered,
   Handles . . . . . . 10.00 to 15.00
Pickle, Handles 22.00
Pitcher, Ice Lip, 2 Qt. . . . 118.00
Plate, 6 In. 8.00
Plate, 7 1/2 In. 8.00
Plate, 9 1/2 In. 15.00
Relish, 3 Sections 28.00
Relish, 4 Sections,
   Glacier 36.00
Sherbet, 5 1/2 Oz.,
   3 1/2 In. . . . . . . 10.00 to 12.00
Sugar 12.00
Sugar &
   Creamer . . . . . 24.00 to 28.00
Tumbler, Footed,
   9 Oz., 4 3/4 In. 19.00

Red
Relish, 2 Sections 55.00

SUNBURST

Crystal dinner sets were made in Sunburst pattern from 1938 to 1941 by Jeannette Glass Company, Jeannette, Pennsylvania.

Berry Bowl, Master,
   8 1/2 In. 95.00
Candlestick, 2-Light 18.00
Candlestick, 2-Light,
   Pair 25.00
Relish, 2 Sections, Oval,
   9 In. 25.00
Sherbet 18.00
Sugar 9.00

SUNFLOWER

Sunflower was made by Jeannette Glass Company, Jeannette, Pennsylvania, in the late 1920s and early 1930s. It is most commonly found in Pink and two shades of Green. The darker green was used for cake plates given as a premium in sacks of flour. Small quantities of Delphite pieces also were made.

Green
Ashtray, 5 In. 12.00
Cake Plate, 3-Footed,
   10 In. . . . . 15.00 to 22.00
Cup 20.00
Cup & Saucer 43.00
Plate, Dinner,
   9 In. . . . . 26.00 to 30.00
Sugar 30.00

Pink
Ashtray, 5 In. 10.00
Cake Plate, 3-Footed,
   10 In. 25.00
Cup . . . . 14.00 to 15.00
Plate, Dinner, 9 In. 35.00
Tumbler, Footed, 8 Oz.,
   4 3/4 In. 40.00

SWANKYSWIG

In October 1933, Kraft Cheese Company began to

market cheese spreads in decorated, reusable glass tumblers. The tumbler was made in a 5-ounce size with a smooth beverage lip and a permanent color decoration. The designs were tested and changed as public demand indicated. Hazel Atlas Glass Company made the glasses, which were decorated by hand by a crew of about 280 girls, working in shifts around the clock. In 1937 a silk-screen process was developed, and the Tulip design was made by this new, faster method. The glasses were made thinner and lighter in weight. The decorated Swankyswigs were discontinued from 1941 to 1946, the war years. They were made again from 1947 through 1958. Since then, plain glasses have been used, although a few specially decorated Swankyswigs were produced.

Antique No. 1
Brown, 3 1/2 In. 6.00
Churn & Cradle,
  Orange 24.00
Spinning Wheel & Bellows,
  Red, 3 1/2 In. 75

❖

When you move, remember that there is no insurance coverage for breakage if the items are not packed by the shipper.

❖

Antique No. 2
Red, 4 1/2 In. 19.00

Band No. 1
Red & Black, 3 3/8 In. 4.00

Band No. 2
Red & Black, 3 3/8 In. 4.00

Band No. 3
White & Blue, 3 1/4 In. . . . 4.00
White & Blue, 3 3/8 In. . . . 4.00

Band No. 6
Red & White, 3 1/2 In. . . . 23.00

Bustlin' Betsy
Blue, 3 3/4 In. 6.50
Green, 3 3/4 In. . . . . 3.00 to 6.50
Orange, 3 3/4 In. 6.00
Red, 3 3/4 In. . . . . . 6.50 to 8.00
Yellow, 3 3/4 In. 24.00

Checkerboard
Green, 3 1/2 In. 13.00

Cornflower No. 1
Blue, 3 1/2 In. 3.25

Cornflower No. 2
Yellow, 3 1/2 In. 4.50

Daisy
Red, Green, White,
  3 3/4 In. . . . . 2.00 to 6.00

Ethnic
India, Poppy Red,
  4 5/8 In. 8.75
Scotland, Burgundy,
  4 5/8 In. 8.75

Forget-Me-Not
Dark Blue, 3 1/2 In. 2.75
Light Blue,
  3 1/2 In. . . . . 2.75 to 3.00
Red, 3 1/2 In. . . . . . 3.00 to 4.00
Red, 3 3/4 In. 2.75
Yellow, 3 1/2 In. 3.00

Galleon
Yellow, 3 1/4 In. 8.00

Kiddie Kup
Elephants & Ducks,
  Red, 3 1/2 In. . . . . . .75 to 3.75
Fawns & Squirrels, Brown,
  3 1/2 In. . . . . 3.75 to 5.00
Kittens & Rabbits,
  Green, 3 1/2 In. 3.75
Kittens & Rabbits,
  Green, 3 3/4 In. 5.00

Ponies & Ducks, Black,
  3 3/4 In. . . . . 4.00 to 5.00
Roosters & Puppies,
  Orange, 3 1/2 In. 5.00
Roosters & Puppies,
  Orange, 3 3/4 In. 4.00
Teddy Bears & Pigs,
  Blue, 3 1/2 In. . . . 3.75 to 7.15
Teddy Bears & Pigs,
  Blue, 3 3/4 In. 6.50

Posy Cornflower No. 1
Light Blue, 3 1/2 In. 3.75
Yellow, 3 1/2 In. 3.00

Posy Cornflower No. 2
Blue, 3 1/2 In. 5.50
Red, 3 1/2 In. 3.25

Posy Jonquil
Yellow, 3 1/2 In. . . . 5.00 to 6.50

Posy Tulip No. 1
Black, 3 1/2 In. . . . . 2.00 to 8.50
Blue, 3 1/2 In. 5.50
Green, 3 1/2 In. 3.00
Red, 3 1/2 In. . . . . 3.50 to 10.00

Posy Tulip No. 2
Black, 3 1/2 In. . . . 3.25 to 14.00
Blue, 3 1/4 In. 5.00
Blue, 3 1/2 In. 15.00
Red, 3 3/4 In. 4.75
Yellow, 3 3/4 In. 4.75

Posy Tulip No. 3
Red, 4 In. 3.00

Posy Violets
Blue & Green, 3 1/2 In. . . . 6.00

Sailboat No. 1
Blue, 3 1/2 In. . . . . 8.75 to 9.75

Sailboat No. 2
Blue, 3 1/2 In. . . . . 6.00 to 9.50
Blue, 4 1/2 In. 5.00
Green, 3 1/2 In. 12.00
Red, 3 1/2 In. 13.00

Star No. 1
Black, 3 1/2 In. 5.75
Blue, 3 1/2 In. . . . . 6.50 to 14.00
Red, 3 1/2 In. 8.00

Texas Centennial
Blue, 3 1/2 In. . . . . 7.00 to 14.00
Red, 3 1/2 In. 14.00

SWEET PEAR
See Avocado

SWIRL DUNCAN & MILLER

Duncan & Miller Glass Company, Washington, Pennsylvania, made a Swirl pattern, too, sometimes called Spiral Flutes. It was made of Amber, Crystal, and Green glass in 1924, and Pink in 1926. A few pieces have been reported with gold trim and in Blue or Vaseline-colored glass.

Amber
Compote, 4 3/8 In. 15.00
Tumbler, Cocktail, Footed,
　2 1/2 Oz., 3 3/8 In. 7.00

Crystal
Plate, Luncheon,
　8 1/2 In. 15.00
Plate, Salad, 7 1/2 In. 4.00

Green
Compote, 6 5/8 In. 25.00
Compote, Silver Rim,
　6 5/8 In. 125.00
Goblet, Water, 7 Oz.,
　6 1/4 In. 22.00
Sherbet, 6 Oz., 4 3/4 In. . . 20.00
Tumbler, Cocktail, Footed,
　2 1/2 Oz., 3 3/8 In. 7.50

Pink
Bouillon, 3 3/4 In. 17.00

SWIRL FIRE-KING

Swirl Fire-King is named for its wide swirled bor-

der. It was made from 1949 to 1962 in Azure-ite (opaque blue-white), Golden Anniversary (22K gold on Ivory), Ivory, Jade-ite, Pink, Rose-ite, Sunrise (red trim), and White (Anchorwhite) with or without Lustre or pastel trim. Other related patterns are listed in the Fire-King section in this book.

Azure-ite
Creamer 10.00
Platter, 12 x 9 In. 24.00

Ivory
Bowl, Vegetable,
　8 1/4 In. 17.00
Cup 8.00
Plate, Salad, 7 3/8 In. 8.00
Platter, 12 x 9 In. 22.00
Saucer 2.00

Rose-ite
Creamer 7.00
Cup & Saucer 14.00
Saucer 4.00

SWIRL HAZEL ATLAS

Swirl, or Swirl Colonial, was made by Hazel Ware, a division of Continental Can Company in the 1960s. Crystal and Milk Glass items were made. See the Moroccan Amethyst and Capri Blue sections for similar Swirl pieces.

Crystal
Bowl, Vegetable,
　7 1/4 In. 17.00
Punch Set, 13 Piece 45.00

Milk Glass
Bowl, Dessert,
　4 7/8 In. . . . . 6.00 to 7.00
Punch Set, Stand,
　8 Piece 75.00

SWIRL JEANNETTE

Swirl, sometimes called Double Swirl or Petal Swirl, was made by Jeannette Glass Company in 1937 and 1938. Ultramarine, in a variety of shades, was the most commonly used color, but Amber, Delphite, Ice Blue, and Pink were also used. Some pieces have a smooth edge, while others have a flower-petal rim.

Pink
Berry Bowl,
　4 7/8 In. 11.00
Bowl, Cereal,
　5 1/4 In. . . . . . . 10.00 to 14.00
Bowl, Footed, Handles,
　10 In. 40.00
Bowl, Salad, Rimmed,
　9 In. 35.00
Butter,
　Cover . . . . . . 226.00 to 240.00
Candlestick, Pair 85.00
Candy Dish,
　3-Footed . . . . . 16.00 to 28.00
Candy Dish,
　Cover . . . . . . 225.00 to 235.00
Coaster,
　3 1/4 In. . . . . . 10.00 to 13.00
Plate, Dinner,
　9 1/4 In. . . . . . 12.00 to 16.00
Plate, Sherbet,
　6 1/2 In. 7.00
Sandwich Server,
　12 1/2 In. 20.00
Sherbet . . . . 15.00 to 18.00

Soup, Dish, Lug
  Handles 45.00

Ultramarine

Berry Bowl,
  4 7/8 In. ...... 15.00 to 17.00
Bowl, 3-Footed,
  2 5/8 x 5 1/2 In. 40.00
Bowl, Cereal,
  5 1/4 In. ...... 16.00 to 19.00
Bowl, Handles, Footed,
  10 In. .... 26.00 to 35.00
Bowl, Salad,
  9 In. .... 24.00 to 32.00
Butter, Cover 375.00
Candlestick, 2-Light 25.00
Candy Dish,
  3-Footed ..... 20.00 to 28.00
Console, Footed,
  10 1/2 In. ..... 25.00 to 35.00
Creamer .... 15.00 to 16.00
Cup .... 12.00 to 16.00
Cup & Saucer 16.00
Plate, 9 1/2 In. 27.00
Plate, Dinner, 9 1/4 In. ... 18.00
Plate, Salad, 8 In. 15.00
Plate, Sherbet,
  6 1/2 In. .... 6.00 to 8.00
Salt & Pepper 50.00
Saltshaker 25.00
Sandwich Server,
  12 1/2 In. ..... 30.00 to 38.00
Saucer .... 3.00 to 5.00
Saucer, Swirl Edge 6.00
Sherbet .... 20.00 to 22.00
Sugar .... 16.00 to 18.00
Sugar &
  Creamer ...... 25.00 to 35.00
Tumbler, Footed,
  9 Oz., 4 5/8 In. 65.00
Vase, Footed,
  8 1/2 In. ...... 25.00 to 28.00

SWIRLED BIG RIB
See Spiral

SWIRLED SHARP RIB
See Diana

SYLVAN

Sylvan is often called
Parrot or Three Parrot
because of the center
pattern on the plates. It
was made by Federal Glass
Company in 1931 and
1932 in Amber, Blue,
Crystal, and Green. The
molds were later used for
the Madrid pattern.

Amber

Berry Bowl,
  5 In. .... 13.00 to 22.50
Cup & Saucer 80.00
Grill Plate, Square,
  10 1/2 In. 60.00
Jam Dish, 7 In. 50.00
Plate, Sherbet,
  5 3/4 In. ...... 22.50 to 35.00
Sherbet .... 31.00 to 35.00
Sherbet, Cone Shape 45.00

Crystal

Butter, Cover Only 75.00
Grill Plate, 10 1/2 In. 32.00
Platter, Oval,
  11 1/4 In. ..... 65.00 to 75.00
Saltshaker, Cover 195.00
Sugar 40.00
Sugar, Cover .. 300.00 to 345.00

Green

Berry Bowl, 5 In. 40.00
Bowl, Vegetable, Oval,
  10 In. .... 70.00 to 85.00
Butter 440.00
Butter, No
  Cover ...... 55.00 to 85.00
Creamer ...... 45.00 to 70.00
Cup 29.00
Cup & Saucer ... 46.00 to 68.00
Grill Plate,
  10 1/2 In. ..... 33.00 to 40.00
Plate, Dinner,
  9 In. .... 58.00 to 70.00

Plate, Salad,
  7 1/2 In. ...... 40.00 to 55.00
Platter, Oval,
  11 1/4 In. ..... 65.00 to 85.00
Salt & Pepper 325.00
Saltshaker 150.00
Saucer .... 17.00 to 30.00
Sherbet 22.50
Soup, Dish,
  7 In. .... 42.00 to 55.00
Sugar, No Cover 52.00
Tumbler, 10 Oz.,
  4 1/4 In. .... 175.00 to 200.00

TALLY HO

Tally Ho was made by
Cambridge Glass Com-
pany, Cambridge, Ohio,
beginning around 1932.
The pressed pattern was
produced plain in several
colors, including Amber,
Carmen (red), Crystal,
Emerald, and Royal Blue,
and used as a blank for
several etchings, including
Elaine, Rose Point, and
Valencia.

Amber

Finger Bowl, Cupped,
  3 In. 16.00
Mug, 14 Oz. 25.00
Punch Bowl, Footed,
  13 In. 65.00

Carmen

Candlestick, 5 In. 45.00
Cup & Saucer 35.00
Mug, 14 Oz. 35.00
Sherbet, Low, 6 1/2 Oz.,
  3 7/8 In. 25.00

Sugar 20.00

Tumbler, 10 Oz.,
4 3/4 In. 30.00

Tumbler, Iced Tea,
10 Oz., 5 5/8 In. 30.00

Tumbler, Water, 8 Oz.,
3 1/2 In. 20.00

Tumbler, Whiskey, 2 Oz.,
2 1/2 In. 30.00

Crystal

Goblet, Claret, 4 1/2 Oz.,
6 3/4 In. 20.00

Goblet, Cocktail, 4 Oz.,
6 1/8 In. 10.00

Goblet, Wine, 2 1/2 Oz.,
6 3/4 In. 20.00

Ice Bucket 40.00

Ice Bucket, Catawba
Etch 325.00

Ice Bucket, Chrome Handle,
Frosted 65.00

Plate, Luncheon,
9 1/2 In. 7.50

Plate, Salad, 8 In. 5.00

Emerald

Goblet, Cocktail, 3 Oz.,
4 In. 16.00

Mug, 14 Oz. 45.00

Saltshaker 35.00

Sugar 20.00

Royal Blue

Bowl, Dressing, 2 Sections,
Crystal Footed
Underplate 325.00

Cup & Saucer 45.00

Tumbler, 10 Oz.,
5 5/8 In. 30.00

TASSEL
See Princess

TEA ROOM

The very Art Deco design of Tea Room has made it popular with collectors; it

is even called Moderne Art by some. The Indiana Glass Company, Dunkirk, Indiana, made it from 1926 to 1931. Dinner sets were made of Amber, Crystal, Green, and Pink glass.

Crystal

Saltshaker 28.00

Sugar, Footed 35.00

Sugar & Creamer, Tray,
Center Handle 135.00

Vase, Ruffled, 9 1/2 In. . . 20.00

Green

Bowl, Salad, Handles,
8 3/4 In. 95.00

Candlestick 55.00

Celery Dish,
8 1/4 In. . . . . . . 40.00 to 45.00

Dish, Sundae, Footed 32.00

Pitcher, 64 Oz.,
10 In. . . . . . . 220.00 to 335.00

Saltshaker . . . . . . 45.00 to 55.00

Sherbet . . . . 32.00 to 40.00

Sugar & Creamer,
Rectangular 150.00

Sugar & Creamer, Tray, Center
Handle . . . . . 185.00 to 195.00

Tumbler, 8 Oz.,
4 1/4 In. 125.00

Tumbler, Footed,
6 Oz., 5 In. 45.00

Tumbler, Footed,
8 Oz., 5 1/4 In. 38.00

Tumbler, Iced Tea, Footed,
11 Oz., 6 1/4 In. 60.00

Vase, Ruffled Edge,
6 1/2 In. 120.00

Vase, Ruffled Edge,
11 In. . . . . . . 175.00 to 295.00

Pink

Candlestick, Pair 145.00

Creamer, 3 1/4 In. 42.00

Creamer, Footed,
4 1/2 In. . . . . . . 20.00 to 25.00

Creamer,
Rectangular . . . 30.00 to 36.00

Cup 60.00

Dish, Banana Split, Footed,
7 1/2 In. . . . . . . 50.00 to 75.00

Dish, Sundae,
Footed . . . . . . 80.00 to 100.00

Goblet, 9 Oz. 98.00

Ice Bucket . . . . . 95.00 to 125.00

Mustard, Cover 100.00

Pitcher,
64 Oz. . . . . . 185.00 to 225.00

Plate, Sherbet, 6 In. 40.00

Relish, 2 Sections 35.00

Salt & Pepper 130.00

Saucer 35.00

Shaker 30.00

Sherbet . . . . 25.00 to 35.00

Sugar, 3 1/4 In. . . 40.00 to 65.00

Sugar,
Rectangular . . . 25.00 to 36.00

Sugar & Creamer 40.00

Sugar & Creamer, Tray, Center
Handle . . . . . 130.00 to 185.00

Tray, Center Handle, For Sugar
& Creamer . . . 85.00 to 145.00

Tumbler, Footed, 6 Oz.,
5 In. . . . . 48.00 to 60.00

Tumbler, Footed, 8 Oz.,
5 1/4 In. 40.00

Tumbler, Malted Milk, Footed,
12 Oz. 35.00

Vase, Ruffled Edge,
6 1/2 In. 75.00

TEAR DROP

Tear Drop, a pattern available in full dinnerware sets, was made by Duncan & Miller Glass Company, Washington, Pennsylvania, from 1934 to 1955. It was made only in Crystal.

Ashtray, 3 In. . . . . . 6.00 to 9.00

Bonbon, 4 Handles,
6 In. 15.00

Bowl, Dressing, 2 Sections,
6 In. 15.00

Bowl, Floral, 3-Footed,
4 x 12 In. 45.00

Bowl, Salad, 12 In. 45.00

Candlestick, 2-Light 40.00

Compote, 4 3/4 In. 14.00
Cup & Saucer 7.00
Dish, Sweetmeat, Center
   Handle, 6 1/2 In. 35.00
Egg Plate, 11 1/4 In. 15.00
Goblet, Champagne, 5 Oz.,
   5 In. . . . . 10.00 to 18.00
Goblet, Cocktail,
   3 1/2 Oz., 4 1/2 In. 15.00
Goblet, Water, 9 Oz.,
   7 In. . . . . 14.00 to 15.00
Goblet, Wine, 3 Oz.,
   4 3/4 In. 18.00
Nappy, Handles,
   5 In. . . . . 10.00 to 12.00
Nappy, Handles, 7 In. 12.00
Nut Dish, 2 Sections, Handles,
   6 In. . . . . 11.00 to 15.00
Olive Dish, 2 Sections,
   6 In. 15.00
Oyster Cocktail, 3 1/2 Oz.,
   2 3/4 In. 8.00
Pickle, 6 In. 15.00
Plate, Bread & Butter,
   4 In. 6.00
Plate, Bread & Butter,
   6 In. 4.00
Plate, Lemon, Handles,
   7 In. 8.00
Plate, Luncheon,
   8 1/2 In. 8.00
Plate, Salad, 7 1/2 In. 5.00
Relish, 2 Sections, Heart
   Shape, 7 1/2 In. 20.00
Relish, 3 Sections, Flower
   Etch, 9 In. 25.00
Relish, 4 Sections, 4 Handles,
   Square, 12 In. 25.00
Relish, 5 Sections,
   12 In. 30.00
Salt & Pepper 25.00
Saucer 2.00
Sherbet 6.00
Sherbet, 5 Oz., 3 1/2 In. . . 20.00
Sugar, Cover 25.00
Sugar &
   Creamer . . . . . . 16.00 to 25.00
Tumbler, Footed, 9 Oz.,
   4 1/2 In. 8.00
Tumbler, Hi-Ball, Footed,
   14 Oz., 6 In. 18.00
Tumbler, Whiskey, 2 Oz.,
   2 1/4 In. 20.00

TEMPO

Cambridge Glass Company's Tempo pattern features a cut design. It was made in Crystal in the 1940s.

Creamer 15.00
Goblet, 9 Oz., 5 In. 15.00
Goblet, Claret, 4 1/2 Oz.,
   5 7/8 In. 45.00
Goblet, Cocktail, 3 Oz.,
   4 7/8 In. 16.00
Goblet, Cordial, 1 Oz.,
   4 1/2 In. 26.00
Goblet, Wine, 2 1/2 Oz.,
   5 1/2 In. 40.00
Oyster Cocktail, 4 1/2 Oz.,
   3 1/8 In. 22.00
Plate, Salad, 7 1/2 In. 24.00
Sherbet, 6 Oz., 3 1/2 In. . . 18.00
Sherbet, 6 Oz., 4 5/8 In. . . 13.00
Sugar 15.00
Tumbler, Iced Tea, Footed,
   12 Oz., 6 1/4 In. 26.00

TERRACE

Terrace was made by Duncan & Miller Glass Company, Washington, Pennsylvania, in 1955 in Amber, Blue, Crystal, and Ruby.

Crystal
Bowl, Dessert, 5 3/8 In. . . 16.00
Bowl, Flared, Footed,
   6 3/4 In. 60.00
Bowl, Flared, Handles,
   9 1/2 In. 50.00
Bowl, Handles,
   10 1/2 In. 30.00
Compote, 3 3/4 In. 30.00
Compote, 7 In. 40.00

Creamer, Footed,
   2 7/8 In. 20.00
Cup & Saucer, Footed,
   2 1/4 In. 25.00
Goblet, Champagne, 5 Oz.,
   4 3/4 In. 18.00
Goblet, Water, 10 Oz.,
   6 5/8 In. 20.00
Goblet, Wine, 3 Oz.,
   5 1/8 In. 30.00
Nappy, Square, 5 1/2 In. . . 25.00
Pitcher, 8 3/4 In. 100.00
Plate, 8 1/2 In. 15.00
Plate, Bread & Butter,
   6 In. 15.00
Plate, Dinner, 10 1/2 In. . . 35.00
Plate, Lemon, 8 1/2 In. . . . 25.00
Plate, Luncheon,
   8 1/2 In. 18.00
Plate, Salad, 7 1/2 In. 24.00
Relish, 5 Sections,
   12 In. 40.00
Saucer 8.00
Sherbet, 5 Oz., 3 In. 16.00
Sugar, Footed, 2 7/8 In. . . 20.00
Sugar & Creamer 50.00
Tumbler, 5 1/2 In. 18.00
Tumbler, Juice, Footed,
   4 3/8 In. 16.00
Tumbler, Water, 10 Oz.,
   5 3/4 In. 18.00

Ruby
Goblet, Champagne, 6 Oz.,
   4 7/8 In. 60.00

THISTLE

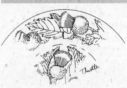

Thistle pattern was made by Macbeth-Evans Glass Company from 1929 to 1930. The pattern pictures large thistles primarily on Pink pieces, but Crystal, Green, and Yellow dishes also were made. Reproductions have been made.

Green

Plate, Luncheon,
8 In. . . . . 20.00 to 28.00
Saucer 15.00

Pink

Bowl, Cereal,
5 1/2 In. . . . . . 30.00 to 35.00
Plate, Luncheon,
8 In. . . . . 22.00 to 25.00

THOUSAND LINE

The Thousand Line pattern gets its name from the numbers (1000–1090) listed in Anchor Hocking Glass Company's catalogs. Collectors also know it as Stars & Bars or Rainbow Stars. It was made from 1941 through the '60s in Crystal and White. Some pieces were decorated with colored satin stains.

Crystal

Bowl, Salad, 10 1/2 In. . . . 30.00
Bowl, Vegetable,
10 7/8 In. 15.00
Cake Plate, 12 In. 15.00
Candleholder, Handle,
5 1/4 In. 10.00
Dish, Jelly, Handle, 6 In. . . 3.00
Relish, 2 Sections, Handles,
10 In. 6.00
Sugar & Creamer . . 5.00 to 8.00

THREADING
See Old English

THREE PARROT
See Sylvan

TIERED BLOCK
See Party Line

TIERED OCTAGON
See Octagon

TIERED SEMI OPTIC
See Party Line

TOWN AND COUNTRY

Eva Zeisel designed glass accessories to match her Town & Country dinnerware line in 1954. A.H. Heisey & Company made the pattern in Crystal, Dawn (charcoal), and Limelight (turquoise). The pattern won a design award in 1955.

Dawn

Plate, 7 1/4 In. 15.00
Plate, 8 3/4 In. 35.00
Platter, 14 In. 30.00
Tumbler, Iced Tea,
5 1/4 In. 35.00

TREE OF LIFE
See Craquel

TROJAN

The Fostoria Glass Company made Trojan. The etched glass dishes were made in Rose from 1929 to 1935, Topaz from 1929 to 1938, and Gold Tint from 1938 to 1944. It also was made in Green. Crystal bases were used on some pieces from 1931 to 1944.

Topaz

Creamer 22.00
Creamer, Tea 51.00
Cup 18.00

Cup & Saucer 24.00
Dish, Grapefruit, Insert . . . 50.00
Finger Bowl 52.00
Goblet, Cocktail, 3 Oz.,
5 1/4 In. 33.00
Plate, Bread & Butter,
6 In. 8.00
Platter, 12 In. 60.00
Saucer 6.00
Sherbet, 6 In. 26.00
Sugar 22.00
Sugar, Tea 46.00
Tumbler, Footed, 5 Oz.,
4 1/2 In. 30.00
Tumbler, Footed, 9 Oz.,
5 1/2 In. 21.00
Whipped Cream Bowl . . . 38.00

TULIP

Tulip pattern pictures the side of a tulip in a very stylized border. It was made by the Dell Glass Company of Millville, New Jersey, during the 1930s. Amber, Amethyst, Blue, Crystal, and Green pieces were made. Fire-King made mixing bowls with tulip decals. Fire-King is listed in its own section in this book.

Amethyst

Tumbler, Whiskey,
1 3/4 In. 35.00

Blue

Ice Tub, 4 7/8 In. 95.00
Tumbler, Juice, 2 3/4 In. . . 40.00
Tumbler, Whiskey,
1 3/4 In. 30.00

Green

Creamer 20.00
Cup 16.00
Plate, 6 In. 9.00
Plate, 10 In. 20.00
Saucer .... 5.00 to 8.00

TURQUOISE BLUE

Turquoise Blue, one of the patterns made by Anchor Hocking Glass Corporation, is a plain pattern named for its color. Mixing bowls were made in 1-pt., 1-qt., 2-qt., and 3-qt. sizes. It was made from 1956 to 1958. Other related patterns are listed in the Fire-King section in this book.

Mixing Bowl, Splashproof,
6 3/4 In. ...... 20.00 to 25.00
Mixing Bowl, Splashproof,
7 3/4 In. 22.00
Mug, Straight Sides 12.00
Relish, 3 Sections,
11 x 8 In. 16.00

TWIST

Twist is one of the most popular patterns by A.H. Heisey & Company, Newark, Ohio. The Art Deco–style pattern includes square, stepped feet and lightning bolt handles. Pieces were made

from 1928 to 1937 in Flamingo (pink), Marigold (deep yellow), Moongleam (green), and Sahara (light yellow). Most pieces are marked with the Diamond H logo.

Flamingo

Bonbon, Handles, 6 In. ... 60.00
Celery Dish, 13 In. 55.00
Cruet, 4 Oz. 140.00
Cup & Saucer, After
Dinner 50.00
Dish, Almond, Footed,
2 1/2 In. 60.00
Dish, Jelly, Handles,
6 In. 70.00
Goblet, Champagne,
5 Oz., 4 3/4 In. 46.00
Ice Bucket, Metal
Handle 200.00
Nappy, 4 1/2 In. 20.00
Plate, Salad, 7 1/8 In. 44.00
Salt & Pepper 150.00
Tumbler, Footed, Cone Shape,
5 Oz., 4 1/2 In. 60.00

Marigold

Goblet, Water, 9 Oz. 100.00

Moongleam

Celery Dish, 10 In. 75.00
Ice Bucket, Metal Handle,
5 1/2 In. 250.00
Pickle, 7 In. 70.00
Plate, Bread & Butter,
5 7/8 In. 25.00

◆◆

Don't light a cabinet filled with glass with light bulbs over 25 watts. Stronger bulbs generate too much heat. There are some new types of bulbs that are brighter and give off less heat.

◆◆

Plate, Luncheon, 8 In. 38.00
Plate, Salad, 7 In. 38.00
Relish, 3 Sections,
13 In. 90.00

Sahara

Cruet, 4 Oz. 185.00

TWISTED OPTIC

Twisted Optic, or line No. 313, is the pattern sometimes confused with Spiral. Be sure to look at the information about that pattern. Imperial Glass Company of Bellaire, Ohio, made Twisted Optic luncheon sets from 1927 to 1930 in Amber, Blue, Canary Yellow, two shades of Green, and Pink.

Blue

Plate, Luncheon, 8 In. 12.00

Canary Yellow

Plate, Luncheon, 8 In. 12.00
Plate, Sherbet, 6 In. 8.00
Sherbet, Underplate 15.00

Green

Sandwich Server, 10 In. ... 9.00

Pink

Basket, 10 In. 55.00
Bowl, 9 In. 26.00
Bowl, Ruffled Edge,
7 In. 18.00
Candy Jar, Cover,
Footed 60.00
Cup & Saucer .... 6.00 to 13.00
Plate, Luncheon, 8 In. 9.00
Sherbet 10.00

Tumbler, 12 Oz.,
5 1/4 In. 14.00

U.S. OCTAGON
See Octagon

VERNON
See No. 616

VERSAILLES

Versailles by Fostoria
Glass Company was made
in many colors during the
years of its production,
1928 to 1944. Azure (blue),
Green, and Rose were
made from 1928 to 1944,
Topaz from 1929 to 1938,
and Gold Tint from 1938
to 1944. Crystal bases
were used with colored
glass from 1931 to 1944.

Azure
Bonbon, Gold Trim 35.00
Compote, 6 1/2 In. 125.00
Sandwich Server, Center
Handle, 11 In. 90.00

Green
Cup 26.00
Dish, Lemon 40.00

Rose
Candlestick, 3 In., Pair . . . 53.00
Candlestick, Scroll, 5 In.,
Pair 110.00
Celery Dish, 11 1/2 In. . . 115.00
Compote, 5 In. 70.00
Dish, Mint, 3-Footed,
4 1/2 In. 35.00
Goblet, Water, 10 Oz.,
8 1/4 In. 75.00

Goblet, Wine, 3 Oz.,
5 1/2 In. 115.00
Plate, Bread & Butter,
6 In. . . . .'. 12.00
Plate, Salad, 7 In. 15.00
Sugar Pail 195.00
Tumbler, Whiskey,
Footed, 2 1/2 Oz. 47.00
Whipped Cream Tub, Metal
Handle, 4 3/4 In. 325.00

Topaz
Ashtray 32.50
Bouillon, Footed,
Underplate 45.00
Bowl, 3-Footed, 12 In. . . . 85.00
Cruet, Footed, Stopper . . 165.00
Cup 25.00
Cup & Saucer 28.00
Plate, Dinner, 10 1/4 In. . . 40.00
Whipped Cream Bowl . . . 45.00

VERTICAL RIBBED
See Queen Mary

VESPER

Vesper was made by the
Fostoria Glass Company
of Ohio and West Virginia
from 1926 to 1934. Din-
ner sets were made in
Amber, Blue, and Green.

Amber
Goblet, Cocktail,
3 Oz. 30.00
Goblet, Water, 9 Oz. 32.50
Plate, Dinner, 9 1/2 In. . . . 30.00
Plate, Luncheon, 8 In. 10.00

Green
Ice Bucket 115.00

VICTORIAN FOSTORIA

Fostoria Glass Company's
Victorian stemware pat-
tern was made from 1933
to 1943, mostly in Crystal.
Combination pieces, with
Burgundy, Empire Green,
Iridescent, Regal Blue,
Ruby, and Silver Mist
bowls and crystal bases,
were made, too.

Empire Green
Goblet, Water, 10 Oz.,
5 5/8 In. 30.00
Goblet, Wine, 3 1/2 Oz.,
4 1/2 In. 26.00

Regal Blue
Goblet, Water, 10 Oz.,
5 5/8 In. . . . .: 85.00
Goblet, Wine, 3 1/2 Oz.,
4 1/2 In. 55.00
Tumbler, Juice, Footed,
5 Oz., 4 1/4 In. 35.00

VICTORIAN HEISEY

A.H. Heisey & Company's
Victorian pattern mimics
the Waffle pressed glass

pattern of the nineteenth century. Heisey made items in Cobalt Blue, Crystal, and Sahara from 1933 to 1953. Goblets were made in Flamingo (pink) and Moongleam (green). Victorian stemware and accessories were reissued in Amber, Azalea (lavender), Crystal, and Verde (olive green) by Imperial Glass Company. Most pieces, even those reissued by Imperial, are marked with the Diamond H logo.

Crystal

Butter, Cover ... 30.00 to 50.00
Finger Bowl 20.00
Goblet, 9 Oz. 30.00
Goblet, Champagne,
   5 Oz. .... 15.00 to 19.00
Goblet, Wine, 2 1/2 Oz. .. 25.00
Plate, 8 In. ...... 30.00 to 35.00
Relish, 3 Sections,
   11 In. 40.00
Sherbet, 5 Oz. ... 20.00 to 25.00
Sugar 30.00
Vase, 4 In. ...... 25.00 to 55.00

VICTORY

The Diamond Glass-Ware Company, Indiana, Pennsylvania, made Victory pattern from 1929 to 1932. It is known in Amber, Black, Cobalt Blue, Green, and Pink. A few pieces have gold trim.

Cobalt Blue

Candlestick, 3 In., Pair .. 155.00
Cup & Saucer ... 42.00 to 58.00

Plate, Luncheon, 8 In. 28.00

Green

Cup & Saucer 12.00

Pink

Bowl, Cereal, 6 1/2 In. 12.00
Dish, Mayonnaise,
   Underplate 38.00
Plate, Luncheon, 8 In. 9.00

VITROCK

Vitrock is both a kitchenware and a dinnerware pattern. It has a raised flowered rim and is often called Floral Rim or Flower Rim by collectors. It was made by Hocking Glass Company from 1934 to 1937 and resembles embossed china. It was made in White, sometimes with fired-on colors, in solid Red or Green, and with decal-decorated centers.

Canister, Cover, Sugar,
   6 1/2 x 5 In. 150.00
Grease Jar, Cover,
   Tulips 40.00
Grease Jar, Metal Cover,
   Red Circle,
   Flowers ...... 48.00 to 56.00
Mug, Red, Little Bo Peep,
   3 1/4 x 3 In. 18.00
Range Set, Blue Circle,
   5 In., 4 Piece 175.00
Range Set, Fired-On Yellow,
   5 In., 4 Piece 160.00
Refrigerator Dish, Cover,
   Red Stripes, 32 Oz.,
   5 3/4 In. 76.00
Shaker, Cover, Flour,
   Tulips 34.00

Shaker, Cover, Pepper,
   Tulips 28.00

VIVID BANDS
See Petalware

WAFFLE
See Waterford

WATERFORD

Waterford, or Waffle, pattern was made by Anchor Hocking Glass Corporation from 1938 to 1944. Crystal and Pink are the most common colors; Yellow and White were used less extensively. Some of the Opaque White pieces also have fired-on pink and green. In the 1950s some Forest Green pieces were made.

Crystal

Ashtray, 4 In. .... 7.00 to 10.00
Berry Bowl,
   4 3/4 In. .... 8.00 to 15.00
Berry Bowl, Master,
   8 1/4 In. ...... 10.00 to 17.00
Bowl, Cereal, 5 1/2 In. 17.00
Butter, Cover ... 26.00 to 29.00
Butter, Cover Only 20.00
Butter, No Cover 6.00
Cake Plate, Handles,
   10 1/4 In. ...... 9.00 to 12.00
Coaster, 4 In. ..... 3.00 to 5.00
Creamer .... 5.00 to 6.00
Cup 8.00
Cup & Saucer .... 8.00 to 12.00

Goblet,
5 1/4 In. . . . . . 17.00 to 25.00

Goblet, 5 5/8 In. 15.00

Pitcher, Juice, Tilted,
42 Oz. 30.00

Plate, Dinner,
9 5/8 In. . . . . . 10.00 to 15.00

Plate, Salad,
7 1/8 In. . . . . . . 6.00 to 10.00

Plate, Sherbet, 6 In. 3.00 to 4.00

Relish, 5 Sections,
13 3/4 In. . . . . . 16.00 to 25.00

Salt & Pepper . . . . 7.00 to 10.00

Sandwich Server,
13 3/4 In. . . . . . 10.00 to 20.00

Saucer . . . . 3.00 to 4.00

Sherbet . . . . 4.00 to 5.00

Sherbet, Ruffled Edge . . . 25.00

Sherbet, Scalloped
Base . . . . 15.00 to 18.00

Sugar 8.00

Sugar, Cover . . . . 10.00 to 18.00

Sugar & Creamer,
Cover . . . . 14.00 to 20.00

Tumbler, Footed, 10 Oz.,
4 7/8 In. . . . . . . 10.00 to 15.00

Pink

Butter, No Cover 95.00

Cake Plate, Handles,
10 1/4 In. . . . . . 20.00 to 35.00

Glassware, old or new, requires careful handling. Wash in moderately hot water and mild detergent. Avoid wiping gold or platinum banded pieces while glasses are hot. Never use scouring pads or silver polish on glass. With an automatic dishwasher, be sure the water temperature is under 180 degrees.

Creamer 20.00

Plate, Sherbet, 6 In. 10.00

Sandwich Server,
13 3/4 In. . . . . . 30.00 to 45.00

Sugar, Cover 60.00

Tumbler, Footed, 10 Oz.,
4 7/8 In. 30.00

WAVERLY

A.H. Heisey & Company, Newark, Ohio, made the Waverly pattern, originally called Oceanic, from 1940 to 1957. The items were made in Crystal and sold plain or with Heisey's popular Orchid and Rose etchings.

Bowl, Crimped, 12 In. . . . 45.00

Bowl, Gardenia, 13 In. . . . 50.00

Candleholder, Epergnette,
6 In. 23.00

Candlestick, 2-Light,
Pair 125.00

Celery Dish, 12 In. 25.00

Chocolate Dish, Cover,
5 In. 45.00

Dish, Mayonnaise, 2 Sections,
Footed, 6 1/2 In. 40.00

Plate, Salad, 8 In. 25.00

Relish, 3 Sections,
3 Handles . . . . . 25.00 to 35.00

Salt & Pepper,
Footed . . . . 33.00 to 43.00

Sugar & Creamer 55.00

Torte Plate,
14 In. . . . . 25.00 to 35.00

WEDDING BAND
See Moderntone

WESTMORELAND
SANDWICH
See Princess Feather

WEXFORD

Wexord is an imitation cut glass pattern made by Anchor Hocking Glass Corporation, Lancaster, Ohio, from 1967 to 1998. Pieces were made in Crystal, Green, Pewter Mist, and with fired-on decorations. Other related patterns are listed in the Fire-King section in this book.

Crystal

Bowl, 5 1/2 In. . . . . 3.00 to 4.00

Bowl, Salad Set, 4 Piece . . 29.00

Bowl, Salad, 5 1/4 In. 8.00

Bowl, Salad, 6 In. 7.50

Bowl, Salad, 9 3/4 In. 10.00

Butter, Cover, 1/4 Lb. 11.00

Canister, 58 Oz., 9 In. 15.00

Centerpiece, Footed,
8 In. . . . . 15.00 to 20.00

Cup, 7 Oz. 2.00

Decanter, Stopper,
32 Oz., 15 In. 16.00

Goblet, 9 1/2 Oz.,
6 1/2 In. 3.00

Ice Bucket, Cover,
10 1/2 In. 27.00

Jar, Cover, 96 Oz. 45.00

Pitcher, 64 Oz., 9 In. 25.00

Plate, Dinner, Scalloped
Edge, 9 1/2 In. 18.00

Punch Bowl,
14 x 8 1/4 In. 40.00

Punch Cup 2.00

Salt & Pepper, 8 Oz.,
4 1/4 In. 15.00

Sherbet, 7 Oz. 2.00

Sugar & Creamer 10.00

Sugar & Creamer,
Cover 20.00

Sugar & Creamer, Cover,
Tray 25.00

Tumbler, Iced Tea,
15 Oz., 6 In. 15.00

Vase, 10 1/2 In. 15.00

WHEAT

Wheat glass was made by Anchor Hocking Glass Corporation from 1962 to 1966. It is part of the Fire-King Ovenware line. It is a white opaque glass decorated with a natural-looking spray of wheat. A few pieces were given added decoration. Anchor Hocking also made transparent glassware with an embossed wheat design. Other companies made glassware with Wheat designs, but only the Anchor Hocking glass is listed here.

Cake Pan, Round, 8 In. . . . 11.00

Casserole, Cover,
1 1/2 Qt. 10.00

Casserole, Cover, 1 Qt. . . . 12.00

Custard Cup,
6 Oz. . . . . 3.00 to 4.00

Plate, Dinner, 10 In. 6.00

Saucer, 5 3/4 In. 1.00

WHIRLPOOL
See Provincial

WHITE SAIL
See White Ship

WHITE SHIP

White Ship, also called Sailboat, Sailing Ship, Ships, or White Sail, is really part of the Sportsman series made by Hazel Atlas Glass Company in 1938. The ships are enamel decorations on Amethyst, Cobalt Blue, or Crystal. The enamel decorations are sometimes in color.

Cobalt Blue

Cocktail Mixer 35.00

Cocktail Shaker 22.00

Ice Bowl 35.00

Tumbler, 9 Oz.,
4 5/8 In. 16.00

Tumbler, Roly Poly,
6 Oz. 10.00

Tumbler, Water, 9 Oz.,
3 3/4 In. 18.00

Crystal

Cocktail Set, 5 Piece 13.00

Pitcher, 32 Oz. 69.00

Plate, Salad, 8 In. 60.00

Tumbler, Water,
9 Oz.,
4 5/8 In. 11.00

WILD BIRD
See Game Bird

WILDFLOWER

Wildflower is another increasingly popular etch made by Cambridge Glass Company. Items were made from 1935 to 1953 in Amber, Crystal, and Emerald. Gold encrusted Ebony accessories can be found, too.

Amber

Cheese Dish, Footed, Gold
Encrusted 75.00

Crystal

Bonbon, Crimped, Handles,
6 In. 35.00

Bowl, Flared, Footed,
Gold Edge, 12 In. 65.00

Bowl, Handles, 13 In. . . . 135.00

Bowl, Salad, Handles,
11 In. 55.00

Candlestick, 2-Light, 6 In.,
Pair 65.00

Candy Dish, Cover,
3 Sections 115.00

Compote, Keyhole Stem,
5 3/8 x 7 1/8 In. 100.00

Dish, Mayonnaise 75.00

Pickle, Oblong,
10 In. 29.00

Plate, Handles, Gold Edge,
12 In. 60.00

Plate, Handles, Gold Encrusted,
13 1/2 In. 85.00

Relish, 2 Sections, Gold
Encrusted, 7 In. 55.00

Sherbet, High, 6 Oz. 29.00

Sherbet, Low, 6 Oz. 15.00

Tumbler, Iced Tea, Footed, Gold
Encrusted, 12 Oz. 28.00

Vase, Flip, 8 In. 195.00

Ebony

Vase, Bud, Gold Encrusted,
10 In. 495.00

WILDROSE
See Dogwood

WILDROSE WITH APPLE BLOSSOM
See Flower Garden with Butterflies

WILLOW

Fostoria Glass Company used Willow etch on stemware and accessories from 1939 to 1944. Only Crystal items are known.

Compote, 4 3/4 In. 46.00
Creamer, Footed,
   4 1/8 In. 28.00
Cup & Saucer,
   After Dinner 35.00
Finger Bowl, 4 5/8 In. . . . 34.00
Goblet, Champagne, 6 Oz.,
   4 7/8 In. . . . . . . 16.00 to 18.00
Goblet, Cocktail, 3 3/4 Oz.,
   4 3/8 In. 18.00
Goblet, Water, 9 Oz.,
   6 1/4 In. 28.00
Oyster Cocktail, 4 Oz. . . . 16.00
Pitcher, 8 5/8 In. 200.00
Plate, Salad, 7 1/2 In. 20.00
Plate, Salad,
   8 In. . . . . 16.00 to 20.00
Sherbet, 6 Oz., 4 7/8 In. . . 14.00
Sugar, Footed, 3 7/8 In. . . 30.00
Tumbler, Footed, 9 Oz.,
   5 1/8 In. 24.00
Tumbler, Iced Tea, Footed,
   12 Oz., 5 3/4 In. 28.00
Tumbler, Juice, Footed,
   5 Oz., 4 1/2 In. 24.00

WILLOW WOM

Dealers have debated the name and origin of this pattern for some time. Is it Willow, Oleander, or Magnolia? To cover all three names, many dealers list it simply as WOM. Collectors may see it listed as WOML, too, because some dealers also consider the name Laurel to be a possibility. The pattern was probably made by Indiana Glass Company in the 1940s. Most items are Crystal, though some pieces have been spotted with stained colors.

Crystal
Bowl, Fruit, 11 1/2 In. . . . 40.00
Creamer 8.00
Sandwich Server,
   13 1/2 In. 40.00
Sugar 8.00

WILLOWMERE

Willowmere etch was used by Fostoria Glass Company on Crystal glassware from 1938 to 1970.

Bowl, Flared, 12 In. 90.00
Bowl, Salad, 2 Sections,
   10 In. 160.00
Bowl, Vegetable, Handles,
   11 In. 70.00
Cake Plate, Handles,
   13 1/8 In. 66.00
Candelabrum, 2-Light,
   Pair 145.00
Cocktail, 3 1/2 Oz.,
   4 3/4 In. 12.00
Creamer, Footed,
   3 1/4 In. 26.00
Creamer, Footed,
   4 1/8 In. 25.00
Cup & Saucer, Footed,
   After Dinner 26.00
Dish, Mayonnaise, 2 Sections,
   6 3/4 In. 55.00
Dish, Mayonnnaise,
   Underplate, Ladle 80.00
Goblet, Champagne,
   6 Oz., 5 5/8 In. 22.00
Goblet, Claret, 4 Oz.,
   5 3/4 In. 80.00
Goblet, Water, 10 Oz.,
   7 1/8 In. 24.00
Goblet, Wine, 3 1/2 Oz.,
   5 3/8 In. 70.00

Oyster Cocktail, 4 1/2 Oz.,
   3 1/2 In. 30.00
Pitcher,
   48 Oz. . . . . . 345.00 to 500.00
Plate, Dinner, 9 1/2 In. . . . 60.00
Plate, Luncheon, 8 3/8 In.   30.00
Plate, Salad, 7 1/2 In. 20.00
Relish, 2 Sections, 8 In. . . 50.00
Relish, 3 Sections,
   12 3/4 In. 55.00
Relish, 4 Sections,
   12 3/4 In. 75.00
Sandwich Server, Center
   Handle, 11 1/4 In. 80.00
Sherbet, 6 Oz., 4 3/8 In. . . 22.00
Sugar, Footed, 3 1/2 In. . . 28.00
Torte Plate,
   14 In. . . . . 55.00 to 80.00
Tray, Muffin, Handles,
   9 1/2 In. 70.00
Tumbler, Footed, 9 Oz.,
   5 1/4 In. 30.00
Tumbler, Iced Tea, 12 Oz.,
   5 3/4 In. 42.00
Tumbler, Juice, Footed,
   5 Oz., 4 5/8 In. 30.00

WINDMILL

Windmill, or Dutch, is a part of the Sportsman series made by Hazel Atlas Glass Company in 1938. It pictures a landscape with a windmill. The windmills are enamel decorations on Cobalt Blue, Crystal, or Amethyst glass.

Cobalt Blue
Cocktail Mixer 40.00
Cocktail Shaker 65.00
Ice Bowl . . . . 35.00 to 38.00

Tumbler, 9 Oz.,
3 3/4 In. 16.00
Tumbler, Old Fashioned, 8 Oz.,
3 1/4 In. . . . . . 30.00 to 35.00

Crystal

Cocktail Mixer 40.00
Cocktail Shaker Set,
5 Piece 135.00
Cocktail Shaker Set,
7 Piece 235.00

WINDSOR

Windsor pattern, also
called Diamond, Smocking,
or Windsor Diamond, was
made by Jeannette Glass
Company, Jeannette,
Pennsylvania, from 1936
to 1946. The pattern is
most easily found in Crystal, Green, and Pink,
although pieces were
made in Amberina, Del-
phite, Ice Blue, and Red.

Crystal

Bowl, Boat Shape,
7 x 11 3/4 In. 39.00
Bowl, Salad, 10 1/2 In. . . . 22.00
Butter, Cover . . . 25.00 to 28.00
Candleholder, 5 In. 38.00
Candlestick, 3 In., Pair . . . 22.00
Candy Jar, Cover 50.00
Chop Plate, 13 5/8 In. 45.00
Creamer . . . . 5.00 to 6.00
Cup & Saucer . . . . . 6.00 to 7.00
Pitcher, 16 Oz.,
4 1/2 In. . . . . . . 18.00 to 25.00
Pitcher, 52 Oz.,
6 3/4 In. . . . . . 12.00 to 13.00
Plate, Dinner,
9 In. . . . . 7.00 to 8.00

Plate, Dinner, Pointed
Edge, 10 1/2 In. 9.00
Platter, Oval, 11 1/2 In. . . . 8.00
Powder Jar,
Cover . . . . 15.00 to 30.00
Relish, 3 Sections,
11 1/2 In. 28.00
Saltshaker 10.00
Saucer 3.00
Sugar, Cover, Holiday
Style 15.00
Sugar, Iridescent 15.00
Sugar & Creamer 52.00
Tumbler, 9 Oz., 4 In. 23.00
Tumbler, 12 Oz., 5 In. . . . 39.00
Tumbler, Footed, 11 Oz.,
5 In. . . . . 10.00 to 11.00

Delphite

Ashtray, 5 3/4 In. 52.00

Green

Bowl, Boat Shape,
7 x 11 3/4 In. . . 45.00 to 60.00
Bowl, Cereal,
5 3/8 In. . . . . . 25.00 to 35.00
Bowl, Vegetable, Oval,
9 1/2 In. 37.00
Butter, Cover . . 95.00 to 130.00
Cake Plate, Footed,
10 3/4 In. . . . . . 30.00 to 35.00
Chop Plate, 13 5/8 In. 38.00
Coaster, 3 1/4 In. 24.00
Creamer . . . . . . 15.00 to 18.00
Cup . . . . 13.00 to 14.00
Cup & Saucer 20.00
Pitcher, 52 Oz.,
6 3/4 In. . . . . . 59.00 to 68.00
Plate, Dinner,
9 In. . . . . 30.00 to 35.00
Plate, Salad, 7 In. 25.00
Plate, Sherbet, 6 In. 8.00
Platter, Oval,
11 1/2 In. . . . . 20.00 to 30.00
Salt & Pepper . . . 59.00 to 60.00
Saltshaker 35.00
Sandwich Server, Handles,
10 1/4 In. 25.00
Saucer 5.00
Soup, Cream, 5 In. 32.00
Sugar . . . . 18.00 to 24.00
Sugar, Cover . . . . 33.00 to 45.00
Tray, Handles,
4 1/8 x 9 In. 33.00

Tumbler, 5 Oz.,
3 1/4 In. . . . . . 35.00 to 39.00
Tumbler, 9 Oz.,
4 In. . . . . 30.00 to 38.00

Ice Blue

Candy Jar, Cover 12.00
Cup 72.00

Pink

Ashtray,
5 3/4 In. . . . . . 43.00 to 45.00
Berry Bowl,
4 3/4 In. . . . . . 12.00 to 13.00
Berry Bowl, Master,
8 1/2 In. . . . . . 22.00 to 30.00
Bowl, 3-Footed,
7 1/8 In. 37.00
Bowl, Boat Shape,
7 x 11 3/4 In. . . 35.00 to 45.00
Bowl, Cereal,
5 3/8 In. . . . . . 32.00 to 40.00
Bowl, Handles,
9 In. . . . . 25.00 to 35.00
Butter, Cover . . . 40.00 to 60.00
Butter, Cover, Diamond . . 90.00
Butter, No Cover 23.00
Cake Plate, Handles,
10 3/4 In. 24.00
Chop Plate,
13 5/8 In. . . . . . 35.00 to 46.00
Compote,
5 1/2 In. . . . . . 20.00 to 35.00
Console, 12 1/2 In. 145.00
Creamer . . . . . . 10.00 to 15.00
Cup . . . . 10.00 to 12.00
Cup & Saucer 18.00
Pitcher, 52 Oz.,
6 3/4 In. . . . . . 32.00 to 40.00
Plate, Dinner,
9 In. . . . . 23.00 to 28.00
Plate, Sherbet,
6 In. . . . . 6.00 to 8.00
Platter, Oval,
11 1/2 In. . . . . 23.00 to 28.00
Salt & Pepper . . . 45.00 to 48.00
Saltshaker 22.00
Sandwich Server, Closed
Handles, 10 In. 45.00
Sandwich Server, Open Handles,
10 1/4 In. . . . . . 16.00 to 20.00
Saucer 5.00
Sherbet . . . . 12.00 to 18.00
Sugar 16.00
Sugar, Cover . . . . 22.00 to 35.00

Sugar & Creamer 30.00

Sugar & Creamer,
Cover 50.00

Tumbler, 5 Oz.,
3 1/4 In. ...... 30.00 to 31.00

Tumbler, 9 Oz.,
4 In. .... 18.00 to 22.00

Tumbler, 12 Oz.,
5 In. .... 38.00 to 40.00

Red
Tumbler, 9 Oz., 4 In. 55.00

WINDSOR DIAMOND
See Windsor

WINGED MEDALLION
See Madrid

X DESIGN

X Design was a Hazel
Atlas Glass Company pat-
tern made from 1928 to
1932. The name indicates
that the pattern has rows
of X's in grids. It was
made in Crystal, Green,
and Pink. Only a table set
was made.

Green
Creamer 16.00
Sugar, Cover Only 10.00

YEOMAN

Yeoman is one of A.H.
Heisey & Company's
longest-lasting patterns. It
was first made in 1915 and
can be found in Alexan-
drite, Cobalt Blue, Crystal,
Flamingo, Hawthorne,
Marigold, Moongleam, and

Sahara. Many companies
used Yeoman blanks for
cuttings, etchings, and
enameled decorations.

Crystal
Bonbon, 6 1/2 In. 38.00

Coaster, 3 1/2 In. 13.00

Compote, Gold Trim,
5 In. 40.00

Cup & Saucer, After
Dinner 32.00

Dish, Banana Split,
7 3/8 In. 26.00

Goblet, Cocktail, 3 In. ... 26.00

Nappy, 4 3/4 In. 24.00

Plate, Luncheon, 8 In. 26.00

Sherbet, 4 1/2 Oz. 26.00

Sugar & Creamer, Engraved
Flowers, Oval 55.00

Tumbler, 8 Oz.,
3 3/4 In. 26.00

Flamingo
Bonbon, Handle, 6 In. ... 40.00

Bowl, Floral, 8 In. 70.00

Compote, 3 3/4 In. 35.00

Cruet, 4 Oz. 70.00

Cup & Saucer, After
Dinner 28.00

Dish, Mayonnaise, Footed,
Handles, 5 1/2 In. 50.00

Goblet, 8 Oz. 30.00

Goblet, 10 Oz. 30.00

Parfait, 5 Oz. 22.00

Plate, Bread & Butter,
6 In. 20.00

Plate, Luncheon, 8 In. 18.00

Plate, Salad, 7 1/8 In. 17.00

Relish, 3 Sections,
13 In. 45.00

Sherbet, 3 1/2 Oz. 22.00

Tumbler, 6 Oz. 26.00

Hawthorne
Saucer 13.00

Moongleam
Candy Dish, Cover,
6 1/2 In. 75.00

Plate, Bread & Butter,
6 In. 30.00

Sherbet, 4 1/2 Oz. 28.00

Sahara
Bonbon, 7 1/8 In. 34.00

Cup & Saucer, After
Dinner 30.00

Goblet, 8 Oz. 35.00

Parfait, 5 Oz. 24.00

Sherbet, 4 1/2 In. 10.00

YORKTOWN

Federal Glass Company
made the Yorktown pat-
tern in the mid-1950s in
Crystal, Iridescent, Smoke,
White, and Yellow. York-
town is often confused
with Heisey's Provincial
pattern. The circular
impressions are more
rectangular on Federal's
pattern.

Crystal
Luncheon Set, Plates, Cups,
Saucers, 24 Piece 125.00

Tumbler, Juice, Footed,
6 Oz., 3 7/8 In. 4.00

Iridescent
Tumbler, Water,
10 Oz., 4 3/4 In. 3.00

Vase, 8 In. 70.00

Yellow
Compote, 10 In. 17.50

Plate, Handle, Metal,
9 1/2 In. 13.00

DEPRESSION GLASS

Clubs and Publications

CLUBS

Akro Agate Collectors Club, *Clarksburg Crow* (NL), 10 Bailey St., Clarksburg, WV 26301-2524, e-mail: rhardy0424@aol.com, website: www.mkl.com/akro/club.

Fenton Art Glass Collectors of America, Inc., *Butterfly Net* (NL), PO Box 384, Williamstown, WV 26187, e-mail: kkenworthy@foth.com, website: fagcainc.wirefire.com.

Fostoria Glass Collectors, Inc., *Glass Works* (NL), PO Box 1625, Orange, CA 92856, e-mail: info@ fostoriacollectors.org, website: fostoriacollectors.org.

Fostoria Glass Society of America, Inc., *Facets of Fostoria* (NL), PO Box 826, Moundsville, WV 26041, website: www.fostoriaglass.org.

Heisey Collectors of America, *Heisey News* (NL), 169 W. Church St., Newark, OH 43055, e-mail: membership@heiseymuseum.org, website: www.heiseymuseum.org.

Michiana Association of Candlewick Collectors, *MACC Spyglass* (NL), 17370 Battles Rd., South Bend, IN 46614, e-mail: cndlwckmom@aol.com, website: http://www.macc-candlewick.org.

National Cambridge Collectors, Inc., *Cambridge Crystal Ball* (NL), PO Box 416, Cambridge, OH 43725-0416, e-mail: NCC_Crystal_Ball@compuserve.com, website: www.cambridgeglass.org.

National Depression Glass Association, *News & Views* (NL), PO Box 8264, Wichita, KS 67208-0264, e-mail: info@ndga.net, website: www.ndga.net.

National Duncan Glass Society, *National Duncan Glass Journal* (NL), PO Box 965, Washington, PA 15301-0965, website: www.duncan-glass.com.

National Fenton Glass Society, *Fenton Flyer* (NL), PO Box 4008, Marietta, OH 45750, e-mail: nfgs@ee.net, website: www.fentonglasssociety.org.

National Imperial Glass Collectors Society, *Glasszette* (NL), PO Box 534, Bellaire, OH 43906, e-mail: info@imperialglass.org, website: www.imperialglass.org.

National Westmoreland Glass Collectors Club, P.O. Box 100, Grapeville, PA 15634, website: www.westmorelandglassclubs.org/nwgcc_mem.html.

Old Morgantown Glass Collectors' Guild, *Topics* (NL), PO Box 894, Morgantown, WV 26507-0894, e-mail: OldMorgantown@aol.com, website: www.oldmorgantown.org.

Promotional Glass Collectors Association, c/o Marilyn Johnston, 528 Oakley, Central Point, OR 97502, website: www.pgcaglassclub.com.

Tiffin Glass Collectors Club, *Tiffin Glassmasters* (NL), PO Box 554, Tiffin, OH 44883, website: www.tiffinglass.org.

Westmoreland Glass Society, Inc., *Westmoreland Glass Society, Inc.* (NL), PO Box 2883, Iowa City, IA 52240-2883, website: www.westmorelandglassclubs.org/wgsi.html.

PUBLICATIONS

Candlewick Collector (NL), 17609 Falling Water Rd., Strongsville, OH 44136.

Glass Messenger (NL), 700 Elizabeth St., Williamstown, WV 26187, e-mail: askfenton@fentonartglass.com, website: www.fenton-glass.com (published by the Fenton Art Glass Company).

DEPRESSION GLASS

References

Birkenheuser, Fred. *Tiffin Glassmasters*. 3 volumes. Privately printed, 1979–1985 (Glassmasters Publications, PO Box 524, Grove City, OH 43123).

Bredehoft, Tom and Neila. *Fifty Years of Collectible Glass, 1920–1970: Tableware, Kitchenware, Barware, and Water Sets*. Volume 1. Iola, Wisconsin: Krause, 2000.

———. *Fifty Years of Collectible Glass, 1920–1970: Stemware, Decorations, Decorative Accessories*. Volume 2. Iola, Wisconsin: Krause, 2000.

———. *Heisey Glass, 1896–1957*. Paducah, Kentucky: Collector Books, 2003.

Brown, O.O. *Paden City Glass Manufacturing Company, Paden City, W. Va.: Catalogue Reprints from the 1920s*. Marietta, Ohio: Antique Publications, 2000.

Chase, Mark, and Michael Kelly. *Collectible Drinking Glasses*. Paducah, Kentucky: Collector Books, 1996, 1999 values.

Clements, Monica Lynn, and Patricia Rosser Clements. *Pocket Guide to Pink Depression Era Glass*. Atglen, Pennsylvania: Schiffer, 2001 (out of print).

Coe, Debbie M., and Philip Hopper, *Anchor Hocking Decorated Pitchers and Glasses*. Atglen, Pennsylvania: Schiffer, 2002.

———. *An Unauthorized Guide to Fire-King Glasswares*. Atglen, Pennsylvania: Schiffer, 1999.

Florence, Gene. *Anchor Hocking's Fire-King and More*. 2 editions. Paducah, Kentucky: Collector Books, 1998–2000.

———. *Collectible Glassware from the '40s, '50s, '60s: An Illustrated Value Guide*. 7 editions. Paducah, Kentucky: Collector Books, 2003.

———. *Collector's Encyclopedia of Akro Agate*. Revised edition. Paducah, Kentucky: Collector Books, 1975, 1992 values (out of print).

———. *Collector's Encyclopedia of Depression Glass*. 16 editions. Paducah, Kentucky: Collector Books, 2003.

———. *Elegant Glassware of the Depression Era*. 10 editions. Paducah, Kentucky: Collector Books, 2002.

————. *Kitchen Glassware of the Depression Years*. 6 editions. Paducah, Kentucky: Collector Books, 2003.

————. *Treasures of Very Rare Glassware of the Depression Years*. Paducah, Kentucky: Collector Books, 2003.

Goshe, Ed, et al. *Depression Era Stems & Tableware: Tiffin*. Atglen, Pennsylvania: Schiffer, 1998.

————. *'40s, '50s, & '60s Stemware by Tiffin*. Atglen, Pennsylvania: Schiffer, 1999.

Hardy, Roger and Claudia. *The Complete Line of the Akro Agate Co.* 2 editions. Privately printed, 1997 (10 Bailey St., Clarksburg, WV 26301–2524).

Heacock, William. *Fenton Glass, The First Twenty-five Years*. Marietta, Ohio: Antique Publications, 1978 (out of print).

————. *Fenton Glass, The Second Twenty-five Years*. Marietta, Ohio: Antique Publications, 1980 (out of print).

————. *Fenton Glass, The Third Twenty-five Years*. Marietta, Ohio: Antique Publications, 1989 (out of print).

Hemminger, Ruth, et al. *Tiffin Glass, 1940-1980: Figurals, Paperweights, Pressed Ware*. Atglen, Pennsylvania: Schiffer, 2001.

Keller, Joe, and David Ross. *Jadite: An Identification & Price Guide*. 3rd edition. Atglen, Pennsylvania: Schiffer, 2003.

Kerr, Ann. *Fostoria: An Identification and Value Guide of Pressed, Blown & Hand Molded Shapes*. Paducah, Kentucky: Collector Books, 1994 (out of print).

Kilgo, Garry and Dale, and Jerry and Gail Watkins. *A Collector's Guide to Anchor Hocking's Fire-King Glassware*. 2nd edition. Privately printed, 1997 (out of print).

Kovar Lorraine. *Westmoreland Glass, 1888–1940*. Volume 3. Marietta, Ohio: Antique Publications, 1997.

————. *Westmoreland Glass, 1950–1984*. 2 volumes. Marietta, Ohio: Antique Publications, 1991.

Kovel, Ralph and Terry. *Kovels' Antiques & Collectibles Price List*. New York: Random House Reference, annual.

Krause, Gail. *The Encyclopedia of Duncan Glass*. Hicksville, New York: Exposition Press, Inc., 1976.

Long, Milbra, and Emily Seate. *Fostoria, Useful and Ornamental: The Crystal for America*. Paducah, Kentucky: Collector Books, 2000 (out of print).

————. *Fostoria Stemware: The Crystal for America, 1924–1943*. Paducah, Kentucky: Collector Books, 1994 (out of print).

————. *Fostoria Tableware: The Crystal for America, 1924–1943*. Paducah, Kentucky: Collector Books, 1999.

————. *Fostoria Tableware: The Crystal for America, 1944–1986*. Paducah, Kentucky: Collector Books, 2000.

————. *Fostoria Value Guide*. Paducah, Kentucky: Collector Books, 2003.

Luckey, Carl F., *Identification & Value Guide to Depression Era Glassware*. 4th edition. Iola, Wisconsin: Books Americana/Krause, 2002.

Mauzy, Barbara. *Kitchen Treasures*. Atglen, Pennsylvania: Schiffer, 2003.

———. *Pyrex: The Unauthorized Collector's Guide*. Atglen, Pennsylvania: Schiffer, 2000.

Mauzy, Barbara and Jim. *Mauzy's Comprehensive Handbook of Depression Glass Prices*. 5th edition. Atglen, Pennsylvania: Schiffer, 2003.

Measell, James, and Berry Wiggins. *Great American Glass of the Roaring 20s & Depression Era*. 2 volumes. Marietta, Ohio: Antique Publications, 1998, 2000.

Measell, James, editor. *Fenton Glass, The 1980s Decade*. Marietta, Ohio: Antique Publications, 1996.

———. *Fenton Glass, The 1990s Decade*. Marietta, Ohio: Antique Publications, 2000.

———. *Imperial Glass Encyclopedia: A–Cane*. Volume 1. Marietta, Ohio: Antique Publications, 1999.

———. *Imperial Glass Encyclopedia: Cape Cod–L*. Volume 2. Marietta, Ohio: Antique Publications, 1999.

———. *Imperial Glass Encyclopedia: M–Z*. Volume 3. Marietta, Ohio: Antique Publications, 1999.

———. *New Martinsville Glass, 1900–1944*. Marietta, Ohio: Antique Publications, 1994 (out of print).

Miller, C.L. *Depression Era Dime Store Glass*. Atglen, Pennsylvania: Schiffer, 1999.

Moore, Mark and Sheila. *Swankyswigs*. Atglen, Pennsylvania: Schiffer, 2003.

National Cambridge Collectors, Inc. *Colors in Cambridge Glass*. Paducah, Kentucky: Collector Books, 1984.

———. *Etchings by Cambridge*. Volume 1. Privately printed, 1997 (out of print).

Newbound, Betty and Bill. *Collector's Encyclopedia of Milk Glass Identification & Values*. Paducah, Kentucky: Collector Books, 1995.

Page, Bob, and Dale Frederiksen. *Tiffin Is Forever*. Privately printed, 1997 (Page-Frederiksen Publishing Company, Replacements, Ltd., PO Box 26029, Greensboro, NC 27420).

———. *Crystal Stemware Identification Guide*. Privately printed, 1997 (Page-Frederiksen Publishing Company, Replacements, Ltd., PO Box 26029, Greensboro, NC 27420).

Piña, Leslie. *Depression Era Glass by Duncan*. Atglen, Pennsylvania: Schiffer, 1999.

———. *Fostoria Designer George Sakier, with Values*. Atglen, Pennsylvania: Schiffer, 1996.

———. *Fostoria: Serving the American Table, 1887–1986, with Price Guide*. Atglen, Pennsylvania: Schiffer, 1995 (out of print).

Piña, Leslie, and Jerry Gallagher. *Tiffin Glass, 1914–1940*. Atglen, Pennsylvania: Schiffer, 1996.

Piña, Leslie, and Paula Ockner. *Depression Era Art Deco Glass*. Atglen, Pennsylvania: Schiffer, 1999.

Ream, Louise, et al. *Encyclopedia of Heisey Glassware: Etchings and Carvings*. 2nd edition. Privately printed, 1994 (Heisey Collectors of America, 160 W. Church St., Newark, OH 43255).

Rogove, Susan Tobier, and Marcia Buan Steinhauer. *Pyrex by Corning*. Marietta, Ohio: Antique Publications, 1993, 1998 values.

Schroy, Ellen T. *Warman's Depression Glass*. 3rd edition. Iola, Wisconsin: Krause, 2003.

Seligson, Sidney P. *Fostoria American: A Complete Guide*. 4th edition. Privately printed, 2001 (4510 Barbados, Wichita Falls, TX 76308).

Six, Dean. *West Virginia Glass Between the World Wars*. Atglen, Pennsylvania: Schiffer Publishing, Ltd., 2002.

Stout, Sandra McPhee. *The Complete Book of McKee Glass*. North Kansas City, Missouri: Trojan Press, 1972 (out of print).

Synder, Jeffrey P. *Morgantown Glass, From Depression Era Through the 1960s*. Atglen, Pennsylvania: Schiffer, 1998.

Venable, Charles, et al. *China & Glass in America, 1880–1980: From Tabletop to TV Tray*. Dallas, Texas: Dallas Museum of Art, 2000.

Walk, John. *The Big Book of Fenton Glass: 1940–1970*. 4th edition. Atglen, Pennsylvania: Schiffer, 2003.

Weatherman, Hazel Marie. *Colored Glassware of the Depression Era*. 2 volumes. Privately printed, 1970 (out of print), 1974. (Weatherman Glassbooks, PO Box 280, Ozark, MO 65721).

———. *Decorated Tumbler*. Privately printed, 1978 (Weatherman Glassbooks, PO Box 280, Ozark, MO 65721) (out of print).

———. *Fostoria: Its First Fifty Years*. Privately printed, 1972 (Weatherman Glassbooks, PO Box 280, Ozark, MO 65721) (out of print).

Wetzel-Tomalko, Mary. *Candlewick: The Jewel of Imperial*. 2 volumes. Privately printed, 1981, 1995 (out of print).

Whitmyer, Margaret and Kenn. *Bedroom & Bathroom Glassware of the Depression Years*. Paducah, Kentucky: Collector Books, 1990 (out of print).

———. *Fenton Art Glass Patterns, 1939–1980*. Paducah, Kentucky: Collector Books, 1999, 2002 values.

Wilson, Chas West. *Westmoreland Glass Identification & Value Guide*. Paducah, Kentucky: Collector Books, 1996.

Yeske, Doris. *Depression Glass: A Collector's Guide*. 6th edition. Atglen, Pennsylvania: Schiffer, 2003.

DEPRESSION GLASS

Factories

FACTORY	LOCATION	DATES
A.H. Heisey & Company	Newark, Ohio	1896–1957
Akro Agate Company	Clarksburg, West Virginia	1914–1951
Bartlett-Collins	Sapulpa, Oklahoma	1914–present
Belmont Tumbler Company	Bellaire, Ohio	1915–1938
Cambridge Glass Company	Cambridge, Ohio	1901–1954; 1955–1958
Central Glass Works	Wheeling, West Virginia	1863–1939
Consolidated Lamp & Glass Company	Coraopolis, Pennsylvania	1893–1933; 1936–1964
Co-Operative Flint Glass Company	Beaver Falls, Pennsylvania	1879–1937
Dell Glass Company	Millville, New Jersey	1930s
Diamond Glass-Ware Company	Indiana, Pennsylvania	1904–1931
Dunbar Flint Glass Corporation/Dunbar Glass Corporation	Dunbar, West Virginia	1913–1953
Duncan & Miller Glass Company	Washington, Pennsylvania	1893–1955
Federal Glass Company	Columbus, Ohio	1900–1980
Fenton Art Glass Company	Williamstown, West Virginia	1906–present
Fostoria Glass Company	Fostoria, Ohio; Moundsville, West Virginia	1887–1986
Hazel Atlas Glass Company/Hazel Ware (division of Continental Can Company)	Washington, Pennsylvania; Zanesville, Ohio; Clarksburg, West Virginia; Wheeling, West Virginia	1902–1956; 1956–1964
Hocking Glass Company/Anchor Hocking Glass Corporation/Anchor Hocking Corporation	Lancaster, Ohio	1905–present (Anchor Hocking Glass Corporation, 1937–1969; Anchor Hocking Corporation, 1969–present)
Imperial Glass Company	Bellaire, Ohio	1904–1984
Indiana Glass Company	Dunkirk, Indiana	1907–2002

FACTORY	LOCATION	DATES
Jeannette Glass Company	Jeannette, Pennsylvania	1898–1983
Jenkins Glass Company	Kokomo, Indiana; Arcadia, Indiana	1900–1932
L.E. Smith Glass Company	Mt. Pleasant, Pennsylvania	1907–present
Lancaster Glass Company	Lancaster, Ohio	1908–1937
Libbey Glass Company	Toledo, Ohio	1892–present
Liberty Works	Egg Harbor, New Jersey	1903–c.1932
Louie Glass Company	Weston, West Virginia	1926–1995
Macbeth-Evans Glass Company	Indiana (several factories); Toledo, Ohio; Charleroi, Pennsylvania; Corning, New York	1899–1936; acquired by Corning
McKee Glass Company	Jeannette, Pennsylvania	1850–1961; acquired by Jeannette Glass Company
Morgantown Glass Works	Morgantown, West Virginia	1900–1972
New Martinsville Glass Manufacturing Company	New Martinsville, West Virginia	1900–1944; acquired by Viking Glass Company
Paden City Glass Manufacturing Company	Paden City, West Virginia	1916–1951
Seneca Glass Company	Fostoria, Ohio; Morgantown, West Virginia	1891–1983
Silex (division of Macbeth-Evans)	Corning, New York	1929–1955; sold to Corning Glass Works
Standard Glass Manufacturing Company (became subsidiary of Hocking/Anchor Hocking in 1940)	Lancaster, Ohio	1924–c.1984
Tiffin Glass Company (Factory R of U.S. Glass Company)	Tiffin, Ohio	1892–1963
U.S. Glass Company	Pennsylvania (several factories); Tiffin, Ohio; Gas City, Indiana; West Virginia	1891–1963
Viking Glass Company/ Dalzell-Viking Glass Company	New Martinsville, West Virginia	1944–1998 (changed name, 1987)
Westmoreland Glass Company	Grapeville, Pennsylvania	1889–1985

CERAMIC DINNERWARE

DINNERWARE

Introduction

There is a difference between the organization of the Depression glass section and this section. Dinnerware items and prices are listed alphabetically by manufacturer, then by pattern name. (Exceptions to this are patterns Autumn Leaf and Willow, which are listed by pattern.) Under the manufacturer's name is a paragraph giving the history of the company. The patterns listed with each manufacturer's name include a sentence or two describing color variations, the years of manufacture, and sometimes the designer's name. Following each pattern name is a list of dinnerware pieces and their prices. Pictures of patterns and marks of patterns and factories are also included. On page 255 there is an index of dinnerware patterns listed in this book. Use this as a cross-reference to help you find patterns and prices under the maker's name. Although hundreds of patterns are included in this list, many patterns were not seen at sales this year and are not included in the price section.

Some companies changed their names during their years of dinnerware production. In both the main price listing and in the References section, we use the company name or trademark name most closely associated with the dishes. For example, Gladding, McBean & Company became Franciscan Ceramics Inc. and eventually was purchased by the Waterford Wedgwood Group. We use the name Franciscan, which has been in use most of the time the dinnerware was made—no matter what the maker's name actually was at the time.

This book has changed to reflect the collecting trends of the twenty-first century. The inexpensive dinnerware sets made in America are the main focus of this section of *Kovels' Depression Glass & Dinnerware Price List*. Also included are sets made in other countries but sold in quantity in America. Azalea pattern, made in Japan, and Liberty Blue, made in England, are two of these entries. Prices listed are for the most popular everyday sets being collected today. Formal dinnerwares made by firms like Lenox or Royal Worcester are not included.

Because dishes were made by many manufacturers, problems arise with variations in vocabulary. Most sugar bowls had covers. Today many have lost their original covers and are sold as open sugars. We don't include the word *open* in the description, but we do indicate if there is a cover. A gravy boat with an underplate is a gravy boat with the plate it rests on. Sometimes the underplate is permanently attached to the gravy boat. A mayonnaise bowl may also have an underplate.

A lug soup is a bowl with a flat handle called a lug. Other soup bowls may have pierced handles or no handles. We list a pickle dish as a pickle and also list a pickle tray. The tray is flat. A snack set is a cup and a matching plate with an off-center indentation for the cup. An after-dinner coffee cup is larger than a demitasse but smaller than a coffee cup. A few mixing bowls have covers, which are very rare. We list the bowls with and without the covers. Sometimes a cover is listed alone. A French baker or fluted baker is a bowl with straight sides. A covered butter dish is listed as "butter, cover." If it is just the cover to a butter dish (and some are listed because they are expensive), the listing says "butter, cover only."

Sometimes collectors use different words to describe the same dish. Oatmeal bowl and cereal bowl are both names for a bowl about 6 inches in diameter. A berry bowl and a fruit bowl may also be the same size, and a plate about 6 inches in diameter can be called a dessert plate, bread plate, or sherbet plate. We list these dishes by the manufacturer's name.

Dealers often use a term like "30s" or "36s" to indicate the size of a dish. When the dinnerware was made, it was packed in barrels. The terms 30s and 36s refer to the number of pieces that fit in a barrel. The larger the number, the smaller the size of the piece. If that is the common way the piece is described today, we have included it in the listing. The height of a pitcher or jug is one indication of size; the number of liquid ounces it holds is also important. We have tried to list both. Wherever possible, we have used both the name of the piece and the size, so the listing is "plate, dinner, 10 in." Although most dinner plates are 10 inches in diameter, a few are smaller, and we have listed the actual size in each case.

The terms "kitchenware" and "dinnerware" are used in the original sense. A dinnerware set includes all the pieces that might have been used on a dinner table, including plates, bowls, platters, tumblers, cups, pitchers, and serving bowls. A kitchenware set has bowls and storage dishes of the type used in a kitchen and does not include dinner plates or cups. Kitchenware includes rolling pins, pie servers, and other kitchen utensils. A few kitchenware bowls are listed, but other pieces are not. Several manufacturers used the term "fine china" to differentiate their informal pottery lines from their more formal china pieces. The term "fine china" is used in this book only if that is what it was called by the factory.

Colors often were given romantic names and, whenever possible, we have used these original factory names. Some colors, such as Camellia (rose), Cadet (light blue), Indian Red (orange), and Dresden (deep blue), are explained in the paragraph descriptions.

It is important to remember that descriptions of any line of dinnerware may include many different names—a manufacturer's name, a trademark name, a pattern name (describing the decorations applied to a dish), and sometimes a shape name (describing the shape of the dish). For example, Taverne is a pattern; Laurel is the shape of the dish decorated with that pattern; and Taylor, Smith & Taylor is the name of the company that made the dinnerware. Sometimes a name refers to both a pattern and a shape; if it does, we explain how the name is used in this book.

Pieces of American dinnerware are constantly being discovered in attics, basements, garage sales, flea markets, Internet sales, and antiques shops. The publications that offer replacement dishes through the mail use descriptions that often include both pattern and shape names. Learn to recognize the shapes and shape names that were used by each maker. Authors of some of the other books about dinnerware have arbitrarily named patterns. Sometimes these pattern names are different in different books, yet describe the same pattern. We have tried to cross-reference these pattern names so you can locate them in any of the books.

We have included a bibliography of books on dinnerware beginning on page 233. The books are listed by manufacturer name unless they are general books on dinnerware or marks. The bibliography lists current books and some important books that are out of print but can be found. There are also many websites on the Internet that picture dinnerware. Some dishes are marked with only the pattern name; others are marked with only the company name; still others are not marked at all. Some of the books we list are filled with photographs that can help you identify your dishes.

Prices listed in this book are actual prices asked by dealers at shows, shops, on the Internet, and through national advertising. It is not the price you would pay at a garage sale or church bazaar (that's where you might find bargains). Prices from matching services were not included because these are higher still. As is true in any type of shopping, you often pay a little extra for immediate availability and expert knowledge. The only reason one pattern has more prices listed than another is because more prices were available for those patterns. It is probably also an indication of the popularity of the pattern. Prices are not estimates. If a high and low are given, we have recorded several sales. There is a regional variation in the prices, especially for the solid-colored wares. In general, these pieces are high-priced in the East and West, lower in the center of the country.

There have been a few reissues of dinnerware. Harlequin was put back into production in 1979 for Woolworth's, the sole distributor. Complete dinner sets were made in the original colors, except that the salmon is a deeper color than the original. The sugar bowls were made with closed handles. Fiesta was reissued by Homer Laughlin China Company in 1986. The original molds and marks were used. The new Fiesta has a china body that shrinks a little more than the semivitreous clay body used before. This means that most new pieces are slightly smaller than old ones. But dinner plates, soup bowls, and cereal bowls were made slightly larger to accommodate modern tastes. New molds were made for these pieces. New dinner plates are $10\frac{1}{2}$ inches in diameter. The new dishes were first made in cobalt blue (darker than the original), black, white, apricot, and rose. Other colors have been added. A few of the pieces have been slightly redesigned since 1986, with variations in handles and bases. A special line was made with added cartoon decorations. A Fiesta look-alike has been made by Franciscan since 1978 under the name Kaleidoscope, and a similar line called Cantinaware has been sold by Target stores. We have tried to indicate in the paragraphs in the price section if any reproductions of a pattern have been made.

This book is a report of prices for pieces offered for sale during the past year. Most of the patterns included in earlier books are found here because collectors still buy these patterns. Many newly popular patterns are also included.

For a list of dinnerware patterns, see the Index.

Depression glass, see pages 1–142.

Plastic dinnerware, see pages 241–253.

AUTUMN LEAF

Autumn Leaf pattern china was made for the Jewel Tea Company beginning in 1933. Hall China Company, East Liverpool, Ohio; Crooksville China Company, Crooksville, Ohio; Harker Potteries, Chester, West Virginia; and Paden City Pottery, Paden City, West Virginia, made dishes with this design. Autumn Leaf has remained popular and was made by Hall China Company until 1978. New limited edition pieces of Autumn Leaf have been distributed by China Specialties, Inc., since 1990 and may be listed here. They are new shapes, not reproductions, and are clearly marked or dated.

Ashtray 75.00
Baker, Fort Pitt, Oval,
  12 Oz. . . . . . 145.00 to 255.00
Baker, French, 4 1/2 In. . . 15.00
Batter Bowl,
  4 x 9 1/4 In. 70.00
Bean Pot, Baby 175.00
Bean Pot, Handle 695.00

Bean Pot, Handles 285.00
Bowl, Cereal,
  6 1/2 In. . . . . . . 12.00 to 15.00
Bowl, Fruit,
  5 1/2 In. . . . . 6.00 to 14.00
Bowl, Salad, 2 Qt. 28.00
Bowl, Vegetable, Oval,
  Cover, 9 3/4 In. 140.00
Bowl, Vegetable, Oval, Cover,
  10 1/2 In. . . . . . 50.00 to 56.00
Bowl, Vegetable, Sections,
  10 1/2 In. . . . 125.00 to 139.00
Bowl Set, 5 1/2 In.,
  2 Piece 14.00
Butter, 1/4 Lb. 300.00
Butter, 1 Lb. . . 500.00 to 600.00
Cake Plate,
  9 1/2 In. . . . . . 35.00 to 63.00
Cake Safe 65.00
Candleholder 45.00
Candy Dish,
  4 5/8 x 5 13/16 In. 600.00
Casserole, 2 Qt. 35.00
Casserole, Cover,
  1 1/2 Qt. 28.00
Casserole, Cover,
  2 Qt. . . . . 70.00 to 95.00
Chocolate Pot, 16 Oz.,
  5 1/2 In. 80.00
Coffeepot, Drip,
  10 1/2 In. 252.00
Coffeepot, Drip, Metal
  Dripper, 13 In. 42.00
Coffeepot, Electric
  Percolator 400.00
Coffeepot, Rayed,
  8 Cup . . . . 55.00 to 70.00
Coffeepot, Rayed,
  9 Cup . . . . 55.00 to 175.00
Coffeepot Set, 4 Piece . . 350.00
Cookie Jar, Rayed 325.00
Creamer . . . . 10.00 to 30.00
Creamer, Ruffled 30.00
Cup, 3 1/2 x 2 1/4 In. 10.00
Cup, After Dinner, 4 In. . . 30.00
Cup, Tea, 2 Piece 11.00
Cup & Saucer 10.00
Cup & Saucer, Ruffled . . . 13.00
Cup & Saucer, St. Denis . . 50.00
Custard Cup . . . . . . 6.00 to 8.00
Dish, 6 3/4 x 2 1/2 x
  3 1/2 In. 55.00
Fork 40.00

Gravy Boat, Underplate,
  9 In. . . . . 39.00 to 75.00
Jam Jar, Underplate,
  Cover, 3 1/2 In. 78.00
Jug, Baby Ball 125.00
Jug, Ball, No. 3 . . 28.00 to 75.00
Jug, Rayed, 2 1/2 Pt. 7.00
Mixing Bowl,
  4 1/2 x 8 3/4 In. 45.00
Mixing Bowl,
  7 1/2 x 4 In. . . . 30.00 to 35.00
Mixing Bowl,
  9 1/2 In. . . . . . . 35.00 to 38.00
Mixing Bowl Set,
  3 Piece . . . . . . 63.00 to 125.00
Mug, Conic 75.00
Mug, Irish Coffee 65.00
Mustard, Underplate,
  Cover . . . . . . 85.00 to 160.00
Pie Bird,
  5 x 2 1/4 In. . . . 30.00 to 40.00
Pie Plate, 9 1/2 In. 28.00
Pitcher, 9 1/2 x 6 7/8 In. . . 100.00
Pitcher, Beer 275.00
Pitcher, Utility,
  2 1/2 Pt 30.00
Plate, Bread & Butter,
  6 In. . . . . 8.00 to 13.00
Plate, Bread & Butter,
  7 1/4 In. 15.00
Plate, Dinner, 10 In. 25.00
Plate, Luncheon, 9 In. 20.00
Plate, Salad, 8 In. 18.00
Platter,
  11 1/4 In. . . . . . 22.00 to 32.00
Platter, 13 1/2 In. 55.00
Reamer 295.00
Rolling Pin 65.00
Salt & Pepper 45.00
Saucer . . . . 2.00 to 10.00
Saucer, Jewel Tea 3.00
Serving Bowl, 7 3/4 In. . . 23.00
Shaker, Pepper,
  2 3/4 In. 15.00
Shaker, Pepper, Range,
  Handle 20.00
Soup, Cream,
  Handles . . . . . . 40.00 to 56.00
Soup, Dish, Flat,
  8 1/2 In. . . . . . 16.00 to 20.00
Spoon Rest, 3 Slots 65.00
Spoon Rest,
  8 1/2 x 6 In. 40.00

Stack Set, 4 Piece 75.00
Sugar . . . . 12.00 to 25.00
Sugar & Creamer,
Boston 110.00
Sugar & Creamer, Cover,
Ruffled Edge 45.00
Syrup, 6 In. . . . . 95.00 to 115.00
Tea Set, Philadelphia,
3 Piece 300.00
Teapot, 4 In. 65.00
Teapot, 5 1/2 In. 125.00
Teapot, 6 Cup, Porcelier . . 35.00
Teapot, Airflow 250.00
Teapot, Aladdin,
11 In. . . . . 40.00 to 99.00
Teapot, Automobile, 4 1/2 x
9 1/2 In. . . . . 425.00 to 495.00
Teapot, Donut 150.00
Teapot, Football, 7 1/2 x
10 1/2 In. . . . 105.00 to 125.00
Teapot, French,
5 1/2 In. 125.00
Teapot, Hook 100.00
Teapot, Long Spout 100.00
Teapot, Musical 125.00
Teapot, Nautilus 198.00
Teapot, Rayed, Long
Spout, 7 In. 67.00
Tidbit,
3 Tiers . . . . . 125.00 to 175.00
Tray, Figure 8 Shape 65.00
Warmer, Round 225.00
Water Server, Norris . . . 125.00

BAUER

John Andrew Bauer, who
had worked in Paducah,
Kentucky, moved to Cali-
fornia in 1909 for his
health. The Bauer pottery
made flowerpots, stone-

ware, and art pottery. In
1923 it became the J.A.
Bauer Company. The
company closed in 1962.
Dinnerware was first
made in 1930. The solid
and brightly colored ware
called "Plain Ware," popular for "casual dining," was
the first American dinnerware of this type, years
before Fiesta ware. Reproductions of Bauer pottery
have been made.

MONTEREY is a solid-color
pottery line made from 1936 to
the early 1940s. The plate borders are a series of separated
rings. The pottery sold full
dinnerware sets with matching
serving pieces. Colors in the set
are mix-and-match. Colors include Burgundy, California
Orange-Red, Canary Yellow,
Green, Ivory, Monterey Blue,
Red-Brown, Turquoise Blue,
and White. Other colors, including Chartreuse, have been
reported.

White
Bowl, Fruit, Footed,
10 In. 125.00
Serving Bowl, Handles,
9 1/4 x 1 3/4 In. 22.00

RING, sometimes called Beehive, is a solid-color pottery
line made from c.1933 to 1962.
Mix-and-match sets were made
in Black, Burgundy, Chinese
Yellow, Delph Blue, Ivory,
Jade Green, Orange Red, and
Royal Blue. Later, Light Brown
and White were used. Papaya

was used from 1941 to 1945.
Other colors reported by collectors are Chartreuse, Gray, Light
Green, Orange, Pale Blue, Pink,
Red Brown, Spruce, and Turquoise. Early dishes had faint
rings, but from 1936 to 1946 the
rings were more distinct.

Burgundy
Soup, Dish,
7 3/4 x 1 1/2 In. 35.00

Chinese Yellow
Cup 9.00
Saucer 18.00

Orange Red
Vase, Handles,
4 1/2 x 5 1/2 In. 75.00

Royal Blue
Cup & Saucer 85.00

MISCELLANEOUS: There are
many other patterns made by
Bauer. Some are listed here.
Bowl, Fruit, La Linda,
Green, 5 In. 18.00
Bowl, Fruit, La Linda,
Pink, 5 In. 18.00
Cookie Jar, Gloss
Pastel Kitchenware,
Yellow 150.00
Cup, Contempo, Indio
Brown, 2 7/8 In. 12.00
Mixing Bowl, Beehive,
7 1/2 x 3 1/2 In. 45.00
Mixing Bowl, Beehive,
9 1/4 x 5 In. 69.00
Mixing Bowl, Gloss Pastel
Kitchenware, Beige,
5 x 3 5/8 In. 13.00
Mixing Bowl, Gloss Pastel
Kitchenware, Pink,
6 3/4 x 4 1/8 In. 18.00
Teapot, Aladdin, Gloss Pastel
Kitchenware, 8 Cup . . . 215.00

◆◆

**Do not use Bauer dishes
in a microwave oven.**

◆◆

BLUE RIDGE

Blue Ridge is a mark used by Southern Potteries, Inc. Collectors use this name to refer to all of the dinnerwares made by Southern Potteries, which worked in Erwin, Tennessee, from 1917 to 1957. Dishes were decorated with decals from 1917 to 1938. Then the factory changed to hand-painted decoration. The pottery made hundreds of different patterns. Because all of the later designs were decorated by hand, there were many variations. Don't be confused by the newly formed Southern Blue Ridge company, which opened in 2002. It is not the same company.

BECKY has large red flowers with yellow centers, green leaves, and green stems on a white background. It was first made in the 1940s.

Bowl, Fruit, 5 1/4 x
   1 1/8 In. . . . . . . 8.00 to 16.00
Cup & Saucer 10.00
Plate, Bread & Butter, 6 In. 4.00
Plate, Dinner, 10 In. 12.00
Platter, 11 3/4 x 8 3/4 In. . 18.00
Platter, 13 3/8 x 10 1/8 In. 30.00

CRAB APPLE is one of the most popular dinnerware patterns made by the pottery. It is decorated with hand-painted clusters of red apples and green leaves. There is a thin red spatter border. The pattern was used after 1930 and discontinued only when the factory closed in 1957.

Plate, Dinner, 9 1/4 In. . . . 20.00
Platter,
   15 1/2 x 11 1/4 In. 50.00

FLOWER has one or two large yellow flowers and two dark green leaves on a white background.

Bowl, Fruit, 5 1/2 In. 5.00
Cup 5.00
Plate, Dinner, 9 1/2 In. 9.00
Sugar & Creamer 14.00

FRUIT FANTASY was introduced in 1944. It is decorated with purple grapes, yellow pears, and red cherries. It has a sponged edge.

Pie Plate, 7 In. 10.00

GREEN BRIAR has yellow-green and brown flowers, green leaves, and green trim. It was made in the Piecrust shape beginning c.1948.

Plate, Dinner,
   9 1/2 In. . . . . . 14.00 to 17.00
Platter 28.00

GREEN LANTERNS has green heart-shaped leaves and brown vines on a white background. It was made on the Candlewick shape.

Gravy Boat 15.00
Plate, Bread & Butter,
   6 In. 5.00
Plate, Dinner,
   9 In. . . . . 6.00 to 9.00
Plate, Salad, 8 In. 5.00
Platter, 11 1/2 In. 20.00

NOCTURNE has red flowers with yellow centers, green leaves, and a red brushed edge. It was made on the Colonial shape and was introduced in the 1940s.

Bowl, Fruit, 5 In. 10.00
Plate, Dinner, 10 1/2 In. . . 20.00
Platter, 11 In. 25.00

POINSETTIA is hand-painted with red poinsettia flowers and dark and light green leaves. It was made on the Colonial shape beginning in 1950.

Bowl, Tab Handle, 7 In. . . 30.00
Plate, Bread & Butter,
   6 In. . . . . 14.00 to 25.00
Plate, Salad, 7 1/4 In. 15.00
Platter, 13 In. 75.00

QUAKER APPLE is decorated with two apples and green leaves on a branch. It has a white background and green brushed trim.

Bowl, Cereal, 6 In. 10.00
Bowl, Fruit, 5 In. 5.00
Cup & Saucer 8.00
Plate, Bread & Butter,
    6 In. 5.00
Plate, Luncheon, 8 In. 12.00
Saucer 4.00

ROOSTERS of many sorts were used as decorations on Southern Potteries pieces. The Rooster crowing from the fence top with a sun and a barn in the distance is a pattern called Cock o' the Morn. Another pattern was known as Cock o' the Walk. Most other patterns picturing the bird are called Rooster by collectors, although Rooster was a giftware line and the dinnerware, on the Clinchfield shape, was known as Game Cock. These pieces have a rooster center and a series of red three-line designs as the border. This pattern pictures a red rooster standing on a sketchy line that looks like a cloud.

Bowl, 5 1/2 In. 28.00
Plate, Bread & Butter,
    6 1/2 In. 65.00
Plate, Dinner, 9 1/4 In. . . . 85.00

RUSTIC PLAID has brown and green bands on a brown sponged background. The pattern was made in the 1950s.

Bowl, Fruit, 5 5/8 In. 5.00
Plate, Bread & Butter,
    6 1/4 In. 7.00
Plate, Dinner, 9 1/2 In. 9.00

STANHOME IVY is one of many ivy-decorated patterns. It was made on the Skyline shape after 1952. It has ivy leaves, clusters of red berries, and brown vines.

Plate, Bread & Butter,
    6 In. 5.00
Plate, Luncheon,
    9 1/2 In. 7.00

SUNNY SPRAY is decorated with a spray of two-tone brown and yellow flowers and dark green leaves. It was made on the Skyline shape c.1950

Plate, Dessert, 6 In. 8.00

Plate, Dinner,
    10 1/4 In. . . . . . 10.00 to 22.00
Plate, Luncheon,
    9 1/4 In. 22.00

YELLOW NOCTURNE has yellow flowers, green leaves, and may or may not have a green brushed edge. It was made on the Colonial shape.

Plate, Bread & Butter,
    6 1/4 In. 21.00
Plate, Salad, 8 In. 12.00

MISCELLANEOUS: There are many other patterns made by Blue Ridge. Some are listed here.

Bowl, Fruit, Bouquet,
    5 In. 4.00
Bowl, Fruit, Cherry Tree
    Glen, 5 In. 10.00
Bowl, Fruit, Petal Point,
    5 1/2 In. 5.00
Bowl, Thorny Mayflower,
    5 In. 5.00
Chocolate Pot, Cover, French
    Peasant, 9 x 7 1/2 In. . . 550.00
Cigarette Box, Cover, Square,
    Butterfly, 4 1/4 In. 100.00
Coffeepot, Ovide, Spiderweb,
    Blue, Gray 125.00
Creamer, Autumn Apple,
    Colonial 20.00
Cup, After Dinner,
    Plume 28.00
Cup & Saucer,
    Green Plaid 15.00
Pie Baker, Cassandra,
    Maroon Border 30.00
Pie Dish, Mt. Vernon 25.00
Pie Plate, Orchard Glory,
    7 In. 18.00
Pie Server,
    Antique Leaf 25.00
Pitcher, Virginia 55.00
Plate, 1980 Olympics,
    8 1/2 In. 10.00
Plate, Bread & Butter,
    Floral, 6 In. . . . 4.00 to 6.00
Plate, Bread & Butter,
    Flower Ring, 6 In. 21.00
Plate, Bread & Butter,
    Green Eyes, 6 In. 5.00

DECADES OF DESIGN

Inexpensive glass was manufactured in massive quantities during the 1920s and '30s by dozens of American factories. The glass was inexpensive because it was manufactured by a new, automated tank-molded method that made it possible to quickly create thin glassware in many different patterns and colors. Overall lacy patterns helped hide any flaws in the glass. Designs were molded on the outside of plates and bowls so the surface that held food was smooth. A twenty-piece set sold for only about $2. The glass, sold in dime stores and department stores, was dubbed "Depression glass" by collectors in the late 1960s. Gradually, the meaning of the term Depression glass broadened to include inexpensive glass made after the Depression, including glass that was pressed to resemble earlier cut glass, glass with enameled or silk-screened decorations, and glass made of dark green, cobalt blue, or other deep colors.

In addition, manufacturers added more shapes to their Depression glass lines as times and attitudes changed. The end of Prohibition in 1933 led to a demand for cocktail shakers, ice buckets, and other liquor-related ware. Small glass statues and figurines, as well as ashtrays and bowls with three-dimensional figural handles, were popular from the 1930s to the '50s. By the '40s, many types of icebox dishes, reamers, canister sets, and other kitchen wares were made. Reproductions began appearing by the '70s.

There are clues that can help date glass dishes. Each style was made to sell in its own era, and as the styles of expensive, handmade glassware (called "Elegant glass" by collectors) changed, the styles and colors of Depression glass changed, too.

During the Depression and afterwards, ceramic dinnerware was made in colors and patterns that complemented popular furniture, glassware, silverware, and table-linen designs. Favorite colors were primarily pastels, cream, and white during the 1920s and early '30s, a period when pottery dishes were made with floral borders that resembled the decorations on expensive porcelain sets. In the 1940s, deep red, blue, and green were favored colors, and dinnerware like Blue Ridge, with hand-painted colorful designs, became popular. By the late '40s, new and modern shapes like Iroquois Casual, designed by Russel Wright, were favored by young families. Plastic dishes in dark or pastel colors were stylish in the 1950s, and avocado green and harvest gold were favored in the '60s for everything from dishes and rugs to refrigerators.

By the mid 1970s, Depression-era glass and dinnerware were out of fashion. Instead, modern shapes, abstract designs, and informal tablewares were popular. But collectors remembered the beautiful table settings at Grandma's house, so they started collecting older pieces. Manufacturers realized that reproductions would sell and were soon copying many of the older designs. Today, both old and new versions of Depression-era dishes can be found—and often the original pieces sell for less than new ones.

1920s

The Depression glass era began in the 1920s. Glass dishes were simple and classic in shape, usually pastel with lacy designs. The companion ceramic dinnerwares were simple shapes with traditional floral borders.

Simple & Classic

This Aunt Polly blue glass sherbet made by the U. S. Glass Co. is 3¼ inches high. It is worth $14.

Beaded Block was a popular pattern made from the 1920s to the '50s by Imperial Glass Co. It was made in at least eleven colors. This clear footed sugar bowl with handles is 4¼ inches high. The asking price is $18.

This clear glass Della Robbia creamer has decorations of raised gold fruit. It was made by the Westmoreland Glass Co. from 1926 to the 1960s and sells today for $12.

Twisted Optic, also
called Line No. 313, came in six
colors. This pink cup costs $6.

Homer Laughlin made Kwaker
pattern dinnerware in the
1920s. The dinner plate with a
decal decoration is worth $6.

Syracuse China's
Wendover pattern
has an elaborate
border. The din-
ner plate sells
for $32.

1930s

During the 1930s, design went in two different directions. Lacy pastel glass continued to be popular, but deep colors and an Art Deco influence made for an opposing, daring look. Ceramic dinnerwares were made for both markets. Buyers could find simple plates with floral borders, as well as brightly colored pottery dishes.

Flowers & Swags

Cherry Blossom was one of the most popular patterns of the 1930s. This 10¼-inch green cake plate (above) has three small feet. Price: $35.

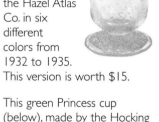

This yellow Florentine No. 1 juice tumbler is 3⅜ inches tall. It was made by the Hazel Atlas Co. in six different colors from 1932 to 1935. This version is worth $15.

This green Princess cup (below), made by the Hocking Glass Co., is covered with swags and flowers. It sells for $13.

Sharon, sometimes called Cabbage Rose, was originally made from 1935 to 1939. Reproductions in new colors were made after 1976. This 1930s 8½-inch yellow bowl can be found for $8.

Georgian, also called Lovebird because of the birds on some pieces, was made by the Federal Glass Co. from 1931 to 1936. This 6-inch green plate is priced $7. Don't confuse it with other patterns called Georgian.

Flowers form the border of this Yellow Rose pattern luncheon plate by Hall China Co. It sells today for $28.

Coors, the famous Colorado brewing company, also owned the Coors Porcelain Co. Coors made dishes from about 1900 to 1943. Its best-known pattern is Rosebud. This 6½-inch maroon plate now brings $18.

Art Deco

Chevron pattern is all straight lines without swags. This 4¼-inch cobalt blue milk pitcher with a very modern look is $18.

Decagon pattern glass, made by the Cambridge Glass Co. in the 1930s, came in nine unusual colors, including black. This etched salad plate is a bargain at $12.

Petalware was made in clear glass in 1930. Within two years, the pattern appeared in opaque Monax or Cremax glass, many with hand-painted or fired-on colored decorations. This Monax saucer with pastel bands sells for $4.

Solid Colors

This ruby-colored Georgian 6-ounce sherbet was made by the Fenton Glass Co. It sells for $8.

Homer Laughlin introduced Riviera pattern pottery dinnerware two years after it started selling Fiesta ware. Riviera dishes were unmarked and were sold by just one retailer, G.C. Murphy Co. This 6¼-inch medium green plate is worth $7.

Fiesta is probably the best-known solid-color pottery dinnerware made since the 1930s. It has been slightly redesigned since then, and many new colors have been added. This salad plate glazed in the original red costs $20.

1940s

During and just after World War II, many people wanted to return to old and familiar dinnerware designs. Colonial scenes, fruit, and flowers were popular decorations on many pottery dishes. But by the late 1940s, a few totally new pottery dinnerware shapes added excitement to the table. Glassware remained light in color, and copies of Victorian milk glass patterns came into fashion.

Fruits & Flowers

Blue Ridge pottery, made by Southern Potteries Inc., was hand-painted in hundreds of different patterns. This 9¼-inch plate in the Betty pattern (below) is only $26.

This Fostoria glass sandwich server (above) is in the etched Chintz pattern. The clear glass 11½-inch piece has a center handle. It is a shape not often made today. The piece is eagerly sought by collectors, who would pay $28 for one.

Stangl Pottery made many dishes decorated with fruit and flowers. This 10½-inch plate in a pattern called Fruit sells for $8.

Nostalgia

What could be more nostalgic than the Wild West. Frankoma Potteries first made Wagon Wheel in 1941, and a few pieces are still being made today. The dishes were actually molded like wheels. This 6½-inch tan plate is $8.

This Paneled Grape milk glass wedding bowl with cover looks Victorian, but it was made by Westmoreland Glass Co. You should be able to find the 8¾-inch piece for $48.

Romantic landscapes and an elaborate border were part of the design for the Vernon 1860 pattern by Vernon Kilns. The brown transfer pattern has hand-painted highlights. A 6½-inch plate sells for $6.

Modern

Vernon Kilns' California Originals pattern, also called California Heritage, was a very modern design for the 1940s. The raisin-purple salt and pepper set with added drip glaze (below) sells for $30.

Looking cool and contemporary, this sapphire blue glass Bubble pattern cup and saucer (below) sells today for $8.

1950s

This decade marked the introduction of designs known as Mid-Century Modern. Streamlined kitchenware enticed new buyers, and ceramic dinnerware was produced in abstract designs. Plastic dishes were considered new and modern. Inexpensive, attractive, and almost unbreakable sets of Melmac and other types of plastic dinnerware were fast sellers, even though the surface scratched and stained with use. Turquoise, yellow, and brown were favored for appliances and textiles. Still, the buyer with more traditional taste found that old, established designs were also available.

New Takes on Old Favorites

This 1950s Forest Green glass bowl in the Hobnail pattern looks like dishes made years before. The 6¼-inch plate with three small feet is $10.

Heather etch by Fostoria could have been a Victorian pattern, but it's a '50s version of the old style. This sugar and creamer (below) lists for $30.

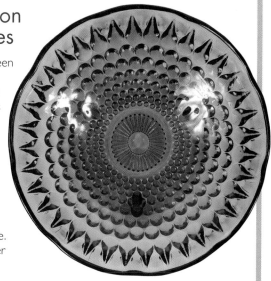

Pink was a popular color for home furnishings in the 1950s, so Windsor Diamond, an old pattern, was reintroduced in shell pink glass in 1957. The 5½-inch compote, made by Jeannette Glass Co., is $23.

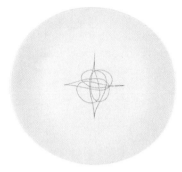

Willow pattern, first made in the eighteenth century, has been copied ever since. This Blue Willow 9-inch plate was made in Japan and sells for just $5.

A modernized version of the Willow pattern was used for plastic dishes by Prolon Plastics. The design was applied as a decal on this dinner plate (below), which is worth $3.

Mid-Century Modern

Eva Zeisel designed the Fantasy pattern for Hall China. It's one of her many modern designs. This dinner plate (below) sells for $25.

Metlox Potteries opened in 1927 but kept up-to-date with new patterns. California Contempora featured an abstract center design that almost shouts "modern." The 10¼-inch plate (below) costs $32 online.

The modern symbols used as a border for Cathay, a dinnerware pattern by Taylor, Smith & Taylor, attracted young buyers. This dinner plate now sells for $13.

Shepherd's Purse is an Iroquois China Co. modern dinnerware pattern used on dishes in the Casual shape, designed by Russel Wright. Wright's Casual line featured unusual shapes, like this slightly oval dinner plate, and interesting innovations, like a stacking sugar and creamer. Price for the plate: $20.

Plastic dishes by Royalon were made in unusual shapes and colors. This lavender gravy boat with two spouts, 7½ inches long, sold at a flea market for $4.

Kitchen Stuff

The useful but plain standard kitchen bowl was transformed into an avocado green Pyrex casserole dish attractive enough to go from oven to table. This 1952 bowl in the Cinderella shape can be found at thrift shops for $6.

A straight-sided modern version of a traditional pottery mixing bowl was made by Watt Pottery in the '50s. This Kitch N Queen bowl, contemporary yet familiar in design, sold well. Today it brings $15.

Buy one of these (below) and use it today. This 10½-inch speckled plastic mixing bowl by Texas Ware is lightweight, attractive, and only $15 at a flea market.

This sleek pottery "queen roaster" in Delphinium blue (below) was a revolutionary idea. It was made by Hall for Westinghouse to go with a new range. The 4½-by-8-inch covered piece can be used in a microwave oven. It sells for $26.

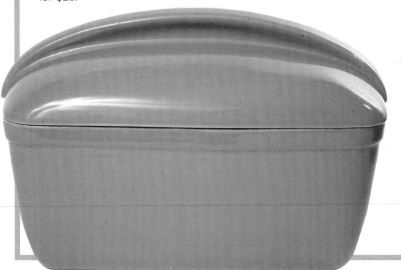

1960s

Color-coordinated dishes were part of the fashion movement in the 1960s. New houses featured avocado or gold kitchens and living rooms. Earth tones that blended with these colors and designs inspired by nature were popular for dinnerware. Plates were often rimless and many had overall center designs instead of border decorations. Textured glassware was popular.

Colors of the Sixties

Capri Blue is the name of the color used for this Swirl pattern cup worth $6.

Nothing is more '60s than avocado green. This textured Soreno iced tea glass (left) can be found for $5.

Harker Pottery Co. made this pattern in about 1966. The lattice-like border was probably the inspiration for the romantic pattern name, Persian Key. The dinner plate, in a green shade popular at the time, costs $13.

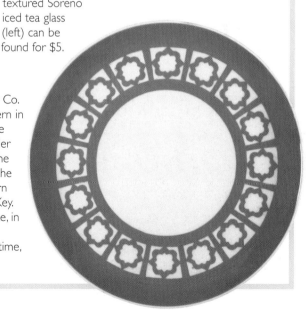

Designs Inspired by Nature

Wheat stalks were the only design on this glass creamer. Price: $8.

Woodland Gold is a Metlox Potteries pattern of the '70s that pictures realistic leaves in earth tones. Like many '70s designs, the plate is rimless and has a large center design. It should cost you $12.

Plate, Bread & Butter,
Sungold No. 2, 6 In. 5.00

Plate, Bread & Butter,
Tulip, 6 1/4 In. 6.00

Plate, County Fair, Peach,
Strawberry, 8 In. 25.00

Plate, County Fair,
Plums, 8 In. 25.00

Plate, Dinner, Chickory,
10 In. 12.00

Plate, Dinner, Christmas
Tree, 10 1/4 In. 13.00

Plate, Dinner, French Peasant,
Woman, 10 In. 125.00

Plate, Dinner, Green
Eyes, 9 1/4 In. 22.00

Plate, Dinner, Ivy,
9 3/8 In. 12.00

Plate, Dinner, Red Nocturne,
10 In. 20.00

Plate, Dinner, Sweet Clover,
10 In. 15.00

Plate, Dinner, Wild Rose,
10 In. 30.00

Plate, Dinner, Windmill,
10 1/2 In. 45.00

Plate, Jubilee Fruit,
Pomegranate, 8 In. 25.00

Plate, Luncheon,
Cherry Tree Glen, 9 In. . 20.00

Plate, Luncheon, Weathervane,
9 1/4 In. 35.00

Plate, Luncheon, Wrinkled
Rose, 9 In. 20.00

Plate, Round, Grape Harvest,
12 In. 40.00

Plate, Salad, Grapes,
8 1/2 In. . . . . . . 20.00 to 30.00

Plate, Salad, Honolulu,
3 Apples, 8 In. 25.00

Plate, Salad, Honolulu,
3 Figs, 8 In. 25.00

Plate, Salad, Honolulu,
Cherries, 8 In. 25.00

Plate, Salad, Rose Chintz,
7 1/8 In. 18.00

Plate, Salad, Rutledge,
7 1/2 In. 15.00

Plate, Salad, Songbirds,
8 5/16 In. 139.00

Plate, Square, Cherry
Bounce, 7 In. 25.00

Platter, Apple Butter,
11 1/2 x 9 1/2 In. 25.00

Platter, Edgemont,
13 In. 30.00

Platter, Lighthearted,
13 In. 25.00

Saltshaker, Figural, Cluckers,
Rooster 70.00

Saltshaker, Moss Rose 4.00

Saucer, Beauty Secret 8.00

Saucer, Celandine, After
Dinner 15.00

Saucer, Chintz, Colonial . . 15.00

Soup, Dish, Waterlily,
7 1/2 In. 20.00

Sugar, Cover, Grandmother's
Garden 30.00

Sugar, Fox Grape 80.00

COORS

The Coors Porcelain Company of Golden, Colorado, was owned by the Coors Brewing Company. Dishes were made from the turn of the century. Coors stopped making nonessential wares at the start of World War II. After the war, the pottery made ovenware, teapots, vases, and a general line of pottery, but no dinnerware—except for special orders. The company is still in business making industrial porcelain.

ROSEBUD, the most popular pattern made by the Coors Porcelain Company, was produced from 1934 to 1942. It is a solid-color pattern with a stylized flower and leaves on the edge of the plates or sides of the cups. It was made in Blue, Green (sometimes called turquoise), Ivory, Maroon, Orange, and Yellow.

COORS
ROSEBUD
U.S.A.

Blue
Bean Pot, Handles 125.00
Tumbler, Handle,
8 1/2 Oz., 3 1/2 In. 95.00

Green
Creamer 55.00
Salt & Pepper 60.00

Maroon
Baker, Oval, Small 65.00
Batter Bowl, 3 1/2 Pt. 95.00
Cake Plate, 11 In. 110.00
Casserole, Medium 75.00
Salt & Pepper 90.00

Orange
Batter Bowl, 3 1/2 Pt. 75.00
Casserole, French 95.00
Teapot, 6 Cup 195.00

Yellow
Bean Pot, Handles 70.00
Pitcher, Batter, 3 1/2 Pt. . . 65.00
Ramekin 70.00

CROOKSVILLE

PANTRY
BAK-IN
by WARE
Crooksville

Crooksville China Company worked in Crooksville, Ohio, from 1902 to

1959. The company made pottery baking dishes, teapots, cookie jars, and other kitchenwares. Semiporcelain and pottery dinnerwares were also made.

APPLE BLOSSOM has pink blossoms and green leaves on a white background. It was made on the La Grande shape and has an embossed rope design around the rim.

Pie Server	25.00
Plate, Salad, 8 In.	8.00
Serving Plate	12.00

DELMAR BEGONIA has a yellow and brown flower, a bud, two large green leaves and two small leaves. It is on the La Grande shape. The same decoration was part of the Gray-Lure line for a pattern called Begonia.

Bowl, Fruit	4.00
Cup & Saucer	10.00
Plate, Bread & Butter, 6 In.	4.00
Plate, Dinner, 9 1/2 In.	9.00 to 10.00

Platter	13.00
Serving Bowl	10.00
Sugar & Creamer	25.00

HIBISCUS pattern is decorated with a red hibiscus and dark and light green leaves.

Bowl, Cereal	6.00
Bowl, Divided, Open Center Handle, Iva-Lure, 11 In.	31.00
Bowl, Fruit	4.00
Bowl, Vegetable, 7 In.	12.00
Cup	5.00
Plate, Bread & Butter, 6 In.	4.00
Plate, Luncheon, 7 In.	10.00
Platter, Gray-Lure, Round, Crimped Edge, 12 In.	6.00
Sugar & Creamer	10.00
Sugar & Creamer, Gray-Lure	24.00

LA GRANDE is a shape made by Crooksville that was decorated with several different decals.

Bowl, Cereal	5.00
Bowl, Fruit	4.00
Casserole, Cover, 1 1/2 Qt.	35.00
Cover, Sugar	4.00
Cup & Saucer	10.00
Gravy, Underplate Only	5.00
Plate, Bread & Butter, 6 In.	3.00 to 4.00
Plate, Dessert, 6 In.	6.00
Plate, Dinner, 9 1/2 In.	10.00
Plate, Luncheon, 7 In.	8.00
Plate, Salad, 8 In.	8.00
Platter, Oval	12.00
Serving Bowl, 8 In.	15.00
Serving Platter, Floral, Square	15.00
Soup, Dish	9.00
Sugar & Creamer	19.00

PETIT POINT HOUSE is a decal of a house, pine tree, flowers, and fence that was used on different shapes and with different borders.

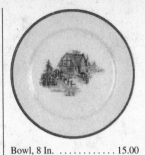

Bowl, 8 In.	15.00
Bowl, 11 In.	59.00
Bowl, Oval, 9 In.	25.00
Creamer	17.00
Cup	12.00 to 18.00
Gravy Boat	9.50
Jug, 56 Oz., 5 3/4 In.	50.00
Pie Plate, 10 In.	8.00
Pitcher, 5 3/4 In.	11.00
Pitcher, Cover, 6 In.	89.00
Plate, 12 1/4 In.	38.00
Plate, Bread & Butter, 6 In.	7.00 to 10.00
Plate, Dinner, 10 In.	15.00 to 33.00
Plate, Luncheon, 9 1/4 In.	14.00
Platter, 11 1/4 In.	29.00
Platter, 13 1/4 In.	40.00
Saucer	6.00 to 12.00
Sugar, Cover	25.00

SILHOUETTE looks just like its name. The 1930s pattern shows a black silhouette of two people eating at a table and a dog begging for food in front of the table. The pieces have platinum trim. The pattern is similar to Taverne by Hall, but Taverne has no dog. Matching metal pieces and glassware were made.

Bowl, 8 In.	4.00
Bowl, Vegetable, Chrome Holder, Handle, 6 3/4 In.	14.00
Casserole, 8 In.	21.00
Casserole, Cover	17.00
Grease Jar, Cover, 5 x 6 In.	12.00

Plate, Dinner,
10 In. . . . . 5.00 to 11.00
Plate, Luncheon, 9 In. 7.00
Sandwich Server,
Handle, Chrome
Holder, 11 1/4 In. 15.00
Soup, Dish, 7 1/2 In. 9.00

SPRING BLOSSOM is decorated with delicate pink and white floral sprays. It was made in the 1940s.

Bowl, Vegetable, Oval,
9 In. 12.00
Plate, Dinner, 10 In. 7.00
Platter, Oval, 11 1/2 In. . . . 4.00
Platter, Oval, 15 1/4 In. . . 11.00
Tureen, Cover 36.00

THEMATIC is an embossed shape that was decorated with various decals. It was made in the 1930s and 1940s.

Bowl, Vegetable, Oval,
9 In. 15.00
Gravy Boat 10.00
Platter, Oval, 15 1/2 In. . . 17.00

WILDFLOWER is decorated with wildflowers and butterflies.

Bowl, Fruit,
5 1/2 In. . . . . 3.00 to 9.00
Bowl, Vegetable,
8 3/4 In. 25.00
Creamer 12.00
Cup & Saucer . . . . 8.00 to 15.00
Plate, Bread & Butter,
6 In. 3.00
Plate, Dinner, 10 1/4 In. . . 12.00
Plate, Salad,
7 3/4 In. . . . . 5.00 to 12.00
Platter, Oval, 11 1/2 In. . . 15.00
Platter, Oval, 13 In. 25.00
Platter, Oval, 15 In. 22.00
Saucer 4.00
Soup, Dish, 6 1/4 In. 5.00
Sugar, Cover 16.00

WINDBLOWN has small pink flowers on graceful windblown stems on a soft pink background.

Bowl, Cereal 6.00
Plate, Dinner, 10 In. 10.00
Serving Bowl 12.00
Sugar & Creamer 24.00

MISCELLANEOUS: There are many other patterns made by Crooksville. Some are listed here.

Bowl, Cereal, Little
Bouquet 3.00
Butter, Square,
Columbia 10.00
Cup & Saucer, Pink &
Yellow, Euclid 10.00
Cup & Saucer, Sun-Lure . . 3.00
Gravy Boat, Underplate,
Petit Point Leaf 22.00
Gravy Boat, Underplate,
Roses 23.00
Pitcher, Mexicana 54.00
Plate, Bread & Butter,
Border Bouquet, 6 In. . . . 4.00
Plate, Bread & Butter, Rose
Band, 6 In. . . . . . . 3.00 to 4.00
Plate, Dinner, Azalea,
9 1/2 In. 10.00
Plate, Dinner, Border
Bouquet, 9 1/2 In. 10.00
Plate, Dinner, Magnolia,
10 In. 8.00
Plate, Luncheon, Autumn,
7 In. 12.00
Plate, Luncheon, Colonial
Couple, 7 In. 5.00
Plate, Luncheon, Rose
Band, 9 In. 8.00
Plate, Luncheon, Rust
Bouquet, 9 In. 7.00
Plate, Salad, Euclid, 8 In. . . 8.00
Platter, Columbia 20.00
Serving Bowl, Gold & Roses,
8 3/4 x 2 1/2 In. 15.00

Serving Plate, Floral 15.00
Soup, Dish, Rose & Gold,
7 7/8 In. 10.00
Sugar & Creamer,
Columbia 24.00

ENOCH WEDGWOOD

Enoch Wedgwood Ltd. is an English factory established in Tunstall, Staffordshire, in 1860. It was called Wedgwood & Co. until 1965. The company is now part of the Waterford Wedgwood Group.

COUNTRYSIDE is a blue and white pattern picturing a castle beside a river with a bridge across it and trees in the foreground. It was made from 1965 to 1980.

Bowl, Fruit, 5 1/4 In. 7.00
Cake Plate, 6 In. 7.00
Cup . . . . 2.00 to 3.00
Cup & Saucer,
2 3/4 & 5 1/2 In. 25.00
Dinnerware Set,
18 Piece 65.00

Plate, Bread & Butter,
6 In. 7.00
Plate, Dessert, 7 In. 9.00
Plate, Dinner,
10 In. . . . . 7.00 to 15.00
Saucer, 5 1/2 In. 5.00

LIBERTY BLUE dishes were
offered by A & P, Grand Union,
and other grocery chains to tie
in with the 1776–1976 bicenten-
nial celebration of America's
independence. They were made
by Enoch Wedgwood Company
of England in the tradition of
the nineteenth-century Staffordshire historical blue china. The
dishes have a floral wreath border and central transfer designs
of scenes from American history. They were sold beginning
in April 1977. There was a different center design on each
plate. Dishes are marked *Liberty Blue* on the back.

Bowl, Fruit,
5 In. . . . . 5.00 to 12.00
Creamer 30.00
Cup & Saucer . . . . 7.00 to 10.00
Gravy Boat,
Underplate . . . . 75.00 to 80.00
Plate, Bread & Butter,
5 3/4 In. . . . . 4.00 to 5.00
Plate, Dinner,
9 3/4 In. . . . . . . 6.00 to 15.00
Plate, Luncheon, 7 In. 10.00
Platter, 12 In. . . 55.00 to 69.00
Platter, 14 In. 95.00
Saltshaker 30.00
Soup, Dish,
6 1/2 In. . . . . . . 25.00 to 28.00

MANCHESTER has a gray central design of stylized hearts
and flowers. It has platinum
trim.

Bowl, Vegetable,
9 1/4 In. 15.00
Bowl, Vegetable, Cover
Only, 8 1/2 In. 15.00
Gravy Boat, Underplate . . . 8.00
Plate, Bread & Butter,
5 3/4 In. . . . . 5.00 to 7.00

Plate, Dessert, 7 In. 9.00
Saucer 4.00
Serving Platter, Oval,
12 x 9 1/2 In. 17.00
Sugar, Cover 18.00

ROYAL BLUE is a blue and
white pattern of flowers and
leaves. It has platinum trim.

Bowl, Fruit, 5 1/4 In. 5.00
Cake Plate, 5 7/8 In. 10.00
Plate, Bread & Butter,
5 3/4 In. 5.00
Plate, Dinner,
10 In. . . . . 10.00 to 12.00
Saucer 4.00
Sugar, Cover 30.00
Sugar & Creamer 30.00
Tea Set, 15 Piece 108.00

MISCELLANEOUS: There are
many other patterns made by
Enoch Wedgwood. Some are
listed here.

Bowl, Dessert, Gold
Medallion, 5 In. 12.00
Bowl, Fruit, Jacqueline . . . 12.00
Cup & Saucer, Yellow,
Jacqueline 30.00
Gravy Boat, Hedge
Rose 20.00
Plate, Dessert, Old Derby,
7 In. 15.00
Plate, Dinner, Madeira,
10 In. 5.00
Plate, Dinner, Royal Homes Of
Britain, Blue, 9 3/4 In. . . 17.00

❖

**Don't put Franciscan
dishes into a hot oven;
they may crack or
break. Turn the heat on
only after placing the
dish in the oven and
turn the heat up slowly.**

❖

Saucer, Royal Homes Of
Britain, 5 5/8 In. 7.00

FRANCISCAN

Franciscan is a trademark
that appears on pottery.
Gladding, McBean and
Company started in Lin-
coln, California, in 1875.
The company acquired
Tropico Potteries, Inc., of
Glendale, California, in
1923. The firm made
sewer pipes, floor tiles,
dinnerwares, and art pot-
tery with a variety of
trademarks. By 1934, all
dinnerware and art pot-
tery was made in Glen-
dale. They made china and
cream-color, decorated
earthenware. The name
used in advertisements
and marks was changed
from Franciscan Pottery
to Franciscan Ware in
1936. In the 1960s, a line
of dishes was made in
Japan for Franciscan. In
1962, Gladding, McBean
and Company merged
with Lock Joint Pipe Com-
pany to become Interpace.
The California pottery
plant was sold by Inter-
pace to Wedgwood Lim-
ited of England, which
renamed it Franciscan
Ceramics Inc. All produc-
tion moved to England.

AMAPOLA, a pattern in the Picnic line, has an orange-yellow background and an overall pattern of large flowers and leaves in related brown and yellow colors. It has an embossed border trimmed in brown. The pattern was introduced in 1973.

Plate, Dinner,
10 3/4 In. . . . . . 12.00 to 17.00
Plate, Salad,
8 3/4 In. . . . . 7.00 to 10.00

ANTIGUA is a pattern in the Whitestone line. It has a wide broken band in yellow and brown tones as a border. Each piece of the band has geometric designs. It was made in Japan in the 1960s.

Cup . . . . 4.00 to 6.00
Plate, Dinner,
10 3/8 In. . . . . . . 8.00 to 16.00
Plate, Salad, 8 1/4 In. 10.00

ANTIQUE GREEN is a plain shape with a greenish border and a narrow band inside the border. It was introduced in 1966.

Creamer 55.00
Cup & Saucer . . . 25.00 to 29.00
Plate, Bread & Butter,
6 1/4 In. . . . . . 11.00 to 15.00
Saucer . . . . 4.00 to 6.00

APPLE pattern dishes were introduced in 1940 and are still being made by Waterford Wedgwood USA. It is a cream-color ware with a raised border of red apples, green leaves, and brown stems. The dishes made in the United States from 1940 to 1984 are lighter in color than those made in England from 1984 to the present.

Ashtray, Individual.
4 1/2 In. . . . . . 15.00 to 19.00
Ashtray, Square,
4 1/2 In. . . . . . 20.00 to 27.00
Bowl, Cereal,
6 In. . . . . 9.00 to 27.00
Bowl, Fruit,
5 1/4 In. . . . . . 10.00 to 15.00
Bowl, Oatmeal, Footed,
5 1/2 In. . . . . . 23.00 to 25.00
Bowl, Vegetable, 2 Sections,
10 3/4 x 7 In. . . 48.00 to 62.00
Bowl, Vegetable,
7 3/4 In. 20.00
Bowl, Vegetable,
8 1/4 In. 27.00

Butter, Cover, 1/4 Lb.,
7 3/4 In. 51.00
Casserole, 1 1/2 Qt.,
6 3/4 In. 60.00
Cigarette Box, Cover,
4 1/2 x 3 1/4 x 2 In. . . . 125.00
Chop Plate,
14 In. . . . . . 140.00 to 195.00
Coaster, 3 3/4 In. 53.00
Coffeepot, 9 7/8 In. 50.00
Compote, 3 1/2 x 6 In. . . . 40.00
Cookie Jar, Cover,
9 1/4 In. 290.00
Creamer,
2 3/4 In. . . . . . 15.00 to 18.00
Cup 4.00
Cup, Tea,
2 3/4 In. . . . . . . 8.00 to 10.00
Cup & Saucer,
2 3/4 In. . . . . . 15.00 to 23.00
Gravy Boat, Attached
Underplate, 8 1/4 x
3 1/2 In. . . . . 35.00 to 74.00
Grill Plate, 3 Sections,
11 In. 95.00
Mixing Bowl, 6 In. 125.00
Pitcher, Milk, 6 1/4 In. . . 100.00
Plate, Bread & Butter,
6 1/2 In. . . . . . 10.00 to 16.00
Plate, Child's,
7 1/4 x 9 In. 195.00
Plate, Dinner,
10 1/2 In. . . . . 10.00 to 25.00
Plate, Luncheon,
9 1/2 In. . . . . . 10.00 to 18.00
Plate, Salad,
8 In. . . . . 15.00 to 22.00
Platter, Oval,
14 In. . . . . 50.00 to 73.00
Relish, 3 Sections,
11 3/4 In. 97.00
Relish, Oval,
10 In. . . . . 26.00 to 40.00
Salt & Pepper, Apples,
2 1/4 In. . . . . . 25.00 to 34.00
Saltshaker 20.00
Saucer, 5 3/4 In. . . . 4.00 to 8.00
Sherbet . . . . 12.00 to 20.00
Soup, Dish, 8 1/2 In. 18.00
Spoon Rest 20.00
Sugar . . . . 20.00 to 30.00
Sugar & Creamer 45.00
Tidbit, 11 1/4 x
6 1/2 In. . . . . . 25.00 to 55.00

Trivet 93.00
Tumbler, 10 Oz.,
    5 1/4 In. ...... 30.00 to 36.00
Tureen, Soup, Cover 450.00

ARCADIA was introduced in 1941. It was part of the Merced line of fine china. The decoration was an inner band of stylized leaves in one of four different colors: Blue, Gold, Green, and Maroon. Each piece has a narrow gold edge.

Blue
Plate, Dinner, 10 1/2 In. ... 49.00
Gold
Cup & Saucer 38.00
Plate, Bread & Butter,
    6 3/8 In. 15.00
Plate, Dinner, 10 1/2 In. .. 24.00
Plate, Salad, 8 3/8 In. 20.00

Going away for the weekend? If you have a car at home, park it at the back of the driveway and lock it. It makes it look as if someone is home and it blocks easy access to a back door.

Saucer 10.00
Green
Cup & Saucer 38.00
Gravy Boat 146.00
Plate, Bread & Butter,
    6 3/8 In. 9.00
Plate, Dinner, 10 1/2 In. .. 49.00
Plate, Salad,
    8 3/8 In. ...... 12.00 to 21.00
Saucer 10.00

AUTUMN pattern is decorated with leaves. Oak leaves of blue, yellow, and brown are scattered near the edges of plates or on the sides of bowls. It was introduced in 1955 as part of the Flair line.

Bowl, Cereal, Handles,
    7 3/8 In. ...... 12.00 to 23.00
Bowl, Fruit,
    5 1/8 In. .... 6.00 to 13.00
Bowl, Vegetable,
    9 3/8 In. ...... 15.00 to 30.00
Bowl, Vegetable, 2 Sections,
    13 3/4 In. ..... 40.00 to 50.00
Butter, No Cover 8.00
Coffee Server, 10 In. 23.00
Coffeepot 45.00
Creamer .... 13.00 to 29.00
Cup .... 4.00 to 5.00
Cup & Saucer .... 7.00 to 16.00
Gravy Boat, Attached
    Underplate 50.00
Pitcher, Milk, 28 Oz.,
    8 1/4 In. 43.00
Plate, Bread & Butter,
    6 1/2 In. .... 4.00 to 7.00
Plate, Dinner,
    10 1/2 In. ...... 7.00 to 22.00
Plate, Salad,
    8 1/4 In. .... 5.00 to 8.00

Platter,
    13 3/4 In. ..... 30.00 to 45.00
Platter, 16 1/2 In. 50.00
Relish, 12 In. 15.00
Saucer .... 3.00 to 5.00
Sugar, No Cover 8.00
Teapot, Cover 75.00

BLUE FANCY is a pattern on a modern white fine china shape. It has a narrow border of blue geometric designs of hearts and scrolls. It was introduced in 1963 as part of the Whitestone line that was made in Japan.

Bowl, Fruit, 5 In. 6.00
Cup & Saucer 9.00
Saucer .... 3.00 to 5.00

BOUQUET is decorated with a central spray of rose, yellow, and blue flowers and a full floral border. There is another Franciscan pattern called Bouquet that has a white, blue, and brown floral spray on a tan background.

Bowl, Cereal, 6 In. 17.00
Creamer 33.00
Cup & Saucer ... 19.00 to 31.00
Plate, Salad, 8 In. 11.00

CAFE ROYAL was introduced about 1980. It is made from the same molds as Desert Rose but is decorated in shades of brown.

Ashtray, Square,
4 3/4 In. 60.00
Baker, 9 1/2 x 8 3/4 In. . . . 79.00
Bowl, Vegetable, Round,
9 In. 30.00
Butter, Cover, 7 3/4 In. . . . 70.00
Cup 14.00
Cup & Saucer . . . . 9.00 to 12.00
Cup & Saucer,
After Dinner 25.00
Mug, 7 Oz., 3 In. 19.00
Pitcher, Large 100.00
Plate, Luncheon,
9 1/2 In. 12.00
Platter, Medium,
14 x 10 1/4 In. 38.00

CANTATA has a center design of blue and purple flowers and green leaves. There is a narrow green border. The pattern was made in Japan from 1965 to 1969 as part of the Whitestone line.

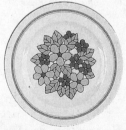

Bowl, Fruit, 5 In. 6.00
Creamer 10.00
Cup & Saucer 7.00

Plate, Bread & Butter,
6 3/8 In. . . . . 3.00 to 5.00
Plate, Dinner,
10 3/8 In. . . . . . . 9.00 to 12.00

CANTON is a fine china pattern introduced in 1950. The pattern is decorated with abstract flowers of gray and black. It is part of the Encanto line.

Creamer 62.00
Sugar, Cover . . . . 75.00 to 85.00

CARMEL, introduced in 1952, is part of the Encanto line of fine china that has a plain rimless plate. The center design is a pink and platinum tulip plant. There is a platinum edge. Some early dishes may not have the edge trim.

Bowl, Vegetable, Oval,
9 In. 86.00
Plate, Bread & Butter,
6 3/8 In. 12.00
Plate, Dinner, 10 1/2 In. . . 41.00

CHEROKEE ROSE came in three variations: wide gold band, thin gold band, and wide green band. The center design is

a bunch of pink roses and green leaves. The first patterns were introduced in 1941, the wide gold band in 1942.

Green Band
Bowl, Vegetable, Oval,
9 3/4 In. 80.00
Cup & Saucer 19.00
Plate, Dinner,
10 5/8 In. . . . . . 20.00 to 40.00
Thin Gold Band
Bowl, Fruit, 6 1/4 In. 14.00
Plate, Bread & Butter,
6 3/8 In. 14.00
Plate, Salad, 8 3/8 In. 22.00
Wide Gold Band
Cup & Saucer 48.00
Gravy Boat, Attached
Underplate 129.00
Plate, Dinner,
10 5/8 In. . . . . . 40.00 to 52.00

CLOUD NINE is a plain white, undecorated plate. It is part of the Whitestone line made in Japan from 1960 to 1969.

Bowl, Fruit, 5 In. 10.00
Creamer . . . . 6.00 to 14.00
Cup & Saucer 12.00
Plate, Bread & Butter,
6 In. . . . . 3.00 to 7.00
Plate, Dinner,
10 3/8 In. . . . . . . 8.00 to 16.00
Plate, Salad, 8 1/4 In. 6.00
Soup, Dish, 6 In. 9.00
Sugar, Cover 17.00

CONCH is one of many patterns picturing sea creatures in the Sea Sculptures line. The Sand or White plate is decorated with an embossed picture of a conch. It was introduced in 1977.

Sand

Casserole, Cover,
Individual 40.00
Cup 12.00
Cup & Saucer 18.00
Plate, Dinner,
10 3/4 In. 24.00
Plate, Luncheon,
9 1/8 In. ...... 15.00 to 21.00

White

Plate, Dinner,
10 3/4 In. ..... 21.00 to 37.00
Plate, Luncheon,
9 1/8 In. ...... 14.00 to 17.00
Saucer 5.00

CONCORD is part of the Merced line that was introduced in 1941. The dishes have a wide gray-green band on the rim and a ring of grapevines near the center. Cups and bowls are gray-green on the outside.

Bowl, Vegetable, Oval,
9 1/4 In. ..... 82.00 to 130.00
Cup & Saucer, Footed ... 30.00
Plate, Bread & Butter,
6 3/8 In. ...... 15.00 to 21.00
Plate, Dinner,
10 1/2 In. ..... 35.00 to 64.00

CORONADO is a solid-color line with a swirl border. It was made in Apple Green, Chartreuse, Coral, Gray, Ivory, Maroon, Turquoise, and Yellow. Most colors were made in two different finishes, glossy and matte. It was made from 1934 to 1954.

Apple Green

Bowl, Fruit, 6 In. 15.00
Cup 10.00

Coral

Bowl, Fruit, 6 In. 15.00
Cup, Coffee 5.00
Cup & Saucer 10.00
Gravy Boat, Attached
Underplate 45.00
Plate, Bread & Butter,
6 1/4 In. 10.00
Plate, Dinner, 10 1/2 In. .. 12.00
Plate, Luncheon,
9 1/4 In. .... 8.00 to 9.00
Platter, Oval, 13 In. 26.00
Relish, 9 1/4 In. 18.00
Salt & Pepper 30.00
Saucer 4.00
Soup, Cream,
Saucer .... 20.00 to 32.00
Soup, Rim,
8 1/2 In. ...... 15.00 to 24.00
Sugar & Creamer 24.00

Ivory

Bowl, Vegetable, Round,
7 1/2 In. ...... 15.00 to 30.00
Chop Plate, 13 3/4 In. 64.00
Creamer,
Footed .... 33.00 to 45.00
Cup .... 8.00 to 9.00
Cup & Saucer ... 11.00 to 18.00
Gravy Boat, Attached
Underplate 10.00
Plate, Bread & Butter,
6 1/4 In. 4.00
Plate, Dinner, 10 3/8 In. .. 16.00
Platter, Oval, 11 1/2 In. .. 10.00
Platter, Oval, 13 In. 10.00
Saucer 8.00
Soup, Rim 24.00

Maroon

Cup & Saucer 13.00
Plate, Luncheon,
9 1/4 In. 13.00
Soup, Cream, Saucer 23.00

Turquoise

Ashtray, 4 1/2 In. 6.00
Creamer, Flat 15.00
Cup 10.00
Cup, Coffee 5.00
Cup & Saucer 13.00

Plate, Bread & Butter,
6 1/4 In. .... 4.00 to 10.00
Plate, Luncheon,
9 1/4 In. .... 9.00 to 14.00
Platter, Oval, 13 1/8 In. .. 30.00
Saucer, 5 1/2 In. ... 3.00 to 4.00
Soup, Cream, Saucer 28.00
Soup, Rim, 8 1/2 In. 24.00

Yellow

Bowl, Cereal, 6 1/4 In. ... 10.00
Bowl, Fruit, 6 In. 8.00
Bowl, Vegetable, Round,
7 1/2 In. 13.00
Chop Plate,
11 3/4 In. ..... 20.00 to 38.00
Creamer, Flat 10.00
Cup & Saucer 10.00
Gravy Boat, Attached
Underplate 56.00
Plate, Bread & Butter,
6 1/4 In. 5.00
Plate, Luncheon,
9 1/4 In. 10.00
Platter, Oval, 13 1/8 In. .. 25.00
Relish, 9 1/4 In. 10.00
Salt & Pepper 15.00
Soup, Rim,
8 1/2 In. ...... 15.00 to 24.00
Sugar, Cover .... 15.00 to 20.00
Teapot .... 50.00 to 60.00

COUNTRY CRAFT, part of the Hacienda line, was made from 1962 to 1989. The line was made to look "hand thrown" and has slight ringed grooves in the surface. The only decoration is a colored rim. It was made in five colors: Almond Cream, Blue, Peach, Raspberry, and Russet (brown).

Almond Cream

Cup, 2 1/2 In. 9.00

Blue

Plate, Salad, 8 3/8 In. 10.00

Russet

Bowl, Cereal, 6 3/8 In. ... 17.00
Creamer .... 15.00 to 33.00
Cup 16.00
Plate, Dinner,
10 7/8 In. ..... 12.00 to 50.00
Plate, Salad, 8 3/8 In. 11.00

CREOLE pattern, part of the Picnic line, is brown with a darker brown rim. It was first offered in 1973.

Bowl, Cereal, 7 1/8 In. 17.00
Bowl, Vegetable,
   9 1/2 In. 45.00
Cup 16.00
Plate, Salad,
   8 3/4 In. 11.00
Platter, Oval,
   12 In. . . . . 45.00 to 49.00

CRINOLINE pattern, part of the Merced line, has a border of pink flowers and ribbons. It is a fine china pattern introduced in 1942. Another pattern was given the same name in 1973. It has yellow flowers.

Bowl, Vegetable, Open . . 58.00
Cup & Saucer 30.00
Plate, Bread & Butter,
   6 3/8 In. . . . . . . 10.00 to 13.00
Plate, Dinner,
   10 5/8 In. . . . . . 24.00 to 28.00
Salt & Pepper 58.00

CYPRESS pattern has white cypress leaves on a plain gray background. It is part of the

---

Flair dinnerware line that was introduced in 1962.

Plate, Dinner,
   10 1/2 In. 14.00
Plate, Salad,
   8 1/4 In. . . . . . . 15.00 to 25.00
Plate, Salad, Crescent,
   8 3/8 In. . . . . . . 17.00 to 25.00

DAISY pattern has a rimless plate with clusters of blue and yellow flowers and gray-green leaves. It is part of the Flair line and was introduced in 1960.

Bowl, Vegetable, 2 Sections,
   13 3/4 In. 62.00
Bowl, Vegetable, Round,
   9 In. 42.00
Butter, No Cover,
   8 In. 51.00
Candy Dish 30.00
Creamer 33.00
Cup & Saucer 19.00
Gravy Boat, Attached
   Underplate 74.00
Plate, Bread & Butter,
   6 1/2 In. 8.00
Platter, Oval, 14 In. 74.00
Relish, 12 In. 35.00
Saucer, 6 In. 5.00
Sugar, Cover 42.00

DAWN, part of the Encanto line, is a plain gray pattern of fine china made with or without a narrow platinum border. It was introduced in 1950.

Cup . . . . 15.00 to 29.00
Cup & Saucer 33.00
Plate, Bread & Butter,
   6 3/8 In. 13.00
Plate, Dinner, 10 1/2 In. . . 25.00
Saucer 5.00

DEL MAR is decorated with a ring of abstract shapes in blue and gray-green. It was made from 1959 to 1969, and is part of the Family-Discovery line of fine china. Another pattern named Del Mar, not included here, was made in 1937. It is decorated with white sailboats and seagulls on a blue ground.

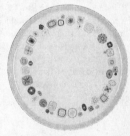

Bowl, Fruit, 5 In. 24.00
Bowl, Vegetable, Divided,
   10 3/4 In. 22.00
Creamer . . . . . . 12.00 to 21.00
Cup & Saucer 14.00
Gravy Boat 34.00
Plate, Dinner,
   10 1/8 In. . . . . . 16.00 to 21.00
Platter, Oval, 13 1/4 In. . . 30.00
Soup, Dish 35.00

DEL MONTE has a gold twisted rope design on the inner rim and gold trim on the outer edge of the plates. Bowls have the gold twisted rope design around the center of the outside. The rope design is inside the cups. It was part of the Merced line, the first fine china line made by Gladding, McBean in 1942.

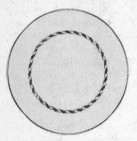

Creamer 60.00
Cup & Saucer,
Demitasse 20.00
Gravy Boat, Attached
Underplate 137.00
Sugar, Cover 81.00

DEL RIO has a pale gray rim with a decoration of a band of stylized white daisylike flowers and thin leaves. The decoration is added as a ring around the center of the outside of pieces like sugars, creamers, and bowls. It is part of the Merced fine china line and was introduced in 1956.

Bowl, Fruit, 5 1/8 In. 33.00
Saucer 11.00

DENMARK, sometimes called Denmark Blue, is a pattern made on English ironstone. It has light and dark blue flowers and decorations on a white background and embossed ridges. It was introduced in 1981.

Butter Chip ..... 16.00 to 20.00
Gravy Boat 69.00
Salt & Pepper 47.00

DESERT ROSE is one of the most popular patterns of earthenware ever sold in America. It was introduced in 1942 and is still being made. The pieces are decorated with large pink five-petal roses with yellow centers. Groupings of three leaves are added to the rose branch. Pieces made today in England are decorated with paler pink and grayer green. Some pieces were made in Portugal and Germany. Matching glasses and tablecloths, clocks, and other items have been made.

Ashtray, 3 1/2 In., Pair ... 50.00
Bowl, Casserole, Cover,
1 1/2 Qt. 50.00
Bowl, Cereal,
6 In. .... 10.00 to 16.00
Bowl, Fruit,
5 1/4 In. .... 4.00 to 6.00
Bowl, Salad,
10 In. .... 75.00 to 115.00
Bowl, Vegetable, 2 Sections,
10 7/8 In. ..... 30.00 to 45.00
Bowl, Vegetable,
9 In. .... 32.00 to 40.00
Butter, Cover, 1/4 Lb.,
7 3/4 In. 45.00
Candlestick, 3 1/2 In.,
Pair .... 80.00 to 95.00
Candlestick, Tulip, 3 In. .. 25.00
Canister, Tea, Cover,
5 3/4 In. 330.00
Casserole, Cover,
1 1/2 Qt. 65.00
Chop Plate, 12 In. 90.00

Chop Plate, 13 In. 95.00
Chop Plate,
14 In. ...... 95.00 to 165.00
Cigarette Box, 4 1/2 x
3 1/2 In. ..... 60.00 to 150.00
Coffeepot, Cover,
7 1/2 In. 95.00
Compote,
4 x 8 In. ...... 68.00 to 90.00
Compote, 6 In. 26.00
Creamer .... 15.00 to 22.00
Cup 11.00
Cup, Jumbo, 4 1/2 In. 30.00
Cup & Saucer .... 5.00 to 18.00
Cup & Saucer, After
Dinner 55.00
Dinner Bell, 6 In. 125.00
Dish, Oval, 3 Sections,
9 In. 195.00
Gravy Boat, Attached
Underplate, 8 1/4 x
5 3/4 In. ...... 38.00 to 74.00
Mixing Bowl,
3 1/2 x 6 In. . 125.00 to 135.00
Mixing Bowl,
4 1/4 x 7 1/2 In. 145.00
Mixing Bowl,
4 3/4 x 9 In. 155.00
Mixing Bowl Set,
3 Piece 495.00
Mug, 7 Oz., 3 In. 20.00
Mug, 10 Oz., 4 1/4 In. ... 45.00
Napkin Ring, 1 1/2 In.,
4 Piece 200.00
Plate, Bread & Butter,
6 1/2 In. .... 4.00 to 20.00
Plate, Dinner,
10 1/2 In. ...... 8.00 to 25.00
Plate, Heart Shape,
5 3/4 In. 145.00
Plate, Luncheon,
9 1/2 In. ...... 18.00 to 22.00
Plate, Salad,
8 1/2 In. .... 5.00 to 26.00
Platter,
12 3/4 In. ..... 27.00 to 55.00
Platter, 14 In. ... 29.00 to 45.00
Platter,
19 In. ...... 275.00 to 300.00
Relish, 11 In. ... 35.00 to 45.00
Salt & Pepper,
2 1/4 In. ...... 24.00 to 38.00
Saltshaker, 2 1/4 In. 13.00
Saucer 4.00

Sherbet,
2 1/2 In. . . . . . . 7.00 to 29.00
Soup, Dish, Footed,
5 1/2 In. . . . . . . 12.00 to 28.00
Soup, Rim, .
8 1/2 In. . . . . . . 15.00 to 30.00
Sugar, 2 x 3 1/4 In. 15.00
Sugar, Cover,
3 In. . . . . 25.00 to 26.00
Sugar &
Creamer . . . . . . 45.00 to 49.00
Teapot 70.00
Tile, Square, 6 In. 65.00
Tureen, Soup, Cover,
7 3/4 In. 625.00

DUET was introduced in 1956. It was a modern shape called Eclipse that was also used for the popular Starburst pattern. It is decorated with two sprigs of a pink flower with gray leaves.

Bowl, Cereal, 7 In. 10.00
Bowl, Fruit, 5 In. 5.00
Bowl, Vegetable, 2 Sections,
8 1/4 In. 20.00
Butter, Cover, 1/4 Lb. 30.00
Casserole, 1 1/2 Qt.,
8 1/2 In. 15.00
Casserole, Cover,
2 1/2 Qt., 11 In. 30.00
Casserole, Individual,
6 In. 15.00
Condiment Tray, 3 Sections,
6 3/4 In. . . . . . . 15.00 to 25.00
Cup 14.00
Cup, Coffee 5.00
Cup & Saucer 5.00
Gravy Boat, Attached
Underplate . . . 13.00 to 15.00
Plate, Dinner, 10 3/4 In. . . 20.00
Platter, 15 In. . . . 15.00 to 25.00
Salt & Pepper, 3 1/2 In. . . 15.00

Sugar & Creamer, 4 In. . . 40.00

DUO TONE was made from 1939 to 1942. Pieces are Blue, Coral, Pastel Green, or Yellow on the front or inside and Ivory on the back or outside.

Blue
Bowl, Fruit, 4 1/4 In. 18.00
Cup & Saucer 23.50
Plate, Bread & Butter,
6 In. 13.50
Plate, Salad,
7 1/8 In. . . . . . . 20.00 to 45.00

Coral
Plate, Salad, 7 1/8 In. 10.00

EL DORADO was one of ten patterns made on the Madeira shape. It was introduced in 1966. Pieces have a sculpted relief floral pattern with a yellow rim or exterior.

Bowl, Cereal, 6 1/4 In. . . . 19.00
Bowl, Vegetable,
Round 50.00
Cup & Saucer 19.00
Plate, Dinner,
10 1/2 In. . . . . . 8.00 to 24.00
Plate, Salad, 8 1/2 In. 11.00
Platter, Small, 11 3/4 In. . . 55.00

EL PATIO was made from 1934 to 1956. The solid-color ware was made in more than twenty colors. In 1939, they introduced Apple Green, Deep Yellow, Flame Orange, Gloss White, Golden Glow, Light Yellow, Mexican Blue, and Redwood. By 1948 Bright Green, Maroon, and Satin Gray were added. Soon after, Bright Yellow

Gloss, Chartreuse Satin, Coral Gloss, Coral Satin, Glacial Blue Gloss, Ivory Satin, and Turquoise Satin were added.

Apple Green
Cup 8.00

Chartreuse
Bowl, Salad, 8 3/4 In. 28.00
Sugar & Creamer 30.00

Cobalt
Sugar & Creamer 35.00

Coral
Bowl, Cereal, 6 In. 10.00
Bowl, Fruit, 5 1/4 In. 7.00
Bowl, Vegetable,
8 1/4 In. . . . . . . 14.00 to 30.00
Creamer, 5 3/8 In. 25.00
Cup & Saucer . . . 10.00 to 15.00
Plate, Bread & Butter,
6 1/2 In. 5.00
Plate, Dinner, 10 1/2 In. . . 14.00
Plate, Salad, 8 In. 9.00
Sugar 14.00
Sugar, Cover 25.00
Sugar & Creamer 35.00

Golden Glow
Gravy Boat, Underplate . . 50.00
Sugar & Creamer 65.00

Ivory Satin
Sugar, Cover 25.00
Teapot 65.00

Maroon
Bowl, Cereal, 6 In. 10.00
Bowl, Fruit, 5 1/4 In. 5.00
Cup & Saucer 15.00
Plate, Bread & Butter,
6 1/2 In. 5.00
Plate, Dinner, 10 1/2 In. . . 20.00
Plate, Salad, 8 In. 5.00
Platter, 11 3/4 In. 30.00

Satin Gray
Bowl, Fruit, 5 1/4 In. 9.00
Creamer, 3 In. 15.00

Cup & Saucer 15.00
Eggcup, 3 1/2 In. 12.00
Plate, Bread & Butter,
    6 1/2 In. 10.00
Plate, Dinner, 10 1/2 In. . . 22.00
Plate, Salad, 8 In. 12.00
Sherbet, Footed,
    3 3/8 x 2 1/8 In. 12.00

Turquoise

Bowl, Cereal,
    6 In. . . . . 5.00 to 10.00
Bowl, Fruit, 5 1/4 In. 10.00
Bowl, Vegetable,
    9 1/4 In. 30.00
Cup & Saucer 15.00
Gravy Boat 55.00
Plate, Bread & Butter,
    6 1/2 In. 5.00
Plate, Dinner, 10 1/2 In. . . 15.00
Plate, Salad, 8 In. 9.00
Platter, 11 3/4 In. 47.00
Platter, 13 In. 45.00
Salt & Pepper 27.00
Soup, Cream 15.00
Sugar, Cover 10.00
Teapot, 6 Cup . . . 58.00 to 65.00

Turquoise Satin

Platter, Oval, 11 3/4 In. . . 47.00
Platter, Oval, 13 In. 45.00

Yellow

Bowl, Cereal, 6 In. 10.00
Bowl, Fruit, 5 1/4 In. 7.00
Cup & Saucer 15.00
Gravy Boat, Underplate,
    5 1/4 x 8 3/4 In. 50.00
Plate, Bread & Butter,
    6 1/2 In. 5.00
Plate, Dinner, 10 1/2 In. . . 20.00
Plate, Salad, 8 In. 9.00

FLORAL is part of the Madeira line of earthenware. It was introduced in 1971. The six-petal flowers are purple, orange, and yellow with leaves in varying shades of green. There is a chartreuse-gray inner border line. A related pattern called Floral was made in England. It has a similar decoration but fewer flowers. These pieces are marked *Made in England*.

Bowl, 7 In. 10.00
Bowl, Cereal, 6 1/4 In. . . . 15.00
Bowl, Vegetable, Round,
    9 3/8 In. . . . . . . 25.00 to 44.00
Butter, Cover, 1/4 Lb. 30.00
Creamer . . . . 20.00 to 30.00
Cup & Saucer 16.00
Plate, Bread & Butter,
    6 3/4 In. 5.00
Plate, Dinner,
    10 1/2 In. . . . . . . 7.00 to 14.00
Plate, Salad,
    8 1/2 In. . . . . 4.00 to 9.00
Platter, Oval, 11 3/4 In. . . 45.00
Platter, Oval,
    13 1/2 In. . . . . . 30.00 to 35.00
Salt & Pepper 20.00
Saucer . . . . 4.00 to 13.00
Sugar & Creamer,
    Cover 40.00

FORGET-ME-NOT has hand-painted blue flowers, green leaves, and green trim. The edges of the plates are slightly scalloped. The pattern was introduced in 1978.

Bowl, Cereal, 7 In. 8.00
Bowl, Fruit, 5 1/4 In. 14.00
Cup 7.00
Cup & Saucer . . . . 8.00 to 18.00
Plate, Bread & Butter,
    6 1/2 In. 10.00
Plate, Salad, 8 1/2 In. 13.00

FREMONT is part of the Merced fine china line made by Gladding, McBean in 1942. It has a white body with a stylized tree in green and brown in the center and a gold line inner border.

Bowl, Fruit, 5 3/8 In. 29.00
Bowl, Vegetable,
    9 In. . . . . 70.00 to 98.00
Cup & Saucer . . . 36.00 to 38.00
Gravy Boat, Attached
    Underplate . . 120.00 to 146.00
Plate, Bread & Butter,
    6 3/8 In. . . . . . . 14.00 to 18.00
Plate, Dinner,
    10 1/2 In. . . . . . 40.00 to 46.00
Plate, Salad,
    8 3/8 In. . . . . . . 20.00 to 23.00
Platter, Oval, 12 1/2 In. . . 90.00
Platter, Oval,
    16 In. . . . . . . 130.00 to 173.00
Soup, Cream,
    Underplate 25.00

FRESH FRUIT looks like hand-painted earthenware. It was first made in 1980, continued in production in England in 1984, and discontinued in 1988. Pieces are decorated with large designs of branches holding fruit. The plates have several fruits with leaves as a border.

Bowl, Cereal,
    6 In. . . . . 11.00 to 19.00
Bowl, Fruit,
    5 1/4 In. 11.00
Cup . . . . 13.00 to 16.00

Cup & Saucer . . . 13.00 to 19.00
Mug, 7 Oz., 3 In. 22.00
Napkin Ring 27.00
Sugar, Cover 36.00

FRUIT, part of the Hacienda line, was made from 1963 to 1984. It is decorated with large center drawings of varied fruits and has a colored border. This fruit pattern is listed here. Other Fruit patterns were also made.

Cup & Saucer 8.00
Plate, Bread & Butter,
6 3/4 In. . . . . 4.00 to 8.00
Plate, Dinner, 10 7/8 In. . . . 9.00

GABRIELLE was made from about 1969 to 1978. The fine china pattern has a lacy band of orange-yellow and gray-green.

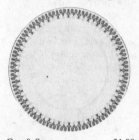

Cup & Saucer 31.00
Plate, Bread & Butter,
6 1/2 In. . . . . 8.00 to 12.00
Plate, Dinner, 10 1/2 In. . . 40.00
Plate, Salad, 8 1/4 In. 17.00

GLENFIELD is a contemporary-looking fine china dinnerware that features wheat stalks and a platinum rim. It was introduced about 1961.

Cup & Saucer 19.00
Sugar, Cover 38.00

GOLD BAND can refer to one of two patterns of fine china. The 1950s version has a plain shape without a rim and was part of the Encanto line. The 1949 pieces, sometimes called Gold Band 301, were made in the Merced line and have a wide rim. Both were trimmed with a narrow gold line at the edge.

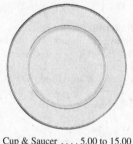

Cup & Saucer . . . . 5.00 to 15.00
Cup & Saucer, After
Dinner 10.00
Plate, Bread & Butter,
6 3/8 In. 3.00
Plate, Dinner,
10 1/2 In. . . . . . 26.00 to 35.00
Plate, Salad, 8 In. 20.00
Saucer, After Dinner 3.00

HACIENDA GOLD, part of the Hacienda line, was introduced about 1965. It was still being made in 1974. The pattern has a center design of an orange-yellow (called gold) circle with a variety of geometric loops and bands. It also has a narrow

orange-yellow band just inside the edge. It is on a body that has tiny grooves, giving it a hand-thrown look.

Bowl, Cereal, 6 3/8 In. . . . 14.00
Bowl, Vegetable, 2 Sections,
11 In. . . . . 20.00 to 34.00
Bowl, Vegetable,
7 3/4 In. 9.00
Bowl, Vegetable,
9 1/4 In. 25.00
Butter, Cover, 1/4 Lb. 20.00
Casserole, Cover,
2 1/2 Qt., 9 1/4 In. 35.00
Creamer . . . . 6.00 to 14.00
Cup 5.00
Cup & Saucer . . . . 6.00 to 15.00
Gravy Boat, Attached
Underplate . . . . 26.00 to 48.00
Mug, 12 Oz., 4 In. 25.00
Pitcher, Milk, 1 Qt.,
6 In. 15.00
Pitcher, Water, 2 1/2 Qt.,
7 1/8 In. 25.00
Plate, Bread & Butter,
6 3/4 In. . . . . 3.00 to 7.00
Plate, Dinner,
10 7/8 In. . . . . . . 7.00 to 13.00
Plate, Salad,
8 3/8 In. . . . . 5.00 to 15.00
Platter, Oval, 11 In. 13.00
Platter, Oval,
14 In. . . . . 22.00 to 47.00
Salt & Pepper . . . 14.00 to 23.00
Saucer . . . . 2.00 to 3.00
Sugar, Cover . . . . 10.00 to 23.00
Sugar, Cover Only 4.00

HACIENDA GREEN is the same as Hacienda Gold except the decorations are green. The interior of the cups and some other pieces in both patterns are glazed in the appropriate color.

Bowl, Cereal, 6 3/8 In. . . . 18.00
Bowl, Vegetable, 2 Sections,
  11 In. 55.00
Bowl, Vegetable,
  7 3/4 In. 14.00
Butter, Cover, 1/4 Lb. 38.00
Casserole,
  Handles . . . . . . 40.00 to 48.00
Coffeepot, Cover,
  7 5/8 In. 25.00
Creamer 21.00
Cup & Saucer . . . . 5.00 to 20.00
Gravy Boat, Attached
  Underplate 55.00
Plate, Bread & Butter,
  6 3/4 In. . . . . 3.00 to 8.00
Plate, Dinner,
  10 7/8 In. . . . . . . 9.00 to 19.00
Plate, Salad,
  8 3/8 In. . . . . 8.00 to 10.00
Platter, Oval, 12 In. 55.00
Platter, Oval,
  14 In. . . . . 64.00 to 120.00
Salt & Pepper . . . 30.00 to 40.00
Saucer . . . . 3.00 to 4.00
Sugar, Cover 38.00
Sugar & Creamer 60.00

HAPPY TALK, part of the White-stone line, is a white earthenware that looks like china. It was introduced about 1959 and made in Japan. The decoration is a scattered gray flower head with six thin petals, scattered pink three-petal flower heads, and a few thin lines suggesting stems. It was discontinued about 1963.

Pitcher, 44 Oz.,
  8 1/4 In. 28.00

Plate, Bread & Butter 9.00
Plate, Dinner,
  10 1/4 In. . . . . . 12.00 to 15.00
Soup, Dish 27.00

HAWAII was part of the White-stone line made from 1967 to about 1969. The design includes rectangular blocks filled with vertical palm leaves in a row. It is orange, yellow, and brown.

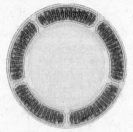

Plate, Dinner, 10 3/8 In. . . 12.00
Platter,
  13 1/4 In. . . . . . 12.00 to 25.00

HERITAGE pattern has a peasantlike inspiration. The black designs on a white body seem to be modern adaptations of colorful Pennsylvania Dutch decorations. It was made from 1960 to 1969.

Bowl, Vegetable, Oval,
  8 1/4 In. 50.00
Coffeepot 77.00
Creamer . . . . . . 15.00 to 30.00
Cup & Saucer . . . 10.00 to 18.00
Gravy Boat, Attached
  Underplate 30.00
Plate, Bread & Butter,
  6 1/8 In. . . . . 8.00 to 10.00

Plate, Dinner,
  10 1/8 In. . . . . . 10.00 to 30.00
Platter, 13 In. 74.00
Saucer 5.00
Soup, Dish, 6 1/4 In. 4.00
Sugar, Cover 29.00

HUNTINGTON is a plain fine china pattern with platinum bands as the only decoration. It was first made in 1948 as part of the Merced line.

Creamer 45.00
Cup & Saucer . . . 24.00 to 36.00
Gravy Boat, Attached
  Underplate 95.00
Plate, Dinner, 10 1/2 In. . . 43.00
Plate, Salad, 8 3/8 In. 23.00
Sugar, Cover 69.00

HUNTINGTON ROSE is part of the Merced fine china line. It was introduced in 1955. It has a single pink rose with gray leaves in the center of a platinum-trimmed plate or on the side of bowls and cups.

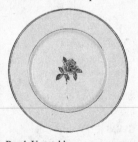

Bowl, Vegetable,
  9 1/2 In. 145.00
Gravy Boat, Attached
  Underplate 195.00

INDIAN SUMMER was made from 1958 to 1969. It is a pattern of scattered maple leaves in the fall colors of orange, yellow, brown, and gray-green on the Family China shape.

Bowl, Fruit, 5 In.	3.00
Bowl, Vegetable, 8 1/4 In.	18.00
Creamer	12.00
Cup	9.00
Cup & Saucer	14.00
Gravy Boat, Attached Underplate	19.00
Plate, Bread & Butter, 6 1/8 In.	4.00
Plate, Salad, 8 3/8 In.	7.00
Platter, 13 In.	24.00
Saltshaker	5.00
Saucer	4.00
Soup, Dish, 6 1/4 In.	3.00

IVY resembles the famous Wedgwood Ivy pattern made in the eighteenth century. It has a hand-painted band of ivy leaves as a border, and it was made from about 1948 to 1983. It was used on the *I Love Lucy* television show.

◆
Don't put china with gold designs in the dishwasher. The gold will wash off. Don't put crazed pottery in the dishwasher. It may be damaged even more.
◆

Bowl, 2 Sections, 8 x 12 1/4 In.	95.00
Bowl, Cereal, 6 In.	13.00 to 17.00
Bowl, Fruit, 5 1/2 In.	7.00 to 19.00
Bowl, Salad, 11 1/4 In.	85.00
Bowl, Vegetable, 7 1/4 In.	35.00 to 48.00
Bowl, Vegetable, 8 1/4 In.	34.00 to 62.00
Chop Plate, 12 In.	85.00 to 95.00
Chop Plate, 14 In.	175.00
Creamer, 4 In.	25.00
Cup	16.00
Cup & Saucer	95.00
Gravy Boat, Attached Underplate, 9 In.	35.00 to 75.00
Mug, 12 Oz., 4 1/4 In.	47.00
Pitcher, 48 Oz., 8 In.	95.00
Plate, Bread & Butter, 6 1/4 In.	7.00 to 12.00
Plate, Dinner, 10 1/4 In.	25.00 to 40.00
Plate, Salad, Crescent	40.00
Platter, 11 1/4 In.	27.00
Platter, 13 In.	78.00
Saucer	4.00
Soup, Dish, Footed, 5 1/2 In.	30.00 to 40.00
Sugar, Cover	53.00 to 60.00
Teapot	290.00
Trivet, Square 6 In.	29.00

JAMOCA is a casual dining pattern typical of its day. It was introduced in 1973 as part of the Picnic line. The dark brown background and orange geometric border and center design made it one of the most popular patterns of the 1970s.

Bowl, Cereal, 7 1/8 In.	14.00
Bowl, Fruit, 5 5/8 In.	13.00
Bowl, Vegetable, 9 1/2 In.	25.00
Creamer	6.00
Cup & Saucer	5.00
Plate, Bread & Butter, 6 3/4 In.	8.00
Plate, Dinner, 10 3/4 In.	10.00
Plate, Salad, 8 3/4 In.	5.00
Platter, Oval, 12 In.	45.00
Platter, Oval, 14 In.	25.00 to 64.00
Saucer	4.00
Sugar, Cover	18.00

LARKSPUR, part of the Flair line, was introduced in 1958. The decoration is a band of leaf and flowerlike shapes in pink, blue, and browns.

Bowl, 2 Sections, Oval, 13 3/4 In.	12.00
Creamer	5.00
Cup	4.00

Plate, Bread & Butter,
6 1/2 In. . . . . 5.00 to 6.00
Relish, Oval, 12 In. 13.00
Saltshaker 10.00
Saucer 5.00
Soup, Lug 4.00

LUCERNE is a white body with two-tone gray scroll-like decorations as a band. It was part of the Cosmopolitan line and was one of the first Franciscan designs made in Japan starting in 1959.

Plate, Bread & Butter,
6 3/8 In. 8.00
Plate, Salad, 8 1/8 In. 11.00

MADEIRA is the name of both a shape and a pattern of earthenware dishes. The pattern is dark brown with an overall center design of pale yellow lines forming flowers and scrolls. It was introduced in 1967.

Bowl, Vegetable, 10 In. . . 33.00
Bowl, Vegetable, 2 Sections,
11 1/8 In. . . . . . 15.00 to 20.00
Butter, Cover, 1/4 Lb. 42.00
Casserole, Cover,
2 1/2 Qt. 30.00

Chip & Dip Set, 2 Piece . . 40.00
Coffeepot 67.00
Creamer . . . . 17.00 to 24.00
Cup . . . . 3.00 to 4.00
Gravy Boat,
Cover . . . . 10.00 to 15.00
Gravy Boat, Underplate . . 55.00
Gravy Boat, Underplate
Only 16.00
Mug, 12 Oz. 8.00
Plate, Bread & Butter,
6 3/4 In. . . . . 4.00 to 7.00
Plate, Dinner,
10 1/2 In. . . . . . 8.00 to 20.00
Plate, Salad,
8 1/2 In. . . . . . . 6.00 to 10.00
Platter, Oval, 12 In. 45.00
Platter, Oval, 13 1/2 In. . . 20.00
Salt & Pepper 34.00
Saucer . . . . 1.00 to 2.00
Sugar, Cover 34.00

MANDARIN is an English-made pattern from the 1970s. The colorful floral border and center design of red, blue, and gray-green is reminiscent of nineteenth-century English designs.

Bowl, Cereal, 6 3/8 In. 17.00
Bowl, Vegetable,
8 1/4 In. 50.00
Plate, Bread & Butter,
6 3/4 In. 8.00
Platter, 12 1/4 In. 55.00
Saucer . . . . 5.00 to 19.00

MARIPOSA is part of the Merced fine china line made by Gladding, McBean in 1949. It is decorated with a bouquet of realistic flowers in natural colors.

Bowl, Fruit, 5 3/8 In. 43.00
Cup & Saucer, After
Dinner 55.00
Plate, Salad, 8 3/8 In. 29.00
Salt & Pepper 98.00
Saucer 14.00
Teapot, Cover 146.00

MAYTIME, part of the same line as Indian Summer, was introduced in 1960. It is decorated with a few pale pink and blue 16-petal flowers.

Platter, 13 In. 19.00

MEADOW ROSE was introduced in 1977. It is a variation of the Desert Rose pattern, but the flowers are yellow instead of pink.

Saucer 4.00
Sugar, Cover 38.00

MELROSE, a fine china pattern, has trailing pink roses and gray-green leaves on the dishes. It was made in the 1960s.

Creamer 38.00
Sugar, Cover 48.00

MERRY-GO-ROUND is another pattern in the Whitestone line, like Hawaii, Antigua, Cantata, and Happy Talk. It was an earthenware made in Japan after 1959. The pattern does not look like a carousel or merry-go-round; it has pink and light green circles and lines as a border.

Casserole, Cover,
1 1/2 Qt. 55.00

METROPOLITAN is a two-tone color line that was introduced in 1940. Pieces are Chocolate Brown, Coral, Gray, Ivory, Mauve, Turquoise, or Yellow on the inside or front and Ivory on the back, outside, lid, or handles. They were made in matte or gloss finish.

Coral
Plate, Dinner,
10 1/4 In. 15.00
Ivory
Cup & Saucer Set, After
Dinner, 6 Piece 228.00
Teapot 125.00
Mauve
Teapot 250.00

MONTECITO ware was made in Celadon, Coral, Eggplant, Gray, Satin Ivory, Turquoise, and Yellow. It was produced from 1937 until 1942. A totally different pattern named Montecito, in the modified Merced line, was introduced after 1957 but is not listed here.

Satin Ivory
Bowl, Fruit, 6 In. 15.00
Salt & Pepper 27.00

MOONDANCE is decorated with what looks like a spiral of ink blots in gray to dark blue. There is also a dark blue band. The fine china pattern was first made in 1972 as part of the Madeira line.

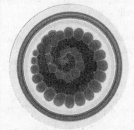

Bowl, Fruit, 5 1/4 In. 15.00

MOUNTAIN LAUREL has a simple design of gold laurel leaves. It is part of the Merced fine china line introduced by Gladding, McBean in 1941.

Creamer 71.00
Sugar, Cover 59.00

NUT TREE is part of the Madeira line. It was made in shades of brown with a center design that looks a little like a snowflake. It was introduced in 1970. The Nut Tree design can be found on the Hacienda shape with a Staffordshire, England, backstamp.

Bowl, Vegetable,
7 3/4 In. 6.00

Bowl, Vegetable,
9 1/2 In. 8.00
Cup 3.00
Plate, Dinner,
10 1/2 In. . . . . . . 8.00 to 12.00
Plate, Salad,
8 1/2 In. . . . . 3.00 to 6.00
Platter, Oval,
13 1/2 In. . . . . . 10.00 to 15.00
Saucer 1.00

OASIS is part of the popular Eclipse line, modern shapes designed in 1955. The pattern is a series of lines, rectangles, and asterisks in blue and black.

Bowl, Fruit, 5 In. 15.00
Bowl, Salad, 12 In. 135.00
Bowl, Vegetable, Oval,
8 1/2 In. 40.00
Chop Plate, 13 1/4 In. 60.00
Cup 15.00
Gravy Boat, Attached
Underplate 50.00
Gravy Boat, Attached
Underplate, Ladle,
2 Piece 95.00
Jelly Server, Handle 40.00
Ladle 50.00
Platter, Oval, 13 In. 50.00
Platter, Oval, 15 In. 60.00
Saltshaker, Tall 50.00
Saucer . . . . 4.00 to 5.00
Syrup, 1 Qt., 5 3/8 In. 75.00

OCTOBER is a hand-painted line decorated with fall-colored leaves and a brown border. It was introduced in 1977.

Bowl, Cereal, 7 In. 14.00
Cup & Saucer 14.00
Saucer 4.00
Sugar, Cover 40.00

OLYMPIC is decorated with realistic violets and leaves. It is part of the Encanto line of fine china and was introduced in 1950.

Ashtray 38.00
Bowl, Fruit, 4 3/4 In. 29.00
Bowl, Vegetable, Oval,
 9 In. 88.00
Creamer 71.00
Plate, Bread & Butter,
 6 3/8 In. 14.00
Plate, Dinner, 10 1/2 In. . . 49.00
Platter, 12 In. 126.00
Platter, 16 In. 173.00
Sugar, Cover . . . . 59.00 to 86.00

PALOMAR, part of the Merced fine china line, was made in many colors, including Cameo Pink, Gray, Jade, Jasper, Robin's Egg Blue, and Yellow. Each color has either platinum or gold trim. It was introduced in 1948.

Gray
Plate, Dinner, 10 1/2 In. . . 40.00

Jade
Bowl, Fruit, 5 3/8 In. 20.00
Platter, 16 In. 150.00
Salt & Pepper 25.00
Soup, Dish, 8 1/4 In. 49.00

Jasper
Plate, Bread & Butter,
 6 3/8 In. 12.00

Yellow
Bowl, Fruit, 5 3/8 In. 25.00

PEBBLE BEACH was first made in 1969. It was part of the Madeira line and is decorated with blobs that formed flowers and a border in earth tones. Several different color combinations were used.

Bowl, Cereal, 6 1/4 In. 6.00
Bowl, Fruit, 5 1/4 In. 11.00
Creamer 4.00
Cup & Saucer . . . . . 4.00 to 8.00
Plate, Dinner,
 10 1/2 In. . . . . . . 8.00 to 12.00

Plate, Salad, 8 1/2 In. 7.00
Saucer 5.00

PICKWICK was introduced in 1965. It was one of the Whitestone patterns made in Japan. The design is orange and yellow fruit and leaves in a wide band around the edge of the plates and bowls.

Bowl, Vegetable, 8 In. . . . 44.00
Cup & Saucer 12.00
Pitcher, Water, 8 In. 40.00
Plate, Dinner, 10 3/8 In. . . 14.00
Platter, 13 1/4 In. 64.00

PICNIC is a shape and a pattern name. The pattern, introduced in 1973, has yellow and green flower heads in a cluster in the center of the plate. There are yellow and green flowers and bands around the edge. Cups and bowls have the band on the outside.

Bowl, Cereal, 7 1/8 In. . . . 12.00
Bowl, Fruit, 5 5/8 In. 10.00
Coffeepot, Cover 80.00
Saucer 4.00

PINK-A-DILLY is decorated with sprigs of pink roses with green leaves. It is one of the Japanese-made Whitestone designs introduced in 1959. It remained in production until about 1969.

Creamer 12.00
Plate, Dinner, 10 3/8 In. . . 13.00

PLATINA is a plain white dinnerware with a swirled or fluted border on plates or on the body of cups and bowls. It has a platinum edge. The design was made in 1959.

Cup & Saucer 43.00
Plate, Dinner, 10 3/4 In. . . 56.00
Soup, Rim, 8 1/8 In. 43.00

PLATINUM BAND is a plain white fine china dinnerware

with a platinum edge. It was introduced in 1949 as part of the Encanto line.

Bowl, Vegetable, Oval,
 9 In. 28.00
Creamer 57.00
Cup 15.00
Cup & Saucer 8.00
Plate, Bread & Butter,
 6 3/8 In. 10.00
Plate, Dinner, 10 1/2 In. . . 38.00
Plate, Luncheon, 9 In. 15.00
Platter, 16 In. 35.00
Saucer 8.00

POPPY is part of the Greenhouse line, a mix-and-match line that includes Daffodil, Sweet Pea, and Blue Bell. All have similar off-center designs of flowers. Poppy has sprigs of yellow or red poppies and leaves. It was introduced in 1975 and discontinued in 1978. Franciscan also made a handpainted poppy pattern from 1950 to about 1955.

Cup . . . . 20.00 to 25.00
Gravy Boat 65.00
Plate, Dinner, 10 3/4 In. . . 20.00

REFLECTIONS, part of the Hacienda line, is a 1982 pattern with a hand-thrown look. The solid-color ware came in Black, Blue, Burgundy, Jade, Lilac, Peach, Sand, Silver Gray, Smoke Gray, and White. Production stopped in the United States in 1984. There was also an English-made pattern called

Reflections made in the 1970s. It has earth-tone blobs filling the center and bands of brown and yellow as a border. It is not listed here.

Jade
Gravy Boat, Attached
Underplate 75.00

Silver Gray
Plate, Dinner, 10 7/8 In. . . 12.00
Platter, Oval, 13 3/4 In. . . 45.00

RENAISSANCE patterns were made on the Del Rey shape by 1957. Renaissance Grey and Renaissance Gold appeared in 1957. Renaissance Platinum was introduced in 1966. Royal Renaissance (blue) was introduced in 1971. Each had a wide, colored border with a lacy design. Renaissance Gold was expensive because the border was actually finished with gold.

Gold
Bowl, Vegetable, Oval,
9 x 6 1/2 In. 190.00
Creamer 110.00
Cup & Saucer 49.00
Plate, Dinner,
10 5/8 In. . . . . . 55.00 to 74.00
Plate, Salad, 8 1/4 In. 42.00
Platter, Oval,
15 1/2 In. 280.00

Grey
Platter, Oval,
15 1/2 In. 149.00

ROSETTE is a 1980s pattern decorated with a band of pink and white flowers. It has a scalloped and beaded edge.

Bowl, Cereal,
6 1/8 In. . . . . . 10.00 to 12.00
Cup & Saucer . . . 15.00 to 18.00
Plate, Dinner,
10 3/4 In. . . . . . 8.00 to 22.00
Platter, Oval, 13 In. 55.00
Sugar, Cover 15.00

ROSSMORE has a small center pattern of pink and light green leafy shapes in a circle. It is a Merced fine china pattern and was first offered for sale in 1945.

Chop Plate, 13 3/8 In. . . . 110.00
Creamer 57.00
Plate, Bread & Butter,
6 3/8 In. 12.00
Plate, Dinner, 10 1/2 In. . . 40.00
Sugar 47.00

SAND DOLLAR is one of many fine china patterns picturing sea creatures that are part of the Sea Sculptures line. The Sand or White plate is decorated with an embossed picture of a sand dollar. It was introduced in 1977.

Sand
Plate, Dinner,
10 3/4 In. . . . . . 18.00 to 25.00

White
Casserole, Cover,
Individual 46.00
Plate, Dinner, 10 3/4 In. . . 27.00
Plate, Luncheon,
9 7/8 In. . . . . . 12.00 to 15.00

SANDALWOOD is a plain solid-color plate in pale tan, the color of sandalwood. It has plat-

inum trim. It was introduced in 1952 as part of the Encanto line.

Plate, Bread & Butter,
6 3/8 In. 12.00
Plate, Dinner, 10 1/2 In. . . 40.00

SIMPLICITY is white ware with plain platinum trim. It is part of a porcelain line introduced in 1961.

Plate, Bread & Butter,
6 3/8 In. 12.00
Platter, 12 1/2 In. 45.00

SPICE, part of the Flair line, is an earthenware design introduced in 1961. It is a pale beige pattern with tan trim and decorations. Plates and some pitchers have a treelike decoration inspired by Pennsylvania Dutch designs. Cups and serving pieces are glazed solid black on the outside.

Bowl, Fruit, 5 1/8 In. 12.00
Bowl, Vegetable,
9 3/8 In. 40.00
Butter, Cover, 1/4 Lb. 12.00
Creamer 15.00
Pitcher, Milk, 1 3/4 Qt.,
9 7/8 In. 50.00
Plate, Bread & Butter,
6 1/2 In. 8.00
Plate, Dinner, 10 1/2 In. . . 15.00
Plate, Salad, 8 1/4 In. 10.00
Platter, 13 1/4 In. 25.00
Sugar, No Cover 15.00
Teapot 75.00

SPRING SONG is decorated with sprigs of pink and blue leaves and a suggestion of Queen Anne's lace. It is a 1959 pattern on the Family China shape.

Creamer 9.00
Cup 6.00
Platter, 13 In. 20.00
Saucer 3.00
Sugar, Cover 13.00

STARBURST, one of the most popular patterns with today's collectors, was made from 1954 to 1985. It is decorated with futuristic starlike forms in turquoise blue and yellow and is part of the Eclipse line. The dish shapes were also very modern.

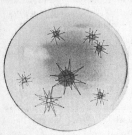

Bowl, Cereal, 7 1/4 In. . . . 30.00
Bowl, Fruit, 5 In. 15.00
Bowl, Salad,
    12 In. . . . . . . 95.00 to 195.00
Bowl, Vegetable, Oval,
    8 3/8 In. . . . . . 50.00 to 65.00
Butter, No Cover 75.00
Creamer 25.00
Cup 15.00
Gravy Boat, Attached
    Underplate . . . . 50.00 to 55.00
Jelly Server, Handle 45.00
Ladle, 5 In. 60.00
Mug, 7 Oz. 75.00
Mug, 12 Oz., 5 In. 45.00
Pitcher, Milk, 1 3/4 Qt.,
    7 1/4 In. 65.00
Pitcher, Water,
    2 1/2 Qt. 195.00
Plate, Bread & Butter,
    6 1/2 In. . . . . 3.00 to 8.00
Plate, Dinner,
    10 3/4 In. . . . . . 12.00 to 25.00
Plate, Luncheon,
    9 1/2 In. 50.00
Plate, Salad, 8 In. 15.00
Platter, Oval, 13 In. 75.00
Platter, Oval, 15 In. 20.00
Saucer 4.00
Shaker, Small 20.00
Sugar, Cover 50.00

SUNDANCE is the same as the Moondance pattern, except it is

decorated in yellow and orange tones. It was made in 1972.

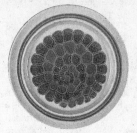

Bowl, Cereal, 6 1/4 In. . . . 12.00
Bowl, Vegetable,
    9 3/8 In. . . . . . . 35.00 to 45.00
Creamer . . . . 12.00 to 22.00
Cup & Saucer . . . 12.00 to 15.00
Plate, Dinner, 10 1/2 In. . . 12.00
Platter, 11 3/4 In. 55.00
Platter, 14 In. 42.00
Sugar 27.00
Sugar, Cover 35.00

TAHITI was introduced in 1965 on the Family China shape. Plates are decorated in shades of brown and tan. The center is lighter than the very dark brown band. There is a row of white dots separating the colors. It came in several different combinations of browns.

Bowl, Vegetable, Oval,
    8 1/4 In. 44.00
Cup & Saucer . . . 12.00 to 14.00
Plate, Bread & Butter,
    6 1/8 In. 5.00
Platter, 13 In. 45.00
Sugar, Cover 38.00

TARA, part of the Cosmopolitan line, is white with platinum trim and a narrow border of gray leaves and flowers. It was made in 1959 in Japan. It remained in production only a short time, perhaps just two years.

Bowl, Cereal, 6 1/8 In. . . . 18.00
Plate, Bread & Butter,
    6 1/4 In. . . . . . . 10.00 to 12.00

Plate, Dinner, 10 1/2 In. . . 21.00
Plate, Salad,
    8 1/8 In. . . . . . . 12.00 to 15.00

TEAK is solid black with solid white interiors for bowls and cups. The pattern is part of the Encanto fine china line and was introduced in 1952.

Bowl, Fruit, 4 3/4 In. 27.00
Sugar, Cover 75.00

TERRA COTTA has a border of rust, brown, and terra-cotta leaves and was made on the Family China shape. It was introduced in 1965.

Gravy Boat, Attached
    Underplate 40.00
Plate, Salad, 8 1/4 In. 12.00

TIEMPO, a modification of the Metropolitan pattern, appeared in stores in 1950. The solid-color pattern has square plates and matching serving pieces. The set came in mix-and-match colors. It was made in Copper, Coral (tan), Hot Chocolate, Leaf (green-black), Mustard, Salt (white), Sprout (lime green), and Stone (gray).

Leaf
Coffeepot, Cover 75.00
Cup 6.00
Sprout
Cup 6.00
Plate, Dinner, 9 3/4 In. . . . 25.00
Stone
Cup 6.00

TRIO is a modern-looking fine china pattern with abstract leaves and dried flowers scattered on the pieces. It was a modification of the Metropolitan pattern and was made from 1954 through 1958.

Coffeepot 67.00
Plate, Bread & Butter,
  6 In. 7.00
Saucer 5.00

TULIP TIME was one of the handmade-looking Hacienda patterns made from 1962 until 1984. The center design is a Pennsylvania Dutch tulip in turquoise and tan. There is a matching rim.

Bowl, Cereal,
  6 3/8 In. 15.00
Bowl, Fruit,
  5 1/4 In. .... 5.00 to 13.00
Bowl, Vegetable, 2 Sections,
  11 In. .... 15.00 to 20.00
Creamer .... 12.00 to 26.00
Cup & Saucer .... 7.00 to 14.00
Gravy Boat, Attached
  Underplate .... 22.00 to 58.00
Pitcher, Milk, 1 Qt.,
  6 In. 24.00
Plate, Bread & Butter,
  6 3/4 In. .... 4.00 to 6.00
Plate, Dinner,
  10 7/8 In. ...... 8.00 to 18.00
Plate, Salad, 8 3/8 In. 10.00
Platter, Oval,
  13 3/4 In. ..... 19.00 to 64.00
Salt & Pepper 34.00
Saucer 4.00
Sugar & Creamer 43.00

WESTWOOD is a white pattern of china with a thin gray inner line, a sprig of three thin leaves, and some golden-yellow berries. It was introduced in 1942 as part of the Redondo line.

Bowl, Fruit, Rim,
  6 1/4 In. 26.00
Chop Plate, 13 1/4 In. 119.00
Plate, Dinner, 10 1/2 In. .. 15.00

WOODLORE has a ring of multicolored mushrooms around the border. It was introduced in 1954.

Bowl, Cereal, Handles,
  7 3/8 In. 10.00
Cup 5.00
Plate, Dinner, 10 1/2 In. .. 12.00
Plate, Salad, 8 1/4 In. 15.00

WOODSIDE has a gold-trimmed rim decorated with pink blossoms and green leaves on brown branches. It was made from 1941 to 1973.

Bowl, Fruit, 5 3/8 In. 29.00
Gravy Boat, Attached
  Underplate 137.00
Sugar, Cover 21.00

FRANKOMA

John Frank established the ceramics department at the University of Oklahoma in Norman, Oklahoma, in 1927. In 1933 he started his own Frank Potteries. He used light-color clay found nearby in Ada to make his pottery. In 1934 the company name was changed to Frankoma Potteries. The operation moved to Sapulpa, Oklahoma, in 1938 and the name became Frankoma Pottery. Red clay was found near the pottery in 1953, and by 1954 all of the pieces were made of red, not light-color, clay. The company is still working. Collectors prize the early pieces made of the light Ada clay, so these pieces cost twice as much as newer red clay pieces.

LAZYBONES was introduced in 1953 and has been made in several different colors including Clay Blue, Desert Gold, Peach Glow, Prairie Green, and Sunflower Yellow.

Desert Gold
Butter, Sapulpa Clay 13.00
Plate, Dinner, Sapulpa
  Clay, 10 In. 7.00
Plate, Salad, Sapulpa
  Clay, 7 In. 4.00

Prairie Green
Bowl, Salad Or Gumbo,
  24 Oz., 7 1/4 In. 15.00
Cup & Saucer,
  2 7/8 In. 12.00
Mug, 18 Oz., 4 In. 9.00
Pitcher, Miniature 15.00
Plate, Dinner, 10 In. 12.00

Woodland Moss
Butter, Cover 15.00

MAYAN-AZTEC pattern was introduced in 1948. It was made in Desert Gold, Prairie Green,

White Sand, and Woodland Moss and has a Mayan geometric border. The names were simplified, and on the 1994 price list, the pattern, called Aztec, was available in Gold, Green, and White.

Desert Gold
Baker, Ada Clay,
Individual 30.00
Dish, Square,
8 1/2 x 2 1/2 In. 45.00
Prairie Green
Bowl, Chili 5.00
Creamer, Ada Clay,
6 Oz., 3 In. 12.00
Dish, Sections,
10 1/2 x 6 In. 20.00
Plate, Dinner, Sapulpa
Clay, 10 In. 7.00
Salt & Pepper, Ringed,
Handle, 4 3/4 In. 15.00

NATIVE AMERICAN was introduced in 1992. It was made in Black, Bone, Forest Green, Navy, Teal, and White with terra-cotta border designs of thunderbirds and other symbols. In 2001 the pattern was renamed Thunderbird. It is still being made, but only in Bone.

Teal
Bowl, 14 Oz., 7 3/4 In. 10.00
Plate, 7 3/4 In. 9.00

PLAINSMAN was originally named Oklahoma. The pattern started in 1948 and is still being made. It is available in Autumn Yellow, Black, Brown Satin, Desert Gold, Flame, Peach Glow, Prairie Green, Robin's Egg Blue, White Sand, and Woodland Moss. The 1994 catalog offered 22 pieces of Plainsman with the simplified color names of Brown, Country Blue, Gold, Green, Forest, and Navy.

Brown Satin
Dish, Sections, Handles,
Sapulpa Clay 12.00
Desert Gold
Dish, Sections, Ada
Clay 25.00
Plate, Bread & Butter,
6 In. 9.00
Plate, Dinner, 10 In. 22.00
Plate, Salad, 7 1/4 In. 18.00
Prairie Gold
Baker, Individual 30.00
Prairie Green
Bowl, 9 Oz., 5 In. 8.00
Bowl, Cereal, 14 Oz.,
5 5/8 In. 12.50
Cup, 7 Oz. 5.00
Plate, Dinner,
10 In. .... 6.00 to 9.00
Plate, Luncheon,
9 In. .... 5.00 to 7.00
Plate, Salad,
7 5/8 In. .... 4.00 to 6.00
Saucer .... 4.00 to 5.00
Sugar, 6 Oz., 3 In. 7.00
Tray, 5 7/8 x 9 1/2 In. 8.00
Woodland Moss
Gravy Boat 20.00

THUNDERBIRD
See Native American

WAGON WHEEL, or Wagon Wheels, was made from 1941 to 1983. A few pieces are still being made. Many of the pieces in this pattern are shaped like wagon wheels. Most pieces were made in Desert Gold and Prairie Green. A few were made in other colors.

Desert Gold
Casserole, Cover,
10 1/2 x 3 In. 28.00
Platter, Ada Clay 30.00
Salt & Pepper,
Ada Clay 25.00
Teapot, 6 Cup 45.00
Prairie Green
Baker, Individual 15.00
Creamer, c.1948,
2 1/2 In. 70.00
Salt & Pepper 25.00
Sugar, Ada Clay 55.00
Turquoise
Salt & Pepper,
Ada Clay 45.00

WESTWIND is a solid-color pattern introduced in 1962. It was made in Autumn Yellow, Peach Glow, Prairie Green, Robin's Egg Blue, White Sand, Woodland Moss, and other colors.

Autumn Yellow
Plate, Dinner, Sapulpa
Clay, 10 In. 7.00
Plate, Salad, Sapulpa
Clay, 7 In. 4.00
Platter, Sapulpa Clay,
11 In. 6.00
Flame
Bowl, Cereal, 14 Oz.,
2 x 5 1/2 In. 7.00
Prairie Green
Bowl, Vegetable, 24 Oz.,
7 3/4 In. 14.00
Plate, Salad, Sapulpa
Clay, 7 In. 5.00
Platter, 11 3/4 x 7 In. 10.00

Woodland Moss

Salt & Pepper 15.00
Sugar 10.00

MISCELLANEOUS: There are many other patterns made by Frankoma. Some are listed here.

Chip & Dip Bowl,
Yellow & Brown,
8 1/4 x 4 1/2 In. 21.00
Cup, Handle, Yellow & Brown,
3 1/2 x 5 1/4 In. 9.00
Lemonade Set, Yellow,
5 Piece 30.00
Platter, Oval, Blue,
17 3/4 In. 40.00
Platter, Yellow & Brown,
9 3/4 x 6 In. 10.00

FRENCH SAXON

French Saxon China Company began making dinnerware and kitchenware in Sebring, Ohio, in 1934, operating out of the old Saxon China Company plant. Saxon China Company, founded in 1911, and French China Company were both owned by the Sebring family and became part of American Chinaware Company in 1929. The company went bankrupt in 1932 and W.V. Oliver bought the Saxon plant. The company was bought by Royal China in 1964. Royal

China changed hands several times before closing in 1986.

GRENADA was made in solid colors of Blue, Green, Tangerine, and Yellow on the Zephyr shape. It was made in the early 1940s.

Blue

Creamer 4.00
Cup 4.00
Soup, Dish 10.00

Tangerine

Bowl, 5 1/2 In. 3.00
Plate, Dinner, 9 In. 7.00

Yellow

Plate, Bread & Butter, 6 In. 1.00
Sugar 5.00

HALL

Hall China Company started in East Liverpool, Ohio, in 1903. The firm made many types of wares. Collectors search for the Hall teapots made from the 1920s to the 1950s. They are listed in this section. Some pieces listed here are identified by the shape name *Pert*. The dinnerwares of the same period, especially Autumn Leaf pattern, are also popular. The Hall China Company is still working. Autumn Leaf pattern dishes are listed in their own category in this book.

ARIZONA has rust-colored leaves and black lines on a white background. It was introduced in 1952 and was made on the Tomorrow's Classic shape designed by Eva Zeisel.

Bowl, 5 3/4 x 4 3/4 x
2 1/4 In. . . . . 8.00 to 10.00
Bowl, Cereal,
6 In. 14.00
Cup & Saucer 12.00
Gravy Boat 65.00
Plate, Bread & Butter,
6 In. 5.00
Plate, Dinner,
11 In. 16.00
Plate, Salad, 8 In. 8.00
Platter, 11 x 10 1/4 In. . . . 45.00
Serving Dish,
9 x 6 3/4 x 2 1/2 In. 40.00

BLUE BOUQUET is a pattern made for Standard Coffee of New Orleans, Louisiana. The coffee company gave Blue Bouquet pattern dinnerware and kitchenware as premiums from the early 1950s to the early 1960s. Although it was made in Ohio, it is most easily found in the South. The pattern is very plain with a thin blue border interrupted by roses. Blue Ridge also made a pattern called Blue Bouquet.

Bowl, Baker, French,
Round, 9 1/4 In. 30.00
Bowl, Vegetable,
9 1/4 In. 45.00
Casserole 70.00
Leftover, Square 189.00
Plate, Bread & Butter,
6 In. 10.00
Platter, 12 In. 40.00
Soup, Dish 30.00
Teapot, Aladdin 150.00

BOUQUET has a large spray of different colored flowers and leaves on a white background. It was made on the Tomorrow's

Classic shape designed by Eva Zeisel.

Baker, 3 1/8 x 8 3/4 x
11 3/4 In. 53.00
Baker, 9 In. 37.00
Bowl, Salad, 12 7/8 In. . . . 50.00
Gravy Ladle 49.00
Platter, 12 In. 50.00
Platter, 15 1/2 In. 65.00

CAMEO ROSE has gray and white decal decorations and gold trim. It was not made by the cameo process used for Cameo Shellware and other designs. New limited edition pieces of Cameo Rose have been distributed by China Specialties, Inc., since 1995 and may be listed here. They are not reproductions and are clearly marked or dated.

Bowl, Fruit, 5 1/4 In. 8.00
Creamer 18.00
Plate, Breakfast,
9 1/4 In. 14.00
Teapot, 6 In. 99.00

CAPRICE, made on the Tomorrow's Classic shape designed by Eva Zeisel, has pink, yellow, and gray flowers and leaves on a white background. It was introduced in 1952.

Creamer, 5 x 4 In. 22.00
Cup & Saucer 10.00
Teapot, 6 x 9 In. 230.00

CHINESE RED is a color used by Hall China Company. This bright red was used on many shapes of dishes. The few listed here are not included in the more recognizable sets.

Casserole, Cover, Pert,
Sani-Grid 45.00
Jar, Drip, Radiance,
4 3/4 In. 89.00
Jug, Ball, No. 3, 2 Qt. 85.00
Jug, Donut, 1930s 285.00
Jug, Pert, Sani-Grid,
7 1/2 In. 50.00
Leftover, Bingo Zephyr,
4 5/8 In. 225.00
Saltshaker, Handle,
Raised Letters 40.00
Shaker, Sani-Grid 30.00
Syrup, Cover, 5 Bands,
5 3/4 In. 149.00
Teapot, 21 Oz. 200.00
Teapot, 6 3/8 In. 389.00
Tureen, Soup,
10 3/8 In. 379.00

CROCUS was made in the 1930s. The decal-decorated dinnerware was sometimes called Holland. The design is a border of oddly shaped crocuses in black, lavender, red, green, and pink. Most pieces have platinum trim. Other firms, including Stangl Pottery and Blue Ridge, had very different-looking dinnerwares called Crocus. New limited edition pieces of Crocus have been distributed by China Specialties, Inc., since 1993 and may be listed here. They are new shapes, not reproductions, and are clearly marked or dated.

Bowl, Vegetable, Round,
Platinum Trim,
9 1/8 x 2 1/2 In. 45.00
Coffeepot, Bellvue,
4 3/4 In. 89.00
Jar, Pretzel, 6 3/4 In. . . . 230.00
Jug, Ball, 7 In. 229.00
Vase, Bud,
6 1/2 x 3 5/8 In. 50.00

FANTASY was designed by Eva Zeisel for the Hall China Company. It is a pattern on Hallcraft's Tomorrow's Classic shape. An abstract line drawing is in the center of the plates.

Serving Bowl,
11 7/8 x 8 3/4 In. 45.00
Soup, Dish, 2 3/4 x 9 In. . . 30.00

GOLDEN GLO is a custommade pattern that has a shiny 24K gold finish over a white or colored glaze. It was introduced in the 1940s and was popular during the 1960s and 1970s. It is still being made. Pieces are marked *Golden Glo.*

Casserole, Cover,
11 1/4 In. 85.00
Coffeepot, Morning,
7 1/2 In. 112.00
Creamer, Sundial, Individual,
Saf-Handle 35.00
Teapot, 6 1/4 In. 149.00

HEATHER ROSE is a decal-decorated Hall Pottery pattern. Both dinnerware and utility ware pieces were made with this decoration. It pictures a realistic-looking pale pinkish purple rose on a stem with many leaves.

Bowl, Cereal, 6 1/4 In. 4.00
Bowl, Dessert, 5 1/4 In. . . . 7.00
Cup, Coffee 4.00
Mug 12.00
Plate, Bread & Butter,
6 3/8 In. 5.00
Plate, Dinner,
10 In. . . . . 4.00 to 10.00

Plate, Luncheon,
9 In. 6.00
Serving Bowl, Gold Trim,
8 1/2 x 2 1/2 In. 6.00

MULBERRY has a branch of purple mulberries and green leaves. It was made in the 1950s.

Bowl, Fruit, 5 3/4 In. 10.00
Cake Plate, 6 In. 10.00
Cup & Saucer 20.00
Plate, Bread & Butter,
6 In. 10.00
Plate, Dinner, 11 In. 22.00

POPPY, sometimes called Orange Poppy by collectors, was made from 1933 through the 1950s. The decals picture realistic groups of orange poppies with a few leaves. New pieces using the Poppy decoration, called Orange Poppy, have been made by China Specialties, Inc., since 1995 and may be listed here. These, unlike the originals, are marked *Limited Edition.* Another Hall pattern called Red Poppy has bright red stylized flowers with black leaves and trim. Poppy is a name used by at least five companies.

Baker, French 35.00
Bowl, Salad, 9 In. 45.00
Coffeepot 45.00
Coffeepot, S Cover 100.00
Drip Jar 45.00
Jug, Ball, No. 3 . . . . 129.00
Jug, Silver Trim,
6 1/4 x 8 1/2 In. 45.00

Pretzel Jar 170.00
Shaker, Radiance,
4 3/4 In. 229.00
Teapot, Streamline,
6 In. 195.00

RED POPPY has bright red flowers and black leaves. The pattern, made in East Liverpool, Ohio, from 1930 through 1950, was a premium item for Grand Union Tea Company. Matching metal pieces, such as wastebaskets and breadboxes, were made, and glass tumblers are known. New limited edition pieces of Red Poppy have been distributed by China Specialties, Inc., since 1993 and may be listed here. They are new shapes, not reproductions, and are clearly marked or dated.

Bowl, 9 1/4 In. 40.00
Bowl, Fruit, 5 1/2 In. 12.00
Bowl, Salad,
9 In. . . . . 30.00 to 35.00
Cake Plate, 12 In. 50.00
Casserole, Cover, Round,
2 Qt. 45.00
Coffeepot 65.00
Cup & Saucer 20.00
Custard Cup 12.00
Drip Jar 30.00
Drip Jar, Cover 35.00
Jug, Radiance,
No. 5 . . . . . . 40.00 to 45.00
Mixing Bowl Set,
3 Piece 65.00
Pitcher, Platinum Trim,
6 1/2 x 8 1/2 In. 47.00
Plate, Bread & Butter,
6 In. 12.00

Plate, Dinner,
9 In. . . . . 18.00 to 22.00
Platter, 13 In. 40.00
Syrup Server 45.00
Teapot 125.00

REFRIGERATOR ware was introduced in the late 1930s. A complete set of refrigerator ware included a water server, one or more leftover dishes, and a covered butter dish. They were made in several different solid colors and shapes. For Westinghouse, Hall made Phoenix (Patrician) in 1938, General (Emperor) in 1939, Hercules or Peasant Ware (Aristocrat) in 1940–1941, and Adonis (Prince) in 1952. Hall also made King and Queen ovenware to match the refrigerator ware. Refrigerator ware was also made for Sears, Montgomery Ward, Hotpoint, and General Electric. In addition, the company made some pieces sold with the Hall name: Bingo in the late 1930s, Plaza in the 1930s to the 1960s, and Norris. Some of the pieces were reintroduced in the early 1980s.

Hotpoint, Leftover,
3 1/2 In. 100.00
Hotpoint, Leftover,
Hercules, Ivory 100.00
Hotpoint, Leftover,
Hercules, Tan 100.00
Hotpoint, Water Server,
Delphinium Blue,
6 1/2 In. 85.00
Westinghouse, Water Server,
Hercules, Tan 129.00
Westinghouse, Water Server,
Phoenix 175.00

RESTAURANT ware, or commercial ware, includes dinnerware made especially for restaurants and other commercial operations. Pieces could be plain or decorated with special logos or wording. The dishes are thicker than those made for home use.

Avocado Green

Bowl, Vegetable,
5 1/2 In. 6.00
Bowl, Vegetable,
9 1/2 In. 5.00

Brown

Bean Pot, Boston,
No. 461, 7 Oz. 3.00
Casserole, No. 550, Oval . . 4.00
Casserole, No. 570-S 4.50
Casserole, Oval 4.00
Custard Cup, No. 351 1/2,
4 Oz. 3.00
Dish, Shirred Egg,
No. 513 . . . . 4.00
Mug, Heavy, No. 1318 . . . . 4.00
Tankard, No. 549, Barnaby's
Bar & Grill 12.00
Tumbler, No. 342 . . . . 7.00

Green

Casserole, No. 570 1/2,
Oval 4.00
Casserole, No. 571 1/2,
Individual 4.00
Casserole, No. 2081,
Oval 4.00
Custard Cup, No. 351 1/2,
4 Oz. . . . . 3.00 to 10.00
Dish, Oval,
6 1/4 x 4 1/4 In. 12.00
Ramekin, No. 362 . . . . 3.00
Soup, Dish, No. 821 . . . . . . 5.00
Teapot, No. 2091 . . . . 6.00

Mauve

Dish, Sugar Packet 5.00

White

Bowl, Oatmeal 4.00
Casserole, Individual,
No. 502, Ridged 4.00
Casserole, No. 527 . . . . 4.50
Mug, Heavy, No. 1318 . . . . 4.00
Ramekin, Ridged,
No. 498 . . . . 3.00

ROSE PARADE has a solid Cadet Blue body with contrasting white knobs and handles. A rose decal was added to the white spaces. Sometimes the flower is pink, sometimes blue.

The pattern was made from 1941 through the 1950s. Serving pieces, not dinnerware sets, were made.

Rose Parade

Bean Pot, Tab Handle 90.00
Creamer, 3 In. 35.00
Teapot, 3 Cup 125.00

ROSE WHITE, first made in 1941, is similar to Rose Parade. The same shapes were used, but the pieces are all white with a slightly different rose-decal decoration. There is platinum trim on many pieces.

Rose White

Bowl, 7 1/2 In. 35.00
Mixing Bowl, 9 In. 46.00

SPRINGTIME has an arrangement of pink flowers as the decoration.

Plate, Salad, 7 1/4 In. 12.00
Platter, Oval,
14 x 10 1/4 In. 34.00
Soup, Dish, 8 1/2 In. 18.00
Bowl, Fruit,
5 1/2 In. . . . . 6.00 to 10.00
Cake Plate,
9 1/2 In. . . . . . . 20.00 to 36.00
Cup 8.00
Plate, Bread & Butter,
6 In. . . . . 4.00 to 10.00
Plate, Dinner,
9 In. . . . . 10.00 to 15.00
Soup, Dish, 8 1/2 In. 14.00

TAVERNE serving pieces were made by the Hall China Company in the 1930s. Matching dinnerware was made by Taylor, Smith & Taylor of Chester, West Virginia. A rolling pin was made by Harker Pottery Company. The silhouetted figures eating at a table are very similar to those seen on the pattern Silhouette, but there is no dog in this decal. In some of the literature, Taverne is called Silhouette. New limited edition pieces of Taverne have been distributed by China Specialties, Inc., since 1993 and may be listed here. They are new shapes, not reproductions, and are clearly marked or dated.

Bowl, Vegetable, Oval,
10 3/8 In. 55.00
Cup & Saucer, Footed . . . 50.00
Pie Plate, 9 1/2 In. 11.50
Utensil Set, 3 Piece 79.00

TEAPOTS of all sizes and shapes were made by the Hall China Company of East Liverpool, Ohio, starting in the 1920s. Each pot has a special design name such as Airflow or Boston. Each shape could be made in one of several colors, often with names like Cadet (light blue), Camellia (rose), Canary (yellow), Delphinium (medium purple-blue), Dresden (deep blue), Green Lustre (dark green), Indian Red (orange), Mahogany (dark brown), and Marine (dark purple-blue). An infuser is an optional piece that was usually sold separately. It held the tea leaves while the water was poured through them. Coffeepots were also made by Hall. New limited edition teapots have been distributed by China Specialties, Inc., since 1992 and may be listed here. They are new shapes, not reproductions, and are clearly marked or dated.

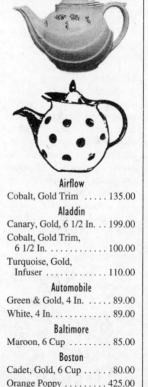

Airflow
Cobalt, Gold Trim 135.00
Aladdin
Canary, Gold, 6 1/2 In. . . 199.00
Cobalt, Gold Trim,
  6 1/2 In. 100.00
Turquoise, Gold,
  Infuser 110.00
Automobile
Green & Gold, 4 In. 89.00
White, 4 In. 89.00
Baltimore
Maroon, 6 Cup 85.00
Boston
Cadet, Gold, 6 Cup 80.00
Orange Poppy 425.00

Cleveland
Cobalt, 6 In. 189.00
Gold, 6 Cup 155.00
Detroit
Athletic Club, Brown,
  4 1/4 In. 189.00
Emerald
Gold Stars, 6 In. 139.00
French
Cadet, 10 Cup 105.00
Globe
Chartreuse, Gold Trim ... 95.00
Los Angeles
Chinese Red, 7 1/4 In. . . 495.00
Cobalt, Gold Trim 95.00
Light Turquoise,
  Gold Trim 80.00
McCormick
Maroon, Infuser,
  7 x 8 3/4 In. 60.00
Moderne
Yellow, 6 Cup 45.00
New York
Chartreuse, Gold,
  8 Cup 150.00
Yellow, 1920s, 6 Cup 50.00
Ohio
Pink, Gold Dot, 6 In. ... 429.00
Parade
Ivory, 6 Cup 85.00
Pert
Chinese Red, Sani-Grid,
  6 Cup 80.00
Plume
Pink 75.00

TOM & JERRY sets were made to serve the famous Christmas punch. A set was usually a punch bowl and six matching cups or mugs.

Black
Mug, 5 Oz. 10.00
Mug, Round, Handle, No. 2044,
  Gold Trim, 2 1/2 In. 3.00
Ivory
Mug, 5 Oz. 10.00

TOMORROW'S CLASSIC was designed by Eva Zeisel for the

Hall China Company's Hallcraft line in 1952. It remained popular until the 1960s. The solid white dinnerware, sometimes decorated with decals, is marked with her name.

Platter, Frost Flowers,
  15 In. 40.00

WILDFIRE has a border of garlands of pink roses and green leaves entwined with blue ribbons on a white background. It has gold trim. It was made as a premium for the Great American Tea Company in the 1940s and 1950s.

Aladdin Teapot, Oval
  Infuser 150.00
Baker, French,
  7 3/4 x 2 1/2 In. 45.00
Berry Bowl 12.00
Bowl, Cereal 15.00
Bowl, Salad,
  9 1/4 In. ...... 30.00 to 45.00
Bowl, Vegetable, Oval,
  10 1/2 x 8 In. 45.00
Bowl, Vegetable, Round . 40.00
Creamer, Pert 25.00
Cup & Saucer 20.00
Plate, Bread & Butter,
  6 In. 10.00
Plate, Dinner, 9 In. 20.00
Plate, Dinner, Gold Trim,
  9 In. 11.00
Plate, Salad, 7 In. 13.00

Platter, Oval 65.00

Salt & Pepper,
Sani-Grid 80.00

Soup, Dish,
8 1/2 In. . . . . . . 22.00 to 30.00

Sugar & Creamer 30.00

Teapot, Sani-Grid,
6 Cup 369.00

MISCELLANEOUS: There are
many other patterns made by
Hall. Some are listed here.

Baker, French, Two-Tone,
Green & Yellow, 7 In. . . 22.00

Baker, French, Two-Tone,
Green & Yellow, 8 In. . . 24.00

Baker French, Serenade,
3 Pt. 28.00

Batter Bowl, Cactus, 5 Band,
4 3/4 x 8 3/4 In. 50.00

Bowl, Fruit, Tulip,
5 1/2 In. . . . . . . 8.00 to 10.00

Bowl, No. 4, Wild Poppy,
7 1/2 In. 50.00

Bowl, Plum Pudding,
Holly, 3 Piece 129.00

Bowl, Salad, China Rose,
No. 547, 24 Oz.,
7 1/2 x 3 In. 12.00

Bowl, Salad, Polka Dot,
Red, 3 x 9 1/2 In. 58.00

Cake Plate, Prairie Grass,
E-Line, 6 5/8 In. 13.00

Casserole, Cover, Blue Garden,
Sundial, No. 4 . . . . 75.00

Coffeepot, Drip-O-Lator, Trellis,
6 Cup, 11 x 10 In. 45.00

Coffeepot, Silhouette Medallion,
10 Cup 145.00

Coffeepot, Step-Down,
Drip-O-Lator, Floral,
7 3/4 x 6 3/8 In. 50.00

Creamer, Floral & Posies,
3 In. 10.00

Creamer, Serenade, Rose
White, Sani-Grid 30.00

Cup, Monticello, Sears 6.00

Dish, No. 521, Green,
9 1/4 In. 5.00

Gravy Boat, Sunglow,
White, Century 40.00

Jug, Water, Ice Lip, Medallion,
Gunmetal, 6 1/2 In. 89.00

Mixing Bowl, Game Bird,
3 Piece 149.00

Mixing Bowl, Medallion,
Ivory, 5 1/4 In. 20.00

Mixing Bowl, Medallion,
Ivory, 6 1/4 In. 25.00

Mixing Bowl, Medallion,
Ivory, 7 1/2 In. 25.00

Mixing Bowl, Serenade,
6 In. 34.00

Mixing Bowl, Serenade,
7 1/2 In. 35.00

Percolator, Electric,
Game Bird 189.00

Pitcher, Tankard Schenley,
White, 64 Oz., 9 In. 50.00

Saltshaker, Canister Style, Wild
Poppy, Radiance 125.00

Soup, Onion, Cover, Yellow
Rose, 5 1/2 In. 45.00

Sugar, Open, Plaza, White,
7 Oz., 2 1/2 In. 12.00

Teapot, Hollywood, Chartreuse,
6 Cup, 7 x 10 In. 56.00

Underplate, Oval, Monticello,
Sears, 5 1/2 x 9 In. 12.00

Water Server, Plaza, Red,
6 5/8 In. 389.00

HARKER

Harker Pottery Company
was incorporated in 1890
in East Liverpool, Ohio.
The Harker family had
been making pottery in
the area since 1840. The
plant was moved in 1931
to Chester, West Virginia.
It closed in 1972. The pottery made a popular line
of dinnerware, including
intaglio or engobe pieces
that were usually marked
Cameo ware.

ALPINE is an intaglio pattern
with white spruce sprays with

turquoise center dots on a pink-
cocoa ground. It was introduced
c.1957.

Plate, Bread & Butter,
6 1/4 In. 5.00

Plate, Salad,
8 1/4 In. . . . . . . 7.00 to 17.50

Platter, Serving,
13 1/2 x 10 1/2 In. 22.50

Soup, Dish 8.50

AMY is decorated with floral
decals and was made in two
versions beginning about 1935.
One has white, orange, and pink
poppies and blue forget-me-
nots and the other has a white
rose, an orange poppy, and blue
forget-me-nots.

Bean Pot, Ivory, Platinum
Trim, 2 3/4 In. 15.00

Plate, Bread & Butter, Triflower,
Bakerite, 6 In. 7.00

Plate, Luncheon, Bakerite,
7 1/4 In. 7.50

Saucer, Triflower,
Bakerite 5.00

CHESTERTON was a pattern
produced from 1945 to 1965.
The pieces have a gadroon border that was left white. Pieces
were then decorated with a
solid color. Hollow ware has
white interiors. Chesterton was
made in Avocado, Celadon,
Charcoal, Chocolate Brown,
Coral, Golden Harvest, Lime,
Pink Cocoa, Pumpkin, Silver-
Gray, Teal, Wedgwood Blue,
White, Yellow, and perhaps
other colors. Teal pieces are
called Corinthian.

Avocado

Bowl, Vegetable, 9 In. . . . 25.00

Celadon

Plate, Bread & Butter,
6 1/2 In. 6.00

Silver-Gray

Bowl, Cereal, Tab Handle,
6 1/2 In. 6.00

Bowl, Fruit, White Gadroon,
5 1/2 In. 7.00

Bowl, Vegetable,
8 3/4 x 2 5/8 In. 35.00

Creamer, 1950s 8.00

Cup & Saucer 9.00

Plate, Bread & Butter,
6 In. 7.00

Plate, Dinner, 9 1/2 In. 8.00

Plate, Salad, Gadroon,
Fluted Trim, Rope
Embossing, 7 1/4 In. 8.00

Plate, Square, 8 1/2 In. 5.00

Platter, Oval, 12 In. 20.00

Salt & Pepper 20.00

Saucer, Round, 6 In. 5.00

Soup, Dish, 1950s,
8 1/2 In. 9.00

Sugar, Cover, 1950s 8.00

Teal

Platter, 12 In. 19.00

COLONIAL LADY has a central
silhouette of a colonial lady on
a white background. It was
made in the 1930s.

Bowl, Red Trim,
5 1/2 In. 6.00

Cup, Red Trim,
3 3/4 x 2 In. 6.00

Dish, Virginia Shape,
5 In. 6.00

DAINTY FLOWER was the
first intaglio pattern made with
a Cameoware backstamp. It
was introduced c.1930 in Blue
and White. Later it was made in

Pink, Teal, and Yellow and on
several different shapes.

Blue

Cup, Jumbo 18.00

Plate, Dinner, Flowers In
Center, 9 3/8 In. 20.00

Platter, Swirl, White Flowers,
12 x 9 In. 25.00

Pink

Bowl, Dessert, 5 In. 7.75

Shaker 15.50

DOGWOOD is an intaglio pattern that was introduced c.1955.

Bowl, Dessert, 5 3/4 In. . . . 6.00

Cup & Saucer 8.50

Plate, Bread & Butter,
7 1/4 In. 6.00

Platter,
11 1/2 x 10 3/4 In. 17.50

Soup, Dish, 7 1/2 In. 8.00

Sugar, Cover 15.00

MODERN TULIP has an orange
tulip with brown and tan leaves
and was introduced c.1940 on
the Modern Age shape. Later,
the design was used on other
shapes.

Bowl, Cereal, 6 1/8 In. 8.75

Bowl, Dessert, c.1940,
5 3/8 In. 6.25

Bowl, Vegetable,
8 1/4 In. 19.50

Custard Cup 6.25

Jar, 5 x 3 5/8 In. 6.25

Jug, Water, Cover, 1939,
8 In. 28.00

Pie Baker,
10 In. . . . . 21.50 to 30.00

Plate, Bread & Butter,
6 1/8 In. 4.75

Plate, Dinner, 9 1/2 In. 8.75

Plate, Square, 6 5/8 In. 8.25

Plate, Utility, 11 In. 26.50

Rolling Pin 110.00

PATE SUR PATE was a backstamp used by Harker.

Blue

Tray, Gold Finished Metal
Handle, 10 3/8 x 3 In. . . 15.00

Gray

Bowl, White Gadroon
Border 7.50

Cup, White Gadroon
Border 6.00

Dish, Oval, 9 In. 15.00

Plate, Luncheon, Gadroon
Border, 8 1/2 In. 8.00

Platter, White Gadroon
Border 15.00

Saucer, 6 1/2 In. 6.00

Teal

Bowl, Fruit, 5 1/2 In. 6.00

Bowl, Vegetable, Oval,
9 1/2 x 6 7/8 In. 20.00

Creamer,
5 3/4 x 2 1/2 In. 18.00

Cup & Saucer . . . . . 5.00 to 8.00

Plate, Bread & Butter,
6 1/4 In. 4.00

Plate, Luncheon, Square,
8 1/2 In. 9.00

Plate, Salad,
7 3/8 In. . . . . 5.00 to 6.00

Platter, 13 3/8 x 10 In. . . . 30.00

Sugar, Cover 25.00

PETIT POINT ROSE is a variation of the Petit Point or Cross
Stitch pattern introduced c.1935.
It is decorated with a decal of a
cross-stitch rose. Other variations are called Petit Point I and
Petit Point II.

Cake Server,
Silver Trim 19.00

Mixing Bowl, 7 In. 16.00

Mixing Bowl, 8 In. 22.50

Mixing Bowl, 9 In. 26.50

Pie Baker, 9 In. 27.50

Plate, Dinner,
  10 In. . . . . 22.50 to 26.50
Plate, Utility, 11 In. 28.50

PINE CONE has a monochromatic design of a pine branch with pine cones and needles on a white background. It was introduced c.1960.

Bowl, Cereal, 6 1/4 In. 7.00

Bowl, Fruit,
  5 1/4 In. . . . . . . 5.00 to 10.00
Plate, Bread & Butter,
  6 1/4 In. 8.00
Soup, Dish 8.00

SPRINGTIME is an intaglio pattern with white flowers and grass on a pink background. It was made about 1959.

Plate, Bread & Butter,
  6 In. . . . . 5.00 to 6.00
Tidbit, 2 Tiers,
  10 x 5 3/4 In. 15.00

STONE CHINA was made in four colors: Blue Mist, Golden Dawn, Shell Pink, and White Cap. It was made in the 1950s.

Shell Pink
Cup 4.50
Cup & Saucer 7.50
Sugar 5.00

WHEAT is an intaglio pattern made for Sears and sold under its Harmony House label c.1961.

Pie Lifter, 9 7/16 In. 19.00
Platter 16.00

Soup, Dish, Oval 8.00
Sugar & Creamer 24.00

WHITE CLOVER is an intaglio dinnerware designed by Russel Wright. It has the very sleek modern shapes inspired by his other design, American Modern, but a sprig of clover decoration was added. It was made in four colors: Charcoal, Coral Sand, Golden Spice, and Meadow Green. The dinnerware was advertised as ovenproof, chip-resistant, and detergent-resistant. The pattern was introduced in 1951 and discontinued in 1955.

Charcoal
Creamer 50.00
Cup, Tea 22.00
Salt & Pepper, Large 10.00
Saucer 7.50

Coral Sand
Bowl, Cereal 25.00
Casserole, No Cover 98.00
Creamer 40.00
Cup, Tea 20.00
Mixing Bowl 90.00
Plate, Bread & Butter,
  6 In. 10.00
Plate, Dinner, 10 In. 15.00
Platter, Barbecue, 11 In. . . 20.00
Salt & Pepper,
  Large . . . . 15.00 to 28.00
Saucer 7.00

Golden Spice
Ashtray 20.00
Plate, Bread & Butter,
  6 In. 8.50
Plate, Salad, 7 3/4 In. 14.00
Saucer 5.50

Meadow Green
Cup & Saucer 15.00
Plate, Bread & Butter,
  6 In. 5.00
Plate, Dinner, 10 In. 15.00

MISCELLANEOUS: There are many other patterns made by Harker. Some are listed here.

Bowl, Cereal, Laurelton,
  Gray, 6 In. 6.00
Bowl, Colonial Couple,
  5 1/4 In. 5.00
Bowl, Colonial Couple,
  Fragonard, 5 1/4 In. 6.00
Bowl, Fruit, Mallow,
  5 1/2 In. 12.00
Bowl, Fruit, Wild Rose,
  Royal Gadroon,
  Gold Trim, 6 In. 8.00
Bowl, Magnolia, 6 In. 5.00
Butter, Rosebud, Heritance,
  Ivory, Gold Trim,
  12 Sides, 1/4 Lb. 25.00
Casserole, Cover Only,
  Red Apple 25.00
Coffeepot, Cover, Olympic,
  Pink, Beige 35.00
Creamer, Embassy,
  Roses 15.00
Creamer, Olympic 6.00
Cup & Saucer, Rosebud,
  Heritance, Gold Trim . . 16.30
Custard Cup, Mallow,
  8 Oz., 2 1/2 In. 15.00
Gravy Boat, Ivy Vine 19.00
Pie Lifter, Silhouette, Horse
  & Trees, 9 3/16 In. 30.00
Plate, Bread & Butter,
  Colonial Couple, Fragonard,
  6 1/4 In. 7.00
Plate, Bread & Butter,
  Mallow, 6 In. 6.00
Plate, Bread & Butter, Rocaille,
  Pink Cocoa, 6 In. 7.00
Plate, Bread & Butter, Rosebud
  Bouquet, 6 In. 6.00

Plate, Bread & Butter,
Sweetheart Rose, Royal
Gadroon, 6 In. 7.00

Plate, Dinner, Laurelton,
Aqua, 10 In. 8.00

Plate, Dinner, Laurelton,
Parchment Beige,
10 In. 8.00

Plate, Dinner, Rosebud,
Heritance, White, Gold Trim,
12 Sides, 10 In. 15.00

Plate, Dinner, White Daisy,
Yellow, 10 In. 15.00

Plate, Round, Cabbage Rose,
Yellow, Gold Trim,
9 1/2 In. 20.00

Platter, Bamboo, 11 In. . . . 15.00

Platter, Godey, 22K Trim,
12 In. 35.00

Platter, Ivy, Small 25.00

Platter, Square, Lovelace,
Gold Trim, 11 In. 27.00

Salt & Pepper, Mallow,
Skyscraper 60.00

Saltshaker, Ivy Vine,
Range 18.00

Serving Bowl, Godey,
22K Trim, 8 5/8 In. 35.00

Soup, Dish, Ivy 18.00

Sugar, Embassy, Ivory,
Rosebuds 20.00

Sugar & Creamer, Cover,
8 Sides, Golden Wheat,
Gold Trim, 5 In. 22.00

Tidbit, Provincial Tulip,
Green 15.00

HARMONY HOUSE

Harmony House was a
mark used on dinnerware
sold by Sears, Roebuck &
Company. Harmony House
dishes were made by vari-
ous factories, including

Hall, Harker, Homer
Laughlin, Laurel Pottery,
Salem China, and Univer-
sal, from 1940 until the
early 1970s. Later pieces
were made in Japan. The
Cattail (Cat-tail) pattern is
listed in this book under
Universal Potteries, Inc.

MODERNE (3545) is a plain
modern dinnerware with a narrow trim.

Creamer 6.00
Gravy, Underplate . . 8.00 to 9.00
Plate, Bread & Butter,
6 3/8 In. 4.00
Plate, Dinner, 10 3/8 In. . . 16.00
Plate, Salad, 7 7/8 In. 6.00

MOUNT VERNON was made
by Hall China for Sears. The
pattern has a blue sprig border,
a center design of blue sprigs
encircling a pink rose, and gold
trim. It was offered for sale
from 1941 to 1959.

Plate, Bread & Butter,
6 1/4 In. 6.00
Platter, 13 1/2 In. 10.00

Soup, Rim 15.00
Sugar & Creamer 10.00

ORIENT is a pattern featuring
branches in an Asian-inspired
design.

Gravy 3.00
Soup, Dish 10.00

PLATINUM GARLAND is a fine
china design made in Japan. It
has a border of platinum stalks
of grass with seed heads.

Gravy . . . . 6.00 to 16.00
Plate, Bread & Butter,
6 3/8 In. 6.00
Plate, Dinner, 10 1/4 In. . . 18.00
Sugar, Cover 8.00
Vegetable, Oval,
10 7/8 In. 34.00

ROSEBUD (3534) is a china
pattern on a modern rimless
shape. It has a center of a rosebud with scattered gray leaves.
It was made in Japan.

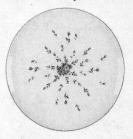

Cup & Saucer 5.00
Plate, Dinner,
10 3/8 In. . . . . . 8.00 to 18.00
Plate, Salad, 7 5/8 In. 8.00
Sugar & Creamer 10.00

HOMER LAUGHLIN

HOMER LAUGHLIN

Homer Laughlin started in 1896 as the Homer Laughlin China Company in East Liverpool, Ohio. It was the continuation of an earlier pottery called Laughlin Brothers. In 1905 the company built a second plant in Newell, West Virginia. Both potteries worked until 1929, when the East Liverpool factory closed. Homer Laughlin is still working in West Virginia. Patterns are listed here by name or by shape.

AMBERSTONE is made on the Fiesta shapes. Fiesta, the popular dinnerware pattern, is made in bright solid colors. In 1967 a new pattern, Amberstone, was created. Pieces were glazed a rich brown, and some have black machine-stamped underglaze patterns. Some pieces were used for supermarket promotions with the backstamp *Genuine Sheffield*. Full sets of dishes were made.

Sheffield ⚜ ™
AMBERSTONE
MADE IN U.S.A.

Cup & Saucer 7.00
Plate, Bread & Butter,
    6 3/8 In. 3.00

BLUE DUCHESS has blue and yellow flowers and green leaves on a white background and a blue band around the edge. It was made in the 1960s on the Vogue shape.

Bowl, Fruit, 5 1/2 In. 3.00
Plate, Bread & Butter,
    6 1/4 In. . . . . 2.50 to 3.00

BRITTANY is a shape made from 1930 to 1958 or later. Many different patterns were made on the Brittany shape.

Bowl, Cranberry, 5 In. 4.50
Bowl, Fruit, Blue,
    5 3/4 In. 3.00
Plate, Dessert, Blue,
    7 1/4 In. 7.00
Saucer, Blue 2.50

CAVALIER
See Eggshell Cavalier

COLONIAL WHITE is undecorated white dinnerware made on the Dover shape. It was introduced in the late 1960s and made until the early 1980s.

Bowl, Dessert, 6 In. 6.50

Plate, Bread & Butter,
    6 1/4 In. 2.50
Plate, Dinner,
    10 In. . . . . 5.00 to 6.50
Plate, Salad,
    7 1/4 In. . . . . 3.00 to 6.50
Saucer 4.00

CRINOLINE has a floral decal center, gray border, and platinum trim. It was made on the Cavalier shape.

Creamer 8.00
Gravy 28.00
Plate, Bread & Butter,
    6 1/4 In. 5.00
Plate, Dinner, 10 1/4 In. . . 16.00
Plate, Salad, Square,
    7 3/4 In. 10.00
Soup, Rim, 8 3/8 In. 15.00

EGGSHELL CAVALIER shape, designed by Don Schreckengost, was made from 1953 to the 1970s. It was decorated in many ways, including solid-color combinations and decals.

Bowl, Cereal,
    5 1/2 In. . . . . 4.00 to 8.00
Bowl, Fruit, Eggshell,
    Rose Melody 3.00
Bowl, Vegetable, Flowers,
    Pink Border, 9 3/4 In. . . 28.00
Cup, Yellow & White,
    Gold Trim 5.00
Gravy Boat, Golden Wheat,
    Gold Border 28.50
Plate, Bread & Butter,
    Eggshell, Rose Melody,
    6 1/4 In. 3.00
Plate, Bread & Butter, White
    Rose, 6 1/4 In. 5.00
Plate, Dinner, Golden Harvest,
    10 In. 6.25
Plate, Salad, Golden Wheat,
    7 1/8 In. 4.25
Platter, Flowers, Pink Border,
    13 1/2 In. 28.00

Saucer, 6 In. 6.50

Saucer, Eggshell, Rose
   Melody 2.50

Saucer, Eggshell, Troy 3.00

Saucer, Somerset 4.00

Soup, Dish, Blue Border,
   8 In. 7.00

Sugar & Creamer 29.00

Teapot, Cover, Golden
   Wheat, 5 3/8 In. 99.00

EGGSHELL GEORGIAN was
made from 1937 to the 1960s.
Dishes were decorated with
many different decals with
wide, colored bands, or with
floral sprigs with narrow bands.
Eggshell shapes were introduced in 1937. Many pieces are
marked with the word *eggshell*
and the name of the shape:
Georgian, Nautilus, Swing, or
Theme. Each shape could have
many different decorations.

Bowl, 8 1/4 In. 5.00

Bowl, Fruit, Ivory &
   Maroon, 5 3/8 In. 4.00

Bowl, Pink & Yellow
   Roses, 8 1/2 In. 29.50

Casserole, Cover,
   Countess, 10 7/8 In. 75.00

Dish, Dessert, Countess,
   5 1/4 In. 7.00

Plate, Bread & Butter,
   6 1/4 In. 4.50

Plate, Bread & Butter,
   Countess, 6 1/4 In. 7.00

Plate, Bread & Butter, Rambler
   Rose, 6 1/4 In. 5.00

Soup, Onion, Pink &
   Yellow Roses 7.00

Sugar & Creamer,
   Countess 33.00

EGGSHELL NAUTILUS is a
shape that was made from 1937
to the 1950s. The nautilus shell
motif can be seen in the handles. The shape was decorated
in many different ways, and
some of the decal decorations
have special pattern names. See
also Nantucket.

Bowl, Fruit, Cashmere,
   5 1/4 In. 4.00

Bowl, Fruit, Flowers,
   5 1/4 In. 5.00

Bowl, Vegetable, Cover,
   Coronet 90.00

Casserole, Cover, White
   Rose 65.00

Creamer 12.00

Plate, Bread & Butter,
   Cashmere, 6 In. 8.00

Plate, Bread & Butter,
   Fruit, Flowers, 6 In. 5.00

Plate, Bread & Butter, Pastel
   Roses, 6 In. 4.00

Plate, Luncheon, Della
   Robbia, 9 In. 8.00

Plate, Salad, Blue Band,
   8 1/8 In. 7.00

Plate, Salad, Jade Rose, Green
   Border, Gold Trim 7.00

Plate, Salad, Pink & Gold
   Roses, 8 1/8 In. 7.00

Sauceboat, Underplate,
   Flowers 30.00

Soup, Dish, Aristocrat,
   8 In. 12.00

Sugar, Cover, Ferndale 5.00

Sugar, Cover,
   Gold Trim 30.00

Teapot, Gold 39.00

EGGSHELL SWING is a shape
made in the 1950s. It was decorated with wide stripes in pas-

tels, floral designs, and decals
picturing Asian or Mexican
figures.

Plate, Bread & Butter,
   Blue Flax, 6 In. 7.00

Plate, Salad, Blue Flax,
   7 In. 7.00

Serving Bowl, Oval,
   Blue Flax, 9 In. 12.00

Serving Bowl, Round,
   Blue Flax, 8 1/2 In. 12.00

Soup, Dish, Blue Flax,
   8 In. 8.00

FIESTA ware was introduced in
1936. It was designed by Frederick Hurten Rhead. The line
was redesigned in 1969, with-
drawn in 1973, and reissued in
1986. The design is characterized by a band of concentric circles beginning at the rim. The
complete Fiesta line in 1937
had 54 different pieces. Rarities
include the covered onion bowl,
the green disk water jug, the 10-
inch cake plate, and the syrup
pitcher. Cups had full-circle
handles until 1969, when par-
tial-circle handles were made.
The original Fiesta colors were
Dark Blue, Fiesta Red, Light
Green, Old Ivory, and Yellow.
Later, Chartreuse, Forest Green,
Gray, Medium Green, Rose,

and Turquoise were added. From 1970 to 1972 the redesigned Fiesta Ironstone was made only in Antique Gold, Mango Red, and Turf Green. Homer Laughlin reissued Fiesta in 1986 using new colors but the original marks and molds. The new colors were Apricot, Black, Cobalt Blue, Rose (pink), and White. Other colors and the years they were introduced are: Yellow, 1987; Turquoise, 1988; Periwinkle Blue, 1989; Sea Mist Green, 1991; Lilac, 1993; Persimmon, 1995; Sapphire, 1996; Chartreuse, 1997, Pearl Gray, 1999; Juniper (dark green), 1999; Cinnabar, 2000; Sunflower, 2001; Plum, 2002; Shamrock, 2002, and Tangerine, 2003. Most Fiesta ware was marked with the incised word Fiesta. Some pieces were hand-stamped before glazing. The word *Genuine* was added to the mark in the 1940s. Dishes in the Fiesta shape with decal decorations are collected by their pattern names. There is also a Fiesta Kitchen Kraft line, a group of kitchenware pieces made in the early 1940s in Blue, Green, Red, or Yellow. These were bake-and-serve wares. Glassware and linens were made to match the Fiesta colors. New limited edition pieces of Fiesta have been distributed by China Specialties, Inc., and may be listed here. They are new shapes, not reproductions, and are clearly marked or dated.

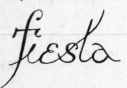

Chartreuse
Plate, Dessert, 6 In. 9.00
Platter, Oval, 12 In. 58.00
Sugar & Creamer 75.00

Cinnabar
Platter, Oval,
  12 1/4 x 9 5/8 In. 38.00

Cobalt Blue
Bowl, Fruit,
  4 3/4 In. . . . . . . 32.00 to 35.00
Bowl, Fruit, 5 1/2 In. 32.00
Bowl, Vegetable, Oval,
  12 In. 50.00
Carafe 75.00
Chop Plate, 12 In. 30.00
Chop Plate, 15 In. 80.00
Cup 25.00
Cup, After Dinner 60.00
Cup & Saucer 17.00
Plate, Dessert, 6 In. 7.00
Plate, Dinner, 10 In. 40.00
Plate, Luncheon,
  9 1/2 In. 17.00
Platter, Oval, 12 In. 85.00
Saltshaker 33.00
Saucer, After
  Dinner . . . . 15.00 to 20.00

Fiesta Red
Ashtray, 5 1/2 In. 125.00
Bowl, Salad, 8 1/2 In. 48.00
Chop Plate, 15 In. 150.00
Cup, After Dinner 60.00
Mug 90.00
Pitcher, Juice, Disk,
  30 Oz. 425.00
Pitcher, Water, Disk,
  2 Qt. 150.00
Pitcher, Water, Ice Lip,
  6 3/8 In. 135.00
Plate, Luncheon, 9 In. 22.00
Relish, 11 In. 260.00
Saucer 12.00
Soup, Cream 60.00

Sugar 100.00
Teapot, Medium,
  6 Cup 175.00

Forest Green
Nappy, 8 1/2 In. 52.00
Plate, Bread & Butter,
  7 In. 14.00
Plate, Deep, 8 1/4 In. 55.00
Platter, Oval, 12 In. 48.00
Soup, Cream 35.00

Light Green
Bowl, Fruit,
  5 1/2 In. . . . . . . 25.00 to 60.00
Chop Plate, 15 In. 100.00
Cup 25.00
Cup, Tea 25.00
Cup & Saucer 20.00
Cup & Saucer,
  After Dinner 85.00
Eggcup 58.00
Pitcher, Water, Disk,
  2 Qt. 75.00
Plate, Luncheon, 9 In. 18.00
Soup, Cream 42.00

Lilac
Candleholder, Tripod,
  Pair 800.00
Vase, 8 In. 400.00

Medium Green
Cup & Saucer 45.00

Mixed Colors
Coffee Set, After Dinner,
  Red Pot, Tom & Jerry
  Mugs, Original Colors,
  7 Piece . . . 1150.00 to 1800.00
Cup & Saucer, 6 Sets . . . 600.00
Cup & Saucer, After Dinner,
  Original Colors,
  6 Sets 1200.00
Salt & Pepper, Green,
  Yellow . . . . . 100.00 to 125.00
Salt & Pepper, Turquoise,
  Cobalt Blue . . . 35.00 to 50.00

Old Ivory
Bowl, Fruit, 5 1/2 In. 32.00
Casserole, French,
  Cover 250.00
Mug, Tom & Jerry,
  Gold Trim 10.00
Plate, Bread & Butter,
  7 In. 10.00
Plate, Dinner, 10 In. 40.00

Plate, Luncheon, 9 In. 15.00
Saucer 5.00
Soup, Cream 60.00

Periwinkle Blue
Candleholder, Bulb
Shape 28.00

Rose
Bowl, Fruit, 5 1/2 In. 52.00
Butter, Cover 17.00
Candleholder, Pyramid
Shape 32.00
Chop Plate, 13 In. 20.00
Plate, Deep, 8 1/2 In. 25.00
Platter, Oval, 15 In. 48.00
Salt & Pepper, 2 3/4 In. . . 19.00
Saucer, After Dinner 85.00
Sugar & Creamer, Cover,
Tray 25.00
Tumbler, Juice, 5 Oz. 65.00

Sea Mist Green
Mug, 10 1/4 Oz. 7.00
Plate, Salad, 7 1/4 In. 8.00

Turquoise
Ashtray, 5 1/2 In. 150.00
Bowl, Fruit, 5 1/2 In. 25.00
Candleholder, Bulb, 4 In.,
Pair 225.00
Casserole, Cover,
7 3/4 In. 75.00
Chop Plate, 13 In. 30.00
Chop Plate,
15 In. . . . . . . 100.00 to 140.00
Coffeepot, After Dinner,
10 1/2 In. 425.00
Coffee Set, Pot, Cups &
Saucers, 13 Piece 1100.00
Eggcup 58.00
Jug, 2 Pt. 125.00
Mug, 2 7/8 In. 7.00
Mug, Tom &
Jerry . . . . 25.00 to 58.00
Pitcher, Water, Disk,
2 Qt. 250.00
Plate, Bread & Butter,
7 In. . . . . 7.00 to 8.00
Plate, Dessert,
6 In. . . . . 5.00 to 9.00
Plate, Dinner, 10 In. 25.00
Plate, Luncheon,
9 In. . . . . 9.00 to 12.00
Platter, Oval, 12 In. 85.00
Salt & Pepper 44.00

Saltshaker 28.00
Saucer 8.00
Soup, Cream 42.00
Teapot, Large, 8 Cup . . . 245.00

Yellow
Bowl, Fruit, 5 1/2 In. 25.00
Bowl, Salad, 7 1/2 In. 85.00
Cake Plate, 11 In. 45.00
Chop Plate, 13 In. 100.00
Cup, After
Dinner . . . . 50.00 to 60.00
Cup, Tea 25.00
Nappy, 8 1/2 In. 40.00
Plate, Bread & Butter,
7 In. 8.00
Plate, Dessert,
6 In. . . . . 5.00 to 9.00
Plate, Dinner, 10 In. 25.00
Plate, Luncheon, 9 In. 12.00
Sauceboat 45.00
Saucer . . . . 4.00 to 8.00
Saucer, After Dinner 10.00
Soup, Cream 42.00

FIESTA KITCHEN KRAFT was a bake-and-serve line made in the early 1940s. It was made in Blue, Green, Red, Yellow, and other colors.

Red
Cake Server 265.00
Spoon 245.00

GEORGIAN
See Eggshell Georgian

GREENBAND is a line of restaurant china. Plates have two green bands on the outside edge of the rim and one thin green band on the inside edge. The mark includes the words *Best China*.

Cup 4.00
Cup & Saucer 7.00
Plate, Dinner, 9 In. 5.00
Plate, Salad, 8 In. 4.50
Saucer 4.00

HACIENDA is a Mexican-inspired pattern introduced in 1938. The dinnerware was made on the Century shape. The decal shows a bench, cactus, and a portion of the side of a Mexican home. Most pieces have red trim at the handles and edge. After 1936, Franciscan also made a dinnerware pattern called Hacienda.

Bowl, 8 1/4 In. 30.00

HARLEQUIN, a solid-color dinnerware, was less expensive than Fiesta. It was made from 1938 to 1964 and sold unmarked in Woolworth stores. The rings molded into the plate are at the edge of the plate well, and the rim is plain. Dishes were made in Chartreuse, Coral, Forest Green, Gray, Green (spruce green), Maroon (sometimes called red), Mauve Blue, Medium Green, Rose, Tangerine (red), Turquoise, and Yellow.

Green
Tumbler, Car Decal,
4 1/4 In. 79.00

Maroon
Candleholder, 1 7/8 In. . . . 250.00
Pitcher, Ball, 22 Oz. 110.00
Tumbler, 4 1/4 In. 55.00

Mauve Blue
Bowl, Casserole,
   8 1/2 In. 45.00
Bowl, Fruit, 5 1/2 In. 29.00
Bowl, Oatmeal, 36s,
   6 1/2 In. 40.00
Candleholder, 1 7/8 In. . . . 250.00
Plate, Bread & Butter,
   6 In. 6.00

Medium Green
Platter, 11 In. 130.00

Rose
Plate, Bread & Butter,
   6 In. 7.00
Saucer, Tea,
   5 7/8 In. . . . . 8.00 to 12.00

Tangerine
Ashtray, 5 1/2 In. 55.00
Nut Dish, 3 In. 20.00
Teapot, 6 1/8 In. 125.00

Turquoise
Ashtray, 5 1/2 In. 50.00
Bowl, Fruit, 5 1/2 In. 7.00
Bowl, Oatmeal, 36s,
   6 1/2 In. 12.00
Cup & Saucer 14.00
Plate, Bread & Butter,
   6 1/4 In. . . . . 4.00 to 6.00
Plate, Salad, 7 1/4 In. 8.00

Yellow
Ashtray, 5 1/2 In. 50.00
Bowl, Fruit, 5 3/4 In. 9.00
Bowl, Oatmeal, 36s,
   6 1/2 In. 18.00
Creamer 10.00
Cup & Saucer . . . . 8.00 to 14.00
Pitcher, Ball, 22 Oz. 125.00
Plate, Bread & Butter,
   6 1/4 In. 6.00
Plate, Dinner, 10 In. 14.00
Plate, Luncheon,
   9 1/4 In. 10.00
Plate, Salad, 7 1/4 In. 8.00

HUDSON is a shape made from 1908 to 1928 that was decorated with various decals. Al-most 70 different pieces were made.

Butter, Domed Cover
   Only 29.00
Casserole, Cover,
   10 x 7 In. 80.00
Gravy Boat, Scalloped
   Edge, Gold Trim 40.00
Platter, Flowers, Scalloped Edge,
   Gold Trim, 14 1/2 In. . . 33.00
Saucer, 5 7/8 In. 5.00

JUBILEE is a 1948 dinnerware shape. The dinnerware called Jubilee is a solid-color line. The colors are Celadon Green, Cream Beige, Mist Gray, and Shell Pink. Jubilee was colored in different ways to produce dinnerware patterns with other names. Jubilee was revived in 1977 and 1978.

Celadon Green
Bowl, Fruit, 5 1/4 In. 4.00
Pitcher, Juice 50.00

Mist Gray
Soup, Coupe, 8 1/4 In. 7.00

KITCHEN KRAFT oven-to-table pieces were introduced in the early 1930s. The pieces were made in plain solid colors or with decals. They were usu-ally marked *Kitchen Kraft, OvenServe.*

Blue
Bowl, Fruit, 5 3/4 In. 7.00
Plate, Bread & Butter,
   6 1/2 In. 7.00

Sugar & Creamer, White
   Handles 30.00

Ivory
Pie Plate, Green Trim,
   10 1/2 In. 30.00

Yellow
Baker, Oval, 6 In. 10.00
Plate, Embossed,
   9 1/2 In. 16.00

MARIGOLD is a scalloped-edge shape made in 1934. Some pieces are plain, some have decal decorations, and some have hand painting on the raised decorations that are part of the plate. Marigold glaze is a pale yellow.

Bowl, Cereal 5.00
Bowl, Vegetable, Cover,
   11 1/2 In. 89.00
Creamer 19.00
Cup 4.00
Gravy Boat, Underplate . . 49.00
Platter, 11 3/4 In. 16.00
Sugar, Cover 32.00

MEXICANA was the first of the Mexican-inspired patterns that became popular as dinnerware in the 1930s. This decal-deco-rated set, designed by Frederick Hurten Rhead, was first offered in 1938. The design shows a collection of orange and yellow pots with a few cacti. The edge of the dish well is rimmed with red or, occasionally, yellow, green, or blue. Almost all of the pieces are Century line, a popu-lar Homer Laughlin dinnerware shape.

Bowl, Vegetable, Oval,
   8 1/2 In. 53.00
Casserole, No Cover 59.00

NANTUCKET is a pattern that appeared in the 1953 Mont-gomery Ward catalog. It has a border of stylized pink and blue flowers and gray leaves.

Gravy Boat, 7 1/2 In. 28.50

NAUTILUS
See Eggshell Nautilus

PRISCILLA is a decal-decorated ware with pale pink roses and sprigs of flowers.

Bowl, Fruit, 5 In. 6.00
Cake Server, 9 5/8 In. 25.00
Cup & Saucer 12.00
Mixing Bowl, 6 In. 24.00
Pie Plate, 9 1/2 In. 20.00
Plate, Dinner,
  9 In. . . . . 10.00 to 18.00
Platter, 13 x 9 1/4 In. 30.00
Serving Bowl, Oval,
  9 1/4 In. 19.00

REPUBLIC was made in the early 1900s and lasted to the 1940s. It is a shape with an embossed scalloped edge decorated in many different ways.

Bowl, Spring Wreath 4.00
Casserole, Cover, Jean,
  Gold Trim, 8 In. 55.00
Creamer, 3 1/2 In. 12.00
Plate, Bread & Butter,
  Jean, 6 1/4 In. 7.00
Platter, Oval, 11 3/4 In. . . 12.00

RHYTHM is a shape that was made in solid colors and with decal decorations from about 1951 to 1958. Solid-color dishes were made in many of the Harlequin colors, including Chartreuse, Forest Green, Gray, Maroon, and Yellow. Other companies also made patterns

named Rhythm, but they are not listed here.

Blue
Underplate, Gold Trim 4.00
Chartreuse
Bowl, Fruit, 5 3/8 In. 4.00
Platter, 11 In. 13.00
Decals
Cup, Golden Wheat 4.25
Cup, Green, Gold, Brown,
  Fantasy 5.00
Plate, Salad, Capri,
  7 1/8 In. 7.00
Gray
Bowl, Fruit, 5 1/4 In. 4.00
Creamer, 3 1/4 In. 7.00
Cup 8.00
Gravy Boat 9.00
Shell Pink
Bowl, Fruit, 5 3/8 In. 5.00
White
Bowl, Fruit, Golden Wheat,
  5 3/8 In. 4.00
Cake Plate, Lotus Hai,
  6 In. 7.00
Plate, Dessert, Golden
  Wheat, 7 1/4 In. 4.00
Platter, Oval, Allegro,
  11 1/2 In. 30.00
Saucer, Golden Wheat,
  6 In. 4.00
Teapot, Sweet Pea,
  Platinum Trim 30.00
Tidbit, Golden Wheat,
  3 Tiers 30.00

RHYTHM ROSE was made from the mid-1940s to the mid-1950s. The pattern features a center rose decal.

Bowl, Vegetable,
  8 7/8 In. 20.00
Jug, Water, 2 Qt. 46.00

Plate, Bread & Butter,
  6 1/8 In. 10.00

RIVIERA, a solid-color ware, was made from 1938 to 1950. It was unmarked and sold exclusively by the Murphy Company. Plates and cup handles are squared. Colors are Ivory, Light Green, Mauve Blue, Red, Yellow, and, rarely, Dark Blue.

Ivory
Butter, Cover Only,
  1/2 Lb. 70.00
Casserole, Cover,
  10 1/4 In. 135.00
Sauceboat, Underplate,
  8 3/8 In. 145.00
Sugar 12.00
Teapot 125.00
Light Green
Cup & Saucer 20.00
Plate, Salad, 7 3/4 In. . . . 15.00
Sugar & Creamer,
  Cover 50.00
Tumbler 75.00
Mauve Blue
Bowl, Vegetable,
  8 1/4 In. 18.00
Casserole, Cover,
  10 1/4 In. . . . . 85.00 to 140.00
Cup & Saucer 20.00
Plate, Bread & Butter,
  6 1/4 In. 7.00
Plate, Deep, 8 In. 24.00
Plate, Dinner, 10 In. 35.00
Plate, Salad, 7 3/4 In. . . . 15.00
Teapot 125.00
Tumbler 75.00

Red

Bowl, Fruit, 5 1/4 In. 12.00

Bowl, Vegetable,
8 1/4 In. . . . . . . 18.00 to 30.00

Butter, Cover Only,
1/2 Lb. 55.00

Butter, Cover, 1/2 Lb. . . . 125.00

Casserole, Cover,
10 1/4 In. 90.00

Cup & Saucer 25.00

Plate, Salad, 7 3/4 In. 18.00

Sugar 12.00

Yellow

Butter, Cover, 1/2 Lb. . . . 125.00

Casserole, No Cover 63.00

Cup & Saucer 20.00

Pitcher, Yellow, Juice . . . 195.00

Plate, Salad, 7 3/4 In. 15.00

Teapot 185.00

Tumbler, Handle 55.00

SHAKESPEARE COUNTRY is a blue and white pattern made on the Brittany shape for Laughlin International, a marketing company in Alliance, Ohio. It has a center picture of an old English village and a blue and white border of leaves or scrolls.

Butter Chip, 4 1/4 In. 20.00

Creamer 7.00

Cup, Tea 4.00

Platter, Oval, 11 In. 45.00

SKYTONE is both a pattern and a shape. The pattern made by Homer Laughlin is plain and light-blue colored. If the dishes have decals, the pieces are known by the name of the decal.

Platter, Serving,
Stardust 18.00

Teapot, 5 x 11 In. 30.00

Teapot, Mini 29.00

STRATFORD has a central floral design, gadrooned edge, and gold trim, and was made on the Liberty shape. It was introduced in 1949 and was distributed by Cunningham & Picket Inc. The distributor's backstamp and the Homer Laughlin mark were used on most pieces.

Bowl, Fruit, 5 3/8 In. 12.00

Cup & Saucer 12.00

Plate, Bread & Butter,
6 1/4 In. 8.00

Plate, Dessert,
7 3/8 In. 8.00

Plate, Salad, 8 1/4 In. 12.00

Soup, Rim, 8 3/8 In. 12.00

Sugar, Cover 32.00

STURBRIDGE has a center design and border of stylized blue flowers and bands on a white background.

Bowl, Cereal, Blue
Flowers, 6 1/4 In. 4.00

Cup, Blue Flowers 4.00

Cup & Saucer, Blue
Flowers 6.50

Plate, Dessert, Blue
Flowers, 7 1/4 In. 4.00

SWING
See Eggshell Swing

VIRGINIA ROSE is the name of a shape of dishes made from 1933 to the 1970s. The shapes are decorated with a variety of decals. The dishes with a design of a spray of roses and green leaves is the pattern most often called Virginia Rose by collectors. If no decal name is mentioned here, it is the Virginia Rose decal design.

Butter, Cover, Moss Rose,
Jade Shape 85.00

Creamer, Fluffy Rose 18.00

Cup, Flowers, Pink &
Purple 7.00

Plate, Bread & Butter,
Gold Rose, 7 In. 5.00

Plate, Bread & Butter, Pink
& Purple, 7 In. 5.00

Plate, Luncheon, Green,
Embossed Rose, 9 In. . . . 6.50

Saucer 4.00

Saucer, Cup, Tea, Gold
Rose 3.00

Saucer, Platinum Flower
Trim 4.00

Saucer, Spring Wreath 4.00

Soup, Dish, Blue Dresden,
8 1/4 In. 18.00

Soup, Dish, Colonial Kitchen,
Rim, 8 1/2 In. 12.00

WELLS is a shape that was made from about 1930 to 1935. Some pieces have special marks that include the word *Wells*. The Wells Art Glaze pieces are solid-color Matte Green, Peach, Rust, or Vellum (ivory). Other pieces on the Wells shape are ivory with decals. Cups have unusual "wing" handles; lids have spiral handles.

Plate, Salad, Yellow Daisies,
　Square, 8 In. 12.00
Platter, Art Glaze, Rust,
　Oval, 11 1/2 In. 35.00

WILLOW is listed in its own category.

YELLOWSTONE is an octagonal shape made from 1926 until 1937 or later. It was decorated with various decals.

Bowl, Fruit, Shaggy
　Tulip, 5 In. 4.00
Casserole, Cover, Caledonian,
　8 Sides, 8 In. 50.00
Casserole, Cover, Ivory,
　Gold Trim, 9 5/8 In. . . . 30.00
Creamer 15.00
Plate, Dinner, 10 In. 12.00
Soup, Dish, Shaggy
　Tulip 7.00

MISCELLANEOUS: There are many other patterns made by Homer Laughlin. Some are listed here.

Bowl, Americana,
　5 3/4 In. 8.00
Bowl, Dessert, Temp Pica,
　6 In. 6.75
Bowl, Fruit, Dixie Rose,
　5 3/8 In. 5.00
Bowl, Fruit, Kwaker, Ivory,
　Black Floral Band 5.00
Bowl, Majestic, 10 In. . . . 45.00
Casserole, Cover,
　Garland 99.00
Casserole, Cover, Kwaker,
　Ivory, Gold Bands 75.00
Creamer, Mt. Vernon 18.00
Cup, Ancient Mariners
　Society, Yesteryear
　Regatta, 1979 . . . . 5.00
Cup, Pastoral, Green 4.00
Cup & Saucer, Gardenia,
　Burgundy 28.50
Cup & Saucer,
　Mt. Vernon 13.00

Gravy Boat, Majestic 25.00
Plate, Bread & Butter,
　Royal Harvest, 6 In. 3.00
Plate, Bread & Butter, Royal
　Joci, Wheat, 7 1/2 In. . . . 5.00
Plate, Bread & Butter, Temp
　Pica, 6 1/4 In. 4.50
Plate, Bread, Athena, 6 In. . 2.50
Plate, Dessert, Dixie Rose,
　7 1/4 In. 5.00
Plate, Dessert, Genesee,
　Gold Trim, 7 1/4 In. . . . 48.00
Plate, Dinner, Mt. Vernon,
　10 In. 15.00
Plate, Dinner, Provincial,
　Blue Flowers, 10 In. 5.00
Plate, Dinner, Spring Garden,
　Duratone, 10 In. 7.00
Plate, Salad, Spring Garden,
　Duratone, 7 1/4 In. 4.50
Platter, Briar Rose,
　14 In. 65.00
Platter, Garland, Bird
　Scene, 11 In. 30.00
Platter, Garland, Flowers,
　11 In. 30.00
Platter, Majestic, Round,
　13 In. 45.00
Saucer, Casualstone 4.00
Saucer, Pastoral, Red 3.00
Sugar, Cover, Kwaker, Ivory,
　Gold Bands 33.00

HULL

Hull pottery was made in Crooksville, Ohio, from 1905. Addis E. Hull bought the Acme Pottery Company and started making ceramic wares. In 1917, A. E. Hull Pottery began making art pottery as well as commercial wares. For a short time, 1921 to 1929, the firm also sold pottery imported from Europe. The dinnerwares of the 1940s (including the Little Red Riding Hood line), the high gloss artwares of the 1950s, and the matte

wares of the 1940s are all popular with collectors. The firm officially closed in March 1986.

LITTLE RED RIDING HOOD is one of the easiest patterns of American dinnerware to recognize. Three-dimensional figures of the little girl with the red hood have been adapted into saltshakers, teapots, and other pieces. The pattern was made from 1943 to 1957.

Butter 480.00
Cookie Jar, 13 1/4 In. . . . 598.00
Creamer 65.00
Salt & Pepper,
　3 1/4 In. . . . . . . 65.00 to 95.00
Teapot 425.00
Wall Pocket 199.00

IROQUOIS

Iroquois China Company was founded in 1905 in Syracuse, New York. The company made mostly hotel china until 1946, when it introduced Russel Wright's Casual pattern. By the 1960s, production was limited to a few patterns, and in 1969 the factory closed.

CASUAL is a dinnerware designed by Russel Wright in 1946. It was a modern solid-color high-fired china that was guaranteed not to chip. The original colors were Ice Blue, Lemon Yellow, and Sugar White. Added later were Aqua, Avocado Yellow, Brick Red, Cantaloupe, Charcoal, Lettuce Green, Mustard Gold, Nutmeg, Oyster, Parsley Green, Pink Sherbet, and Ripe Apricot. Some pieces are listed here by their decal decorations.

Avocado Yellow

Berry Bowl . . . . . 13.00 to 15.00
Bowl, Cereal,
  5 In. . . . . 10.00 to 15.00
Bowl, Vegetable, 10 In. . . 45.00
Butter, Cover Only,
  1/2 Lb. 70.00
Casserole, Cover Only . . . 45.00
Casserole, Cover,
  Sections 50.00
Casserole, No Cover,
  2 Qt. 32.00
Casserole, Pinched Cover,
  2 Qt. . . . . 43.00 to 60.00

Coffeepot, No Cover 65.00
Creamer,
  Stacking . . . . . 13.00 to 15.00
Cup, Loop Handle 9.50
Cup & Saucer 10.00
Cup & Saucer, Loop
  Handle . . . . . . 15.00 to 30.00
Gravy Boat, Cover Only . . 78.00
Plate, Bread & Butter,
  6 1/2 In. . . . . 5.00 to 6.50
Plate, Dinner,
  10 In. . . . . 10.00 to 15.00
Plate, Luncheon,
  9 1/2 In. 15.00
Plate, Salad, 7 1/2 In. 8.00
Platter,
  12 3/4 In. . . . . 25.00 to 33.00
Platter, 14 1/2 In. 35.00
Salt & Pepper, Stacking . . 25.00
Saucer 4.00
Soup, Dish,
  5 3/8 x 2 3/4 In. 30.00
Sugar & Creamer,
  Stacking 25.00

Cantaloupe

Cup 35.00
Cup & Saucer 50.00

Charcoal

Berry Bowl 20.00
Bowl, Cereal 28.00
Butter, No Cover 70.00
Casserole, No Cover,
  2 Qt. 58.00
Creamer, Stacking 30.00
Cup, Loop Handle 18.00
Plate, Bread & Butter,
  6 1/2 In. 10.00
Plate, Luncheon, 9 In. 26.00
Salt & Pepper, Stacking . . 68.00

Gay Wings

Bowl, Cereal 20.00
Cup 18.00
Plate, Bread & Butter,
  6 1/2 In. 7.50
Plate, Dinner, 10 In. 28.00
Platter, 13 In. 35.00
Saucer 7.50
Sugar, Cover 50.00

Ice Blue

Bowl, Cereal, 5 In. 11.00
Bowl, Vegetable,
  Sections, 10 In. 38.00

Butter 45.00
Casserole, Cover Only . . . 45.00
Casserole,
  Open . . . . 25.00 to 38.00
Coffeepot, Cover Only . . . 90.00
Creamer 32.00
Creamer, Stacking 14.00
Cup 6.00
Cup, Loop Handle 12.00
Cup & Saucer . . . . 8.00 to 32.00
Plate, Bread & Butter,
  6 1/2 In. . . . . 4.00 to 5.50
Plate, Luncheon, 9 In. 12.00
Plate, Salad, 8 In. 18.00
Platter, 12 3/4 In. 30.00
Platter, 14 1/2 In. 30.00
Saltshaker, Stacking 17.00
Saucer 4.00
Soup, Gumbo 55.00
Sugar & Creamer,
  Stacking 30.00

Lemon Yellow

Berry Bowl 18.00
Bowl, Cereal 15.00
Bowl, Fruit 13.00
Casserole, No Cover 50.00
Cup 15.00
Cup & Saucer 20.00
Mug, Redesigned 90.00
Plate, Bread & Butter,
  6 1/2 In. . . . . . . 10.00 to 11.00
Plate, Dinner,
  10 1/8 In. . . . . . 11.00 to 15.00
Plate, Salad,
  7 3/8 In. . . . . . . 15.00 to 18.00
Salt & Pepper, Stacking . . 60.00
Saucer 5.50
Sugar 50.00
Teapot, Cover 245.00

Lettuce Green

Berry Bowl 18.00
Creamer 40.00
Cup 16.00
Cup, Loop Handle 17.00
Plate, Bread & Butter,
  6 1/2 In. 9.00
Saucer 5.00
Soup, Dish 55.00

Mustard Gold

Cup 20.00
Plate, Salad, 7 3/8 In. 25.00

Nutmeg

Berry Bowl . . . . . 10.00 to 15.00
Bowl, Cereal 15.00
Butter,
Cover . . . . . 150.00 to 165.00
Butter, Cover Only 90.00
Carafe 175.00
Coffeepot,
Cover . . . . 75.00 to 135.00
Cup, Loop Handle 11.00
Cup & Saucer 15.00
Plate, Bread & Butter,
6 1/2 In. . . . . 5.00 to 10.00
Plate, Dinner, 10 1/8 In. . . 14.50
Plate, Luncheon, 9 In. 19.00
Plate, Salad, 8 In. 17.00
Platter,
12 3/4 In. . . . . . 30.00 to 42.00
Platter, 14 1/2 In. 53.00
Saucer 4.00
Soup, Dish,
5 3/8 x 2 3/4 In. 30.00
Sugar & Creamer,
Stacking 30.00

Oyster

Bowl, Sections 70.00
Casserole, Cover Only . . . 60.00
Cup, Loop Handle 20.00
Plate, Bread & Butter,
6 1/2 In. 10.00
Plate, Luncheon, 9 In. 20.00
Salt & Pepper, Stacking . . 75.00
Saucer 9.00
Sugar & Creamer 75.00

Parsley Green

Bowl, Fruit, 5 1/2 In. 12.00
Bowl, Vegetable, Round,
8 In. 55.00
Plate, Bread & Butter,
6 1/2 In. 6.00
Plate, Luncheon,
9 1/2 In. 10.00
Sugar & Creamer,
Stacking 45.00

Pink Sherbet

Bowl, Vegetable, Open,
8 In. 32.00
Butter, Cover 110.00
Chop Plate 60.00
Creamer, Stacking 15.00
Mug 80.00
Platter, 12 3/4 In. 35.00

Platter, 14 1/2 In. 43.00
Salt & Pepper, Stacking . . 28.00
Sugar & Creamer,
Stacking 30.00

Ripe Apricot

Berry Bowl 15.00
Bowl, Cereal 13.00
Bowl, Sections 40.00
Butter 40.00
Casserole, Cover Only . . . 40.00
Casserole, No Cover 38.00
Coffeepot, Cover 150.00
Creamer 32.00
Creamer, Stacking 14.00
Cup, Loop Handle 10.00
Plate, Bread & Butter,
6 1/2 In. 5.50
Plate, Luncheon, 9 In. 19.00
Plate, Salad, 8 In. 17.00
Platter, 14 3/4 In. 30.00
Salt & Pepper, Stacking . . 25.00
Saucer 4.00
Soup, Dish 42.00
Soup, Gumbo 55.00
Sugar 35.00
Sugar & Creamer,
Stacking 30.00

Sugar White

Berry Bowl 16.00
Bowl, Sections 58.00
Carafe 295.00
Casserole, Cover,
Sections 75.00
Casserole, No Cover 58.00
Creamer, Stacking 27.00
Cup 17.00
Plate, Dinner,
10 In. . . . . 18.00 to 25.00
Saucer 7.00
Sugar 55.00
Teapot, Cover 200.00

White Violets

Bowl, Cereal 25.00
Cup 25.00

IMPROMPTU is a 1956 shape designed by Ben Seibel. It was offered in solid-color Bridal White and seven original patterns. The china was guaranteed not to chip or break.

Aztec

Saucer, Gold & Orange
Triangles 4.00

Beige Rose

Bowl, Cereal,
2 1/4 x 7 1/8 x 6 In. 9.00
Bowl, Fruit, Footed,
2 1/2 x 5 1/4 In. 9.00
Bowl, Vegetable, 9 1/2 x
8 3/8 x 2 3/8 In. 22.00
Creamer, 5 3/4 In. 18.00
Plate, Salad, 8 In. 9.00
Platter, 11 1/2 x 8 In. 26.00
Platter,
13 1/4 x 10 3/4 In. 28.00
Sugar, Cover,
2 1/4 x 5 7/8 In. 20.00

Sugar White

Plate, Dinner, 10 In. 7.50

LAZY DAISY has five blue and citron yellow daisies on a white background. The reverse side of the dishes are citron yellow. It was designed by Ben Seibel.

Bowl, Vegetable,
10 1/2 x 9 In. 35.00
Plate, Dinner, 10 In. 9.00
Platter, 12 In. . . . 12.50 to 16.00
Platter, 15 1/2 In. 55.00
Pot, Cover, 1 Qt. 65.00
Sugar, Cover 25.00

ROSEMARY has three long-stemmed roses on a white background. The reverse side is gray-green. It was designed by Ben Seibel.

Bowl, Salad, 7 In. 15.00
Creamer 25.00
Cup & Saucer 15.00
Plate, Salad, 8 In. 10.00
Platter, 11 In. 25.00
Platter, 13 In. 35.00

JOHNSON BROTHERS

Brothers Frederick and Alfred Johnson started their pottery business in Stoke-on-Trent, England, in 1883. The company made ironstone and semi-porcelain dinnerware with printed underglaze decorations. In 1968, Johnson Brothers became part of the Wedgwood Group (which became the Waterford Wedgwood Group in 1995).

FRIENDLY VILLAGE is made by Johnson Brothers, Ltd. of Hanley, England, now part of the Waterford Wedgwood Group. The pattern has been made since 1953 and is still being made. It is decorated with a black transfer design tinted in pastel colors and features scenes of rural life.

Bowl, Fruit, Village
   Scenes 12.00
Bowl, Square, Covered
   Bridge, 6 1/4 In. 13.00
Chop Plate, 14 In. 150.00
Mug, 3 1/4 In. 12.00
Plate, Bread & Butter, Sugar
   Maples, 6 In. . . . . 6.00 to 7.00
Plate, Salad, Covered
   Bridge, 7 1/2 In. 12.00
Saucer, Harvest Time 4.00
Teapot,
   8 3/4 x 9 1/2 In. 130.00
Tumbler, Covered Bridge,
   4 1/8 x 3 1/8 In. 5.00

KNOWLES

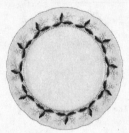

Edwin M. Knowles China Company was founded in Chester, West Virginia, in 1900. The offices were located in nearby East Liverpool, Ohio. In 1913, a new factory was built in Newell, West Virginia. The company closed in 1963. The name was purchased by another company and has appeared on plates since 1977.

LEAF DANCE has green leaves and dots around the rim and a scalloped edge.

Bowl, Cereal 6.00
Bowl, Fruit 4.00
Cup & Saucer 9.00
Gravy Boat 12.00
Plate, Bread & Butter,
   6 In. 4.00
Plate, Dessert, 6 In. 5.00
Plate, Dinner, 10 In. 9.00
Serving Bowl, Oval 8.00
Sugar & Creamer 17.00

MARION is a ribbed shape with octagonal flat pieces that was introduced c.1930. It was made in solid Green and Pink and in Ivory with decal decorations.

Green
Bowl, 6 x 6 In. 7.00
Cup, 6 Oz. 5.00
Saucer, 5 7/8 In. 5.00

PEONY has pink flowers with yellow centers and gray-green leaves. It has a scalloped rim and gold trim.

Bowl, Fruit 3.00

Plate, Bread & Butter,
6 In. 6.00

Plate, Dinner, 10 In. 10.00

WHEAT is a 1954 pattern with a simple design of wheat stalks.

Bowl, 5 1/4 In. 2.00

Chop Plate, Handles,
Round, 13 3/4 In. 15.00

Plate, Bread & Butter,
6 In. 3.00

Plate, Dinner, 9 In. 5.00

Plate, Luncheon, 7 In. 4.00

Saucer 2.00

Soup, Dish, 7 1/2 In. 4.00

WINSLOW is a floral pattern with a scalloped rim and gold trim.

Bowl, Fruit 5.00

Cup & Saucer 12.00

Plate, Bread & Butter,
6 In. 5.00

Plate, Dinner, 10 In. 12.00

Platter 20.00

Serving Bowl 10.00

Soup, Dish 9.00

MISCELLANEOUS: There are many other patterns made by Knowles. Some are listed here.

Bowl, Horizontal Ribs,
Yellowware, 10 In. 8.00

Creamer, Floral 9.00

Platter, Floral 12.00

Platter, Handles, Yorktown,
Green, 12 1/2 In. 21.00

Sauceboat, Floral 18.00

Serving Bowl, Floral 12.00

Sugar, Cover, Fruit 63.00

METLOX

Metlox Potteries was founded in 1927 in Manhattan Beach, California. The company originally made ceramic fittings for neon signs. Metlox's first dinnerware was made in 1931. In 1958, the company bought molds and rights to the trademark *Vernonware* from Vernon Kilns. The factory closed in 1989.

ANTIQUE GRAPE is a pattern introduced by Metlox Potteries in 1964. The firm had been making a pattern called Sculptured Grape with a raised grapevine border in natural colors. Antique Grape is the same shape but, according to a company brochure, has "carved grapes and leaves raised on a soft beige antique finish against a warm white background." It was made until at least 1975.

Bowl, Vegetable 71.00

Bowl, Vegetable,
Cover 104.00

Platter, Medium 54.00

Creamer 29.00

Cup & Saucer .... 6.75 to 12.00

Gravy Boat, Underplate .. 10.00

Plate, Bread & Butter,
6 In. 5.00

Plate, Salad, Poppytrail,
7 5/8 In. 8.00

Saucer, 6 1/8 In. ... 2.25 to 4.00

Sugar 9.00

Sugar, Cover,
3 x 3 1/4 In. 25.00

AUTUMN BERRY was pictured in the 1979 Metlox brochure. The pattern features brown leaves and berries.

Plate, Dinner, 10 In. 20.00

Saucer 4.00

CALIFORNIA APPLE has two red apples on a branch. It was a Poppytrail pattern made on the Ivy shape. The pattern was introduced in 1949.

Bowl, Vegetable,
Sections 14.00

Chop Plate,
13 In. .... 22.50 to 25.00

Plate, Bread & Butter,
6 1/2 In. .... 3.00 to 6.00

Plate, Dinner, 9 3/8 In. 6.25

CALIFORNIA AZTEC is made on the Freeform shape. It is white with a wiggly black line as the design. It was introduced in 1955.

Bowl, Vegetable, 7 In. 8.50

Bowl, Vegetable,
Sections 250.00

CALIFORNIA DEL REY was in the 1955 Metlox brochures. It is made on the Confetti shape. California Del Rey is blue and white; California Confetti is pink and white. Both patterns look like bits of confetti were dropped on the plates. Pieces like pitchers and sugar bowls are white on the inside, solid color on the outside.

Bowl, Cereal, 6 7/8 In. 16.00

Plate, Bread & Butter,
6 1/2 In. . . . . 6.00 to 8.00
Plate, Salad,
8 In. . . . . 10.00 to 14.00

CALIFORNIA FRUIT is a Poppytrail pattern that includes six different fruits, each on a different item.

Cup 11.00
Teapot 75.00

CALIFORNIA IVY was one of the most popular patterns made by Metlox. It was introduced in 1946. The pattern was named for its ivy vine border.

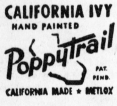

Bowl, Vegetable, Round,
9 1/4 In. 40.00
Butter, Cover, 1/4 Lb. 50.00
Chop Plate 10.00
Cup & Saucer 7.00
Gravy Boat 4.00
Plate, Bread & Butter,
6 1/2 In. . . . . 4.00 to 5.00
Plate, Luncheon,
9 3/8 In. 7.00

Salt & Pepper 28.00
Teapot, Cover,
6 1/2 x 10 5/8 In. 90.00

CALIFORNIA PROVINCIAL dinnerware pictures a maroon, green, and yellow rooster in the center. It has a border made up of a wavy line and dots. It was made beginning in 1950. A similar design, with a different border, was called Red Rooster. Green Rooster is another name for California Rooster.

Ashtray, Square, 6 In. 59.00
Ashtray, Square, 10 In. . . 101.00
Bowl, 6 In. 6.00
Bowl, Vegetable 45.00
Bread Box 85.00
Bread Tray, Handles,
10 1/2 In. 16.00
Butter, Cover 33.00
Canister, Flour 80.00
Chop Plate, 12 In. 65.00
Cigarette Box, 5 x 3 In. . . . 8.50
Coaster,
3 3/4 In. . . . . . . 20.00 to 24.00
Condiment Set,
9 Piece 175.00
Creamer 28.00
Cup 10.00
Cup & Saucer 21.00
Gravy Boat 50.00
Mug, 5 In., Pair 34.00
Pepper Mill 59.00
Pitcher, 6 1/2 In. 31.00
Pitcher, Water, 2 1/2 Qt.,
10 In. 165.00
Plate, Bread & Butter,
6 In. . . . . 4.00 to 8.00
Plate, Dinner,
10 In. . . . . 6.50 to 15.00
Plate, Salad, 7 1/2 In. . . . 10.00
Platter, Oval,
13 1/2 In. . . . . . 21.00 to 30.00
Salt & Pepper . . . . 6.00 to 15.00
Saucer . . . . 3.00 to 5.00
Soup, Dish 20.00
Sugar, Cover 40.00
Sugar & Creamer 13.00

Teapot 150.00
Tureen, Ladle,
16 x 9 7/8 x 9 In. 566.00

CALIFORNIA STRAWBERRY has red strawberries, avocado green leaves, and avocado green trim. The outside of the hollowware is avocado green. Lids have strawberry knobs. It is a Poppytrail pattern that was introduced in 1961.

Bowl, Cereal, 5 3/8 In. . . . 10.00
Bowl, Cereal, 5 5/8 In. . . . 14.00
Bowl, Sections,
9 In. . . . . 35.00 to 45.00
Canister Set, Covers,
4 Piece 60.00
Creamer 18.00
Cup 8.00
Cup & Saucer 5.00
Gravy Boat 35.00
Mug . . . . 18.00 to 20.00
Plate, Bread & Butter,
6 1/2 In. . . . . 6.00 to 7.00
Plate, Dinner,
10 In. . . . . 6.00 to 20.00
Plate, Salad, 8 In. 5.00
Platter, 13 In. 18.00
Saltshaker 10.00
Saucer 2.00
Soup, Dish,
6 3/4 In. . . . . . . 4.00 to 13.00
Sugar, Cover 20.00
Sugar & Creamer 10.00

CALIFORNIA TEMPO is featured in the 1961 catalog. It is a solid-color pattern made with yellow, blue, or chartreuse on the front, walnut brown on the back.

Bowl, 6 In. 6.00
Bowl, Vegetable,
Round 22.50
Cup & Saucer, 6 In. 12.00
Plate, Dinner,
10 1/4 In. . . . . . . 7.00 to 20.50
Plate, Salad, 8 In. 8.00
Platter, Oval, 13 1/4 In. . . 25.00

CAMELLIA has a border of pink camellias and green leaves in relief on a creamy white background. It was made in two versions, one with a brown border and one with an olive border. It was introduced in 1946.

Bowl, Fruit, 6 In. 13.00
Cup, Prouty 10.00
Plate, Bread & Butter,
6 In. 8.00
Saucer 4.00

COLORSTAX is a pattern that was made to mix and match. Pieces were made in solid colors and could be bought in any combination. Chocolate, Fern Green, Forest Green, Midnight Blue, Sand, Sky Blue, Terra-Cotta, White, and Yellow were used. These 1970s dishes were dishwasher, oven, and microwave safe.

COLORSTAX
Sky Blue
Butter, Cover 8.00
Platter, 13 1/4 In. 26.00
Terra-Cotta
Creamer, 4 x 4 3/4 In. 12.00
Cup & Saucer 7.00

Plate, Salad, 8 In. 8.00
Salt & Pepper 12.00

DELLA ROBBIA shape was made in 1965. Vernon Della Robbia, seen in the 1974 catalog, was this shape with a brown, green, and beige border of leaves and flowers.

Bowl, Vegetable,
Cover 104.00
Casserole 56.00
Coffeepot, Antiqua 67.00
Baker, Oval,
12 1/8 x 9 1/4 In. 36.00
Bowl, Fruit, 6 1/2 In. 12.00
Bowl, Vegetable,
2 Sections, 12 1/8 In. . . . 55.00
Bowl, Vegetable,
Cover, 7 1/4 x 5 In. 35.00
Bowl, Vegetable,
Round, 9 1/2 In. 28.00
Bowl, Vegetable, Round,
10 1/2 In. . . . . . 24.00 to 32.00
Butter, Cover 28.00
Casserole, Cover 66.00
Coffeepot, Cover,
10 1/2 In. 85.00
Creamer,
10 Oz. . . . . 18.00 to 21.00
Cup & Saucer, 8 Oz.,
6 1/2 In. 11.00
Gravy Boat 55.00
Plate, Bread & Butter,
6 1/2 In. 7.00
Plate, Dinner, 10 5/8 In. . . 11.00
Plate, Salad, 7 5/8 In. 9.00
Platter, 9 5/8 In. 34.00
Platter,
11 1/8 In. . . . . 20.00 to 57.00
Platter, 14 1/2 In. 26.00
Saucer 4.00
Sugar, Cover 28.00

FRUIT BASKET has a basket of fruit and flowers in the center, a border of brushstrokes, scalloped edges, and fluting. It is a Vernonware pattern made on the San Fernando shape and was introduced in 1961.

Bowl, Fruit, 6 In. 13.00
Chop Plate, 14 1/4 In. 35.00

Cup & Saucer 7.00
Gravy Boat, Underplate . . 30.00
Plate, Dinner, 10 3/4 In. . . 10.00
Platter, Oval, 13 In. 18.00
Platter, Oval, 14 In. 7.00

HOMESTEAD PROVINCIAL is one of the Poppytrail patterns by Metlox Potteries. The designs are based on Early American folk art themes. Homestead Provincial is dark green and burgundy. Other patterns are the same design but in different colors. Colonial Homestead is red and brown, and Provincial Blue is blue.

Ashtray,
6 1/2 x 6 1/2 In. 22.00
Bowl, 6 In. 12.00
Bowl, Salad Set,
11 1/4 In., 3 Piece 75.00
Bowl, Vegetable,
2 Sections, Rim 55.00
Chop Plate, Round,
11 3/4 In. 25.00
Chop Plate, Round,
12 In. 55.00
Creamer, Cover . . 8.00 to 30.00
Cup & Saucer 15.00
Plate, Bread & Butter,
6 In. 7.00
Plate, Dinner, 10 In. 25.00
Plate, Luncheon, 9 In. 18.00
Plate, Salad, 7 1/2 In. 12.00
Platter, 13 1/2 In. 45.00
Saltshaker, Stopper 13.00
Saucer 4.00
Sugar 26.00
Sugar, Cover 30.00

LA MANCHA is a Poppytrail pattern on the American Tradition shape. It was made in Gold, Green, or White with black borders. It may or may not have a large black flower in the center.

Gold
Cup & Saucer 12.00
Green
Creamer, 9 Oz.,
5 1/2 In. 16.00

Cup & Saucer 10.00
Plate, Salad, 8 3/4 In. 9.00
Platter, Oval,
   11 7/8 x 8 7/8 In. 25.00

White
Bowl, Cereal, 6 1/4 In. 7.00
Cup 5.00
Plate, Dinner, 10 1/2 In. . . . 5.00
Platter, 14 1/2 In. 25.00
Saucer 2.00

LOTUS is a shape introduced in 1974. The First Series was made in Lime, Pink, White, and Yellow. It was discontinued in 1975 and reintroduced in 1977. Several new colors were added when the Second Series was introduced in 1979. Four patterns of Decorated Lotus were also made c.1980 to 1985.

Lime
Bowl, Cereal, 6 3/4 In. . . . 10.00
Plate, Dinner, 11 In. 9.00
Plate, Salad, 8 1/2 In. 8.00

Peach
Bowl, Fruit, 5 7/8 x 2 In. . . 9.00

Pink
Plate, Dinner, 11 In. 9.00

Yellow
Plate, Bread & Butter,
   6 In. 12.00
Plate, Dinner,
   11 In. . . . . 9.00 to 24.00

MARGARITA was featured in the 1971 brochure. It is a hand-painted golden-yellow pattern on a burnt orange background.

Bowl, Cereal, 5 1/2 In. . . . 13.00
Bowl, Sugar, Cover 25.00
Bowl, Vegetable,
   9 1/2 In. 25.00
Creamer 15.00
Cup & Saucer 10.00
Plate, Dinner, 10 In. 12.00
Plate, Salad, 8 In. 8.00
Platter, 13 In. 30.00
Salt & Pepper 30.00
Saucer 3.00

NAVAJO pattern has a turquoise and light brown decoration on the border and solid pieces in turquoise and light brown. It was the first design made on the Navajo shape.

Bowl, Cereal 6.00
Bowl, Vegetable,
   8 3/4 In. 15.00
Bowl, Vegetable, Oval,
   Divided, 16 3/4 In. 13.00
Butter, Cover . . . 10.00 to 18.00
Cup & Saucer 7.00
Plate, Dinner,
   10 1/2 In. . . . . 3.00 to 6.50
Platter, 14 3/4 x
   9 1/4 In. . . . . . . 8.00 to 11.00
Soup, Dish 5.00
Sugar & Creamer 10.00

PEPPER TREE is a 1957 pattern decorated with a leaf pattern in bronze-green and sun-gold.

Bowl, Vegetable,
   8 3/4 x 2 In. 14.00
Creamer 23.00
Cup, Green, Satin Finish . . 7.00
Gravy Boat 56.00
Plate, Bread & Butter,
   Green, 6 1/2 In. 7.00
Platter, 11 In. 55.00
Saucer, Green 3.00
Vase, 6 1/4 In. 16.00

PROVINCIAL BLUE is a Metlox Potteries pattern that was made from 1950 to about 1968. It is decorated with blue scenes of farm life. A similar pattern, Homestead Provincial, features the designs in other colors.

Lazy Susan Set, 10 1/2 x 9 In.,
   6 Piece 175.00
Candleholder, Handle 3.00
Canister, Coffee, Cover . . 95.00
Canister, Sugar, Cover . . . 45.00
Canister, Tea, Cover 85.00
Cruet Set, 5 Piece 150.00
Cup & Saucer 12.00
Mustard, Cover,
   4 3/4 x 3 1/8 In. 55.00
Plate, Dessert, 6 3/8 In. . . . 2.00
Plate, Dinner, 10 In. 20.00
Teapot, 7 Cup 45.00

PROVINCIAL FRUIT pattern was made in 1965. It is part of the Poppytrail line. Another pattern called Provincial Fruit was made by Purinton, but it is not listed here.

Butter 34.00
Plate, Salad, 7 3/4 In. 12.00
Soup, Dish, 8 In. 8.00

RED ROOSTER is a pattern in the Poppytrail line made beginning in 1955. It is easy to identify because the center design is a large red rooster. Some pieces are made in solid red and some look as if they have rivets. California Provincial is a similar design with a different border. Another similar pattern is called Rooster Bleu.

Bowl, 2 Sections,
   Beaded Handle,
   8 1/2 x 5 1/2 In. 75.00
Bowl, Cereal, 7 In. 13.00
Bowl, Dessert, Rim,
   6 In. 10.00
Bowl, Fruit,
   6 In. . . . . 10.00 to 14.00
Bowl, Porridge, Handle . . 25.00
Bowl, Vegetable,
   8 x 2 1/2 In. 65.00

Bowl, Vegetable, Round,
  10 x 2 1/2 In. . . 35.00 to 40.00
Bowl, Vegetable, Sections,
  Red, 8 1/2 x 5 1/2 In. . . . 75.00
Butter 65.00
Butter, Red,
  8 x 2 1/2 In. 65.00
Canister, Coffee, Cover . . 60.00
Canister, Flour, Cover . . . 75.00
Canister, Sugar, Cover . . . 35.00
Canister, Tea, Cover 90.00
Carafe, Coffee, Cover,
  44 Oz., 6 Cup 100.00
Coaster 15.00
Coffeepot, Cover 100.00
Creamer . . . . 15.00 to 25.00
Cruet, Cover Only 5.00
Cup 8.00
Dish, Hen On Nest Cover,
  6 1/2 x 7 1/2 In. 39.00
Gravy Boat, 6 1/2 In. 45.00
Mustard, No Cover 10.00
Plate, Bread & Butter,
  6 In. 5.00
Plate, Dinner,
  10 In. . . . . 10.00 to 15.00
Plate, Salad,
  7 1/2 In. . . . . . . 8.00 to 12.00
Salt & Pepper 30.00
Saltshaker, Red,
  4 x 2 In. 22.00
Saucer 3.00
Serving Bowl, Red,
  8 x 2 1/2 In. 65.00
Shaker, Pepper, Red,
  4 x 2 In. 22.00
Soup, Dish,
  8 In. . . . . 20.00 to 23.00
Soup, Rim,
  8 In. . . . . 10.00 to 13.00
Sugar 13.00
Sugar, Cover 25.00
Sugar & Creamer,
  Cover 60.00

SAN FERNANDO is a Vernon-ware pattern made by Metlox beginning in 1966. It is amber and golden brown decorated with a scroll design. Some pieces have a brown exterior and amber interior.

Bowl, Cereal, 6 7/8 In. . . . 13.00

Cup & Saucer, Brown
  Scalloped Border 2.50
Plate, Bread & Butter,
  6 5/8 In. 6.00
Platter, Scalloped Edge . . 12.00
Salt & Pepper 12.00
Saucer 4.00

SCULPTURED DAISY was made in 1964 as part of the Poppytrail line. The pattern features raised white daisies and green leaves.

Cookie Jar 125.00
Bowl, 12 1/2 x 4 1/4 In. . . 75.00
Bowl, Fruit, 6 1/2 In. 13.00
Bowl, Vegetable, Sections,
  Round, 7 In. . . . 30.00 to 35.00
Bowl, Vegetable, Sections,
  Round, 9 In. 30.00
Butter, Cover 21.00
Canister Set, Covers, 3 1/4 to
  5 3/4 In., 4 Piece 91.00
Chip & Dip, 12 In. 71.00
Creamer . . . . 20.00 to 24.00
Cup . . . . 7.00 to 9.00
Cup & Saucer 12.00
Gravy Boat,
  Fastand . . . . . . 32.00 to 58.00
Pitcher, 2 Qt. 13.00
Plate, Bread & Butter,
  6 In. . . . . 5.00 to 6.00
Plate, Dinner, 10 1/2 In. . . 12.00
Plate, Salad,
  7 1/2 In. . . . . 7.00 to 8.00
Platter,
  11 3/4 In. . . . . . 35.00 to 65.00
Platter, Oval,
  14 1/4 In. . . . . . 32.00 to 85.00
Platter, Round,
  8 7/8 In. 55.00
Salt & Pepper 25.00
Saucer . . . . 2.50 to 4.00
Sugar, Cover . . . . 22.00 to 32.00

Sugar & Creamer 13.00
Teapot, Cover, 7 Cup 75.00

SCULPTURED GRAPE is a pattern made by Metlox Potteries as part of the Poppytrail line from 1963 to 1975. The pattern has a raised grapevine colored blue, brown, and green.

Casserole, Cover, 1 Qt.,
  9 x 4 1/4 In. 68.00
Bowl, Cereal, 7 1/2 In. . . . 13.00
Bowl, Fruit,
  6 1/2 In. . . . . . . 11.00 to 20.00
Bowl, Vegetable, 2 Sections,
  9 1/2 In. . . . . . . 23.00 to 55.00
Bowl, Vegetable,
  8 1/2 In. 35.00
Bowl, Vegetable,
  9 1/2 In. 22.00
Butter, Cover 30.00
Canister, 7 1/2 In. 20.00
Canister, Cover,
  5 1/2 In. 40.00
Casserole, Cover, 6 In. . . . 30.00
Casserole, Cover,
  8 1/2 In. 80.00
Compote, 4 3/4 x
  8 1/2 In. 41.00
Creamer . . . . 18.00 to 26.00
Cup 10.00
Cup & Saucer 8.00
Gravy Boat, Attached
  Underplate . . . . 22.00 to 35.00
Plate, Bread & Butter,
  6 1/4 In. . . . . 4.00 to 12.00
Plate, Dinner, 10 1/2 In. . . 22.00
Plate, Salad,
  7 1/2 In. . . . . . . 10.00 to 14.00
Platter, 12 3/8 x 9 In. 12.00
Platter, Oval, 12 In. 7.50
Platter, Oval,
  14 1/2 In. . . . . . 23.00 to 50.00
Salt & Pepper . . . 25.00 to 26.00
Saucer, 6 1/4 In. . . . 3.00 to 6.00
Soup, Rim,
  8 1/4 x 1 3/4 In. 14.00

Sugar 10.00
Sugar, Cover . . . . 25.00 to 34.00
Sugar & Creamer 12.00

SCULPTURED ZINNIA is a
pattern made from 1964 to
1980 as part of the Poppytrail
line. The Sculptured Zinnia
shape was made in three color
variations named Lavender
Blue, Memories, and Sculptured
Zinnia.

Bowl, Cereal,
7 3/8 In. . . . . . . 12.00 to 13.00
Bowl, Fruit,
6 3/8 In. . . . . . . 11.00 to 12.00
Bowl, Vegetable 30.00
Butter, Cover 50.00
Casserole, Cover,
9 1/2 In. 40.00
Creamer . . . . . . 20.00 to 26.00
Cup 9.00
Cup & Saucer, 7 Oz.,
6 1/8 In. 10.00
Plate, Bread & Butter,
6 In. 7.00
Plate, Dinner, 10 1/4 In. . . 13.00
Plate, Salad, 7 1/2 In. 9.00
Platter, 12 In. 35.00
Platter, 14 In. 40.00
Salt & Pepper 20.00
Saltshaker, 3 7/8 In. 8.00
Saucer . . . . 3.00 to 4.00
Sugar, Cover 8.00
Sugar & Creamer 22.00

TRUE BLUE is a 1974 Vernon-
ware pattern. It has scalloped
edges and fluted details. There
is a blue floral design on an off-
white background.

Coffeepot 67.00
Creamer, 8 Oz. 25.00
Pitcher, Medium, 1 Qt. . . . 55.00
Bowl, Vegetable,
Scalloped Edge, Fluted,
8 1/4 In. 35.00
Casserole, Cover,
1 1/4 Qt. 80.00
Creamer, 8 Oz. 29.00
Gravy Boat, Fastand 28.00
Mug, 8 Oz. 24.50
Pitcher, 1 Qt. 55.00
Platter, Oval, 12 3/8 In. . . 55.00
Salt & Pepper 25.00
Saucer 4.00
Sugar, Cover, Scalloped
Edge, Fluted, 8 Oz. 32.00

VINEYARD is a pattern shown
in the 1974 brochure. It is decorated with a border of grapevine
leaves in fall tones with blue
grapes.

Bowl, Vegetable, Sections,
11 1/4 In. 55.00
Bowl, Cereal,
7 In. . . . . 7.50 to 14.00
Bowl, Fruit,
6 In. . . . . 11.00 to 12.00
Bowl, Vegetable,
8 1/2 In. 35.00
Bowl, Vegetable, Cover,
9 In. 16.00
Bowl, Vegetable, Oval,
11 In. 50.00
Butter, Cover 55.00
Casserole, Cover,
7 1/2 In. 8.00
Creamer 22.00
Cup 10.00
Gravy Boat, Attached
Underplate . . . . 35.00 to 65.00
Pitcher, 6 In. 21.00
Plate, Bread & Butter,
6 5/8 In. 7.00
Plate, Dinner, 10 1/2 In. . . 13.00
Plate, Salad, 7 1/4 In. 9.00
Platter, Oval, 11 1/4 In. . . 64.00
Platter, Oval, 13 3/4 In. . . 40.00
Salt & Pepper 25.00
Saucer, 6 In. . . . . . . 2.50 to 3.00
Soup, Dish, 8 In. 4.00

Sugar 16.00
Teapot, 8 3/4 In. 21.00

WOODLAND GOLD is from
the 1970s. It features leaves in
fall colors.

Platter, Oval, 11 In. 55.00
Bowl, Cereal, 5 5/8 In. . . . 13.00
Butter, Round 45.00
Creamer 23.00
Cup & Saucer 7.00
Gravy Boat . . . . . 56.00 to 65.00
Plate, Bread & Butter,
6 3/8 In. 6.00
Plate, Salad, 8 In. 5.00
Platter, Oval,
13 1/4 In. 8.50
Salt & Pepper 6.00
Sugar, Cover . . . . 28.00 to 32.00
Sugar, Cover Only 5.00

YORKSHIRE was made in sev-
eral different solid colors in
both glossy and satin glazes.
Plates have a swirled rim, and
cups and serving pieces are
swirled on the outside. The pattern was introduced in 1937 as
part of the Poppytrail line.

Bowl, Cereal, Lug
Handle 20.00

Bowl, Fruit, 6 In. 8.00

Chop Plate 50.00

Coffeepot, Art Deco
Yellow, Wooden
Handle, 8 1/2 In. 33.00

Plate, Bread & Butter,
6 In. 6.00

Plate, Luncheon, 9 In. 10.00

Salt & Pepper 25.00

Soup, Dish, Mauve,
8 3/4 In. 10.00

MISCELLANEOUS: There are
many other patterns made by
Metlox. Some are listed here.

Bowl, Vegetable, Sections,
Oval, Sculptured Berry,
10 3/4 x 6 In. 58.00

Platter, Round, Calico,
Medium 55.00

Bowl, Fruit, Sculptured
Berry, 6 In. 22.00

Bowl, Salad, Classic Flower,
Cream, 7 1/8 In. 8.00

Bowl, Vegetable, Colonial
Heritage, 8 x 2 3/8 In. .. 30.00

Creamer, Golden Fruit,
6 Oz. 18.00

Cup & Saucer, Classic
Flower, Cream 12.00

Cup & Saucer, Quail
Ridge 4.00

Cup & Saucer, Sculptured Berry,
3 1/4 x 3 1/4 In. 20.00

Gravy Boat, Quail Ridge . 10.00

Gravy Boat, Underplate,
Gold Dahlia,
7 1/2 In. x 3 5/8 In. 16.00

Plate, Bread & Butter, Colonial
Heritage, 6 1/2 In. 8.00

Plate, Bread & Butter, Del Rey,
Gray Ground, 6 1/4 In. .. 8.00

Plate, Bread & Butter,
Vernon Rose, 6 5/8 In. .. 6.00

Plate, Dessert, Autumn
Leaves, 6 In. 5.00

Plate, Dinner, Colonial
Heritage, 10 In. 11.00

Plate, Dinner, Vernon
Rose, 10 3/4 In. 20.00

Plate, Dinner, Wild Poppy,
10 3/4 In. ..... 10.00 to 12.00

Plate, Salad, Del Rey,
8 In. 14.00

Plate, Salad, Wild Poppy,
8 In. .... 6.00 to 9.00

Platter, Oval, Gold Dahlia,
13 x 10 In. 18.00

Platter, Oval, Quail Ridge,
14 In. 10.00

Salt & Pepper, Heavenly
Days 13.00

Saucer, Butterscotch,
6 3/8 In. 6.00

Saucer, Classic Flower, Ribbed
Border, Gold Band 3.00

Saucer, Grape Arbor 4.00

Saucer, Vernon Rose 4.00

Sugar, Cover, Golden Fruit,
8 Oz. 18.00

Sugar & Creamer, Quail
Ridge 15.00

NORITAKE

Noritake porcelain was
made in Japan after 1904
by Nippon Toki Kaisha.
The best-known Noritake
pieces are marked with
the M in a wreath for the
Morimura Brothers, a
New York City distribut-
ing company. This mark
was used until 1941.

AZALEA pattern by Noritake
was made for Larkin Company
customers from 1918 to 1941.
Larkin, the soap company, was
in Buffalo, New York. Each
piece of the white china was
decorated with pink azaleas and
green leaves.

Butter, Insert, 5 1/2 In. ... 40.00

Butter, Liner, 2 Square Handles,
Wreath M Mark 100.00

Cake Plate, 9 1/2 In. 40.00

Celery Dish, Open Handles,
12 3/4 In. 225.00

Dish, Mayonnaise, Underplate,
Spoon, Footed 145.00

Pickle, No. 121, Plastic
Fork, 5 1/2 In. 24.00

Plate, Dinner, 10 In. 15.00

Platter, 11 1/2 In. 40.00

Platter, 13 1/2 In. 40.00

Relish, Sections,
8 1/4 In. 40.00

Sugar & Creamer, Gold Trim,
Blue Mark, c.1915 ..... 45.00

Sugar & Creamer, Pink &
Gold Beading & Trim,
Crown Mark 150.00

Underplate, No. 3,
5 3/8 In. 12.00

ROSEVILLE has a large pink
rose, small blue flowers, taupe
leaves, and gold trim. It was
made in the 1960s.

Bowl, Dessert, 5 1/2 In. ... 4.50

Bread & Butter,
6 3/8 In. .... 4.50 to 7.00

Cup & Saucer .... 9.75 to 16.00

Plate, Dinner, 10 In. 20.00

Plate, Salad, 8 In. 10.00
Saucer 3.00
Soup, Dish 16.00
Sugar 26.00
Sugar, Cover 38.00

TREE IN THE MEADOW is another pattern made for the Larkin Company in the early 1900s.

Bowl, Shrimp 225.00
Coffeepot, 6 1/2 In. 350.00
Platter, Oval, 11 5/8 In. . . 40.00
Saltshaker, 6 1/2 In. 45.00

PURINTON

Purinton Pottery

Purinton Pottery Company was incorporated in Wellsville, Ohio, in 1936. The company moved to Shippenville, Pennsylvania, in 1941 and made a variety of hand-painted ceramic wares. By the 1950s, Purinton was making dinnerware, souvenirs, cookie jars, and florist wares. The pottery closed in 1959.

APPLE, sometimes called Open Apple by collectors, was made by Purinton in the early 1940s. It was designed by William Blair. The hand-decorated pattern features an open apple colored red with yellow and brown highlights. The stems and leaves are green, blue, and dark brown. The trim colors are red, cobalt blue, or blue-green. If the decoration is a closed apple, it is part of the Fruit pattern.

Bean Pot, Cover,
    3 1/2 In. . . . . . . 18.00 to 44.00
Bowl, Vegetable, Divided,
    11 In. 38.00
Butter, Rolled Handle,
    7 In. 53.00
Canister, Cover Only 19.00
Canister, Sugar, Cover,
    9 In. 25.00
Canister, Tea, Cover 25.00
Canister Set, Covers,
    5 Piece 71.00
Chop Plate, 12 In. 70.00
Creamer, Cover 10.00
Cruet, 6 In. 40.00
Cruet Set, Oil & Vinegar,
    5 In., 2 Piece 41.00
Cup 6.50
Jelly & Jam Dish, Divided,
    Jelly & Jam On Center
    Handle . . . . 53.00 to 75.00
Jug, Kent, 4 1/2 In. 8.00
Mug, Beer, 16 Oz., 5 In. . . 68.00
Pitcher, 5 In. 33.00
Pitcher, Long Spout,
    7 In. 13.00
Platter, 12 x 9 In. 23.00
Salt & Pepper, Jug Shape, Cork
    Stoppers, 2 1/2 In. 15.00
Sandwich Server, 12 In. . . 53.00
Shake & Pour, 4 1/2 In. . . 37.00

❖

Put foam or paper plates between the china plates stacked for storage.

❖

Snack Plate, Cup Indent,
    8 1/2 In. 9.00
Sugar & Creamer 10.00
Teapot,
    6 1/2 In. . . . . . . 75.00 to 90.00
Tidbit, 3 Sections,
    9 1/2 In. 21.00
Tumbler, 3 In., 6 Piece . . . 30.00
Vase, 5 In. 42.00
Wall Pocket,
    3 3/4 x 4 1/2 In. 38.00

FRUIT was made from 1936 to about 1950. It pictures a variety of large fruits.

Bowl, Cover, 6 1/2 In. . . . 29.00
Canister Set, Covers, 8 In.,
    4 Piece 60.00
Coffee & Tea Set,
    4 Piece 60.00
Jug, 2 Qt. 35.00
Jug, Dutch, 2 Pt.,
    5 3/4 In. 7.00
Oil & Vinegar, Square,
    5 In. 50.00
Pitcher, 16 Oz.,
    4 1/2 In. 10.00
Relish, 3 Sections,
    Wooden Center Handle,
    Apple, Grapes, 10 In. . . 45.00
Salt & Pepper,
    4 1/4 In. . . . . . . 10.00 to 30.00
Teapot, Individual,
    2 Cup, 4 In. 50.00

INTAGLIO has an incised design on a colored background of Black, Blue, Brown, Coral, Golden Brown, Green, or Turquoise. It was made from 1936 to 1959.

Brown
Baker, 7 In. 22.00

Bowl, 8 In. 5.00
Casserole, Cover, Oval,
  Handles, 7 In. 55.00
Cookie Jar, Square, Wooden
  Cover, 9 1/2 x 6 In. 75.00
Jam Jar, Cover 50.00
Mug, 4 In. 18.00
Mug, Beer, 16 Oz., 5 In. . . 16.00
Plate, Bread & Butter,
  6 3/4 In. 6.50
Plate, Dinner, 9 3/4 In. . . . 13.00
Plate, Salad, 8 1/2 In. 10.00
Platter, 12 In. 25.00
Relish, 2 Sections,
  10 In. 30.00
Saucer 4.00
Sugar, Cover 20.00

IVY was made with either a red or yellow flower and was produced in the early to mid-1940s.

Red Blossom

Creamer, 3 1/2 In. 15.00
Jug, Dutch, 6 In. 55.00
Jug, Honey, 6 1/4 In. 35.00
Pitcher, 4 1/2 x 5 1/2 In. . . 15.00
Teapot, 4 Cup, 5 In. 25.00

Yellow Blossom

Creamer, 5 In. 9.00
Jug, Kent, 4 1/2 In. 6.50
Teapot, 6 Cup, 6 In. 12.00

NORMANDY PLAID is a red plaid pattern made from 1936 to 1959.

Canister Set, Lazy Susan,
  4 Sections,
  10 x 10 In. 190.00
Jug, 2 Qt., 7 1/2 In. 110.00
Salt & Pepper 6.75
Sugar, Cover 7.00

MISCELLANEOUS: There are many other patterns made by Purinton. Some are listed here.

Honey Jug, Morning Glory,
  6 1/2 In. 20.00
Planter, Basket, Mountain
  Rose, 6 1/4 In. 60.00
Teapot, Mountain Rose,
  2 Cup . . . . 25.00 to 50.00
Watering Can, Red
  Tulip 29.00

RED WING

Red Wing Pottery, Red Wing, Minnesota, was a firm started in 1878. The company first made utilitarian pottery. In the 1920s art pottery was made. Many dinner sets and vases were made before the company closed in 1967.

BOB WHITE was made from 1956 to 1967. It was one of the most popular dinnerware patterns made by the factory. The pattern, a modern hand-painted design, shows a stylized bird and background. It was part of the Casual line.

Bob White
BY RED WING
detergent proof
oven proof
14 8

Cup 15.00
Cup & Saucer 9.00
Pitcher, 60 Oz. 45.00
Plate, Dinner, 10 1/2 In. . . . 9.00
Plate, Salad, 7 1/2 In. 22.00
Salt & Pepper 22.00
Teapot 63.00
Tray, 24 In. 51.00

CRAZY RHYTHM was a hand-painted abstract pattern of dots, lines, and combs on a tan and brown flecked background. It was made on the Futura shape beginning in 1960.

Bowl, Salad, 12 In. 31.00
Plate, Dinner, 10 1/2 In. . . 18.00
Relish, 2 Sections 35.00

LOTUS was made in the Concord shape introduced in 1941. A large lotus flower in pale cream with black leaves is shown on the plates.

Cup 12.00
Cup & Saucer . . . . 9.00 to 16.00
Plate, Bread & Butter,
  6 1/2 In. 6.00
Soup, Cream, Open 12.00
Soup, Rim 12.00

LUTE SONG is a pattern decorated with stylized pictures of musical instruments in pastel colors. Unlike most Red Wing patterns, the dishes are china, not pottery. Lute Song was one of eight patterns made in 1960.

Creamer 15.00
Cup & Saucer 10.00
Plate, Dinner, 10 1/2 In. . . 13.00
Plate, Salad, 7 1/2 In. 10.00
Sugar, Cover 15.00

MAGNOLIA has a white magnolia with pale green leaves on the plate. It was introduced in 1947 as part of the Concord line.

Creamer 20.00
Plate, Bread & Butter,
    6 3/8 In. 6.00
Plate, Dinner,
    10 1/2 In. . . . . . 16.00 to 19.00
Platter, Oval,
    13 1/2 In. 50.00
Relish, 3 Sections,
    12 3/8 In. 24.00
Teapot, Cover 125.00

MERRILEAF has a design of translucent beige and gray-green leaves and wheat. It is a china pattern made about 1960.

Bowl, Cereal 17.00
Cup & Saucer 15.00
Plate, Dinner,
    10 1/2 In. 20.00
Plate, Salad, 7 1/2 In. 11.00

PEPE has a hand-painted modern design of lines, dots, and shapes in shades of pink, orange, and yellow-green. It is part of the Duo-Tone or Cylinder line and was introduced in 1962.

Bowl, Vegetable, Divided,
    Oval, 12 1/2 In. 60.00
Creamer 11.00
Cup 5.00
Cup & Saucer 18.00
Plate, Bread & Butter,
    6 1/4 In. 8.00
Plate, Dinner,
    10 1/4 In. . . . . 10.00 to 17.00
Plate, Salad, 7 In. 8.00
Sugar, Cover 11.00

POMPEII is an abstract design that looks like bottles, vases, and a dish in light browns and turquoise. It is part of the Duo-Tone or Cylinder line and was introduced in 1962.

Bowl, Vegetable, 8 In. . . . 10.00
Cup & Saucer 17.00
Plate, Dinner, 10 3/8 In. . . 14.00
Plate, Salad,
    7 1/2 In. . . . . . . 7.00 to 10.00
Platter, Cylinder Shape . . . 20.00

RANDOM HARVEST is a dinnerware pattern that is colorfast and ovenproof. It was made in the 1960s. The leafy design is hand-painted in brown, copper, coral, green, and turquoise on a flecked dish.

Bowl, Cereal 12.00
Bowl, Salad, 12 In. 30.00
Casserole, Cover 58.00
Creamer 25.00
Cup & Saucer 17.00
Gravy Boat 9.00

Plate, Dinner,
    10 1/2 In. 14.00
Plate, Salad, 8 1/2 In. 10.00
Platter, 13 In. 28.00
Salt & Pepper 32.00
Sugar 25.00
Tidbit, 3 Tiers 55.00

TAMPICO has hanging melons, a hanging wine bottle, and brown leaves on a flecked background. It was introduced in 1956.

Bowl, Vegetable, Round,
    9 In. 40.00
Cup 12.00
Plate, Bread & Butter,
    6 1/2 In. 7.00
Plate, Dinner, 10 1/2 In. . . 20.00
Platter, Oval, 13 1/4 In. . . 35.00
Salt & Pepper 39.00

TOWN & COUNTRY was designed by Eva Zeisel in 1947 and was made until 1954. Pieces are decorated with glossy or matte glaze. Sets were sold in mixed colors. Colors include Chalk White, Chartreuse, Dusk Blue, Forest Green, Gray, Metallic Brown, Peach, Rust, and Sand. Pieces have been reissued in Black, Lime, and White.

Chartreuse

Soup, Dish, Lug 65.00
Sugar, Cover Only 30.00

Dusk Blue

Bowl, Vegetable, Round,
 8 3/4 In. 70.00
Creamer 35.00
Mixing Bowl 200.00
Sugar 50.00

Forest Green

Bowl, Vegetable, Round,
 8 3/4 In. 70.00
Plate, Dinner, 10 5/8 In. . . 45.00
Plate, Salad, 8 In. 30.00

Peach

Bowl, Cereal, 5 3/4 In. . . . 40.00
Plate, Dinner, 10 5/8 In. . . 50.00
Plate, Salad, 8 In. 30.00
Relish, 8 3/4 In. 44.00

MISCELLANEOUS: There are many other patterns made by Red Wing. Some are listed here.

Creamer, Midnight Rose . 25.00
Egg Plate, Blossom
 Time 225.00
Server, Cover, Blossom
 Time 65.00

REGAL CHINA

FINE CHINA

Regal China Corporation was founded in Antioch, Illinois, around 1938. The company was bought by Royal China and Novelty Company in the 1940s. Regal made Jim Beam bottles, cookie jars, kitchen canisters, and salt and pepper shakers called Huggers or Snuggle Hugs designed by Ruth Van Tellingen Bendel. The company closed in 1992.

OLD MCDONALD'S FARM is a line of accessories featuring figures of barnyard animals and farmers.

Creamer, Rooster 150.00
Salt & Pepper, Boy &
 Girl, 3 1/2 In. 120.00
Sugar, Cover, Hen 175.00
Teapot, Duck 295.00

VELLUM is decorated with various decals of pastel flowers. Some have a metallic trim.

Creamer 9.00
Cup & Saucer 30.00
Gravy Boat, Attached
 Underplate 22.00
Plate, Bread & Butter,
 6 3/8 In. 8.00
Plate, Salad,
 8 3/8 In. . . . . 8.00 to 10.00
Serving Bowl, Oval,
 9 1/2 In. 16.00
Soup, Rim,
 8 1/2 In. . . . . . . 9.00 to 18.00

ROSEVILLE

Roseville Pottery Company was organized in Roseville, Ohio, in 1890. Another plant was opened in Zanesville, Ohio, in 1898. Many types of pottery were made until 1954. Later lines were often made with molded decorations, especially flowers and fruit. Most pieces are marked *Roseville*. Only a few dinnerware patterns were made. Many reproductions made in China have been offered for sale the past few years.

RAYMOR is a stoneware made by the Roseville Pottery in 1952 and 1953. It was designed by Ben Seibel. Pieces were made in Autumn Brown, Avocado Green, Beach Gray, and Terra Cotta (rust) in either a plain or mottled version and in Contemporary White. Some Avocado pieces are mistakenly called black. Later, Chartreuse and Robin's Egg Blue were added to the line.

Bowl, Fruit, Lug
 Handles, 5 In. 11.00
Bowl, Salad, 11 1/2 In. . . . 40.00
Bowl, Vegetable, 9 In. . . . 35.00
Cup 11.00
Plate, Bread & Butter,
 6 In. 8.00
Platter, Oval, 14 In. 60.00
Sugar, Cover 30.00

Don't use a repaired plate for food. It could be a health hazard.

ROYAL

Royal China Company began operating in the old E.H. Sebring China Company plant in Sebring, Ohio, in 1934. The company made semiporcelain dinnerware, cookware, and advertising premiums. Jeannette Glass Corporation bought the factory in 1969. Royal changed ownership several times before closing in 1986.

BUCK'S COUNTY features a country scene center with a stylized flower and leaf border. The center scenes vary, but the border remains the same. The design is brown on a yellow background.

Plate, Bread & Butter,
  6 1/2 In. 6.00
Plate, Dinner,
  10 In. .... 8.00 to 10.00
Saucer 3.00
Soup, Dish,
  8 1/2 In. 15.00

COLONIAL HOMESTEAD was introduced about 1951 and was

offered by Sears, Roebuck & Company through the 1960s. It was designed by Gordon Parker and features scenes from a colonial home. The scenes are in green and vary depending on the item, but all have wide green borders.

Ashtray 15.00
Bowl, Cereal,
  6 3/8 In. ...... 14.00 to 18.00
Bowl, Fruit, 5 1/2 In. 10.00
Bowl, Fruit, Lug Handles,
  5 1/2 In. 40.00
Bowl, Vegetable,
  9 In. .... 9.00 to 25.00
Casserole, Cover 75.00
Chop Plate,
  12 In. .... 18.00 to 24.00
Creamer .... 7.00 to 14.00
Cup & Saucer .... 8.00 to 10.00
Gravy Boat 25.00
Gravy Ladle, White 70.00
Mug, Coffee 40.00
Pie Plate, 10 In. 40.00
Plate, Bread & Butter,
  6 1/2 In. 6.00
Plate, Dinner,
  10 In. .... 7.00 to 15.00
Plate, Luncheon,
  9 In. 18.00
Plate, Salad, 7 In. 14.00

Platter, Oval,
  13 x 10 In. 35.00
Platter, Round, 13 In. 50.00
Platter, Tab Handle,
  10 1/2 In. 14.00
Salt & Pepper 40.00
Saucer, 6 1/4 In. ... 3.00 to 8.00
Soup, Dish,
  8 1/2 In. .... 6.00 to 12.00
Sugar, Cover .... 10.00 to 24.00
Teapot, Drop Spout 110.00
Teapot, Flat Spout 90.00

CURRIER & IVES was made from 1949 until about 1983. It was designed by Gordon Parker and is based on the old Currier & Ives prints. Early pieces were date coded. It is white with decal decorations in Blue, Brown, Green, or Pink. The pattern was popular as a store premium. Some serving pieces were made by Harker Pottery Company.

Blue
Ashtray, 5 1/2 In. 10.00
Bowl, Cereal, Schoolhouse
  In Winter,
  6 1/4 In. ...... 16.00 to 20.00
Bowl, Cereal, Tab Handle,
  Suburban Retreat 50.00
Bowl, Fruit, Old Farm
  Gate, 5 1/2 In. ... 5.00 to 6.00

Bowl, Vegetable, Family
Welcome, Dad Is Home,
10 In. 26.00

Bowl, Vegetable, Maple
Sugaring, 9 In. 15.00

Butter, Road, Winter 40.00

Butter, Summer Top,
Winter Bottom 60.00

Casserole, Scrolled Tab
Handles 175.00

Casserole, White Dome,
Fashionable
Turnouts . . . . 90.00 to 110.00

Chop Plate, Rocky Mountains,
12 In. 45.00

Chop Plate, Winter In
The Country, Getting Ice,
12 In. . . . . 25.00 to 28.00

Coffee Mug, Fashionable
Turnouts, 2 5/8 In. 35.00

Creamer, American Express
Train . . . . 4.00 to 16.00

Cup 6.00

Cup, Tea . . . . 3.00 to 4.00

Cup, Tea, Medium Duty,
Star Of Road 15.00

Cup & Saucer 8.00

Egg Plate, Hostess Series,
10 1/4 In. 150.00

Gravy Boat, Spouted, Road,
Winter 25.00

Gravy Boat, Tab Handle,
Road, Winter 40.00

Gravy Boat, Underplate Only,
Old Oaken Bucket 22.00

Gravy Ladle . . . . 40.00 to 75.00

Hostess Set, Cake Plate, 9 Piece,
Box . . . . 60.00 to 150.00

Hostess Set, Getting Ice,
10-In. Cake Plate 35.00

Mug, 2 5/8 x 3 3/4 In. 14.00

Mug, Express Train,
10 Oz., 3 1/4 In. 75.00

Mug, Star Of The Road, 7 Oz.,
2 1/2 x 3 3/4 In. 20.00

Pie Baker, 10 In. 75.00

Pie Baker, Christmas
Snow, 10 In. 50.00

Pie Baker, Homestead In
Winter, 10 In. 50.00

Pie Baker, Maple Sugaring,
10 In. 65.00

Pie Baker, Sleigh Race,
10 In. 18.00

Plate, Bread & Butter,
6 1/2 In. . . . . 4.00 to 6.00

Plate, Calendar, 1973,
10 In. 35.00

Plate, Calendar, 1974,
10 In. 40.00

Plate, Calendar, 1978,
10 In. 35.00

Plate, Calendar, 1984,
10 In. 40.00

Plate, Calendar, 1985,
10 In. 40.00

Plate, Dinner, Country Life,
10 In. 10.00

Plate, Dinner, Old Grist Mill,
10 In. . . . . 15.00 to 19.50

Plate, Luncheon, Old Grist
Mill, 9 In. 19.00

Plate, Salad, Birthplace Of
Washington, 7 1/4 In. . . 16.00

Plate, Serving, Hostess
Series, 7 In. 20.00

Platter, Old Inn Winter,
Oval, 13 x 10 In. 35.00

Platter, Snowy Morning,
13 In. 125.00

Platter, Tab Handles, Rocky
Mountains, 11 In. 19.00

Salt & Pepper 35.00

Salt & Pepper, Open
Carriage 45.00

Saltshaker 25.00

Saucer, Low Water In
Mississippi,
6 /14 In. . . . . 1.00 to 4.00

Soup, Dish,
8 1/2 In. . . . . . . 12.00 to 14.00

Soup, Dish, Early
Winter 12.00

Sugar, Handleless, On
The Mississippi 40.00

Sugar, On The
Mississippi . . . 17.00 to 26.00

Sugar & Creamer,
Cover 22.50

Sweet Server, Wood Stand,
10 & 13 In. 175.00

Teapot, Clipper Ship Dread-
nought . . . . . 135.00 to 150.00

Brown

Pie Baker, American Farm
Scene, 10 In. . . 18.00 to 22.00

Pie Baker, American Homestead
Winter, 10 In. 18.00

Green

Platter, Early Winter Scene,
Oval, 9 x 12 In. 23.00

Pink

Bowl, Cereal, Schoolhouse In
Winter, 6 3/8 In. 25.00

Bowl, Vegetable, Family
Welcome, Dad Is
Home, 10 In. 45.00

Bowl, Vegetable, Home Sweet
Home, 10 In. 45.00

Bowl, Vegetable, Maple
Sugaring, 9 In. 25.00

Chop Plate, Getting Ice,
12 1/4 In. 80.00

Chop Plate, Rocky Mountains,
11 In. 300.00

Chop Plate, Winter In
The Country, Getting Ice,
12 In. 50.00

Creamer, American Express
Train . . . . 25.00 to 100.00

Cup, Tea, Scrolled Handle,
Star Of The Road 20.00

Gravy Boat, Road,
Winter 45.00

Gravy Boat, Underplate only,
Old Salem Bucket 45.00

Plate, Dinner, Memory
Lane, 10 In. 15.00

Plate, Dinner, Old Grist
Mill, 10 In. 16.00

Plate, Salad, 7 3/8 In. 22.00

Platter, Old Inn, Winter,
Oval, 13 x 10 In. 55.00

Platter, Rocky Mountains, Tab
Handles, 10 1/2 In. 35.00

Platter, Snowy Morning,
13 In. 175.00

Saucer, Low Water In
Mississippi, 6 1/4 In. . . . 3.00

Soup, Dish, Early Winter,
8 1/4 In. 16.00

Sugar, No Cover, On
The Mississippi 35.00

Plain White

Gravy Ladle, Footless, Hole
In Handle 50.00

FAIR OAKS is a transfer-decorated pattern that is primarily
brown on white. It pictures a
boy and his dog herding cows
and other assorted tranquil

country scenes. The pattern has its own oak-leaf-shaped mark. It was made after the 1940s.

Bowl, Cereal, Tab Handle,
  6 3/8 In. . . . . . 20.00 to 35.00
Bowl, Vegetable, 9 In. . . . 15.00
Bowl, Vegetable, 10 In. . . 25.00
Butter, Cover 40.00
Casserole, Cover 100.00
Creamer 5.00
Cup, Tea 6.00
Cup & Saucer 15.00
Gravy Boat, Spout 30.00
Gravy Boat, Underplate
  Only 30.00
Gravy Ladle 50.00
Plate, Bread & Butter,
  6 1/2 In. 6.00
Plate, Dinner, 10 In. 10.00
Plate, Salad, 7 1/4 In. . . . 18.00
Platter, Oval, 11 x 9 In. . . 40.00
Platter, Oval, 13 x 10 In. . . 40.00
Platter, Round, Tab
  Handles, 10 1/2 In. 25.00
Salt & Pepper 40.00
Saucer, 6 1/4 In. 5.00
Soup, Dish, 8 1/4 In. 10.00
Sugar, Cover 20.00
Teapot, Cover . . 80.00 to 100.00

MEMORY LANE is a rose on white transfer-decorated pat-

tern. Plates picture a log cabin in the woods. Scenes on other pieces vary, but all pieces have yellow flower borders. Memory Lane has its own oak-leaf-shaped mark.

Ashtray, 5 1/2 In. 12.00
Bowl, Cereal, 6 3/8 In. . . . 20.00
Bowl, Vegetable, 9 In. . . . 16.00
Bowl, Vegetable, 10 In. . . 25.00
Butter, Cover 45.00
Casserole, Cover 90.00
Chop Plate, 12 In. 30.00
Cup, Tea 5.00
Cup & Saucer 12.50
Gravy Boat, Underplate . . 24.00
Gravy Ladle 50.00
Mug, Coffee 35.00
Pie Plate, 10 In. 35.00
Plate, Bread & Butter,
  6 1/2 In. 15.00
Plate, Dinner, 10 In. 15.00
Plate, Luncheon, 9 In. . . . 18.00
Plate, Salad, 7 1/4 In. . . . 18.00
Platter, Oval,
  10 x 13 In. 38.00
Salt & Pepper 35.00
Soup, Rim, 8 1/4 In. 17.50
Sugar & Creamer,
  Cover 22.00
Teapot, Cover 90.00
Tumbler, Juice,
  3 5/8 In. 30.00
Tumbler, Old Fashioned,
  Set Of 4 . . . . 75.00

OLD CURIOSITY SHOP is a 1940s pattern. It has a green scenic center design and an elaborate border. The Cavalier shape was used.

Bowl, Cereal,
  6 3/8 In. . . . . . . 18.00 to 40.00
Bowl, Fruit,
  5 1/2 In. . . . . 4.00 to 7.00
Bowl, Vegetable, 9 In. . . . 16.00
Bowl, Vegetable, 10 In. . . 26.00
Butter, Cover 40.00
Casserole, Cover 75.00
Chop Plate,
  12 In. . . . . 25.00 to 80.00
Creamer 8.00
Cup 6.00
Cup, Tea 4.00
Gravy Boat 25.00
Gravy Ladle 50.00
Mug, Coffee 20.00
Pie Plate, 10 In. 75.00
Plate, Bread & Butter,
  6 1/2 In. 5.00
Plate, Dinner, 10 In. 10.50
Plate, Luncheon, 9 In. . . . 24.00
Plate, Salad, 7 1/4 In. . . . 18.00
Platter, Oval,
  13 x 10 In. 40.00
Salt & Pepper 40.00

Saucer 1.00
Sugar & Creamer,
  Cover . . . . 22.00 to 40.00
Teapot, Droop Spout . . . 100.00

STAR GLOW was made in the 1960s and features golden snowflakes on a white ground.

Bowl, Cereal,
  6 1/4 In. . . . . 8.00 to 15.00
Bowl, Fruit,
  5 1/2 In. . . . . 3.00 to 6.00
Chop Plate,
  12 In. . . . . 20.00 to 30.00
Plate, Bread & Butter,
  6 1/2 In. 6.00
Plate, Dinner,
  10 In. . . . . 8.00 to 10.00
Plate, Luncheon, 9 In. 10.00
Plate, Salad,
  7 In. . . . . 12.00 to 18.00
Saucer . . . . 2.00 to 4.00
Soup, Coupe, 7 7/8 In. . . . 12.00

SUSSEX is a brown transferware pattern sometimes called Royal Sussex. It has flowers in the center and a border.

Cup, Tea 7.00
Cup & Saucer 4.00
Plate, Bread & Butter,
  6 1/2 In. 4.00
Plate, Dinner, 10 In. 9.00
Soup, Dish, 6 1/4 In. 8.50

WILLOW is listed in its own category.

SALEM

Salem China Company produced white granite and semiporcelain dinnerware in Salem, Ohio, from 1898 to 1967. Many of Salem's patterns made in the 1930s and 1940s were designed by Viktor Schreckengost or his brother, Don. Manufacturers in England, China, and Japan made dinnerware with the Salem label from 1968 until c.2000.

ARISTOCRAT has a center decal of flowers. The wide borders are dark colors like blue or maroon and have gold filigree decorations.

Cup & Saucer, Red 12.00
Plate, Bread & Butter,
  Red, 6 In. . . . . 6.00 to 8.00
Plate, Dinner, Cobalt
  Blue, 10 In. 15.00
Soup, Rim, Red 12.00

BASKET PETIT POINT has a petit point basket of flowers on a white ground. It was made with and without a gold inner ring. The pattern was made on the Victory shape designed by Viktor Schreckengost in 1938.

Bowl, Fruit, 6 1/4 In. 7.50
Casserole, Cover, 9 In. . . . 78.00
Cup 8.00
Plate, Bread & Butter,
  6 1/2 In. 4.50
Plate, Dinner,
  9 1/2 In. . . . . 8.00 to 13.50
Plate, Salad, 7 1/4 In. 6.50
Platter, 11 1/4 In. 19.00

Saucer 3.75
Teapot, Cover,
  9 1/2 In. 135.00

BISCAYNE has small white flowers with pink centers and green and blue leaves on a white background. It was made in the late 1950s and early 1960s. A similar pattern called Biscayne was made by Paden City.

Cup & Saucer 7.50
Gravy Boat, Solid Blue . . . 7.00
Plate, Bread & Butter,
  6 In. 3.00
Plate, Luncheon, 9 In. 7.00
Shaker 4.00
Sugar & Creamer,
  Cover 18.00

BRIAR ROSE is a shape that was introduced in 1932. It was made with various decal decorations. It was first made by American China Corporation, which went bankrupt and was bought by Salem China Company.

Bowl, Fruit, 6 In. 6.00
Bowl, Vegetable, 9 In. . . . 15.00
Butter, Oval, 7 In. 8.00
Cup & Saucer 6.00
Plate, Bread & Butter,
  6 In. 6.00
Plate, Dinner, 9 In. 10.00
Platter, 11 1/2 In. 25.00
Sugar, Open 10.00

CENTURY was made in the solid colors of Birch Gray, Cedar Coral, Lime Yellow, and Pine Green and with decal decorations. The Century shape was also used for special orders for various groups.

Bowl, Fruit, Gold Trim,
  6 In. 8.00
Plate, Bread & Butter,
  6 1/2 In. 5.75
Plate, Salad, 7 1/4 In. 8.50
Saucer, Gold Pattern 6.00

COLONIAL COUPLE pictures a colonial couple dancing. It has a maroon rim and 23K gold trim.

Bowl, Cereal, 6 1/4 In. 8.00
Bowl, Fruit, 5 1/2 In. 6.50
Plate, Dinner,
  10 In. . . . . 11.00 to 14.00
Plate, Ribbed Inner Edge,
  6 1/2 In. 9.00
Soup, Dish, 8 1/2 In. 8.50

DAYBREAK has turquoise and brown leaves and stylized starbursts on a white background.

Cup & Saucer 5.00
Plate, Bread & Butter,
  6 In. 6.00
Plate, Dinner, 10 In. 10.00
Soup, Dish, 8 In. 7.00
Sugar, Open 6.00

DOMINION has a bouquet of flowers on a white background and was made on the Victory shape designed by Viktor Schreckengost in 1938.

Bowl, Dessert, 5 3/8 In. . . . 7.00
Bowl, Vegetable,
  8 7/8 x 2 1/2 In. 22.00
Cup & Saucer 18.50
Plate, Bread & Butter,
  6 In. 3.50
Plate, Dinner, 10 In. 17.00
Soup, Dish, 8 3/8 In. 11.00

DUTCH PETIT POINT has a petit point scene of a Dutch couple in the center and a gold sunburst border. It was introduced in 1934 on the Century shape.

Bowl, Dessert, 5 1/2 In. . . . 9.50
Bowl, Fruit, 6 1/4 In. 13.50
Cup & Saucer 15.50
Plate, Bread & Butter,
  6 1/4 In. 8.25
Plate, Dinner, 9 In. 14.00
Saucer, Gold Trim,
  Boy & Girl 5.00
Soup, Cream 14.00

ENGLISH VILLAGE was made to resemble the old blue and white Staffordshire transfer-decorated plates. Various scenes are pictured. The plates have a floral border. Pieces have a special mark.

Bowl, Cereal 14.00
Creamer 23.00
Cup & Saucer 22.00
Plate, Bread & Butter,
  6 1/2 In. 30.00
Plate, Dinner, 9 3/4 In. . . . 28.00

SERENADE is a simple shape with wheat-like sprays. It is marked with the word *Serenade* and a treble clef.

Creamer, Pink 6.00
Cup, Teal 4.00
Cup & Saucer 9.00
Plate, Dinner, Pink,
  10 In. 8.00
Serving Bowl,
  Turquoise 10.00
Tea Set, Platinum Trim,
  3 Piece 40.00

SHEFFIELD has a small bouquet and blue laurels in the center and blue laurel branches on the rim.

Bowl, Dessert, 5 1/2 In. . . . 7.00
Bowl,
  Vegetable . . . . 20.00 to 25.00
Cup & Saucer 13.00
Plate, Bread & Butter,
  6 1/2 In. 5.00
Plate, Dinner, 9 5/8 In. . . . 14.00
Platter, Oval,
  11 3/4 x 9 3/8 In. 25.00
Saucer, 6 In. 5.00

Soup, Dish, 8 1/2 In. 13.00
Sugar, Cover 25.00

SILVER ELEGANCE is an ironstone pattern with platinum trim made in England or America.

ENGLISH IRONSTONE
● SALEM
ENGLAND
Silver Elegance

Bowl, Dessert, Silver
  Trim 5.00
Plate, Bread & Butter,
  6 In. 6.00
Plate, Salad, Silver Trim,
  7 In. 7.00
Saucer 5.00

SOUTHWIND is a pattern on the Free Form shape designed by Viktor Schreckengost in the 1940s. It has turquoise, orange, and green-gold leaves on black branches against a white background.

Cup 10.00
Plate, Dinner, 10 1/4 In. . . 11.00

WHIMSEY has a nosegay of five-petaled flowers and leaves and platinum trim.

Bowl, Cereal, 6 In. 9.00

MISCELLANEOUS: There are many other patterns made by Salem. Some are listed here.

Bowl, Cereal, Autumn
Leaves, 6 1/8 In. 5.00

Bowl, Cereal, Whimsical
Christmas, 6 1/2 In. 7.00

Bowl, Fruit, Northstar,
5 In. 5.00

Bowl, Vegetable, Cover Only,
Minuet, 8 1/2 In. 15.00

Chop Plate, Lug Handles, Wild
Rice, 11 1/4 In. 9.00

Creamer, Heirloom,
6 x 2 1/2 x 3 1/2 In. 8.00

Creamer, Minuet 8.00

Cup, Coffee, Blue
Diamonds 4.00

Cup, Coffee, Minuet . . . . . : 5.00

Cup, Coffee, Spring Valley,
Majesticware 5.00

Cup, Tea, Tricorne Streamline,
Mandarin 8.50

Cup & Saucer,
Georgetown 15.00

Cup & Saucer, Whimsical
Christmas 6.00

Plate, Bread & Butter,
Blue Diamonds, 6 In. . . . 6.00

Plate, Bread & Butter,
Dogwood, 6 In. 6.00

Plate, Dinner, Blue
Diamonds, 10 In. 8.00

Plate, Dinner, Bridal
Bouquet, 10 1/4 In. 9.00

Plate, Dinner, Dogwood,
10 In. 10.00

Plate, Dinner, Georgetown,
10 1/4 In. 28.00

Plate, Dinner, Mardi Gras,
10 In. 7.50

Plate, Dinner, Northstar,
10 In. 8.00

Plate, Dinner, Whimsical
Christmas, 10 1/2 In. . . . 12.00

Plate, Luncheon, Northstar,
9 In. 7.00

Plate, Salad, Dogwood,
7 In. 8.00

Plate, Salad, Minuet,
7 1/8 In. 6.00

Plate, Salad, Whimsical
Christmas, 8 In. 8.00

Plate, Serving, Tab
Handle, Ranchstyle,
Lime Yellow 10.00

Platter, Handles, Northstar,
11 3/4 In. 21.00

Platter, Maple Leaf,
13 In. 30.00

Platter, Parsley,
12 x 9 1/2 In. 20.00

Platter, Rust Tulip, Victory,
11 1/2 x 8 3/4 In. 12.00

Saucer, Autumn Leaves . . . 2.50

Saucer, Georgetown,
6 1/8 In. 7.50

Saucer, Northstar 2.50

Soup, Dish, Blue Diamonds,
7 1/2 In. 8.00

Soup, Dish, Dogwood,
8 1/2 In. 10.00

Sugar, Cover, Indian
Tree 17.50

Sugar, Cover, Parsley,
6 1/2 x 3 1/2 In. 35.00

Sugar, Cover, Shangri La,
Wild Rice 7.00

Sugar, Cover,
Simplicity 10.00

Sugar, Cover, Tricorne
Streamline 10.00

SHAWNEE

Shawnee
U. S. A.

Shawnee Pottery was
started in Zanesville,
Ohio, in 1937. The com-
pany made vases, novelty
ware, flowerpots, planters,
lamps, cookie jars, and
dinnerware. Shawnee pro-
duced pottery for George
Rumrill during the late
1930s. The company
closed in 1961.

CORN KING is an unusual
pattern. Dishes are three-
dimensional representations of
ears of corn. This novel idea
became a popular reality when
Corn King pattern was sold by
Shawnee in 1946. The green
and yellow pieces ranged from
dinner plates to small salt and

pepper shakers. Corn King has
darker yellow corn kernels and
lighter green leaves than a later
pattern called Corn Queen.

Bowl, Cereal, No. 94,
6 1/2 In. . . . . . . 13.00 to 45.00

Bowl, Vegetable, No. 95,
9 In. . . . . 16.00 to 30.00

Butter, Cover . . . 20.00 to 51.00

Casserole, Cover,
No. 73 . . . . 63.00 to 75.00

Casserole, Cover,
No. 74, 11 In. 26.00

Cookie Jar, Cover,
10 1/2 In. . . . 180.00 to 195.00

Creamer, No. 70,
5 In. . . . . 13.00 to 18.00

Cup, No. 90 . . . . 25.00

Cup & Saucer 54.00

Mixing Bowl, No. 6,
6 1/2 In. . . . . . . 24.00 to 29.00

Mixing Bowl, No. 8,
8 In. . . . . 37.00 to 53.00

Mug, No. 69,
8 Oz. . . . . 31.00 to 37.00

Pitcher, No. 71,
8 1/2 In. . . . . . . 39.00 to 60.00

Plate, Corn Tray,
8 x 3 1/2 In. . . . . . 4.25 to 7.00

Plate, Dinner, No. 68,
10 In. . . . . 11.00 to 21.00

Plate, Salad, No. 93,
7 In. 30.00

Platter, No. 96,
11 3/4 In. . . . . . 52.00 to 61.00

Salt & Pepper, 3 1/4 In. . . . 9.00

Salt & Pepper,
5 In. . . . . 16.00 to 25.00

Saltshaker, 3 1/2 In. 9.00

Sugar, Cover,
No. 78 . . . . 34.00 to 50.00

Sugar & Creamer 40.00

Sugar & Creamer, Cover, Gold
Trim . . . . 22.00 to 60.00

Teapot,
No. 65 ..... 100.00 to 192.00
Teapot,
No. 75 .... 91.00 to 96.00

CORN QUEEN is similar to Corn King pattern. The shapes are the same, but the corn kernels are a lighter yellow. It was made from 1954 to 1961.

Bowl, Vegetable, No. 95,
9 x 7 In. 81.00
Cookie Jar, Cover,
No. 66 .... 103.00
Creamer, No. 70 .... 27.00
Creamer, White Corn,
4 3/4 In. 11.00
Cup 29.00
Mixing Bowl, No. 5,
5 In. .... 18.00 to 30.00
Mixing Bowl, No. 6,
6 1/2 In. ...... 12.00 to 13.00
Mixing Bowl, No. 8,
8 In. .... 15.00 to 30.00
Mug, No. 69 .... 17.00 to 20.00
Mug, Underplate,
No. 69 & 91 ... 23.00 to 31.00
Pitcher, No. 71,
8 1/2 In. 103.00
Pitcher, Syrup, 4 3/4 In. .. 45.00
Plate, No. 68,
10 In. .... 20.00 to 21.00
Salt & Pepper 5.25
Salt & Pepper,
3 1/8 In. 13.00
Saltshaker, 3 1/2 In. 9.00
Sugar 3.00
Sugar, Cover .... 21.00 to 41.00

SOUTHERN POTTERIES
See Blue Ridge

STANGL

Stangl Pottery traces its history back to the Fulper Pottery, Flemington, New Jersey. In 1910, Johann Martin Stangl started working at Fulper. He bought into the firm in 1913, became president in 1926, and in 1929 changed the company name to Stangl Pottery. The pottery made dinnerwares and a line of bird figurines. The company went out of business in 1978.

AMBER GLO is a pattern made in 1954. It was designed by Kay Hackett. The flames are orange, the background gray.

Bowl, Vegetable, 8 In. 22.00
Gravy Boat ..... 18.00 to 19.00

COLONIAL is a solid pattern line. Colonial Blue, Persian Yellow, and Silver Green were introduced in 1924. Rust, Surf White, and Tangerine were added in 1935. Aqua Blue was added in 1937, and the white was renamed Satin White. Some sets of dishes were sold in mixed colors.

Aqua Blue
Plate, Dinner, 10 In. 10.00
Sugar, Cover, 10 In. 10.00

Silver Green
Plate, Salad, 8 In. 15.00

Tangerine
Saucer 5.00

COUNTRY GARDEN is decorated with various stylized flowers in red, blue, and yellow and has narrow bands of dark

turqoise and green on the rim. The pattern was made from 1956 to 1974.

Bread Tray 40.00
Coaster, 5 In. 8.50
Cup 9.00
Plate, Dinner, No. 3943,
10 In. 25.00
Platter, 14 In. 80.00
Salt & Pepper, 3 In. 25.00

FRUIT & FLOWERS pattern, No. 4030, was made from 1957 to 1974. The design shows a mixed grouping of flowers, leaves, grapes, and fanciful shapes. Pieces have a colored border.

Bowl, Vegetable, Sections,
10 1/2 In. 50.00
Chop Plate, 14 1/2 In. 37.00
Cup 10.00
Cup & Saucer 18.00
Gravy Boat 25.00
Plate, Bread & Butter,
6 In. 12.00
Plate, Dinner, 10 In. 44.00
Plate, Luncheon,
9 In. 20.00
Platter 60.00
Salt & Pepper, 4 In. 35.00

Saucer 8.00

Serving Bowl, Sections,
   10 x 8 In. 47.00

Soup, Dish, 5 1/2 In. 6.00

Tidbit, 10 In. 15.00

GOLDEN BLOSSOM, made
from 1964 to 1974, is decorated
with brown blossoms and
orange leaves.

Cup 5.00

Cup & Saucer 10.75

Mug, 3 1/8 In. 15.00

Plate, Dinner,
   10 In. . . . . 10.75 to 12.00

Tidbit, 10 In. 12.00

MAGNOLIA pattern has a center design of a burgundy magnolia flower. The pattern, No.
3870, was made from 1952 to
1962.

Bowl, Fruit,
   5 1/2 In. . . . . . . 22.00 to 25.00

Chop Plate, 14 1/2 In. 37.00

Platter, 10 In. 9.00

Soup, Dish 25.00

PROVINCIAL is a bordered
plate with a floral center made
from 1957 to 1967.

Plate, Bread & Butter,
   6 In. 5.00

Plate, Dinner, 10 In. 15.00

Plate, Salad, 8 In. 10.00

Soup, Dish, 5 1/2 In. 10.00

TOWN & COUNTRY pattern
was made in a variety of colors
in the 1970s. The design looks
like the sponged stoneware
made in the nineteenth century.

Black, Blue-Green, Brown,
Honey Beige, and Yellow were
used.

Bowl, 5 3/8 In. 25.00

Coffeepot, 6 1/2 In. 38.00

Creamer, 3 1/2 In. 35.00

Platter, 14 3/4 In. 145.00

MISCELLANEOUS: There are
many other patterns made by
Stangl. Some are listed here.

Bowl, Vegetable, Oval,
   Sections, Fruit, 10 In. . . 45.00

Bowl, Vegetable, Thistle,
   8 In. 45.00

Cake Plate, Metal Base,
   Chicory, 10 In. 20.00

Candle Warmer, Terra
   Rose, Blue 12.00

Casserole, Blueberry,
   8 In. 35.00

Cup, Blueberry 10.00

Plate, Dinner, Chicory,
   10 In. 30.00

Plate, Dinner, Thistle,
   10 In. 22.00

Plate, Salad, Thistle,
   8 In. 12.00

STEUBENVILLE

Steubenville Pottery Com-
pany operated in Steuben-
ville, Ohio, from 1879 to
1959. The company made
granite ware, semiporce-
lain dinnerware, and toilet
seats. When the Ohio fac-
tory closed, the molds and
equipment were moved to
a Canonsburg, Pennsylva-
nia, factory that continued
to use the Steubenville
mark in the 1960s.

AMERICAN MODERN, de-
signed by Russel Wright, was
the most popular dinnerware
pattern made in the 1950s. It
was made by Steubenville from
1939 to 1959. The original
dishes were made in Bean
Brown (a shaded brown), Chartreuse, Coral, Granite Gray,
Seafoam (blue-green), and
White. The brown was replaced
with Black Chutney (dark
brown) during World War II.
Cantaloupe, Cedar Green, and
Glacier Blue were added in the
1950s. Matching linens and
glassware were made. Wright
designed dinnerware in modern
shapes for many companies,
including Iroquois China Company, Harker Pottery Company,
Steubenville Pottery, Paden
City Pottery (Justin Tharaud
and Sons), Sterling China Company, Edwin M. Knowles China
Company, and J.A. Bauer Pottery Company.

Bean Brown

Casserole, Stick
   Handles 90.00

Chop Plate, 13 In. 45.00

Cup & Saucer 28.00

Plate, Salad, 8 In. 28.00

Saucer 9.00

Soup, Dish, Tab
   Handles 30.00

Black Chutney

Baker, 10 3/4 In. 53.00
Bowl, Fruit, Lug,
  6 1/4 In. 18.00
Bowl, Vegetable, 10 In. . . 35.00
Chop Plate, 13 In. 50.00
Cup . . . . 10.00 to 13.00
Gravy Boat 32.00
Plate, Bread & Butter,
  6 1/4 In. 5.50
Plate, Dinner,
  10 In. . . . . 8.00 to 12.00
Plate, Salad, 8 In. 18.00
Salt & Pepper 23.00
Saltshaker 10.00
Saucer 5.00
Soup, Dish, Lug 23.00
Sugar 27.00

Cedar Green

Baker, 10 3/4 In. 25.00
Bowl, Vegetable, 10 In. . . 45.00
Bowl, Vegetable,
  Sections 145.00
Casserole, Cover 55.00
Casserole, Stick
  Handles 95.00
Coffeepot 500.00
Coffeepot, No Cover . . . 105.00
Creamer 32.00
Cup . . . . 10.00 to 19.00
Plate, Bread & Butter,
  6 1/4 In. 10.00
Saltshaker, 5-Hole 19.00
Saucer 6.50
Soup, Dish, Lug 25.00

Chartreuse

Baker, 10 3/4 In. 45.00
Bowl, Vegetable, Cover,
  12 In. 50.00
Bowl, Vegetable,
  Sections 85.00
Casserole, Stick
  Handles 38.00
Celery Dish, 13 In. 30.00
Chop Plate,
  13 In. . . . . 35.00 to 38.00
Creamer 18.00
Cup & Saucer, After
  Dinner . . . . 23.00 to 32.00
Gravy Boat 19.00
Pitcher,
  Water . . . . 95.00 to 120.00

Plate, Bread & Butter,
  6 In. . . . . 5.00 to 5.50
Plate, Dinner, 10 In. 16.00
Platter, 13 1/4 In. 18.00
Salt & Pepper 25.00
Saltshaker, 5-Hole 11.00
Saucer 5.00
Soup, Dish 15.00
Stack Server 300.00
Sugar 20.00

Coral

Bowl, Fruit, Lug,
  5 1/2 In. . . . . . . 15.00 to 18.00
Bowl, Salad 98.00
Bowl, Vegetable,
  10 In. . . . . 20.00 to 25.00
Bowl, Vegetable, Cover,
  12 In. 50.00
Bowl, Vegetable,
  Sections 95.00
Carafe 270.00
Casserole, Stick Handle . . 38.00
Celery Dish . . . . 23.00 to 30.00
Chop Plate, 13 In. 38.00
Coffeepot 60.00
Creamer 18.00
Cup . . . . 7.00 to 13.00
Cup & Saucer 9.00
Cup & Saucer, After
  Dinner 32.00
Gravy Boat 25.00
Pickle, Liner 18.00
Pitcher,
  Water . . . . . 100.00 to 125.00
Plate, Bread & Butter,
  6 In. . . . . 2.50 to 5.00
Plate, Dinner,
  10 In. . . . . 10.00 to 15.00
Plate, Salad,
  8 In. . . . . 14.00 to 18.00
Platter,
  13 1/4 In. . . . . . 22.00 to 28.00
Salt & Pepper 20.00
Saucer 10.00
Soup, Dish,
  Lug . . . . 15.00 to 20.00
Sugar, Cover . . . . 18.00 to 20.00
Teapot 125.00

Glacier Blue

Platter, 13 1/4 In. 50.00

Granite Gray

Baker, 10 3/4 In. 45.00

Bowl, Fruit, Lug,
  6 1/4 In. 18.00
Bowl, Salad 98.00
Bowl, Vegetable,
  10 In. 28.00
Bowl, Vegetable, Cover,
  12 In. 50.00
Bowl, Vegetable,
  Sections . . . . 105.00 to 145.00
Celery Dish 30.00
Chop Plate, 13 In. 38.00
Creamer 18.00
Cup 13.00
Cup, After Dinner 16.00
Cup & Saucer 13.00
Cup & Saucer, After
  Dinner 32.00
Gravy Boat 25.00
Pickle, Liner 18.00
Pitcher, Water 95.00
Plate, Bread & Butter,
  6 1/4 In. 5.50
Plate, Dinner,
  10 In. . . . . 12.00 to 16.00
Platter, 13 1/4 In. 28.00
Saltshaker 11.00
Saucer . . . . 3.00 to 5.00
Sugar 22.00
Teapot 125.00

Seafoam

Bowl, Vegetable, 10 In. . . 35.00
Bowl, Vegetable, Cover,
  12 In. 40.00
Casserole, Stick
  Handles 50.00
Creamer 29.00
Cup 19.00
Cup & Saucer, After
  Dinner 45.00
Plate, Bread & Butter,
  6 1/4 In. 8.00
Plate, Dinner, 10 In. 16.00
Platter, 13 1/4 In. 40.00
Salt & Pepper 30.00
Saltshaker 15.00
Saucer 7.50
Sugar 30.00

White

Bowl, Fruit, Lug,
  6 1/4 In. 15.00

Creamer 30.00

Cup 25.00

Cup & Saucer, After
  Dinner 60.00

Gravy Boat 42.00

Plate, Bread & Butter,
  6 1/4 In. 5.50

Plate, Dinner,
  10 In. . . . . 12.50 to 15.00

Salt & Pepper 43.00

Saucer 4.50

Teapot 45.00

CONTEMPORA was designed
by Ben Seibel for Raymor. It
came in Charcoal, Fawn, Mist
Gray, and Sand White.

Bowl, Cereal,
  6 1/2 In. 13.50

Bowl, Fruit, 5 7/8 In. 11.00

Bowl, Salad, Fawn 45.00

Bowl, Vegetable, Oval,
  8 5/8 x 7 In. 35.00

Creamer 20.00

Cup 11.00

Cup & Saucer 18.00

Gravy Boat, 9 1/2 In. 38.00

Plate, Bread & Butter,
  7 In. 8.00

Plate, Dinner, 10 1/8 In. . . 11.00

Platter, Oval, 14 In. 60.00

Shaker 19.50

Shaker, Pepper,
  Charcoal 20.00

Sugar, Cover 30.00

FAIRLANE was made from
1959 to 1962. It is a white dinnerware decorated with pink
wildflowers with blue petals at
the bottom and green leaves.

Bowl, Cereal,
  6 In. . . . . 5.00 to 6.00

Bowl, Fruit, 5 1/2 In. 5.00

Butter, Cover . . . . 9.00 to 15.00

Cup 4.00

Gravy Boat . . . . . . 6.00 to 13.00

Plate, Bread & Butter,
  6 1/2 In. 4.00

Plate, Dinner,
  10 1/2 In. . . . . . . 7.50 to 10.00

Plate, Salad,
  7 1/4 In. . . . . 3.00 to 5.00

Platter, 14 In. . . . 10.00 to 16.00

Salt & Pepper 10.00

HARVEST has a wide border of
fruit and flowers, scalloped
edges, and a black rim.

Bowl, Vegetable 55.00

Creamer 15.00

Platter . . . . 20.00 to 25.00

Sauceboat, Stand,
  9 1/4 In. 40.00

Serving Bowl, Oval 20.00

OLIVIA is decorated with floral
decals on a white background.
It has slightly scalloped gadrooned edges. Olivia was
introduced in 1926.

Soup, Dish, Saucer,
  Handles 20.00

Bowl Set, Fruit, 5 Piece . . 20.00

Cup & Saucer 16.00

Plate, 7 In. 15.00

ROSE POINT (Rosepoint) is an
all-white pattern with a wide
border of raised roses and a
scalloped edge. It was first
made by Pope-Gosser. Salem
bought the molds in 1958 when
Pope-Gosser closed.

Plate, Luncheon,
  9 1/4 In. . . . . 3.00 to 9.00

Plate, Salad, 8 1/2 In. 7.00

Saucer, 6 1/4 In. . . . 1.00 to 4.00

Soup, Dish, 8 In. 12.50

WOODFIELD dishes are shaped
like leaves and are colored in
many of the shades used for
American Modern dishes, made
by Steubenville. Full dinner sets
were made.

Dove Gray

Cup 5.00

Snack Set,
  4 1/4 x 2 1/2 In. 10.00

Tea & Toast Set,
  8 Piece 30.00

Golden Fawn

Cup & Saucer 7.50

Plate, Bread & Butter,
  6 In. 4.00

Jungle Green

Cup & Saucer 7.50

Sugar & Creamer 22.00

Tea & Toast Set,
8 Piece 32.00

MISCELLANEOUS: There are
many other patterns made by
Steubenville. Some are listed
here.

Cup & Saucer, Yellow
Pinecone 6.00

Dinner Set, Patio Retro,
4 Piece 11.00

Plate, Bread & Butter, Adam
Antique, 6 In., 5 Piece . . 85.00

Plate, Dinner, Yellow
Pinecone 7.00

Soup, Dish, Yellow
Pinecone 8.00

Teapot, Adam Antique,
9 x 8 x 4 3/4 In. 20.00

SYRACUSE

SYRACUSE
1871 *China*

The Farrar Pottery was
established in 1841 in
Syracuse, New York, by
W.H. Farrar. It soon be-
came the Empire Pottery
Company, and in 1871 it
was acquired by Onon-
daga Pottery Company. In
1891 the firm started to
make Syracuse China. The
name of the company was
changed to Syracuse China
Corporation in 1966. The
corporation merged with
Canadian Pacific Invest-
ments, Ltd., in 1978. The
Susquehanna-Pfaltzgraff
Company bought it in
1989. It was purchased by
Libbey, Inc., in 1995. The
company closed its con-
sumer division in 1970 and
now makes dinnerware
only for the food service
industry.

APPLETON is decorated with
swags of blue and yellow roses
on an ivory ground. Plates have
a wide rim, scalloped edge, and
gold trim. It was made on the
Federal shape.

Plate, Bread & Butter,
6 1/2 In. 8.00

Sugar & Creamer,
Cover 45.00

ARCADIA, made from 1928 to
1932, is decorated with garlands of roses. Dishes are ivory
with gold trim.

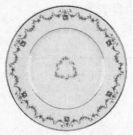

Cup & Saucer 34.00

Plate, Bread & Butter,
6 1/4 In. 10.00

Plate, Dinner,
9 3/4 In. . . . . . . 13.00 to 30.00

Saucer 10.00

Soup, Dish 8.00

ATHENA, made from 1937 to
1970, has a black ropelike border and gold trim.

Plate, Bread & Butter,
6 1/4 In. 13.00

Plate, Dinner, 10 In. 34.00

Soup, Rim, 8 7/8 In. 25.00

BRACELET is a pattern introduced in 1941. It is a white dinnerware with gold trim.

Cup & Saucer, Espresso . . 33.00

Gravy Boat 115.00

Plate, Bread & Butter,
6 In. 14.00

Plate, Dinner, 10 In. 43.00

Platter, 14 In. 131.00

Platter, Round,
Medium 107.00

Saucer 6.00

Saucer, After Dinner 8.00

BRIARCLIFF pattern was introduced in 1938 and continued in
production until 1969. It is decorated with pastel yellow, pink,
and blue flower clusters.

Bowl, Vegetable, Oval,
10 3/4 In. . . . . . 38.00 to 74.00

Cup & Saucer 17.50

Plate, Bread & Butter,
6 1/4 In. 9.00

Platter,
12 1/8 In. . . . . . 50.00 to 90.00

Platter, Medium 110.00

Sugar, Cover 7.00

CELESTE has a rim with scattered blue leaves. It has platinum trim. It was made from
1954 to 1969.

Cup & Saucer 14.00

Plate, Bread & Butter,
6 1/4 In. 12.00

Sugar, Cover 70.00

CHAMPLAIN, made from 1950
to 1966, is trimmed with gold.
The rim is fluted and the design
is green leaves.

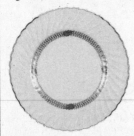

Plate, Bread & Butter,
6 3/8 In. 9.00

Plate, Dinner, 10 3/8 In. . . 19.00

CORALBEL, made from 1937 to 1970, has green and platinum lines as an inner border. The center of the plate is decorated with green and pink flowers that resemble lilies of the valley. It was made on several different shapes.

Bowl, 5 1/8 In. 10.00
Cup & Saucer 17.50
Cup & Saucer, Virginia
  Shape 18.00
Plate, Bread & Butter,
  6 1/2 In. 8.00
Plate, Bread & Butter, Virginia
  Shape, 6 1/4 In. 8.00
Plate, Luncheon, Virginia
  Shape, 8 In. 18.00
Plate, Salad,
  7 1/2 In. . . . . . . 12.00 to 18.00
Soup, Dish 20.00
Soup, Rim 20.00

DIANE features encrusted gold trim and an inner gold border. It was made from 1937 to 1970.

Cup & Saucer 18.00
Plate, Bread & Butter,
  6 1/4 In. 8.00
Plate, Luncheon, 9 In. 25.00
Plate, Salad, 8 In. 18.00

FINESSE has an off-center decoration of sprigs of gray and pink. It was made from 1956 to 1970.

Plate, Dinner, 10 In. 12.00
Serving Dish, Sections . . . 20.00
Sugar, Cover 38.00

GARDENIA was made from 1950 to 1966. It has a fluted rim, gold trim, and a border of large gardenias.

Plate, Dinner, 10 In. 36.00
Soup, Cream, Saucer 41.00

LYRIC has inner and edge platinum trim. The design pictures a leaf sprig and dots. It was made from 1952 to 1970.

Plate, Bread & Butter,
  6 In. . . . . 8.00 to 12.00
Plate, Dinner, 10 In. 40.00
Plate, Salad, 7 1/2 In. 20.00
Sugar, Cover 70.00

MEADOW BREEZE has a pale gray-blue border and curving thin leaves and twigs of brown and gray-blue for a center design. It has platinum trim. The pattern was made from 1952 to 1970.

Cup & Saucer 34.00
Gravy Boat 137.00

MONTICELLO has gold trim and a plain, wide rim. It was made from 1928 to 1952.

Cup & Saucer 18.00
Gravy Boat 128.00
Plate, Bread & Butter,
  6 1/4 In. 8.00
Plate, Salad, 8 In. 15.00
Saucer 9.00

ORCHARD is decorated with apple blossoms, leaves, and branches. Plates have a wide rim, scalloped edge, and gold trim.

Plate, Bread & Butter,
  6 1/2 In. 8.00
Plate, Dinner, 10 1/2 In. . . 30.00
Plate, Salad, 8 In. 18.00

PENDLETON pattern is made with a red and blue vine border, an inner red rim, and gold trim. It was made from 1938 to 1969.

Plate, Bread & Butter,
  6 1/2 In. 14.00
Plate, Salad, 7 1/2 In. 19.00

SHERWOOD was made from 1940 to 1970. The design has a formal berry and leaf border in blues and dark yellow. It has gold trim.

Cup & Saucer 18.00
Gravy Boat 115.00
Plate, Bread & Butter,
  6 1/2 In. 14.00
Plate, Dinner,
  10 In. . . . . 30.00 to 43.00
Plate, Luncheon, 8 In. 18.00
Plate, Salad, 7 1/2 In. 19.00
Saucer 9.00
Sugar, Cover 75.00
Sugar & Creamer,
  Cover 45.00

STANSBURY was introduced in 1938 and discontinued in 1969. The pattern features trailing flowers in pale pinks, green, and grays. It has gold trim.

Bowl, Vegetable,
  Oval . . . . 35.00 to 86.00
Plate, Bread & Butter,
  6 1/2 In. 14.00

SUZANNE pattern has a border strewn with pink, blue, and yellow flowers. The edge has gold trim. It was introduced in 1938 and discontinued in 1970.

Bowl, Vegetable,
  Cover 203.00
Bowl, Vegetable, Oval . . . 73.00
Gravy Boat 115.00
Plate, Bread & Butter,
  6 1/2 In. 13.00

Platter, Large 152.00
Platter, Medium 117.00
Platter, Small 108.00
Sugar, Cover 75.00

VICTORIA was made from 1939 to 1970. The center of the plate pictures a realistic rose with buds and leaves. A few small buds are placed on the border. The ivory plate has a fluted shape and gold trim.

Bowl, Vegetable, Oval,
   10 1/2 In. 35.00
Bowl, Vegetable, Round,
   8 3/4 In. 40.00
Gravy Boat,
   Underplate . . 125.00 to 128.00
Plate, Dinner, 10 In. 43.00
Plate, Salad, 7 1/2 In. 19.00
Platter, Medium 131.00
Platter, Small 108.00
Soup, Dish,
   1 5/8 x 7 7/8 In. 15.00
Sugar, Cover 75.00

WINDSOR has small floral bouquets on an aqua and pink band and gilt trim.

Cup & Saucer 18.00
Plate, Bread & Butter,
   6 1/2 In. ....8.00 to 13.00
Plate, Luncheon, 9 In.....23.00
Platter, 12 In. 23.00

WOODBINE was made from 1956 to 1970. The decoration features an off-center branch of pink and green maple leaves.

Bowl, Round 13.00
Creamer 21.00
Cup & Saucer 6.00
Plate, Bread & Butter,
   6 1/2 In. 6.00
Plate, Dinner, 10 In. 12.00

TAYLOR, SMITH & TAYLOR

Taylor, Smith & Taylor produced dinnerware in Chester, West Virginia, from 1901 to 1981. The company produced an extensive number of patterns. In 1973, Anchor Hocking purchased the company and started marking the dinnerware *Anchor Hocking*.

AUTUMN HARVEST was made on the Versatile shape.

Bowl, Cereal 8.00
Bowl, Fruit,
   5 1/8 In. ....4.00 to 11.00
Bowl, Vegetable,
   9 1/4 In. ......18.00 to 20.00
Creamer 11.00
Cup ....4.00 to 10.00
Plate, Bread & Butter,
   6 1/2 In. 3.00
Plate, Dinner, 10 In. 7.00

BOUTONNIERE has a group of blue flowers that resemble bachelor buttons as the design.

Bowl, Fruit, 5 In. 3.00
Creamer 20.00
Cup & Saucer 7.00
Plate, Bread & Butter,
   6 5/8 In. 3.00
Plate, Dinner,
   10 In. ....7.00 to 10.00
Sauceboat 8.00

LAZY DAISY is a pale green dinnerware with a border of realistic white daisies and leaves.

Plate, Bread & Butter,
   6 1/2 In. ....6.00 to 13.00
Plate, Dinner, 10 1/2 In. . . 16.00
Platter, Oval, 13 1/2 In. ..20.00
Soup, Dish ......9.00 to 17.00
Sugar, Cover ....22.00 to 30.00

LU-RAY has a slightly speckled, solid-color glaze. It was made from 1938 to 1961. Pastel colors include Chatham Gray, Persian Cream (yellow), Sharon Pink, Surf Green, and Windsor Blue.

Chatham Gray
Cup 10.00
Plate, Bread & Butter,
   6 In. 10.00
Plate, Salad, 9 In. 15.00
Saucer, 5 In. ......6.00 to 9.00
Soup, Dish 30.00

Persian Cream
Bowl, Fruit, 5 In. 6.00
Bowl, Salad, 9 1/2 In. 55.00
Platter,
   11 1/2 In. .....13.00 to 18.00

Platter, Round 20.00

Sharon Pink

Cup & Saucer 10.00

Plate, Bread & Butter,
6 1/4 In. . . . . 3.00 to 7.00

Plate, Dinner, 10 In. 20.00

Plate, Luncheon,
9 1/4 In. 18.00

Salt & Pepper 18.00

Saucer, 6 In. . . . . . 2.00 to 11.00

Surf Green

Berry Bowl 5.00

Bowl, Fruit, 5 In. . . 6.00 to 7.00

Bowl, Salad,
9 1/2 In. 75.00

Cup & Saucer . . . . 8.00 to 12.00

Plate, 6 In. . . . . 3.00 to 4.00

Plate, 9 In. 10.00

Saucer, 6 In. . . . . . 3.00 to 11.00

Soup, Dish,
7 1/4 In. . . . . . . 10.00 to 15.00

Windsor Blue

Berry Bowl, 6 In. 5.00

Bowl, Fruit, 5 In. . . 6.00 to 7.00

Bowl, Tab
Handle . . . . . . 19.00 to 20.00

Cup & Saucer 18.00

Plate, Bread & Butter,
6 In. . . . . 3.00 to 4.00

Plate, Dinner, 10 In. 20.00

Plate, Luncheon,
9 In. . . . . 10.00 to 25.00

Platter, 11 1/2 In. 6.00

Salt & Pepper 18.00

Saucer, 6 In. . . . . . . 2.00 to 3.00

Soup, Dish,
7 1/4 In. . . . . . . 13.00 to 18.00

Sugar 5.00

PEBBLEFORD was made on the Versatile shape, which included a plain round coupe shape. It has a speckled glaze in Burnt Orange, Granite Gray, Honey (beige), Marble White, Mint Green, Pink, Sand (pumpkin), Sunburst Yellow, Teal, and Turquoise. Every piece was made in every color. There are two different styles of teapots and sugar bowls.

Granite Gray

Bowl, 5 In. 6.00

Cup 8.00

Plate, Bread & Butter,
6 In. 4.00

Plate, Dinner, 10 In. 15.00

Mint Green

Cup & Saucer 9.00

Plate, Dinner, 10 In. 9.00

Pink

Plate, Bread & Butter,
6 In. 6.00

Plate, Dinner, 10 In. 20.00

Plate, Salad, 8 In. 6.00

Sugar, Cover 20.00

Sand

Platter, Oval, 13 In. 20.00

Turquoise

Cup 8.00

Plate, Dinner, 10 In. 15.00

REVEILLE pattern pictures a red rooster in a Pennsylvania Dutch design. It was made about 1960. Some small pieces like saucers do not show the rooster.

Bowl, Vegetable 12.00

Plate, Dinner, 10 In. 12.00

Platter, 13 In. 20.00

Saucer 3.00

TAVERNE dinnerware was made by Taylor, Smith & Taylor of Chester, West Virginia. Matching serving pieces were made by the Hall China Company of East Liverpool, Ohio, in the 1930s. A rolling pin was made by Harker Pottery Company. The silhouetted figures eating at a table are very similar to those seen on the pattern Silhouette, but there is no dog in this decal. In some of the literature, Taverne is called Silhouette. Reproductions using the Taverne decoration have been made. These, unlike the originals, are marked *Limited Edition.*

Creamer 50.00

Drip Jar 55.00

Mug 55.00

Plate, Bread & Butter,
6 1/4 In. 6.00

Salt & Pepper 140.00

Sugar 58.00

Teapot 225.00

VISTOSA is a solid-color dinnerware made about 1938. The plates have piecrust edges, and the other pieces have some bands or ridges. The glaze colors are Cobalt Blue, Deep Yellow, Light Green, and Mango Red. Pieces were marked with the name Vistosa and the initials T.S. & T. Co. U.S.A.

Cobalt Blue

Saucer, 6 In. 7.00

Mango Red

Saucer, 6 In. 7.00

Sugar & Creamer 7.00

WILD QUINCE is part of the Ever Yours line.

Bowl, Cereal, 6 1/2 In. 8.00
Creamer 18.00
Cup & Saucer 11.00

WOOD ROSE is part of the Ever Yours line.

Casserole,
Cover . . . . 18.00 to 20.00
Cup & Saucer 8.00

UNIVERSAL

Universal Potteries, Inc., operated in Cambridge, Ohio, from 1934 to 1976. The company made semi-porcelain dinnerware and kitchenware until 1960.

See Harmony House for additional patterns and information.

BALLERINA was a very modern shape and had solid-color glazes. It was made from 1947 to 1956. A later line was decorated with decal designs. The original solid-color Ballerina dinnerware was offered in Dove Gray, Jade Green, Jonquil Yellow, and Periwinkle Blue. In 1949, Chartreuse and Forest Green were added. By 1955, Burgundy, Charcoal, and Pink were added, while some other colors had been discontinued. There was also a line called Ballerina Mist, which had a pale background and decal decorations. It may be marked with the backstamp *Ballerina* or *Ballerina Mist*.

Burgundy
Cup & Saucer 8.00
Plate, Bread & Butter,
6 1/2 In. 5.00

Charcoal
Sugar, Cover 15.00

Chartreuse
Cup & Saucer 5.00
Plate, Dinner, 10 In. 18.00
Sugar 8.00

Dove Gray
Cup & Saucer 8.00
Plate, Dinner, 10 In. 18.00
Plate, Luncheon, 9 In. 7.50
Plate, Serving,
Tab Handle 10.00
Sugar, Cover 15.00

Jade Green
Saucer 4.00

Jonquil Yellow
Plate, Bread & Butter,
6 In. 6.00

Periwinkle Blue
Plate, Dinner, 10 In. 18.00

Pink
Plate, Dinner, 10 In. 18.00

CATTAIL (CAT-TAIL) pattern dishes were found in many homes in America in the 1940s. Sears, Roebuck & Company featured the pattern from 1934 to 1956. It was made by the Universal Potteries. The red and black cattail design was used for dinnerware and matching tinware, kitchenware, glassware, furniture, and table linens. Another pattern by Universal was also called Cattail. It has a realistic green and brown design. The red and black pieces are listed here. New limited edition pieces of Cat-tail have been distributed by China

Specialties, Inc., and may be listed here. They are new shapes, not reproductions, and are clearly marked or dated.

Casserole, Cover	25.00
Cup & Saucer	42.00
Custard Cup	25.00
Mixing Bowl, 6 In.	15.50
Mixing Bowl, 7 In.	20.00
Mixing Bowl, 8 In.	25.00
Mixing Bowl, 10 1/2 In.	30.00
Pie Baker, 10 In.	20.00
Plate, Dinner, 9 7/8 In.	40.00
Soup, Dish, Flat	50.00

VERNON KILNS

Vernon Kilns was the name used by Vernon Potteries, Ltd. The company, which started in 1931 in Vernon, California, made dinnerware and figurines until it went out of business in 1958. The molds were bought by Metlox, which continued to make some patterns. Collectors search for the brightly

colored dinnerware and the pieces designed by Rockwell Kent, Walt Disney, and Don Blanding.

BROWN EYED SUSAN was made by Vernon Kilns from 1946 to 1958. It has yellow flowers and a brown border.

Bowl, Fruit, 5 1/4 In.	9.00
Bowl, Vegetable, Oval, 9 3/4 In.	36.00
Butter, Cover	50.00
Casserole, Cover, Handles, 5 1/2 In.	45.00
Chop Plate, 12 In.	20.00
Chop Plate, 13 5/8 In.	43.00
Cup	12.00
Cup & Saucer	14.00 to 18.00
Cup & Saucer, After Dinner	30.00
Plate, Bread & Butter, 6 1/2 In.	10.00
Plate, Dinner, 10 1/2 In.	23.00
Plate, Luncheon, 9 1/2 In.	6.00 to 14.00
Plate, Salad, 7 1/2 In.	5.00 to 15.00
Platter, 13 1/2 In.	25.00
Salt & Pepper	19.00
Saltshaker	7.00
Sauceboat	32.00
Saucer	2.00
Serving Bowl, Round, 9 In.	18.00
Teapot	80.00

CALICO is one of the plaid patterns made from 1949 to 1958. It is pink and blue plaid with a blue border. Other plaids are Gingham (green and yellow), Homespun (cinnamon, green, and yellow), Organdie (brown and yellow), Tam O'Shanter (rust, chartreuse, and dark green), and Tweed (yellow and gray-blue).

Casserole, Chicken Pie, Cover, Stick Handle	50.00
Casserole, Cover, Handle, 4 In.	50.00
Creamer	20.00
Gravy Boat	30.00
Soup, Rim, 8 In.	26.00

CASUAL CALIFORNIA, a very popular solid-color dinnerware, was made from 1947 to 1956. It was made in Acacia Yellow, Dawn Pink, Dusk Gray, Lime Green, Mahogany Brown,

Mocha Brown, Pine Green, Sno-white, and Turquoise Blue.

Acacia Yellow
Cup & Saucer 14.00

Dawn Pink
Butter 30.00

Lime Green
Casserole, Cover, Chicken Pie,
Stick Handle 40.00
Chop Plate, 13 In. 37.00
Pitcher, 2 Qt., 11 In. 70.00

Mocha Brown
Pitcher, 1/4 Pt. 22.00
Pitcher, 1/2 Pt. 22.00
Pitcher, 1 Pt. 24.00

Pine Green
Cup & Saucer 14.00
Pitcher, 1/4 Pt. 50.00

CORONADO, made from 1935 to 1939, was used as a grocery promotion. It was glazed Blue, Brown, Dark Blue, Light Green, Orange, Pink, Turquoise, or Yellow.

Brown
Cup 8.00

Orange
Plate, Bread & Butter,
6 1/2 In. 7.00

Turquoise
Cup 8.00
Plate, Bread & Butter,
6 1/2 In. 7.00
Soup, Dish, 7 1/2 In. 20.00

Yellow
Plate, Bread & Butter,
6 1/2 In. 7.00
Plate, Luncheon,
9 1/2 In. 9.00
Salt & Pepper 22.00

EARLY CALIFORNIA is a solid-color line of dinnerware

made in the late 1930s. The dishes, in Blue, Brown, Green, Orange, Pink, Turquoise, or Yellow, were made to be used as mix-and-match sets. The dishes are marked with the name of the pattern.

Blue
Plate, Bread & Butter,
6 In. 3.50
Saucer 3.00

Brown
Cup & Saucer 12.00
Saltshaker 9.00

Pink
Chop Plate,
12 In. . . . . 18.00 to 32.00
Creamer, Round, 3 In. . . . 15.00

Turquoise
Eggcup 20.00

GINGHAM is one of the plaid patterns made from 1949 to 1958. It is green and yellow plaid with a dark green border. Other plaids are Calico (pink and blue), Homespun (cinnamon, green, and yellow), Organdie (brown and yellow), Tam O'Shanter (rust, chartreuse, and dark green), and Tweed (yellow and gray-blue).

Bowl, Vegetable, 2 Sections,
11 1/2 In. 26.00
Bowl, Vegetable,
8 7/8 In. 26.00
Butter, Cover Only 18.00
Casserole, Cover 30.00
Coffeepot 35.00
Jug, 1 Pt. 23.00
Mixing Bowl, 5 In. 33.00
Mixing Bowl, 7 In. 44.00
Mixing Bowl, 8 In. 47.00
Pitcher, 1/2 Pt., 5 In. 80.00
Pitcher, Streamline,
11 In. 65.00
Plate, Bread & Butter,
6 1/2 In. 7.00
Plate, Dinner,
10 1/2 In. 12.00
Plate, Luncheon,
9 1/2 In. 7.00
Plate, Salad, 7 1/2 In. 6.00
Platter, Oval, 14 In. 38.00
Saucer 3.00
Soup, Rim 12.00
Sugar, Cover 18.00

HEAVENLY DAYS was made from 1956 to 1958. Pieces are decorated with aqua, mocha, and pink geometric designs.

"Heavenly Days"

Bowl, Vegetable,
7 1/2 In. 16.00
Creamer 15.00
Gravy Boat 23.00
Plate, Bread & Butter,
6 In. 8.00
Platter, 11 In. 22.00
Platter, 13 1/2 In. 24.00
Saucer 4.00
Sugar, Cover 21.00

HOMESPUN is a cinnamon, green, and yellow plaid pattern with a reddish brown border made from about 1948 to 1958. Other related plaids are Calico (pink and blue), Gingham (green and yellow), Organdie (brown and yellow), Tam O'Shanter (rust, chartreuse, and dark green), and Tweed (yellow and gray-blue). Some of the Vernon Kilns molds were bought by Metlox and the patterns remained in production.

Bowl, 8 1/2 In.		24.00
Bowl, Fruit, 5 1/2 In.		8.00
Bowl, Vegetable, Sections, 10 In.		25.00
Butter, Cover Only		22.00
Butter Chip, 2 1/2 In.		36.00
Carafe, Stopper		45.00
Chop Plate, 12 In.		30.00
Creamer		12.00
Cup, Tea		11.00
Cup & Saucer		12.00 to 14.00
Jug, Bulb Bottom, 1 Pt.		35.00
Mixing Bowl, 7 In.		35.00
Mixing Bowl, 8 In.		39.00
Plate, Bread & Butter, 6 1/2 In.		3.00 to 7.00
Plate, Bread & Butter, Metlox, 6 In.		6.00
Plate, Dinner, 10 1/2 In.		16.00
Plate, Luncheon, 9 1/2 In.		9.00 to 10.00
Plate, Salad, 7 1/2 In.		7.00
Platter, 12 In.		19.00 to 29.00
Saucer, 6 In.		3.00 to 4.00
Soup, Dish, 8 1/2 In.		24.00

LOLLIPOP TREE is a pattern that features abstract pastel lollipops. It was made from 1957 to 1958.

Bowl, Vegetable, 9 In.		20.00
Cup		10.00
Plate, Bread & Butter, 6 In.		11.00
Platter, 13 1/2 In.		55.00
Sugar, Cover Only		10.00

MAY FLOWERS was made from 1942 to 1955. The pieces picture a large floral spray.

Chop Plate, 14 In.		63.00
Creamer		10.00
Cup, Tea		18.00
Gravy Boat		30.00
Platter, Oval, 13 1/2 In.		43.00
Salt & Pepper		10.00
Sauceboat		5.00
Saucer		1.00
Serving Bowl, Oval, 10 In.		33.00
Sugar		20.00
Sugar, Cover		25.00

NATIVE CALIFORNIA was made in solid pastel colors of Aqua, Blue, Green, Ivory, Pink, and Yellow. It was made on the Melinda shape from 1942 to 1947.

Aqua

Plate, Dinner, 10 1/2 In.		16.00
Plate, Salad, 7 1/2 In.		8.00
Saucer		5.00

Blue

Plate, Dinner, 10 1/2 In.		16.00

Yellow

Chop Plate, 12 In.		20.00
Relish, 4 Sections, Leaf Shape, 14 In.		60.00

ORGANDIE is one of several different plaid patterns made in the 1940s and 1950s. It is an overall brown pattern with a yellow and brown plaid border. Other related plaids are Calico (pink and blue), Gingham (green and yellow), Homespun (cinnamon, yellow, and green), Tam O'Shanter (rust, chartreuse, and deep green), and Tweed (yellow and gray-blue). Organdie was originally the name for a group of plaid designs made in 1937 that are not listed here. One of these was Coronation Organdy (gray and rose).

Bowl, Round, 8 1/2 In.		17.50
Bowl, Vegetable, 9 In.		20.00 to 28.00
Carafe, Stopper		45.00
Casserole, Chicken Pie, Stick Handle		43.00
Casserole, Individual, 4 In.		25.00
Casserole, Round, Handles		40.00

Chop Plate, 12 In. 24.00
Coaster, Ridged,
   3 3/4 In. 25.00
Creamer, Cover 20.00
Creamer, Round 12.00
Cup 10.00
Cup & Saucer . . . . 7.00 to 11.00
Cup & Saucer, After
   Dinner 25.00
Eggcup,
   Double . . . . 25.00 to 30.00
Mixing Bowl, 5 In. 35.00
Mixing Bowl, 7 In. 38.00
Mug, Straight Sides,
   3 1/2 In. 26.00
Pitcher, 2 Qt. 45.00
Plate, Dinner, 10 1/2 In. . . . 5.00
Plate, Luncheon,
   9 1/2 In. 7.00
Plate, Salad, 7 1/2 In. 5.00
Platter, Oval, 10 1/2 In. . . 23.00
Salt & Pepper . . . 10.00 to 18.00
Saucer 3.00
Sugar & Creamer 18.00

RAFFIA is a pattern made about
1950. It is green brushed with
brownish red to give a textured
effect. Barkwood and Shantung
are the same pattern in different
colors.

Bowl, Vegetable, Sections,
   10 In. 18.00
Chop Plate, 13 In. 12.00
Cup & Saucer 4.00
Gravy Boat 23.00
Pitcher, 6 1/2 In. 35.00
Plate, Bread & Butter,
   6 In. 4.00
Plate, Dinner, 10 In. 4.00
Plate, Salad, 8 In. 5.00
Platter, Oval, 11 In. 12.00
Salt & Pepper 11.00
Saucer, 6 In. 2.00
Soup, Chowder, Lug
   Handle, 6 In. 6.00
Soup, Dish, 8 In. 7.50
Sugar, Cover 10.00

SHADOW LEAF has red and
green flowers on a green
swirled background. It is the

same design as Trade Winds,
but in different colors. It was
made from 1954 to 1955.

Cup, Tea 8.00
Pitcher, 1/2 Pt., 5 In. 60.00
Pitcher, 1 Qt. 60.00

TAM O'SHANTER is one of
many plaid patterns made
between 1949 and 1958. It is a
rust, chartreuse, and dark green
plaid with forest green border.
Other related plaids are Calico
(pink and blue), Gingham
(green and yellow), Homespun
(cinnamon, yellow, and green),
Organdie (brown and yellow),
and Tweed (yellow and gray-
blue).

Cake Plate, 6 1/2 In. 7.00
Casserole, Cover, Chicken
   Pie, Stick Handle 37.00
Chop Plate, 12 In. 35.00
Cup 10.00
Cup & Saucer 12.00
Gravy Boat . . . . . 25.00 to 35.00
Jug, 1 Pt. 15.00
Jug, 1 Qt. 60.00
Pitcher, 1/2 Pt. 50.00
Pitcher, 1 Qt. 60.00
Plate, Salad, 7 1/2 In. 7.00
Platter, Oval, 12 1/2 In. . . 25.00
Platter, Oval, 14 In. 36.00
Shaker, Pepper 8.00
Sugar, Cover 15.00

TICKLED PINK is a pattern
made from 1955 to 1958. It features small squares and crosses
in pink and charcoal on most
pieces. Cups, lids, and a few
serving pieces are made of solid
pink. The pattern and name
rights were purchased by Met-

lox Potteries in 1958 and Tickled Pink continued to be produced.

Bowl, Vegetable, 2 Sections,
   9 1/2 In. 24.00
Bowl, Vegetable, 9 In. . . . 19.00
Chop Plate, 13 In. 30.00
Creamer, 4 1/4 In. 10.00
Cup & Saucer 12.00
Plate, Bread & Butter,
   6 In. 6.00
Saucer 5.00
Shaker, Pepper 10.00

TWEED is one of the plaid patterns. It was made between
1950 and 1955. It is a yellow
and gray-blue plaid with a border. Other related plaids are Calico (pink and blue), Gingham
(green and yellow), Homespun
(cinnamon, yellow, and green),
Organdie (brown and yellow),
and Tam O'Shanter (rust, chartreuse, and dark green).

Bowl, Vegetable,
   8 7/8 In. 38.00
Chop Plate, 13 3/4 In. 50.00
Cup & Saucer 15.00
Pitcher, 1/2 Pt., 5 In. 77.00
Plate, Bread & Butter,
   6 1/2 In. 7.00
Plate, Dinner, 10 1/2 In. . . 18.00
Plate, Luncheon,
   9 1/2 In. 17.00

MISCELLANEOUS: There are
many other patterns made by
Vernon Kilns. Some are listed
here.

Casserole, Cover, Santa
   Anita, 9 1/2 In. 75.00

Chop Plate, Bits Of Old
New England, Tapping
For Sugar, 12 In. 55.00

Chop Plate, Santa Maria,
12 In. 65.00

Coffeepot, Ultra
California 110.00

Creamer, Modern
California 15.00

Cup, Tea, Blossoms 11.00

Cup & Saucer,
Monterey 30.00

Pitcher, Sherwood,
1 Qt. 45.00

Plate, Salad, Dolores,
7 1/2 In. 15.00

Salt & Pepper, Gayety . . . 19.00

Salt & Pepper, Modern
California 10.00

Salt & Pepper, Mojave . . . 13.00

Saltshaker, Monterey 10.00

Sauceboat, Dolores 39.00

Serving Bowl, Dolores,
Oval, 10 In. 33.00

W.S. GEORGE

W.S. George ran the Ohio
China Company in the
1890s. He purchased the
East Palestine Pottery
Company in East Palestine,
Ohio, in 1903 and
renamed it the W.S.
George Pottery Company.
It closed about 1960.

BOLERO is a shape made both
with and without decal decorations. A fluted coupe shape was
made c.1933 to c.1939, when
the line was restyled. The later
round shape is usually found
today. Bolero Faience was
made in Alabaster, Lemon Yellow, and Turquoise beginning
in 1934. It is rarely found today.

Bowl, Salad, Colonial Couple,
7 1/4 In. 11.00

Cake Plate, Tab
Handles 12.00

Casserole, Red Chinese
Design 35.00

Creamer 10.00

Cup, Flora 5.00

Plate, Bread & Butter,
6 3/4 In. 5.00

Plate, Bread & Butter, Colonial
Couple, 6 1/4 In. 7.50

Plate, Dinner, 9 1/4 In. . . . 10.00

Plate, Luncheon, 8 In. 10.00

Platter, 11 3/4 In. 20.00

Platter, 12 In. 18.00

Platter, Meat, Oval, Roses,
Lilies, 13 3/4 In. 24.00

Platter, Tab Handle, Colonial
Couple, 12 In. 20.00

Saucer, Colonial Couple,
5 3/4 In. 5.00

Soup, Dish, Deep, Colonial
Couple, 8 In. 13.00

DERWOOD is a shape that was
decorated with various decals.

Bowl, Cereal 4.00

Bowl, Flowers, 1 Pt. 7.50

Bowl, Fruit, 5 1/2 In. 5.00

Cake Plate, 6 1/4 In. 10.00

Cup & Saucer 9.00

Dish, Oval 17.00

Plate, Bread & Butter,
6 1/4 In. . . . . 3.00 to 5.00

Plate, Dinner, Blue Band,
10 In. 10.00

Plate, Salad, 7 1/2 In. 12.00

Platter, Orange Poppy,
11 1/4 x 14 3/4 In. 75.00

Sauceboat . . . . . . 14.00 to 15.00

Soup, Dish 7.00

LIDO is a shape made in the
1930s and early 1940s. It was
made in Canarytone, an ivory-
colored glaze, or White with
various decal decorations.
Pieces are marked with the
name of the line, manufacturer,
and color.

Canarytone

Bowl, 5 3/4 In. 4.75

Bowl, Fruit, Rust Floral . . . 6.00

Plate, Bread & Butter,
Rust Floral, 6 1/2 In. 6.00

Platter, Floral,
11 1/2 In. 12.00

Platter, Floral, 13 In. 15.00

Saucer, Rust Floral 4.00

White

Bowl, Dessert, Platinum
Trim, 5 1/2 In. 3.00

Bowl, Oval, 9 1/2 In. 10.00

Bowl, Vegetable, Cover,
2 3/4 x 10 1/4 In. 45.00

Platter, 10 x 7 3/4 In. 18.00

PETALWARE, or Petal, is the
name some collectors use for
Georgette. It is a round shape
with panels, or "petals," that
form a scalloped edge. Decal-
decorated Petalware was made
beginning in 1933 and is hard to
find today. Solid-color pieces
were made beginning in 1947.

Aqua

Bowl, Cereal, 6 1/4 In. 9.75

Bowl, Dessert, 5 1/2 In. . . . 6.75

Cup 6.00

Plate, Dinner, 9 3/8 In. 6.00

Saucer 2.00

Soup, Dish, 8 In. 11.50

Blue

Bowl, Cereal, 6 1/4 In. 9.75

Bowl, Dessert, 5 1/2 In. . . . 6.75

Bowl, Vegetable 15.50

Cup 6.00

Cup, After
Dinner . . . . 8.75 to 9.75

Plate, Bread & Butter,
6 1/2 In. 4.50

Plate, Dinner, 9 3/8 In. 6.00

Plate, Salad, 7 1/2 In. 5.50

Saucer . . . . 8.50 to 12.00

Saucer, After Dinner 7.50

Saucer, Jumbo, Mother,
Gold Edge 8.25

Sugar, Cover Only 6.75

Dark Green

Bowl, Cereal, 6 1/4 In. 9.75

Bowl, Dessert, 5 1/2 In. . . . 6.75

Cup, After Dinner 8.75

Plate, Bread & Butter,
  6 1/2 In. 4.50
Plate, Dinner, 9 3/8 In. 6.00
Saucer 2.00
Saucer, After Dinner 7.50
Saucer, Jumbo, Father 7.50

Gray
Bowl, Cereal, 6 1/4 In. 9.75
Bowl, Fruit, 5 1/2 In. 11.00
Plate, Salad, 7 1/2 In. 5.50
Serving Bowl, Scalloped
  Edge 17.00
Serving Dish, Scalloped
  Edge, Oval, 9 x 7 In. . . . 18.00
Soup, Coupe, Scalloped
  Edge, 7 3/4 In. 8.00
Soup, Dish, 8 In. 11.50

Light Green
Bowl, Vegetable 15.50
Saucer 12.00
Sugar, Cover,
  4 1/2 x 2 1/4 In. 25.00

Maroon
Bowl, Vegetable 15.50
Plate, Bread & Butter,
  6 1/2 In. 4.50
Plate, Dinner, 9 3/8 In. 6.00

Pink
Bowl, Cereal, 6 1/4 In. 9.75
Bowl, Dessert,
  5 1/2 In. 6.75
Bowl, Vegetable 15.50
Cup 6.00
Cup, After Dinner . . 8.75 to 9.75
Plate, Bread & Butter,
  6 1/2 In. 4.50
Plate, Dinner, 9 3/8 In. 6.00
Plate, Salad, 7 1/2 In. 5.50
Saucer 2.00
Saucer, After
  Dinner . . . . 7.50 to 8.50
Soup, Dish, 8 In. 11.50
Sugar, 4 1/2 In. 9.75
Sugar, Cover Only 6.75

Yellow
Bowl, Vegetable 15.50
Cup, After Dinner . . 8.75 to 9.75
Plate, Salad, 7 1/2 In. 5.50
Platter, 13 In. 27.00
Saucer . . . . 2.00 to 8.50
Saucer, After Dinner 7.50

Soup, Dish, 8 In. 11.50
Sugar, Cover Only 6.75

RADISSON was made from the 1920s to the 1940s. The shape has a scalloped edge. Pieces are decorated with small groups of flowers or bands of color, or are undecorated with or without gold trim.

Bowl, Dessert, Twyla,
  5 In. 7.50
Bowl, Oval, Twyla,
  9 In. 14.00
Bowl, Vegetable, Garland,
  9 x 3 In. 22.00
Bowl, Vegetable, Oval,
  Twyla, 9 3/8 In. 24.00
Creamer, Twyla 15.00
Cup, Tea 4.00
Dish, Fruit, Garland,
  5 In. 8.00
Plate, Bread & Butter,
  6 In. . . . . 3.00 to 10.00
Plate, Dinner, Garland,
  10 In. 15.00
Plate, Dinner, Twyla,
  9 3/4 In. 9.50
Plate, Luncheon, Pink
  Roses, 9 In. 7.50
Plate, Salad, Twyla, 7 In. . . 6.50
Platter, Oval, Twyla,
  11 1/2 In. 25.00
Platter, Oval, Twyla,
  13 1/2 In. 35.00
Soup, Dish, Black Line,
  Pink Roses 6.00
Sugar, Cover, Twyla 18.50

RANCHERO, a shape designed by Simon Slobodkin, was introduced in 1933. It was made in plain colors and with various decal decorations.

Bowl, Speckled Gold,
  Monogram 15.00

Bowl, Vegetable, Pussy
  Willow, 9 x 3 In. 20.00
Casserole, Pussy Willow,
  Handles, 1 Qt. 30.00
Creamer, Monogram,
  Gray 10.00
Plate, Dessert, Pussy Willow,
  White, 6 1/4 In., Pair . . . 12.00
Plate, Dinner, Wampum,
  10 In. 9.00
Saucer, Coupe Shape, Shortcake,
  Ivory, 6 1/4 In. 5.00
Soup, Rim, Wampum,
  8 In. 15.00
Teapot, 5 x 8 1/2 x 6 In. . . 40.00

SHASTA is an asymmetrical shape made in the mid-1950s. It was decorated with various decals.

Plate, Dessert, Primavera,
  6 In. 4.50
Plate, Luncheon,
  Primavera 7.50
Soup, Dish, Pinehurst,
  7 3/4 In. x 1 1/4 In. . 8.00 to 10.00

WATT

Watt Pottery was started in 1922 in Crooksville, Ohio, by William J. Watt and his sons. They made oven-safe kitchenware in 1935. Most of its dinner-wares were not made un-til the 1950s. The pottery was destroyed by fire in 1965. Pieces were usually marked with an impressed number indicating shape. The company used the impressed numbers 04 through 07 for nappies, low bowls that we would call mixing bowls today. Numbers 5 through 14 were used for the large mixing bowls.

AMERICAN RED BUD, also called Bleeding Heart or Teardrop, was decorated with hanging red buds, green leaves, and brown stems. It was introduced in the mid-1950s.

Baker, Square, Cover,
  No. 84 .... 800.00
Bean Cup, No. 75 .... 30.00
Bean Pot, Cover,
  No. 502 .... 140.00
Bowl, Salad, No. 74 ..... 45.00
Canister, Tea, Cover,
  No. 82 .... 232.00
Casserole, Cover,
  No. 66 .... 135.00
Casserole, Cover,
  No. 67 .... 10.00
Mixing Bowl Set,
  3 Piece 81.00
Mixing Bowl Set,
  4 Piece ..... 159.00 to 164.00
Pitcher, No. 15 .. 33.00 to 50.00
Salt & Pepper, Barrel, No. 45
  & No. 46 ... 155.00 to 200.00

APPLE is the most popular Watt pattern. It is sometimes called Red Apple. Dinnerware sets and kitchenware were made beginning in 1952. There are several variations within the Apple pattern, including 2-leaf, 3-leaf, Reduced Apple (looks like a red heart), Open Apple (shows the core), and Double Apple. There are some price differences between the pattern variations.

Baker, No. 67,
  3-Leaf 27.00
Baker, No. 96 .... 16.00
Bean Pot, Cover,
  No. 76 .... 41.00 to 81.00
Berry Bowl, No. 22,
  3-Leaf 22.00
Bowl, Advertising,
  Lennox South Dakota,
  4 1/2 In. 125.00
Bowl, Advertising,
  W.O. Kienas Markesan,
  Wisconsin Phone 25 .. 125.00
Bowl, No. 602, 3-Leaf ... 10.00
Bowl, No. 603, 3-Leaf 8.50
Bowl, Salad, No. 73 ..... 34.00
Bowl, Salad, No. 74,
  2-Leaf 38.00
Bowl, Spaghetti,
  No. 39 ..... 135.00 to 150.00
Bowl, Spaghetti, No. 39,
  Open Apple 786.00
Casserole, Cover,
  No. 110 .... 300.00
Casserole, Cover,
  No. 601 .... 115.00 to 140.00
Cookie Jar, Cover Only,
  No. 503 .... 10.00
Cookie Jar, Cover, 8 In. .. 77.00
Ice Bucket, Cover,
  No. 59, 3-Leaf 118.00
Mixing Bowl, No. 6 ..... 95.00
Mixing Bowl, No. 8,
  Ribbed .... 25.00 to 60.00
Mixing Bowl, No. 9 .... 175.00
Mixing Bowl, No. 63 ... 100.00
Mixing Bowl, No. 63,
  2-Leaf 49.00
Mixing Bowl, No. 64 ... 125.00
Mixing Bowl, No. 64,
  2-Leaf 19.00

Mixing Bowl,
  No. 65 ..... 100.00 to 145.00
Mixing Bowl, No. 73,
  3-Leaf .... 55.00 to 70.00
Mug, No. 121,
  3-Leaf ..... 100.00 to 160.00
Nappy, No. 04, 3-Leaf ... 51.00
Nappy, No. 04, Ribbed ... 95.00
Nappy, No. 05,
  3-Leaf .... 50.00 to 70.00
Nappy, No. 06,
  3-Leaf .... 30.00 to 50.00
Nappy, No. 06, Open
  Apple 98.00
Nappy, No. 07,
  3-Leaf .... 35.00 to 89.00
Nappy, No. 07, Ribbed .. 110.00
Pitcher,
  No. 15 ..... 100.00 to 165.00
Pitcher, No. 15,
  3-Leaf .... 63.00 to 69.00
Pitcher,
  No. 16 ..... 120.00 to 250.00
Pitcher, No. 16,
  3-Leaf ...... 66.00 to 120.00
Pitcher, No. 17,
  3-Leaf ..... 100.00 to 185.00
Pitcher, No. 62 .. 55.00 to 95.00
Salt & Pepper,
  Hourglass, No. 117 &
  No. 118 .... 250.00 to 255.00
Sugar, No. 98 .... 224.00

AUTUMN FOLIAGE was made from 1959 to 1965. It has brown leaves on brown stems. It is also called Brown Leaves.

Mixing Bowl, No. 8 ..... 36.00
Nappy, No. 05 .... 57.00
Pitcher,
  No. 15 ...... 75.00 to 107.00
Pitcher, No. 17 .... 90.00
Shaker, Pepper, Hourglass,
  No. 118 .... 90.00
Sugar, No. 98 .... 183.00

DUTCH TULIP was introduced in 1956. The design shows a black stylized tulip with green and red leaves on a cream-color dinnerware.

Baker, No. 67 .... 24.00
Bowl, No. 58 .... 81.00
Creamer, No. 62 .... 140.00
Ice Bucket, No. 59 ..... 163.00
Pitcher, No. 15 .... 128.00
Saltshaker, Barrel,
   No. 45 .... 450.00

KITCH-N-QUEEN was introduced in 1955. The kitchenware pieces are cream-colored with a wide mauve band centered between two narrow turquoise bands.

Bowl, Salad, No. 73 ..... 56.00
Mixing Bowl, No. 5 ..... 21.00
Mixing Bowl, No. 6 ..... 20.00
Mixing Bowl, No. 7 ..... 15.00
Mixing Bowl, No. 9 ..... 22.00
Mixing Bowl, No. 12 .... 20.00
Mixing Bowl,
   No. 14 .... 40.00 to 70.00
Mixing Bowl, Ribbed,
   No. 8 .... 36.00
Nappy, No. 600 .... 25.00
Nappy Set, No. 05,
   06 & 07, 3 Piece 81.00

PANSY, or Rio Rose as it was called in Watt advertising, was first produced in the 1950s. It was the first hand-painted Watt pattern and comes in many variations: Raised Pansy or Wild Rose, Cut-Leaf or Bull's Eye, Pansy, Old Pansy, and Cross Hatch.

Berry Bowl, No. 22 ..... 23.00

Bowl, Lug Handles,
   No. 18 .... 10.00
Bowl, Spaghetti,
   No. 25 .... 150.00
Bowl, Spaghetti, No. 25,
   Cut-Leaf 24.00
Bowl, Spaghetti, No. 39 .. 52.00
Bowl, Spaghetti, No. 39,
   Cut-Leaf 80.00
Casserole, No. 8, 4 Tab
   Handles 10.00
Chop Plate, No. 105,
   Cut-Leaf 105.00
Cookie Jar, Cover, No. 91,
   Raised Pansy 76.00
Cookie Jar, Cover,
   No. 91 .... 71.00
Mixing Bowl, No. 6,
   Cross Hatch 47.00
Mixing Bowl, No. 8 ..... 15.00
Mixing Bowl, No. 9 ..... 30.00
Pie Plate, No. 33 .... 85.00
Pitcher, No. 17 .... 148.00
Plate, Dinner, No. 101,
   Cut-Leaf 50.00

ROOSTER pattern was introduced in 1955. It was made until at least 1958. Pieces picture a black, green, and red rooster standing in green grass.

Baker, No. 85 .... 515.00
Casserole, Cover,
   No. 18 .... 150.00
Pitcher, No. 15 .. 36.00 to 56.00
Pitcher, No. 62 .... 115.00

STARFLOWER was made in the early 1950s in several variations. One type has either four-petal or five-petal red flowers with green leaves on a cream background. Other variations have two or three green leaves.

Similar patterns with different names were made in several color combinations.

Berry Bowl,
   No. 22 ...... 15.00 to 19.00
Bowl, No. 1 .... 50.00
Bowl, Salad,
   No. 55 ..... 75.00 to 100.00
Bowl, Salad, No. 55,
   5-Petal 75.00
Bowl, Spaghetti, No. 24 .. 21.00
Casserole, Cover, 2 Tab
   Handles, No. 18 ...... 103.00
Casserole, Cover,
   No. 54 .... 245.00
Chop Plate, 5-Petal 125.00
Chop Plate,
   No. 31 ..... 100.00 to 125.00
Cookie Jar, No. 21,
   5-Petal 225.00
Ice Bucket, Cover,
   No. 59, 5-Petal 185.00
Mixing Bowl, No. 5 ..... 21.00
Mixing Bowl,
   No. 7 .... 65.00 to 75.00
Mixing Bowl, No. 9,
   5-Petal 31.00
Mixing Bowl, No. 12 ... 100.00
Nappy, No. 05 .... 34.00
Nappy, No. 06 .... 55.00
Pitcher, No. 15 .... 23.00
Pitcher, No. 16 .. 21.00 to 35.00
Pitcher, No. 17 .... 110.00
Pitcher, No. 17, 5-Petal .. 82.00
Plate, Luncheon, No. 43,
   Pink Flower 58.00
Salt & Pepper 150.00
Saltshaker, Hourglass,
   No. 117 .... 75.00

TULIP pattern was sold in Woolworth stores. It was made about 1963. The pattern features a red and a blue tulip with green leaves.

Bowl, Salad, No. 73 ..... 39.00
Mixing Bowl, No. 64 ... 175.00
Mixing Bowl, No. 65 ... 190.00
Pitcher,
No. 16 ..... 145.00 to 178.00
Pitcher, No. 17,
Ice Lip ..... 195.00 to 240.00
Saltshaker, No. 45 ..... 450.00

WILLOW

Willow pattern pictures a bridge, figures, birds, trees, and a Chinese landscape. The pattern was first used in England by Thomas Turner in 1780 at the Caughley Pottery

Works. It was inspired by an earlier Chinese pattern. The pattern has been copied by makers in almost every country. It was made in the United States by Homer Laughlin China Company, Sebring, and others. Pieces listed here are blue unless another color is mentioned. Blue and pink willow were made by the Royal China Company of Sebring, Ohio, from the 1940s through the 1960s.

Ashtray, Royal China 18.00
Berry Bowl, Pink, Royal
China, 5 1/4 In. 10.00
Berry Bowl, Royal China,
5 1/4 In. 8.00
Bowl, Cereal, Cavalier, Royal
China, 6 1/2 In. 6.00
Bowl, Cereal, Pink, Royal
China, 6 1/4 In. 16.00
Bowl, Cereal, Red, Royal
China, 6 1/2 In. 6.50
Bowl, Cereal, Royal China,
6 1/4 In. 14.00
Bowl, Cereal, Tab Handle,
Royal China, 6 1/4 In. .. 40.00
Bowl, English Ironstone
Tableware, 6 In. 9.00
Bowl, Green, Royal
China, 10 In. 40.00
Bowl, Pink, Buffalo
Pottery, 8 In. 50.00
Bowl, Tab Handle, Pink,
Royal China, 6 1/4 In. .. 45.00
Bowl, Vegetable, Oval, Homer
Laughlin, 8 5/8 In. 50.00
Bowl, Vegetable, Pink, Royal
China, 9 In. 24.00
Bowl, Vegetable, Pink, Royal
China, 10 In. 35.00
Bowl, Vegetable, Royal
China, 9 In. 20.00
Bowl, Vegetable, Royal
China, 10 In. 24.00
Butter, Cover, Royal
China 50.00
Butter Chip, Buffalo Pottery,
1916, 3 3/4 In. 39.00

Casserole, Cover, Royal
China 90.00
Charger, Pink, Royal
China, 13 1/4 In. 60.00
Chop Plate, Cavalier, Royal
China, 11 1/2 In. 18.00
Chop Plate, Green, Royal
China, 12 1/4 In. 50.00
Chop Plate, Green, Royal
China, 13 1/4 In. 80.00
Chop Plate, Pink, Royal
China, 12 1/4 In. 32.00
Chop Plate, Royal China,
11 1/2 In. 28.00
Chop Plate, Royal China,
12 1/4 In. 24.00
Chop Plate, Royal China,
13 1/4 In. 65.00
Coffee Cup, Handle Design,
Royal China 16.00
Creamer, Pink, Royal
China 12.00
Creamer, Royal China ... 10.00
Cup, Tea, Blue, Hall,
2 3/8 x 2 1/4 In. 50.00
Cup, Tea, Handle Design,
Royal China 6.00
Cup, Tea, No Handle Design,
Royal China 5.00
Cup, Tea, Pink, Handle
Design, Royal China 8.00
Cup & Saucer, Royal
China 7.00
Dinner Set, English Ironstone
Tableware, 12 Piece ... 40.00
Gravy Boat, Pink, Royal
China 30.00
Gravy Boat, Underplate,
Royal China 20.00
Gravy Ladle, White, Fair
Oaks, Royal China 50.00
Grill Plate, Brown, Royal
China, 11 1/8 In. 40.00
Grill Plate, Royal China,
10 3/8 In. 40.00
Pie Baker, Royal China,
10 In. 50.00
Plate, Black, Royal China,
9 1/4 In. 20.00
Plate, Bread & Butter, Pink,
Royal China, 6 1/2 In. ... 7.00
Plate, Bread & Butter, Royal
China, 6 1/4 In. .. 4.00 to 5.00
Plate, Cavalier, Bread & Butter,
Royal China, 6 1/2 In. ... 4.00

Plate, Cavalier, Dinner, Royal
China, 10 In. 10.00

Plate, Cup & Saucer,
Tillson, England,
3 1/2 In., 5 3/4 In. 80.00

Plate, Dinner, Pink, Royal
China, 10 In. 16.00

Plate, Dinner, Royal China,
10 In. . . . . 14.00 to 40.00

Plate, Luncheon, Pink,
Royal China, 9 In. 20.00

Plate, Luncheon, Royal
China, 9 In. . . . 10.00 to 25.00

Plate, Salad, Royal China,
7 1/4 In. 14.00

Plate, Tillson, England,
8 In. 80.00

Platter, Black, Royal China,
8 3/4 x 11 In. 25.00

Platter, Handles, Royal
China, 11 1/2 In. 50.00

Platter, Oval, Pink, Royal
China, 13 x 10 In. 35.00

Platter, Oval, Royal China,
13 x 10 In. 40.00

Platter, Royal China,
12 1/4 In. 25.00

Platter, Tab Handle, Royal
China, 10 1/2 In. 20.00

Salt & Pepper, Handle
Design, Royal China . . . 40.00

Salt & Pepper, No Handle
Design, Royal China . . . 30.00

Salt & Pepper, Royal
China 40.00

Saucer, Pink, Royal China,
6 In. . . . . 6.00 to 10.00

Saucer, Royal China 5.00

Snack Plate, Royal China,
9 In. 40.00

Soup, Dish, Flat, Royal
China, 8 1/4 In. 12.00

Soup, Dish, Royal China,
7 1/4 In. 8.00

Soup, Dish, Royal China,
8 1/4 In. . . . . . . 12.00 to 14.00

Sugar, Cover, Pink, Tab Handle,
Royal China 25.00

Sugar, Cover, Royal
China 15.00

Sugar, Loop Handle, Cover,
Pink, Royal China 20.00

Sugar & Creamer, English
Ironstone Tableware,
Marked Old Willow . . . 35.00

Teapot, Droop Spout, Royal
China 80.00

Teapot, Flat Spout, Royal
China 70.00

CERAMIC DINNERWARE

Clubs and Publications

CLUBS

Blue & White Pottery Club, *Blue & White Pottery Club* (NL), 224 12th St. NW, Cedar Rapids, IA 52405.

Butter Pat Patter Association, *The Patter* (NL), 265 Eagle Bend Dr., Bigfork, MT 59911-6235.

Currier & Ives Dinnerware Collectors, *Currier & Ives Dinnerware Collectors' Newsletter* (NL), 29470 Saxon Rd., Toulon, IL 61483, website: www.royalchinaclub.com (Currier & Ives dinnerware by Royal China Company).

Eva Zeisel Collectors Club, *Eva Zeisel Times* (NL), 695 Monterey Blvd., # 203, San Francisco, CA 94127, e-mail: patmoore@evazeisel.org, website: www.evazeisel.org.

Frankoma Family Collectors Association, *Pot & Puma* (NL), *Prairie Green Sheet* (NL), PO Box 32571, Oklahoma City, OK 73123-0771, e-mail: fcca4 nancy@aol.com, website: www.frankoma.org.

Hall China/Jewel Tea Collector's Club, *Quarterly Newsletter of the Hall China Collector's Club & Jewel Tea & Other Tea Company China* (NL), PO Box 361280, Cleveland, OH 44136, e-mail: chandler-10@msn.com, website: www.chinaspecialties.com.

Homer Laughlin Collectors Club, *The Homer Laughlin Glaze* (NL), PO Box 1093, Corbin KY 40702-1093, e-mail: info@hlcca.org, website: www.hlcca.org.

International Willow Collectors, 503 Chestnut St., Perkasie, PA 18944, e-mail: willowpd@enter.net, website: www.willowcollectors.org.

National Autumn Leaf Collectors Club, *Autumn Leaf Newsletter* (NL), PO Box 7929, Moreno Valley, CA 92552-7929, e-mail: diannamark@aol.com, website: nalcc.org.

Red Wing Collectors Society, *Red Wing Collectors Newsletter* (NL), PO Box 50, Red Wing, MN 55066, website: www.redwingcollectors.org.

Stangl/Fulper Collectors Club, *Stangl/Fulper Times* (NL), PO Box 538, Flemington, NJ 08822, e-mail: cpm426@ameritech.net.

Watt Collectors Association, *Watt's News* (NL), 1431 4th St. SW, PMB 221, Mason City, IA 50401, e-mail: wattcollectors@yahoo.com.

PUBLICATIONS

McCoy Lovers NM Express (NL), 8934 Brecksville Rd., Suite 406, Brecksville, OH 44141-2318, e-mail: nmxpress@aol.com, website: www.nmxpress.com (McCoy pottery).

National Blue Ridge Newsletter (NL), 144 Highland Dr., Blountville, TN 37617-5404.

Purinton News & Views (NL), PO Box 153, Connellsville, PA 15425, e-mail: jmcmanus@hhs.net.

CERAMIC DINNERWARE

References

China Identification Kit. Replacements, Ltd. Privately printed, continuously updated (PO Box 26029, Greensboro, NC 27420).

Chipman, Jack. *Collector's Encyclopedia of California Pottery.* 2nd edition. Paducah, Kentucky: Collector Books, 1998.

Cunningham, Jo. *Collector's Encyclopedia of American Dinnerware.* Revised edition. Paducah, Kentucky: Collector Books, 1999.

————. *The Best of Collectible Dinnerware.* Atglen, Pennsylvania: Schiffer, 1995.

Duke, Harvey. *Official Price Guide to Pottery and Porcelain.* 8th edition. New York: House of Collectibles, 1995 (out of print).

From Kiln to Kitchen: American Ceramic Design in Tableware. Springfield: Illinois State Museum, 1980 (out of print).

Gates, William C. Jr., and Dana E. Ormerod. "The East Liverpool, Ohio, Pottery District: Identification of Manufacturers and Marks." *Historical Archaeology* 16 (1982). Washington, D.C.: The Society for Historical Archaeology (out of print).

Keller, Joe, and David Ross. *Russel Wright Dinnerware, Pottery & More: An Identification and Price Guide.* Atglen, Pennsylvania: Schiffer, 2000.

Kerr, Ann. *Collector's Encyclopedia of Russel Wright: Identification & Values.* 3rd edition. Paducah, Kentucky: Collector Books, 2002.

Kovel, Ralph and Terry. *Kovels' Antiques & Collectibles Price List.* New York: Random House Reference, annual.

————. *Kovels' Know Your Collectibles.* New York: Crown Publishers, 1981, updated 1992.

————. *Kovels' New Dictionary of Marks—Pottery & Porcelain, 1850 to the Present.* New York: Crown Publishers, 1986.

Lehner, Lois. *Lehner's Encyclopedia of U.S. Marks on Pottery, Porcelain & Clay.* Paducah, Kentucky: Collector Books, 1988 (out of print).

Piña, Leslie. *Pottery: Modern Wares, 1920–1960.* Atglen, Pennsylvania: Schiffer, 1994.

Pratt, Michael. *Mid-Century Modern Dinnerware: Ak-Sar-Ben Pottery, Denwar Ceramics, Iroquois China Company, Laurel Potteries of California, Royal China Company, Stetson China Company.* Atglen, Pennsylvania: Schiffer, 2002.

Snyder, Jeffrey B. *Depression Pottery.* Atglen, Pennsylvania: Schiffer, 1999.

Venable, Charles, et al. *China & Glass in America, 1880–1980: From Tabletop to TV Tray.* Dallas, Texas: Dallas Museum of Art, 2000.

BAUER

Snyder, Jeffrey B. *Beautiful Bauer: A Pictorial Study with Prices.* Atglen, Pennsylvania: Schiffer, 2000.

Chipman, Jack. *Collector's Encyclopedia of Bauer Pottery: Identification & Values.* Paducah, Kentucky: Collector Books, 1998.

Tuchman, Mitch. *Bauer Classic American Pottery.* San Francisco, California: Chronicle Books, 1995.

BEN SEIBEL

Racheter, Richard G. *Tableware Designs of Ben Seibel, 1940s–1980s.* Atglen, Pennsylvania: Schiffer, 2003.

BLUE RIDGE

Newbound, Betty and Bill. *Best of Blue Ridge Dinnerware: Identification & Value Guide.* Paducah, Kentucky: Collector Books, 2003.

Ruffin, Frances and John. *Blue Ridge China Today: A Comprehensive Identification and Price Guide for Today's Collector.* Atglen, Pennsylvania: Schiffer, 1997.

———. *Blue Ridge China Traditions.* Atglen, Pennsylvania: Schiffer, 1999.

COORS

Carlton, Carol and Jim. *Collector's Encyclopedia of Colorado Pottery.* Paducah, Kentucky: Collector Books, 1994 (out of print).

Schneider, Robert. *Coors Rosebud Pottery.* Privately printed, 1984 (out of print).

ENOCH WEDGWOOD

Coe, Debbie and Randy. *Liberty Blue Dinnerware.* Atglen, Pennsylvania: Schiffer, 2002.

FRANCISCAN

Elliot-Bishop, James F. *Franciscan, Catalina, and Other Gladding, McBean Wares: Ceramic Table and Art Ware, 1873–1942.* Atglen, Pennsylvania: Schiffer, 2001.

Enge, Delleen. *Franciscan Ware*. Paducah, Kentucky: Collector Books, 1981 (out of print).

Enge, Delleen, and Merrianne Metzger. *Franciscan: Plain & Fancy*. Privately printed, 1996 (121 E. El Roblar Dr., Suite #10, Ojai, CA 93023).

Page, Bob, and Dale Frederiksen. *Franciscan: An American Dinnerware Tradition*. Privately printed, 1999 (Replacements, Ltd., PO Box 26029, Greensboro, NC 27420).

Snyder, Jeffrey B. *Franciscan Dining Services: A Comprehensive Guide with Values*. 2nd edition, revised. Atglen, Pennsylvania: Schiffer, 2002.

FRANKOMA

Bess, Phyllis and Tom. *Frankoma and Other Oklahoma Potteries*. 3rd edition. Atglen, Pennsylvania: Schiffer, 2000.

Schaum, Gary V. *Collector's Guide to Frankoma Pottery, 1933–1990*. Gas City, Indiana: L-W Book Sales, 1997.

HALL

Duke, Harvey. *Superior Quality Hall China: A Guide for Collectors*. Privately printed, 1977 (out of print).

Miller, C.L. *Jewel Tea Sales and Houseware Collectibles with Value Guide*. Atglen, Pennsylvania: Schiffer, 1995.

———. *The Jewel Tea Company: Its History and Products*. Atglen, Pennsylvania: Schiffer, 1994.

Snyder, Jeffrey B. *Hall China*. Atglen, Pennsylvania: Schiffer, 2002.

Whitmyer, Margaret and Kenn. *Collector's Encyclopedia of Hall China*. 3rd edition. Paducah, Kentucky: Collector Books, 2001.

HARKER

Colbert, Neva W. *Collector's Guide to Harker Pottery U.S.A.: Identification and Value Guide*. Paducah, Kentucky: Collector Books, 1993 (out of print).

HOMER LAUGHLIN

Cunningham, Jo. *Homer Laughlin: A Giant Among Dishes, 1873–1939*. Atglen, Pennsylvania: Schiffer, 1998.

———. *Homer Laughlin China: 1940s & 1950s*. Atglen, Pennsylvania: Schiffer, 2000.

Fiesta, Harlequin, Kitchen Kraft Dinnerware: The Homer Laughlin China Collectors Association Guide. Atglen, Pennsylvania: Schiffer, 2000.

Gonzalez, Mark. *Collecting Fiesta, Lu-Ray & Other Colorware*. Gas City, Indiana: L-W Book Sales, 2000.

Huxford, Sharon and Bob. *Collector's Encyclopedia of Fiesta, plus Harlequin, Riviera, and Kitchen Kraft.* 9th edition. Paducah, Kentucky: Collector Books, 2001.

Jasper, Joanne. *The Collector's Encyclopedia of Homer Laughlin China: Reference & Value Guide.* Paducah, Kentucky: Collector Books, 1993, 2002 values.

Nossaman, Darlene, and Jo Cunningham. *Homer Laughlin China: An Identification Guide to Shapes & Patterns.* Atglen, Pennsylvania: Schiffer, 2002.

Page, Bob, Dale Frederiksen, and Dean Six. *Homer Laughlin: Decades of Dinnerware.* Replacements, Ltd. Privately printed, 2003.

Racheter, Richard. *Post 86 Fiesta: Identification and Value Guide.* Paducah, Kentucky: Collector Books, 2001.

Snyder, Jeffrey B. *Fiesta: The Homer Laughlin China Company's Colorful Dinnerware.* 4th edition. Atglen, Pennsylvania: Schiffer, 2002.

HULL

Hull, Joan Gray. *Hull: The Heavenly Pottery.* 7th edition. Privately printed, 2000 (1376 Nevada SW, Huron, SD 57350).

Roberts, Brenda. *Collector's Encyclopedia of Hull Pottery.* Paducah, Kentucky: Collector Books, 1980, 2003 values.

Snyder, Jeffrey B. *Hull Pottery: Decades of Design.* 2nd edition. Atglen, Pennsylvania: Schiffer, 2003.

Supnick, Mark and Ellen. *Collecting Hull Pottery's Little Red Riding Hood.* Gas City, Indiana: L-W Book Sales, 1998.

JOHNSON BROTHERS

Finegan, Mary J. *Johnson Brothers Dinnerware Pattern Directory & Price Guide.* 2nd edition. Privately printed, 2003 (Marfine Antiques, PO Box 3618, Boone, NC 28607).

E.M. KNOWLES

Gonzalez, Mark. *Collecting Fiesta, Lu-Ray & Other Colorware.* Gas City, Indiana: L-W Book Sales, 2000.

MCCOY

Hanson, Bob, Craig Nissen, and Margaret Hanson. *McCoy Pottery,* 3 volumes. Paducah, Kentucky: Collector Books, 1996, 2002–2003 values.

Snyder, Jeffrey B. *McCoy Pottery.* 3rd edition, revised. Atglen, Pennsylvania: Schiffer, 2002.

———. *McCoy Pottery: A Field Guide.* Atglen, Pennsylvania: Schiffer, 2002.

METLOX

Gibbs, Carl Jr. *Collector's Encyclopedia of Metlox Potteries: Identification and Values.* 2nd edition. Paducah, Kentucky: Collector Books, 2001.

NORITAKE

Brewer, Robin. *Noritake Dinnerware: Identification Made Easy.* Atglen, Pennsylvania: Schiffer, 1999.

PURINTON

Bero-Johnson, Jamie, and Jamie Johnson. *Purinton Pottery with Values.* Atglen, Pennsylvania: Schiffer, 1997.

Dole, Pat. *Purinton Pottery.* Privately printed, 1984 (out of print).

———. *Purinton Pottery.* Book 2. Privately printed, 1990 (out of print).

Morris, Susan. *Purinton Pottery.* Paducah, Kentucky: Collector Books, 1994.

RED WING

Dollen, B.L. *Red Wing Art Pottery Identification & Value Guide, 1920s–1960s.* Paducah, Kentucky: Collector Books, 1997.

Dollen, B.L. and R.L. *Red Wing Art Pottery.* Book 2. Paducah, Kentucky: Collector Books, 1998.

———. *Collector's Encyclopedia of Red Wing Art Pottery.* Paducah, Kentucky: Collector Books, 2001.

Reiss, Ray. *Red Wing Art Pottery.* Volume 2. Chicago: Property Publishing, 2000.

———. *Red Wing Art Pottery, Including Pottery Made for RumRill: Classic American Pottery from the 30s, 40s, 50s & 60s.* Chicago: Property Publishing, 1996.

———. *Red Wing Dinnerware Price and Identification Guide.* Chicago: Property Publishing, 1997.

Simon, Dolores. *Red Wing Pottery with RumRrill.* Paducah, Kentucky: Collector Books, 1980.

ROSEVILLE

Bassett, Mark. *Introducing Roseville Pottery.* 2nd edition, revised. Atglen, Pennsylvania: Schiffer, 2001.

———. *Understanding Roseville Pottery.* Atglen, Pennsylvania: Schiffer, 2002.

Bomm, Jack and Nancy. *Roseville in All Its Splendor.* Gas City, Indiana: L-W Book Sales, 1998.

Huxford, Sharon and Bob. *The Collector's Encyclopedia of Roseville Pottery.* 2 volumes. Paducah, Kentucky: Collector Books, 1976 and 2001, 2001 values.

Mollring, Gloria and James. *Roseville Pottery Collector's Price Guide.* 6th edition. Privately printed, 2000 (PO Box 22754, Sacramento, CA 95822).

SHAWNEE

Curran, Pamela Duvall. *Shawnee Pottery: The Full Encyclopedia with Value Guide.* Atglen, Pennsylvania: Schiffer, 1995.

Mangus, Jim and Bev. *Shawnee Pottery: An Identification & Value Guide.* Paducah, Kentucky: Collector Books, 1994.

Supnick, Mark E. *Collecting Shawnee Pottery.* Gas City, Indiana: L-W Book Sales, 2000.

Vanderbilt, Duane and Janice. *The Collector's Guide to Shawnee Pottery.* Paducah, Kentucky: Collector Books, 1992 (out of print).

STANGL

Duke, Harvey. *Stangl Pottery.* Radnor, Pennsylvania: Wallace-Homestead, 1993 (out of print).

Rehl, Norma. *Collectors Handbook of Stangl Pottery.* Privately printed, 1979 (out of print).

————. *Stangl Pottery.* Part 2. Privately printed, 1982 (out of print).

Runge, Robert C. Jr. *Collector's Encyclopedia of Stangl Dinnerware.* Paducah, Kentucky: Collector Books, 2000.

SYRACUSE

Reed, Cleota, and Stan Skoczen. *Syracuse China.* Syracuse, New York: Syracuse University Press, 1997.

TAYLOR, SMITH & TAYLOR

Gonzalez, Mark. *Collecting Fiesta, Lu-Ray & Other Colorware.* Gas City, Indiana: L-W Book Sales, 2000.

Meehan, Kathy and Bill. *Collector's Guide to Lu-Ray Pastels.* Paducah, Kentucky: Collector Books, 1995 (out of print).

UNIVERSAL

Smith, Timothy J. *Universal Dinnerware and Its Predecessors.* Atglen, Pennsylvania: Schiffer, 2000.

VERNON KILNS

Nelson, Maxine. *Collectible Vernon Kilns: An Identification & Value Guide.* Paducah, Kentucky: Collector Books, 1994 (out of print).

————. *Versatile Vernon Kilns.* Book 2. Paducah, Kentucky: Collector Books, 1983 (out of print).

WATT

Morris, Sue and Dave. *Watt Pottery: An Identification and Value Guide.* Paducah, Kentucky: Collector Books, 1993.

Thompson, Dennis, and W. Bryce Watt. *Watt Pottery: A Collector's Reference with Price Guide.* 2nd edition, revised. Atglen, Pennsylvania: Schiffer, 2003.

WILLOW

Lindbeck, Jennifer A. *A Collector's Guide to Willow Ware.* Atglen, Pennsylvania: Schiffer, 2000.

Rogers, Connie. *Willow Ware Made in the U.S.A.: An Identification Guide.* Privately printed, 1996, 2000 values (1733 Chase Ave., Cincinnati, OH 45223).

PLASTIC
DINNERWARE

PLASTIC DINNERWARE

Introduction

Plastic dinnerware is just starting to interest collectors. Many pieces have the information about the maker as part of the mold, and it can be read on the bottom of each piece. Plastic dinnerware is listed here by manufacturer.

Plastic dishes were first made in the late 1920s. American Cyanamid Corporation developed a urea formaldehyde material that was similar to the British plastic called Beetleware. The earliest American Beetleware was given away as a premium with products like Wheaties and Ovaltine. American Beetleware was inexpensive to produce, but it didn't stand up to normal use. The dishes faded and cracked after repeated contact with water.

The formula for melamine was originally developed in 1834 by a Swiss scientist. The plastic wasn't used for dishes until 1937, when a food company used it to make trays for serving hot meals to factory workers. During World War II, the U.S. Navy bought more than a million pounds of melamine to make injection-molded dishes. American Cyanamid was the major producer of the powder that was used in the injection-molding process.

In 1944 American Cyanamid commissioned designer Russel Wright to create a line of melamine dishes for the average home. Wright's first design was called Meladur. By the 1950s, melamine dishes, commonly called Melmac, were advertised as an "accident-proof" substitution for pottery dinnerware. In the 1953 Sears catalog, a 16-piece set of Melmac cost almost twice as much as a similar 16-piece set of semi-porcelain dinnerware.

Melamine dishes scratched and stained easily, and the dinnerware wasn't truly unbreakable. By the late 1970s, Melmac lost its popularity.

Collectors pay most for items by well-known designers, like Russel Wright and Joan Luntz. The dinnerware is usually sold in sets or mixed lots. "Mixed color" listings in this section refer to mixed sets of solid-color dishes. "Speckled" means the plastic itself has dots of different colors. "Decal" refers to printed decorations, usually on solid white dishes.

There is a bibliography for books about plastic on page 253. There are also many sites on the Internet that offer pictures and information about plastic dinnerware.

Depression glass, see pages 1–142.

Ceramic dinnerware, see pages 241–253.

AZTEC

The Aztec Company was located in St. Louis, Missouri. The design of the medium-weight dinnerware line suggests the line was produced in the mid-1950s. Dishes are in deep colors, including Brown, Gray, Green, Mustard Yellow, Salmon, and Turquoise; and pastel colors, including Blue, Pink, White, and Yellow. Some colors are speckled, and a Beige set with a floral pattern was made. Dishes are marked *Aztec* and *Melamine Dinnerware.*

Speckled Green
Salad Set, Open Handles,
9 Piece 20.00

Speckled Rust
Bowl, Vegetable, Open Handles,
12 In. . . . . 13.00 to 16.00

Speckled Tan
Bowl, Vegetable, Open
Handles, 12 In. 14.00

BOONTON

The Boonton Molding Company, of Boonton, New Jersey, made heavy-weight Melmac dishes in 1948 for institutional use. In 1951, designer Belle Kogan worked with the company to produce dinnerware for the home. Later patterns, like Crown Patrician, Normandy Rose, and Somerset, are lighter weight. The company's ads listed the colors Butter Yellow, Charcoal, Cranberry Red, Forest Green, Golden Yellow, Oyster White, Pewter Gray, Powder Blue, Seafoam Green, Shrimp Pink, Stone Gray, Tawny Buff, and Turquoise

---

Blue. Decals, including Normandy Rose, were used on white dishes. Some pieces were made in speckled colors. The company continued to make dinnerware until 1977. Dishes are marked *Boonton, Boontonware, Boontonware Belle,* and *Melmac.*

Butter Yellow
Sugar & Creamer, Cover . 10.00

Cranberry Red
Mixing Bowl, Fluted Border,
7 In. 14.00
Sugar & Creamer,
Cover . . . . 10.00 to 14.00

Forest Green
Celery Dish, 6 In. 11.00

Mixed Color Set
Dinner Set, Plates, Bowl,
Cups, Saucers, Pastels,
16 Piece 16.00

Oyster White
Cup 3.00

Pewter Gray
Cup 5.00

Seafoam Green
Bowl, Vegetable, 2 Sections,
Handles, 10 In. 5.00
Dinner Set, Plates, Cups,
Saucers, 16 Piece 14.00
Platter, 12 In. 4.50

Shrimp Pink
Bowl, Vegetable, 2 Sections,
Handles, 10 In. 10.00
Bowl, Vegetable, Cover,
Handles, 10 In. 13.00
Butter, Cover,
1/4 Lb. . . . . 5.50 to 8.00

Speckled Chartreuse
Mixing Bowl, Fluted
Border, 7 In. 14.00

Speckled Powder Blue
Mixing Bowl, Fluted
Border, 7 In. 31.00

Speckled White
Butter, Cover, 1/4 Lb. 4.00

BROOKPARK

Brookpark dinnerware was made by International Molded Products, of Cleveland, Ohio, from 1950 to 1962. The Arrowhead line was designed by Joan Luntz in 1950 and won a Good Design Award from the Museum of Modern Art. Modern Design dinnerware, also designed by Luntz, features square dishes. Brookpark's dinnerware was made in Black, Burgundy, Chartreuse, Emerald, Pearl Gray, Pink, Stone, Turquoise, White, and Yellow. In 1956, Brookpark introduced the Fantasy line, the first decal-decorated melamine dinnerware. Other decorated lines are Bluebells, Contemporary, Delicado, Dual-Tone, Elegance, Flower Box, Gaiety, Golden Pine, Magic Carpet, Only a Rose Pavilion, Pink Hyacinth, Town and Country, and Tropicana. Desert Flower is a Brookpark line with an impressed floral decoration. Mixing bowls were made in speckled colors. Dishes are marked *Brookpark, Efficiency Ware, Ever Ware, International Molded Plastics Inc.,* and with pattern names.

Arrowhead
Bowl, Vegetable, 2 Sections,
 Turquoise, 10 In. 7.50

Fantasy
Dinner Set, Turquoise, Abstract
 Decal, 37 Piece 61.00

Modern Design
Bowl, Vegetable, 2 Sections,
 Chartreuse, 10 In. 11.00
Bowl, Vegetable, 2 Sections,
 White, 10 In. 4.00
Bowl, Vegetable, Pink,
 2 Sections, 10 In. 10.00
Dinner Set,
 Chartreuse, 20 Piece . . . 39.00
Dinner Set, Pink,
 16 Piece 13.00
Sugar & Creamer, Pink . . 10.00

Speckled
Mixing Bowl, Blue, Fuchsia,
 Green, 8 1/2 In. 22.00
Mixing Bowl, Blue, Red,
 Green, 6 In. 10.50
Mixing Bowl, Chartreuse, Red,
 Yellow, 11 3/4 In. 40.00
Mixing Bowl, Green, Pink,
 White, 8 1/2 In. 15.00
Mixing Bowl, Rust, Orange,
 Tan, 11 3/4 In. 18.00
Mixing Bowl Set, Nesting, Blue,
 Pink, White, 3 Piece . . . 90.00
Mixing Bowl Set, Nesting,
 Green, Blue, 3 Piece . . . 40.00
Mixing Bowl Set, Nesting,
 Yellow, Purple, Orange,
 3 Piece 67.00

COLOR-FLYTE

Color-Flyte and Color-Flyte Royale medium-weight dishes were made by Branchell (a division of Lenox Plastics) in St. Louis, Missouri, and San Francisco, California, beginning in 1952. It was sold by door-to-door salesmen. The dinnerware was produced in mottled colors: Glade Green, Glow Copper, Mist Gray, and Spray Lime. Royale colors were Charcoal Gray, Flame Pink, Gardenia White, and Turquoise Blue. Some of the plates were sold with decal decorations, including Golden Grapes, Golden Harvest, Lady Fair, Rosedale, Sweet Talk, and Tip Top. The dishes are marked *Branchell, Color-Flyte, Melmac,* and *Royale.*

Glow Copper
Platter, 13 3/4 In. 7.00
Salad Fork & Spoon 9.00

Mist Gray
Bowl, Vegetable, 2 Sections,
 10 1/2 In. 5.00

Platter, 13 3/4 In. 5.00

Mixed Colors
Dinner Set, Plates, Cups,
Saucers, Bowls,
   43 Piece 20.00
Tumbler Set, 5 Piece 17.00
Tumbler Set, 7 Piece 23.00

Spray Lime
Bowl, Vegetable,
   2 Sections, 10 1/2 In. 13.00
Gravy Boat 10.00
Salt & Pepper 27.00

HARMONY HOUSE

Harmony House melamine dishes were made by Plastic Masters, of New Buffalo, Michigan, for Sears, Roebuck & Company. The Talk of the Town line first appeared in the 1953 catalog and was produced in Chartreuse, Dawn Gray, Mint Green, and Victorian Red. Other solid-color lines are Avalon (Blue, Ivory, Pink, and Yellow), Catalina (Bronze Green, Inca Gold, Malibu Coral, and Spice Beige), Catalina Translucent (Light Federal Gold, Light Malibu Coral, Ming Blue, and Parchment Beige), New Talk of the Town (Clay Beige, Frosty Pink, Medium Federal Gold, and Medium Sage

Green), and Today (Aquamarine, Dawn Gray, Spice Beige, and Sunshine Yellow). Many decal-decorated patterns, like Autumn Leaves, Crocus, Floral Lace, Frolic, Golden Spears, Mademoiselle, Patio Rose, and Province, were introduced after 1957 and continued to be made through the 1960s. Dishes are marked *Harmony House, Melmac,* and with pattern names.

Avalon
Dinner Set, Pink,
   19 Piece 10.00
Dinner Set, Pink Roses,
   32 Pieces 95.00

Catalina
Bowl, Dessert 4.00
Creamer 8.00
Sugar, Cover 8.00

Patio Rose
Dinner Set, Plates, Bowls,
Platter, Cup, Saucers,
   42 Pieces 21.00

Talk Of The Town
Bowl, Vegetable, 2 Sections,
Pink, 9 In. 3.00
Dinner Set, Mixed Colors,
   24 Pieces 57.00

HOLIDAY

Holiday medium-weight dinnerware was manufactured by Kenro Company of Fredonia, Wisconsin.

Kenro also produced the Debonaire pattern. The speckled dishes came in Blue, Pink, Red, Salmon, Turquoise, White, and Yellow. Decorated patterns included Gale Art, Orchid Spray, and Seneca. An op-art black and white checkered set was designed by Tom Strobel and produced in a limited edition. Dishes are marked *Holiday by Kenro.*

Salmon
Bowl, Salad, 9 In. 10.00
Bowl, Vegetable, 2 Sections,
   9 In. 4.00

Yellow
Bowl, Vegetable, 2 Sections,
   9 In. 4.00

INSULATED PLASTIC

In the mid-1950s, the plastics industry introduced colorful insulated (thermal) tumblers, pitchers, mugs, and dishes. The drinking items were advertised as preventing condensation, thus avoiding rings on the furniture. The mugs, pitchers, and serving dishes could keep drinks and food hot or cold. One popular, unmarked design features a woven straw insert, similar to burlap, between a layer of Lucite and opaque colored plastic. Marked lines include Bolero by Thermo-Temp, Cornish, Raffiaware by Thermo-Temp, Sunfrost, Therm-O-Bowl by Reinecke, Thermo-Serv by West Bend, and Vacron.

Bolero

Beverage Set, Pitcher, Tumblers, Mixed Colors 15.00

Bowl, 3-Footed, Turquoise, 48 Oz. 15.50

Bowl Set, 3-Footed, Mixed Colors, 12 Oz., 6 Piece . 15.00

Bowl Set, Mixed Colors, 6 Piece 7.00

Ice Bucket, Cover, Turquoise 10.50

Mug Set, Mixed Colors, 8 Oz., 8 Piece 48.00

Pitcher, Cover, Turquoise, 8 3/4 In. 7.00

Tumbler Set, Iced Tea, Mixed Colors, 12 Oz., 8 Piece 31.00

Cornish

Beverage Set, Pitcher, Cover, Tumblers, Mixed Colors, 7 Piece 7.00

Mug Set, Mixed Colors, 4 Piece 12.00

Tumbler Set, Mixed Colors, 5 In., 4 Piece 4.00

Raffiaware

Bowl, Cover, Avocado Green, Box, 3 Qt. 7.00

Mug Set, Mixed Colors, 12 Piece 15.50

Pitcher, Turquoise 5.00

Sherbet Set, Pink, 6 Piece . . 5.00

Tumbler Set, Handles, Mixed Colors, 12 Oz., 5 Piece 20.00

Tumbler Set, Iced Tea, Mixed Colors, Brass Holder, 9 Piece 38.00

Tumbler Set, Iced Tea, Mixed Pastel Colors, 6 Piece . . 20.00

Straw Weave

Beverage Set, Turquoise Cloth, Pitcher, Tumblers, Ice Bucket, Cover, 8 Piece 31.00

Bowl Set, Cereal, Mixed Rim Colors, Brass Holder, 7 Piece 10.00

Bowl Set, Mixed Rim Colors, 4 Piece 5.50

Ice Bucket, Cover, Tan Rim 6.00

Ice Set, Tan Rim, 4 Piece . . 6.00

Mug Set, Mixed Rim Colors, 4 Piece 12.00

Pitcher, Cover, Tan Rim . . . 5.50

Tumbler Set, Iced Tea, Mixed Cloth Colors, 8 Piece . . 30.00

Tumbler Set, Mixed Rim Colors, 4 Piece 8.00

Tumbler Set, Mixed Rim Colors, Brass Holder, 7 Piece . . 20.00

Thermo-Serv By West Bend

Beverage Set, Daisies, Pitcher, Tumblers, Mugs, Ice Bucket, Cover, Tray, 11 Piece . . 20.00

Condiment Set, Metallic Gold Cups, Wooden Holder . . . 5.00

Mug Set, Metallic Gold & Black, 4 Piece 11.00

Tumbler Set, Iced Tea, Metallic Brown, 6 Piece 11.00

Tumbler Set, Tahitian Scene, Box, 6 Piece 15.00

Vacron

Mug Set, Pink, 6 Piece . . . 10.50

Pitcher, Cover, Chrome Finial, Yellow 5.50

MALLO-WARE

P.R. Mallory Plastics Inc. of Chicago, Illinois, made

Mallo-Ware. The medium-weight dinnerware was produced in Avocado, Beige, Burgundy, Chartreuse, Gold, Gray, Light Blue, Light Green, Pink, White, Yellow, and a decorated line called Moonglow. Dishes are marked *Mallo-Ware, Melmac,* and with shape numbers.

Beige

Sugar & Creamer 3.00

Chartreuse

Dinner Set, Plates, Bowls, Cups, Saucers, 38 Pieces 18.50

Light Blue

Dinner Set, Plates, Bowls, Platter, Cups, Saucers, 32 Piece 15.50

Platter, 15 1/2 In. 10.00

Yellow

Bowl, Vegetable, Handles . 6.00

PROLON

Prolon Plastics was a division of Prophylactic Brush Company of Florence, Massachusetts. Early Prolon dishes are heavier and were probably created for institutional use. Later styles, like Beverly, Cadence, and Florence, are lighter weight and more graceful. The Florence dinnerware line, designed by George Nelson Associates, won the

House Beautiful Classic Award in 1955. Colors include Burgundy, Dark Green, Dawn (beige-gray), Gray, High Noon (mustard yellow), Lime Green, Midnight (black), Olive Green, Rust Red, Sunset (red), Turquoise, White, and Yellow. Decorated lines include Artiste, Bazaar, Designers, Grant Crest, Hostess, Potpourri, Vista, and World of Color. Dishes are marked *Melmac, Prolon, Prolon Ware,* and with pattern names. Institutional dinnerware marked *Prolon* is still being made by Lincoln Foodservice Products Inc. in Fort Wayne, Indiana.

Florence

Bowl, Vegetable, Yellow,
  Oval, Handles, 11 In. . . 15.00
Butter, Cover, White 3.00
Dinner Set, Turquoise &
  White, Plates, Bowls, Cups,
  Saucers, Sugar, Creamer,
  42 Piece 40.00
Gravy Boat, White 9.50
Sugar & Creamer, Cover,
  White, Gold Decal 5.50

Prolon Ware

Creamer, Light Blue 4.00
Cup & Saucer, Ivory 3.00
Dinner Set, Mixed Pastel Colors,
  Plates, Cups, Saucers, Bowls,
  70 Piece 46.00
Sugar & Creamer,
  Chartreuse 10.50
Sugar & Creamer,
  Ivory 10.00

Never leave a key under the doormat.

ROYALON

Royalon Inc. of Chicago, Illinois, was a subsidiary of Royal China Inc. of Logansport, Indiana. Royalon's lines included Brookpark by Royalon, Candlelight, Hallmark, Roymac, Windsor, and World's Fair House. The lines were made in Beige, Pink, Purple, Turquoise, White, and Yellow, and were decorated with decals like Aristocrat, Crescendo, Jasmine, Romance, San Marino, and Violets. The Shenandoah line is decorated with apples. Dishes are marked *Melmac, Romac, Royalon,* and with pattern names.

Decal

Dinner Set, Flowers,
  Roymac, Box,
  45 Piece 36.00
Dinner Set, Roses, Plates,
  Bowls, Cups, Saucers, Sugar,
  Creamer, Gravy Boat,
  44 Piece 35.00
Dinner Set, Violets, Plates,
  Bowls, Cups, Saucers,
  21 Piece 45.00
Platter, Turkey Decal, Roymac,
  21 In. 22.00

Purple

Salt & Pepper, Cone
  Shape, 4 In. 15.00

Turquoise

Creamer 3.00

Cup 3.00
Gravy Boat 6.00
Sugar, Cover 9.00

White

Bowl, Vegetable,
  2 Sections 5.00

Yellow

Creamer 10.00

RUSSEL WRIGHT

Designer Russel Wright was a pioneer in melamine dinnerware. In 1945 he worked with American Cyanamid on prototype dishes for institutional use. His first line was Meladur, which was marked with his signature from 1949 to 1953. Wright's Residential line was made for domestic use by Northern Industrial Chemical Company, Boston, Massachusetts, and received the Good Design Award from the

Museum of Modern Art in 1953 and 1954. Residential dishes are opaque with a mottled effect created by overlapping two colors. Original colors are Black Velvet (black with aluminum dust), Copper Penny (brown with copper dust), Gray, Lemon Ice, and Sea Mist. Additional colors are Light Blue, Salmon, and White. The Home Decorators line was introduced in 1954 and came in Blue, Pink, Salmon, White, and Yellow with Bow Knot and Leaf decorations. Flair was introduced in 1959 in solid colors and with Arabesque, Golden Bouquet, Ming Lace, Spring Garden, and Woodland Rose decorations. Wright's Ideal Adult Kitchen Ware for children and for "refrigerator-to-table" use is also listed here, although the dishes are made of polyethylene, not melamine. Dishes are marked *Russel Wright, Northern,* and with pattern names.

Flair

Plate, Dinner, Ming Lace, Spring
Green, 9 3/4 In. 45.00

Home Decorators

Bowl, Vegetable, Pink,
9 In. 20.00
Plate, Dinner, Pink, White
Flowers, 10 1/2 In. 7.50
Platter, Pink, White
Flowers 11.00
Soup, Dish, Blue 15.00
Sugar, Cover, Pink 9.00
Tumbler, Yellow 5.50

Ideal Adult's Kitchen Ware

Creamer, Coral 12.50
Cup, Yellow 7.50
Gravy Boat, Coral 15.00

Don't put a runner or a vase on your wooden table if it is in sunlight. Eventually the finish will fade around the ornaments and leave a shadow of the items on the wood.

Pickle, Chartreuse 15.00
Plate, Dinner, Chartreuse . . 7.50
Plate, Dinner,
Glacier Gray 7.50
Saucer, Bean Brown 6.00
Sugar, Cantaloupe 12.50
Tea Set, Mixed Colors,
9 Piece . . . . , 20.50
Teapot, Cantaloupe 25.00
Teapot, Coral 25.00

Residential

Bowl, Fruit, Handle, Black
Velvet, 5 In. 65.00
Bowl, Vegetable, 2 Sections,
Copper Penny, 11 In. . . . 75.00
Bowl, Vegetable, 2 Sections,
Light Blue, 11 In. 17.50
Bowl, Vegetable, 2 Sections,
Sea Mist, 11 In. 25.00
Bowl, Vegetable, Lemon
Ice, 9 In. 20.00
Creamer, Lemon Ice 30.00
Creamer, Salmon 20.00
Creamer, Sea Mist 30.00
Cup & Saucer, Black
Velvet 17.50
Cup & Saucer, Salmon . . . 15.00
Plate, Bread & Butter,
Gray 5.00
Plate, Dinner, Salmon 10.00
Platter, Salmon, 14 In. . . . 25.00
Soup, Dish, Lug Handle,
Gray 17.50

Sugar & Creamer,
Light Blue 25.00
Tumbler, Light Blue,
8 Oz. 35.00
Tumbler Set, Mixed Colors,
10 Piece 150.00

STETSON

Stetson Chemicals had factories in Lincoln and Chicago, Illinois. The company made various lines, including Contour, Riviera, and Sun Valley. The dinnerware was made in Butterscotch, Light Green, mottled Orange, Pink, Turquoise, White, and Yellow. The dishes are marked *Melmac, Stetson,* and with pattern names.

Contour

Bowl, Fruit, Pink 2.00
Bowl, Vegetable, 2 Sections,
Pink, 9 In. . . . . 10.00 to 11.00

Sun Valley

Bowl, Vegetable, 2 Sections,
Turquoise, 9 In. 10.00
Sugar & Creamer, Cover,
Pink 5.50
Sugar & Creamer, Cover,
Yellow 10.00

TEXAS WARE

Texas Ware heavyweight dinnerware was made by Plastics Manufacturing Company in Dallas, Texas. The most common items are the speckled mixing bowls. Dallas Ware was an institutional line. Rio Vista was introduced in 1952 in Bone White, Chinese Red, Ebony Black, Sage Green, Stone Gray, and other colors. San Jacinto was introduced in 1953 and was made in Bone White, Dresden Blue, Dusty Rose, Jonquil Yellow, Sage Green, Sandalwood, and Sea Green. In 1957 Plastics Manufacturing Company introduced the first tone-on-tone items. The San Jacinto line won a Good Design Award from the Museum of Modern Art for Gray on White, Sandalwood on White, White on Sage Green, and Yellow on Dusty Rose items. Decal decorations included Angles, Autumn Leaves, Avant Garde, Bon Vivant, Bouquet, Classics, Epicure, Flourish, Happenings, Marco Polo, Park Avenue, Shasta Daisy, Trend, and Westwood. Dishes are marked *Plastics Manufacturing Company, PMC, Texas Ware,* and with pattern names. Plastics Manufacturing Company is still in business.

Decal

Dinner Set, Blue Band, Plates, Bowls, Mugs, Tumblers, Box, 16 Piece 22.50

Dinner Set, Daisy, Plates, Cups, Saucers, Bowls, 33 Piece 10.00

Dinner Set, Ivy, Plates, Cup, Saucers, Bowl, Platter, 55 Piece 25.00

Dinner Set, Lilac, Plates, Cups, Saucers, Bowls, 59 Piece 23.00

San Jacinto

Bowl, Vegetable, 2 Sections, Bone White, 9 In. 9.00

Dinner Set, Mixed Colors, 16 Piece 13.00

Speckled

Mixing Bowl, Chartreuse, White, Blue, No. 111, 8 In. 13.00

Mixing Bowl, Dark Blue, Green, Yellow, White, No. 125, 11 In. 47.00

Mixing Bowl, Gray, Black, Cream, Red, No. 125, 11 In. 26.00

Mixing Bowl, Gray, Tan, White, No. 111, 8 In. 10.00

Mixing Bowl, Green, Yellow, White, No. 118, 10 In. ... 28.00

Mixing Bowl, Pink, Peach, Blue, No. 118, 10 In. 11.00

Mixing Bowl, Pink, Peach, Red, No. 125, 11 In. ... 31.00

Mixing Bowl, Pink, Peach, White, No. 125, 11 In. ... 15.00

Mixing Bowl, Yellow, Tan, White, No. 111, 8 In. 15.50

WATERTOWN

Watertown Manufacturing Company was located in Watertown, Connecticut. The company's lines included Balmoral, Lifetime Ware, Monterey, and Woodbine. Woodbine, introduced in 1952, was the first plastic dinnerware with a raised design. The heavyweight dinnerware was made in Beige, Bermuda Coral, Black, Canyon Yellow, Caribbean Blue, Chartreuse, Cocoa, Grenada Green, Light Blue, Palisades Gray, Pink, Red, Sahara Sand, and Yellow. Decal decorations include Cathay, Country Gardens, Promenade, Puffs, and Wheat. Dishes are marked *Watertown* and with pattern names.

Lifetime Ware

Butter, Cover, Canyon Yellow 6.00

Butter, Cover, Pink 4.00

Creamer, Pink 4.00

Dinner Set, Pink, Plates, Bowls, Cups, Saucers, 43 Piece 40.00

Mug, Grenada Green, 4 Piece 15.00

Plate, Bread & Butter, Canyon Yellow 2.00

Plate, Luncheon, Sahara Sand, 7 In. 3.00

PLASTIC DINNERWARE

References

Alexander, Brian S. *Spiffy Kitchen Collectibles.* Iola, Wisconsin: Krause, 2003.

Goldberg, Michael J. *Collectible Plastic Kitchenware and Dinnerware, 1935–1965.* Atglen, Pennsylvania: Schiffer, 1995.

Wahlberg, Holly. *1950s Plastic Design: Everyday Elegance.* Atglen, Pennsylvania: Schiffer, 1999.

Zimmer, Gregory R., and Alvin Daigle Jr. *Melmac Dinnerware.* Gas City, Indiana: L-W Book Sales, 1997.

Ceramic Dinnerware
Patterns and Factories Index

This is an alphabetical list of the dinnerware patterns and factories listed in this book. Factory names are in capital letters.

Kovels' New Dictionary of Marks

Pottery and Porcelain 1850 to the Present

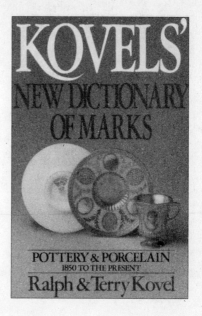

- Provides the quickest, easiest way to identify more than 3,500 American, European, and Oriental marks
- Arranged by symbol and alphabetically according to name
- Each mark is illustrated and accompanied by factory, city, and country of origin, material used, color mark, date mark was used, and name of current company
- Includes the vocabulary of marks, fakes and forgeries, and a cross-referenced index

304 pages, hardcover, $19.00 • ISBN 0-517-55914-5

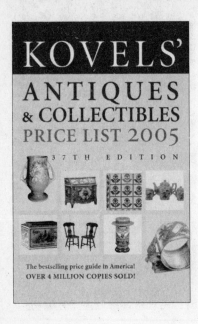

Kovels' Antiques & Collectibles Price List 2005

37th Edition

The bestselling price guide in America!

- 50,000 actual retail prices gathered from shops, shows, sales, auctions, and the Internet—no estimated prices—and every price is reviewed for accuracy

- Hundreds of photographs of genuine antiques and vintage collectibles—from Empire furniture to Barbie dolls

- Great tips on restoring and preserving your antiques and collectibles

- Company histories and hundreds of identifying marks and logos of artists and manufacturers

- Special 16-page color section

  Comprehensive index, extensive cross-references

96 pages, paperback, $16.95 • ISBN 0-375-72068-5

Kovels' Library

Kovels' Depression Glass,
8th Edition
1-4000-4663-7 • $16.00

Kovels' American Antiques
1750-1900
0-609-80892-3 • $24.95

Kovels' Antiques and
Collectibles, 37th Edition
0-375-72068-5 • $16.95

Kovels' Bottles Price
List, 12th Edition
0-609-80623-8 • $16.00

Kovels' Know Your
Collectibles, Updated
0-517-58840-4 • $16.00

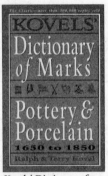

Kovels' Dictionary of
Marks: Pottery & Porcelain
0-517-70137-5 • $19.00

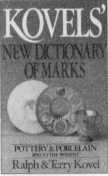

Kovels' New Dictionary
of Marks
0-517-55914-5 • $19.00

Kovels' Yellow Pages,
2nd Edition
0-609-80624-6 • $19.95